Other Books by the Author

Second World War Photo Intelligence
Prelude To Pearl Harbor
To Fool A Glass Eye
Asia From Above
V-Weapons Hunt
Axis Warships
The Normandy Invasion
Evolution of Airborne Ops
Chasing SAM

First published in Great Britain in 2016 by
PEN & SWORD AVIATION
an imprint of
Pen & Sword Books Ltd,
47 Church Street,
Barnsley, South Yorkshire
S70 2AS

ISBN 978 1 47388 349 9

A CIP record for this book is
available from the British Library.

Typeset by CHIC GRAPHICS

Printed and bound in Great Britain by TJ International

Pen & Sword Books Ltd incorporates the Imprints of
Pen & Sword Aviation, Pen & Sword Family History, Pen & Sword Maritime, Pen &
Sword Military, Pen & Sword Discovery, Wharncliffe Local History, Wharncliffe True
Crime, Wharncliffe Transport, Pen & Sword Select, Pen & Sword Military Classics,
Leo Cooper, The Praetorian Press, Remember When, Seaforth Publishing
and Frontline Publishing.

For a complete list of Pen & Sword titles please contact
PEN & SWORD BOOKS LIMITED
47 Church Street, Barnsley, South Yorkshire, S70 2AS, England
E-mail: enquiries@pen-and-sword.co.uk
Website: www.pen-and-sword.co.uk

CONTENTS

ACKNOWLEDGEMENTS

As usual, my wife and tireless caregiver/editor, Mary Ellen and Susan Strange, friend and NARA researcher extraordinaire (www.StrangeArchives.com). Others who made specific contributions are cited in footnotes.

DEDICATION

To:
All those who served their country from vaults without windows
and kept their secrets.

FOREWORD

Even casual readers of World War II history will know of Barbarossa, code name for the German invasion of the Soviet Union begun on 22 June 1941. It was the largest single military operation ever mounted, involving 800,000 men on one side and just under three million on the other. Sheer hubris of an attack along an 1800 mile front is astounding.

I'm not going to attempt to retell the story of Barbarossa. It's been covered at length and in depth in books by commanders and soldiers who were there and serried ranks of historians who weren't. Think about what you know about that momentous operation. Names like Leningrad, Stalingrad and Sevastopol spring to mind. You may know of Gorki, Kiev, Kazan, Rostov and others but chances are all you have are words. Do you have any idea what any of them LOOKED like, what they looked like to Intelligence Services of the advancing German army?

This isn't a book about strategy, soldiers, tactics or equipment. My Barbarossa survivors are photographs, mostly aerial photoreconnaissance. It is a book about materials collected for use by military Intelligence between 1941 and 1945. Almost all of the photos included here are from German sources captured during and at the end of WW II. Others are from retired US Army and Navy Intelligence imagery holdings. A few pictures from open sources (magazines, newspapers, non-DoD archives) have been added to fill out the story in places.

I will show you examples of what German army and Luftwaffe Intel personnel saw, what they used for planning, what their targeting materials looked like, and what tactical operations sources looked like in their field headquarters. As a former aerial photo interpreter (PI) I know what the imagery means—I can read them. I know what the target materials mean—I've made studies like them. These pages will use Luftwaffe aerial reconnaissance and ground photos taken by soldiers and combat photographers to show you what terrain, selected places and situations in the Soviet Union looked like during the conflict. Those will be photos collected by the Allies at the end of WW II.

During early days of the Cold War, PIs and targeteers in Britain and the US exploited many of those same German aerial and ground photos for reasons identical to their original use.[1] They were invaluable for Target Studies and maps. It is no surprise that this imagery survived into the 1960s. After that, survival became more problematic. Intelligence is perishable and other sources were coming into play.

This book is about Barbarossa but ultimately it is about the photos—and I will tell you how they survived into the present. I'll tell you what I see on that imagery as if you and I were sitting in my study going through stacks of prints.[2]

Roughly 80 per cent of the images are negs I had printed nearly four decades ago. When I decided to write this book I was fortunate to meet Ms Susan Strange, a professional researcher at NARA. She has been my eyes at the Archives. She sends me plots I need to see and scans the images I want to look at. Her help has been invaluable in filling gaps in my collection.

Finally, while writing this I realized it is possible to respect, even admire, professionalism, skill, courage, determination and sacrifice on both sides—without approving of the either's politics.

---

[1] In 1977 I assisted FBI prosecutions of war criminals using WW II German aerial imagery of Poland, searching for possible mass grave sites matching witness descriptions.

[2] 1:250,000 scale maps available on-line at www.lib.utexas.eud/maps/ams/eastern_europe were an invaluable source for using this imagery. They are the same maps used to plot GX in the 1950s.

Chapter I

INTRODUCTION

By inclination, Intelligence organizations are peopled by pack-rats. Everything that comes in is kept because it may be of use in the future. That works for a given conflict, but Intelligence is perishable. When the 'old stuff' obviously has less (if any) usefulness it is usually stuck in boxes and filed. The bulk of it, and there is a LOT, is sometimes eventually destroyed. Old Intelligence materials are like old buildings. If they survive long enough to be considered 'historic' they may be kept. If not they will be removed to make room for newer items.

During World War II, German Intelligence collected a large volume of ground and aerial photos, including those of their invasion of the Soviet Union.

German Photo Interpreters (PIs) were experienced and, evidence shows, quite good.

Many senior German officers regularly relied on aerial imagery.

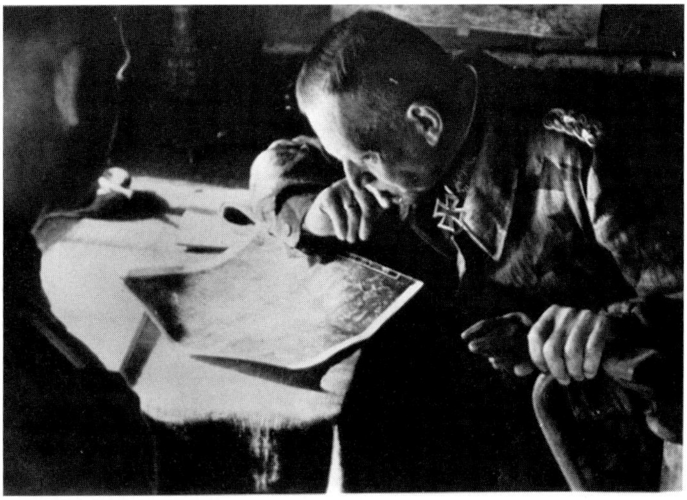

Some of that material was captured by the Allies at the end of World War II and quickly recognized as a valuable source of Targeting and Cartographic Intelligence for the Cold War.[1] Some of the ground shots showed key buildings, construction of bridges, location of factories and rail yards.

Luftwaffe imagery of Russia was the only source of aerial photo coverage prior to the U-2 in 1957 and Corona satellites in the 1960s.

Twenty tons of German photoreconnaissance results and ground photography were found in eleven different locations in Germany. In June 1945 the mother lode, the German Army Print Library, was found in a barn 8 miles south west of Salzburg.[2] A few of those boxes of original German contact prints contained paper traces showing where the mission went. That was something we had to know, so the prints were taken to the Aeronautical Chart and Information Center (ACIC) in St Louis, MO and plotted at a scale of 1:250,000. Those plots, made in the Standard Indexing System (SIS), were the retrieval tools for the imagery.

---

[1] The print collection was dubbed GX (for captured German). A small amount of German print and cut neg targeting material found separately was labeled DT (it got the name Dick Tracy) and was mostly German Target Materials. I'm grateful to Chris Going (Cambridge Architectural Research) and Wing Commander Mike Mockford (RAF ret.) for details of the finds.

[2] The first mission I PI-ed was a 1960 flight over China and my team had to make several SIS plots. Working with acetate ink was messy and one mistake and you had to start all over but the indexing system worked well.

All US aerial imagery flown anywhere in the world was indexed that way.

Still photos were filed and retrieved by content/subject. Some included a ‘Frisket’, a piece of film with date, location and subject that would be printed with the image negative. Others had finding tools that were gone by the time I was involved, making those images unlocatable in a search and findable only at random.

SIS Plots were on 20” x 24” transparencies showing where frames of aerial imagery fell on a map. Normally every fifth frame was shown so a flight trace could be seen. Vertical plots are shown as squares or rectangles. Low Obliques[3] are drawn as closed convex polygons. High Obliques always show the horizon so are drawn as open-ended convex polygons.

A Standard Indexing System overlay was made for each camera position with frames falling in each mission in a Degree Square (one degree of Lat x one degree of Long) shown by corner tics on the overlay below. The center line is 30’ of Long.

One recce mission could generate dozens of SIS plots. SIS Plots were filed in large metal-clad binders which were stacked on shelves in wooden boxes specially made to hold them. A busy Degree Square could have more than one SIS Book.

Want to see if someplace had coverage? Go to the Film Library and locate the proper Degree Square plot book. Fold pages back till you got to the date range you wanted and slip the appropriate map underneath. You could see what the imagery covered and decide what you wanted to look at, or have the photo lab copy for you.

MAPPING CHARTING & RECONNAISSANCE STANDARD PLOTTING FORM
U S AIR FORCE
ORGN. & SORTIE
FOCAL LENGTH
ALTITUDE (S)
SCALE (APPROX.)
EXP. THIS DE. SQ
TOTAL EXP.
REMARKS
MAP SCALE 1:250,000 (MAP REF.)
DATE (D.M.Y.) 1942
TIME (G.M.T.)
COUNTRY (S) USSR
QUALITY ☒EXCELLENT ☐GOOD ☐FAIR ☐POOR
SNOW COVER (EXP. & %)
CLOUD COVER (EXP. & %)
O.P. FILE NO.
OVERLAY FILE NO.
GEO. REF.
☐SECRET ☒CONFIDENTIAL ☐UNCLASSIFIED
Roll 324
SG
ADDITIONAL SECURITY INFORMATION
PREPARED BY
AIRFIELD
6

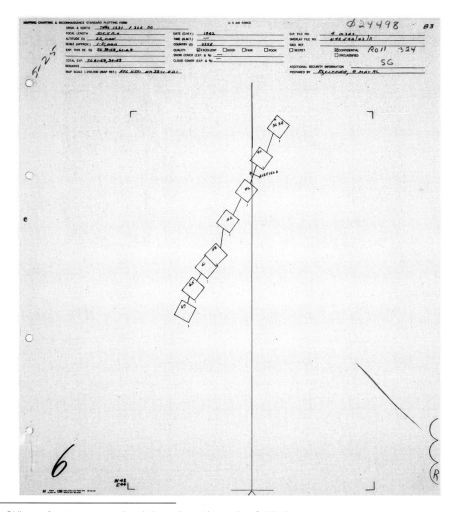

3 High and Low Oblique refers to camera angle pointing at the earth, not aircraft altitude.

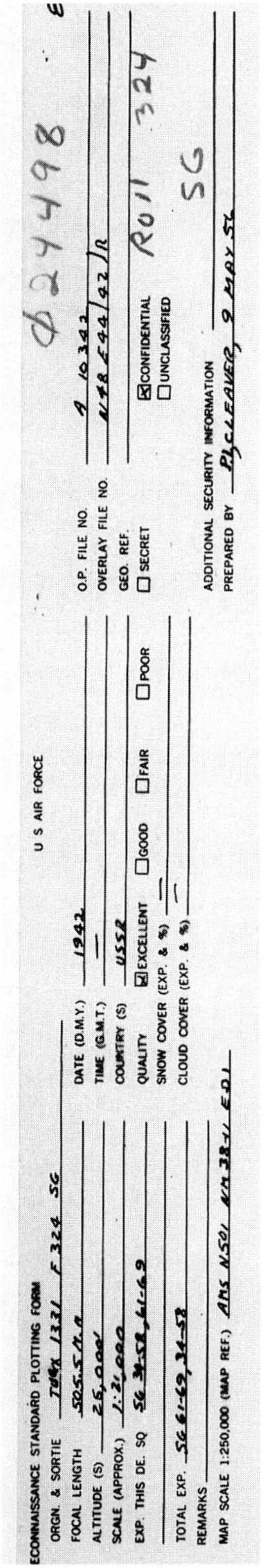
ECONNAISSANCE STANDARD PLOTTING FORM
U S AIR FORCE
ORGN. & SORTIE 1331 F 324 SG
FOCAL LENGTH
ALTITUDE (S) 25,000'
SCALE (APPROX.) 1:21,000
EXP. THIS DE. SQ SG 34-58, 61-69
TOTAL EXP. SG 61-69, 34-58
REMARKS
MAP SCALE 1:250,000 (MAP REF.)
DATE (D.M.Y.) 1942
TIME (G.M.T.)
COUNTRY (S) USSR
QUALITY EXCELLENT GOOD FAIR POOR
SNOW COVER (EXP. & %)
CLOUD COVER (EXP. & %)
O.P. FILE NO.
OVERLAY FILE NO.
GEO. REF.
SECRET CONFIDENTIAL UNCLASSIFIED
ADDITIONAL SECURITY INFORMATION
PREPARED BY
Roll 324
SG

This plot is for a run over Stalingrad (48N44E). The location of Stalingradski Landing Ground is noted. The SIS Plot header (enlarged below) told mission/sortie, date, focal length and altitude (needed to compute imagery scale), exposure range, when the plot was made (in this case May 1956) and by whom.

SIS header enlarged.

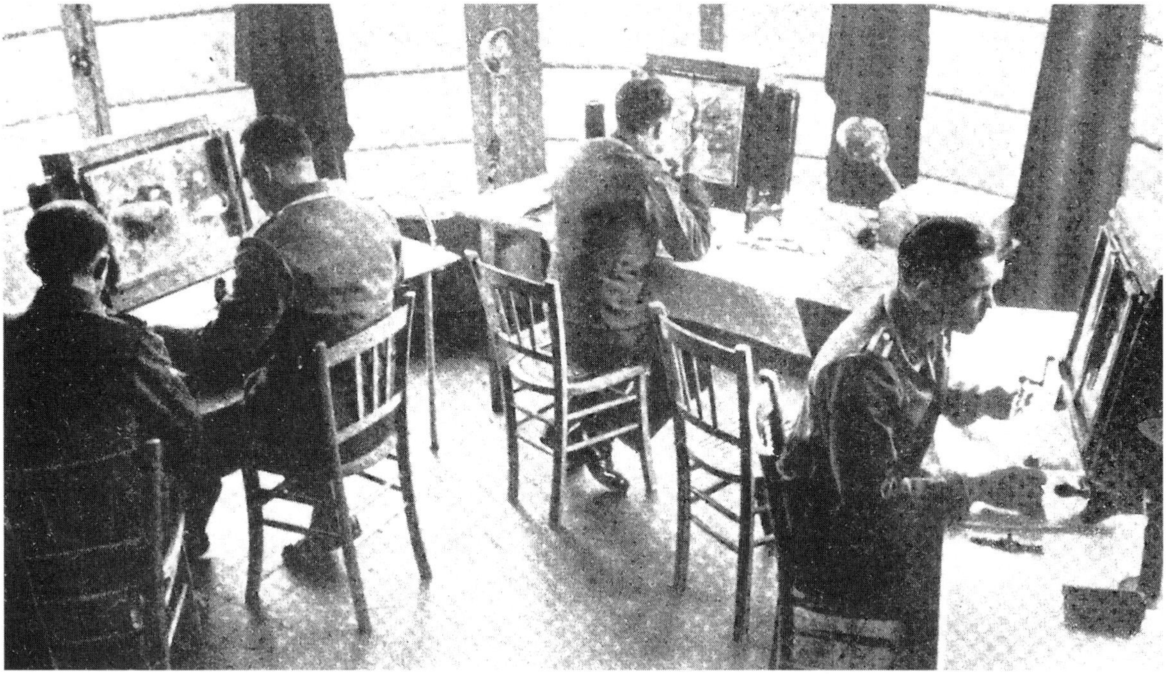

German PIs working off original negatives. Most German roll film was sprocketed and 11.9" wide.[4] American lab and PI equipment was designed for 9.5" roll film and we didn't have German light-tables or lab equipment.

Thus GX could only be viewed using prints or reproductions from copy cameras. Repeated handling would have soon destroyed the prints, so, one frame at a time, to cameras reduced image size and transferred them, US standard copy film—thousands of cans of 500' rolls of film. For two decades military intelligence and cartographic requirements for coverage of the Soviet Union were serviced by that film. From 1945 to 1957, GX was the only thing we had over some areas. After the U-2 and Corona, GX was still valuable to provide 'comparative cover', a way to see what had changed from then to now. Eventually satellites were frequent enough to provide their own comparative cover.

In 1976 I was assigned as Deputy of the Defense Intelligence Agency (DIA) Division with custody of all DoD imagery. By the time I became involved calls, for Luftwaffe coverage were few and far between. I lived what came next and here's the way I remember it.

When DIA was formed in October 1961 my Division had inherited original roll negatives from Air Force, Army and Navy repositories. Our mission was to retrieve, copy and deliver whole missions or selected exposures to military units needing the images. Film went back to the 1930s, but the bulk was WW II. Our film custody was mostly a paper transfer of Army and Navy material already stored in the General Services Administration Federal Record Center, Suitland, MD.[5] More than 100,000 cans of aerial film[6] from Southeast Asia ballooned the collection to strain the Records Center and probably +90% of the film we held hadn't been withdrawn for use in years.

In 1977 GSA asked DIA to reduce cost by culling our holdings. At the same time, silver price was very high and aerial film has a silver halide emulsion that could be recovered. A win-win situation, the brass thought. It was the Carter Administration and cost saving was a fetish, so we were pressured by our hierarchy. Nearly dormant GX film was a prime candidate.

I was concerned. I had degrees in Geography and History and had read everything I could on WW II and

---

[4] I've seen German cut-negs but, as far as I know no original German negative roll film has ever been found.

[5] Most Navy film came from the old Torpedo Factory in Alexandria, VA. Korean War imagery in particular suffered badly from leaking tape splices caused by storage proximity to steam pipes.

[6] A surprising percentage of it was junk; duplicate cover (recce planes flew in pairs), cloud cover or missions with camera malfunctions.

knew what could be seen on aerial film, so I was aware of the treasures that might be on those rolls. I was loath to destroy material without knowing what it was. The fact that no one had called for a roll or box of film recently didn't mean it had no value. By coincidence, one of our researchers had recently withdrawn a roll of old film to satisfy a request from one of the military commands and found it was on highly flammable nitrate base. The National Archives recently had a fire caused by nitrate base film (I think it was old newsreels) so everyone was sensitive to the problem. The boss directed a screening program to physically look at all the older film, searching for more nitrate so those rolls could be converted to safety film. That screening resulted in discovery of numerous rolls of film with obvious historic significance.

I spent time with people from the National Archives Modern Military Branch to create lists of things they'd like to see retained.

I began looking at our computer print-outs for significant locations and almost immediately found Pearl Harbor and Wake Island days before the 1941 attacks, pre-war Philippines, D-Day and other names I recognized. We contacted The National Archives and arranged to move rolls of the most obviously historic imagery from GSA storage to what is now called the National Archives and Records Administration.

In an attempt to convince the head-shed that wanton destruction of unscreened rolls of old imagery to save cost was a bad idea, I made over two hundred 30" x 40" displays using some of the best photos I'd found.

19 JUN44
BERLIN
B17 SLID UNDER ANOTHER BOMBER
AIRCRAFT DID NOT PULL OUT

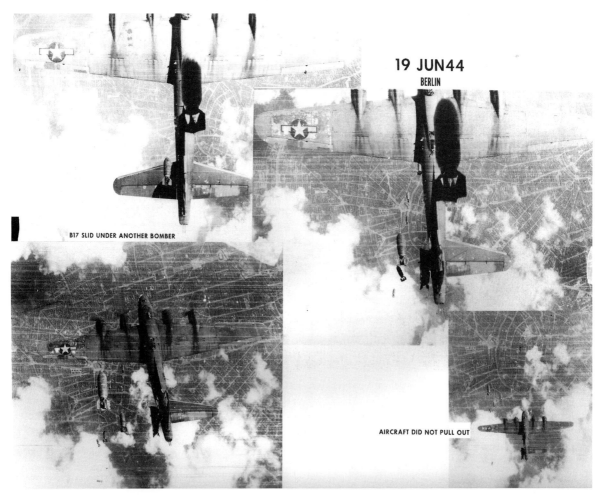

My display board of a USAAF bombing tragedy in Europe.

My displays mounted on the walls of our building attracted much attention.[7] Some people in our Division didn't like what I was doing because they felt it took effort away from our primary mission, but the boss knew what we were finding was good public relations for DIA and DoD. As interest grew, I was 'unofficially' helped by other people in the organization who shared my enthusiasm for our nation's history. Film researchers and photo lab technicians who had experienced WW II first hand kept an eye out for items of special value. Some of them also provided useful information and added 'corporate memory' to the investigation. Bless them all for their foresight and wisdom.

Our efforts stalled the push for destruction but didn't end it. Fortunately the boss, a former Naval Officer and NPIC analyst, agreed with what I was trying to do and was a formidable bureaucrat who knew how to keep our 'brass' wolves at bay.[8]

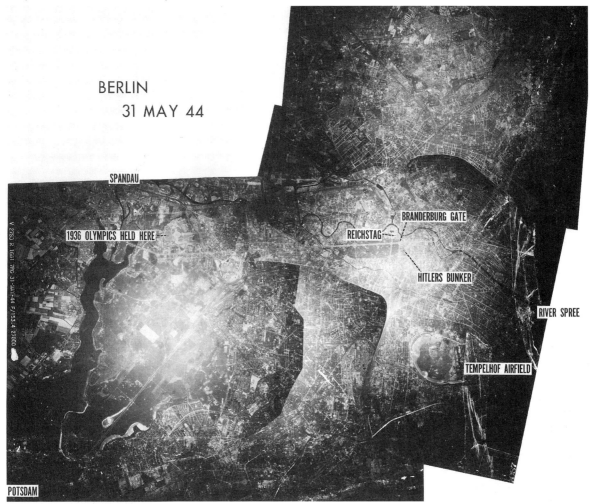

BERLIN
31 MAY 44
SPANDAU
1936 OLYMPICS HELD HERE
BRANDERBURG GATE
REICHSTAG
HITLERS BUNKER
RIVER SPREE
TEMPELHOF AIRFIELD
POTSDAM

I made a mosaic of Berlin using five exposures.

Displays like these began to get attention and helped show value of the imagery.

I next learned of over a thousand boxes of cut negatives. Most were copies of attachments from briefings, Attaché Reports, photos from foreign sources (mostly British) and captured documents. Most were 4" x 5" or 8" x 10".

---

7 They were seen by Charles Scribner, Jr. during a tour of our facility and my first book, *World War II Photo Intelligence* (1981) resulted. Some of those displays are included in the chapters that follow.

8 Paul LaBar was a superb manager and rare boss who knew how to use a Deputy to extend his reach and show initiative. We made an excellent team and he taught me a lot.

Military Intelligence has an insatiable need to collect photos and documents on the off-chance that something will be meaningful when put with some other piece as yet to be collected, or for some future operation. As war loomed in Europe in the late 1930s, actual collection methods and opportunities were limited so military attachés, agents and librarians in military offices of all the future belligerents were furiously cutting items from newspapers and books, gathering post cards and photos, taking trips and covertly snapping pictures of things that might be important (bridges, RR Stations, air landing fields, military garrisons, factories) in territories they expected might soon be denied to them. Our pre-war aerial photo coverage of foreign soil was almost non-existent.

It was important to learn where things were in other countries, what they were and what they looked like—military installations, industry, transportation, equipment, you name it. Well into the 1940s, Military Intelligence in the United States, with the exception of spies and intercepting, decoding/deciphering message traffic, was essentially a library function, filing away anything that came to hand for use by staff officers from other branches. Except for actual spies, Intelligence was barely a career. In the US, experts, when required, would be called in from industry and aerial photography was mainly for cartography, not intelligence.

People we would recognize today as analysts or intelligence professionals were few and far between in America until well into WW II. Intelligence analysis, such as it was (except for signals intelligence), was done by 'operators'. Pilots, ship drivers Naval and Army planners, infantry officers, and their civilian counterparts, did their own research and analysis. The same Intel amateurs were assigned to various embassies as attachés collecting most of the information in the field. In fact, well into the 1950s US military personnel considered an assignment in Intelligence was a 'career killer'.

If an office in the War Department or Navy Department had a problem; a plan needed shaping or updating, a VIP was going on a trip, or a threat assessment was wanted, the action officer went to the appropriate Intel library and pawed through the files for anything of use.

Here is how the system worked for images. Every scrap of imagery collected (ground photos, aerial photos, drawings, graphs etc.) was printed and filed separately on page-sized pieces of cardstock with appropriate explanations of when, where and what the image was. Hard copy images were cross-filed with copies in as many places as there were topics on the material. For example: Germany, airfield, a certain aircraft, an adjoining aircraft factory and electric power or rail lines resulted in the same image filed in seven different places in different library safes—perhaps with duplicates in other offices—but each card and negative had the same 'accession number'. When an action officer wanted copies of an image he sent an order to the photo lab citing its number. The proper negative was pulled from photo files where they were stored sequentially. Copies were made and forwarded to the requester. US Army and Navy photo labs held thousands of those negatives. Photo lab people holding those files didn't know, or care, what the images were—they just filed, retrieved, reproduced and refiled them. Those were the cut-negs I was looking at.

Of course army and navy files used different but similar systems for identification of negatives and accession numbers. Apparently the army (and possibly the Air Corps) used at least two different numbering schemes over the years.

Once WW II began, other sources came into the system. Cut negatives (copy negs) of the 'best' frames from photoreconnaissance and bombing missions in combat theaters; copies of briefing materials and images from other nations (particularly Britain) were added. As the war began to wind down, there was a flood of ground shots and captured images, mostly from German sources. The number of negatives in the system grew significantly but the accession number system held up.

Sometime after the war, probably in the late 1950s, emphasis changed and I guess someone determined that the WW II and pre-war material was no longer relevant. Many of the places in Europe and Asia had been considerably changed by the war. Perhaps someone needed the space in the Pentagon or thought that the original materials were 'held elsewhere so we can get rid of our copy'. Whatever the reason, the accession number file system was scrapped. Card files with positive print images and all the pertinent information were destroyed and hundreds of safes reused or sent to salvage. The negatives were put in standard 12" x 15" boxes and retired to the Federal Records Center. Anyone who's seen the end of *Raiders of the Lost Ark* knows the drill; acres of shelving with boxes stacked to the ceiling—and it was a high ceiling. Upon its creation the DIA also inherited custody of those files, sight-unseen. We also got the USAF/USN civilian researchers, photo lab equipment and personnel who serviced those files. When called to our/my attention, most of those boxes of history and junk had remained unopened, gathering dust for over thirty years—I suspect in part because the retrieval tools were gone.

No one knew what was in those boxes, so I began drawing four or five from the Federal Records Center each a day, working through my lunch period and staying after work to look at the contents, which could be anything from a few hundred to over a thousand cut negatives per box. Many were negs of graphics used in DoD publications dating from the early 1940s. Perhaps the published documents were in someone's file somewhere?

Clearly this might be a treasure trove, but it was equally clear that there was little wheat and a lot of chaff in those boxes. The biggest problem (aside from the sheer size of the task) was that few of the negatives had anything on them to identify date, location, subject or its significance. That information had been on the now long-gone cards. Again fortune smiled as my PI training and memory let me recognize a lot of the material by origin or location or (the more obvious) type of subject. I was also able to identify dupes, but a lot of it was unknown and unidentifiable. Sadly, many negatives were unusable because of over or under exposure during copying. Other negatives had faded; the base reticulated (acetate base 'crazed' making the image unusable). Some images had kept on developing into nothing because of improper washing during processing. Others were torn by rough handling or otherwise destroyed.

The photo below was in the first box I opened—and it amused me. Why would an attaché forward that to Washington in a report? Was it a covert place to meet someone? A spy hangout? Did the Attaché have a quota of images to deliver? I never learned why this one was important enough to keep in someone's file, but it had been dutifully cataloged and indexed. I quickly learned it was typical of the 'junk' regularly submitted.

Area 5--COLOMBIA--R--**--BUENAVENTURA--TOWN-HOTEL BOGOTA--*--N 0355 W 7711--*--
RESTRICTED
927.89

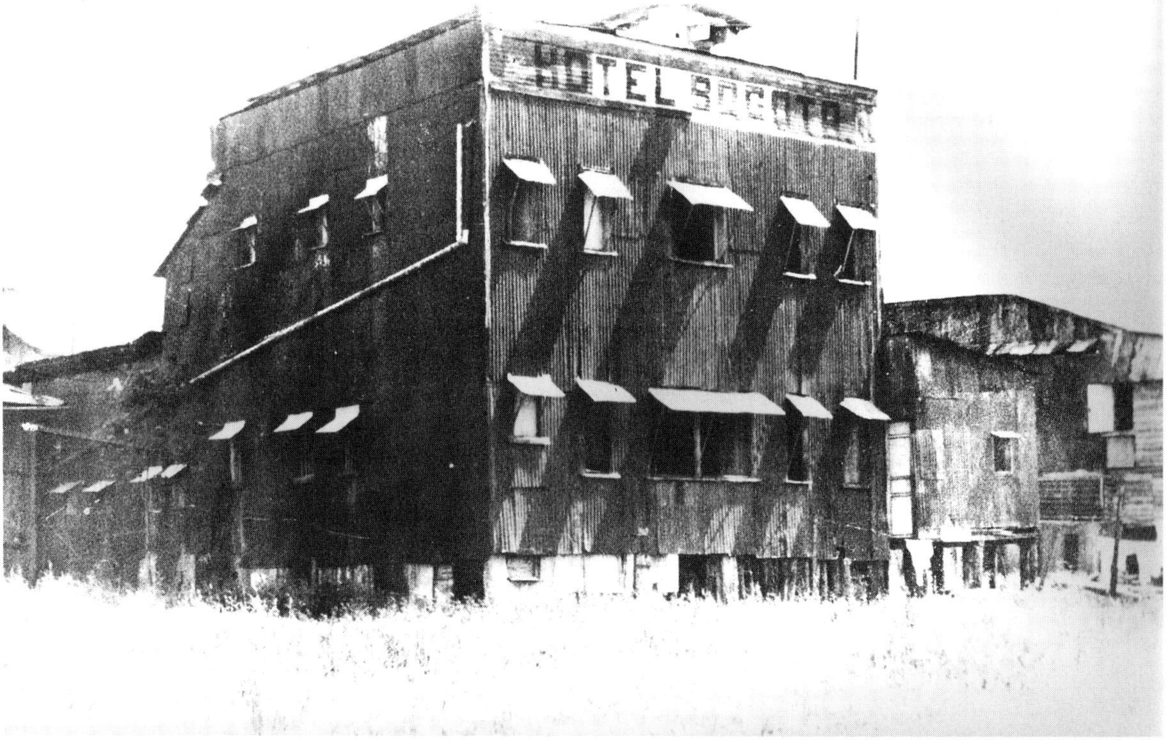
HOTEL BOG

After five dozen shots of Lorelei Rock and Christ of the Andes, I realized those cut-neg files were 98 per cent trash and multiple duplicates of trash but kept plowing on and gradually came upon a number of images that were clearly 'keepers'.

There were examples of pre-war German preparations, such as a 15cm sFH18 heavy howitzer battery. Those don't look like field uniforms so the photo may be from an exercise before Poland was invaded. There were a few good ground shots taken by German soldiers in the field (many had their own cameras). You'll see some of those in the following pages.

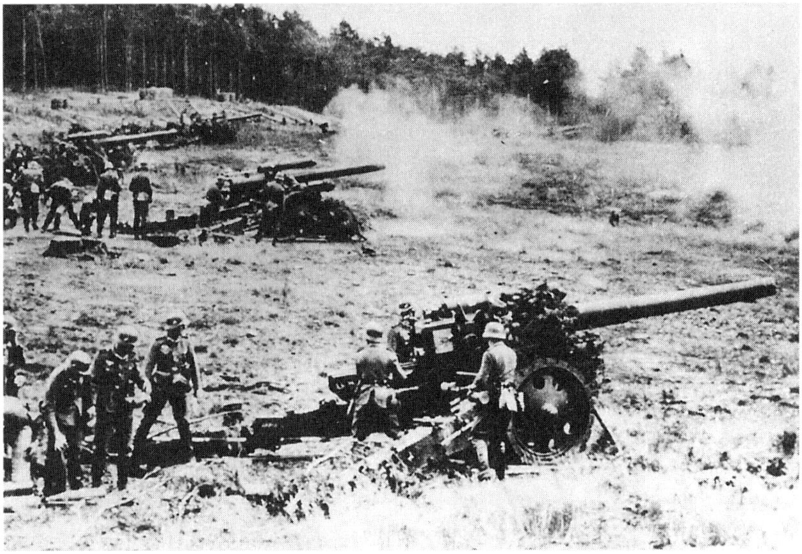

This troop of Pz II's maneuvering is also probably pre-Poland.

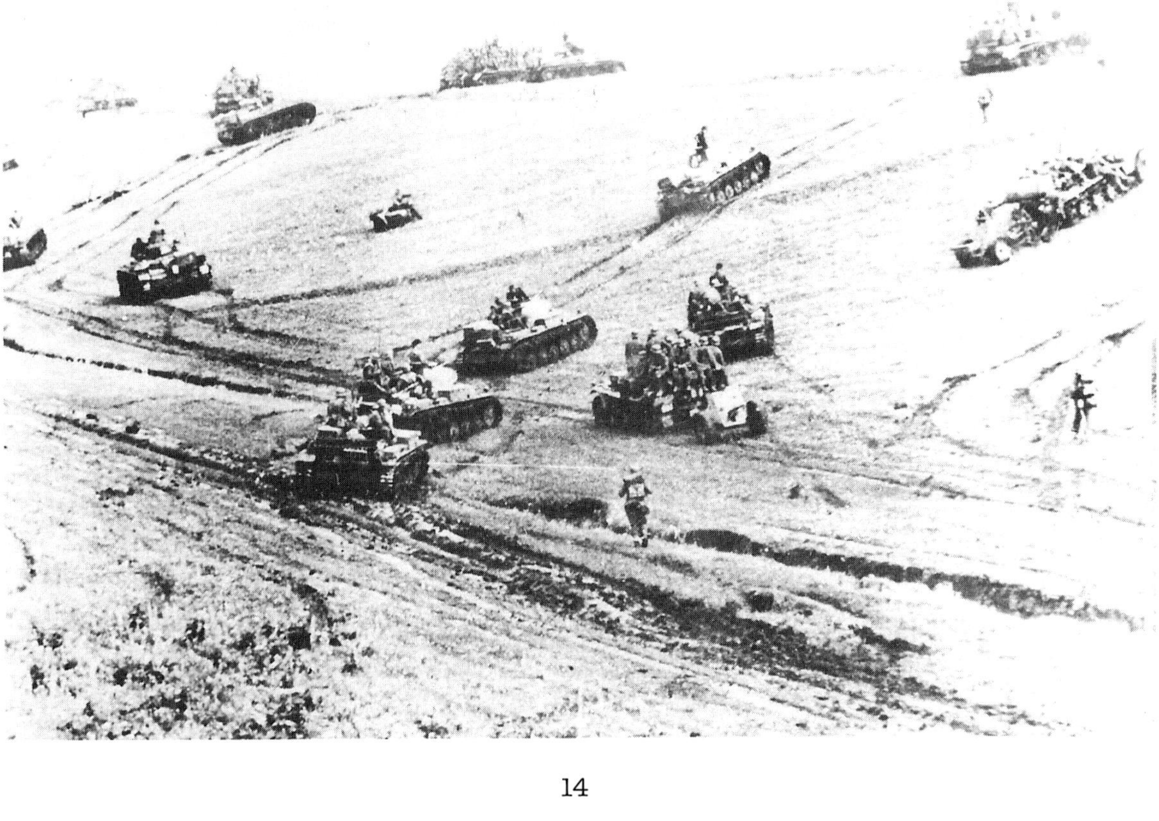

Copies of many of those cut negs have been used in my earlier books and some of the ground shots are included in these pages. Ultimately the thousand-plus boxes boiled down to three or four that I sent to the Archives (mostly Allied and German equipment from North Africa and RAF photos of their bombing).

Meanwhile, transfer of historical roll film to NARA was progressing slowly and pressure from GSA was still mounting, then, at one our staff meetings, a researcher offered, 'Why not just burn the German prints?'

The boss and I about came out of our chairs.

GERMAN PRINTS?

FIRST GENERATION CONTACT PRINTS! (i.e., made from original negatives). Imagery doesn't get any better than that.

Neither Paul nor I knew they existed. We dealt in NEGS. Our lab was equipped to efficiently copy individual frames or whole rolls of film[9]. Use of German prints pre-dated both our assignments to the Division. GX prints had never been mentioned in any of our staff or production meetings. We learned they hadn't been used for at least two decades, probably not since before transfer to DIA, and only the old timers knew about them since we'd been answering the dwindling number of requests for USSR coverage using the ACIC roll film copies of the GX prints.

I went over to the Records Center the next day to look at the GX print collection.

It was a revelation. A treasure trove for a photo interpreter. Over a million original German prints. I half expected to find Brünnhilde sleeping in those stacks with her spear.

There were tens of thousands of original German one-foot square gray boxes in various thicknesses depending upon the number of prints—one box per camera per mission (usually one to three cameras on a mission). Those often remarkably sharp 11.9" x 11.9" prints, made from original negatives going back to 1938. Most German imagery, particularly early in the war, was of excellent quality.

German cameras were designed for mapping precision and their lenses were outstanding, but those cameras were a LOAD. A Dornier Do 17 could carry two cameras, one with a long lens (as at left below) another with a shorter wide angle lens. A Ju 88 could carry three. Wide German film was also heavier than ours, limiting numbers of exposures per mission. In some larger German PR planes crew members could change film magazines in flight, thereby extending the coverage.

Left is a size comparison with RAF cameras of the same focal-length.

---

[9] This was before the days of digital scanning.

PHOTOGRAPHIC EQUIPMENT **Section VII**

Stock No. 3609-84-0000-135-207A-1
1. Nomenclature: Camera, aerial.
2. Foreign Nomenclature: Riehienbilder Rb 75/30.
3. Country of Origin: Germany.
4. Manufacturer: Unknown.
5. Identification Numbers:
   Fl. No: 38702 Gerat No: 135-207A-1
6. Models Available: As Illustrated.
7. Documents: See "Instructions for Ordering."
8. Description: Camera is magazine loaded, electric motor driven. Used for automatic topographic and panoramic photography. Lens: Carl Zeiss 1:6.3 F=75 cm. Lens is a Carl Zeiss 4 component, cryolite coated. Filter is a "D" (orange) mounted by a bayonet type mounting. Picture size is 30 X 30 cm. Reference is made to the Rb 50/30 as to the operations of the various accessories. Camera comes boxed with mounting.

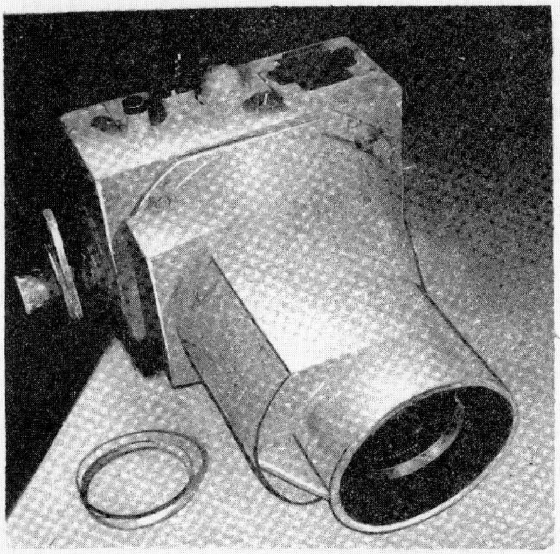

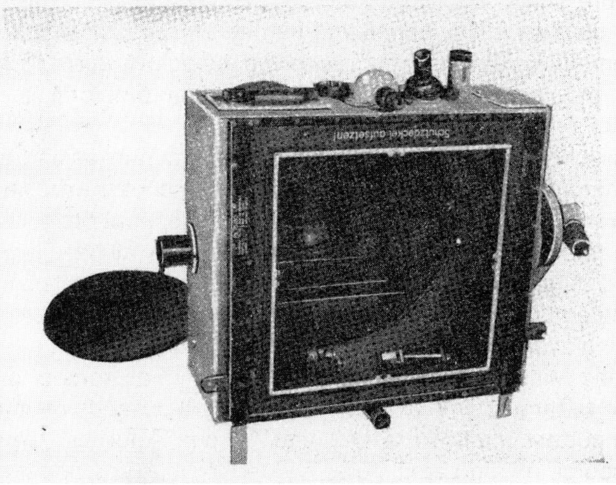

One of the most used German aerial cameras.

Opening sample boxes, I saw amazing images, complete reconnaissance missions over Soviet cities and industrial areas; London during the blitz; Leningrad and Stalingrad during their sieges. I saw the docks where *Titanic* was built, ports above the Arctic Circle, North Africa from Morocco to Egypt and most of the Soviet Union west of the Urals. Howard Carter couldn't have been more excited when he found Tut. Fortunately the boss was a photo scientist and he instinctively knew there would be more 'information' in prints just one generation from the original negatives than on the third generation grainy, contrasty roll copy film we had been using. A series of scientific tests he directed proved him correct.

We decided to try to save the prints for history.

I quickly made displays featuring GX imagery to advertise its value. Leningrad was an obvious choice for a composite. My Stalingrad mosaic (included later in this book) was displayed in the main National Archives Building foyer in Washington for a Modern Military Branch Symposium. It was 30" high and 8 feet wide, using 28 frames of GX, at their original size, plus ten still photos to show Stalingrad at the time of German assault.

You'll see more of both cities later in this book, and more of my mosaics.

We checked with the only potential users of GX at the time (NPIC/CIA, Strategic Air Command and US Air Forces Europe) and no one objected to destruction of the film IF we would guarantee continuing service of the occasional request. Had we failed, the National Archives would have eventually wound up with German aerial reconnaissance imagery on grainy, contrasty 1946 roll copy film and the rare prints would have been gone. As it was, we destroyed hundreds of rolls of copy film for space and silver recovery, and arranged for transfer of the print collection to NARA to protect it from future DoD Philistines. To honor our servicing promise to Commands we negotiated an agreement that we could pull needed boxes of GX from NARA for copying (to keep specific points of interest secret).

Our hierarchy was happy, we were happy. As shelf space cleared, GSA could see happy on the horizon… and NARA had a headache as civilians found out about the collection.

The organization Paul LaBar and I managed is gone. Files of cut and roll negatives (if they still exist) now belong to some other agency. People who helped me research and print the negatives are long since retired, replaced by folks who may not have the same sense of worth for historic imagery and don't know what we did. I can't help but believe that history was fortunate in the accident of all of us coming together in that unit at that moment in time thirty years ago with that challenge and that perspective.

As in my other books, I hope these photos will encourage increased use of similar material as a primary source for military history. Aerial photographs taken before, during and after a battle or campaign are a most neglected resource for understanding what happened. A major reason for that is few historians are trained or qualified to do anything more than a superficial presentation of the imagery. PIs have a saying, 'Everybody thinks they're a PI', but real photo interpretation is far more complex than just looking at a photo and recognizing the obvious. It involves understanding the nuances captured on frames collected for reconnaissance, pre-strike analysis, damage assessment or target identification. It requires understanding the use of objects in a contextual framework, shadows, changes in tone and texture, and subtle indications of something happening or recently passing over that ground. When you can read those things in aerial photos, they become an incredibly rich source of information—vignettes of history frozen in time.

This book is a compilation of photos coming from the German Invasion of the Soviet Union, a book that will let you see what other authors write about. Some of these photos were taken by German propagandists or journalists, some by individual soldiers, many are from aerial photoreconnaissance. A few came from books published at the time and third nation news sources. They all have two things in common; they were captured/found/acquired during WW II and all were entered into Allied Intelligence files where I found them. When the Cold War heated up, a German ground or aerial shot of a bridge, dam or factory taken in 1941-43 might be the only thing available for target study. During the Cold War, attachés and tourists (sometimes referred to as 'Wandering Minstrels') were sneaking photos of all sorts of subjects but the coverage was meager and of little use to targeting. WW II shots taken by thousands of sources were important to let us see changes. More important, before the U-2 and Corona satellites, German vertical reconnaissance imagery was the only source of large area views needed for mapping and targeting the USSR.

Notes on the text. If I name a place or piece of equipment, I'm sure of it. Less than 100 per cent positive is PROBABLE. Best guess is POSSIBLE.

Where feasible, images are oriented with north to page top. Exceptions are obliques; where reading contemporary captions makes that inappropriate or where I needed to turn the images to get more picture on a page. Except for my 'display boards' I have added no words to photos. Writing or annotations on photos are as I found it and probably original to Intelligence use before and during WW II. I have added arrows to identify points noted and explained in my text.

I have selected ground and aerial photos I found note-worthy—and hope you will too. Some capture moments; others weeks or months. Some are just plain interesting. They all tell a little story, but I'm not going to go into any more explanation than necessary to put the images in context. This book is mainly for people who already know the history of Barbarossa. It is aimed at giving readers a different look at some of the war's events or places—or simply sharing pictures that appealed to me. The judgments and opinions stated are those of a PI and long-time Intelligence Officer. I'll tell you what I see on the images.

This collection of survivors and the rest of its GX fellows came within a gnat's whisker of being destroyed in 1977-78. I believe their survival is evidence of the right people in the right place at the right time doing something special. If not for a remarkable GS-15 who understood and provided support and skills to fend off bureaucratic pressure, and an Air Force Lt. Col. with PI experience and a love of history, large segments of WW II military imagery history could have been destroyed on the altar of cost-cutting.

What follows are some aerial and ground photo Barbarossa survivors that caught my eye four decades ago and some material new to me included with help from Susan Strange.

Chapter II

PREPARING FOR INVASION

Getting ready to wage war requires a lot of spade work. You have to know as much as possible about the enemy. Where is he strong? What weapons does he use? How big is his force? Where are his logistic and manufacturing centers?

From what I saw, German Intelligence had been collecting material on the Soviet Union for years, much of it from local libraries and periodicals. Typical is the shot below of Balaklava Bay with the ruins of a fort built by Genoese traders in the fourteenth century.

Another shot of the bay where British and French armies landed and their fleets anchored during the Crimean War (1853-56).

The objective was to outflank Sevastopol and thus control the Black Sea, but the Germans attacked the same objective from the land so none of these photos had any use during Operation Barbarossa—but German Intel kept them. So did we.

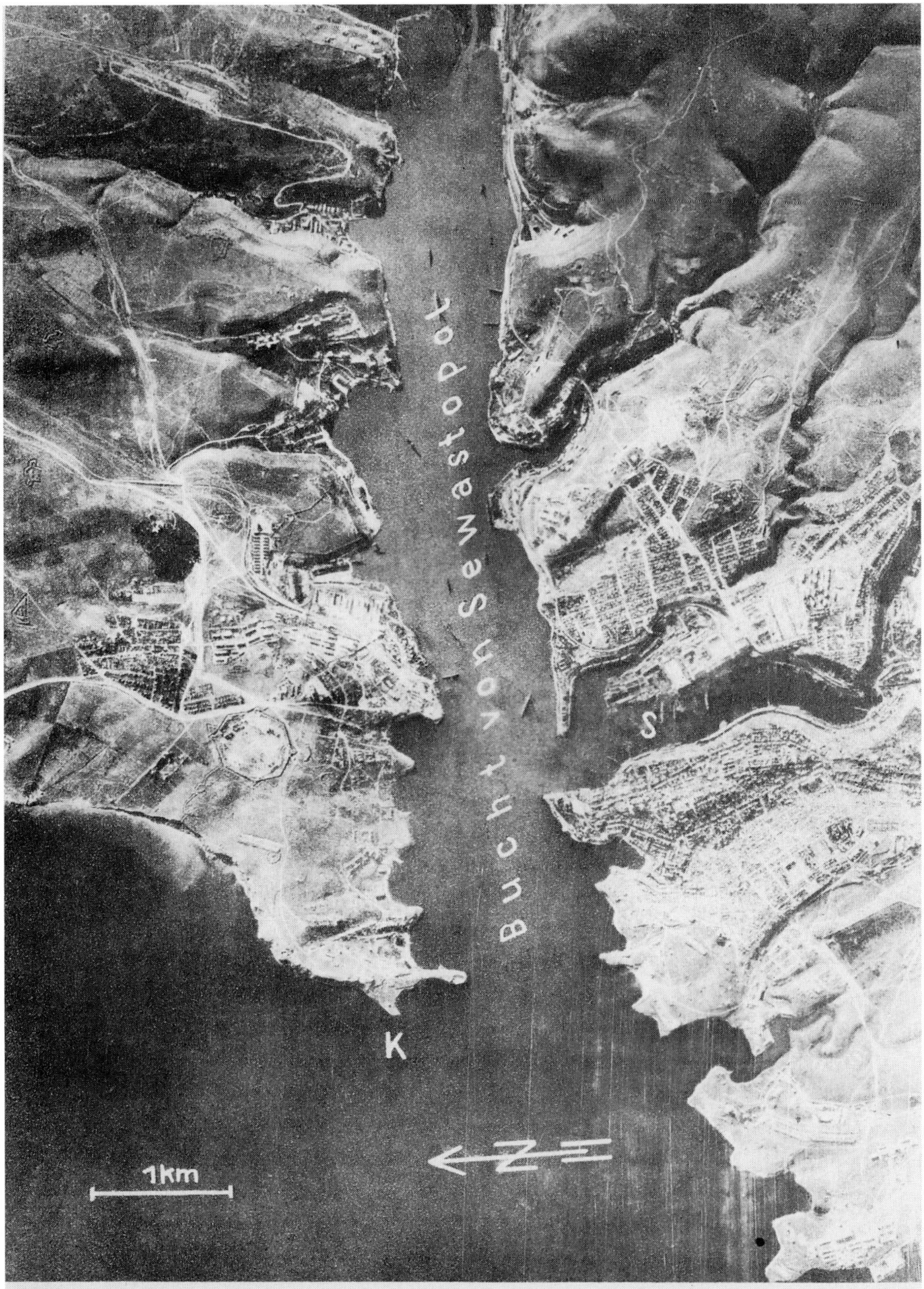
Bucht von Sewastopol
S
K
1km
N

a **Sewastopol.** Übersichtsbild der Bucht von Sewastopol mit Kap Konstantin (K) und d
nach S abzweigenden Südbucht (S), die von der Stadt Sewastopol umgeben wird.

A good look at the configuration of Severnaya Bay. From a book, probably around WW I. Seaward defensive forts are at 'K' and the Naval Base at 'S'.

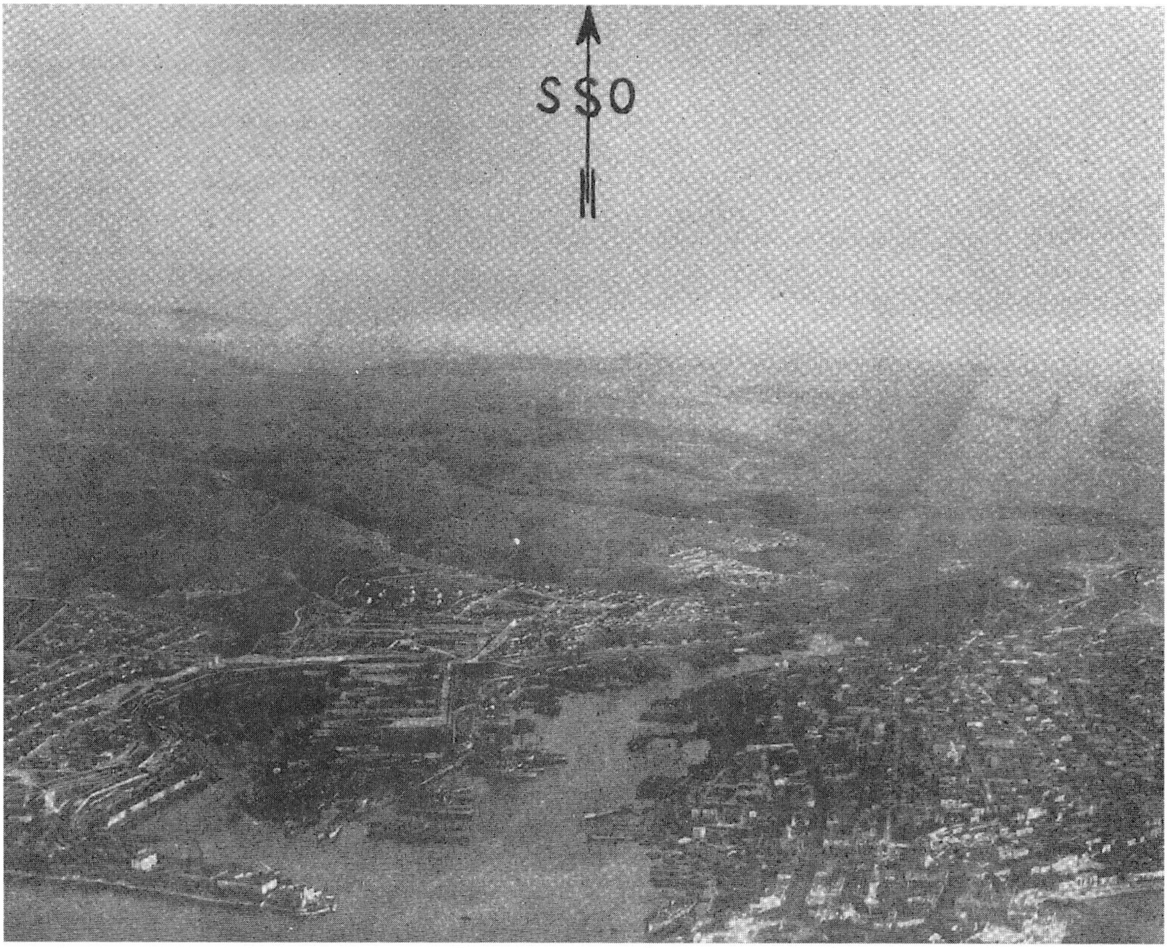
SSO
N

Looking south-southeast up Severnaya Bay at the broken-eroded Crimean terrain that would have to be crossed to take the city. The undated photo is clearly from before the war. I count at least twenty merchant ships in the harbor, and no naval vessels.

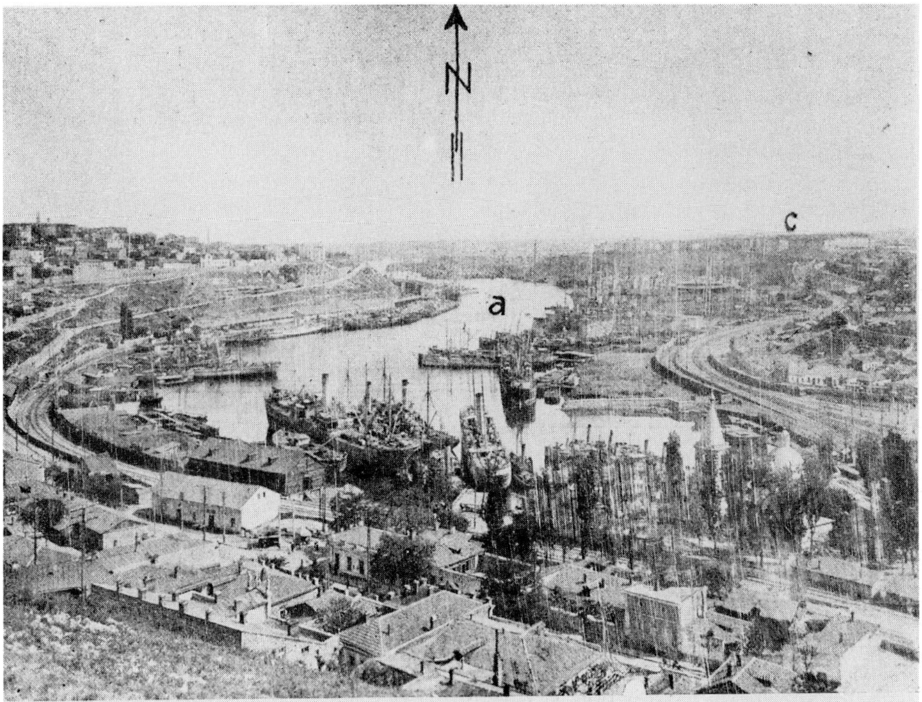
N
a
c

Abb. 14 **Sewastopol.** Blick vom innersten Teil der Südbucht (a) zur Hauptbucht. Rechts die hochgelegenen Kasernen (c). (Weltkriegsaufnahme).

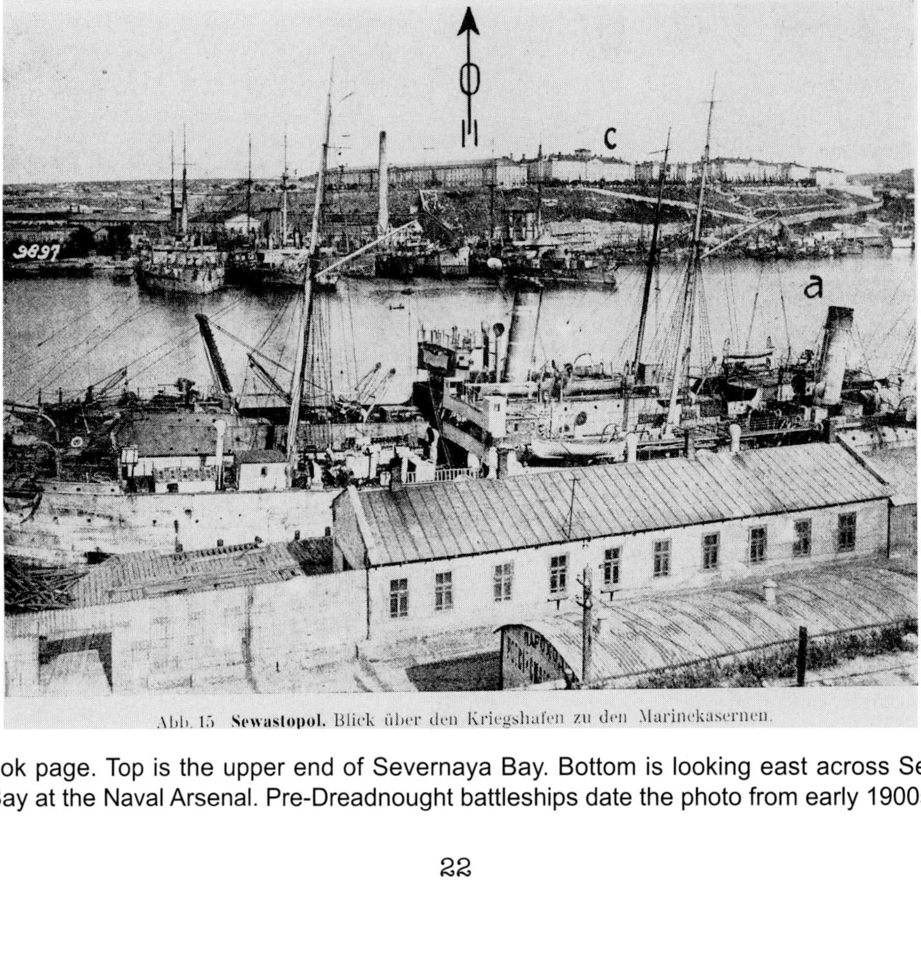
O
c
a
9897

Abb. 15 **Sewastopol.** Blick über den Kriegshafen zu den Marinekasernen.

Another book page. Top is the upper end of Severnaya Bay. Bottom is looking east across Sevastopol's Pivdenna Bay at the Naval Arsenal. Pre-Dreadnought battleships date the photo from early 1900s.

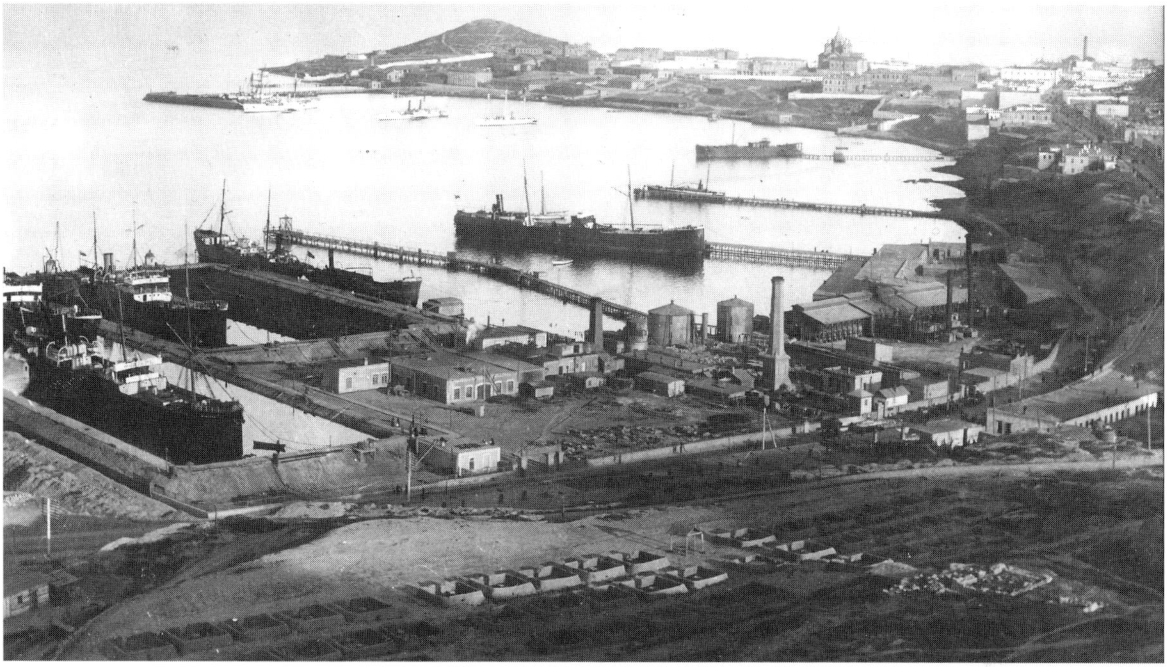

Caspian Sea oil port of Baku, probably post WW I. This was a major German objective.

Below, the upstream Dnieper River Bridge at Kiev. German forces wanted this intact.

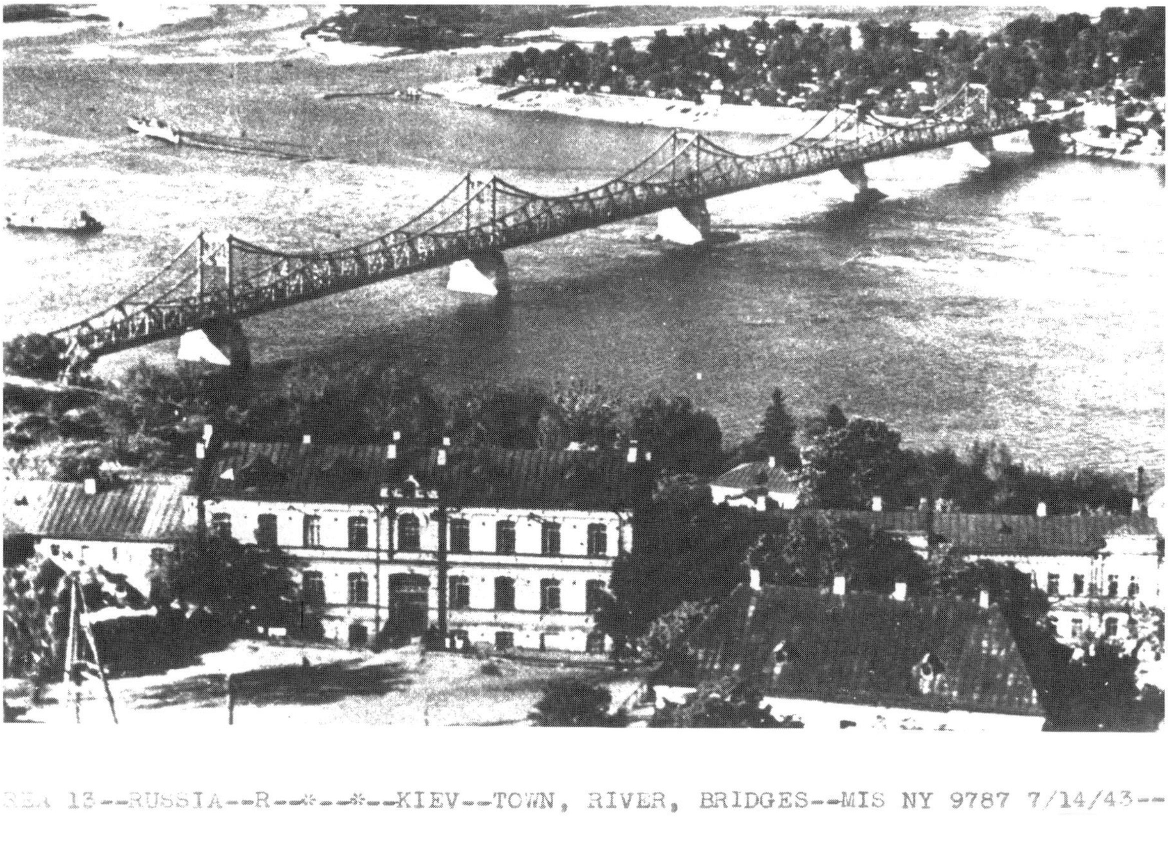

SEA 13--RUSSIA--R--*--*--KIEV--TOWN, RIVER, BRIDGES--MIS NY 9787 7/14/43--

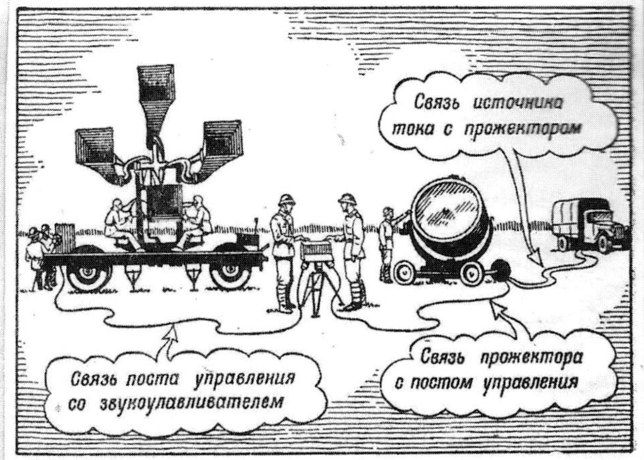
Связь источника тока с прожектором
Связь поста управления со звукоулавливателем
Связь прожектора с постом управления

Рис. 306. «Прожзвук Сперри» дает согласованную работу звукоулавливателя и прожектора

„Scheinwerfer-Horchgerät Sperri" (mit Anschluß an) vereinbart
von Horchgerät und Scheinwerfer

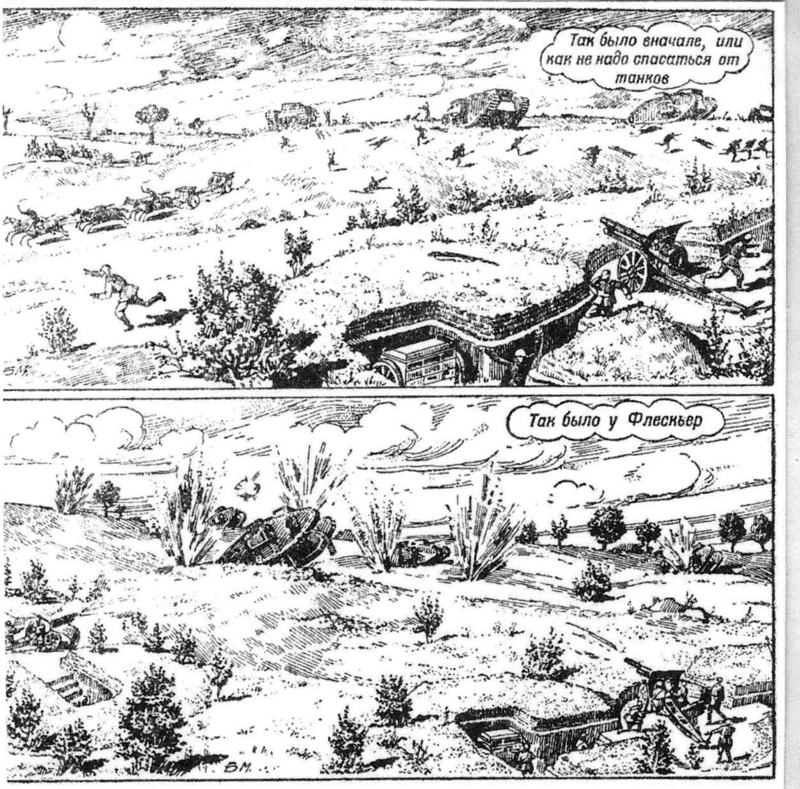
Так было вначале, или как не надо спасаться от танков
Так было у Флескьер

Рис. 346. Танки и артиллерия в сражении у Камбрэ

Panzer und Artillerie im kampf bei Cambrai

Over their years of association with Soviet military as Germany covertly rearmed and trained in Russia, German Intel acquired and translated manuals. This case discusses sound and searchlight aircraft detection and, below, anti-tank tactics. The translator noted examples were from November 1917, Cambrai, France.

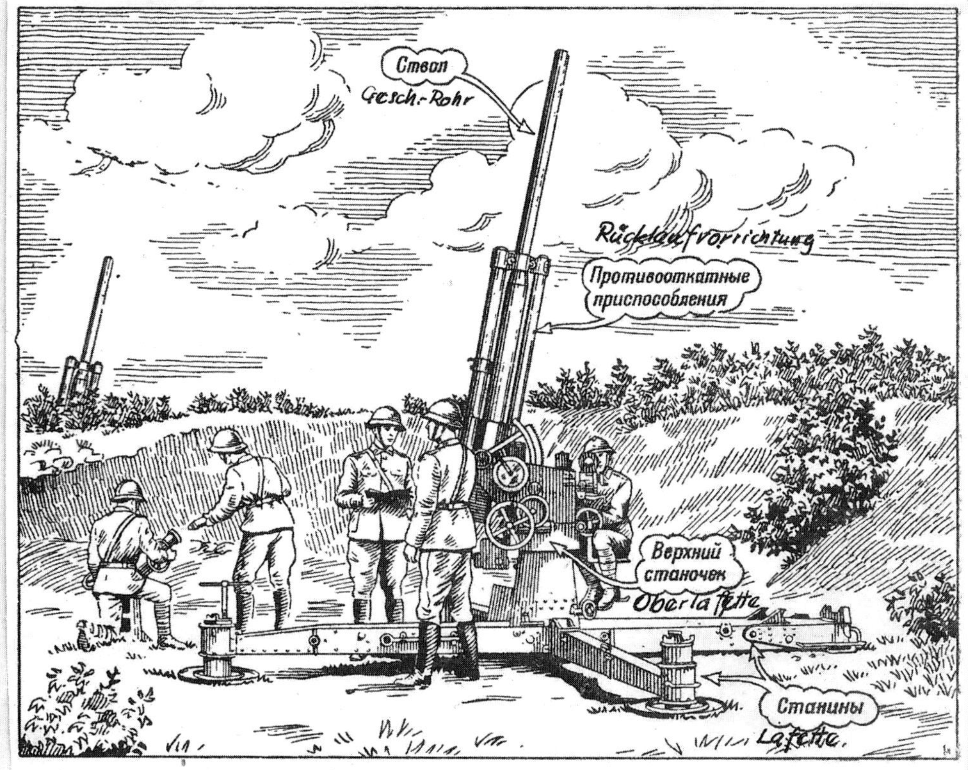
Ствол
Gesch.-Rohr
Rücklaufvorrichtung
Противооткатные приспособления
Верхний станочек
Oberlafette
Станины
Lafette

Рис. 298. Зенитное орудие готово к бою

Flugzeug-Abw.-Geschütz, feuerbereit

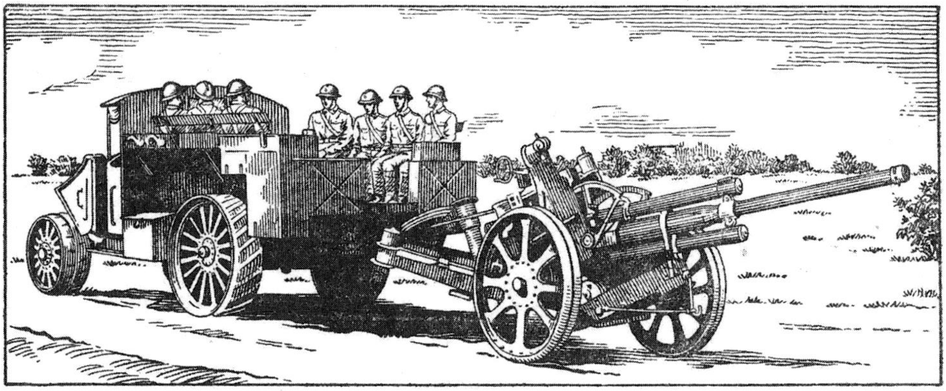

Рис. 296. Современная зенитная пушка на походе

Neuzeitliche Flak auf dem Marsch

This page of the Soviet manual shows an anti-aircraft gun and what looks to be an anti-tank gun being towed with its crew in the truck. The truck wheels are interesting and show a tractor influence.

Рис. 264. Ложная батарея

Schein-Batterie

Pz.-Abw.-Schacht

Противотанковый колодец

Станина *Lafette*

Противотанковый колодец

Pz.-sicherer

Сошник *Sporn*

Рис. 279. Противотанковая пушка на огневой позиции

Pz.-Abwehr-Kanone in Feuerstellung

Top: Howitzers in camouflaged positions.
Below, firing position for an anti-tank gun. The observers/spotters hole is interesting.

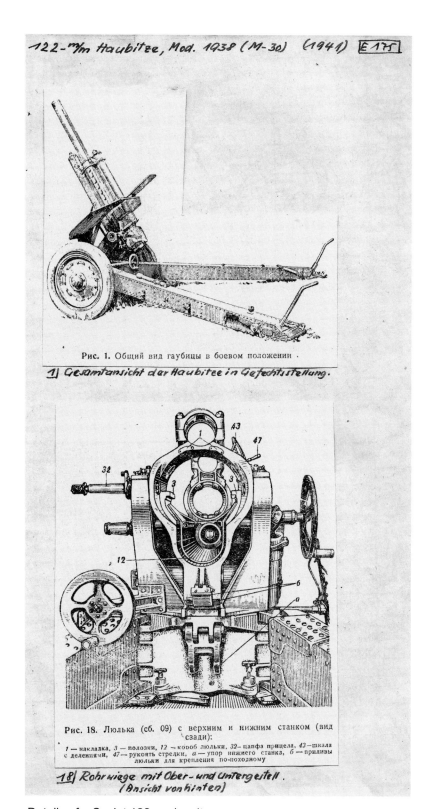

122-ᵐ/m Haubitze, Mod. 1938 (M-30) (1941) E 175

Рис. 1. Общий вид гаубицы в боевом положении.

1) Gesamtansicht der Haubitze in Gefechtsstellung.

Рис. 18. Люлька (сб. 09) с верхним и нижним станком (вид сзади):

1 — накладка, *3* — полозки, *12* — короб люльки, *32* — цапфа прицела, *43* — шкала с делениями, *47* — рукоять стрелки, *а* — упор нижнего станка, *б* — приливы люльки для крепления по-походному

18) Rohrwiege mit Ober- und Untergestell.
(Ansicht von hinten)

Details of a Soviet 122mm howitzer.

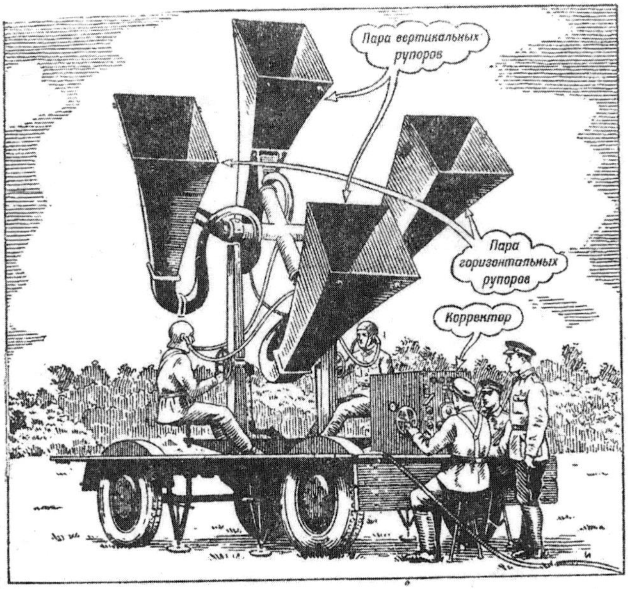
Пара вертикальных рупоров
Пара горизонтальных рупоров
Корректор

Рис. 302. Звукоулавливатель «Сперри»

Richtungshörer „Sperry"

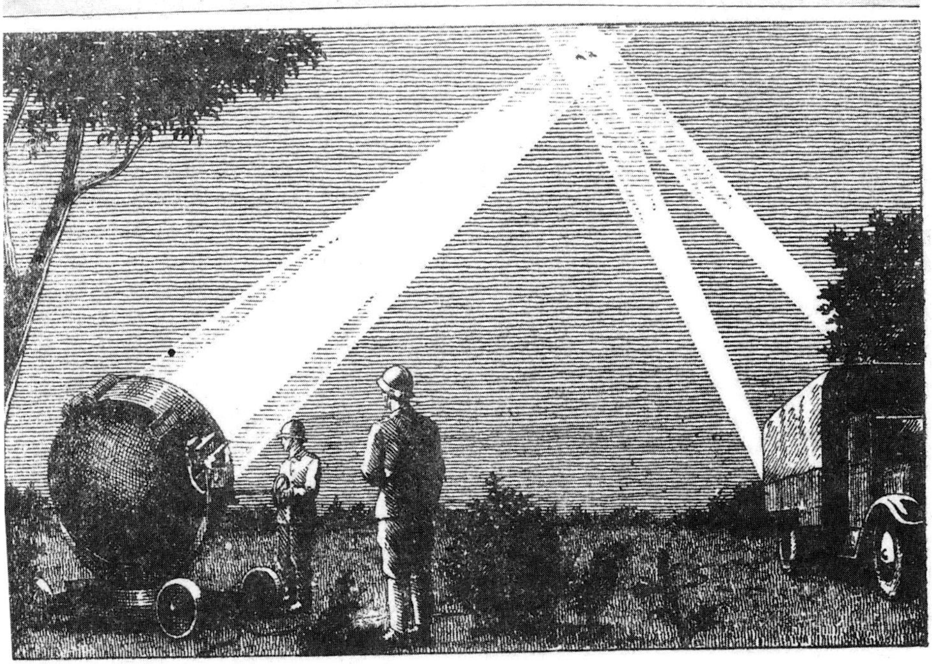

Рис. 305. Прожекторы «поймали» самолет

Scheinwerfer nehmen ein Flugzeug „gefangen".

Use of a sound ranging system and searchlights to locate aircraft at night.

TB-3, Kampf- und Transportflugzeug.

Abspringende Fallschirmjäger.

I D 569

Page from a German study on Soviet heavy bombers. The 1930s open cockpit Tupolev TB-3 (ANT-6) could cruise at just under 100mph and climb to 12,000 feet. It was the world's first four-engine, cantilever-wing bomber but was no longer considered viable for front line service. TB-3s were used as cargo transports and platforms for paratroops. The plane was retired in 1939—then brought back for Barbarossa.

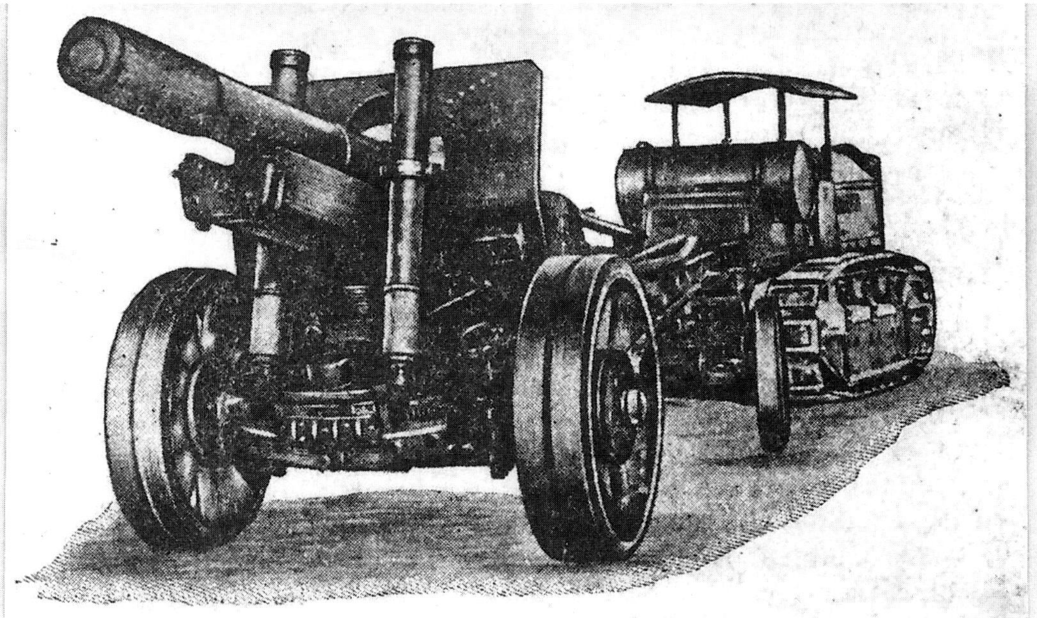

Рис. 3. 152-*мм* гаубица-пушка обр. 1937 г. в походном положении.

152 m/m Kan.-Haubitze Modell 1937 in Fahrstellung

A Soviet 152mm howitzer, limber and prime mover from a Soviet document that wound up in German hands… then ours.

Below, M1937 152mm howitzers with limbers and Voroshilovets Prime Movers, Red Square, probably May Day, 1939 or 40.

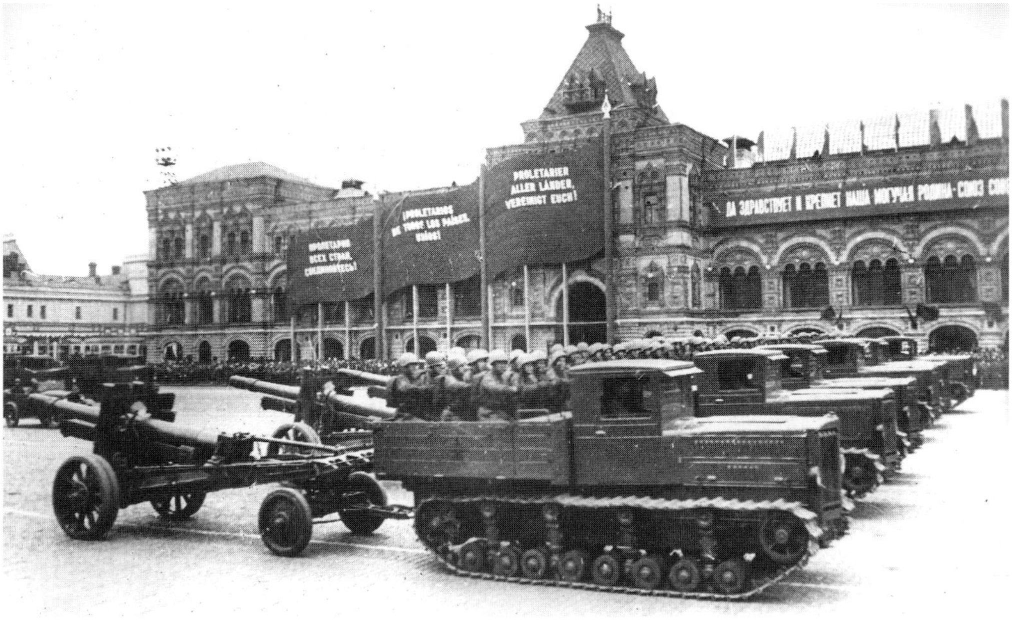
PROLETARIER ALLER LÄNDER, VEREINIGT EUCH!

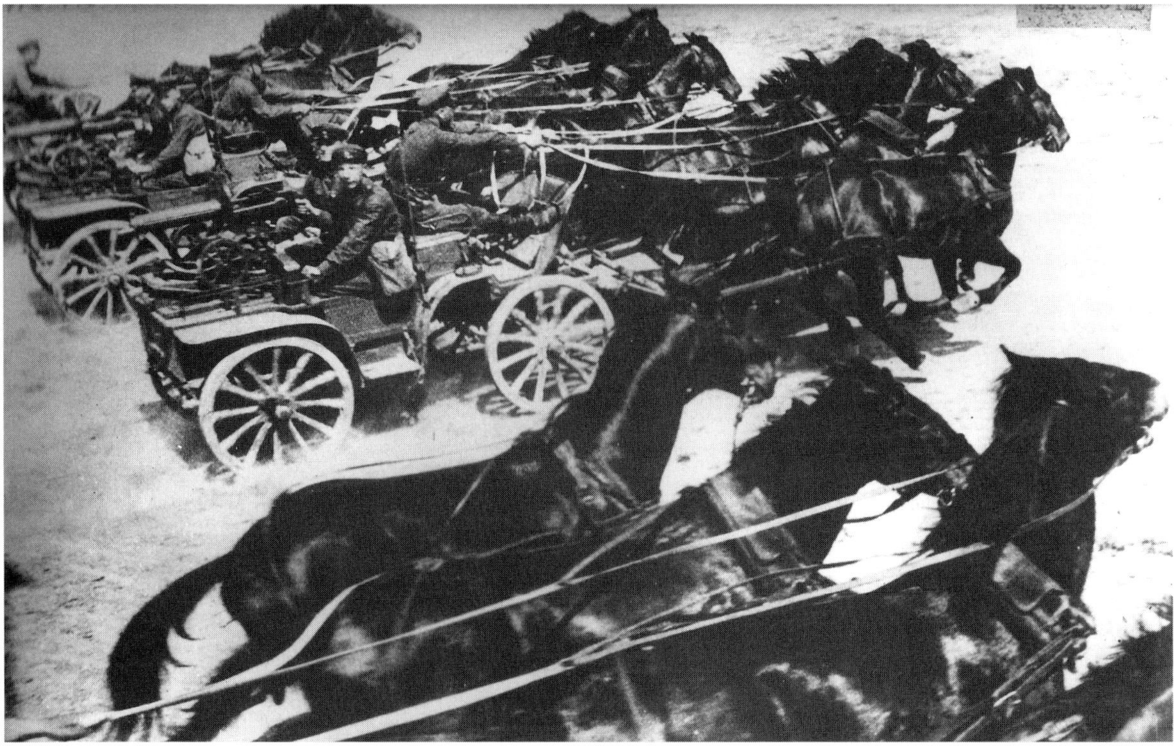

More action in Red Square. Four-horse teams pulling carts with three-man squads for PM M1910 Maxim 7.62mm machine guns. Definitely pre-war. The 1910 Maxim was more often seen with a shield.

Below, a unit of Maxim heavy machineguns parading in Red Square, May 1941. In later pages you'll see how I know the date—and, be sure to remember those wide black marks on the pavement.

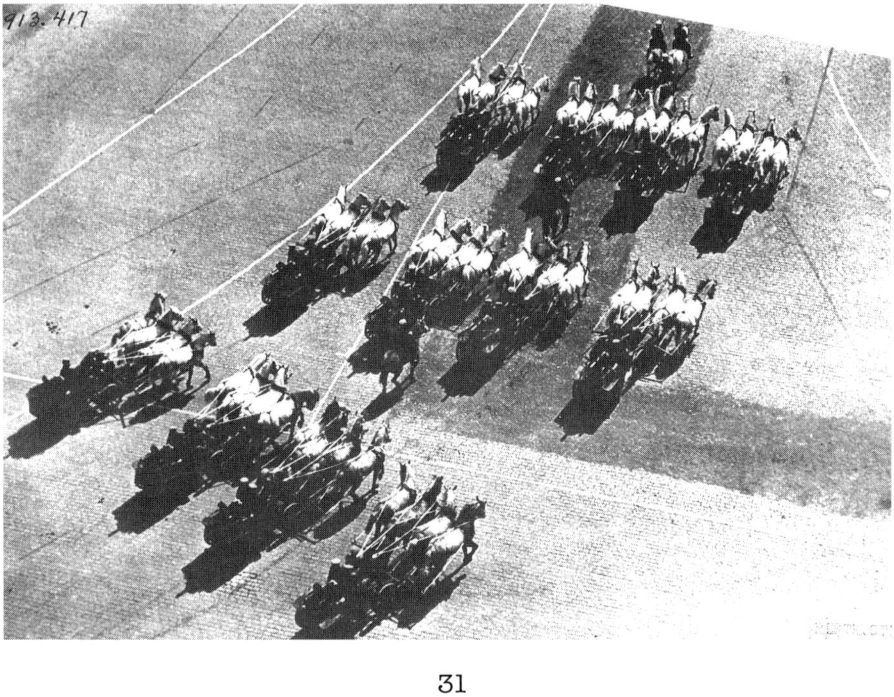
913.417

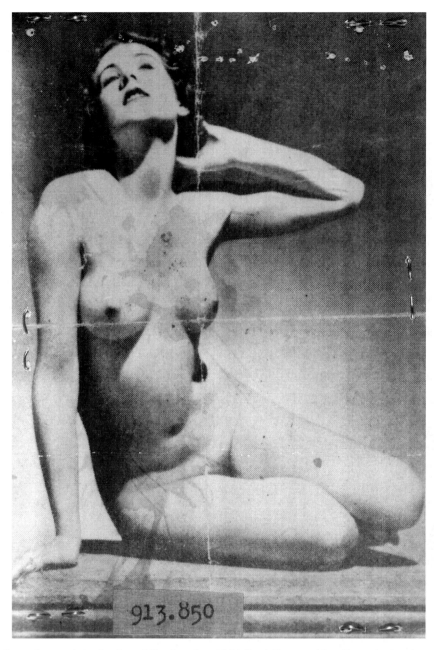

913.850

Two cut negatives deeper into the box following the 1941 Red Square May Day photo above, I ran across this negative. She has an Army Air Corps accession number and was originally a paper print that was obviously folded, probably carried in someone's wallet. At some time the print was stapled onto a heavier paper or card and copied to make the 8" x 10" negative I found. Staples at either side give an idea of original size.

Someone, probably an Attaché, forwarded her photo to Intelligence in Washington.

Who was she? What was she? Does she have anything to do with the Invasion?

Perhaps the person carrying the photo was the important connection. Why was this photo put in US Intelligence files? Why was it filed near/with pre-war photos from Moscow?

I never got answers to any of those questions.

Kronstadt Naval Base, covert German collection of 24 July 1938.

For several years before World War II began, the Luftwaffe had a program of covert aerial photoreconnaissance of key locations in potential enemy countries. Usually posing as civil airliners, specially outfitted He 111s were a favorite vehicle. I have seen examples of similar GX collection over the UK, Netherlands, Belgium and France as well as the Soviet Union.

Naturally the main Soviet naval anchorage in the Baltic was a target.

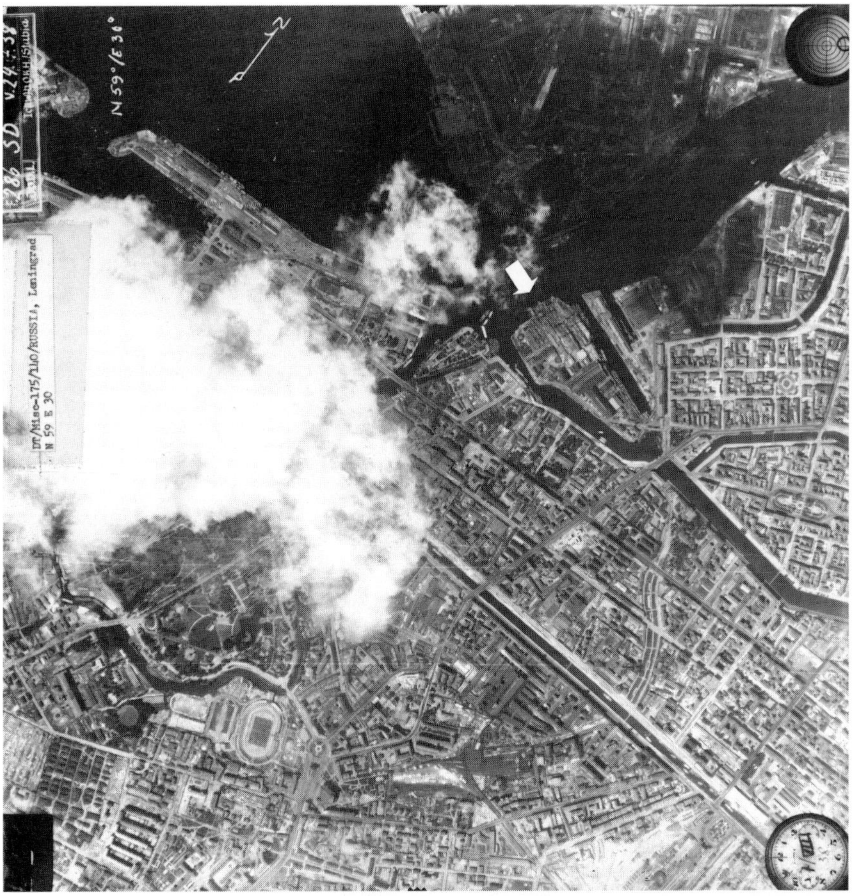
N 59°/E 30°
DT/Misc-175/140/RUSSIA, Leningrad
N 59 E 30

Leningrad shipyards covertly photographed, 24 July 1938. Baltic yards are under cloud. South of the river, Marti yard (arrow) doesn't yet show the aircraft carrier hull we'll see later.

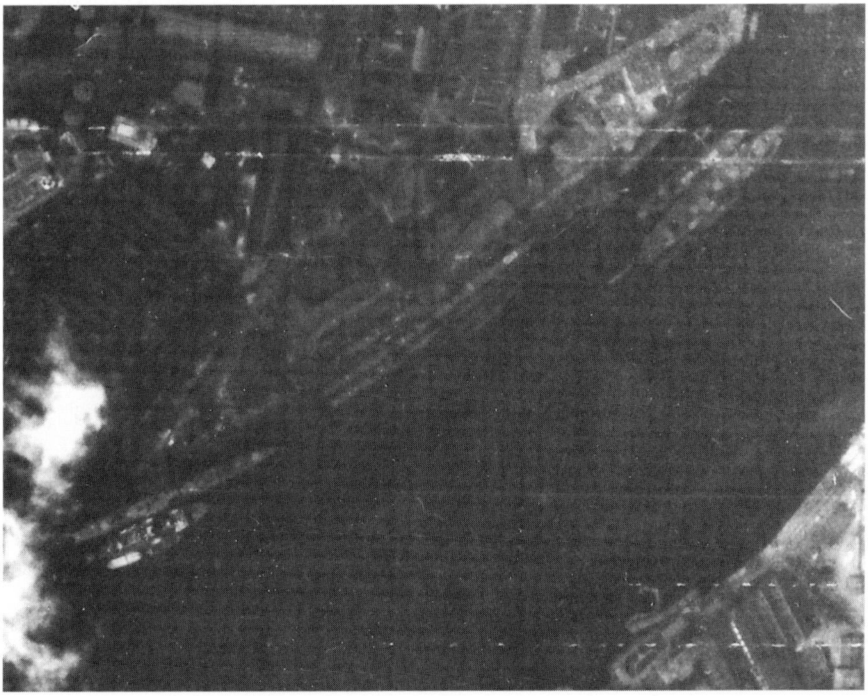

Right, enlargement shows a Soviet *Gangut-Class* battleship in the Neva River.

Sowjet-Ostseeflotte

a) Wasserverdrängung (normale) b) Höchstgeschwindigkeit c) Hauptartillerie d) Torpedorohre.
e) Abmessungen: größte Länge × größte Breite × Tiefgang bei normaler Wasserverdrängung in m. f) Fertigstellung. *) Umbau bzw. Modernisierung.

Schlachtschiffe und Kreuzer

Schlachtschiff
Oktjabrskaja Rewoluzia
a) 23 464 t, b) 22.48 Kn, c) 12 – 30 cm, 16 – 12 cm, 6 – 7.6 cm, d) 4 TR 45 cm ↓, e) 184.8 × 26.9 × 9.1 m, f) 1914/1934*)

Kreuzer
(Kirow-Klasse)
a) 8545 t, b) 35.94 Kn, c) 9 – 18 cm, 6 – 10 cm, d) 6 TR 53.3 cm III, e) 191 × 17.7 × 5.75 m, f) 1938/41
a)   Kirow
b)   Maksim Gorki

Minenkreuzer
Marti
a) 5664 t, b) 18.7 Kn, c) 4 – 13 cm, 7 – 7.6 cm, d) keine TR, e) 122.3 × 15.39 × 6.54 m, f) 1896/1936*)

Zerstörer

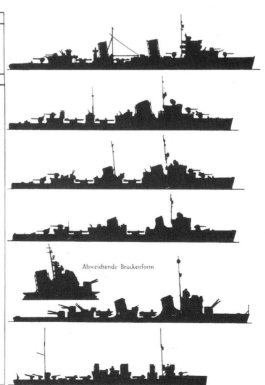

Flottillenführer
(Leningrad-Klasse)
a) 2225 t, b) 43 Kn, c) 5 – 13 cm, 2 – 7.6 cm, d) 8 TR 53.3 cm IIII, e) 127.5 × 11.7 × 3.66 m, f) 1936/37
Namen: Leningrad, Minsk

Zerstörer
a)   Gnewny-Klasse
a) 1657 t, b) 39 Kn, c) 4 – 13 cm, 2 – 7.6 cm, d) 6 TR 53.3 cm III, e) 112.5 × 10.2 × 3.27 m, f) 1939/41
Namen: Grosjaschtschi
b)   Storoshewoj-Klasse
a) 1686 t, b) 38.2 Kn, c) 4 – 13 cm, 2 – 7.6 cm, d) 6 TR 53.3 cm III, e) 112.5 × 10.2 × 3.5 m, f) 1939/41
Namen: Slawny, Strojny, Strogi, Vize-Adm. Drosd, Straschny, Silny, Swirepy
c)   Zerstörer Opytny
(ex Sergo Ordshonikidse)
a) 1570 t, b) 42 Kn, c) 3 – 13 cm, 2 – 7.6 cm, d) 8 TR 53.3 cm IIII, e) 113.5 × 10.2 × 2.9 m, f) ca. 1939
d)   O-Klasse
(Projekt Nr. 30)
a) ca. 2000 t, b) 38–40 Kn, c) 6 – 13 cm, 2 – 7.6 cm, d) 10 TR 53.3 cm IIIII, e) ca. 118 × ? × ?
e)   Dreischornstein-Klasse
(alte Zerstörer)
a) ca. 1300 t, b) 26–31 Kn, c) 4 – 10 cm, 1 – 7.6 cm, d) 9 TR 45 cm III, e) ca. 100 × ca. 9.5 × ca. 3 m, f) 1915/1925*)
1 Zerstörer, Namen: ?

Abweichende Brückenform

U-Boote

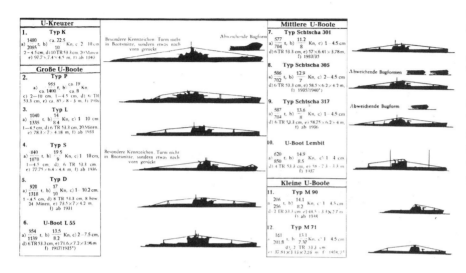

a) Wasserverdrängung über Wasser / getaucht • b) Höchstgeschwindigkeit über Wasser / getaucht • c) Hauptartillerie • d) Torpedorohre •
e) Abmessungen: größte Länge • größte Breite • Tiefgang bei voller Beladung • f) Fertigstellung • g) Umbau bzw. Modernisierung

U-Kreuzer	
1.	**Typ K**
a) 1480 / 2095 t, b) ca. 22.5 / 10 Kn, c) 2 – 10 cm, d) 10 TR 53.3 cm, 20 Minen, e) 97.7 × 7.4 × 4.5 m, f) ab 1940	
Große U-Boote	
2.	**Typ P**
a) 955 / ca. 1400 t, b) ca. 19 / ca. 8 Kn, c) 2 – 10 cm, 1 – 4.5 cm, d) 6 TR 53.3 cm, e) 85 × 8 · 3 m, f) 1936	
3.	**Typ L**
a) 1040 / 1335 t, b) 14 / 8.4 Kn, c) 1 – 10 cm, 1 – 4.5 cm, d) 6 TR 53.3 cm, 20 Minen, e) 78.3 × 7 × 4.18 m, f) ab 1933	
4.	**Typ S**
a) 840 / 1070 t, b) 19.5 / 9 Kn, c) 1 – 10 cm, 1 – 4.5 cm, d) 6 TR 53.3 cm, e) 77.75 × 6.4 × 4.4 m, f) ab 1936	
5.	**Typ D**
a) 920 / 1318 t, b) 17 / 10 Kn, c) 1 – 10.2 cm, 1 – 4.5 cm, d) 8 TR 53.3 cm, 8 bzw. 24 Minen, e) 73.5 × 7 / 4.2 m, f) ab 1931	
6.	**U-Boot L 55**
a) 954 / 1139 t, b) 13.5 / 8.2 Kn, c) 2 – 7.5 cm, d) 6 TR 53.3 cm, e) 71.6 × 7.2 × 3.96 m, f) 1917 (1935*)	

Mittlere U-Boote	
7.	**Typ Schtscha 301**
a) 577 / 704 t, b) 11.2 / 8 Kn, c) 1 – 4.5 cm, d) 6 TR 53.3 cm, e) 57 × 6.41 × 3.78 m, f) 1933/35	
8.	**Typ Schtscha 305**
a) 586 / 702 t, b) 12.9 / 7 Kn, c) 2 – 4.5 cm, d) 6 TR 53.3 cm, e) 58.5 × 6.2 × 4.2 m, f) 1935 (1940*)	
9.	**Typ Schtscha 317**
a) 587 / 704 t, b) 13.6 / 8 Kn, c) 1 – 4.5 cm, d) 6 TR 53.3 cm, e) 58.75 × 6.2 × 4 m, f) 1937	
10.	**U-Boot Lembit**
a) 620 / 850 t, b) 14.9 / 8.5 Kn, c) 1 – 4 cm, d) 4 TR 53.3 cm, e) 58 – 7.3 – 3.3 m, f) 1937	

Kleine U-Boote	
11.	**Typ M 90**
a) 206 / 256 t, b) 14.1 / 8.2 Kn, c) 1 – 4.5 cm, d) 2 TR 53.3 cm, e) 44.5 × 3.4 × 2.7 m, f) ab 1938	
12.	**Typ M 71**
a) 161 / 201.8 t, b) 13.1 / 7.37 Kn, c) 1 – 4.5 cm, d) 2 TR 53.3 cm, e) 37.81 × 3.13 × 2.28 m, f) 1934/37	

Besondere Kennzeichen: Turm nicht in Bootsmitte, sondern etwas nach vorn gerückt

Abweichende Bugform

Abweichende Bugformen

Abweichende Bugform

The next four photos of Kronstadt Naval Base were covertly collected from a ship heading for Leningrad, probably sometime in the mid-1930s. PA/TM markings show they were from Target Material files. Below, rounding the south end of the base, three old (bow rake says WW I or earlier) destroyers/patrol boats were moored with hulls overlapping.

PA/TM-2/32E

36

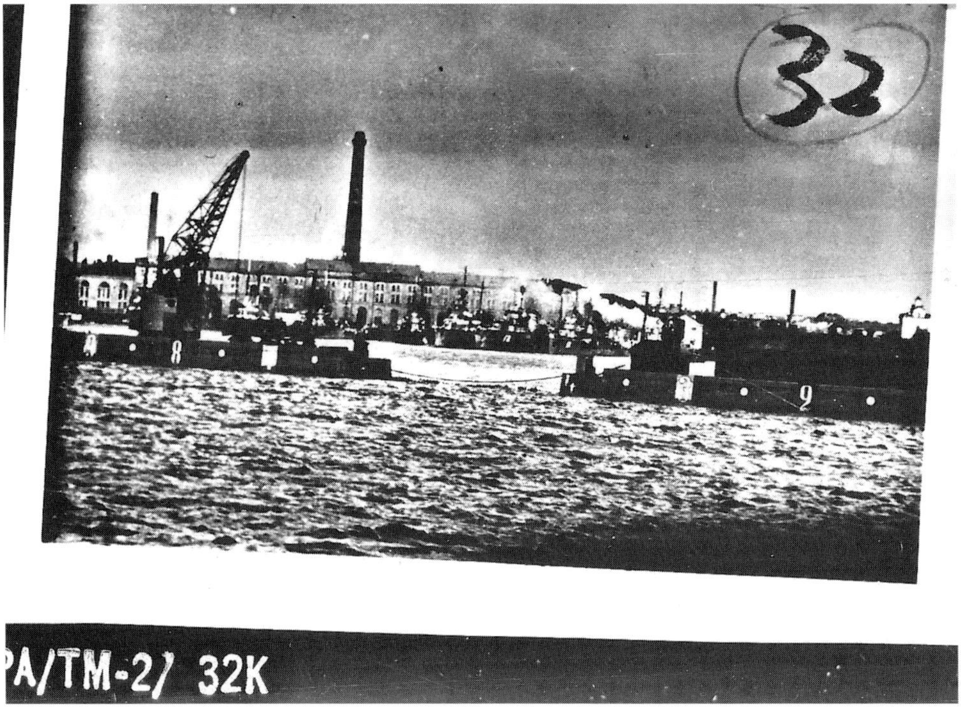
32
PA/TM-2/ 32K

Left, rounding the east end of Kronstadt harbor, looking northwest at destroyer moorings.

Below, harbor facilities. Markings match the Kronstadt breakwater but I can't match it to a specific location or 'look direction'.

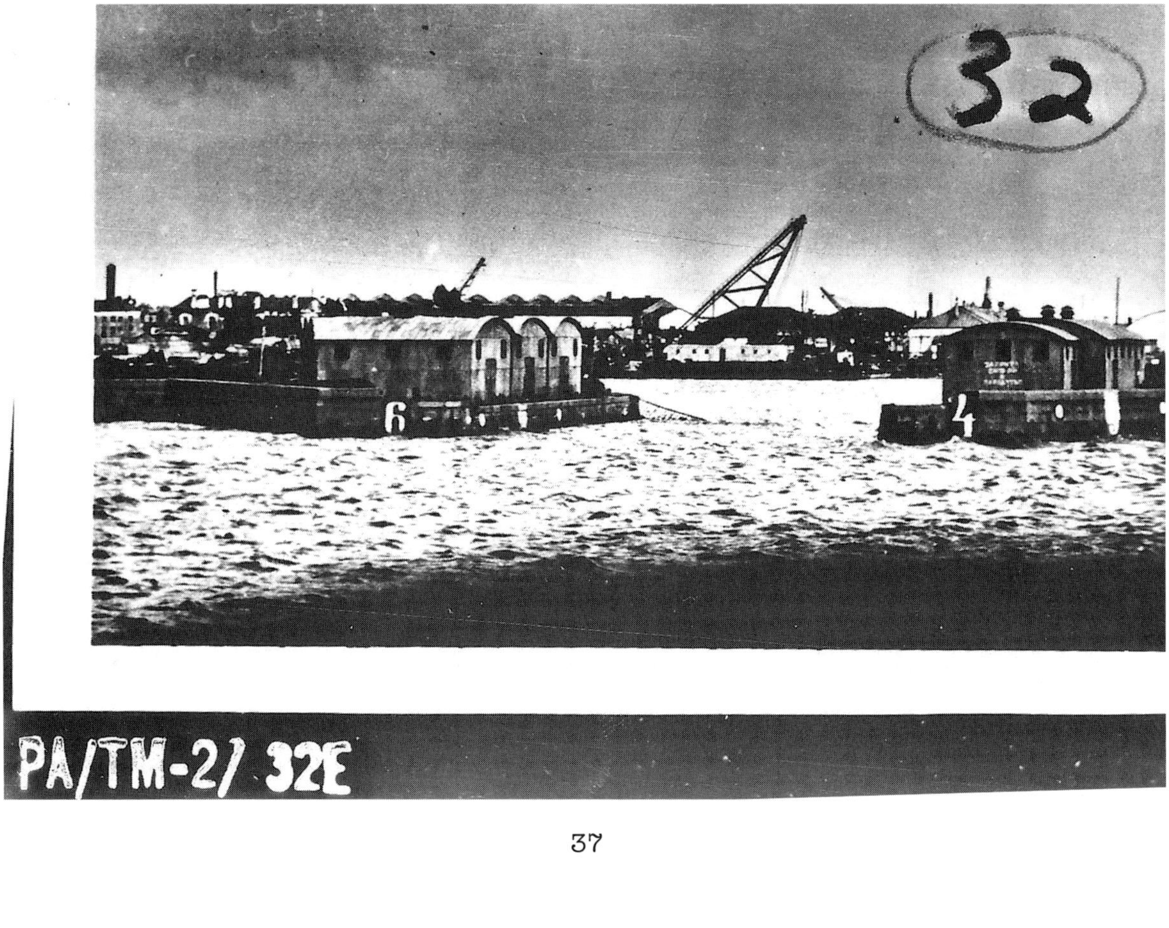
32
PA/TM-2/ 32E

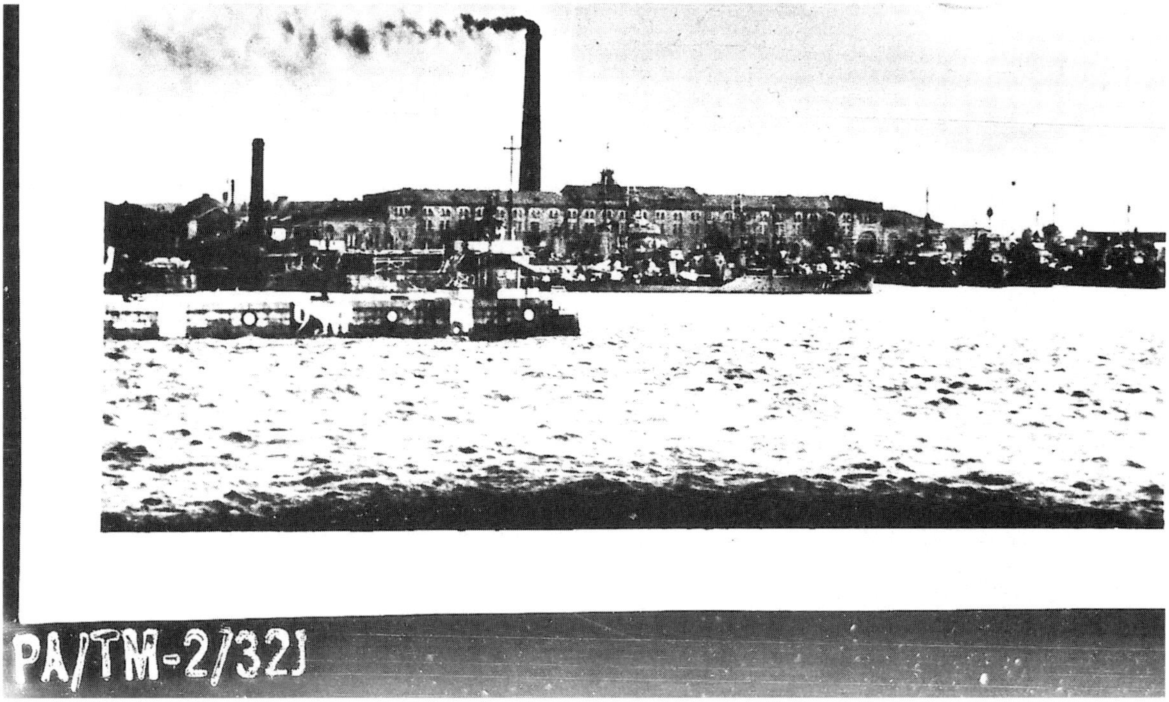
PA/TM-2/32J

Kronstadt, looking west while rounding Kotlin Island. On the right, at least four destroyers are moored facing out. We see the side of a probable *Taifun-Class* torpedo boat moored with the side facing us. It overlaps another vessel, probably of the same class.

Below, is German heavy cruiser, *ex-Lutzow*, sold to the Soviets as part of the 1939 Nazi-Soviet Pact that carved up Poland. The incomplete CA was taken to Leningrad and renamed *Petropavlovsk.* Only its two lower turrets have their twin 8" guns but the ship was reportedly used as a floating battery against the German Invasion in 1942, and again in 1944. The Luftwaffe photographed their former cruiser at Leningrad on 1 June 1942, moored in an out-of-the way ship basin southeast of the city.

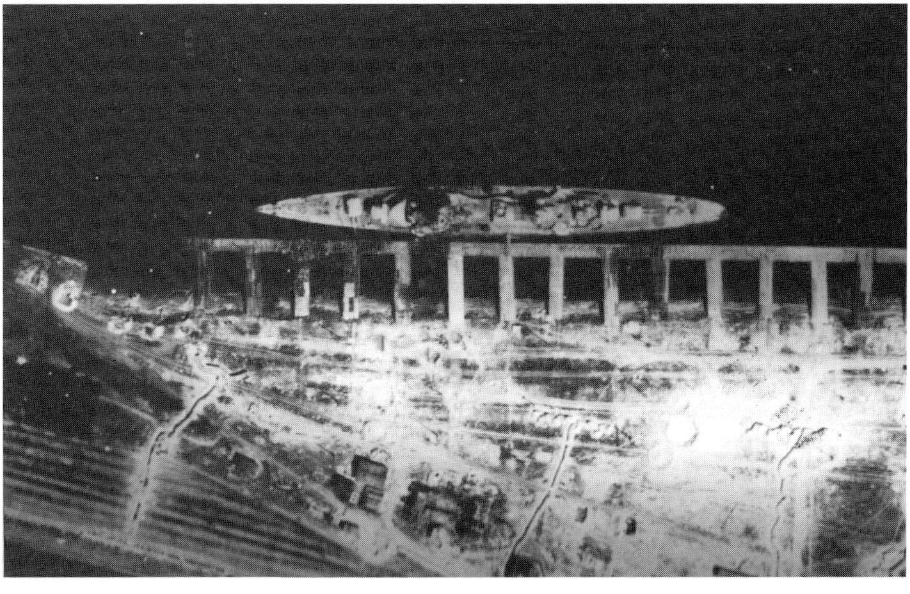

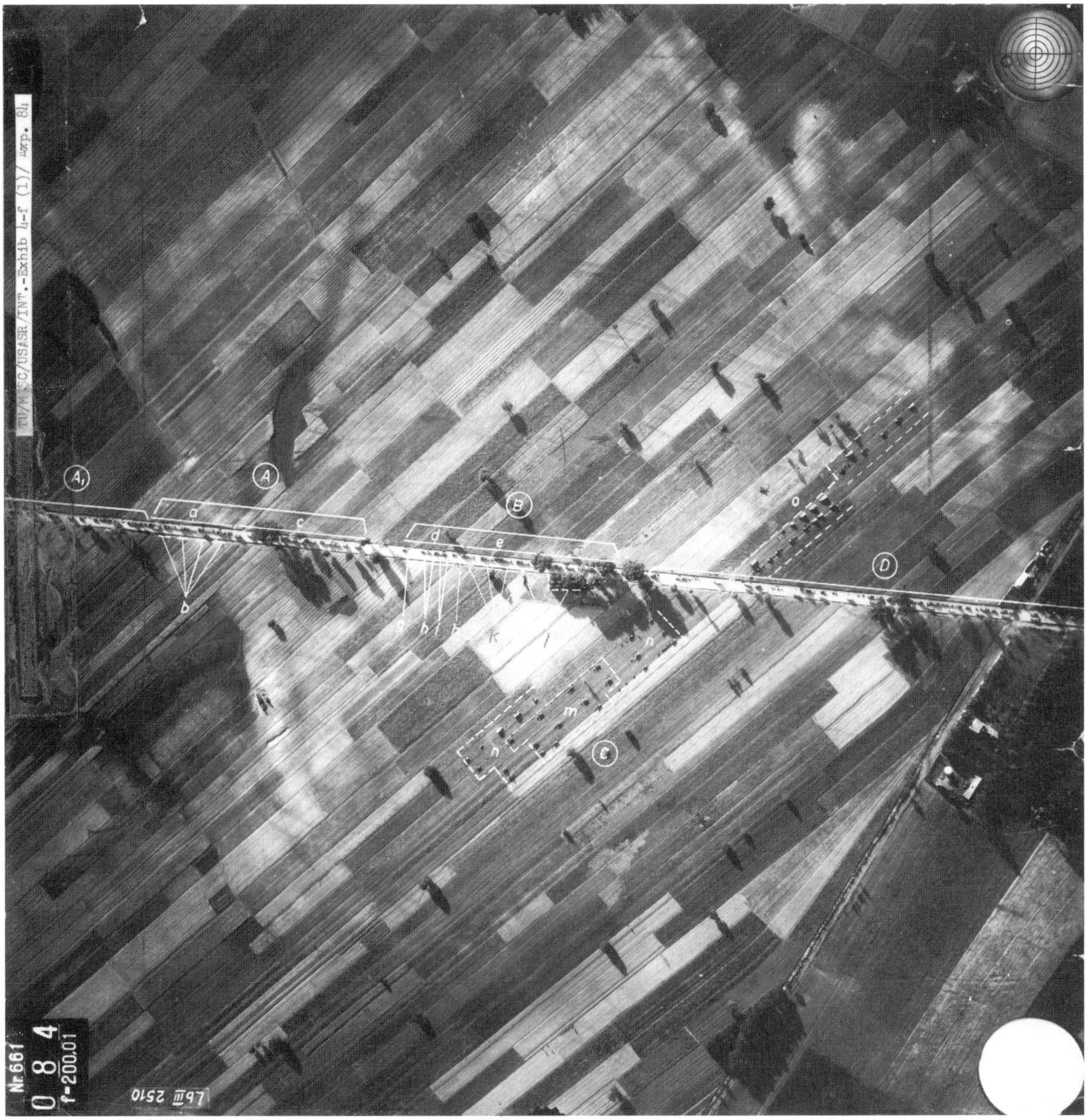
Nr.661
0 8 4
f=200.01

On 1 September 1939, one week after Hitler and Stalin agreed to divide Poland between them, Germany invaded. This is 13 September near Jedlnia, 40 miles south of Warsaw.

It shows a German artillery and Panzer column heading for the Vistula (10 miles east). The column is moving from right to left (north is down). Four days after this photo was taken the Soviets invaded Poland.

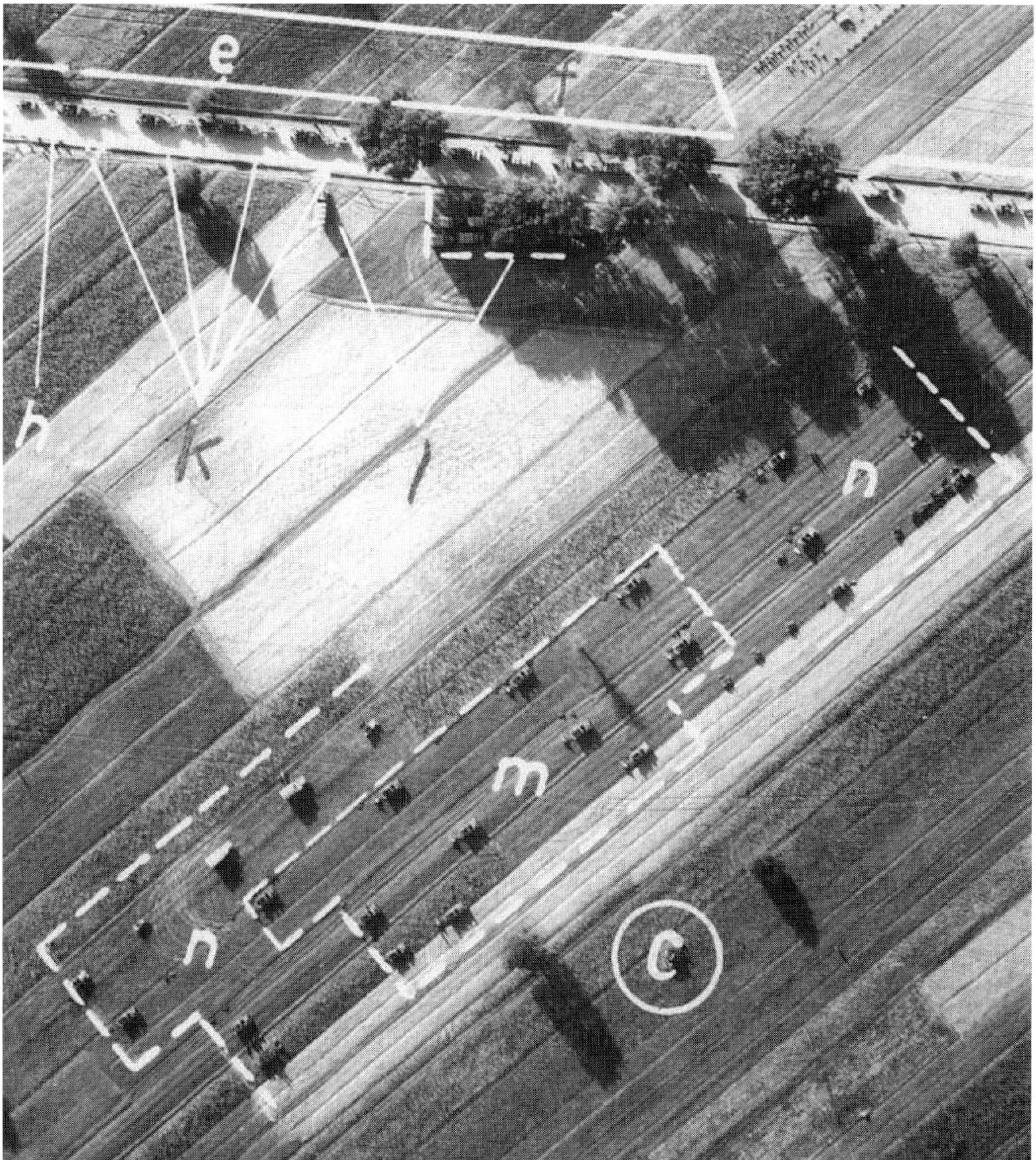
e
f
h
k
l
n
m
n
c

Enlargement of the previous photo. I expected to see use of horses but everything is mechanized. Triple-tows are: prime mover-caisson-gun.

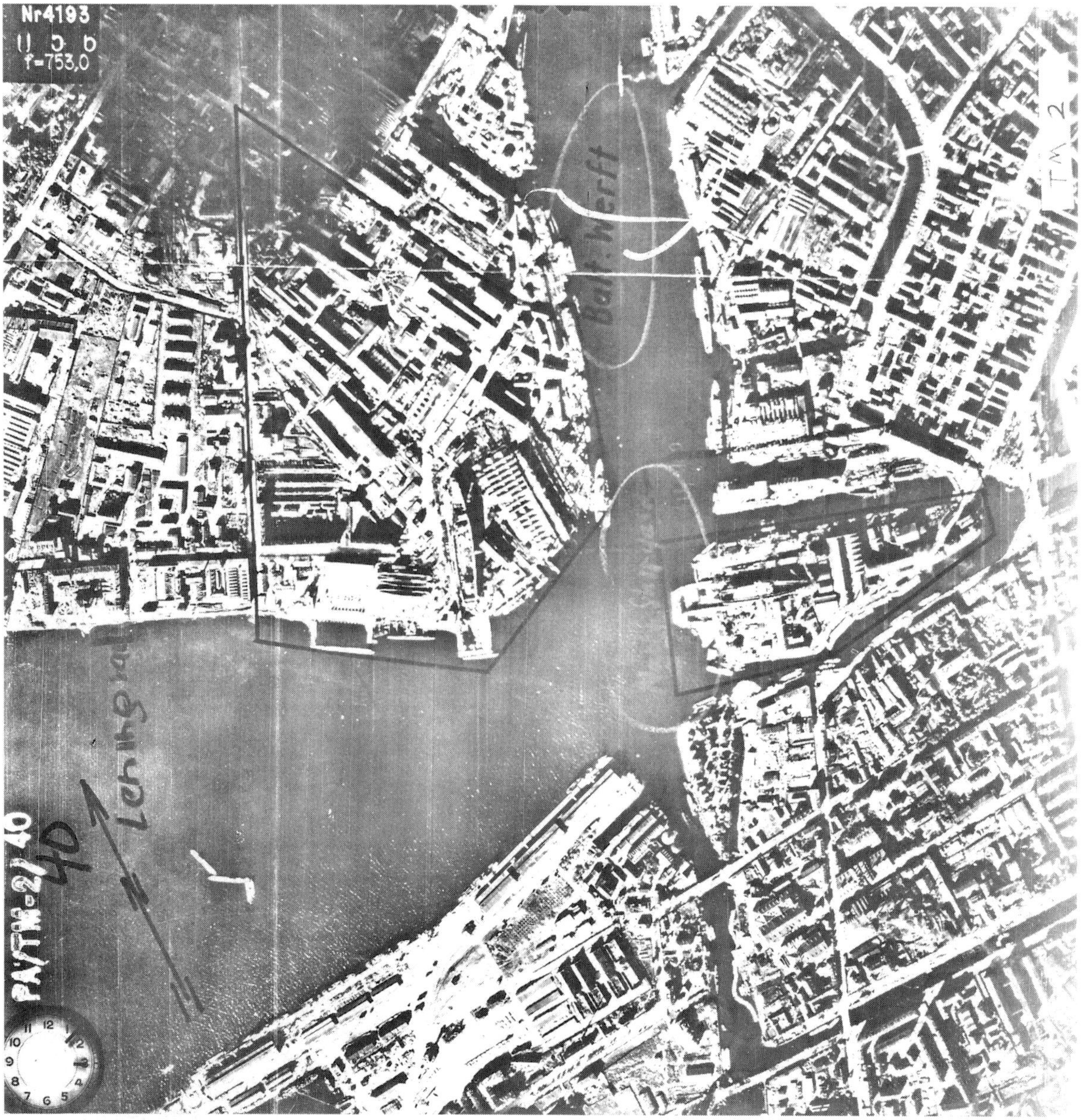
Nr4193
f=753,0
TM 2
PA/TM-2/40

Leningrad coverage in 1940. Writing is the work of German PIs. Baltic Shipyard is on the left. My left arrow shows what a German PI called a 787' long battleship hull in building ways. Marti Yards are on the right and that arrow indicates a 656' long aircraft carrier hull under construction (it may be a battlecruiser conversion). German Intelligence watched those two hulls like a hawk.

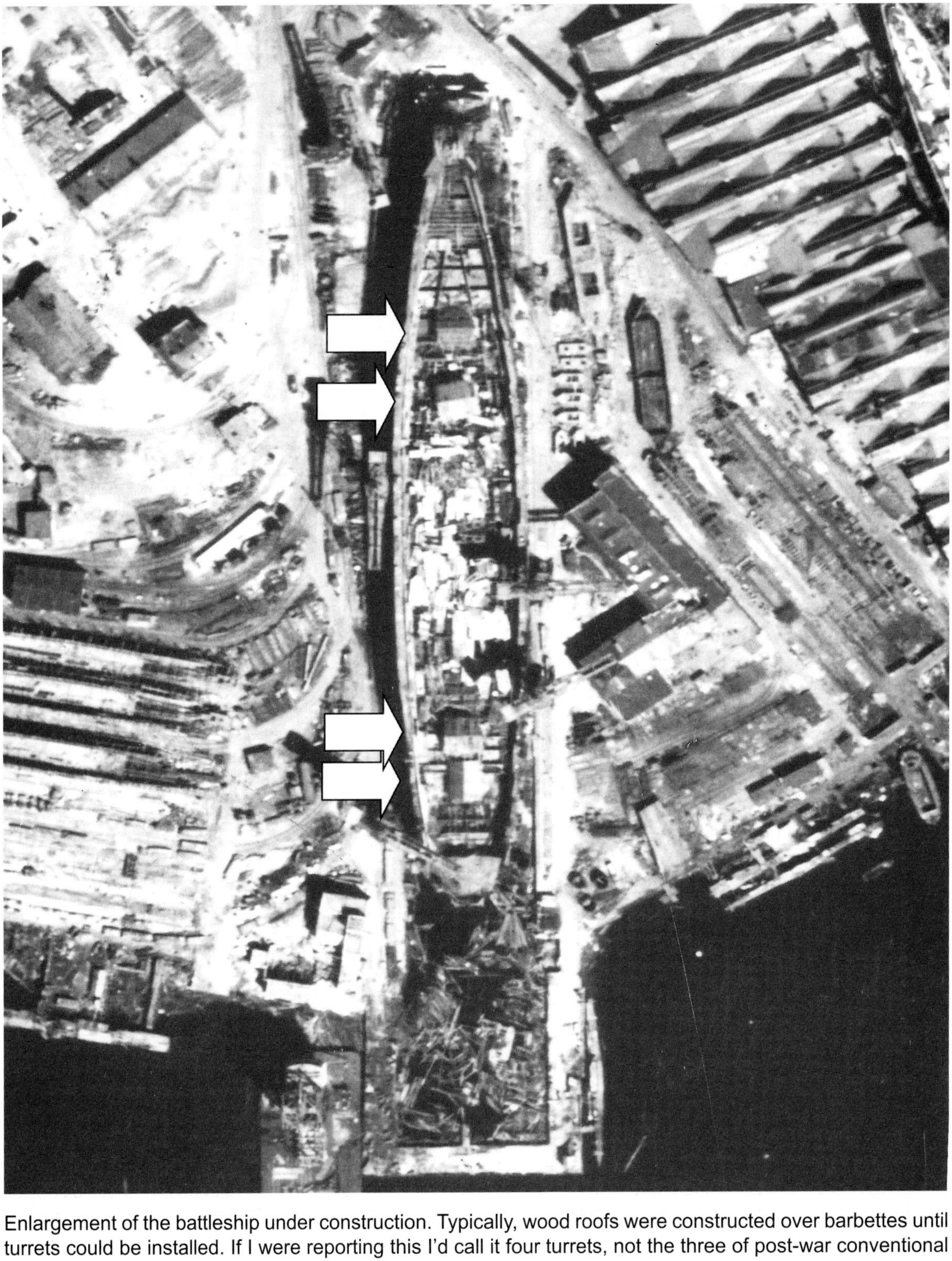

Enlargement of the battleship under construction. Typically, wood roofs were constructed over barbettes until turrets could be installed. If I were reporting this I'd call it four turrets, not the three of post-war conventional wisdom.

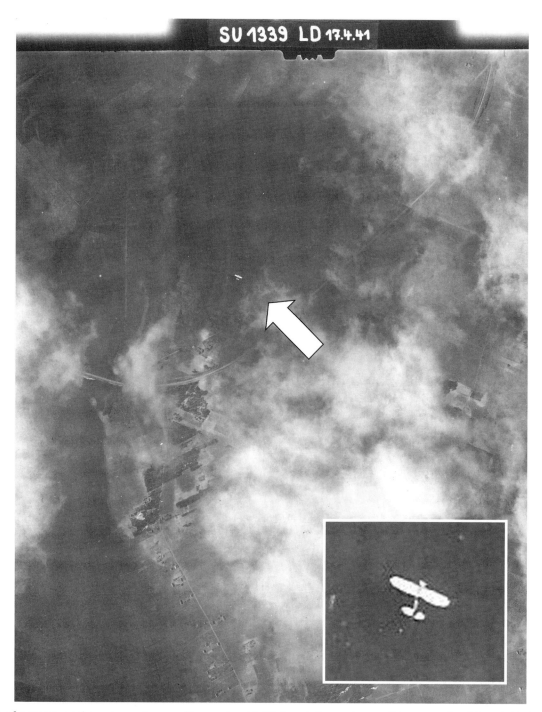

One of our researchers came to my office and said, 'Colonel, I've got something you should see'. He had a 17 April 1941 GX roll copy neg on a light table, running it down to identify a place someone wanted printed.

Directly below the Luftwaffe plane was a tiny black blob on the neg that enlarged to be a Soviet Polikarpov I-152 (ceiling 29K). The German plane was at 35K altitude. The researcher rolled film and we watched that Red fighter pace the recon plane for almost 100 frames deeper into the Soviet Union.

This German recce mission over Russia was two months before the invasion.

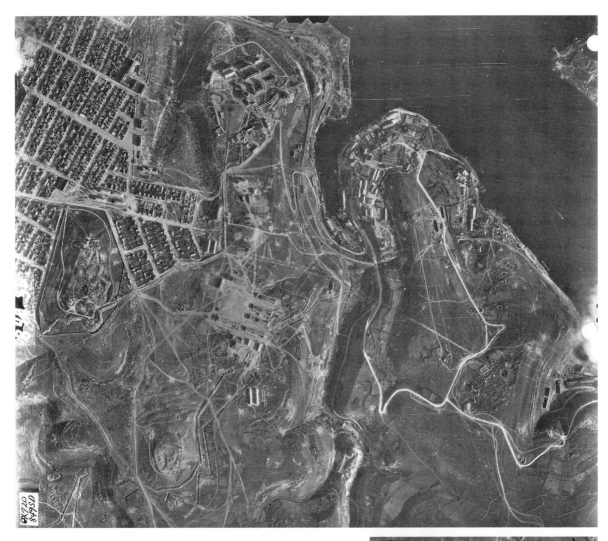

Almost a month before invasion, Luftwaffe was back over Sevastopol, probably flying from Romania. This good quality 7 May 1941 imagery shows the city (upper left) and some military installations/forts south of Severnaya Bay.

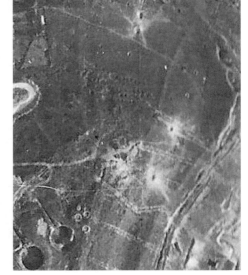

Enlargement shows obvious bomb craters suggesting the photo date is wrong.

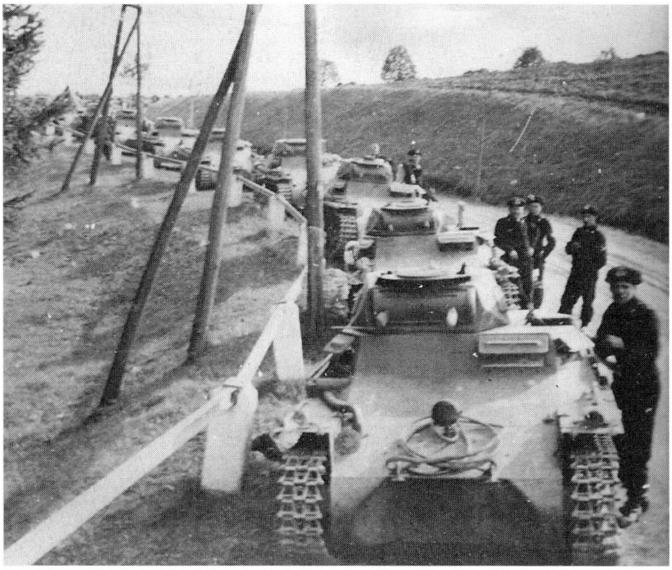

German Pz I tanks lined up, may not be for Barbarossa. Could be the 1 September 1939 invasion of Poland.

With only two machine guns Pz Is were seriously under-armed and armored by 1941. They were still useful for reconnaissance and as scout cars.

Note: Tanks, self-propelled artillery, assault guns, tank destroyers, half-tracks, scout cars and armored cars are collectively called AFVs—Armored Fighting Vehicles.

Stalin had more planes than Hitler and nimble Polikarpov I-15 fighter planes were effective in Spain in 1936-7. By 1941 they were outclassed by newer Messerschmitt Bf 109s.

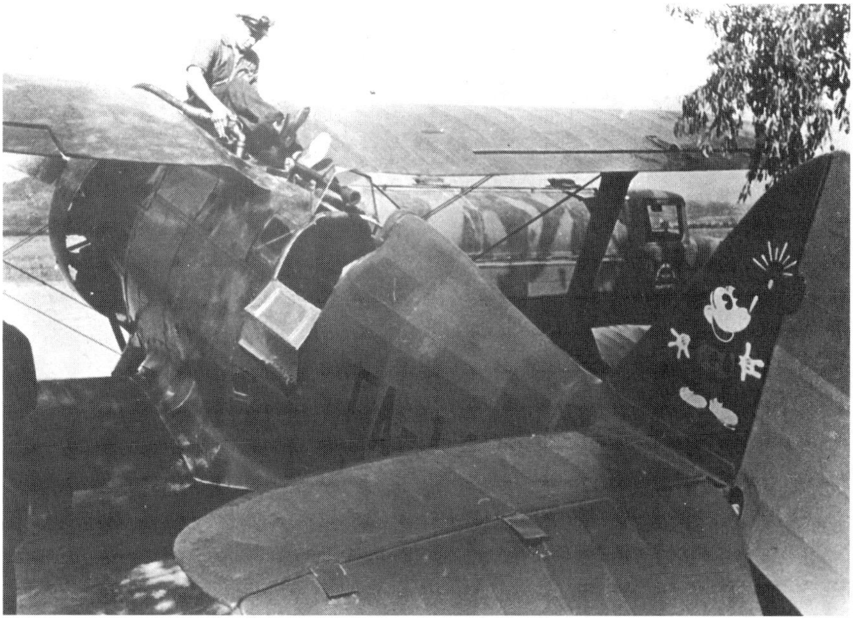

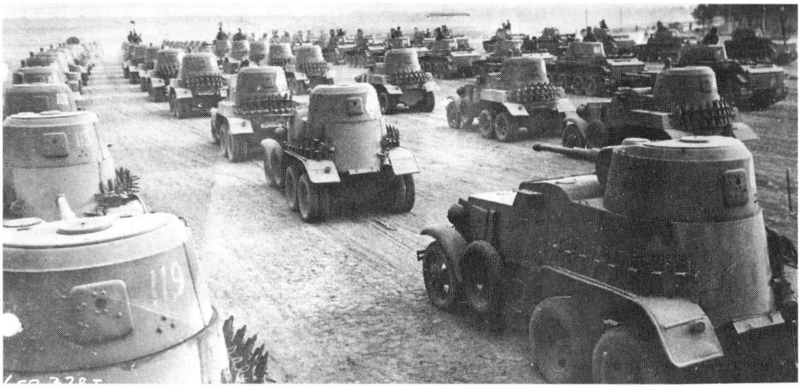
119

Soviets had 20,000 armored vehicles but most weren't competitive by 1941. Below, BA-10 armored cars and BT-7 tanks.

Chapter III

INVASION 1941

Germany had recently successfully intimidated Austria, invaded and easily dominated Czechoslovakia, Poland, Denmark, Norway, The Netherlands, Belgium and France. Only England had denied them. In the years before war began again in Europe, no intelligence activity had much more than the word of spies, stolen communications, reports from attaches and materials culled from libraries. Only Britain and Germany were exploiting the strategic value of modern aerial photography over potential enemies—both covertly.

Stalin and Hitler signed a Non-Aggression Pact in August 1939, then invaded Poland and each took half. That pact lasted twenty-two months and I'm surprised two such paranoid dictators trusted each other that long. The Soviet Union had plenty of warning that a German invasion was imminent, but they were rolled over. German forces were successful beyond their dreams.

Hitler used 3,350 tanks for his invasion, many of them Pz IVs—a fine tank for its day but under-gunned with a low velocity 50mm main gun. Though outnumbered four-to-one, the Panzers were better (the superlative T-34s were just being introduced), and Stalin's tanks were scattered. Hitler's armor was concentrated. The Soviets also had more aircraft but the Luftwaffe organization and equipment were more effective. Many German Infantry, Armor and Air commanders and staff had recent combat experience—successful combat experience. Most important, Germany had a cadre of well-trained non-commissioned officers and Infantry warfare is essentially at the Squad level. All the Soviets had was experience fighting against 'White Army' counter revolutionaries.

In 1936-38 Stalin conducted a purge of 'politically unreliable' officers, losing many of his most competent field commanders. There is some evidence that Stalin was tricked into the purge by German disinformation. In any case he, was forced to rely on Communist Party loyalists of questionable background, education and skill in battle. The Wehrmacht had a well-qualified, highly professional officer corps with experience and tradition behind them.

Below, early morning, 22 June 1941. German troops crossing a bridge in occupied Poland entering Soviet Poland. It is hard to see how the Soviets wouldn't be aware of a force that size building up on their doorstep.

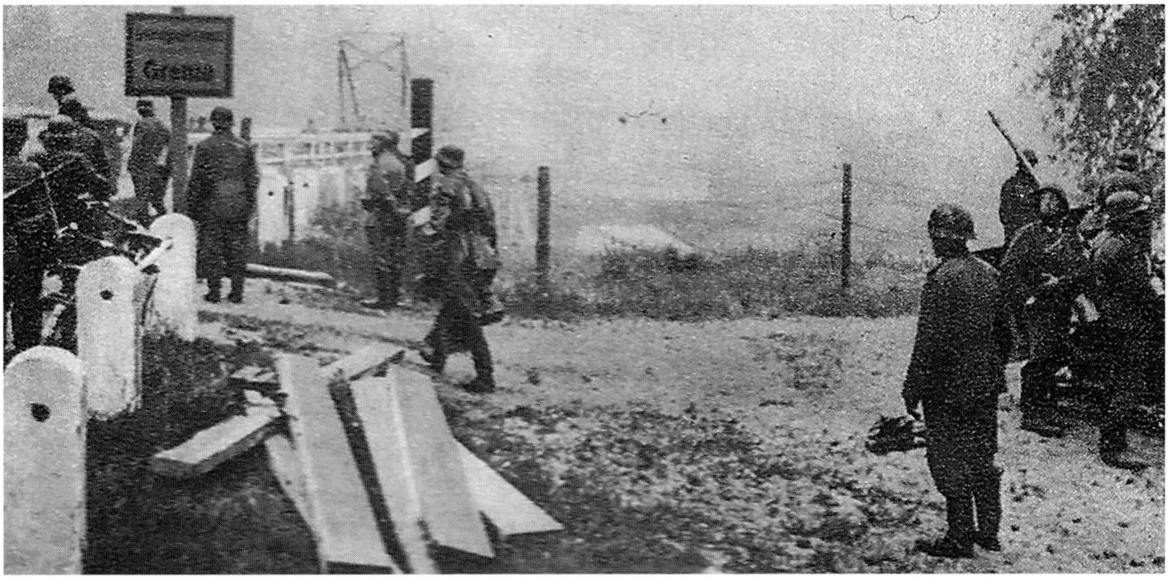

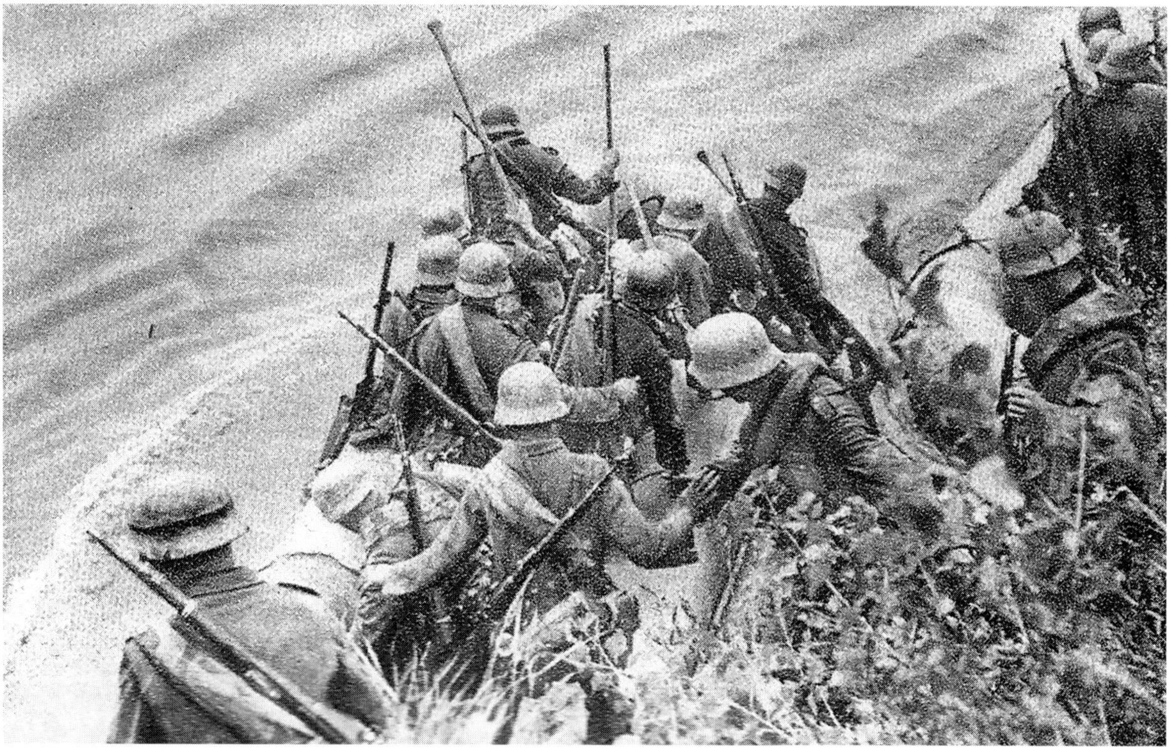

Crossing the Danube into Soviet territory from ally Romania. Others following Hitler's lead and furnishing forces to attack the Soviet Union were: Italy, Slovakia, Finland and Hungary.

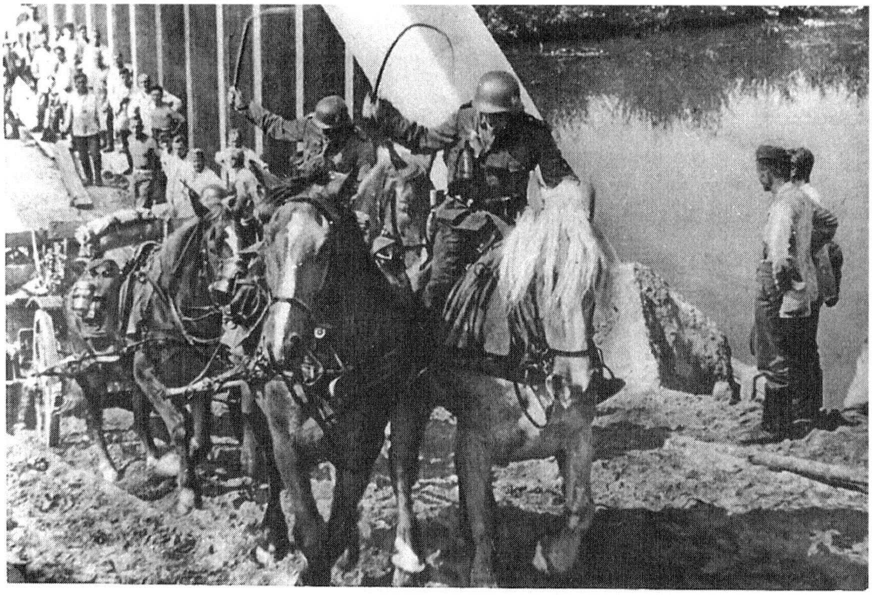

Getting supplies over the Bzura River in front of a crowd. West of Warsaw, June 1941.

11 Bruecke ueber die Bzura N von Platek

913.331

A Polikarpov I-153 Chaika (Sea Gull), upgraded version of the I-15 fighter (note retractable landing gear), under camouflage netting and a pilot ready to fly. A starter truck was used to spin the prop until the motor kicked over.

Introduced in 1938, well after most other nations had gone to monoplanes, I-153s remained in use for much of the war, more often as bombers than fighters. When Barbarossa began I-15/I-153s made up a third of available Soviet Air Force fighters. They claimed responsibility for some 800 kills in the first two months of war but the plane gave up at least 100 knots airspeed to competing German Bf 109Fs and many German pilots had combat experience over Spain, Poland and Britain while Stalin's purges in the '30s had eliminated many good Soviet pilots. By August their numbers were decimated.

Within days of Barbarossa's kick-off most of the Red Air Force was swept from the skies over advancing German troops or destroyed on the ground.[1]

By 1942 all the Polikarpov fighters were hopelessly outclassed by German Messerschmitt and Focke-Wulf aircraft in everything but turn radius.

---

[1] In the first nine days of Barbarossa 3,200 Soviet planes were destroyed on the ground and 1,400 in the air.

48

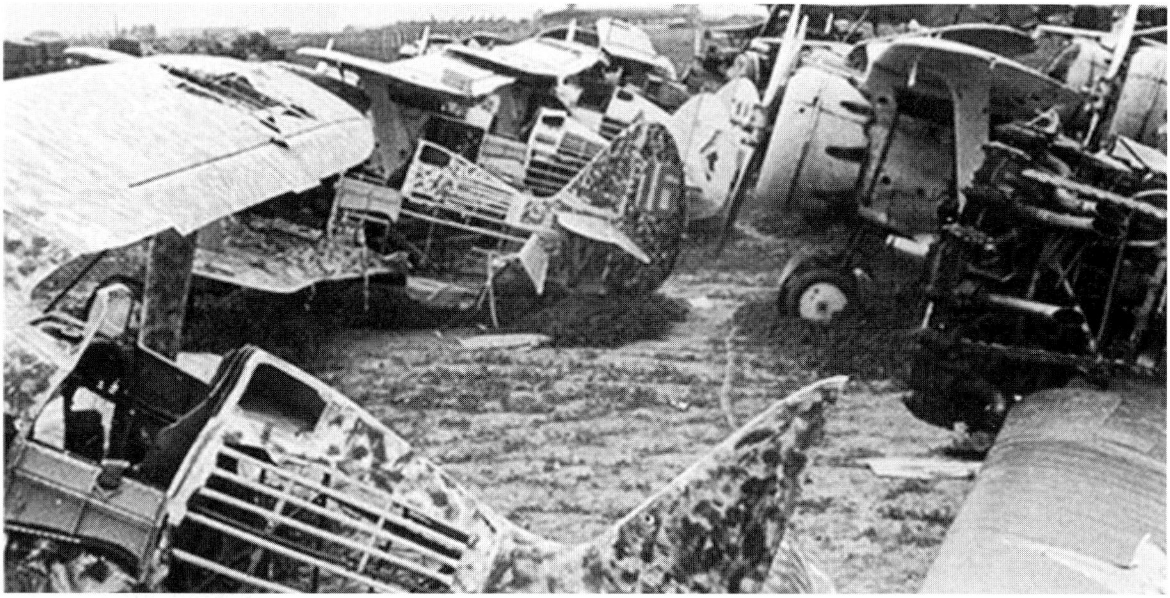

Minsk, 1941. Straight-wing fighters are Polikarpov I-15bis/I-152. Gull-wing aircraft are I-153 fighters. These were destroyed 400 miles east of the Barbarossa start line.

Below, destruction at a Soviet airfield in Lithuania in the first days of war. Wings in the foreground appear to be from Polikarpov I-16 (Soviets didn't usually put national markings on the upper surface). A Tupolev SB-2M medium bomber is at right. In the distance above it is a Tupolev ANT-40. Moving left, the bi-planes (one facing away, the other looking left) are possibly Polikarpov I-5s (fighters from 1930s) or I-15bis. That cross on a wing at left is the Lithuanian Air Force national marking.

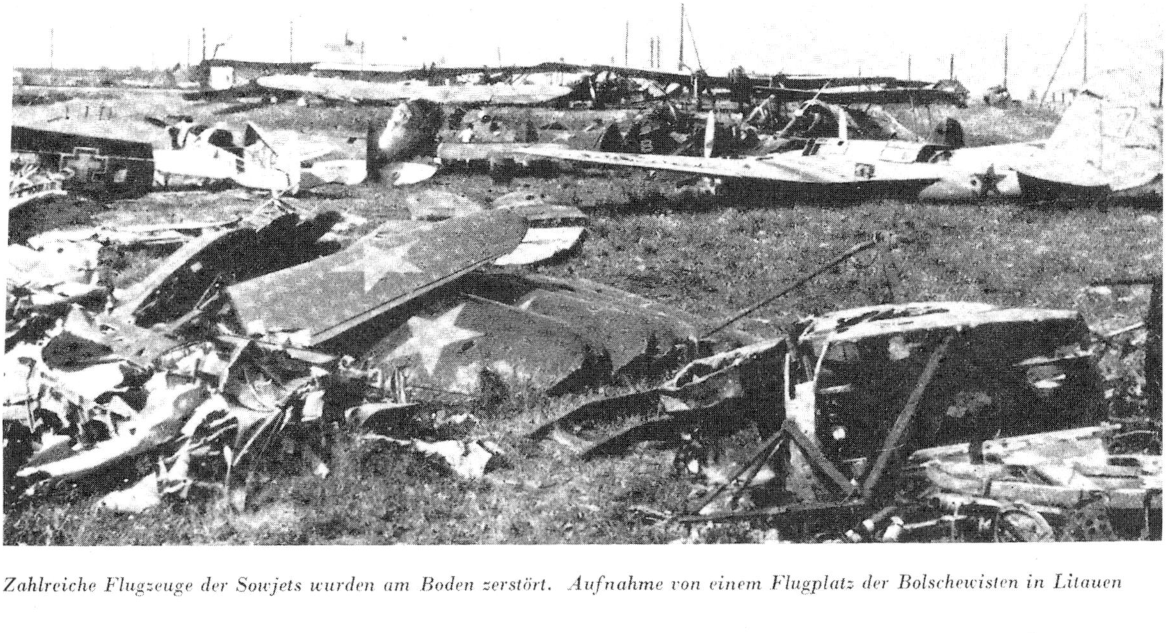

Zahlreiche Flugzeuge der Sowjets wurden am Boden zerstört. Aufnahme von einem Flugplatz der Bolschewisten in Litauen

Numerous Soviet planes destroyed on the ground. Picture of a Soviet air field in Lithuania.

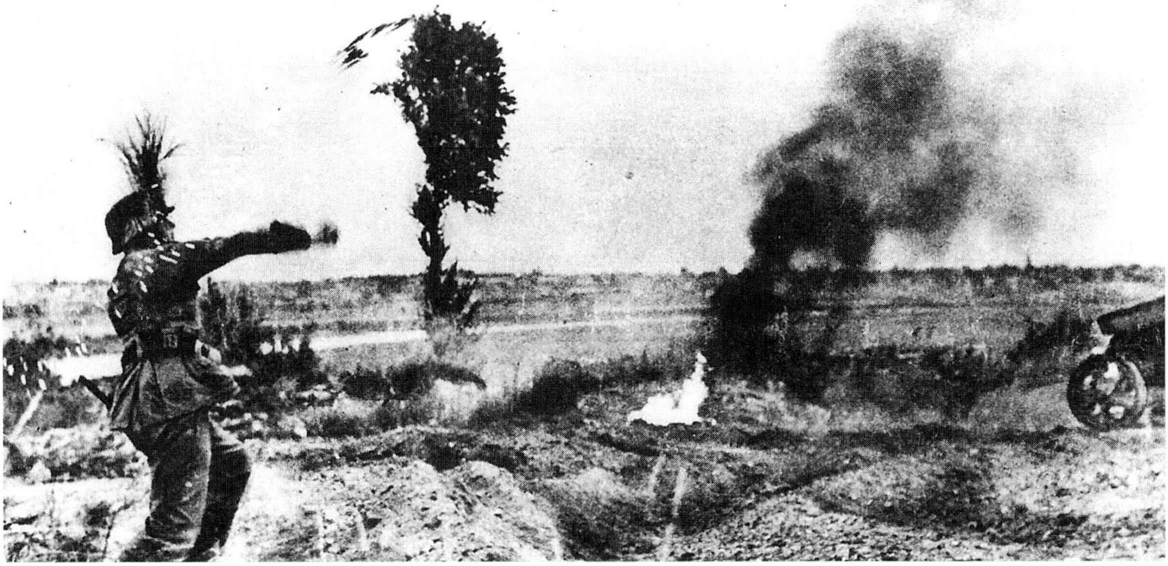

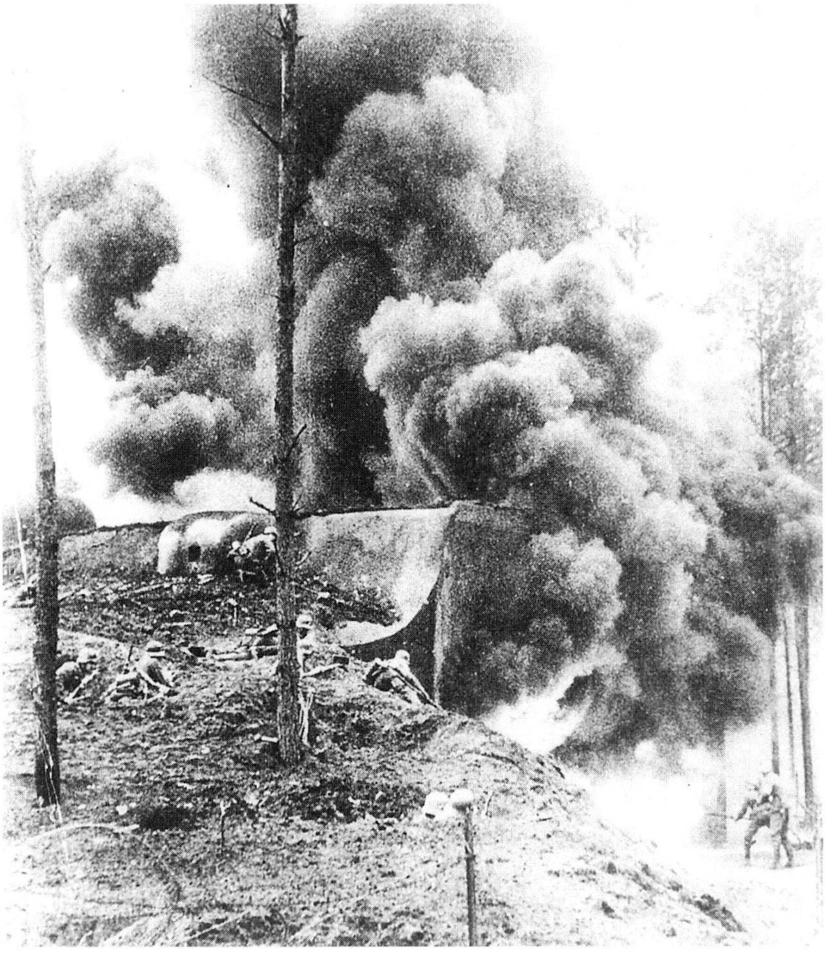

Throwing a Molotov cocktail and flame-throwing a bunker. I like both of these pictures but I am always skeptical of 'combat' photos where the camera man is too close to the action, not looking at it from behind. Both photos were undated but I found them in boxes with material clearly from Barbarossa. Either photo could actually be of training or the Invasion of Poland.

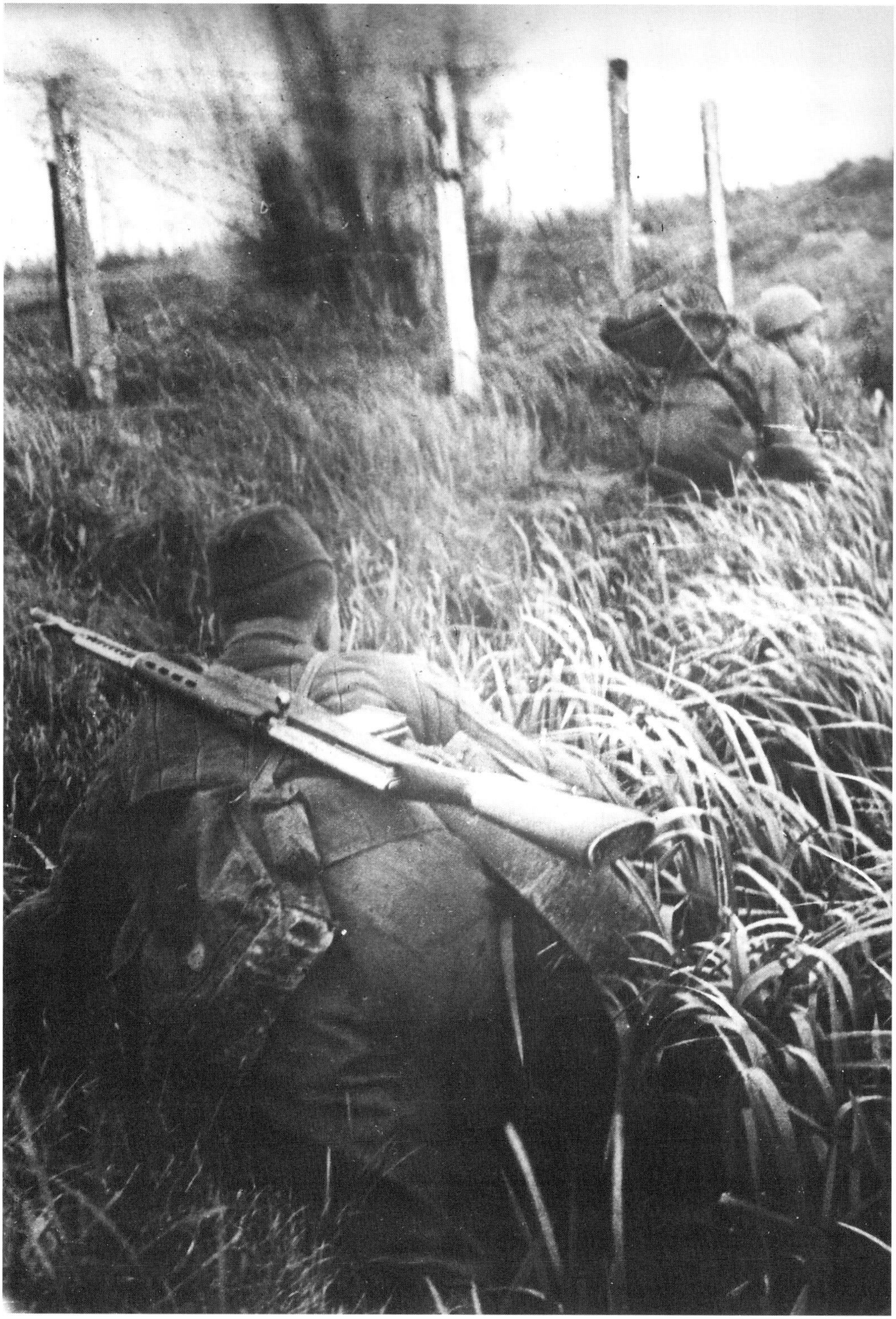

Troops with packs, 1940 Tokarev SVT semi-automatic rifles slung and explosions going off inside what appears to be a wire-marked 'safe area' make this smack of publicity photography during a training exercise.

Two days into Barbarossa German 4th Panzer Group met Soviet 3rd and 12th Mechanized Corps in a massive armored engagement northeast of Raseiniai, Soviet Occupied Lithuania. From 23 to 27 June, various tank and mechanized columns moving east sought to cross rivers and Soviets attempted to block crossings. The Soviet force was larger but German units better handled. German armor was mainly Pz IV Infantry support tanks and Pz IIIs designed as tank killers. Other AFV were Pz.Kpfw 38(t) mediums and Pz.Kpfw 35(t) light tanks inherited from the take-over of Czechoslovakia, all superior to the mass of Soviet BT-7s and T-26s.

The Soviets also fielded three tanks the Germans didn't know about; the superlative T-34 medium and a battalion of monster KV-1 and KV-2 heavy tanks with armor German 37mm anti-tank guns couldn't even dent. Light Soviet tanks didn't fare well in the battle and were sparingly used during the rest of Barbarossa.

The foreground tank is a Pz.Kpfw 38(t). Those behind it are Pz.Kpfw 35(t). Armor and gun size/muzzle velocity made these Czech tanks useful but obsolescent.

If the Soviet 'heavies' hadn't run out of gas and ammunition, battles around Raseiniai might have ended differently. As it was, when the Soviets withdrew east they'd lost 704 of 749 tanks and Germans still had most of the 245 they'd started with.

Soviet Northwest Frontier defenses were in shambles.

Surprisingly, there is no GX coverage of this epic battle. Missions were flown in this area in April 1941, all above 35K altitude implying covert collection. The Soviets had no fighters with the speed and rate of climb to intercept at that altitude.

I had high hopes of seeing aerial recon of the battle, at least to see what the ground looked like either before or after the event, but it was not to be. I told Susan the area I needed and she sent me SIS plot microfilm for the proper Degree Square. There was only one mission near the Raseiniai action—19 June 1941. Five days before the battle and two days before the invasion German recon mission collected spot photography on three locations just east of the Dubysa River, six exposures at each location. Could be crossings. Could be Soviet tank lagers. Boy, I really wanted to see those three spots.

Sadly, that GX box couldn't be found at NARA II. Misfiled? Misappropriated? It's an old library axiom that three moves equals one fire and I know the GX collection has moved three times—DoD holdings in Suitland, MD Records Center—to NARA storage in Alexandria, VA—to NARA II in College Park, Maryland.

Perhaps no strategic GX photo missions were flown over the battle area because German Commanders felt they were getting enough information on the ground. Perhaps the Luftwaffe didn't have complete control of the air or perhaps because they were filling the air with attack sorties supporting the tank battle. There may have been tactical aerial photo sorties flown, but to my knowledge none of that film has survived.

Meanwhile, 275 miles south-southeast, near Brody in Ukraine, another massive armored clash was being fought at the same time (23-30 June 1941). Six German Mechanized Corps comprised of heavy Infantry (Grenadiers) and 750 tanks, mostly German but augmented with appropriated Czech, French and British tanks, were moving east. They were opposed by 3,500 Soviet tanks, including a few T-34 and KVs. Infantry on both sides took heavy losses. One German Grenadier Division lost 8,000 of its 11,000 strength. The Germans lost 200 tanks. Soviets lost 800 tanks, mostly to Luftwaffe action.

Susan again researched the coordinates I asked for and we discovered the plots in that Degree Square begin with 'Part II' and 1943 imagery. Plots for everything earlier are missing. Either the people microfilming SIS Plots before they were destroyed skipped a Degree Square Book or it was microfilmed out of order and can only be found now at random.

Bummer!

German soldiers looking over an abandoned Soviet Klimenti Voroshilov KV-2 tank. It doesn't appear disabled—probably abandoned when it ran out of fuel or ammunition. The size of its 152mm howitzer gun dictated that ungainly turret, and turrets determine tank size. This tank had armor impervious to German 37mm Pz III and anti-tank weapons. Note the wide tread needed to carry the tank's 57 tons. Wide tread was a feature that would prove more advantageous as winter arrived.

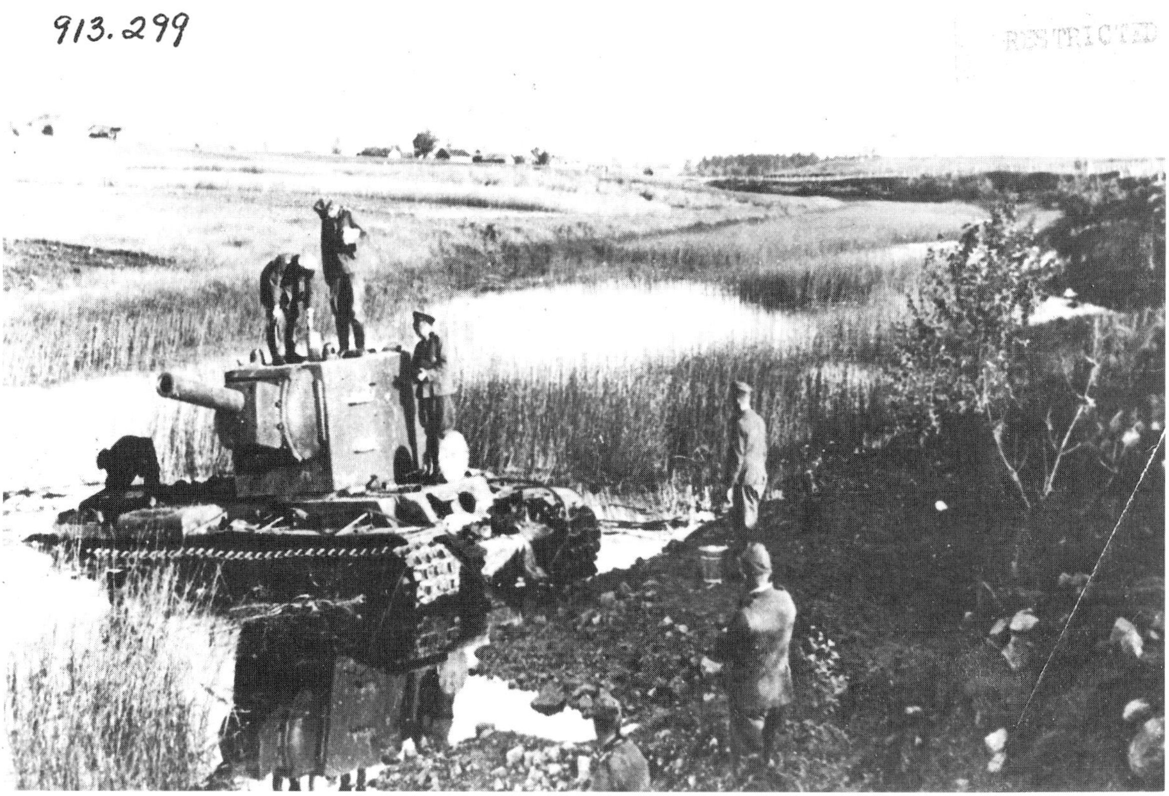
913.299
RESTRICTED

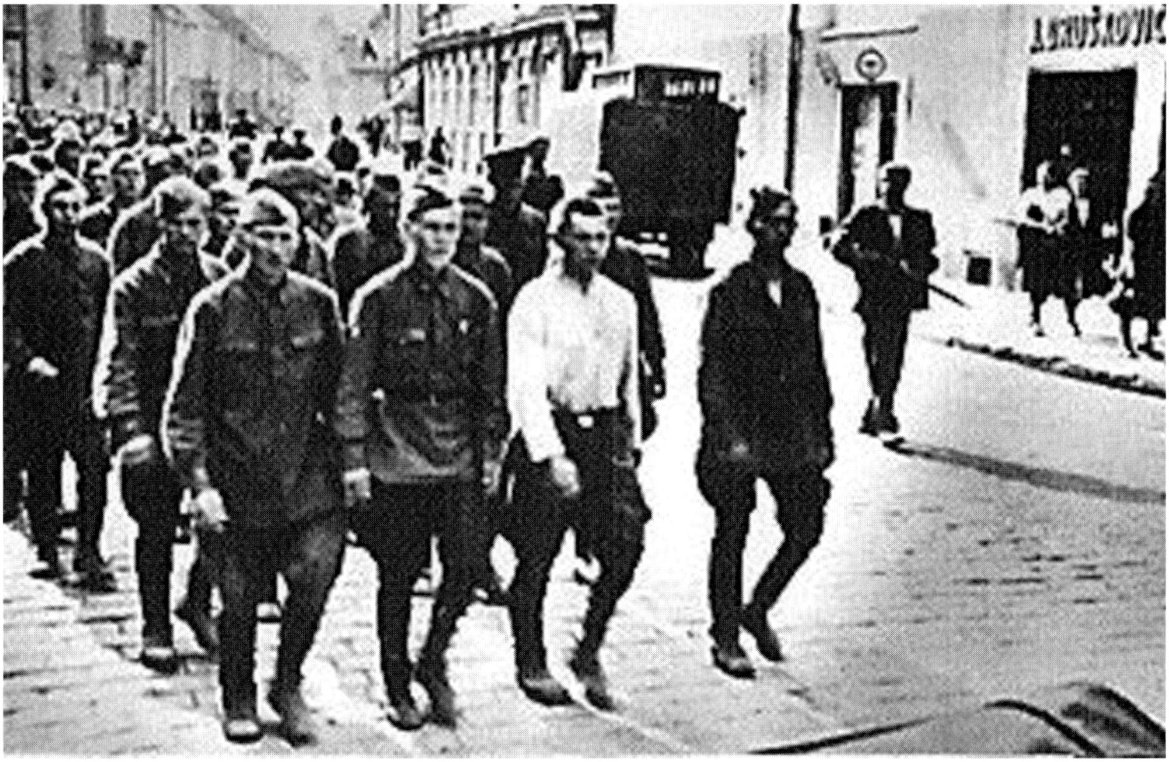

Soviet prisoners at Kunas, Lithuania. It appears they are being herded by civilian collaborators.

Below, newly captured Soviet soldiers passing a disabled and burning BT-7 tank. Location and date unspecified.

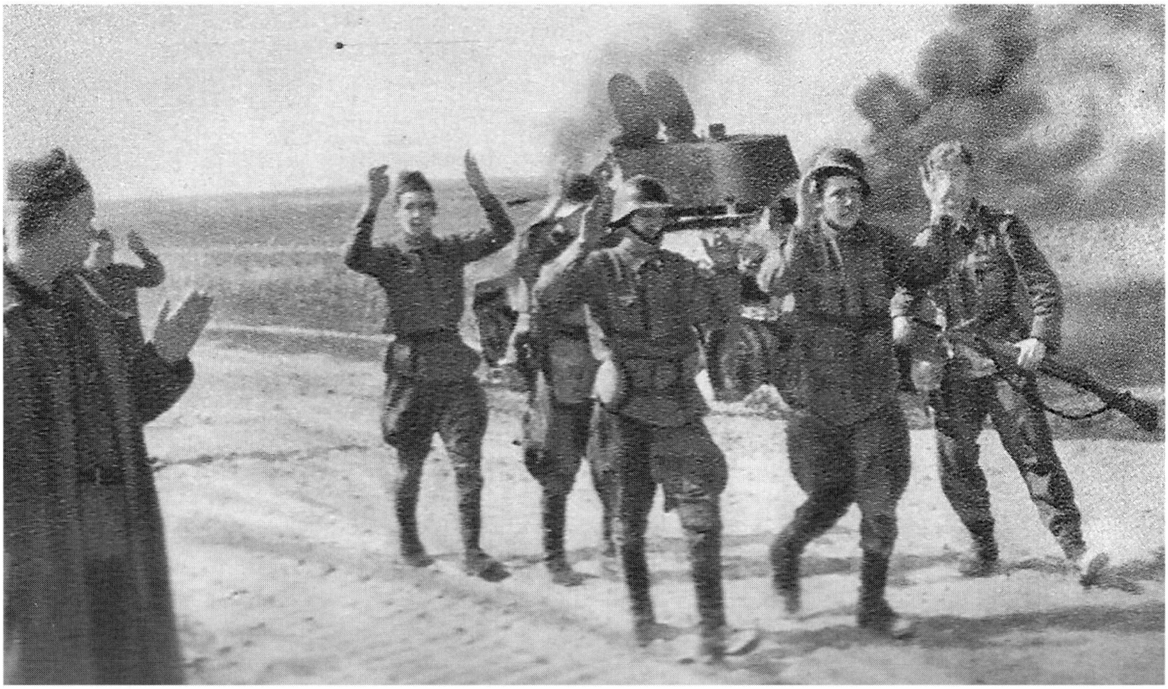

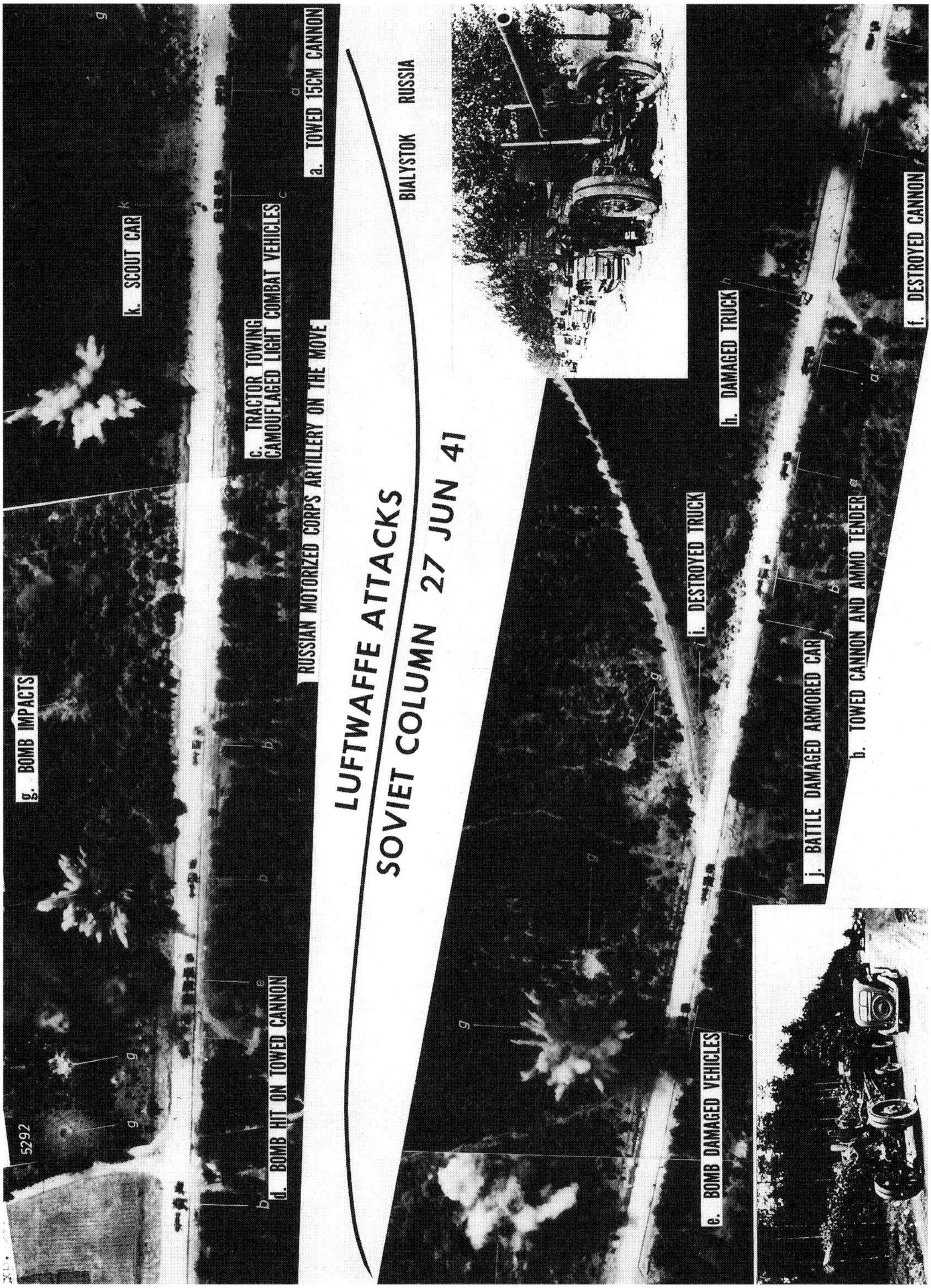
LUFTWAFFE ATTACKS
SOVIET COLUMN 27 JUN 41
BIALYSTOK RUSSIA
RUSSIAN MOTORIZED CORPS ARTILLERY ON THE MOVE
a. TOWED 15CM CANNON
b. TOWED CANNON AND AMMO TENDER
c. TRACTOR TOWING CAMOUFLAGED LIGHT COMBAT VEHICLES
d. BOMB HIT ON TOWED CANNON
e. BOMB DAMAGED VEHICLES
f. DESTROYED CANNON
g. BOMB IMPACTS
h. DAMAGED TRUCK
i. DESTROYED TRUCK
j. BATTLE DAMAGED ARMORED CAR
k. SCOUT CAR
5292

My wall display mosaic of a retreating Soviet heavy artillery unit being attacked (rather badly) by low-flying horizontal bombers near Bialystok five days into Barbarossa. At the time this would have been 150 miles east into Soviet occupied Poland.

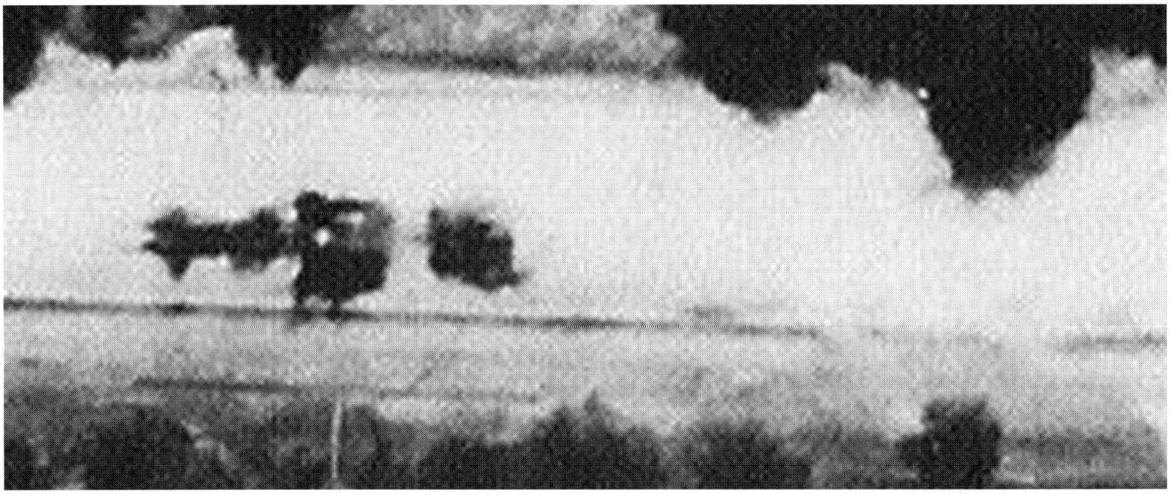

Enlargement from the mosaic shows prime movers, caisson/crew transports, limbers and 150mm howitzers (traveling left to right).

This looks like an Infantry Mess Company caught by the Luftwaffe fording the Bzura River. Except for two shapes that look like civilian roadsters in the middle of the ford, all vehicles are horse-drawn. I see no dead animals but two surviving horses are standing patiently and pathetic on the far bank. The location is 50 miles west of Warsaw.

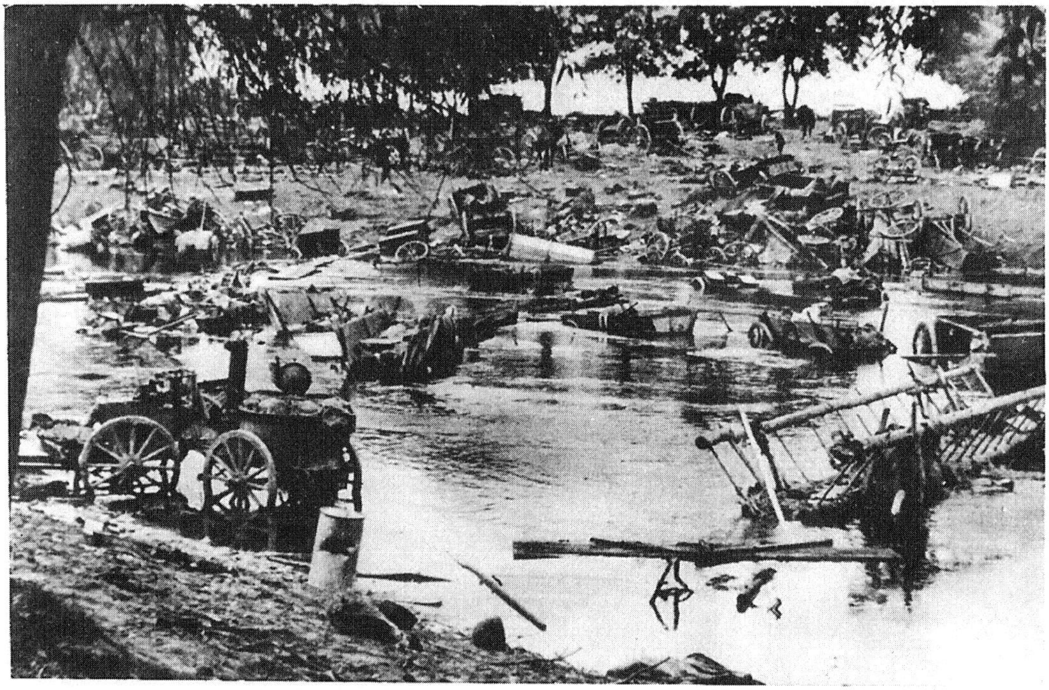

Furt an der Bzurabei Ktery
S von Kutno

Horses provided much of the mobility for both sides and suffered terribly throughout the war. What these were hauling has been taken away. There is bigger pile-up of vehicles on the road behind them and I see a horse standing back there and in the field to the right.

At first I thought the figure at right might be an undertaker but after looking at this highly magnified over and over I now believe it is a Polish woman. Though what she's raking or digging escapes me. Burying bodies? The juxtaposition of her calmly going on with her work is surreal.

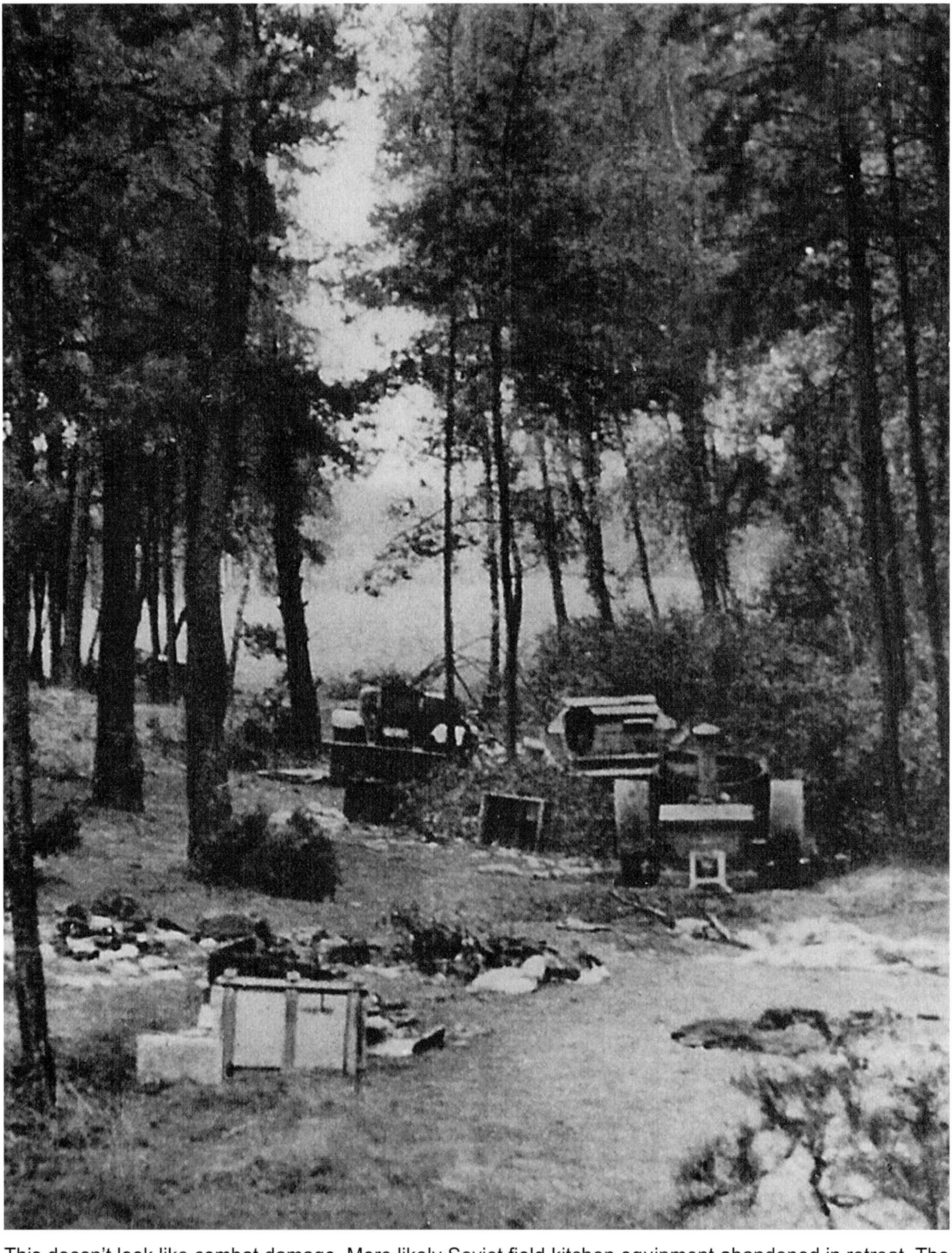

This doesn't look like combat damage. More likely Soviet field kitchen equipment abandoned in retreat. The site has also apparently been looted.

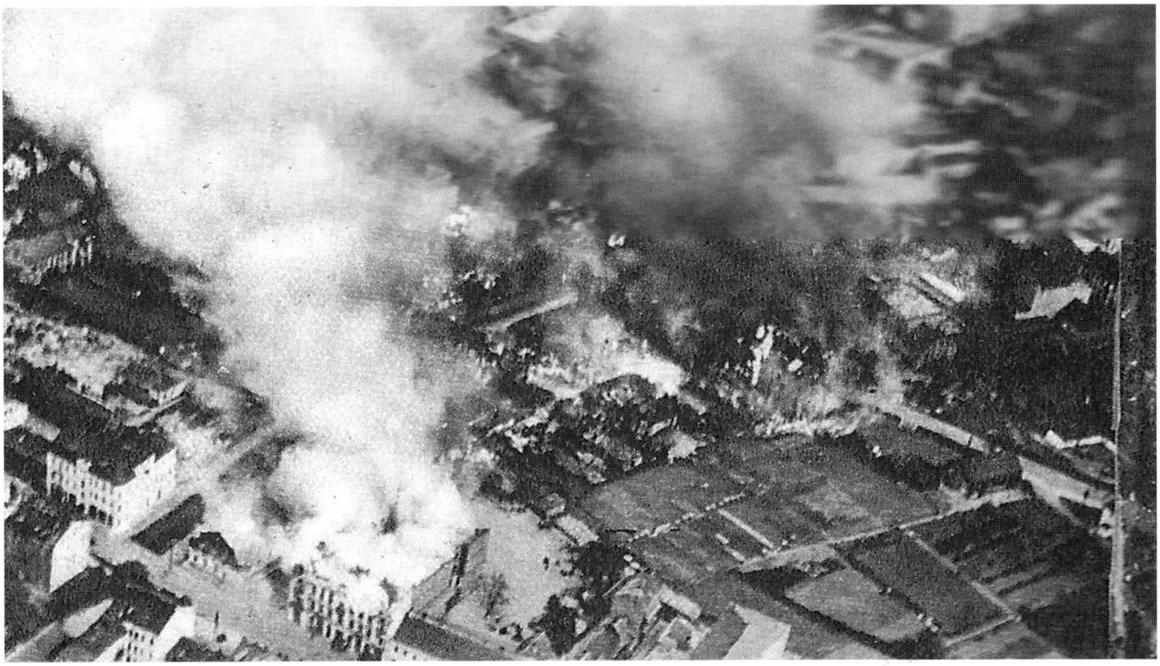

Bialystok after bombing. At the time of Barbarossa this was in Soviet-occupied Poland, twenty miles west of the actual Soviet border.

You'll see a number of photos like the one below in the following pages. German soldiers took photos with personal cameras and German Intelligence obtained copies. We got those at the end of the war. When I found them, many of the photos were attached to small paper diagrams showing taking location and sometimes a note explaining content. Most comments are in German (probably from German Intelligence) but most have an AMS series N501 map series reference (in this case NN 37-7). Additional notes may have been added by Germans working with US Intelligence during post-war processing.

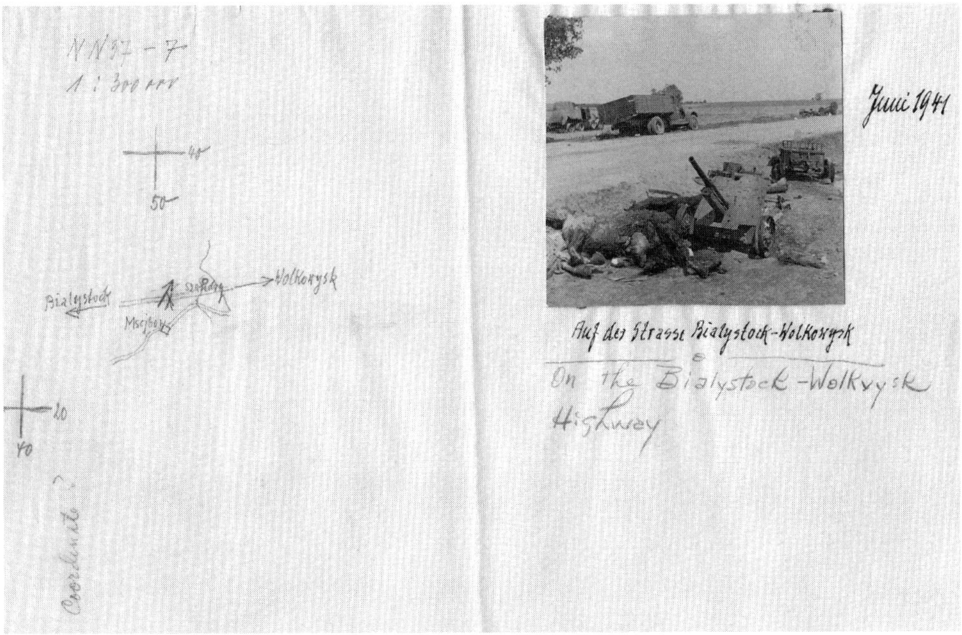
Juni 1941
Auf der Strasse Bialystock-Wolkowysk
On the Bialystock-Wolkvysk Highway

Enlargement of the photo above. June 1941, a dismembered/burned horse and Soviet 45mm M1937 (53-K) anti-tank gun with burned tyres, east of Bialystok. Its caisson is a few feet farther down the road. Looking over the AT gun shield we see the handle, shield and barrel of a M1910 Maxim heavy machine-gun facing away from the camera.

A burned Soviet BA-10 armored car is across the road.

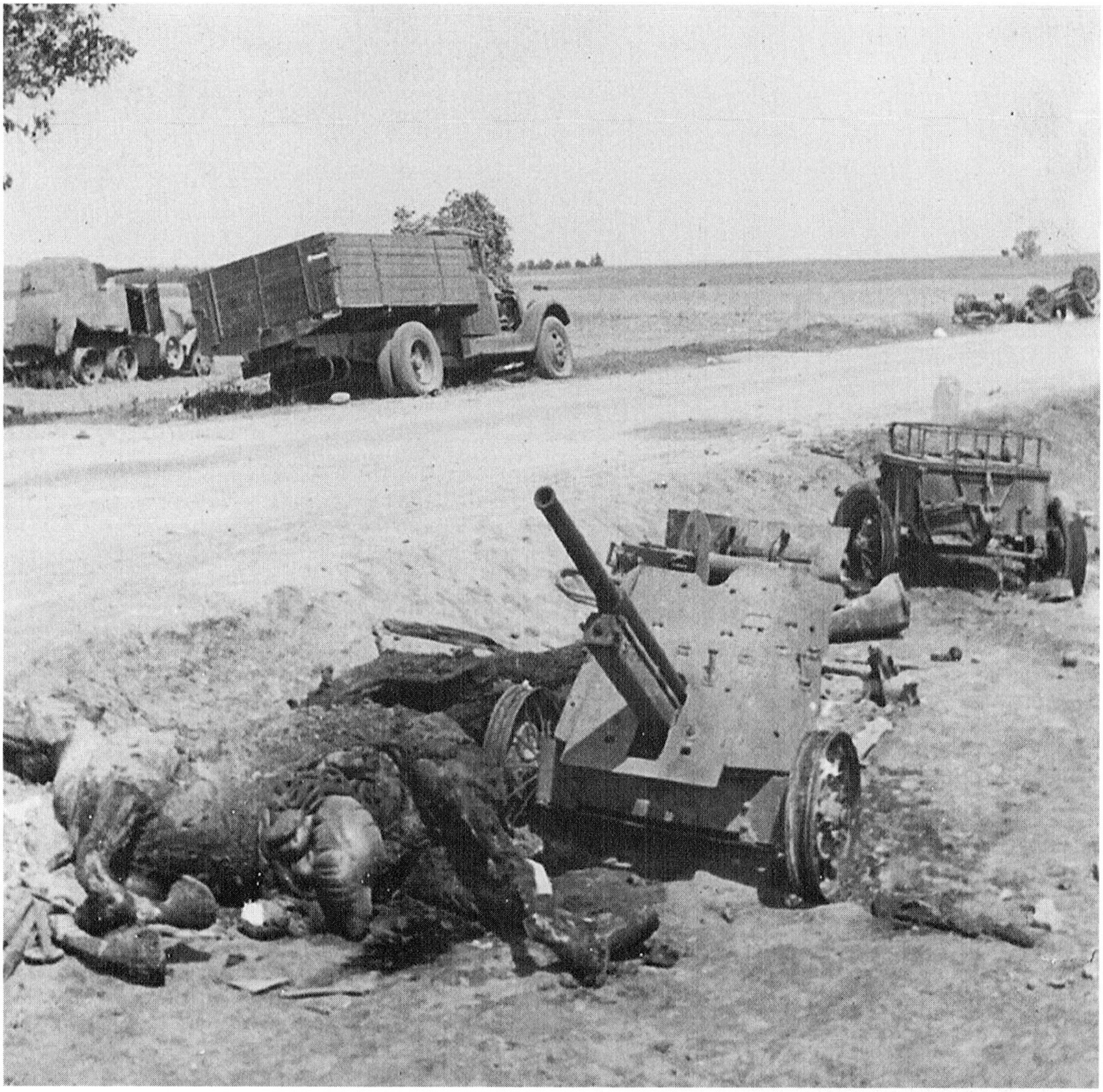

This bit of Intelligence is actually incorrect in several ways. The highway east of Bialystok leads to Wolkowysk (now Volkvysk), forty miles away. The map reference is for a Degree Square 360 miles further east. The proper map reference for this event is NN 34-9. The sketch map appears correct.

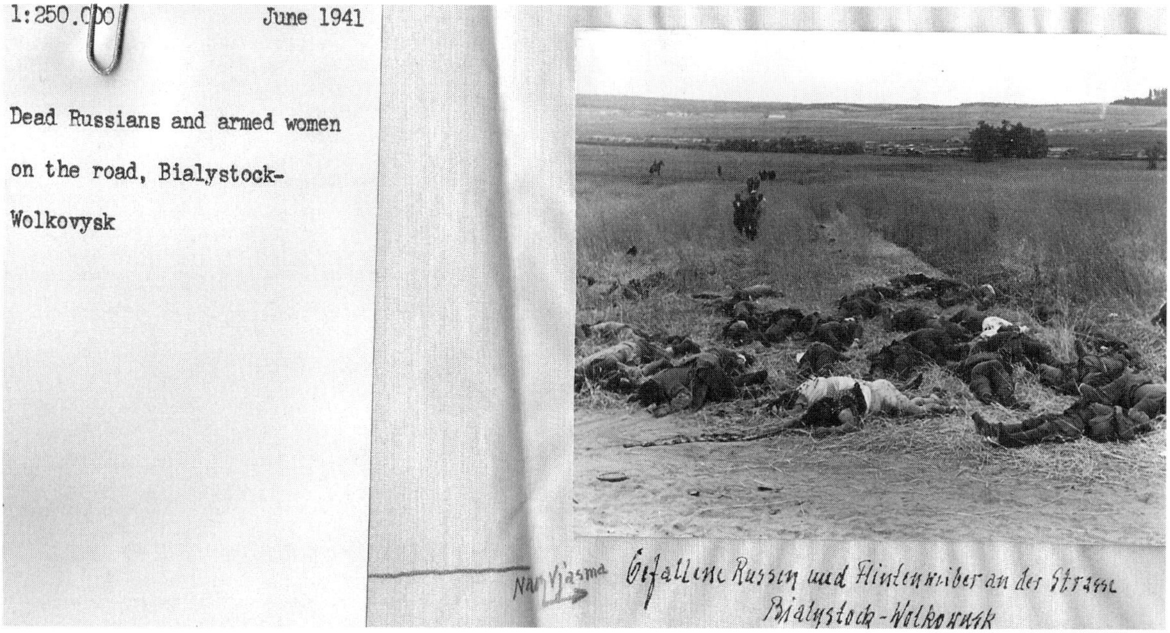
1:250.000
June 1941
Dead Russians and armed women
on the road, Bialystock-
Wolkovysk
Nach Vjasma
Gefallene Russen und Flintenweiber an der Strasse
Bialystock-Wolkowysk

Above, filed near the previous photo, probably taken by the same soldier in the same area..

Enlargement of above. If these were partisans they picked a terrible place to ambush German troops. Based upon bare flesh showing, I see one woman and two possibles (left rear and another a little to right). The photo implies female bodies were given special examination. People from the small settlement just beyond the trees are coming through the wheat, perhaps to claim bodies.

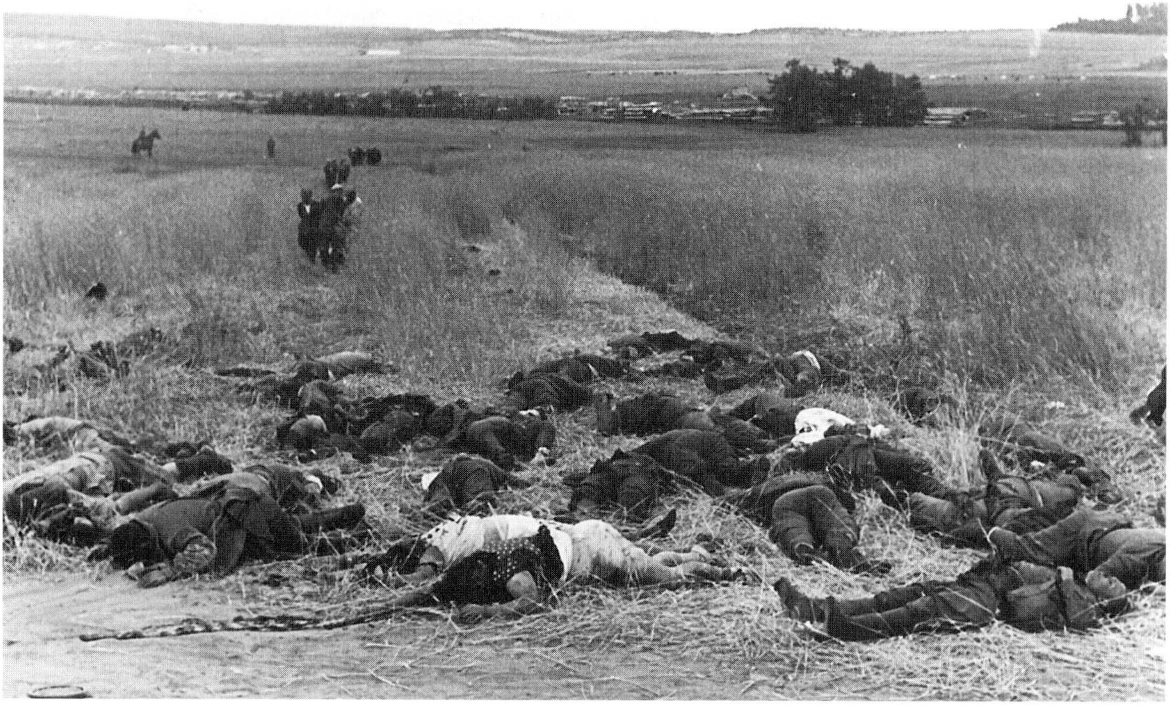

Left, I count twenty plus uniformed men in the ditch, a ruined car mounting machine-guns, and a field gun in the ditch farther back looks like work of the Luftwaffe taking out a would-be road block.

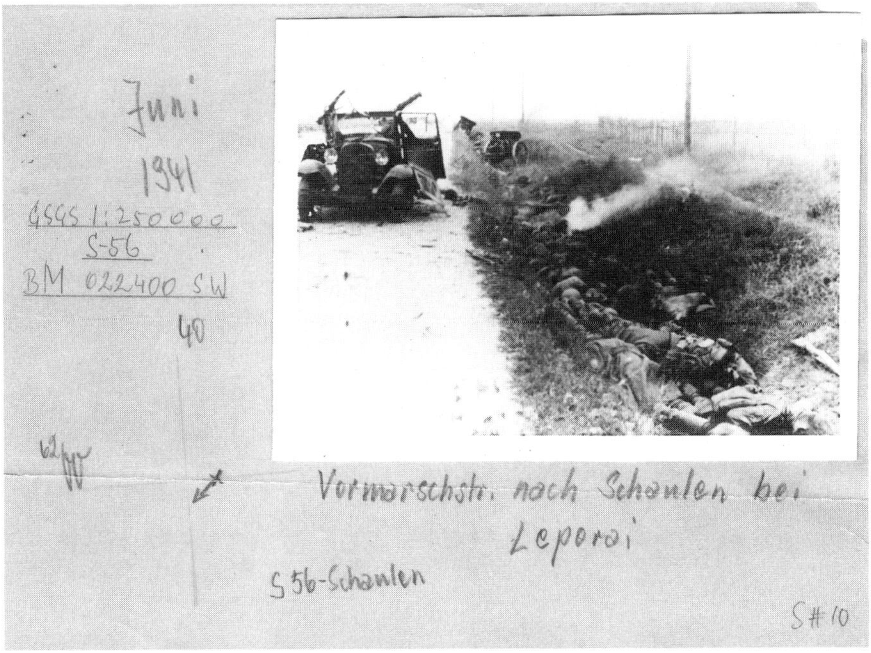

Juni
1941
GSGS 1:250000
S-56
BM 022400 SW
40
Vormarschstr. nach Schaulen bei
Leporai
S56-Schaulen
S#10

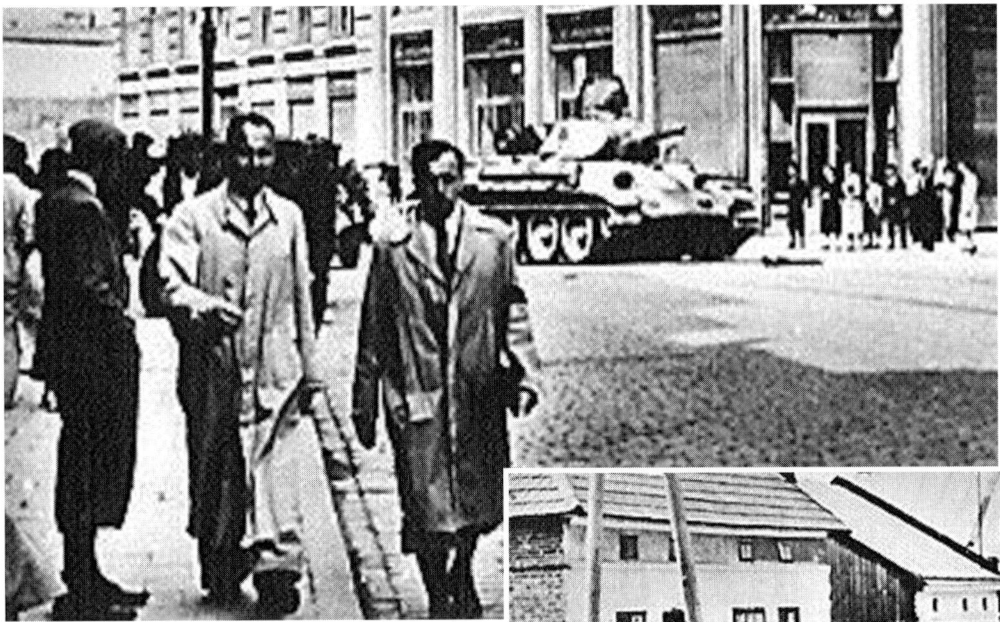

June 1941, ten miles NW of Panevezys, Lithuania. Lvov, 30 June 1941. An abandoned T-34 tank in the background.

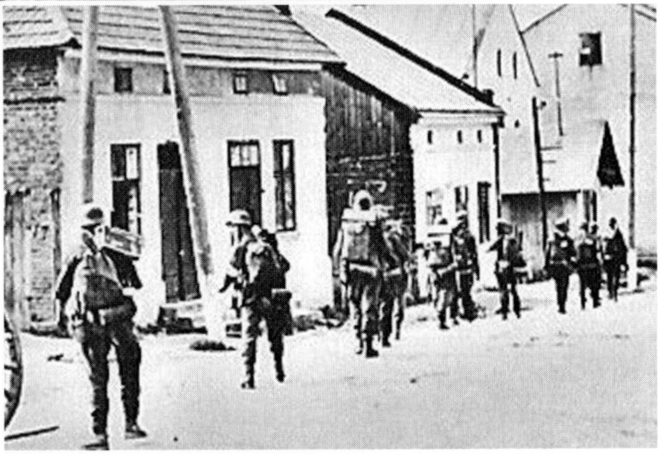

Right, Infantry mop up in Ivana Franko, 30 June 1941.

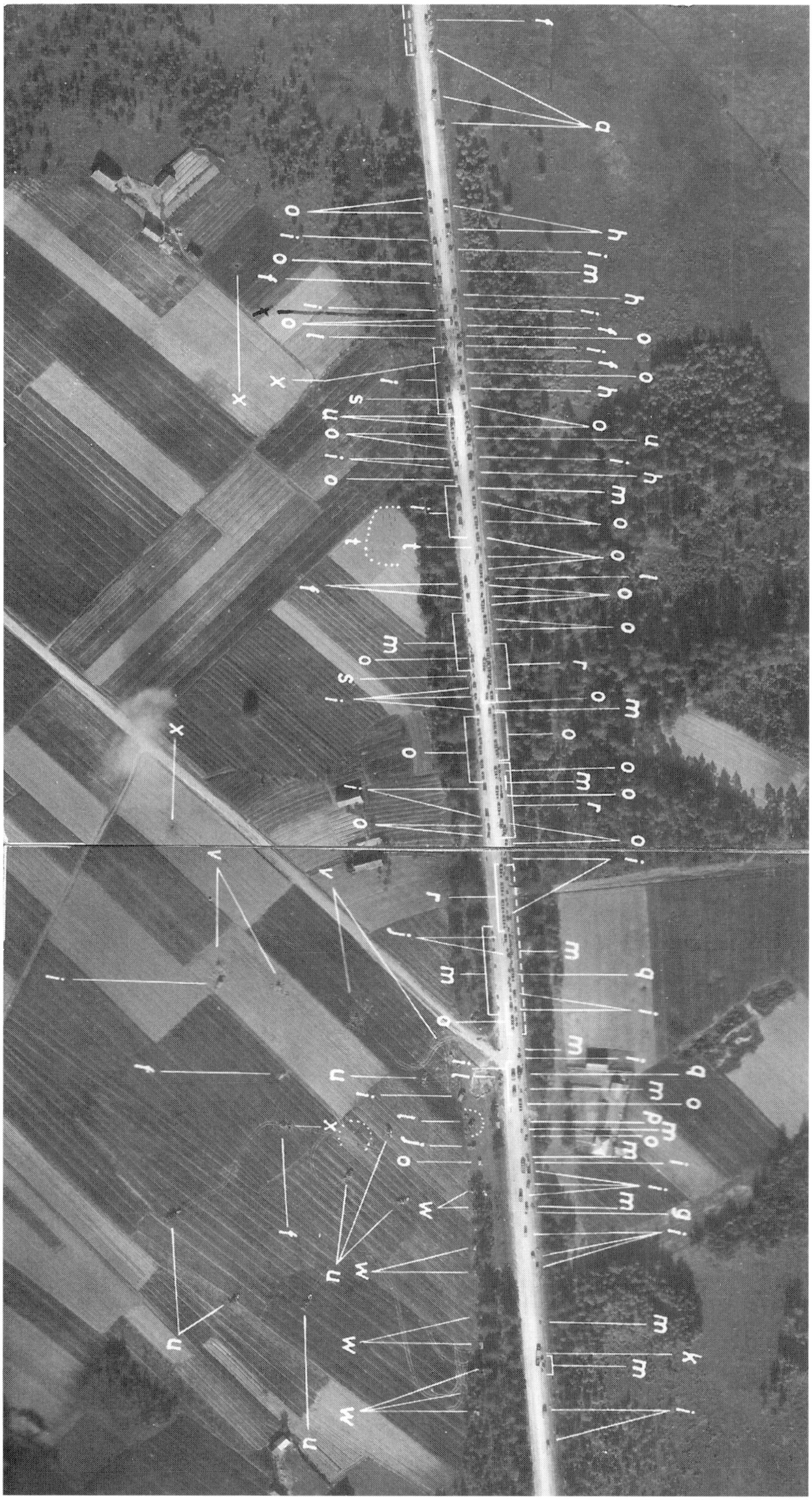

Frames three and four of a four photo run over a German Panzer Battle Group on the road east of Pinsk, 24 June 1941. Mixed in with Pz.Kpfw III and IVs are captured Soviet BT 7, T 60 and Bronieford armored vehicles.

The accompanying report (next page) gives no hint why such a detailed analysis of a friendly unit was required.

Perhaps it was a training exercise for new PIs?

In any case, the PI work is remarkable and detailed to the point of being anal. Since they were reporting on a friendly column it looks like these PIs were just showing off how good they were. Pretty darn good, it seems.

CONFIDENTIAL

Beobachter: Ltn. Schuntermann 1.(F) 122	Kennung u. Anford.Nr. I/B III/9/ 621o - 6213		
Film: F.1o139 ohne Laufzettel	Bildnummer: ~~175-178~~ 6210-6213	Brennweite: 5o cm	
Aufnahmeort: Rollbahn im Raume Pinsk-Luniniec-Shlobin/UdSSR.			Karte: ---
Aufn. Datum: 24.VI.1941	Uhrzeit: 17,o5	Maßstab etw. 1: 3 ooo	

55. Sendung

(17)

Deutsche gemischte Kampfgruppe und verlassener feindlicher
motorisierter Fahrzeugverband auf ~~der Rollbahn~~ einer Straße im Osten.

[redacted] RUSSIA/Shlobin TU/MISC/Data Sheet/6210-6213

mot. Truppen

Auswertung :

a). Deutscher Panzerkampfwagen,Typ Pz. IV
z.T. mit einachsigem Muni-Anhänger

b). Zg.-Kw. mit einachsigem Anhänger
ansch. Geschützstaffel einer leichten mot. Feldhaubitz-Batterie

c). ansch. Panzerkampfwagen russischer Herkunft (BT)

d). ansch. Panzerspähwagen russischer Herkunft (Bronieford)

e). leichter russischer Panzerkampfwagen Typ T. 6o (5,5 to.)

f). leichte Pzkw. oder gepanzerte Spezialfahrzeuge
Typ nicht feststellbar

g). Lkw. mit einachsigen Anhängern

h). Deutscher Panzerkampfwagen,Typ ansch. Pz. III

i). Lkw. aller Größen

j). Spezialfahrzeuge

k). schw. Lkw. 7 to. mit 2 achsigem Anhänger

l). durch Waffenwirkung zerstörte mot. Fahrzeuge aller Art

m). Reitertrupps

n). Pkw. bzw. Kübelsitzwagen,teilw. mit einachsigem Anhänger

p). Deutscher leichter Panzerspähwagen

q). Zg.-Kw. mit angehängtem leichten Feldgeschütz

r). 3 Regts.-Panzerjägerzüge (bestehend aus 3 x 4 Pkw.
mit angehängter Pak)

s). Kräder mit Beiwagen

t). abgesessene Mannschaften auf der Straße und im Gelände

u). leichte Flak auf Selbstfahrlafette mit einachsigen Muni-Anhängern auf der Straße und im Gelände

v). Kanonen-Batterie in feldmäßiger Feuerstellung,ohne jede Tarnung (4 Geschütze)

w). mot. Fahrzeuge und Troß der Batterie am Waldrand getarnt abgestellt
Ausgeprägte Fahrspuren lassen den Standort der Batterie schon aus großen Höhen erkennen.

x). Bombentreffer und Einschläge

y). gestapeltes Straßenbaumaterial

An der Rollbahn stehende Bäume wurden z.T. umgefahren.

Breite der Rollbahn etwa 12 m

Marschrichtung : südwest

CONFIDENTIAL

Photo Interpretation Report on the previous imagery.

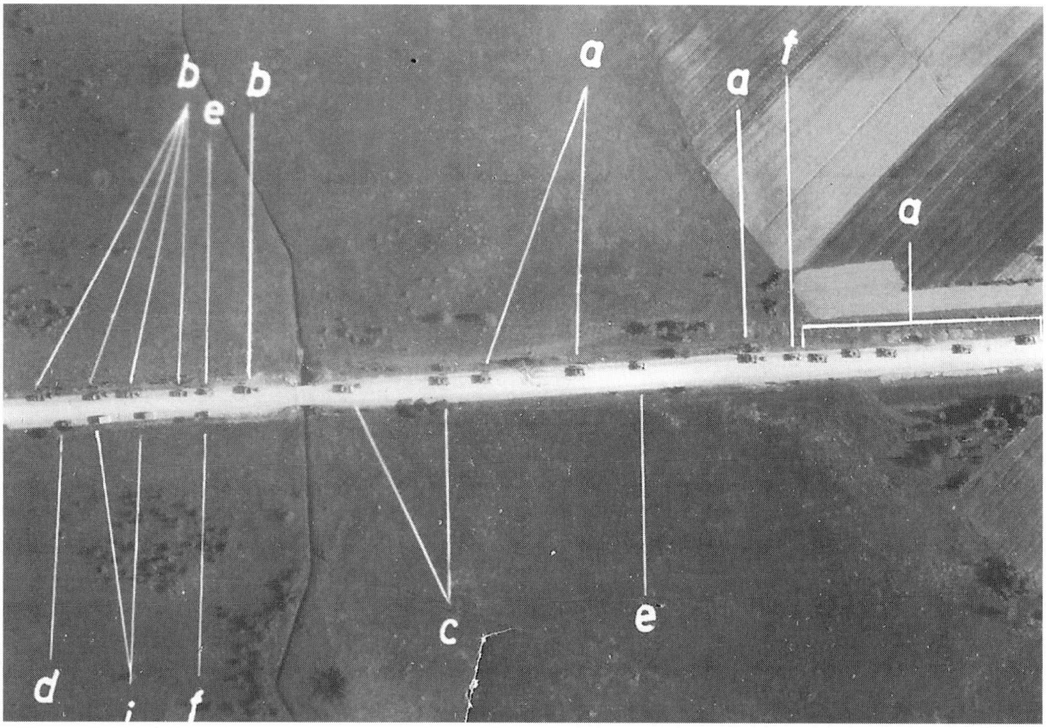
b
e
b
a
a
f
a
d
c
e

Enlargement of frame one of the previous series. Soviet BT-7s tanks(c), Bronieford armored cars (d), and T 60 tanks (e), rolling with German Pz IVs (a).

Polikarpov I-153 pilot remaining onboard during bombing-up suggests a turn-around mission. The ‘circle star’ was an early war Soviet national marking. The bomb is 50 kg.

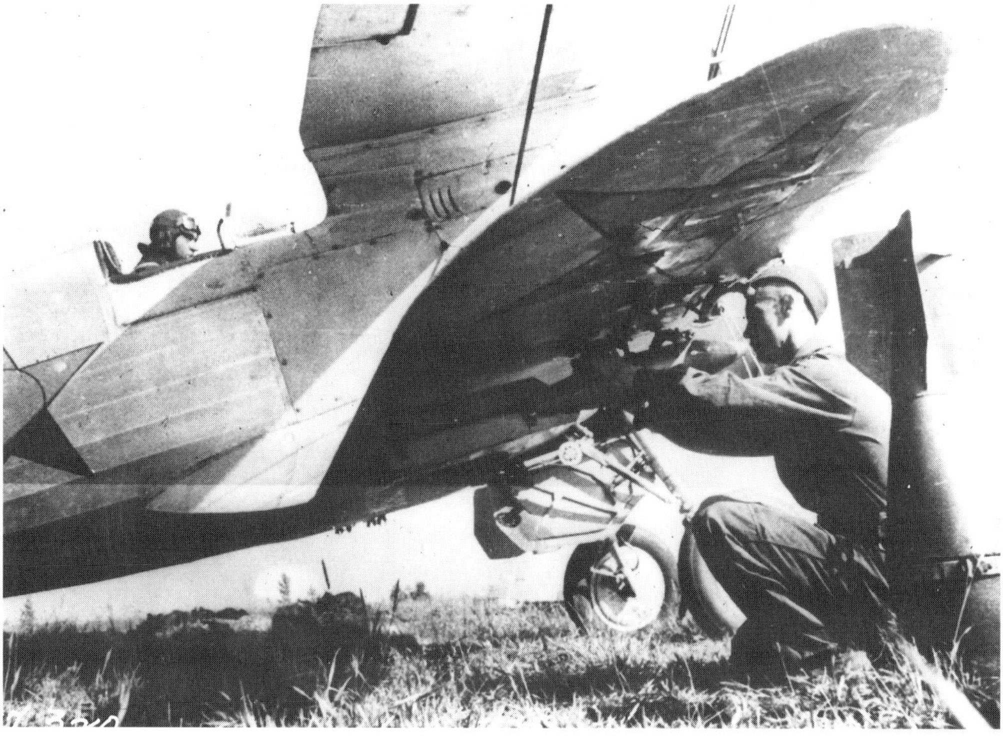

NO 35-10 #22

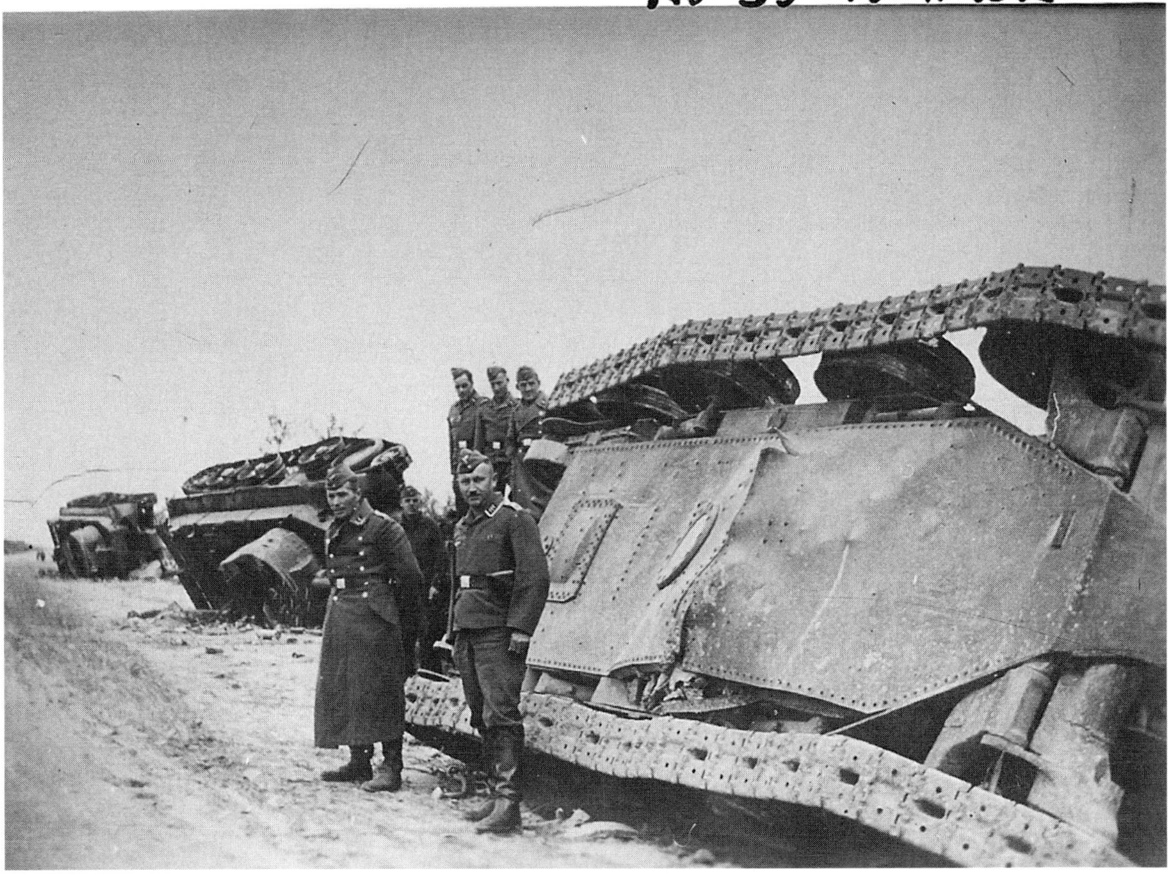

Above, three 12.5 ton BT-5 tanks tipped over by German tanks or engineers.

NO 35-10 # 23

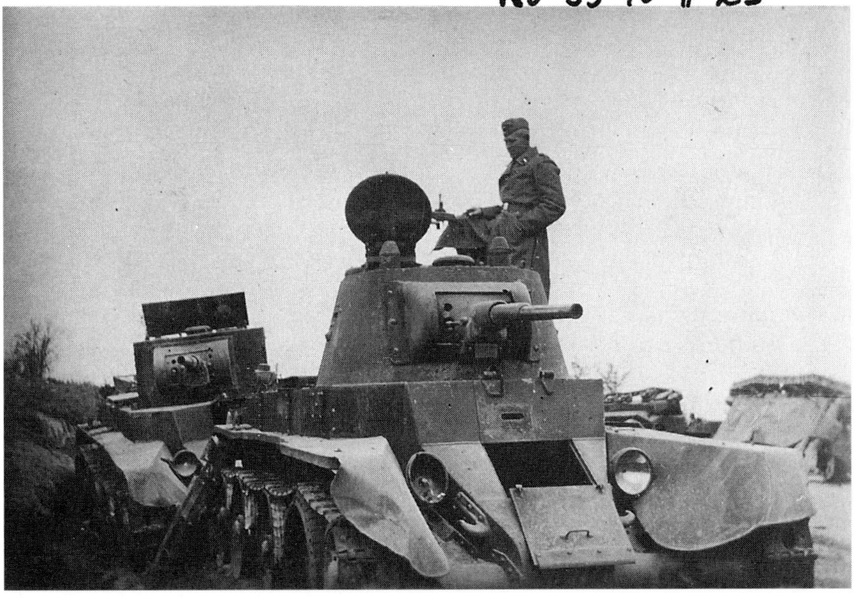

Left, examining an abandoned Soviet BT-7. A BT-5 is behind it and the three tipped-over BT-5s are across the road. NO 35-10 is the Degree Square for Riga.

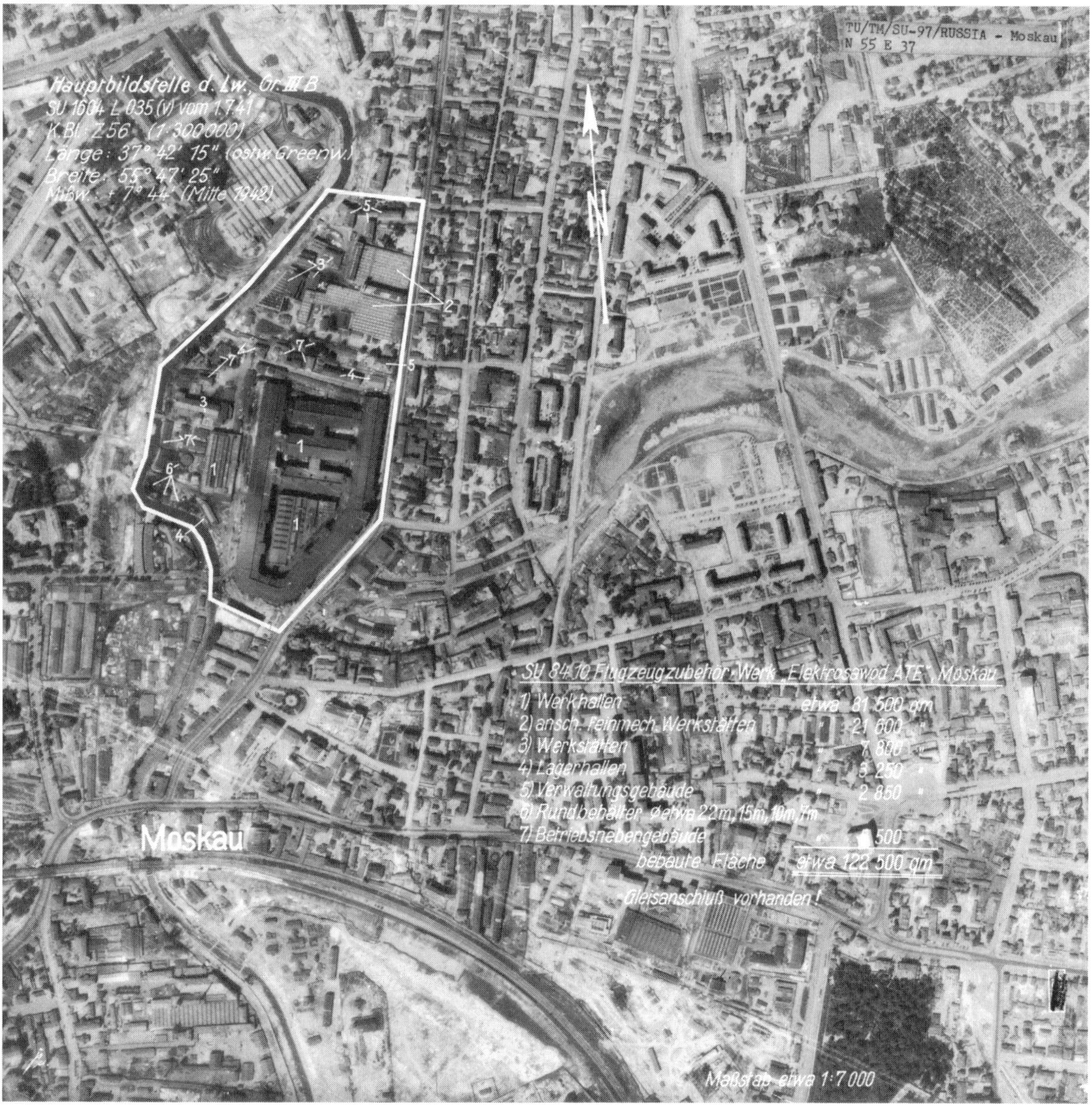
TU/TM/SU-97/RUSSIA - Moskau
N 55 E 37
Hauptbildstelle d. Lw., Gr. III B
SU 1604 L 035 (v) vom 1.7.41
K.Bl.: Z 56 (1:300 000)
Länge: 37° 42' 15" (östl. Greenw.)
Breite: 55° 47' 25"
Mißw.: + 7° 44' (Mitte 1942)
N
SU 84 10 Flugzeugzubehör-Werk „Elektrosawod ATE", Moskau
1) Werkhallen etwa 81 500 qm
2) ansch. feinmech. Werkstätten 21 600
3) Werkstätten 7 800
4) Lagerhallen 3 250
5) Verwaltungsgebäude 2 850
6) Rundbehälter ø etwa 22m, 15m, 10m, 7m
7) Betriebsnebengebäude 500
bebaute Fläche etwa 122 500 qm
Gleisanschluß vorhanden!
Moskau
Maßstab etwa 1:7 000

While troops on the ground surged forward, Luftwaffe aerial reconnaissance continued to catalog potential targets far ahead of the FEBA (Forward Edge of the Battle Area). In this example an aircraft parts plant in Moscow, 1 July 1941.

Annotations at lower right explain the detailed analysis of the plant including Fabrication Buildings (1, 2 & 3), Admin building (5), fuel tanks (6) and an Operations Building (7).

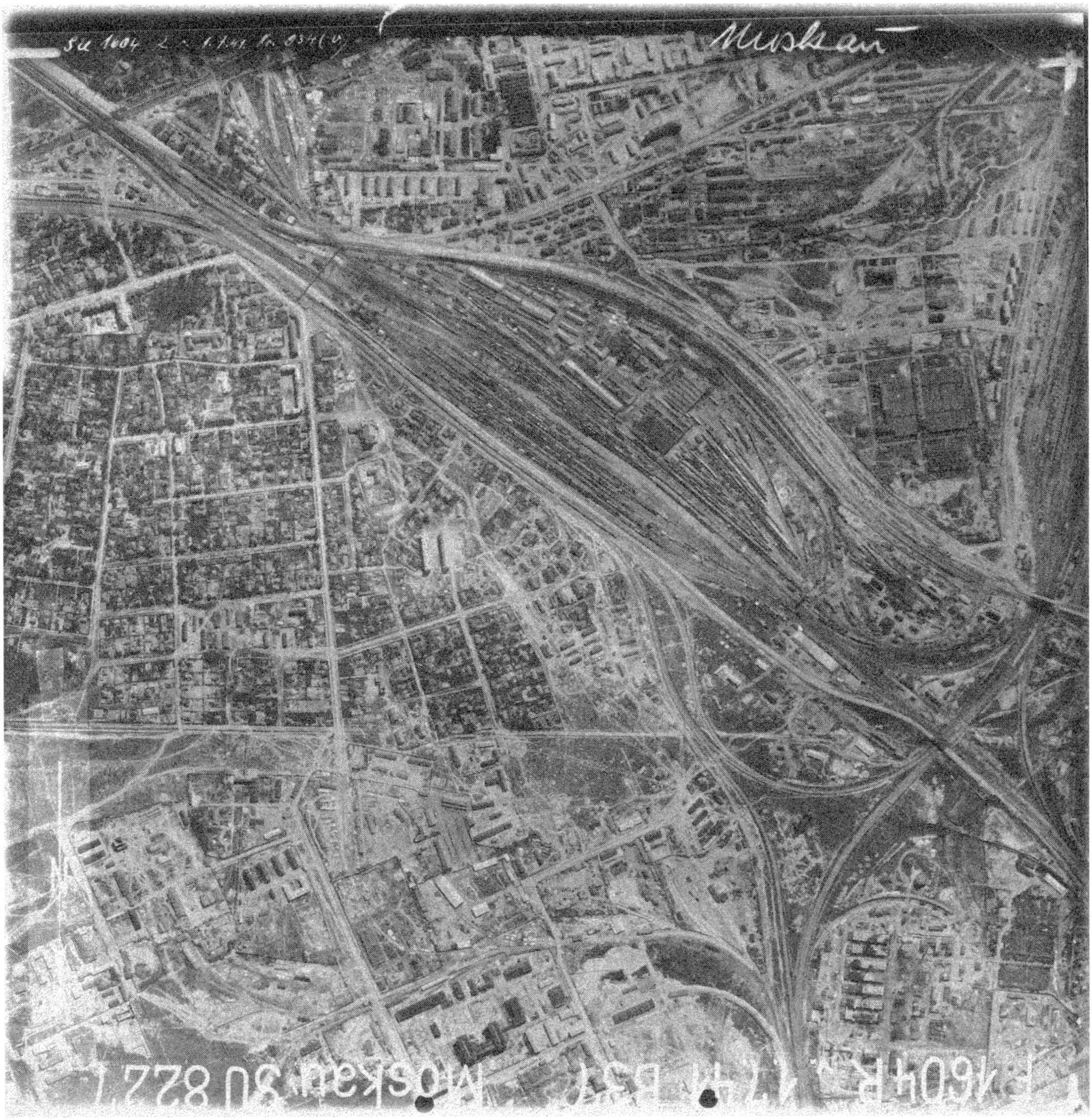

Another Moscow photo from 1 July 1941. This is a major rail yard in the Perevo District, four miles east of Red Square. It would have been a major target for the German advance in WW II—and US planners during the Cold War. The yard is easily identified today on Google maps.

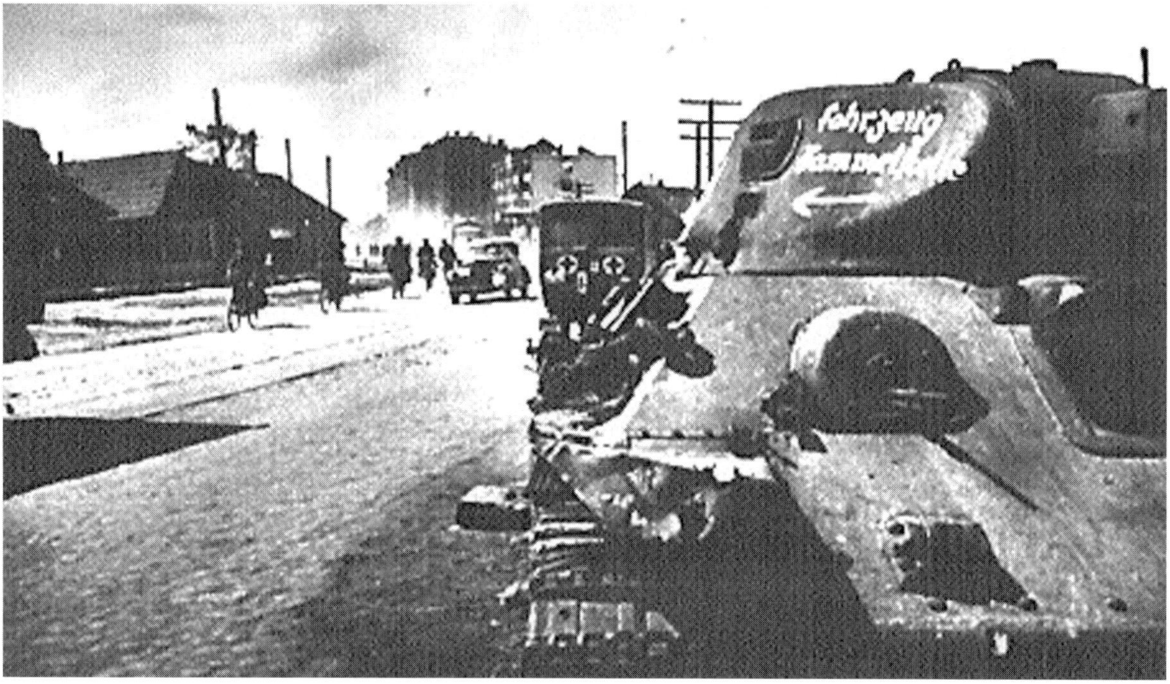
Fahrzeug

T-34 tank used as a signpost, Minsk, 10 July 1941. It says 'Vehicle' something. Sorry, I can't make out the rest.

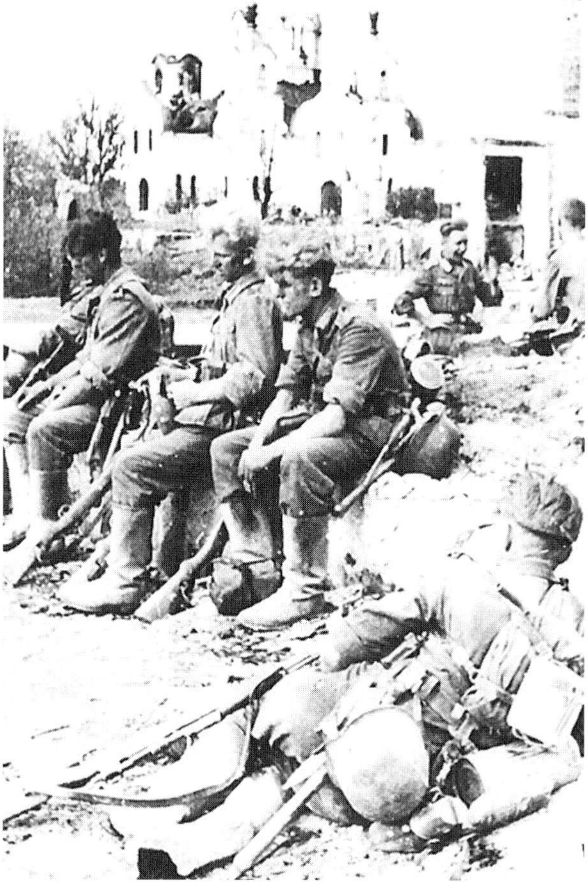

This is what dog-tired looks like in combat. Vitebsk, 13 July 1941.

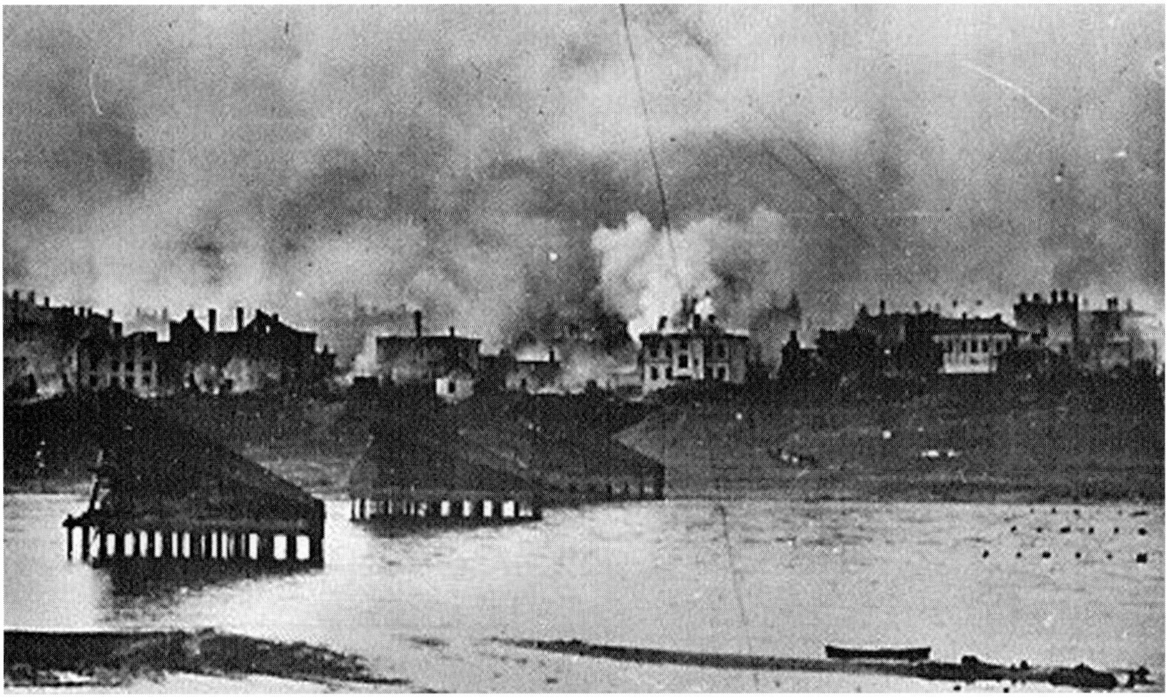

Above, bridge over Western Dvina River destroyed, Polatsk, Belarus, 15 July 1941.

Below, 90 miles NNE of Minsk, Stalin's statue pulled down, Polatsk, 16 July 1941.

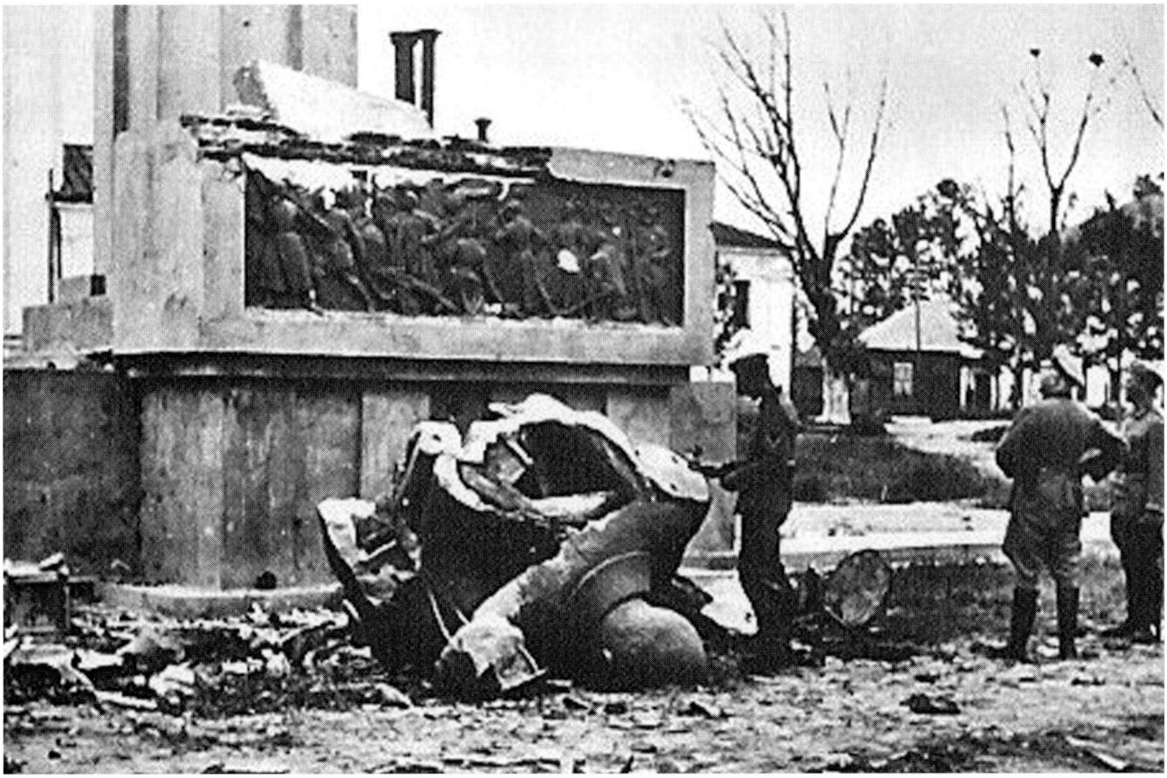

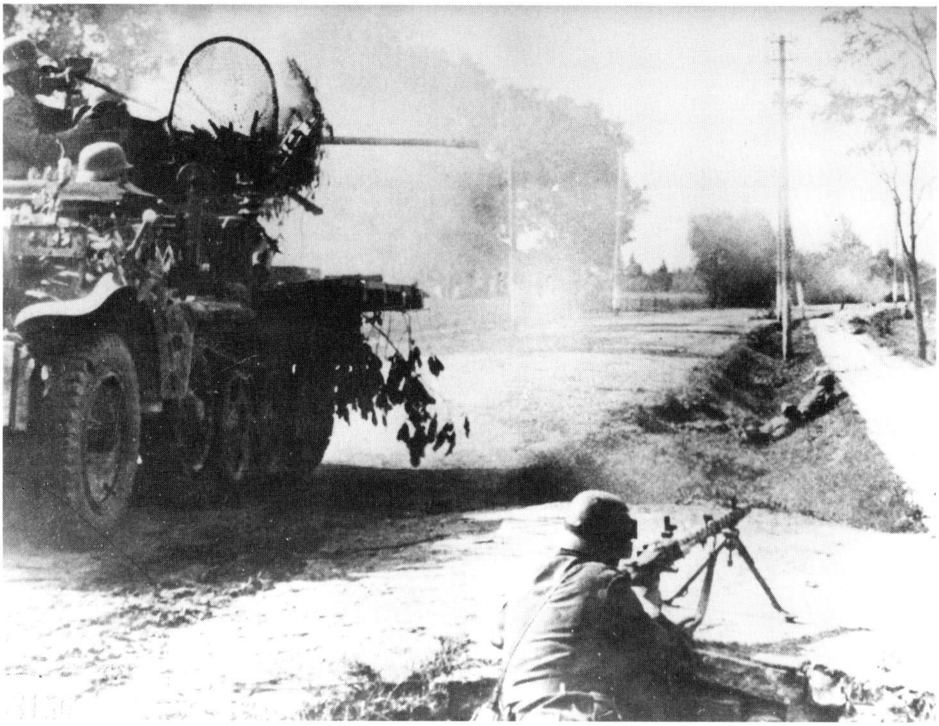

An SdKfz 10 half-track mounting a Flak 30, 20mm anti-aircraft gun, supporting infantry. The light machine gun is an early version MG34. Photo date and location unknown but probably from Barbarossa based upon where I found it in retired photo files.

Below, reinforcements entering Vitebsk, 17 July 1941.

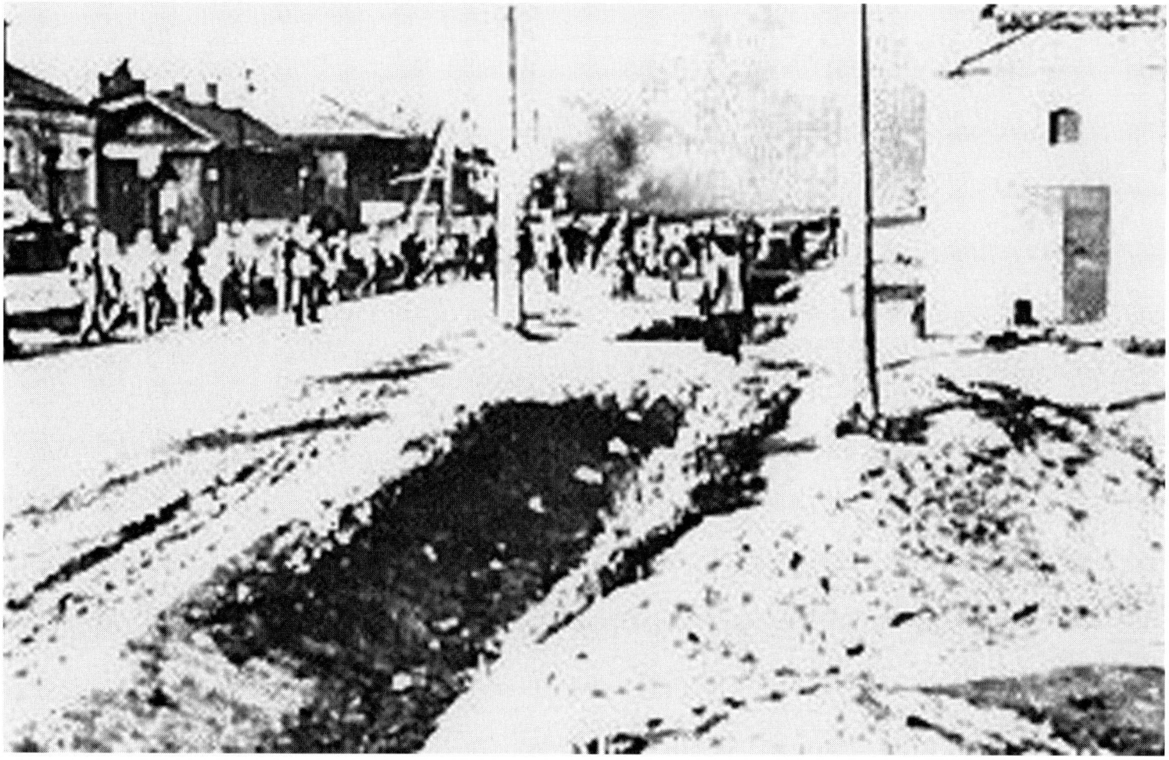

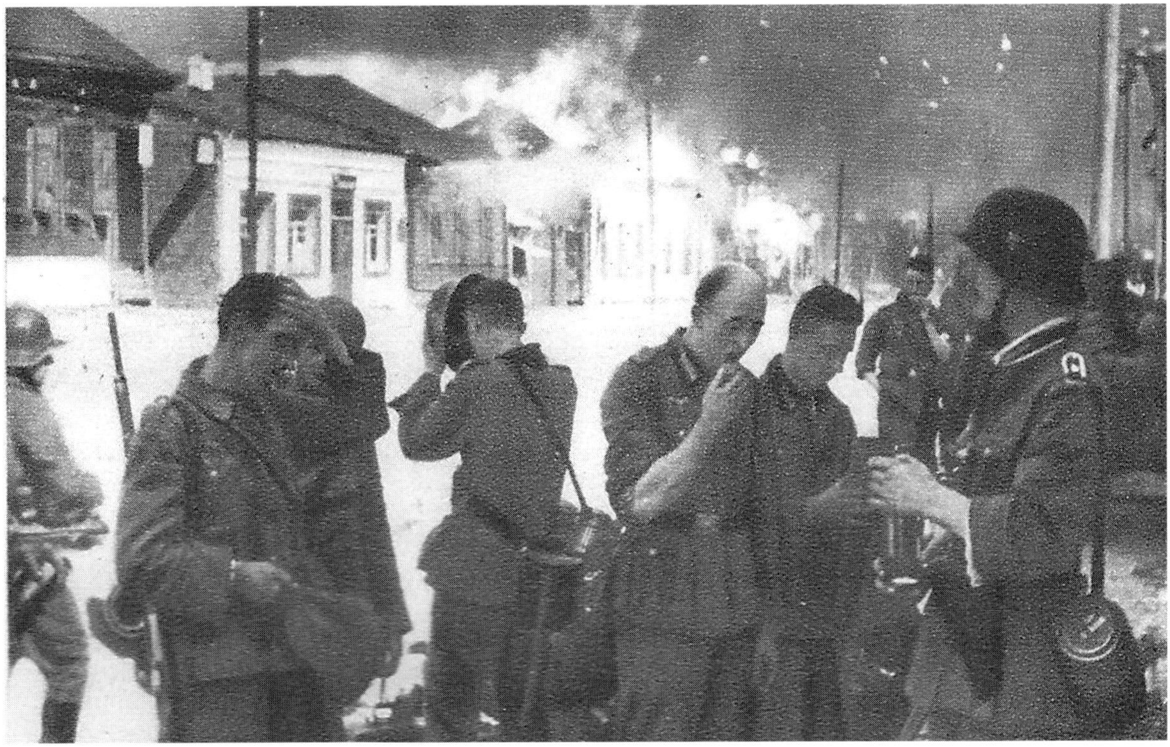

Above, 'Take Five' in an unnamed burning town.

A Soviet I-153 fighter squadron briefing.

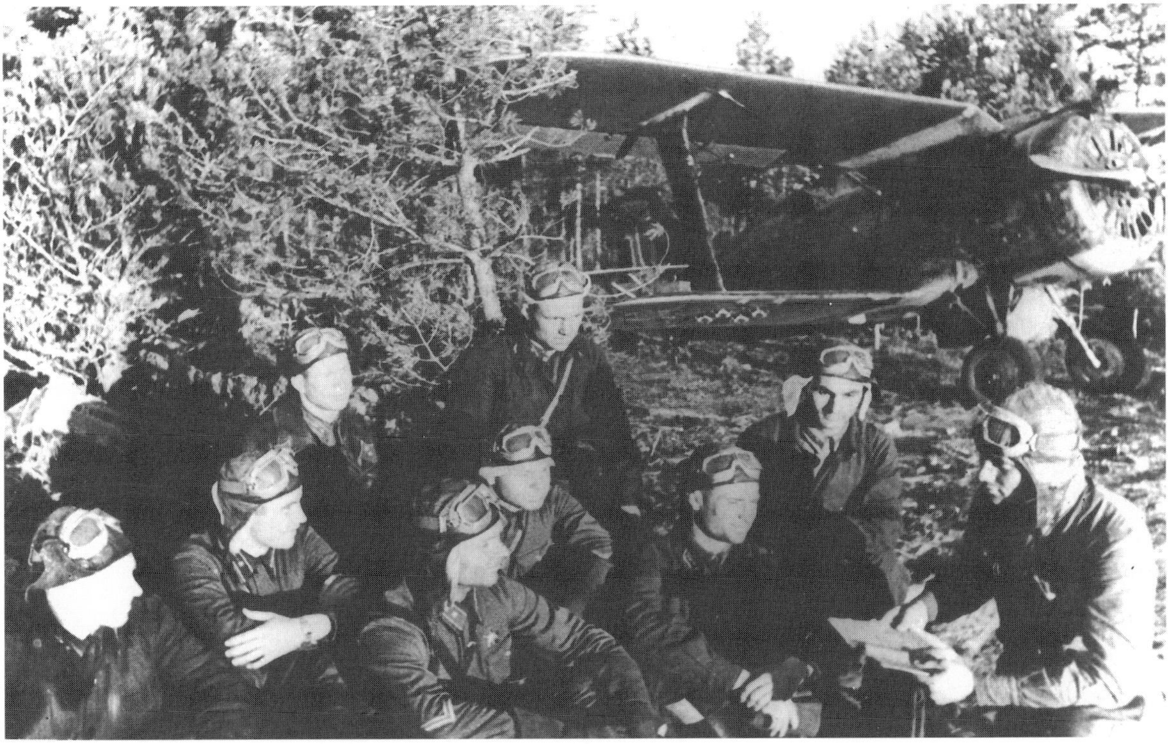

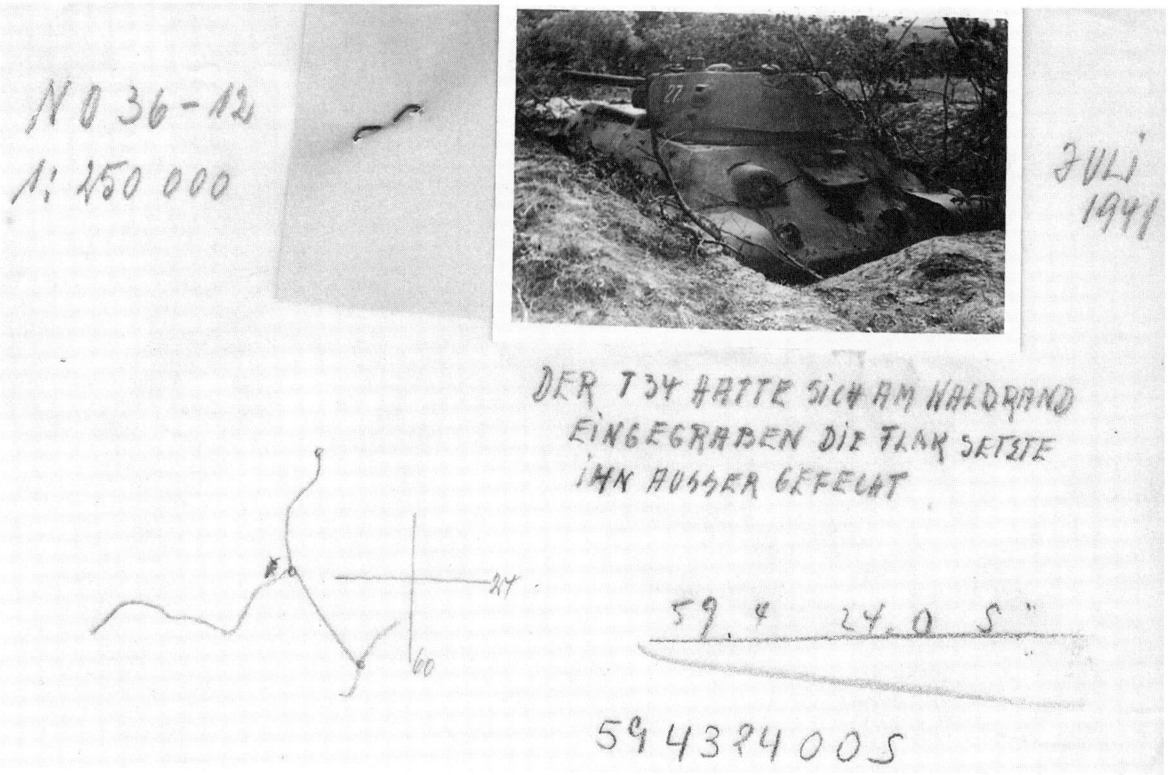
NO 36-12
1: 250 000
JULI 1941
DER T34 HATTE SICH AM WALDRAND EINGEGRABEN DIE FLAK SETZTE IHN AUSSER GEFECHT
24
60
59.4 24.0 S

Soviet T-34 hull-down as a strong point (likely inoperable), near Kalinin, July 1941. This photo shows the sloping armor and 76.2mm main gun that made the T-34 such a formidable weapon.

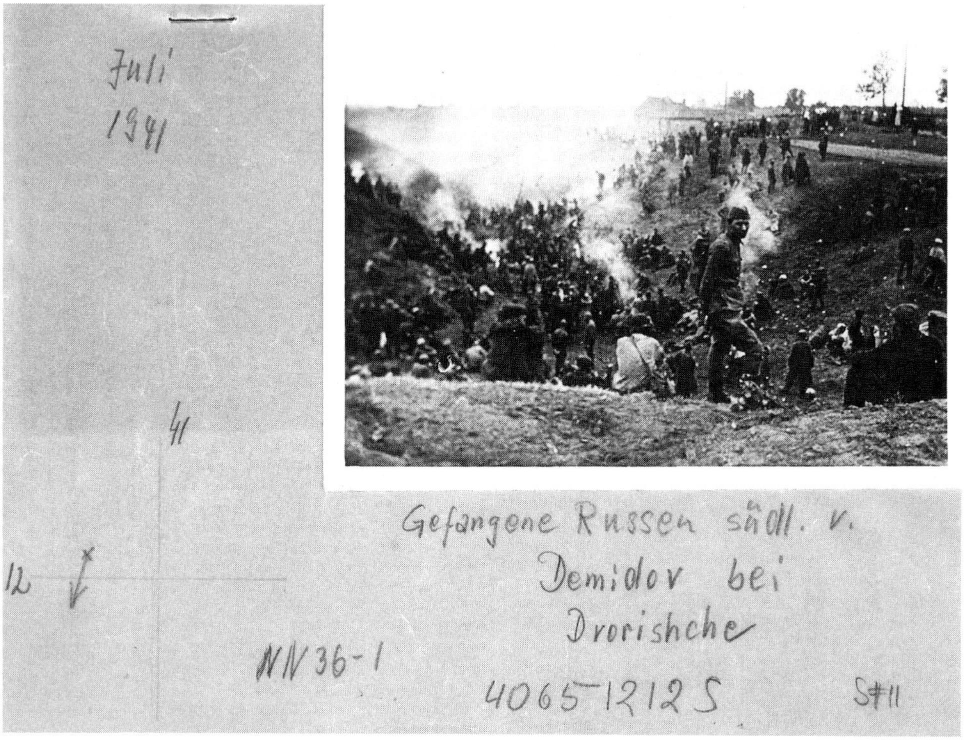
Juli 1941
41
12
Gefangene Russen südl. v. Demidov bei Drorishche
NN 36-1
4065 1212 S
S#11

Soviet PoWs in a valley 30 miles north of Kiev, July 1941.

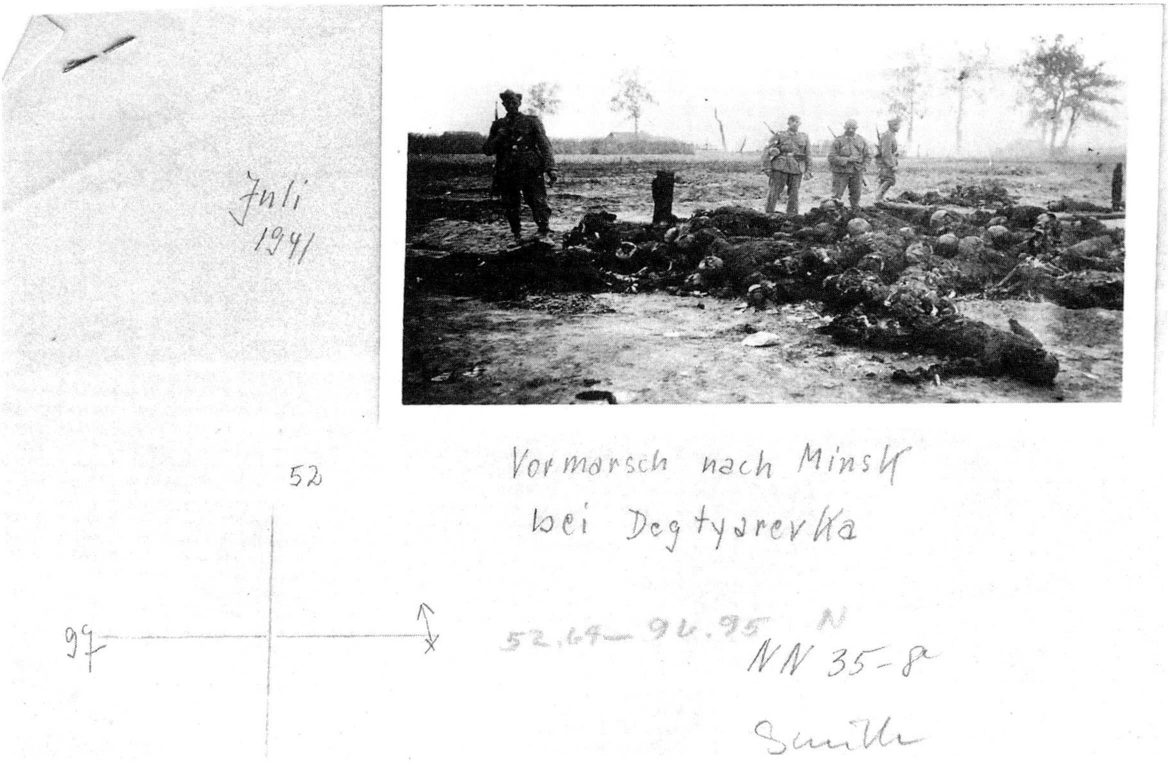
Juli 1941
Vormarsch nach Minsk
bei Degtyarevka
52
97
NN 35-8
Smith

July 1941 three miles west of Minsk. Who are those burned/decomposed bodies? I don't see weapons, helmets, military uniforms or boots. Who piled them up like that? It looks recent. Less than a month into invasion was this German or the remains of some Soviet action?

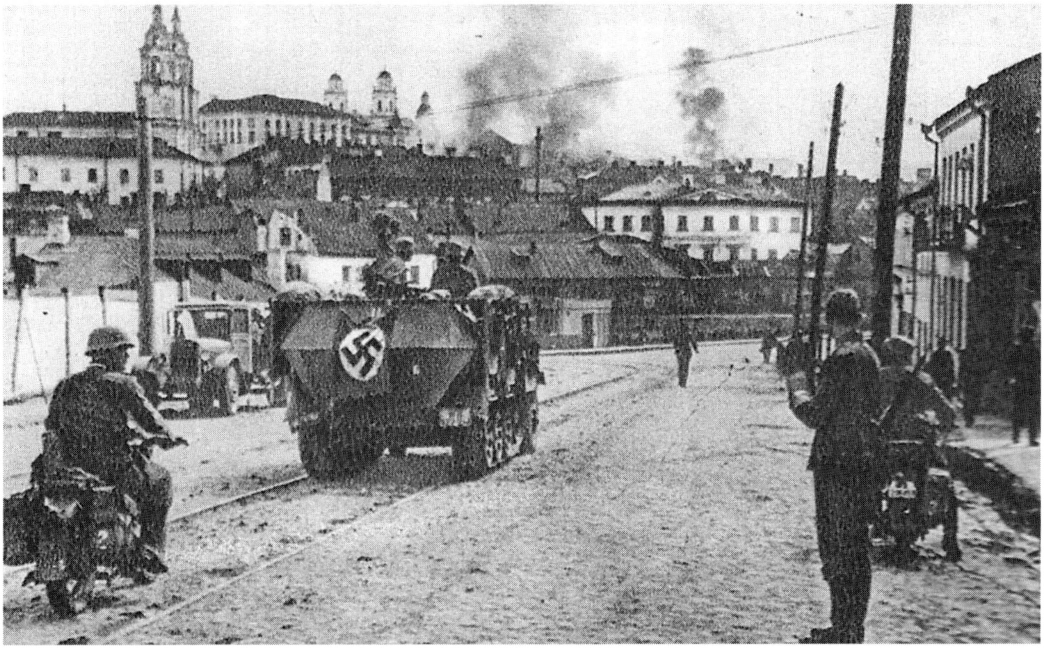

A German SdKfz3-251 half track and motorcycle in burning Minsk.

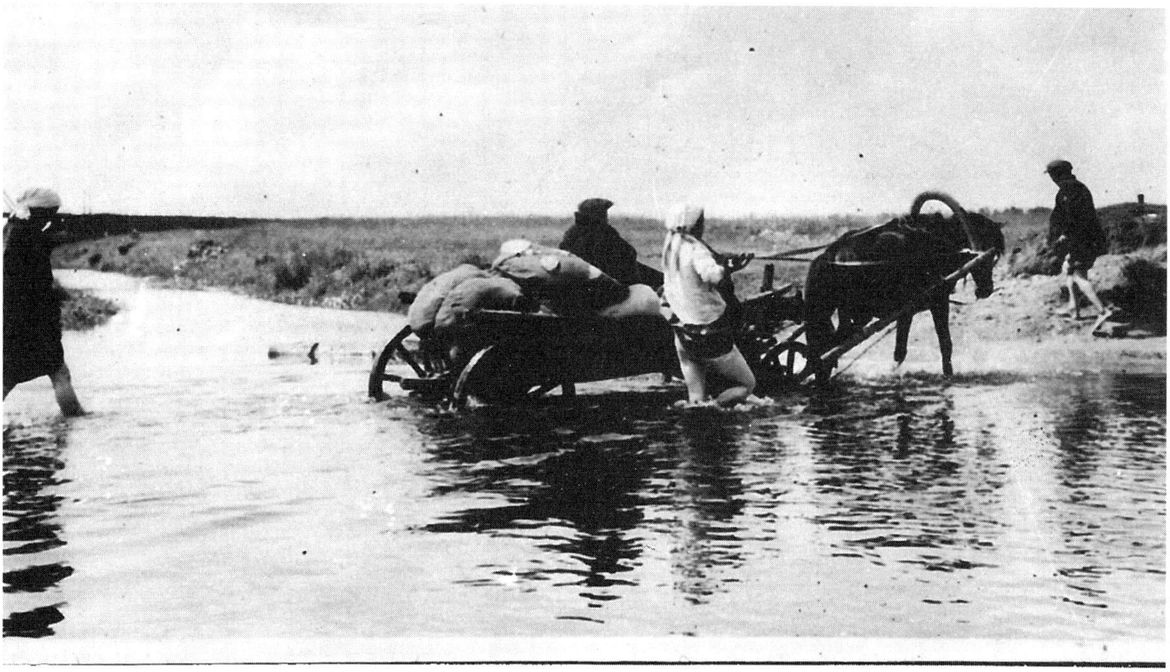

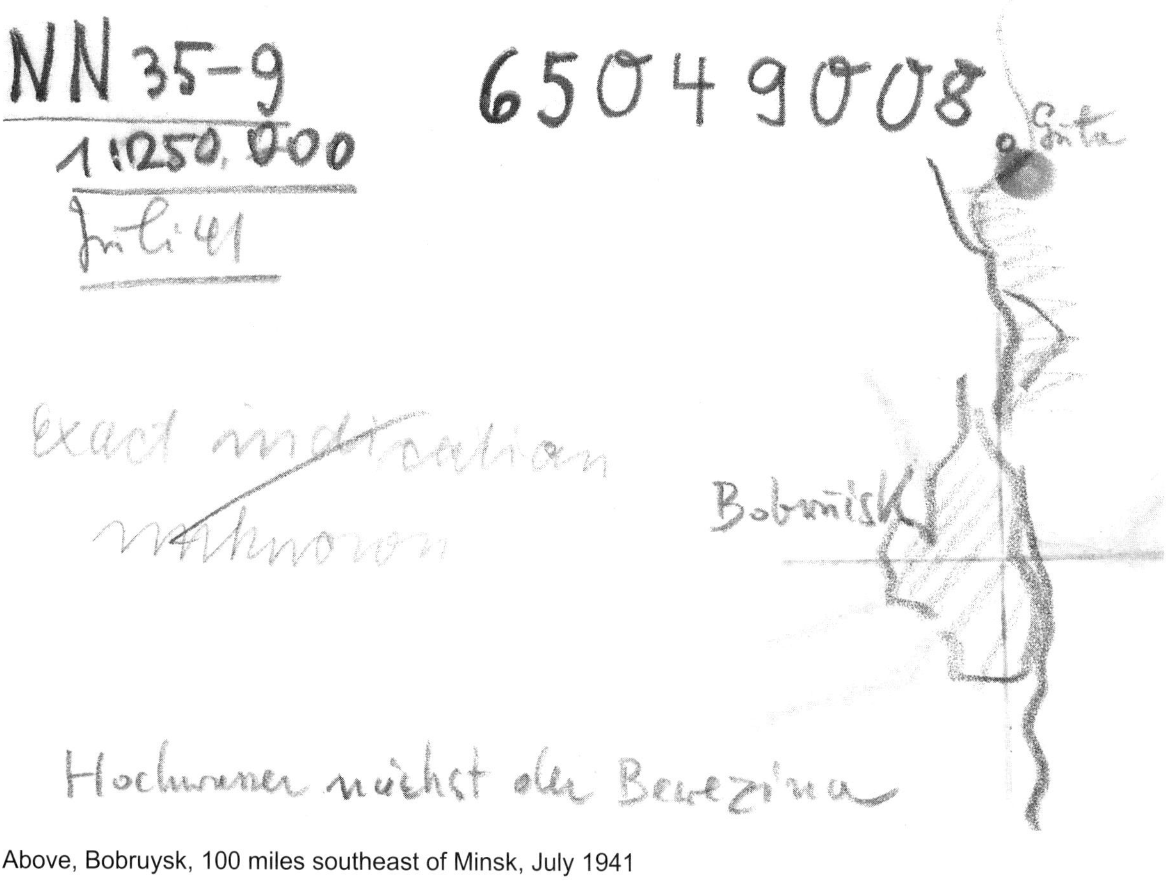
NN 35-9
1:250,000
Juli 41
65049008
exact indication unknown
Bobruisk
Hochwasser nächst der Berezina

Above, Bobruysk, 100 miles southeast of Minsk, July 1941

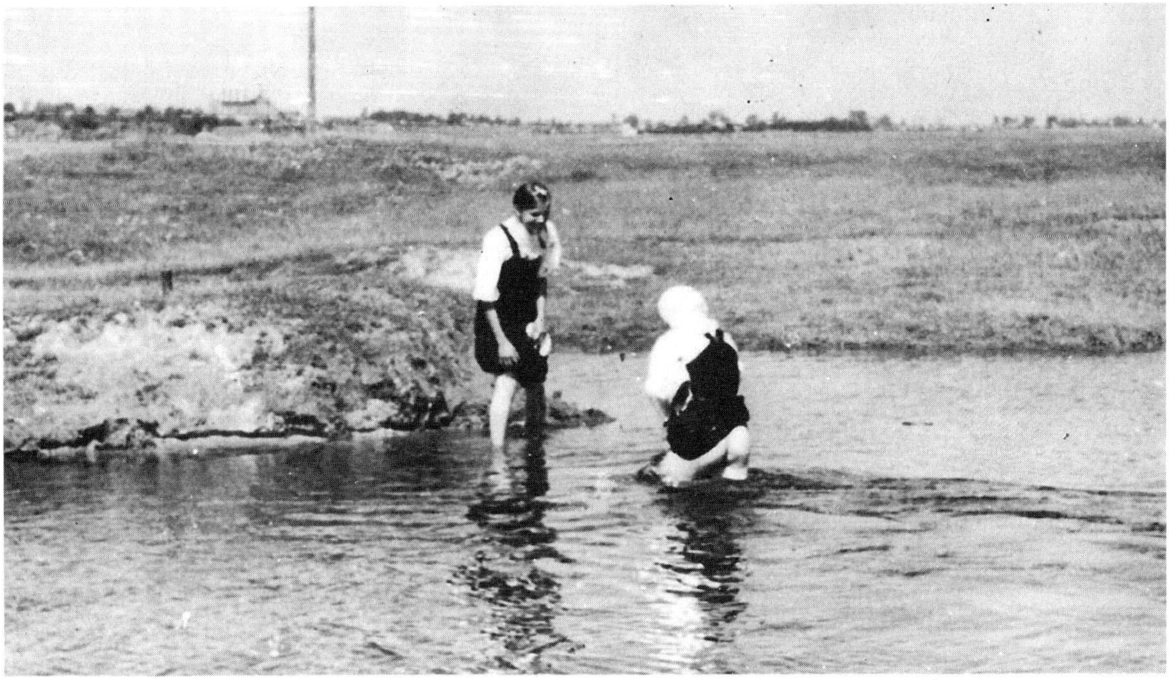

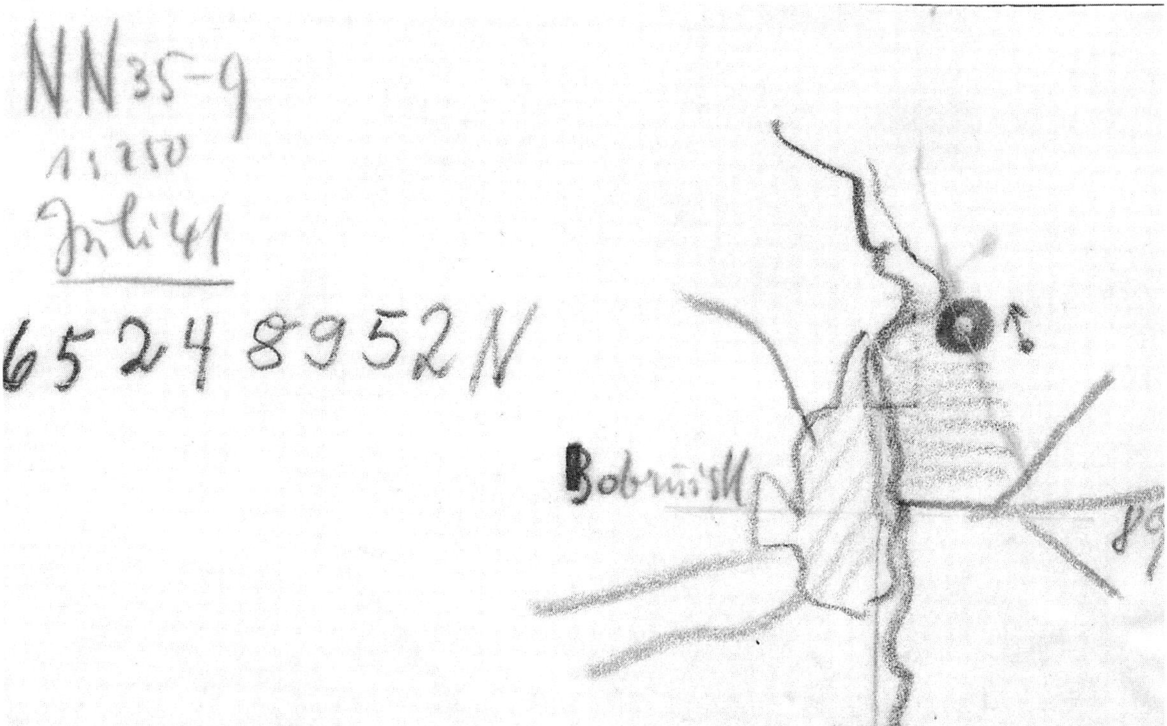
NN35-9
Juli 41
65248952N
Hochwasser

A pretty girl and an unexpected display. No soldier could resist taking that photo. Bobruysk, Belarus, July 1941.

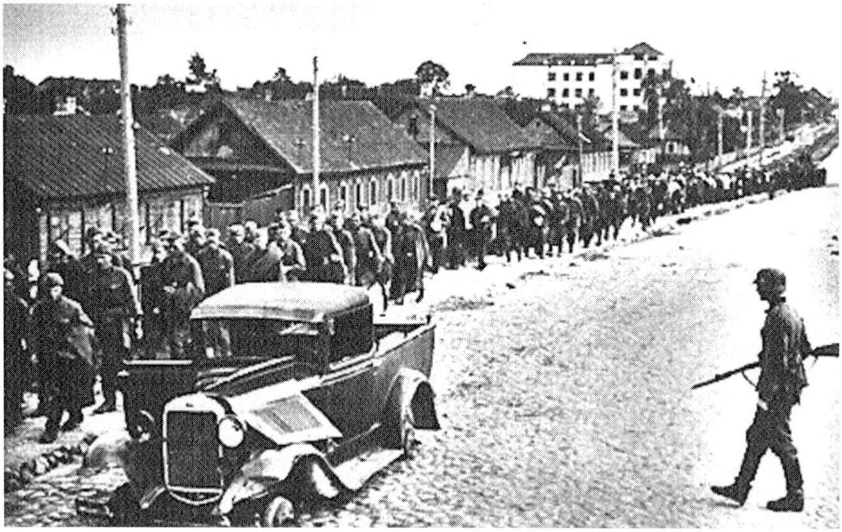

Soviet PoWs at Minsk, 2 July 1941.

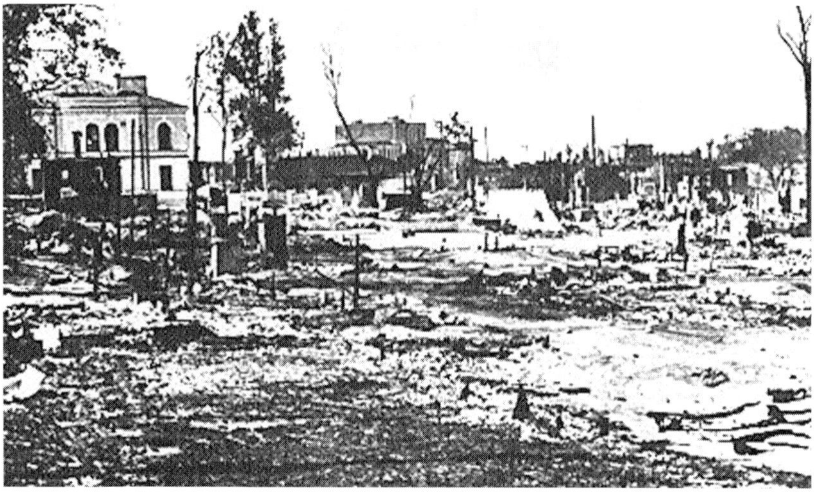

Destruction in Minsk, 3 July 1941.

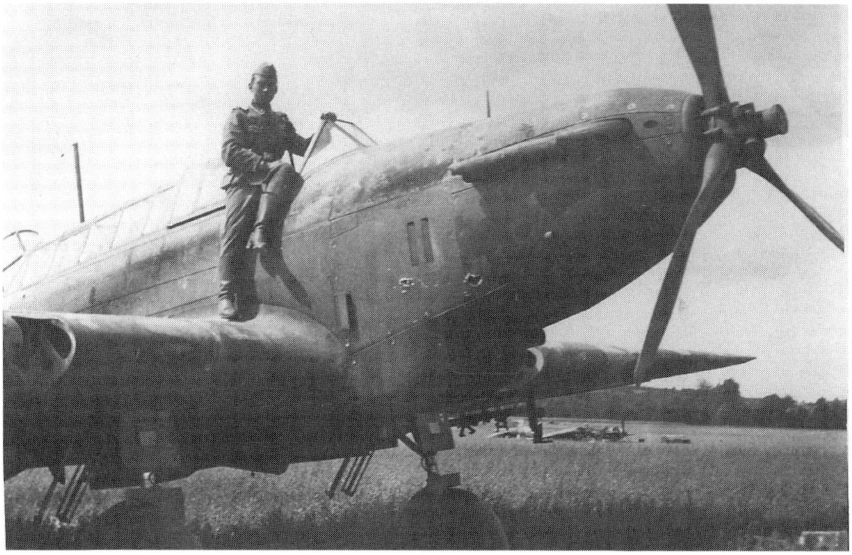

Summer, 1941, a German soldier examines a prize. What is a Fairey Battle light bomber doing on an airfield at Roslavl, half way between Minsk and Moscow?

That looks like an Ilyushin DB-3 wrecked in the background.

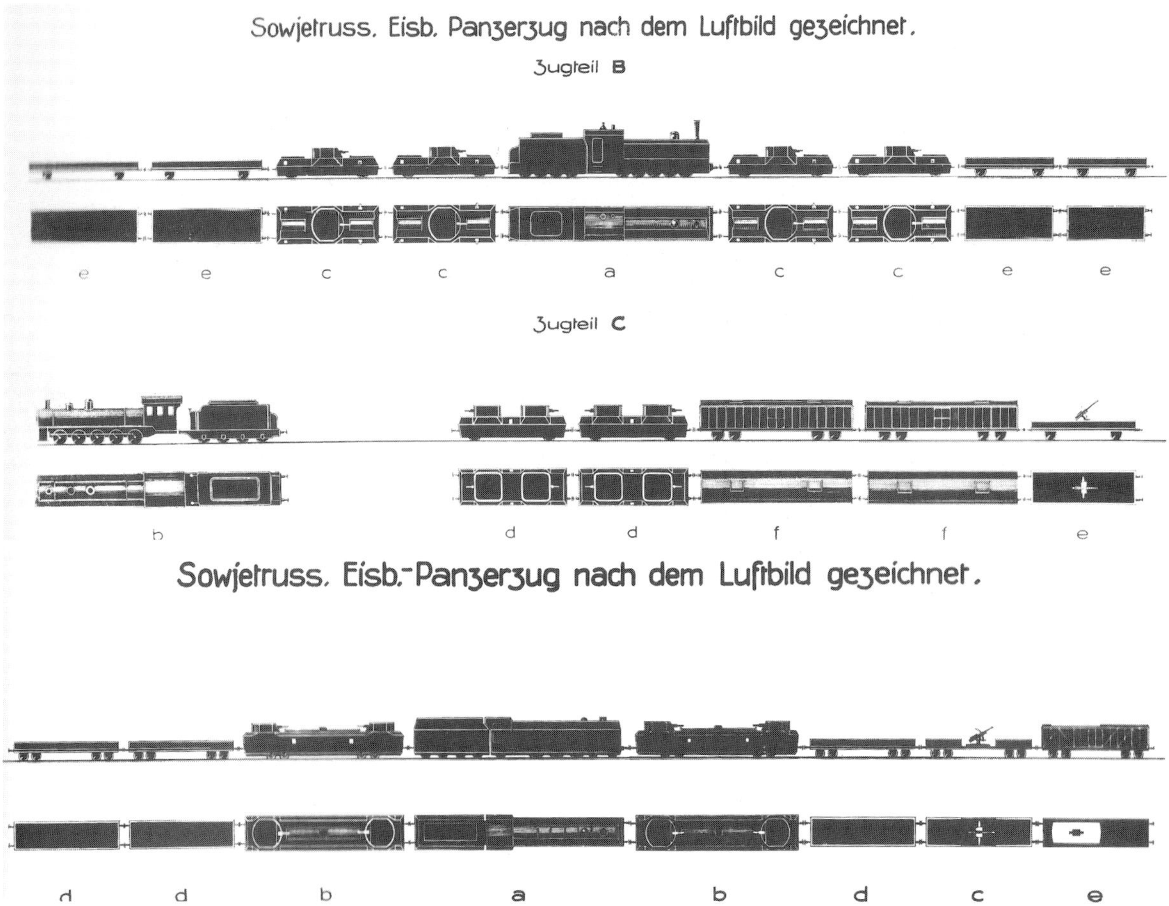
Sowjetruss. Eisb. Panzerzug nach dem Luftbild gezeichnet.
Zugteil B
e e c c a c c e e
Zugteil C
b d d f f e
Sowjetruss. Eisb.-Panzerzug nach dem Luftbild gezeichnet.
d d b a b d c e

The Soviets had used armored trains since shortly after WW I. German Intelligence produced the above recognition guide for three versions of weapons rail cars.

Below, a Soviet armored engine and weapons car with two turrets—lower version in the graphic above.

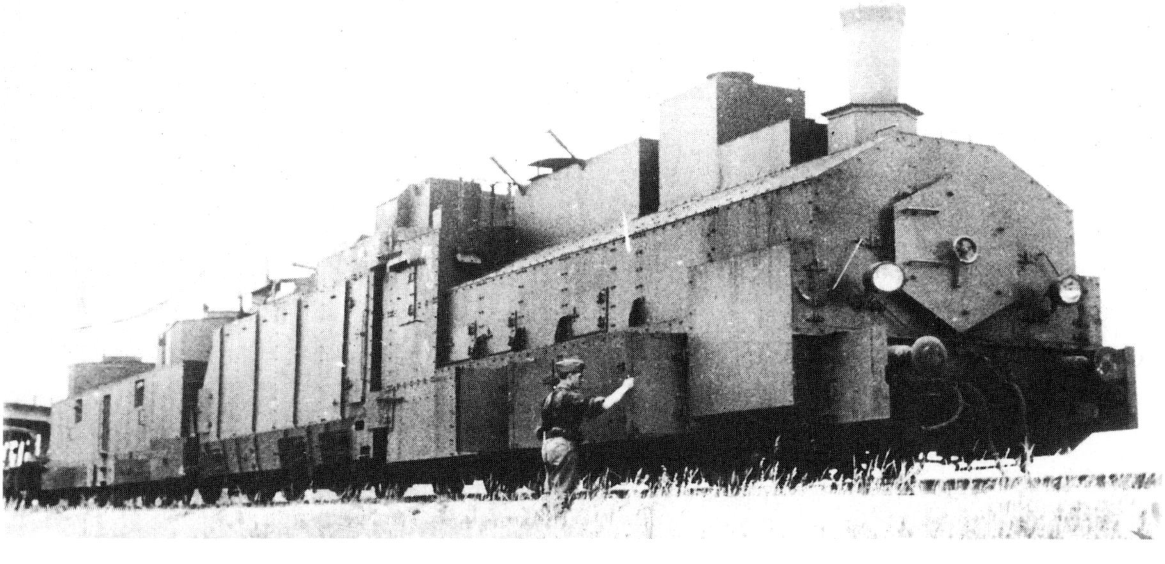

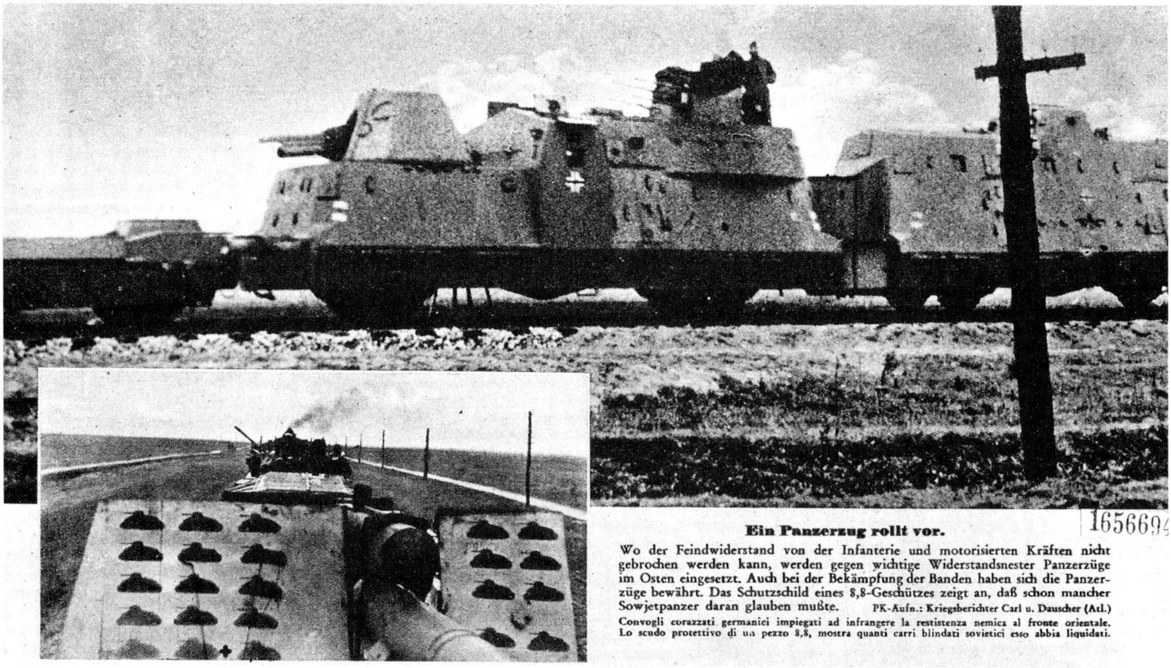

1656694

Ein Panzerzug rollt vor.

Wo der Feindwiderstand von der Infanterie und motorisierten Kräften nicht gebrochen werden kann, werden gegen wichtige Widerstandsnester Panzerzüge im Osten eingesetzt. Auch bei der Bekämpfung der Banden haben sich die Panzerzüge bewährt. Das Schutzschild eines 8,8-Geschützes zeigt an, daß schon mancher Sowjetpanzer daran glauben mußte. PK-Aufn.: Kriegsberichter Carl u. Dauscher (Atl.)

Convogli corazzati germanici impiegati ad infrangere la restistenza nemica al fronte orientale. Lo scudo protettivo di un pezzo 8,8, mostra quanti carri blindati sovietici esso abbia liquidati.

In response the Germans brought in their own armored train, Panzerzug BP42 (possibly taken from Poland). In the inset, this one claimed 23 Soviet tank kills with the 88mm gun behind that shield (but we don't see the gun in photos taken from the side). The bottom lines of text are in Italian, so the photo was apparently a magazine release.

Below, a look at the entire train, definitely the same one as above. It's easy to see how a train would be effective moving and employing artillery on open plains in Belarus and Ukraine.

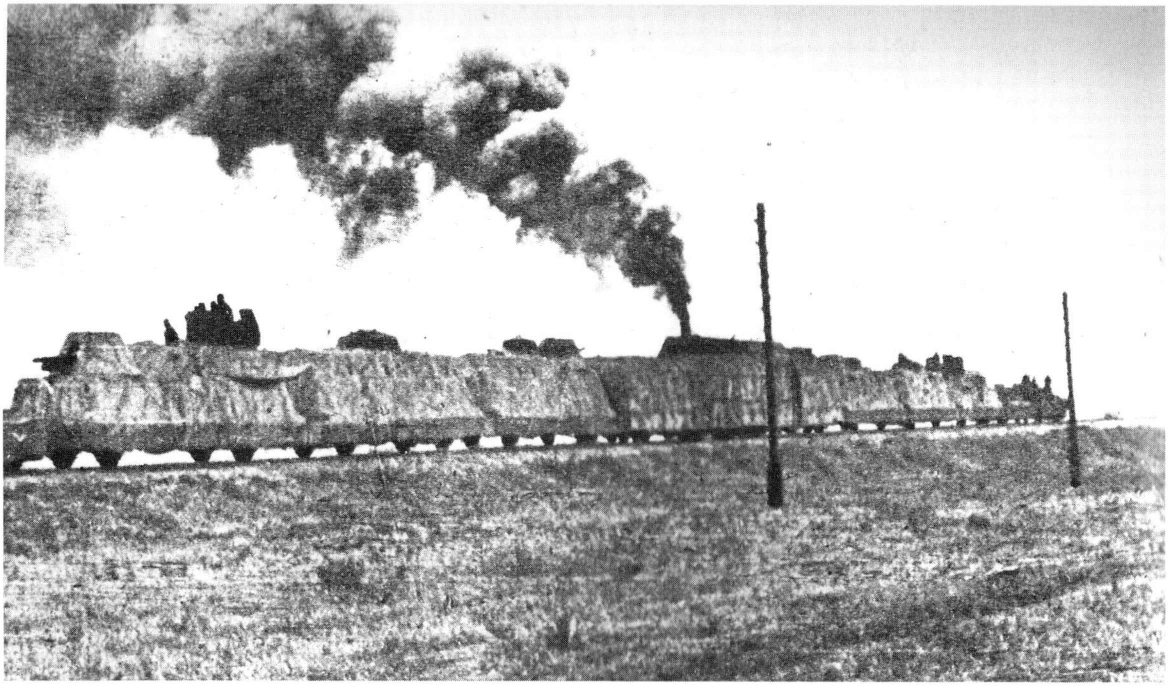

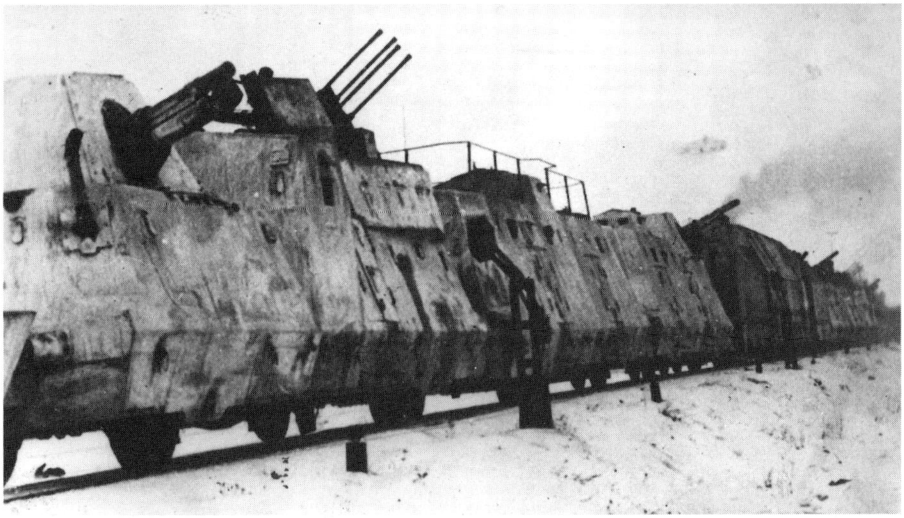

A closer look in winter paint. The four turret guns are probably 10.5cm howitzers and there are at least two Flak 20, four barrel 20mm AA guns.

Engine and tender were protected from weapons up to 20mm.

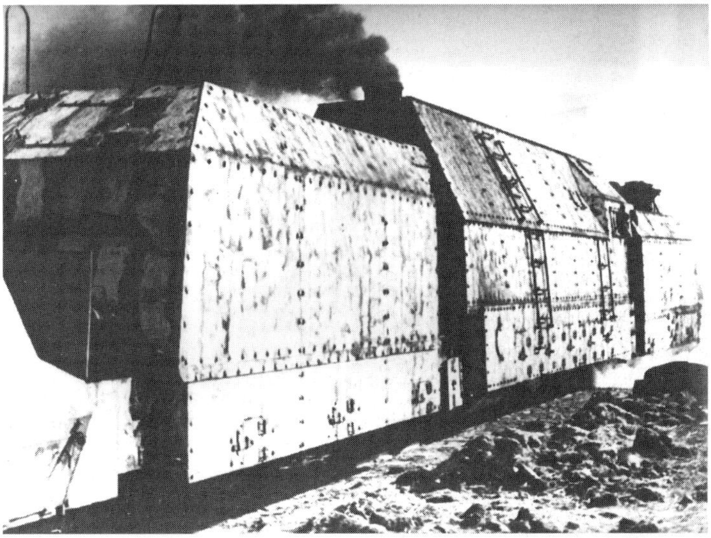

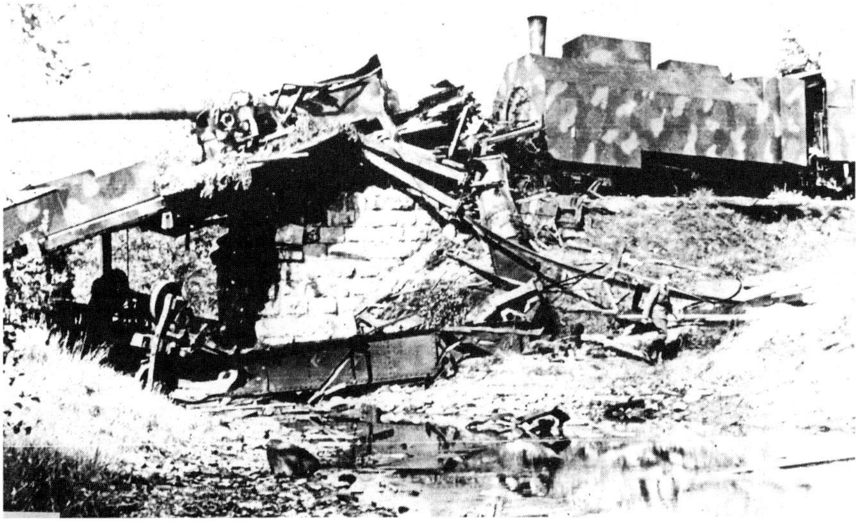

Left—there was one sure way to stop an armored train.

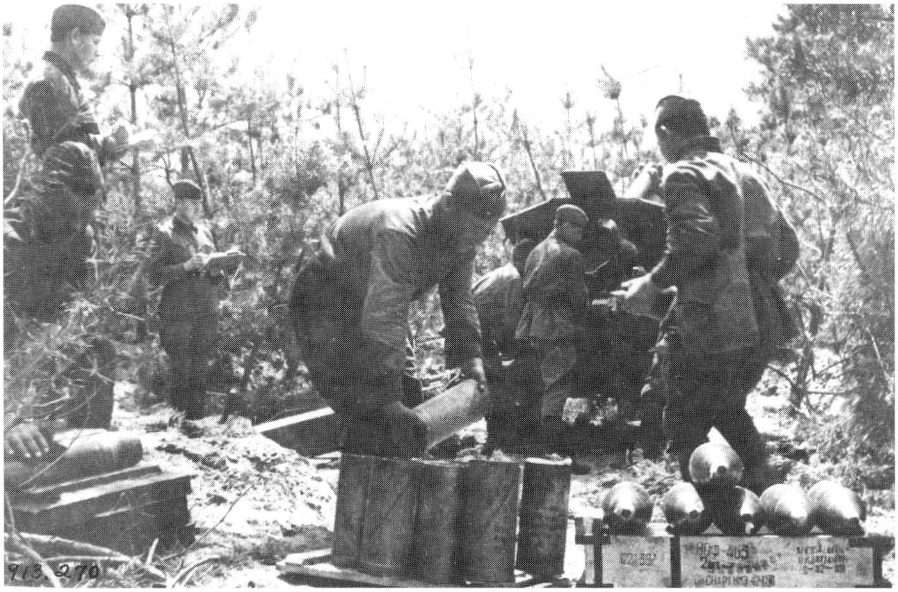

Soviet artillery, a 122mm M1938 (M-30). The round is two parts—powder and projectile.

The Luftwaffe regularly imaged Moscow. The triangular building just right of center is the Kremlin and right of it is Red Square. Annotation '4' and the circle are bomb hits (miniscule damage was done).

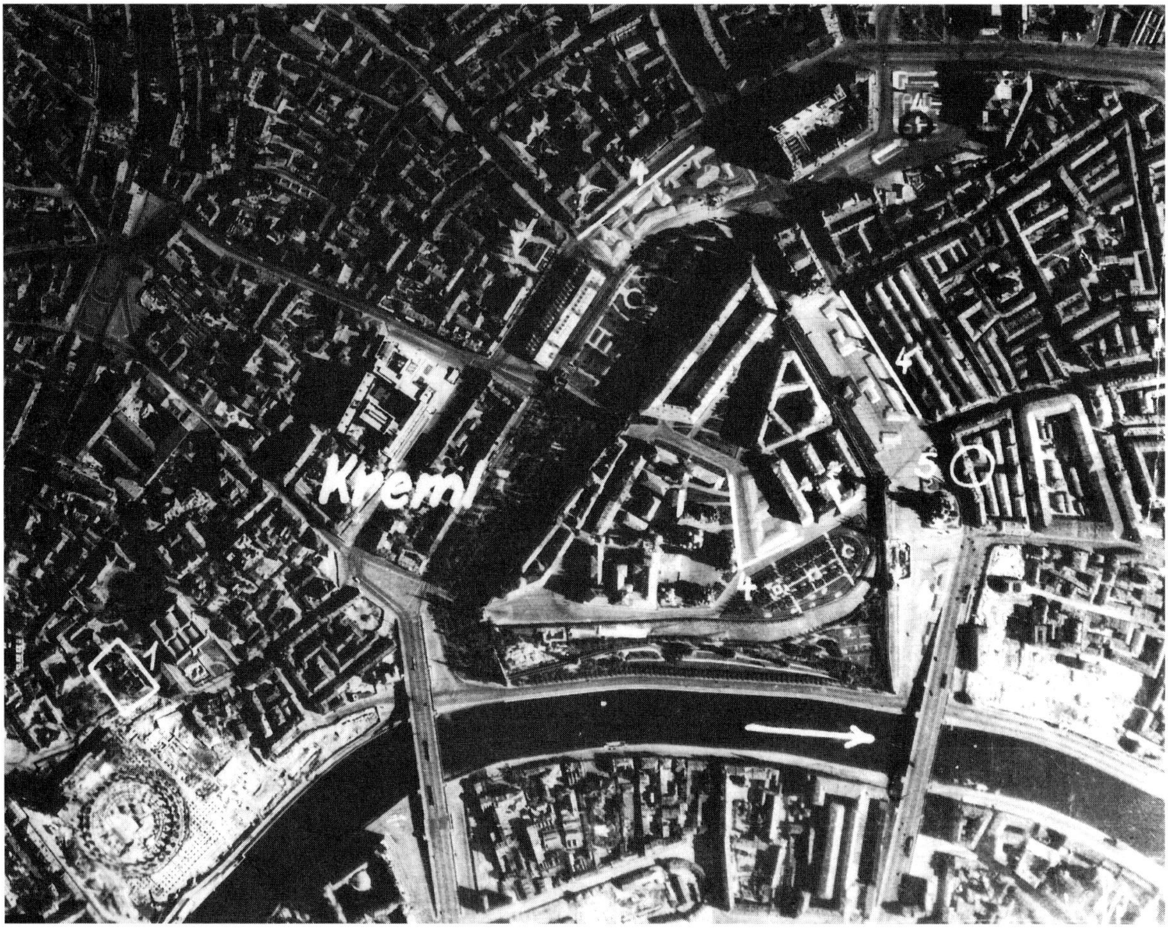
Kreml

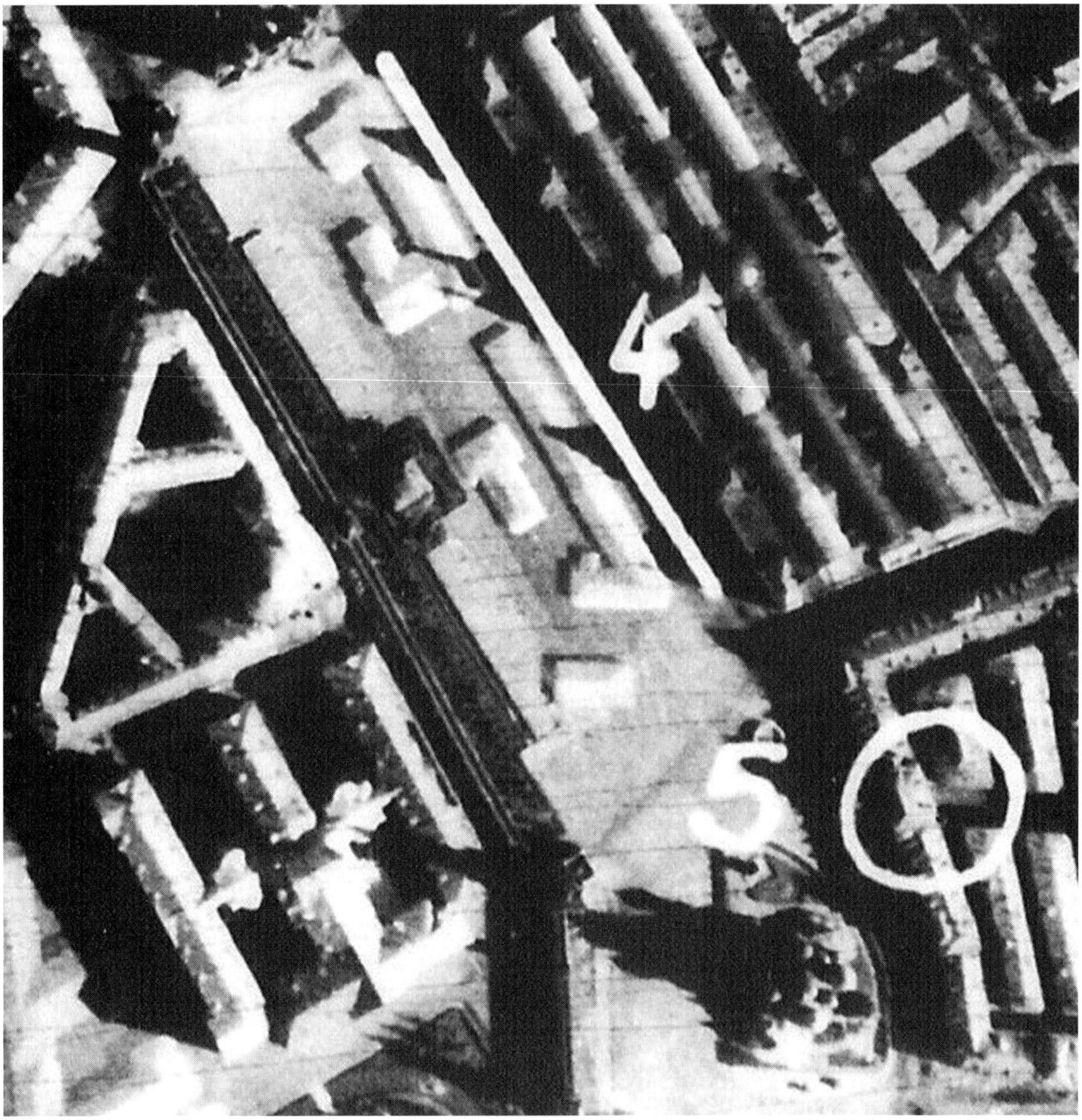
4
5

Enlargement of the previous image. Just right of the Kremlin (the triangular building), Lenin's Mausoleum juts out into Red Square which runs up and left from Saint Basil's Cathedral (below annotation 5).

Remember that Chapter II photo of a horse-drawn machine-gun unit in Red Square on 1 May 1941? Here is the reason for those strange dark lines on the pavement. The Soviets were attempting to camouflage Red Square, making it look like just another part of the city to confuse Luftwaffe bombers. Those 'building' shapes, including shadows, are flat. Of course shadow length and direction are different from surrounding buildings, which blows the effect.

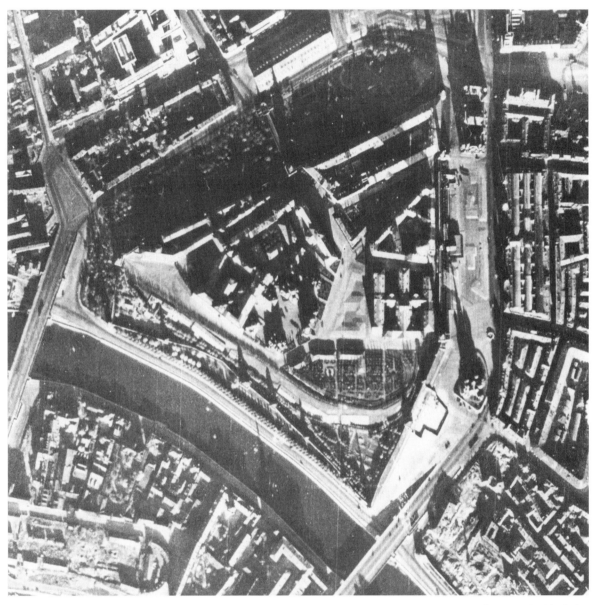

The absurdity of that painted camouflage on open flat surfaces was more obvious on 5 October 1941. Saint Basil's shadow almost touches Lenin's Tomb. Another area of bogus buildings is left of Red Square (left and down from the Kremlin). That is the square in front of Ivan the Great's Bell Tower.

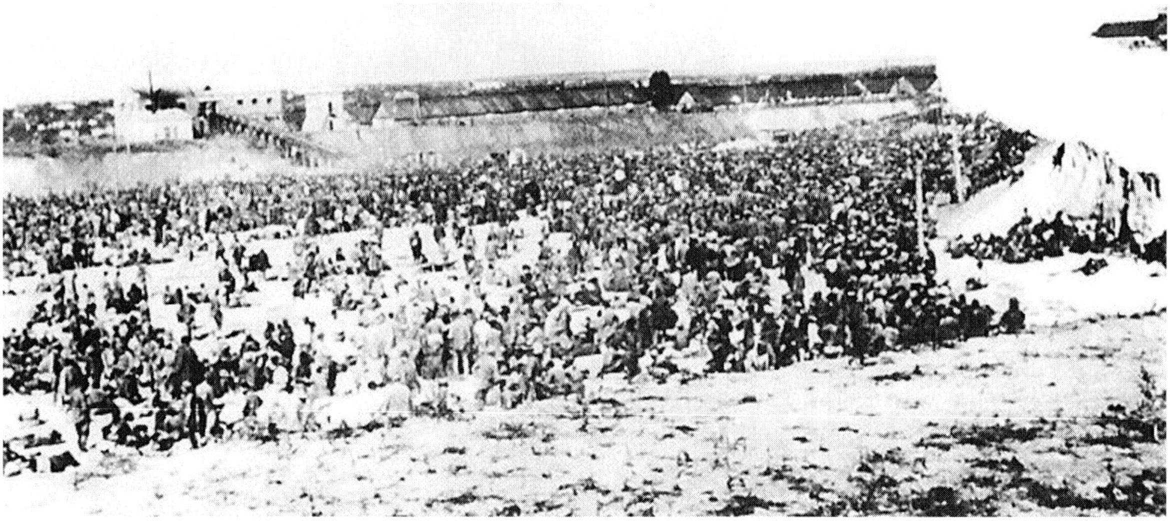

Near Uman, 50,000 Soviet prisoners,
14 August 1941.

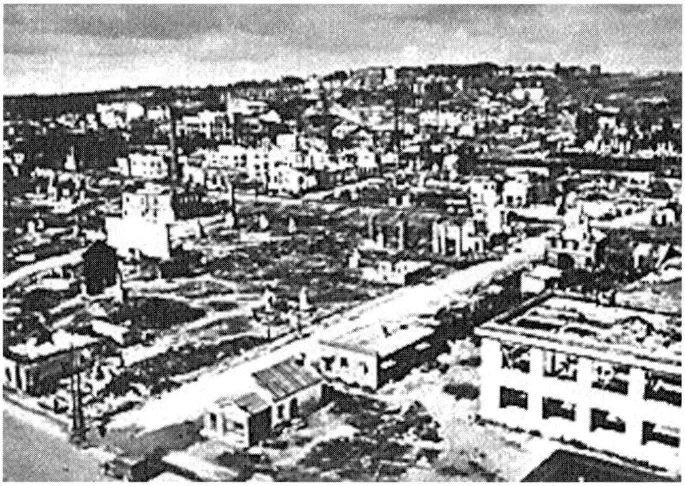

Smolensk destroyed,
29 August 1941.

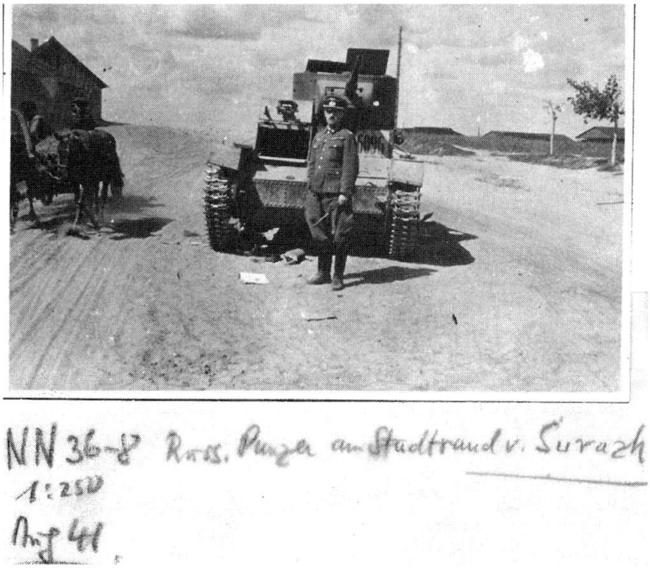
NN 36-8 Russ. Panzer am Stadtrand v. Surazh
1:250
Aug 41

German officer posing with an abandoned Soviet T 26 light tank near Roslavl, August 1941. Horses and peasants at left couldn't care less.

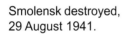

Karte: 1 : 250000 Blatt: NN 36-4 ORSHA Aufnahme August 1941

38
607
AUTOBAHN N. SMOLENSK
606
40

266

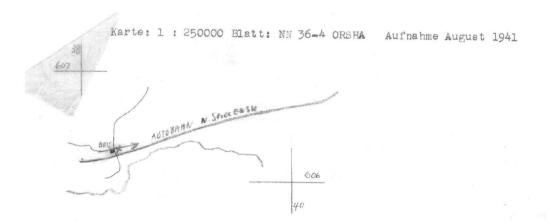

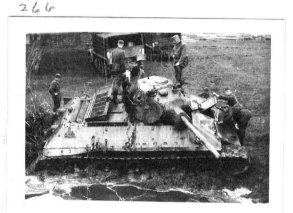

Im Sumpf festgefahrener Russ. Panzer T34 bei BELEI, noerdl. der Autobahn MINSK-MOSKVA (SMOLENSK)

3834 0630 E

August 1941, 200 miles northeast of Minsk, German soldiers inspect an abandoned T-34, which was new to them. Its 76.2mm gun had more range and penetration power than Pz IV's short barrel 50mm. A German caption says the tank was bogged in a swamp, but muck on the turret and tow cables running to background half-tracks suggest it was on its side in the water and has just been righted.

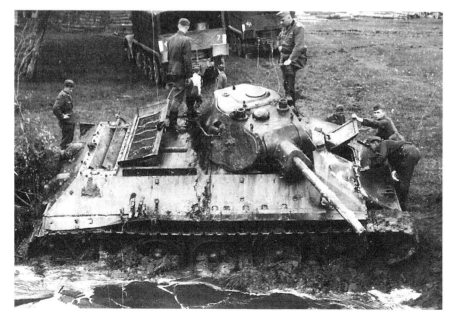

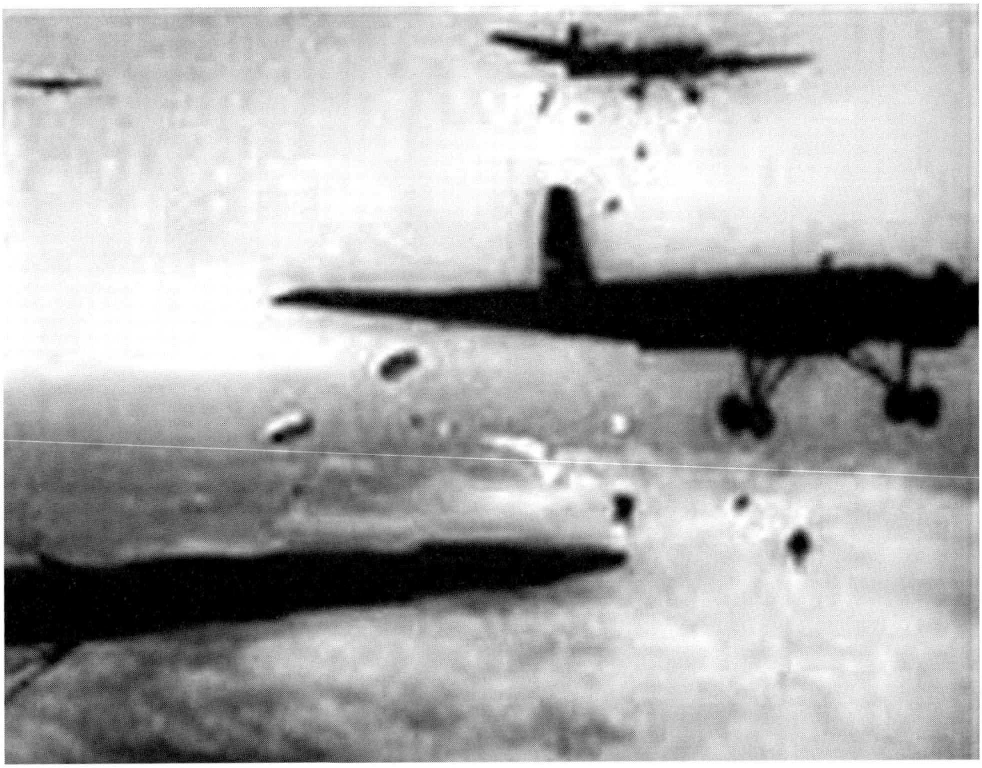

Just as ground troops were being thrown into impossible, even hopeless, situations in a panic to at least slow the German onslaught, vastly outclassed Soviet aviation was struggling back with anything that could get into the air. Venerable TB-3s were put back in operation. Red Air Force had over 500 TB-3s and used them mainly as night bombers and for para-drops of men and supplies.

Below, at least four giant Tupolev TB-3s on an unnamed base, probably during Barbarossa. Sending these dinosaurs against the Luftwaffe was sheer desperation but they fought at Smolensk, Moscow, Leningrad, Stalingrad and Kursk. At the end of WW II only ten TB-3s were still flying.

The single-engine light bomber at right is probably an equally obsolete Sukhoi Su-2.

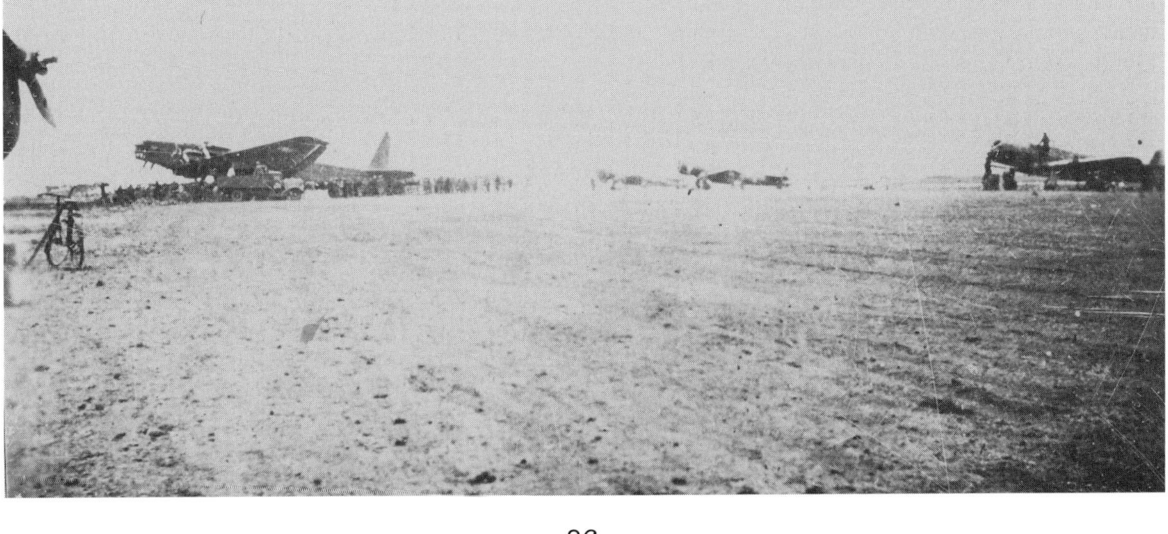

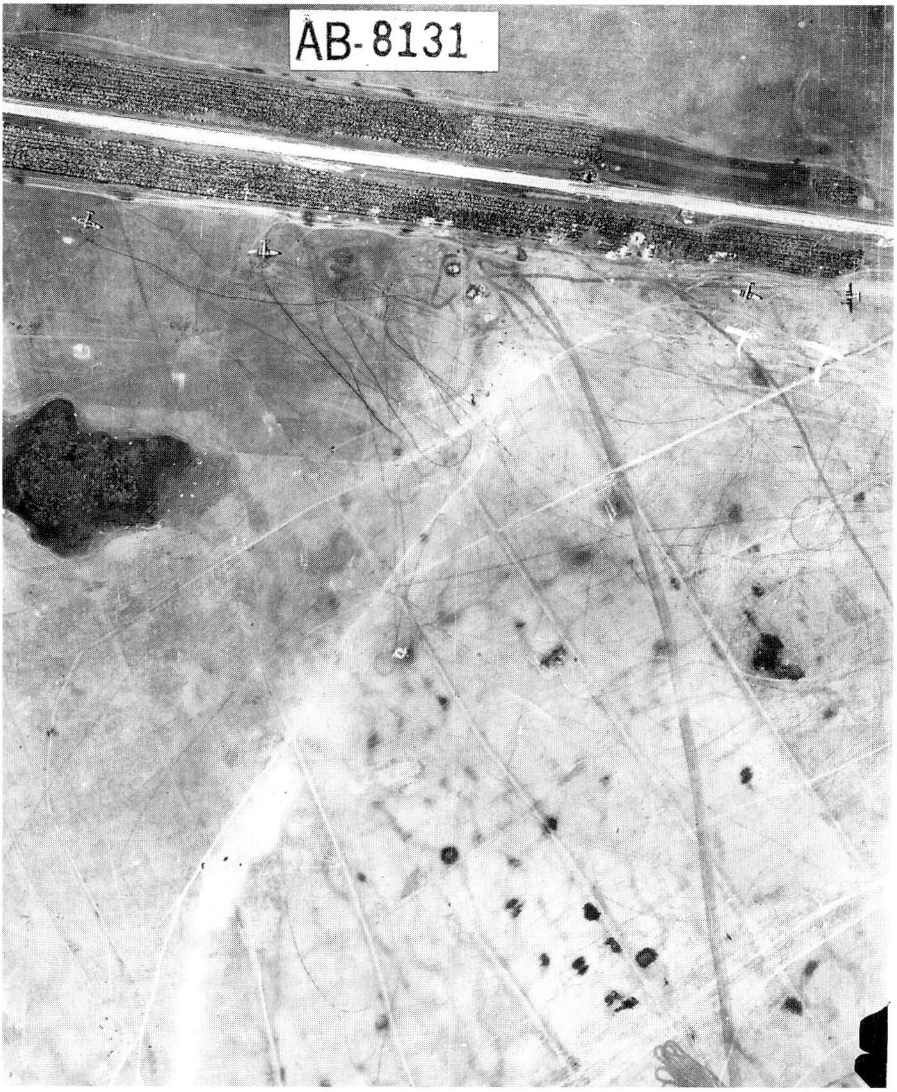
AB-8131

An unnamed field 150 miles west of Moscow, summer 1941. Four TB-3s are at the top, two with 'X' from a PI which usually indicated something destroyed. Below is the best look I found of TB-3s from overhead. Its 137 foot wingspan was 33 feet longer than a B-17.

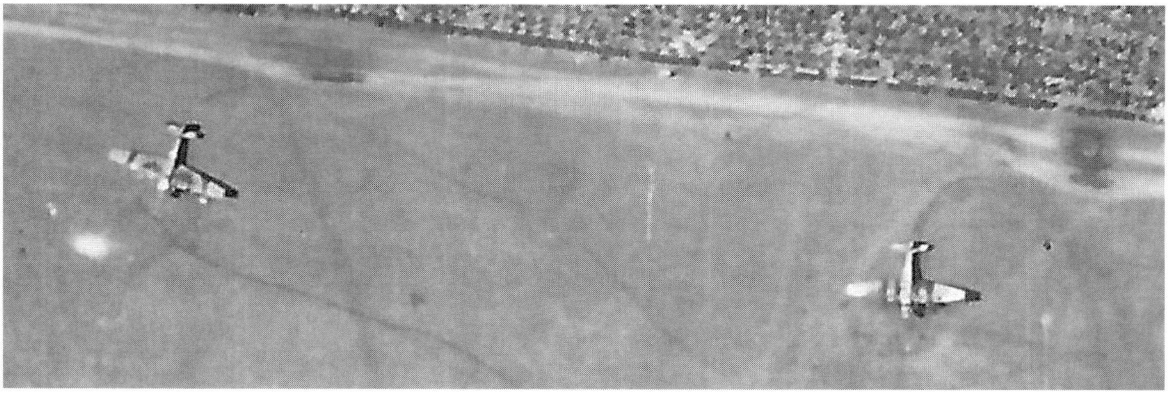

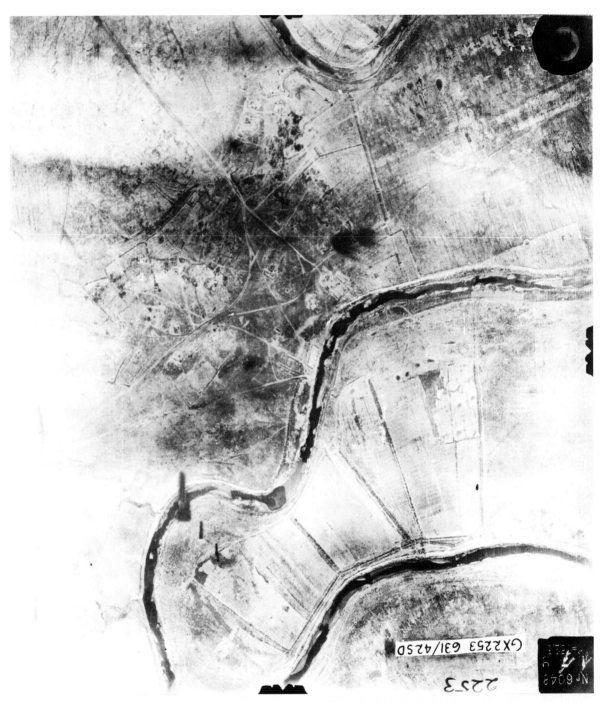

I don't know where this is, or when, much less the target. This photo is included because of its rarity. I can count on one hand the number of Barbarossa aerial photos I've seen showing actual bombing (which was often photographed over England). This appears to have been taken with a reconnaissance camera but the altitude seems low and recon sorties weren't routinely armed. Bombing accuracy from a recon altitude of 30-35,000 feet would be poor at best.

Five bombs in sequence rules out a Ju-87 and they are falling, not tumbling as from a He-111. My best guess for a bomb-capable camera-capable aircraft is the Ju-88.

Right, troops entering Kiev 20 September 1941. Success and confidence show in their stride.

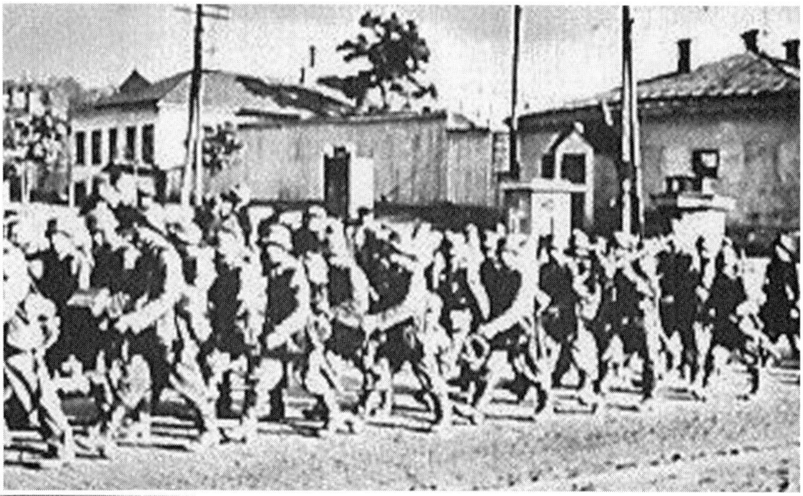

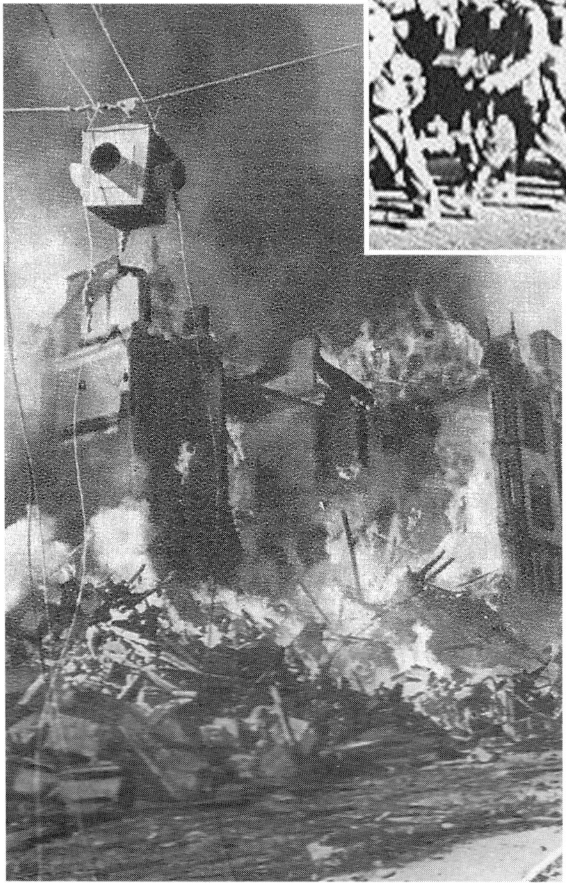

Kiev, 9 September 1941.

Burning Soviet depots, Kiev, 20 September.

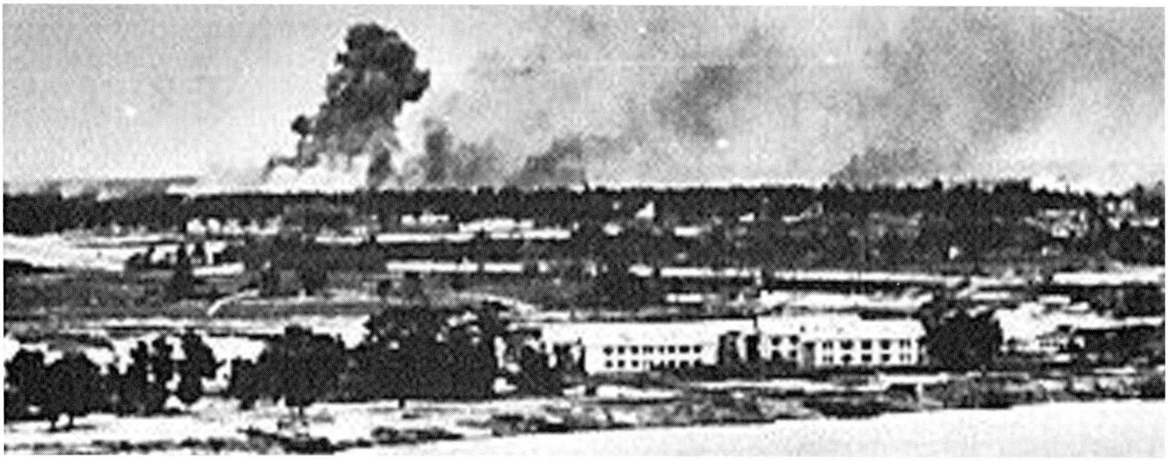

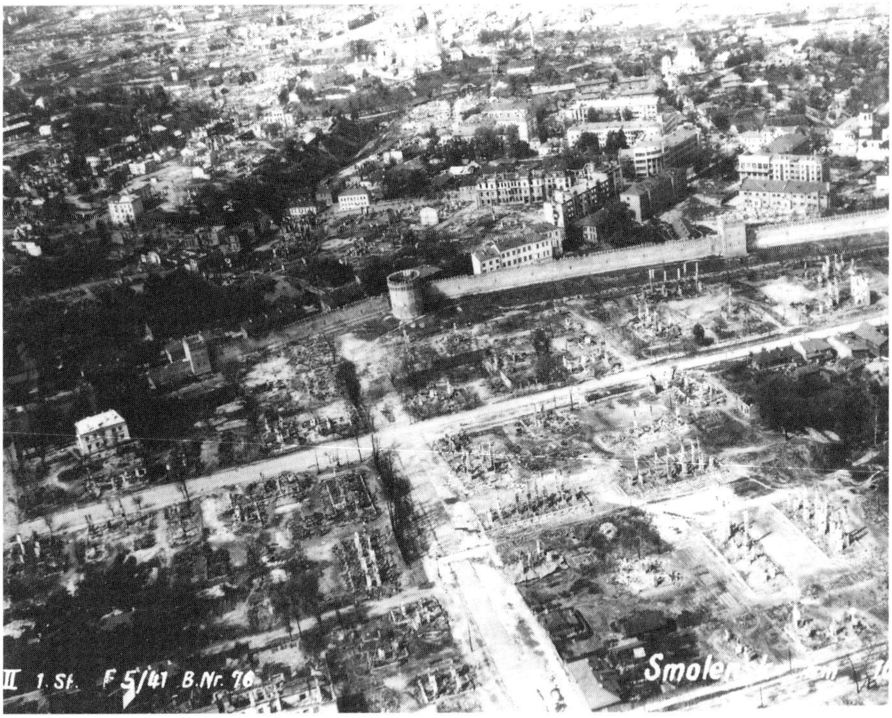
1. St. F 5/41 B.Nr. 76

Only chimneys stand in the ruins of this part of Smolensk, 8 October 1941.

Below, it looks like the soldier at left, and probably the one in front of our photographer, are also taking pictures of hanged partisans. The Intel analyst was interested in bridge construction.

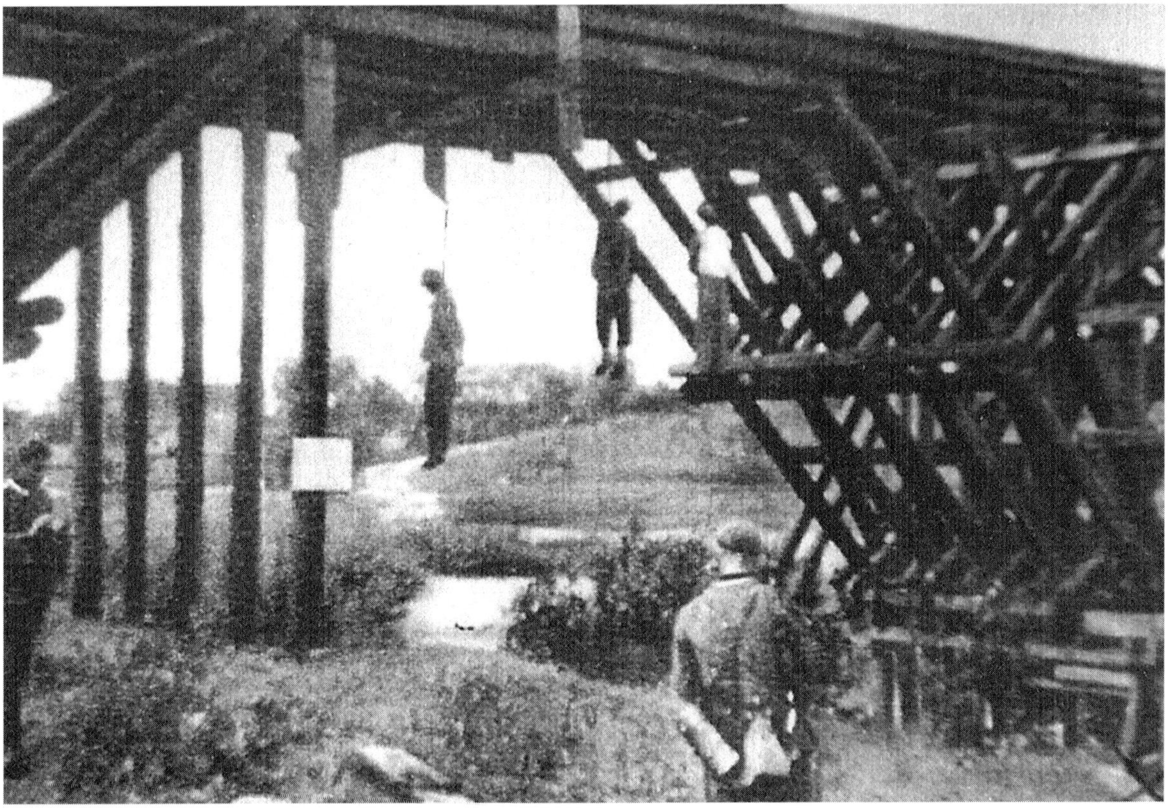

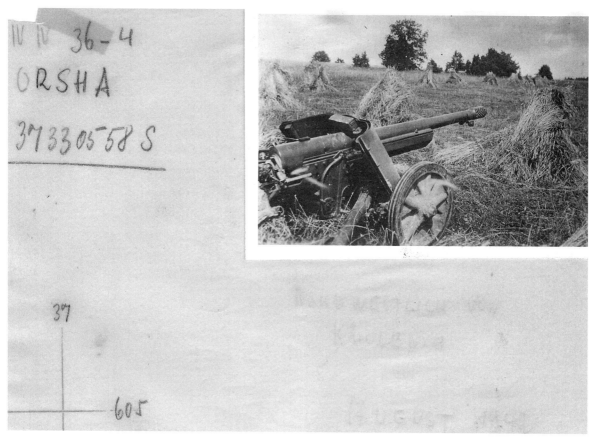

IV IV 36-4
ORSHA
37330558 S
37
605

Above, German 7.5cm Pak 97/38 anti-tank gun in a wheat field near Orsha, Belarus.

8.8 cm Flak in Stellung. Um einen Durchbruch mehrerer eingeschlossener Sowjet-Divisionen zu verhindern, wurde im Verband einer Panzerdivision Flakartillerie eingesetzt

8.8 cm antiaircraft artillery in position. Antiaircraft artillery was attached to a panzer division unit in order to prevent the break-through of several encircled Soviet divisions.

From: M/A. Berlin, Germany   Report #18,717   Oct. 15, 1941.

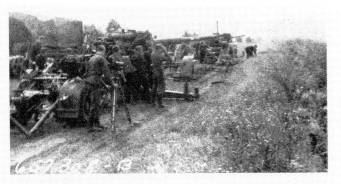

US Attaché Report, Berlin, 13 October 1941, on using an 88mm AA gun as an anti-tank weapon.

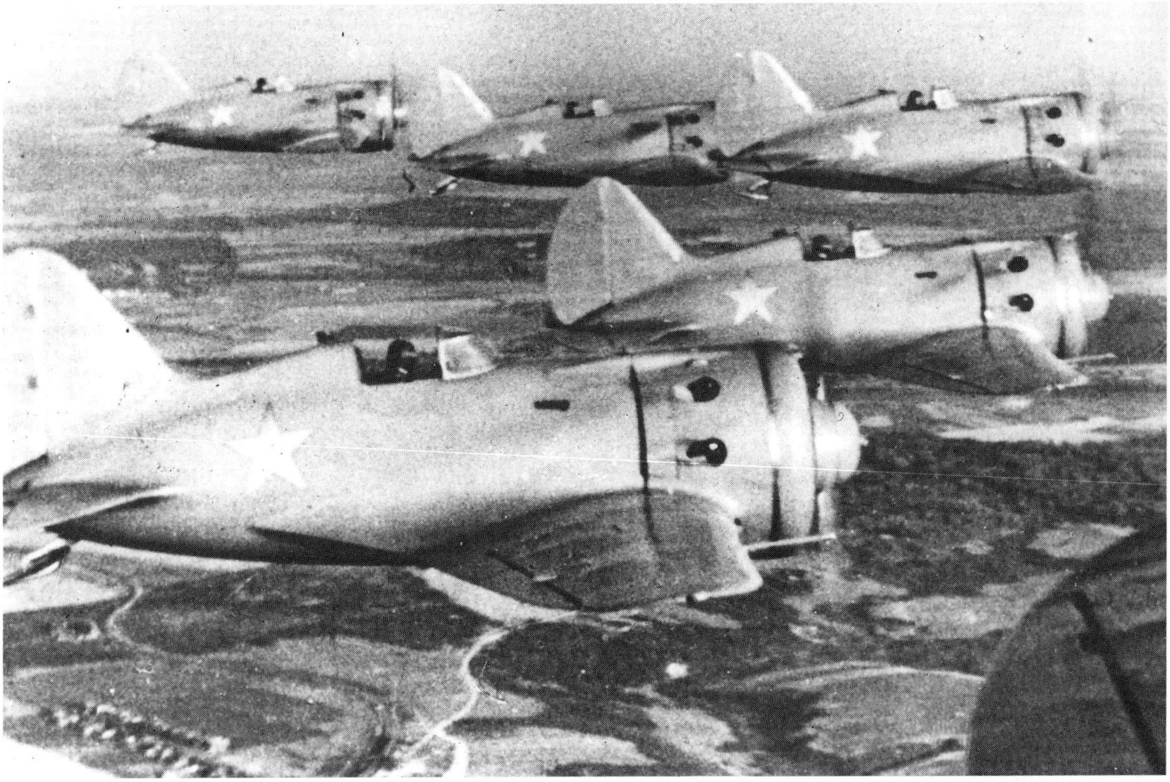

Soviet aviation was fighting back desperately in 1941. A Polikarpov I-16 in skilled hands could hold its own. The first cantilevered wing, retractable landing gear fighter, the Rata (Rat) was highly maneuverable. Dubbed Rata or Mosca in Spain (rat or fly) where it did well, in 1942 it wasn't able to rat-race with Bf 109Fs and half of the I-16s were destroyed by August. This is a photo of a pre-war Red Air Force demonstration team.

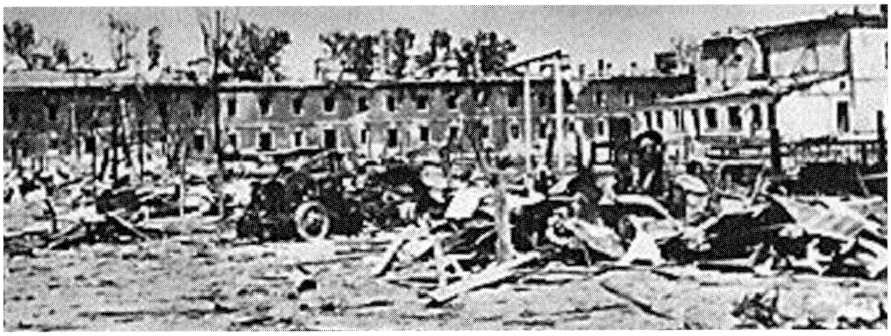

Citadel at Brest destroyed by the Luftwaffe, 30 June 1941.

Below, an armored regiment advances into Borisov, 30 June 1941.

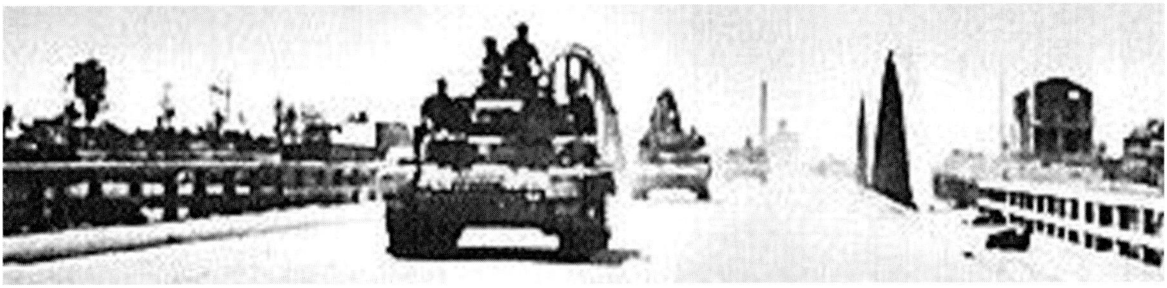

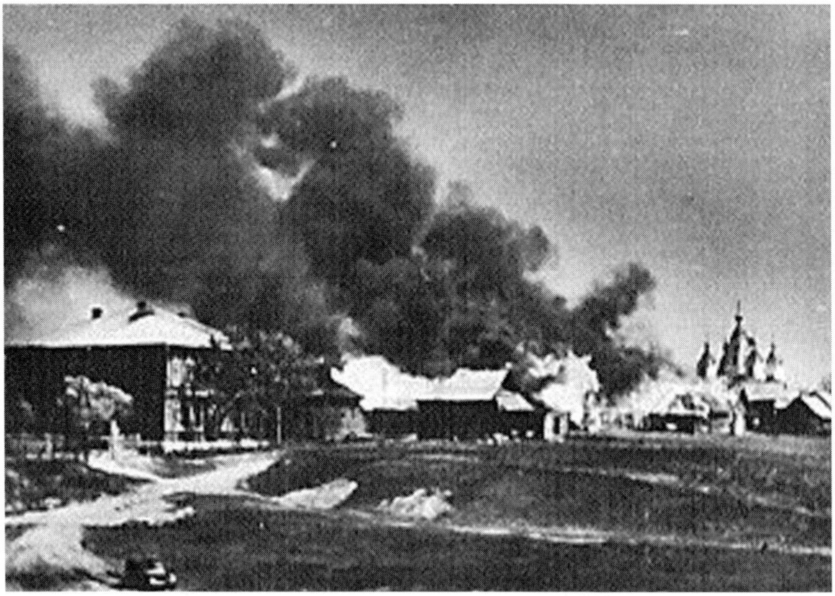

Demidov, 17 miles north of Kiev, 14 July 1941.

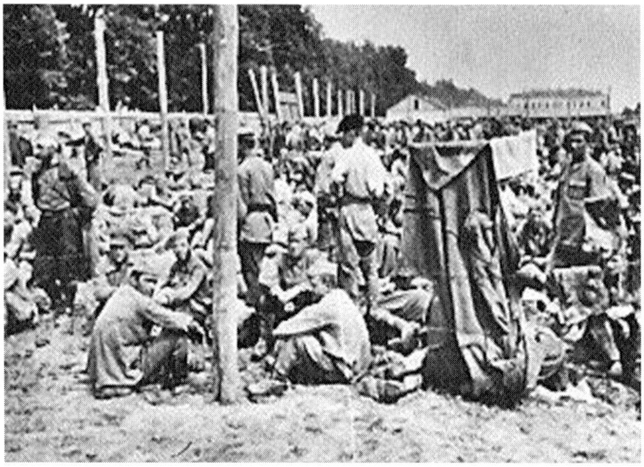

6,000 prisoners at Vinnitsa, 28 July 1941.

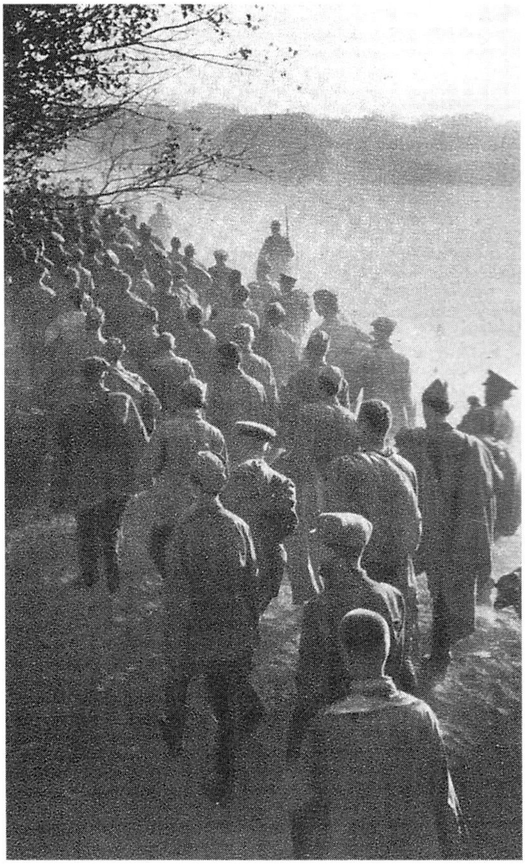

PoWs at Smolensk.

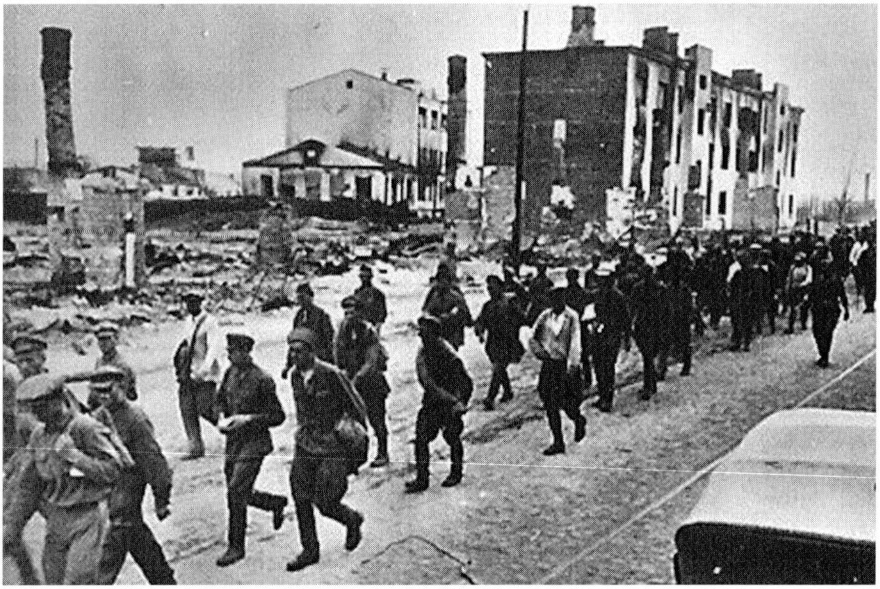

PoWs in destroyed Vitebsk, 17 July 1941.

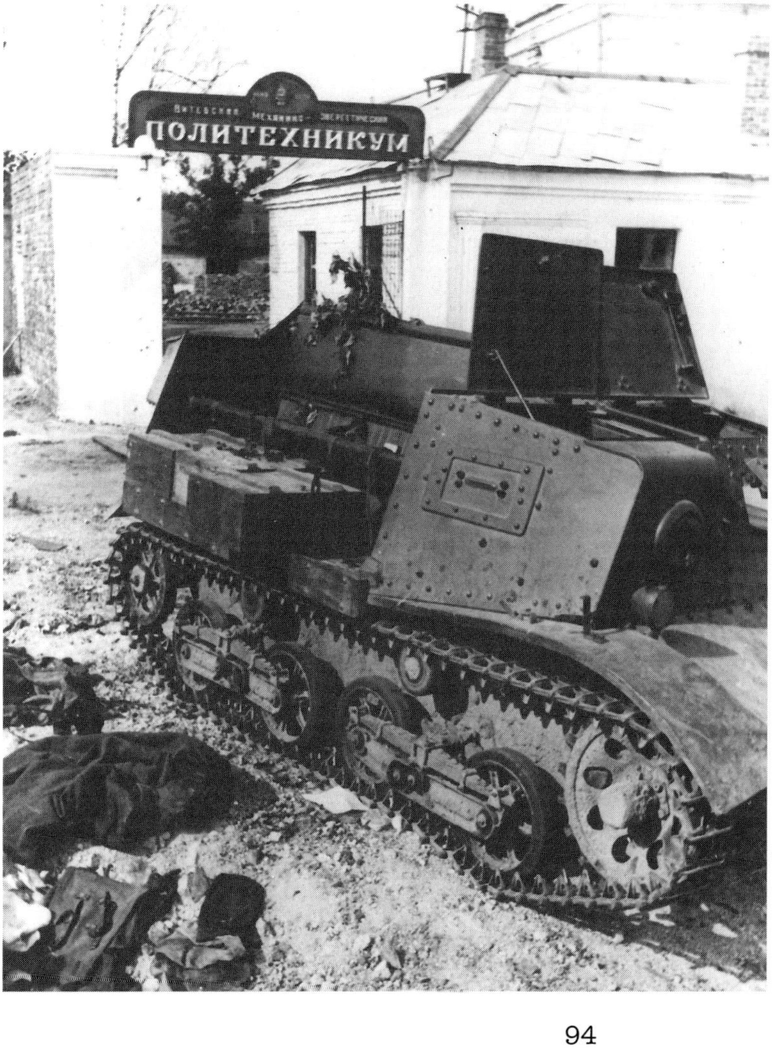
ПОЛИТЕХНИКУМ

An abandoned Soviet T-20 tankette, Vitebsk, July 1941.

German light anti-aircraft gun on guard at Riga, 7 July 1941. Probably a 20mm Flak 38.

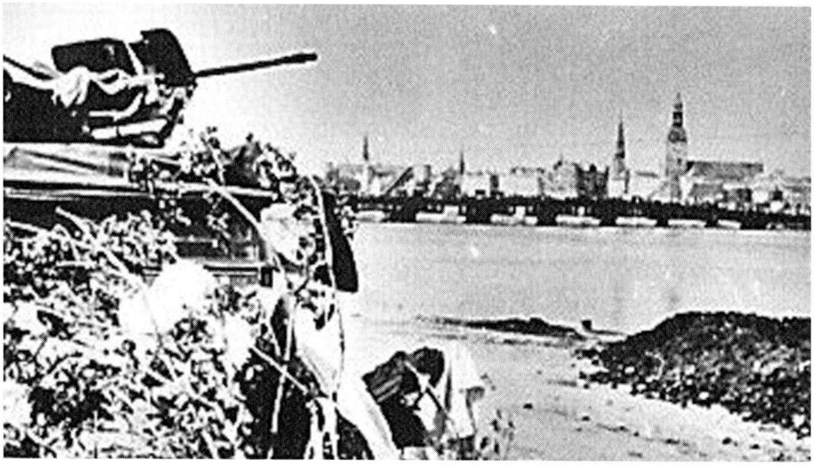

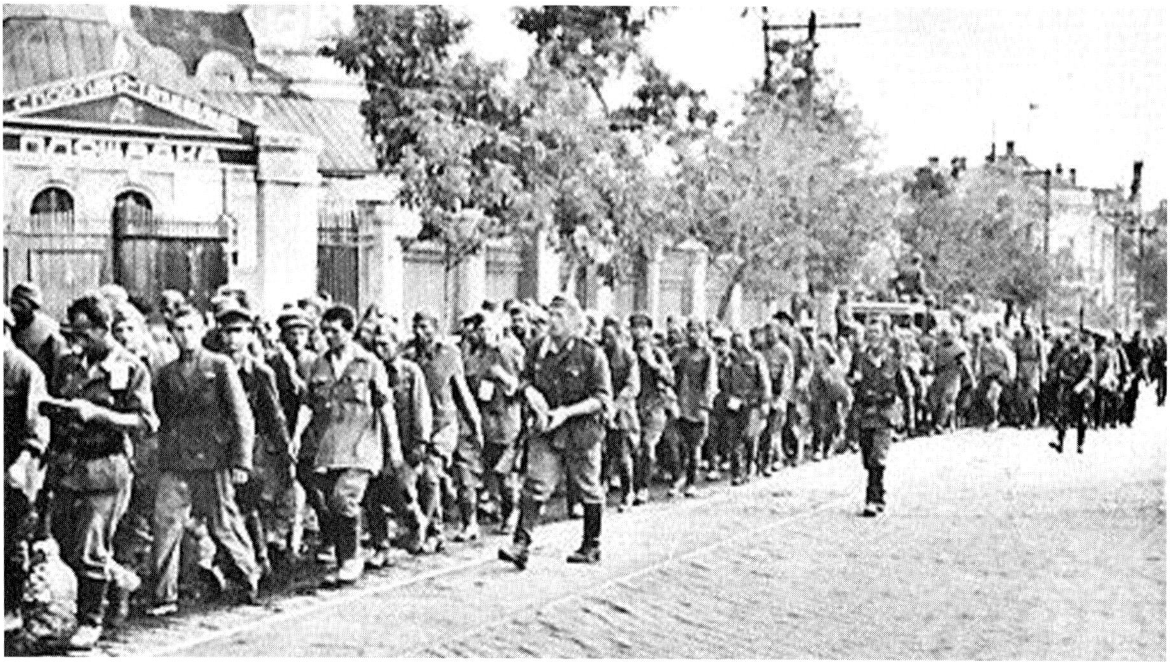

Above, Soviet PoWs, Kirovograd. Guards with slung rifles appear unconcerned with being so outnumbered.

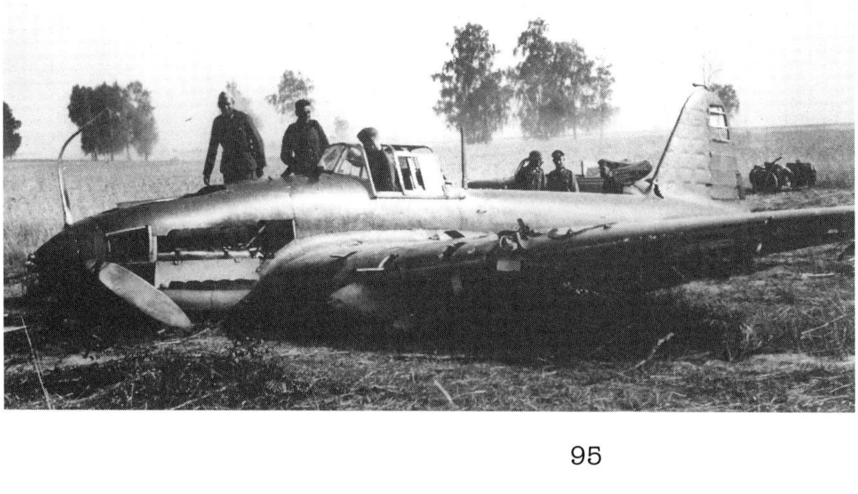

Left, German soldiers examine a downed Interleukin IL-2 Stormivik. One of the most effective ground attack aircraft of the war—a real tank killer. Over 36,000 were built, more than any other WW II aircraft. This is an early war single-seat version.

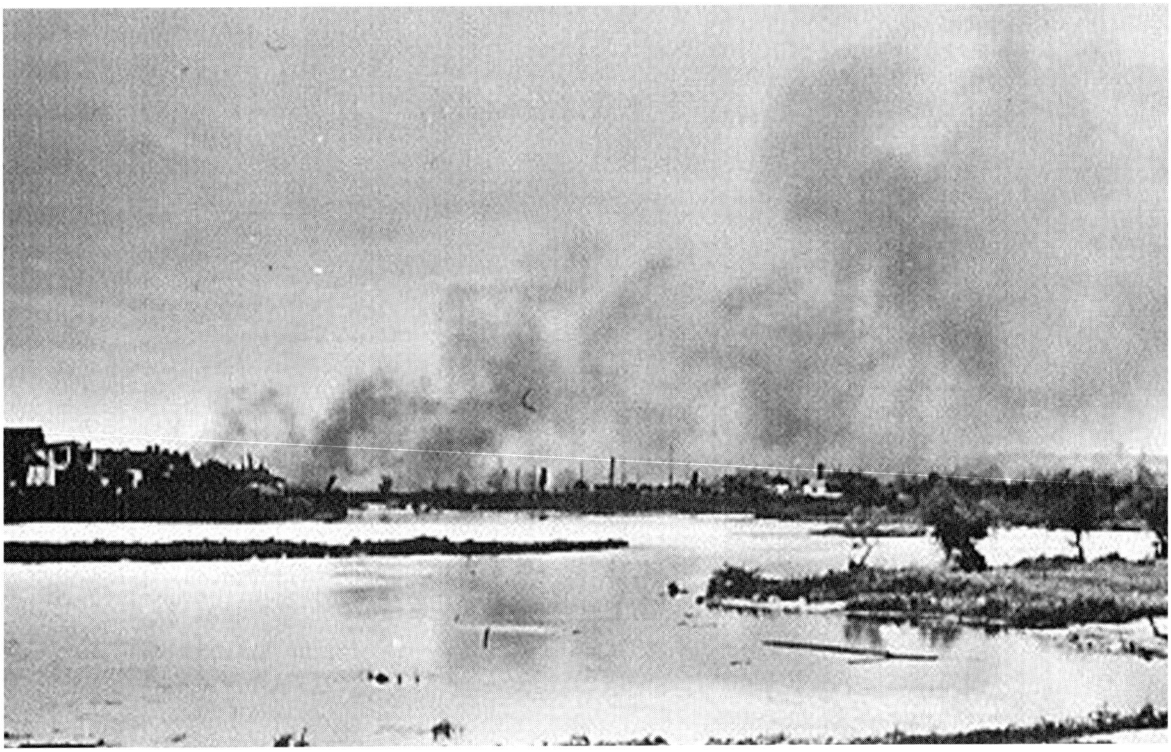

Vinnitsa, burning supplies, 28 July 1941.

Soviet prisoners, probably near Kiev, Fall 1941.

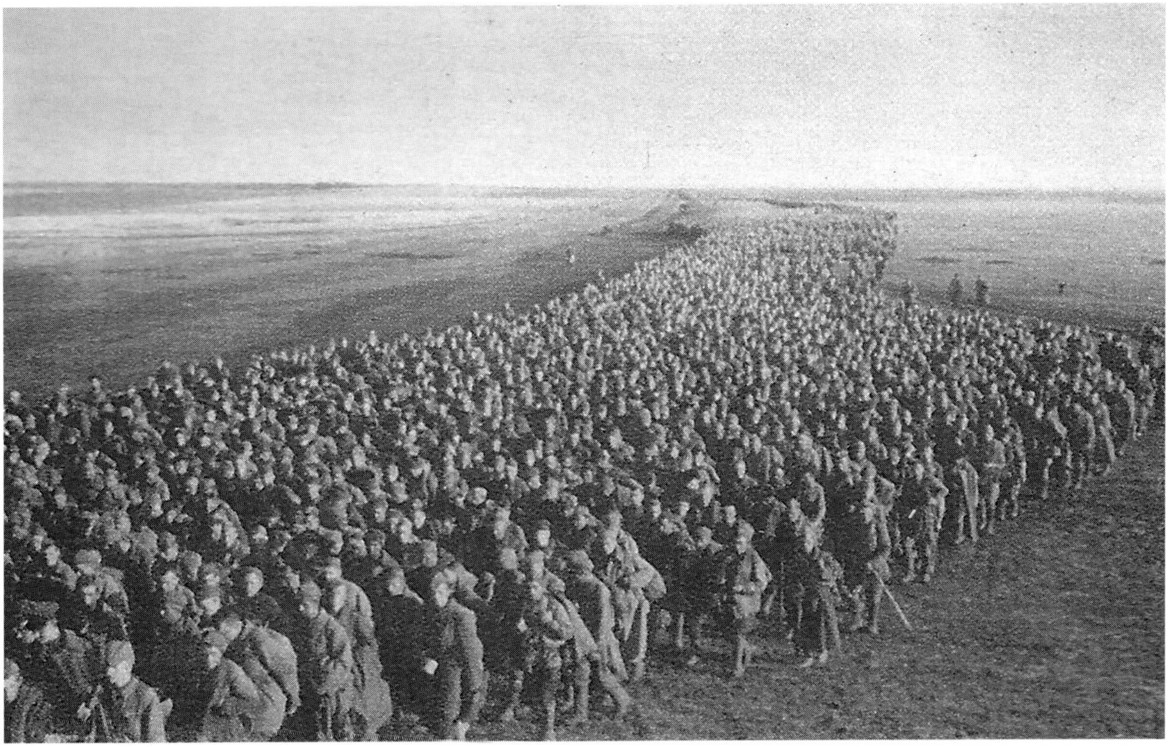

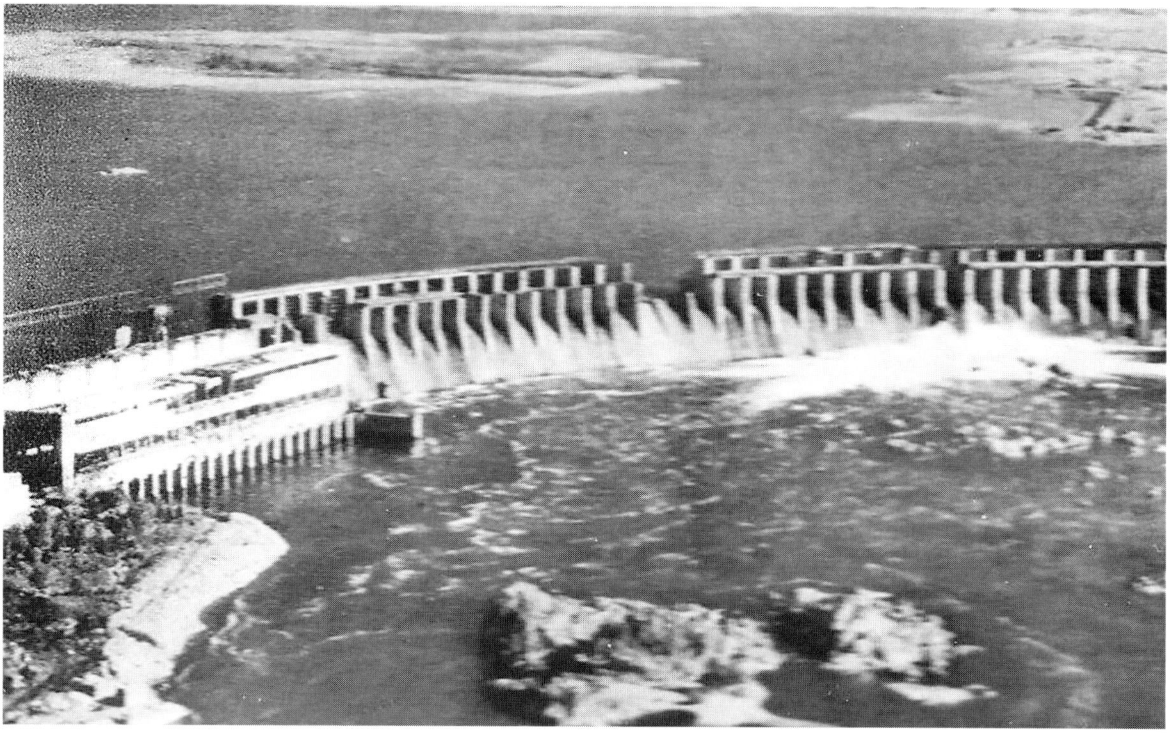

This negative was marked, Hydro-electric dam, Dnipropetrovsk, the one below, marked Zaporozhye. They are the same dam and the second location is correct. When completed in 1932, this was the largest Soviet electric producer, one of the world's largest.

German troops reached here on 16 August 1941. Soviet Engineers blew the bridge and dam on 18 August. The resulting downstream flood killed many German and Soviet soldiers and more Ukrainian civilians (note flooded trees in right foreground. In this photo the blown gap has widened. Tall towers on each side of the Dnieper carry electric cables over the river.

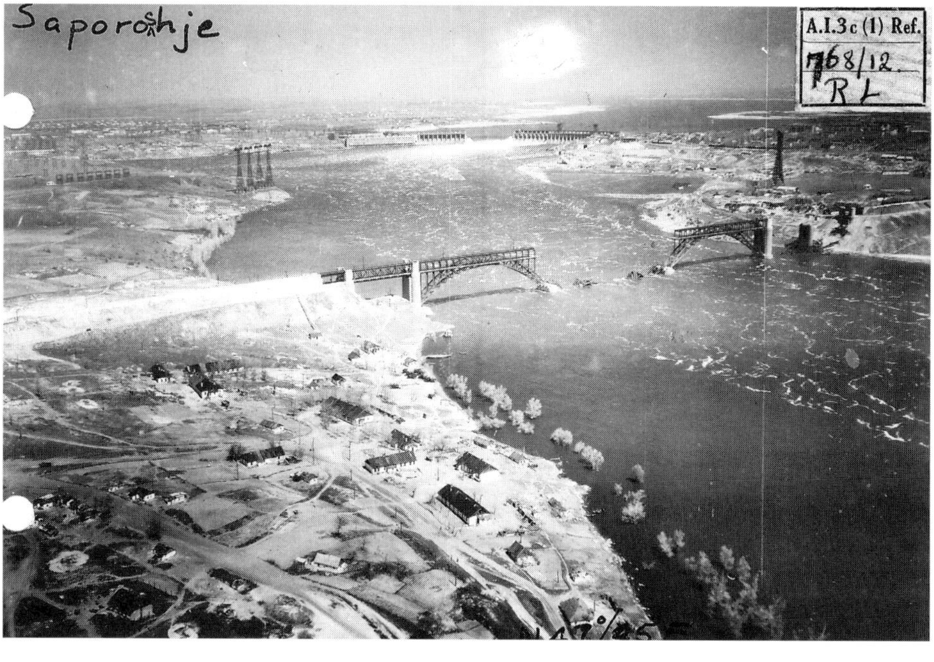

Saporoshje
A.I.3c (1) Ref.
768/12.
RL

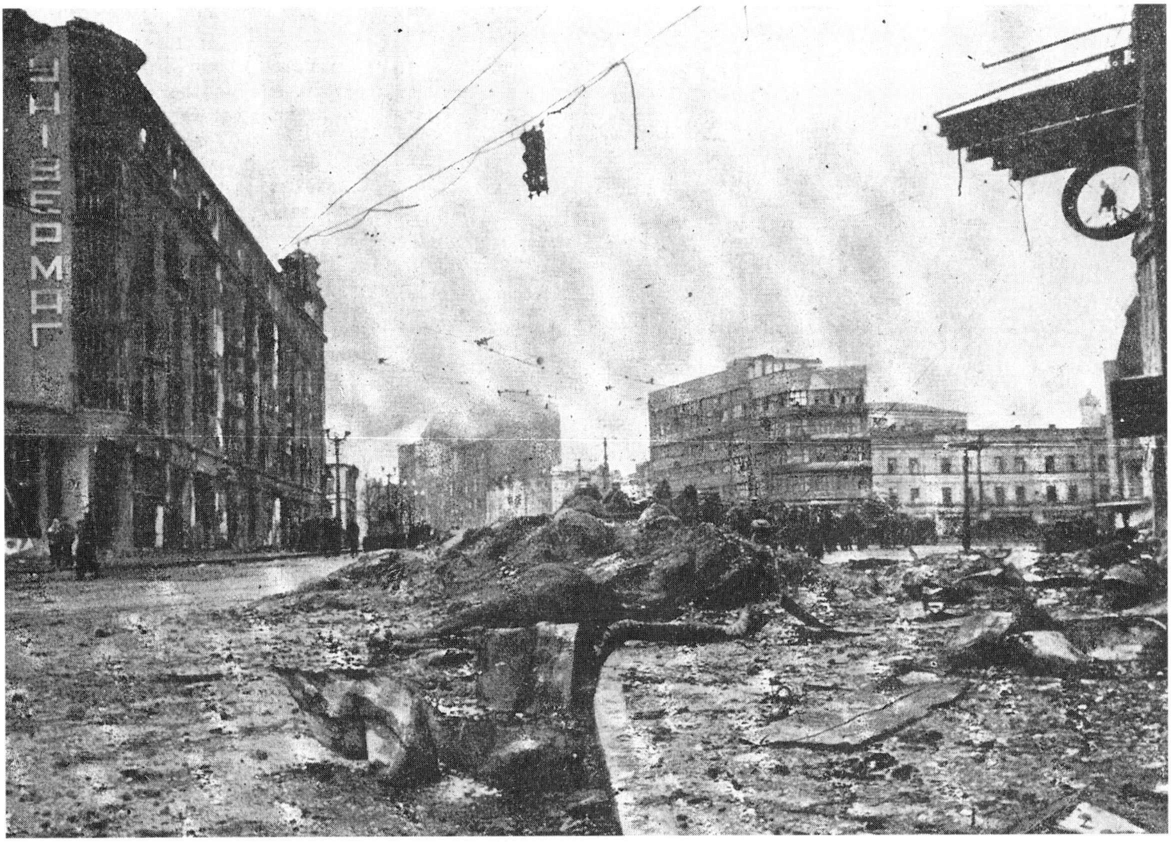

A square in Kharkov, German troops with horse-drawn wagons, fall 1941.

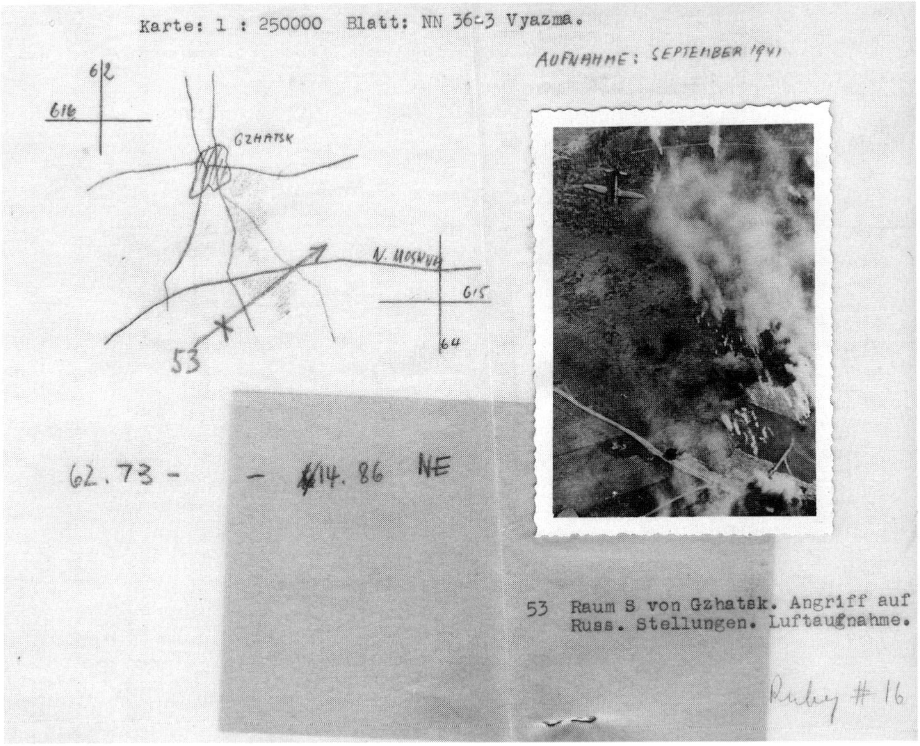
Karte: 1 : 250000 Blatt: NN 36-3 Vyazma.
AUFNAHME: SEPTEMBER 1941
GZHATSK
N. MOSKVA
53
62.73 - - 14.86 NE
53 Raum S von Gzhatsk. Angriff auf Russ. Stellungen. Luftaufnahme.
Ruby #16

Left, Stukas firing 2cm rockets at a Soviet defense position on road to Moscow, September 1941. Gzhatsk (now Gagarin) is 100 miles west of Moscow.

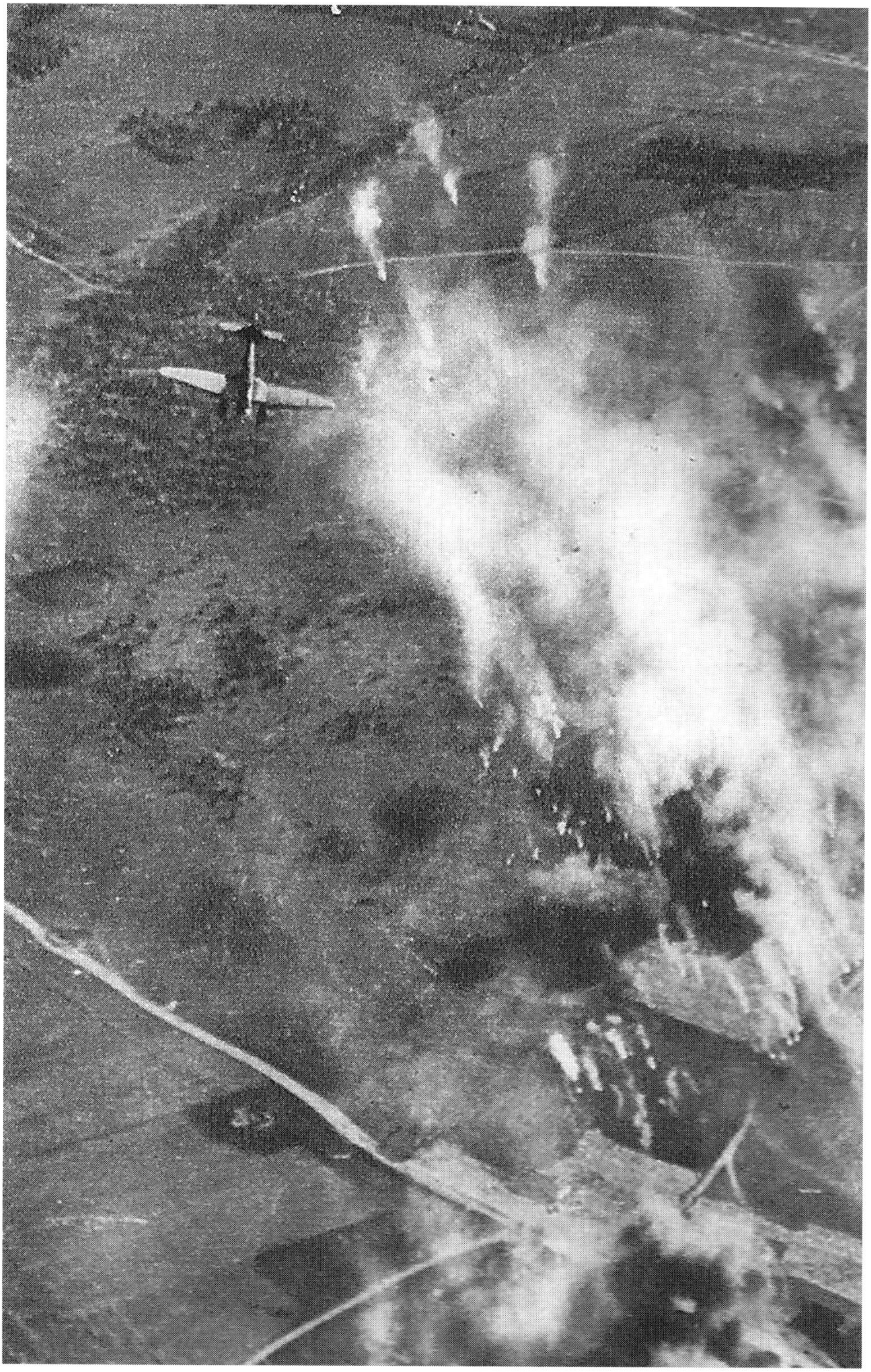

A better version of the preceding photo shows rockets in flight. We don't see the target(s) but they are probably defenses on the Moscow road.

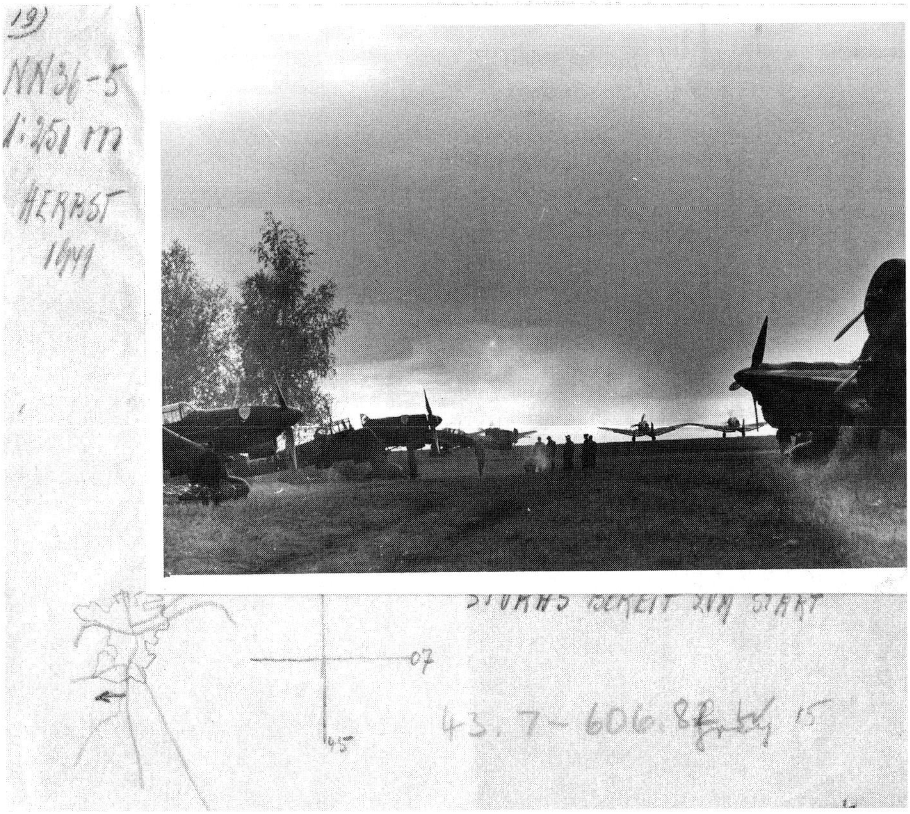
NN36-5
HERBST
1941
STUKAS BEREIT ZUM START

An ad hoc Ju 87 airstrip near Smolensk, fall 1941. Two-bladed props at right are on a Ju-52.

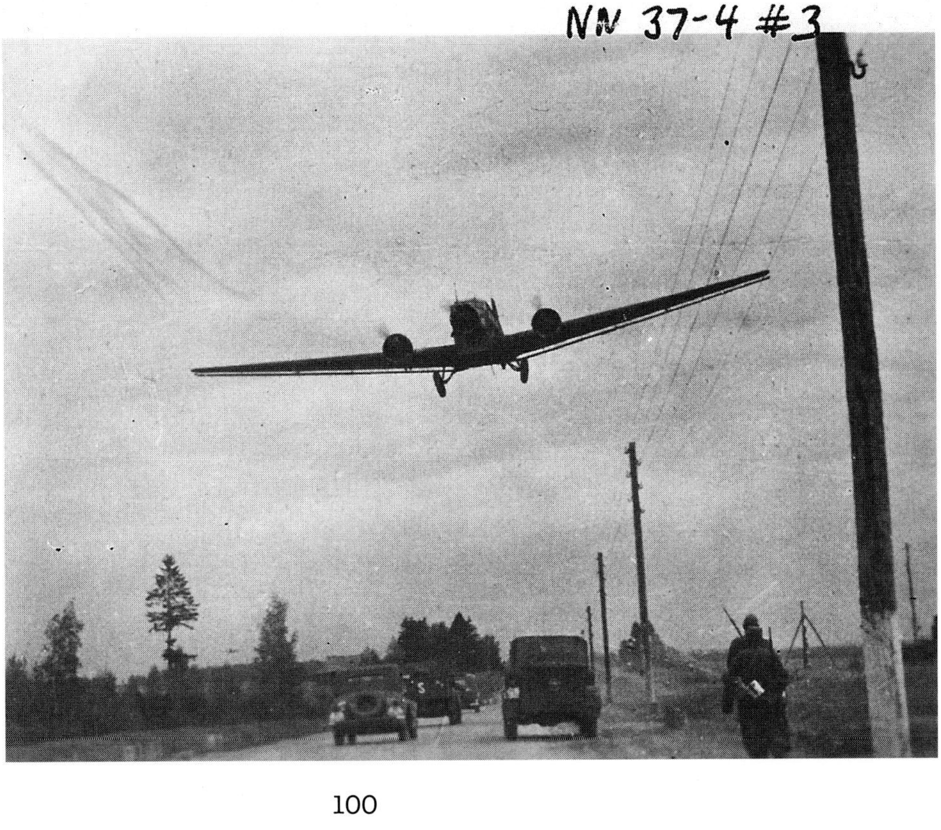
NN 37-4 #3

Right, a Ju-52 following the road for navigation. Juchnow, 93 miles southwest of Moscow 10 October 1941.

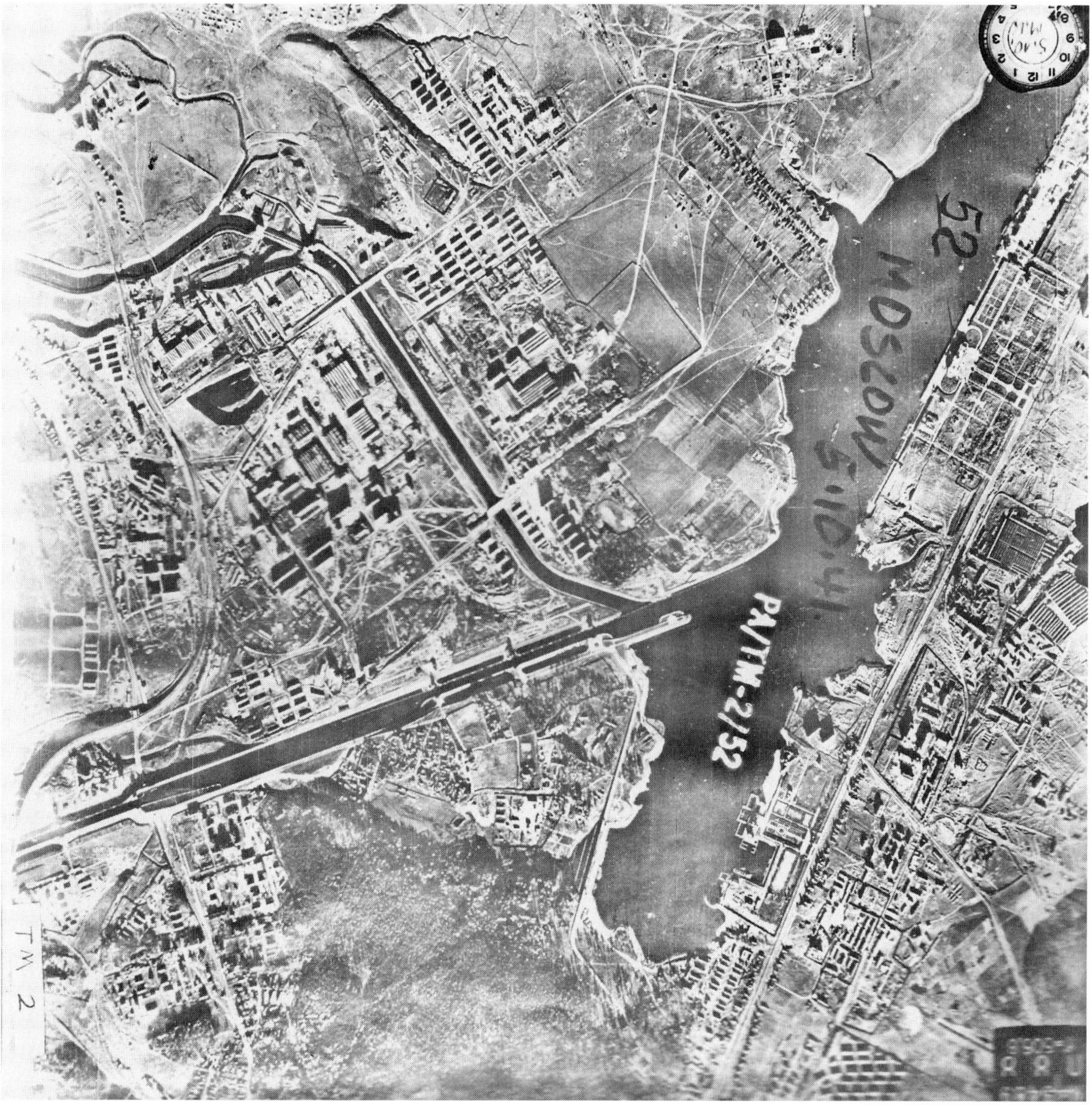
52
MOSCOW 5.10.41
PA/TM-2/152
TM 2

Luftwaffe aerial reconnaissance kept reaching out to catalog Soviet industry and other key installations. Moscow, five miles northwest of Red Square, 5 October 1941. Notes and markings show this imagery was used for target study by German Intelligence and by Cold War warriors.

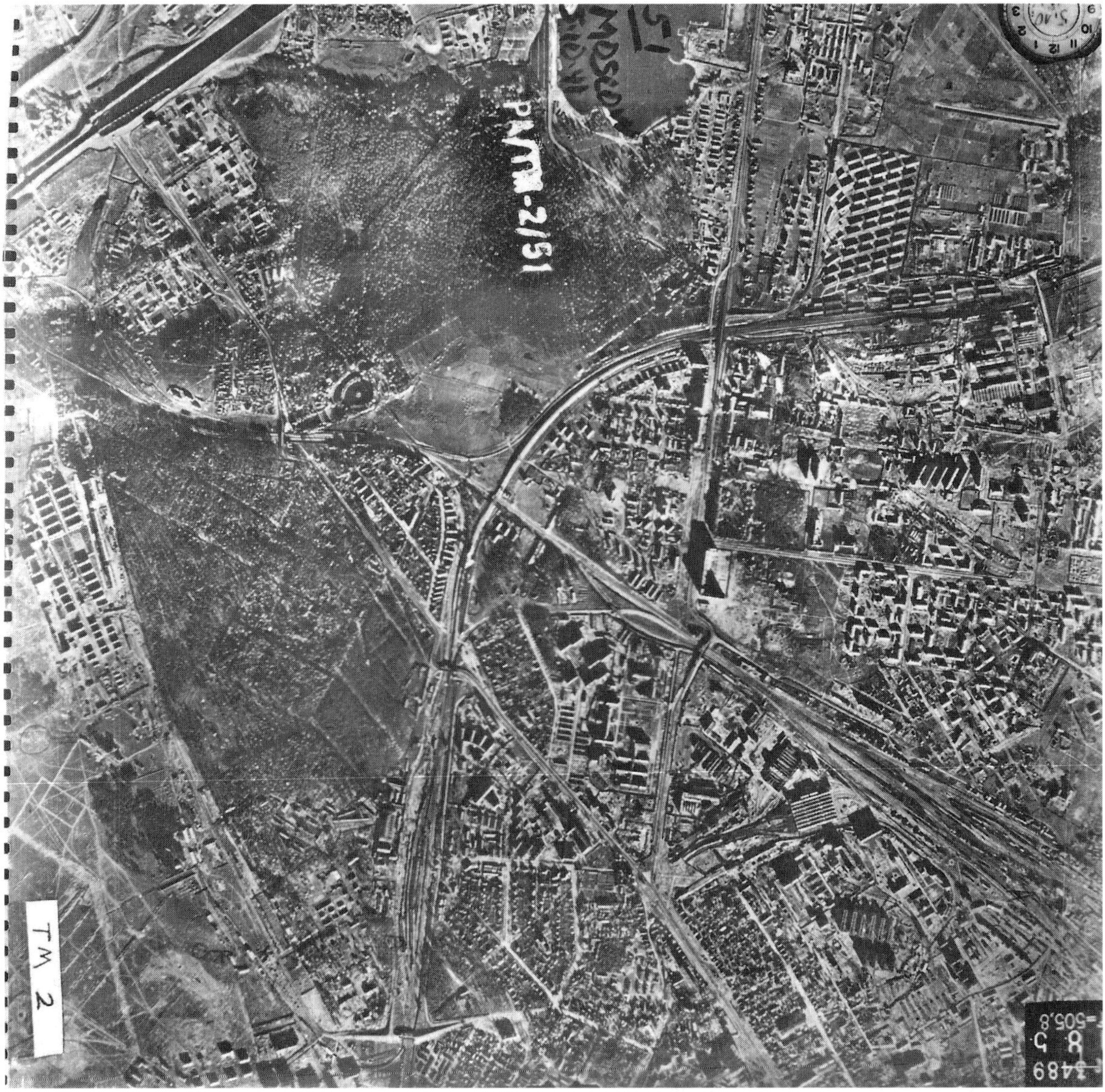
TM 2

Voykovsk District, just southeast of the preceding photo. Major rail yards are always targets, 5 October 1941.

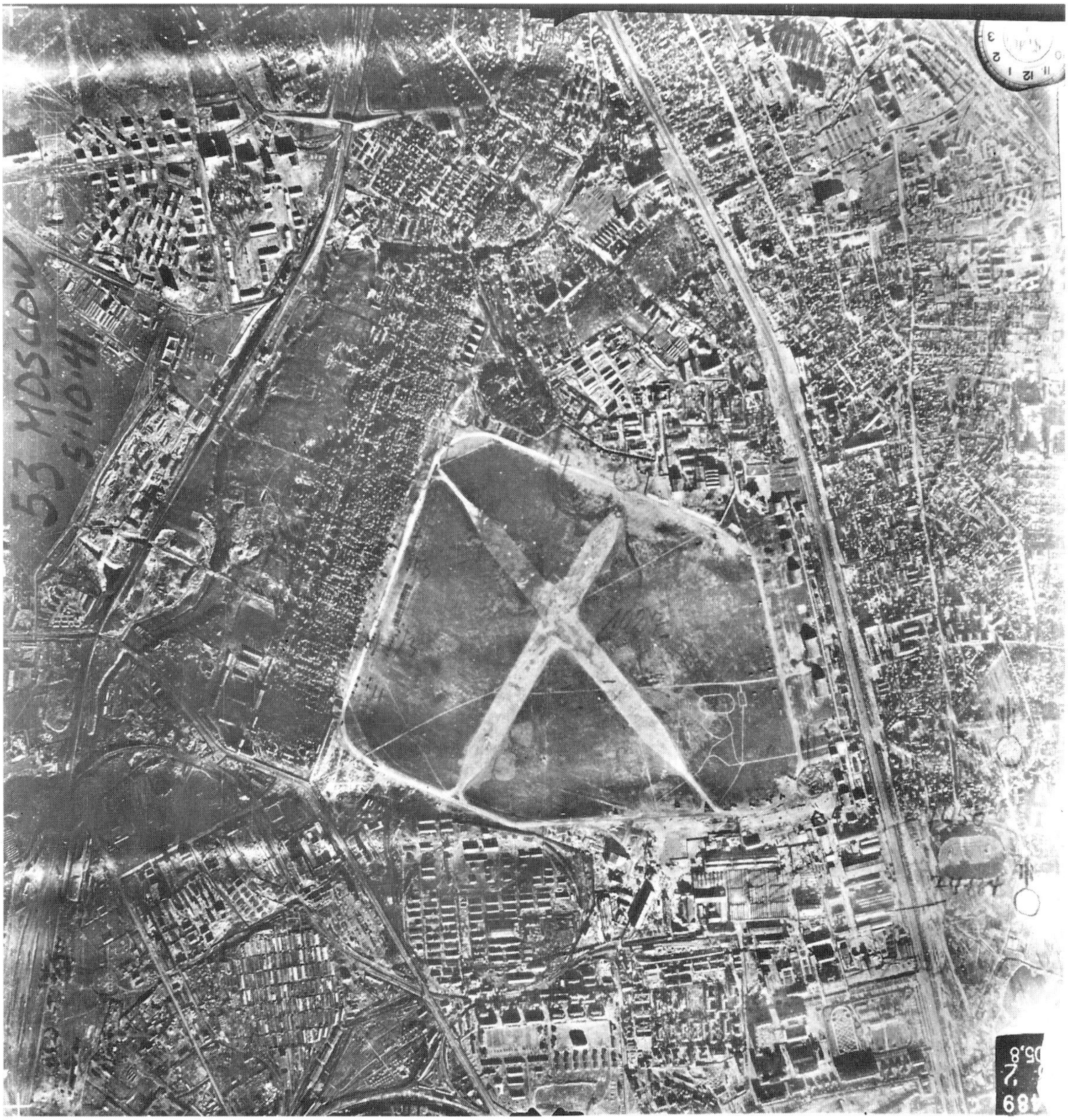

Khodynka Airport, Moscow's only airport until 1933. It is in the Khoroshyovsky District, four miles northwest of Red Square, 5 October 1941. These shapes can still be distinguished on today's Google maps.

Hauptbildstelle d. Lw., Gr. III B
SU 311 SK 055 (v)(Lfl.2)v.29.10.41
K.Bl.A 58 (1:300000)
Länge: 39°51'00" (o.G.)
Breite: 57°39'00"
Mißw.: +8°58' (Mitte 1943)

Jaroslawl

SU 66 7 Gummikombinat

SU 50 710 Kraftwerk

1) Kessel-u.Maschinenhaus etwa	3 000 qm	
2) Trafo-u Schalthaus	900	»
3) Freiluftschaltanlage	1 500	»
4) Schrägaufzug		
Länge etwa 250 m		
5) Tanklager für Sprit Ø 8-20 m		
6) Pumpstation etwa	250	»
7) Destillationsgebäude	1 900	»
8) Skrubber	»	
9) Kondensationsabteilung	650	»
10) Gasabteilung	3 200	»
11) Verdampferstation	400	»
12) Gasometer Ø etwa 18m		
13) Kälteanlage	700	»
14) Polymerisationsgebäude	5 000	»
15) Aufarbeitung	2 100	»
16) Butadienkontaktfabrik	550	»
17) Hydr. Druckanlagen	3 250	»
18) Cordfabrikationshallen	35 300	»
19) Webereihallen	9 450	»
20) Hallen z Fertigherstellung	27 700	»
21) Verwaltungsgebäude	3 550	»
22) Lagergebäude	12 500	»
23) Betriebs-u Nebengeb.	12 600	»
bebaute Fläche etwa	124 500 qm	
Ausdehnung insg.	685 000 qm	
Gleisanschluß vorhanden		

Maßstab etwa 1:9200   4695

In 1943 Luftwaffe Intelligence used this 29 October 1941 imagery to produce a Detailed PI Report on the Rubber Plant at Jaroslavl. I don't doubt that US Intelligence in the 1950s used this imagery for target study.

Chapter IV

NORTHERN SEAS

BALTIC FORTRESS

At the Baltic's eastern reaches are Leningrad (Saint Petersburg) and its naval base at Kronstadt, home to the Red Fleet. The Baltic also being home and haven for Hitler's Kriegsmarine, an active Soviet Baltic Fleet threat could not be ignored. With few maritime interests, originally Soviet leadership saw little need for a navy. So, by the late 1930s heavy ships were largely obsolescent, barely post-*Dreadnought* legacies from the Tsar. But late 1930s new construction was worrisome to Germany. Two Leningrad-built *Kirov-Class* heavy cruisers were afloat, and two more building. A battleship and aircraft carrier were on the way. As we've already seen, all that was carefully watched by agents and photo interpreters.[1]

Threat-in-being naturally took precedent over threat under construction, so the Naval Base was hit first. Below, photo coverage fifteen days after Barbarossa kicked off. Both Soviet battleships are present, one inside the breakwater, one outside. The Naval Base is on Kotlin Island, 12 miles west of the Neva River's mouth.

20
Kronstadt
7.7.41
PA/TM-2/20A

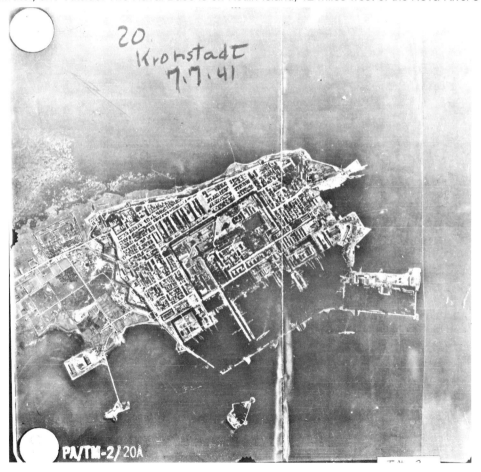

1 With 180mm (7.1") main guns Kirov's were at the low end of heavy cruisers. Two more Kirov's were built on the Black Sea.

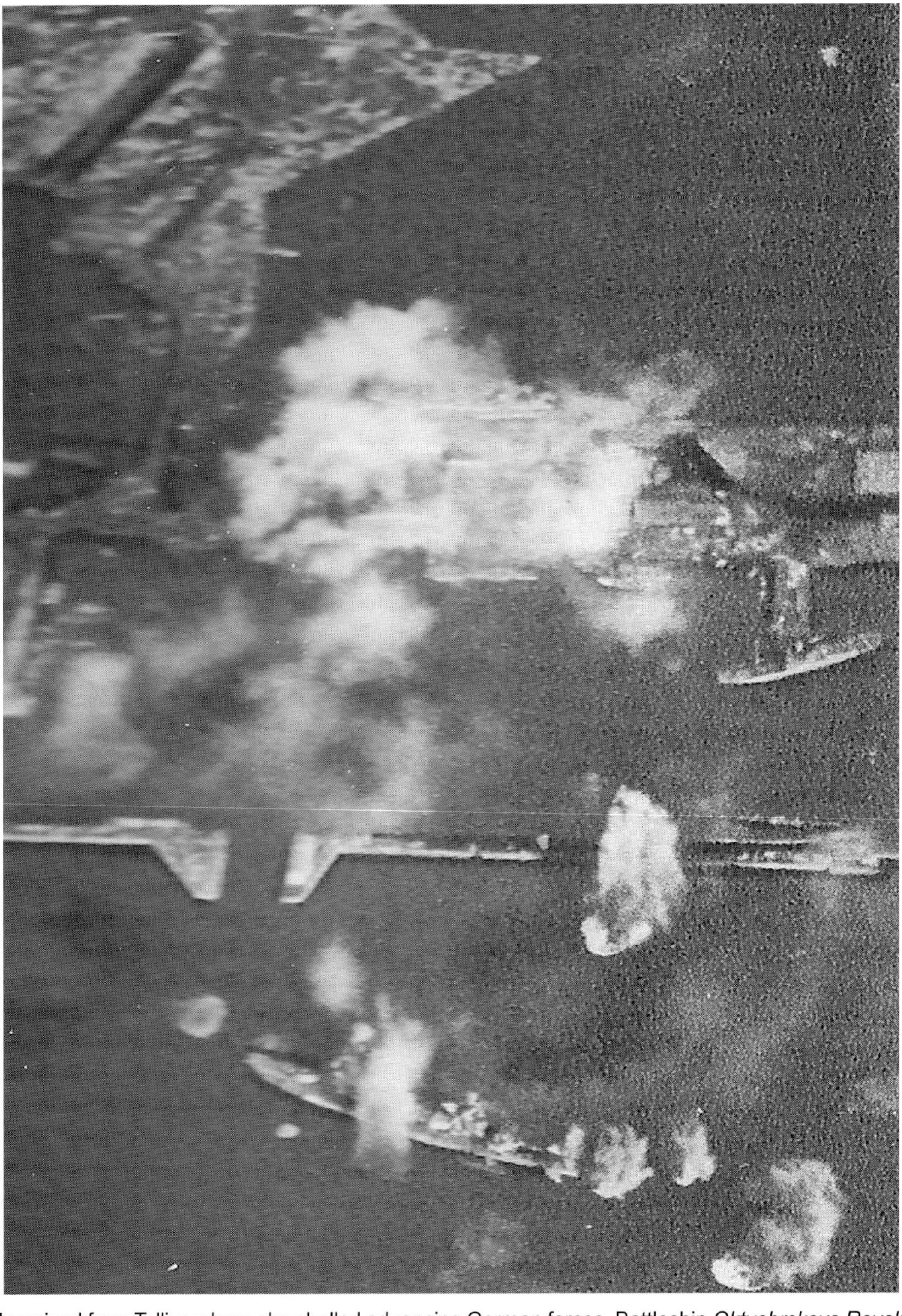

Newly arrived from Tallinn where she shelled advancing German forces, Battleship *Oktyabrskaya Revolutsiya* (*October Revolution*) under attack by Ju 87 dive bombers.

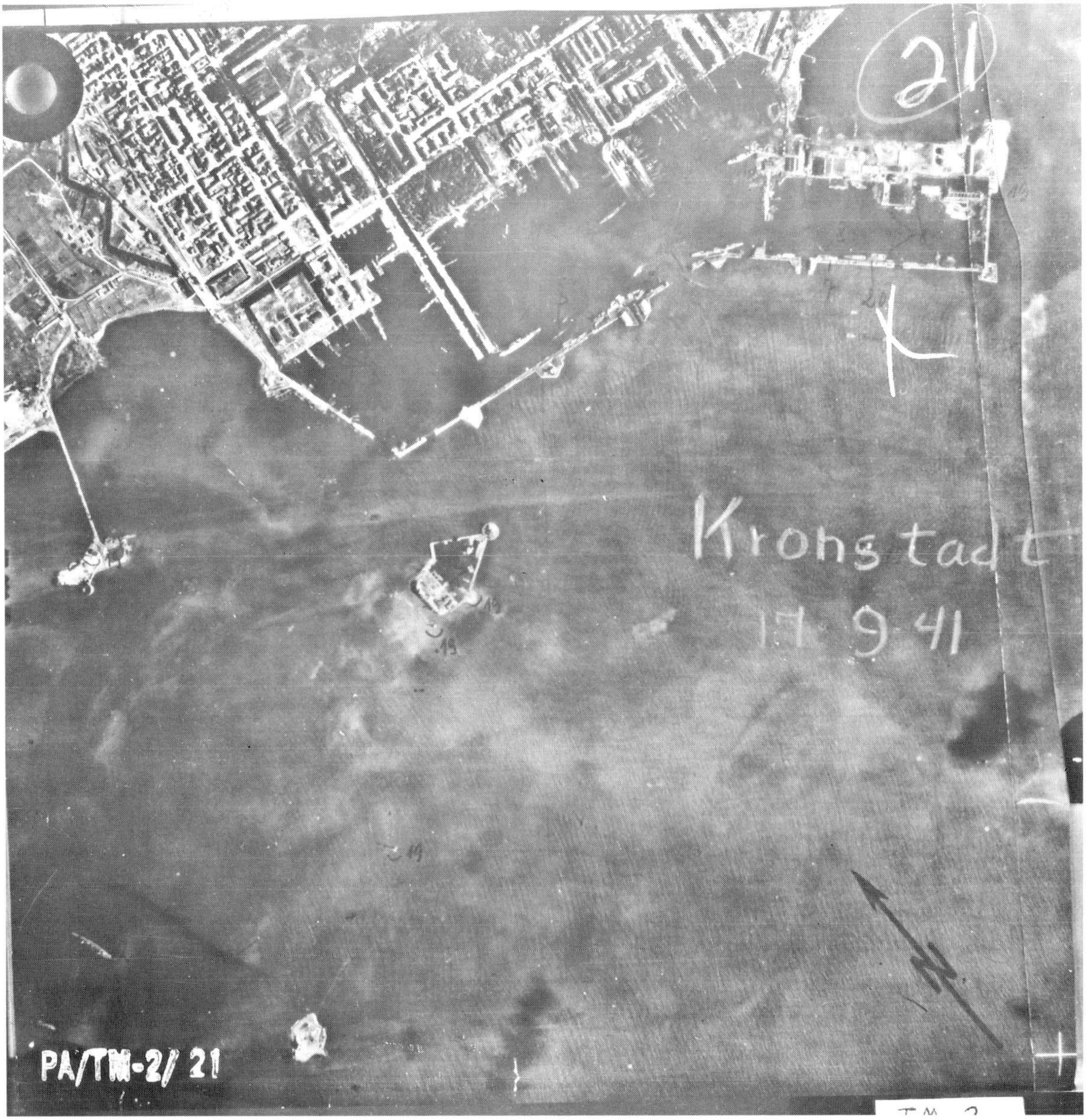
21
Kronstadt
17 9 41
PA/TM-2/ 21

Kronstadt Naval Base covered on 17 September 1941. Annotations in white are not original. They were probably made by Allied PIs as GX (in this case probably DT) imagery was copied and cataloged in 1946-50. My guess is the 'X' outside the breakwater at upper right indicates battleship *October Revolution* isn't present on this coverage. Both *Gangut-Class* battleships were of pre-WW I vintage but capable of providing on-shore fire support for defending Soviet units with their twelve 12" (305mm) guns, making them prime targets for Luftwaffe bombing.

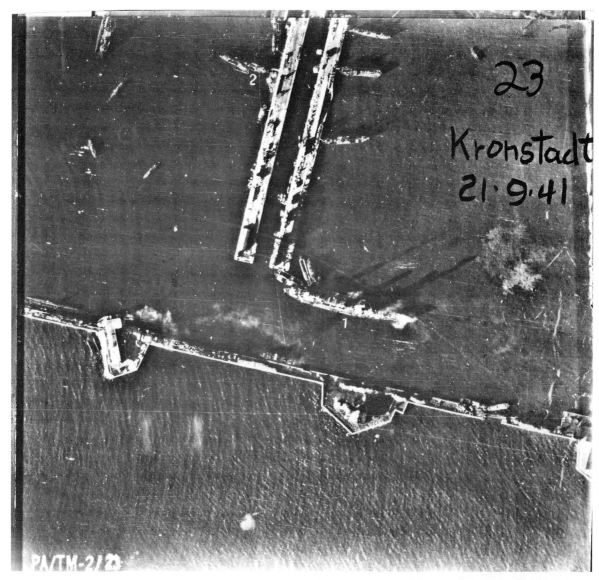

Battleship *Marat*, 21 September 1941. Note tall shadows for superstructure and mast and compare with the next photo. German concentration on the old battleships was not a concern for their power at sea—a modern German heavy cruiser could run rings around them. It was fear of them as mobile, floating gun batteries supporting Soviet Infantry as German forces advanced into the Baltic States and on Leningrad.

In this case white annotations are original and black were added post-war.

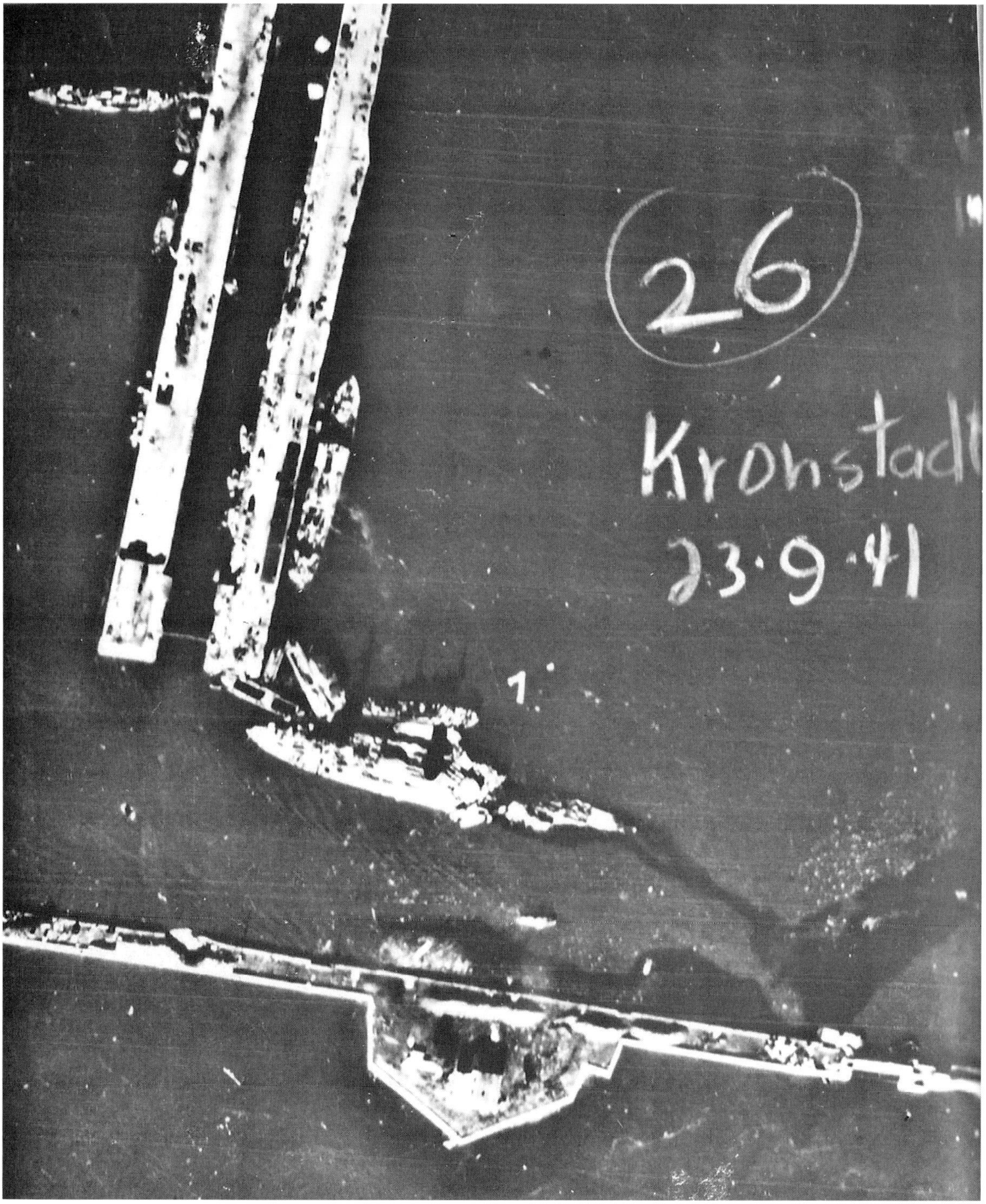
26
Kronstad
23·9·41
1.

Marat was hit hard by Stukas, 22 September 1941. We see her one day later, down at the bow and leaking oil. Fortunately the bottom is shallow. It looks like heavy damage to the hull portside of the forward turret and shadow indicates her forward superstructure is toppled. She'd had a new false-bow put on in the 1930s and it appears that construction failed.

Grease pencil scrawl is post-war.

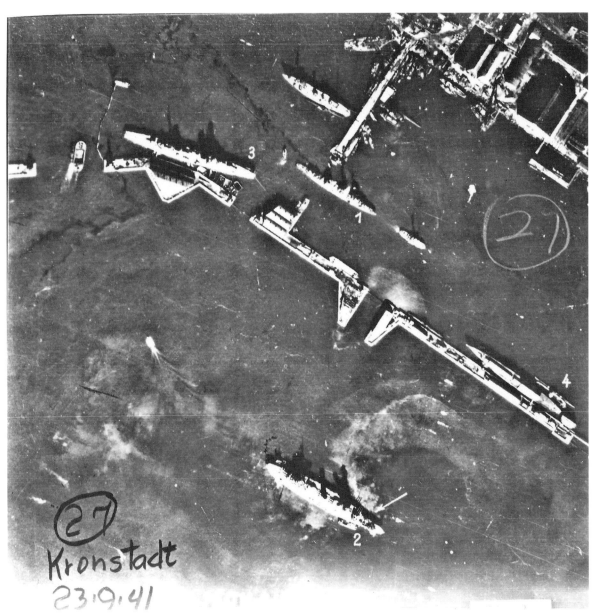

Kronstadt
23.9.41

Sister *Gangut-Class* BB, *October Revolution* (annotation '2'), was hit and had two turrets damaged on 21 September. Two days later a German PI arrow correctly points to damage. In unusual annotation sequence, a destroyer is '1' and a *Kirov* cruiser '2'. I believe '4' is the Tsar's 401 foot-long, 1895 yacht *Standart*, renamed *Marti* and converted into a minelayer for the war.

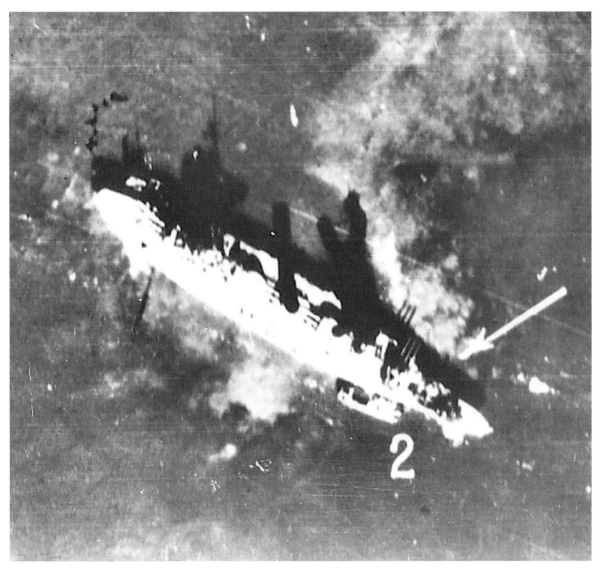

Enlargement of 23 September 1941 imagery shows superstructure intact but guns in the forward turret are trained to port (almost due east). Perhaps that was for balance or to use the barrels as cranes to rig work on a damaged hull. Swirling water indicates the tide is ebbing.

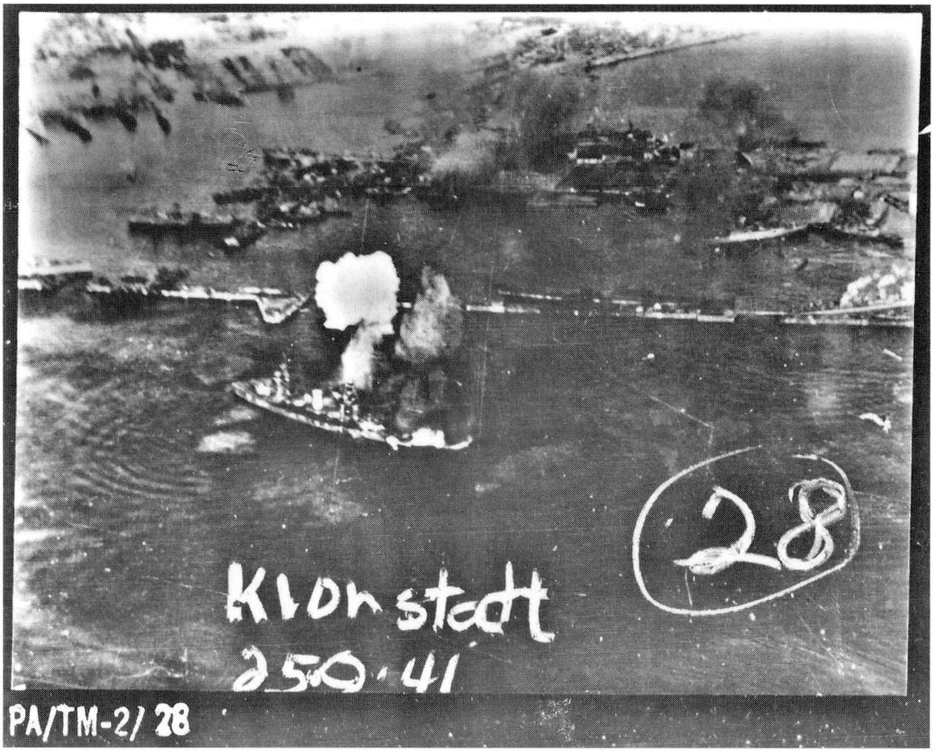
Kronstadt
28
PA/TM-2/ 28

October Revolution hit again on 25 and 26 September.

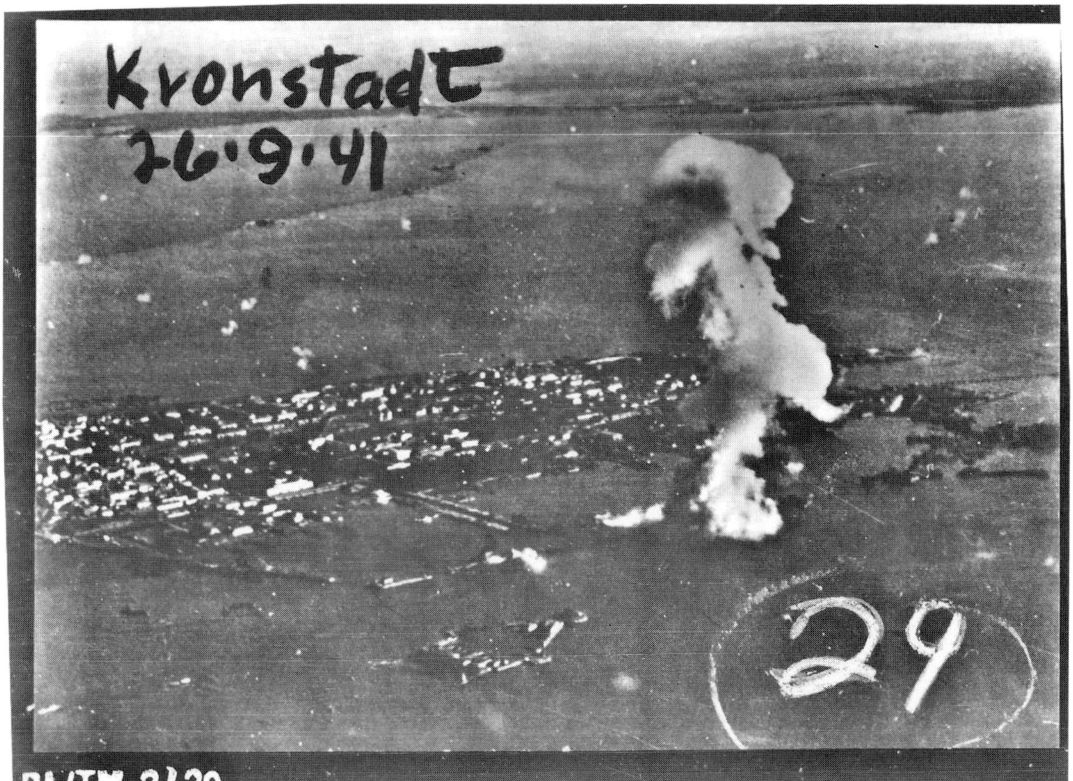
Kronstadt
26·9·41
29
PA/TM-2/29

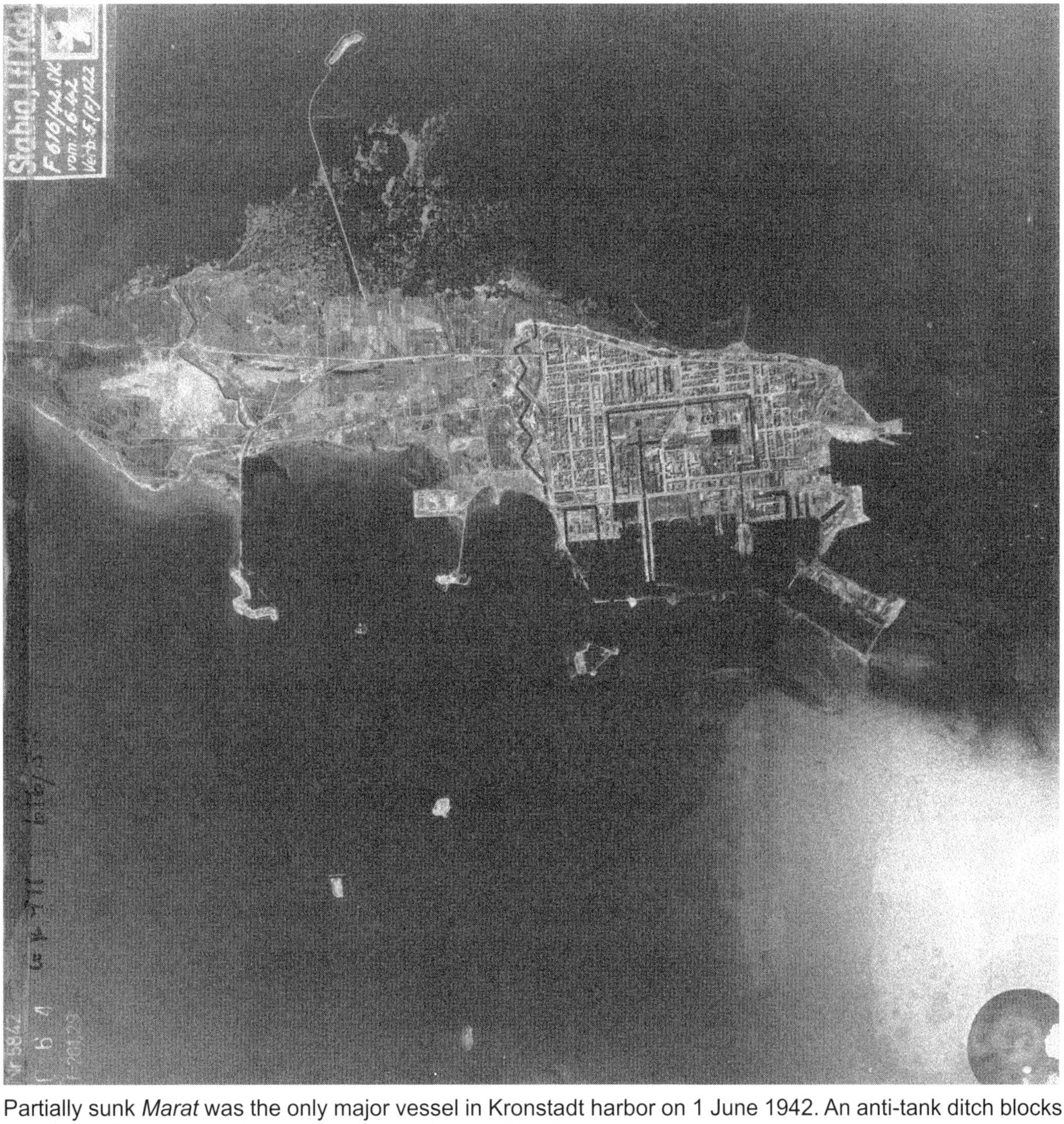

Partially sunk *Marat* was the only major vessel in Kronstadt harbor on 1 June 1942. An anti-tank ditch blocks movement into the naval base from the rest of the island.

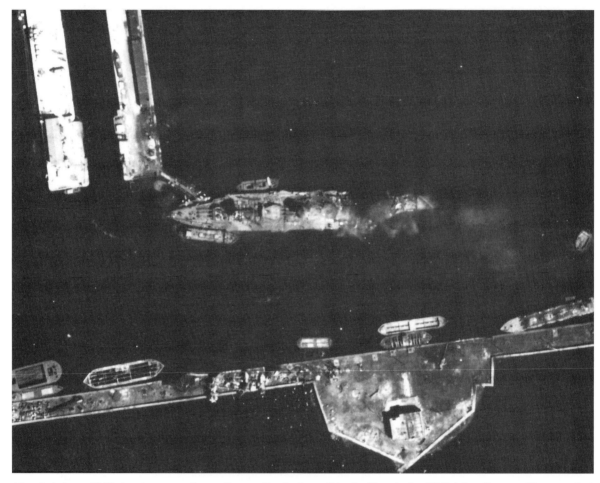

Marat, 1 June 1942, her bow may be resting on the bottom. It looks like she's still fighting fires and her combat career is probably over. Surprisingly, her 12" guns haven't been pulled for use elsewhere.

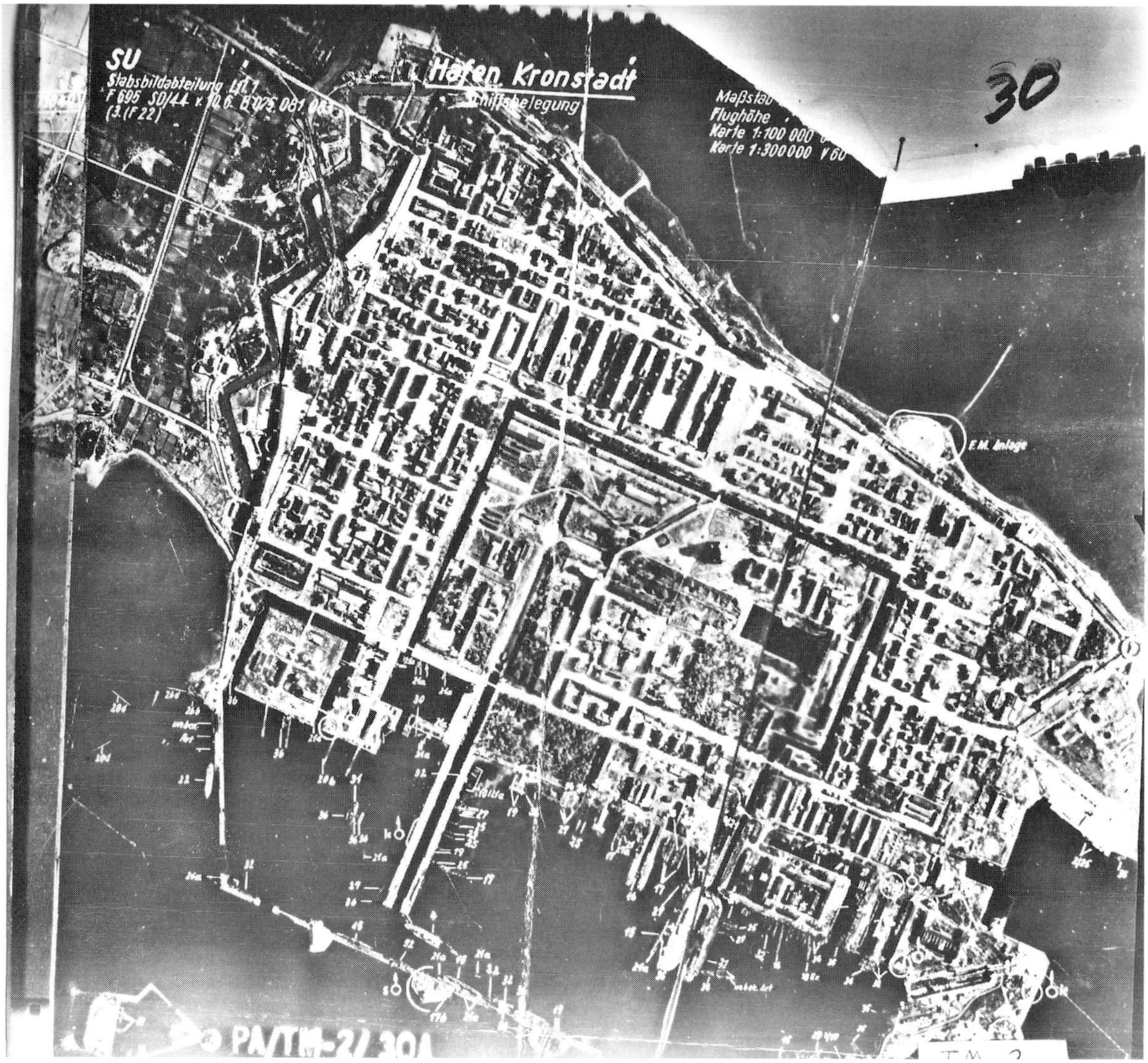
SU
Hafen Kronstadt
30
Karte 1:100 000
Karte 1:300000

A German target mosaic using 10 May 1944 imagery. *Marat* is still in the same location at the end of the mole (annotation '4'). Small white circles indicate bomb hits and even the most insignificant vessels have been catalogued as to type if not specific ship name (I don't have the report).

As we see often in this book, German PIs were quite good and kept grinding out detailed reports long after the knowledge could be of any use to German operational forces.

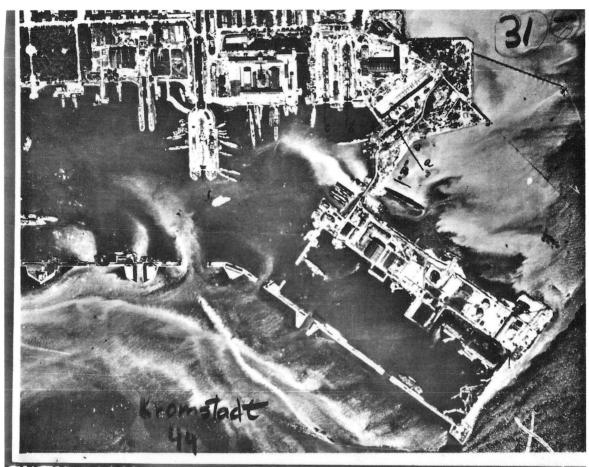

Kronstadt was still being covered frequently in late 1944. Swirling white are waves. At far left center are two ships moored side-by-side (neither with a warship's hull shape) where *Marat* was partially sunk two years earlier, suggesting the battleship has been moved. There are several black annotations indicating PI interest in the facilities—to what end is obscure.

LENINGRAD

Left is Baltic Sea, right about a mile is the Neva River. The ship channel runs south to sheltered maritime basins. In 1941 German PIs were interested in something named Kanonerski Werk at the Neva end of the canal. Two of the boats at the upper end basin appear to be ice-breakers.

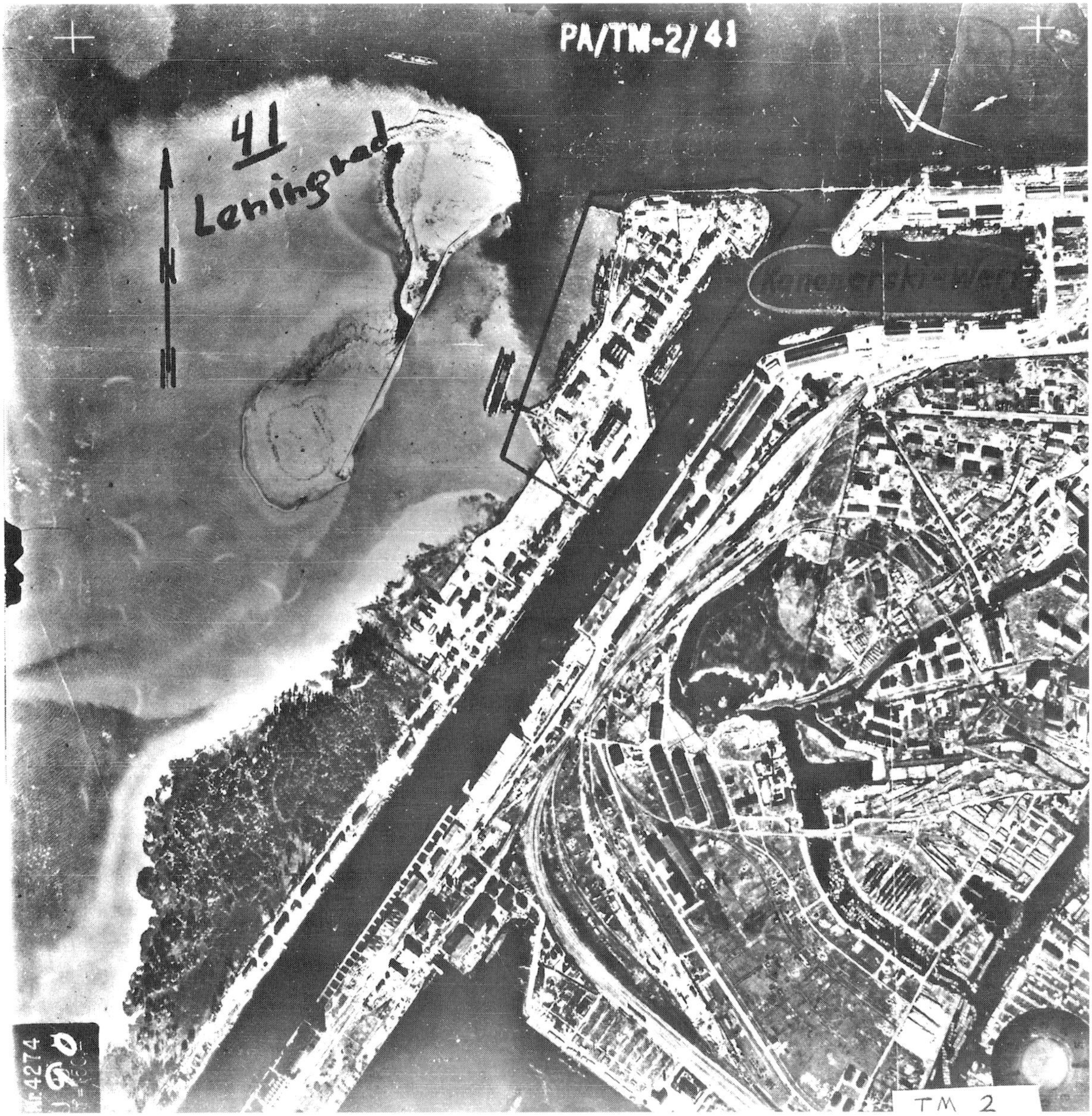
PA/TM-2/41
41
Leningrad
N
Kanonerski-Werk
4274
TM 2

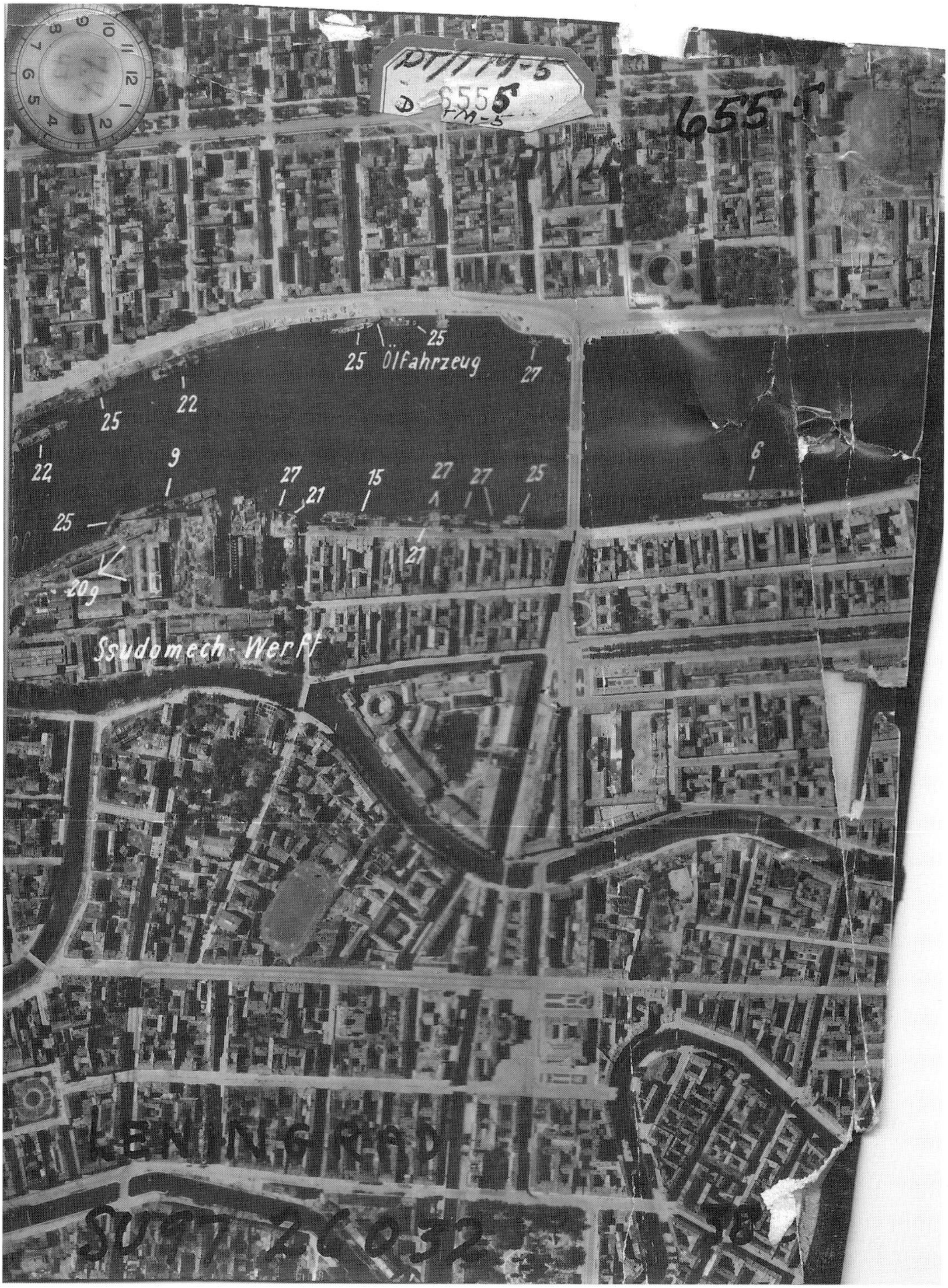
DT/TM-5
D 6555
TM-5
655
25
25 Ölfahrzeug
27
22
25
22
9
27
21
15
27
27
25
6
25
21
20
9
Ssudomech-Werft
LENINGRAD
SU97 Z6032
38

This photo is centered on the first bridge upstream on the lower Neva River. Again we note forensic reporting on craft in the Neva, 7 February 1941. The paper label at top was added by American Intelligence post-war and indicates this as Dick Tracy imagery used for targeting.

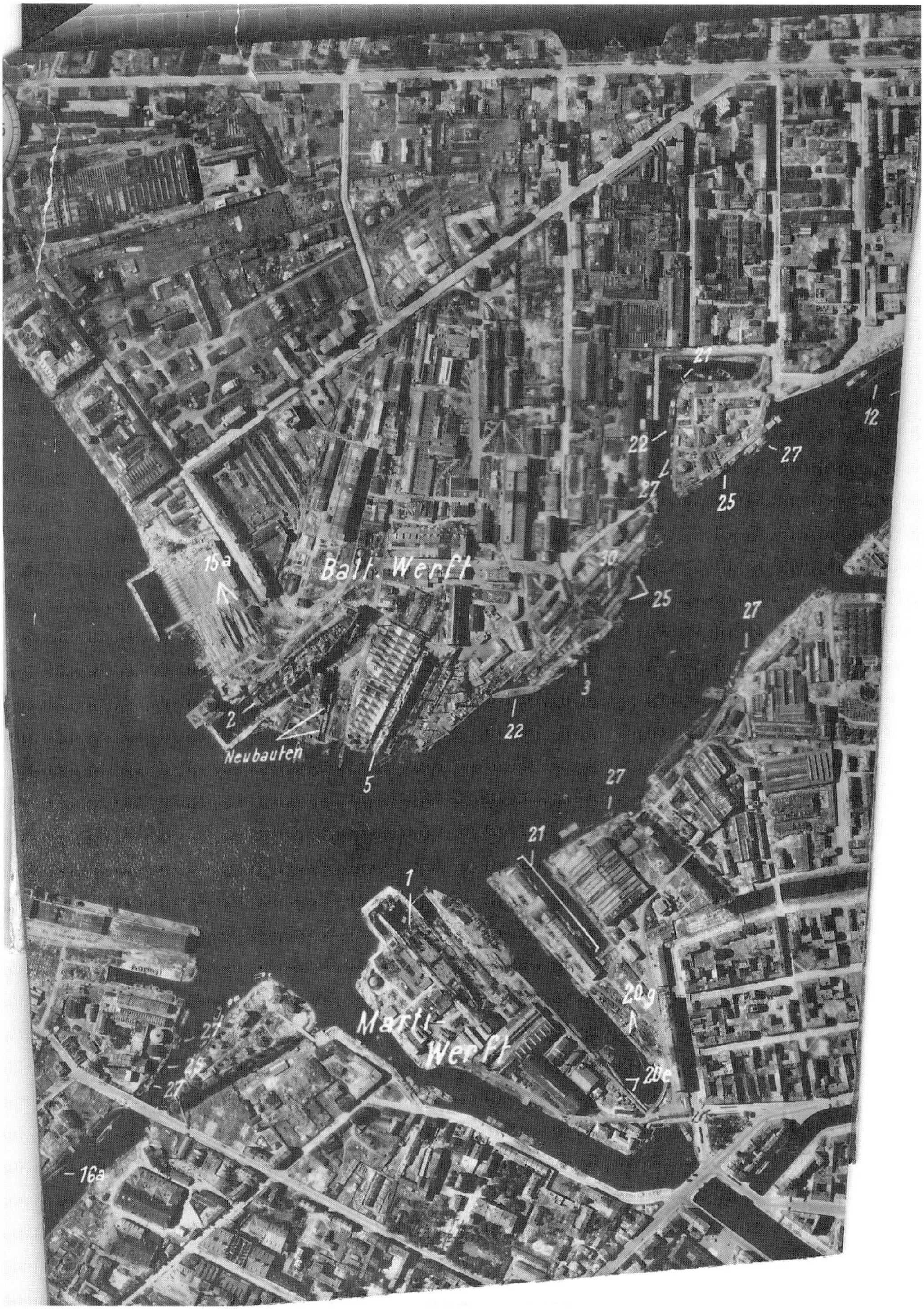
Balt Werft
15a
2
Neubauten
5
22
3
30
25
27
12
21
1
Marti-Werft
20g
20e
16a

About a half mile down the lower Neva from the previous photo, 7 July 1941. This is the Neva mouth. Annotation '2' in Baltic Shipyards is battleship *Sovetskaya Soyuz* (*Soviet Union*). Marti Shipyards, on the south bank, has the aircraft carrier (annotation '1'). Annotation '5' is a *Kirov* cruiser. Construction appears to have continued on all three despite the German invasion.

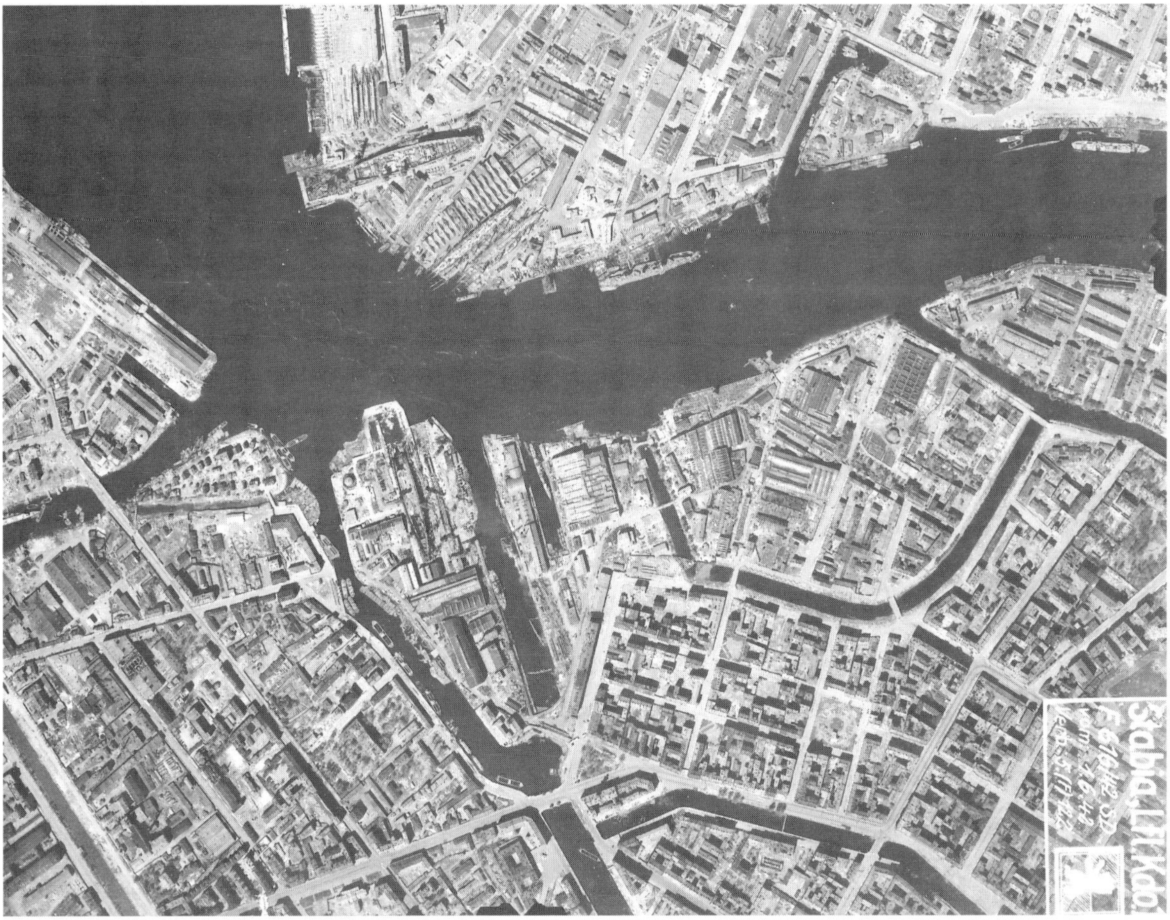

Imagery of 1 June 1942 gave a better quality look at the two capitol ships and a *Kirov* cruiser in work. Battered *October Revolution* is quayside a few yards up river. Except for possibly turret three, her main guns have been pulled, enlargement below.

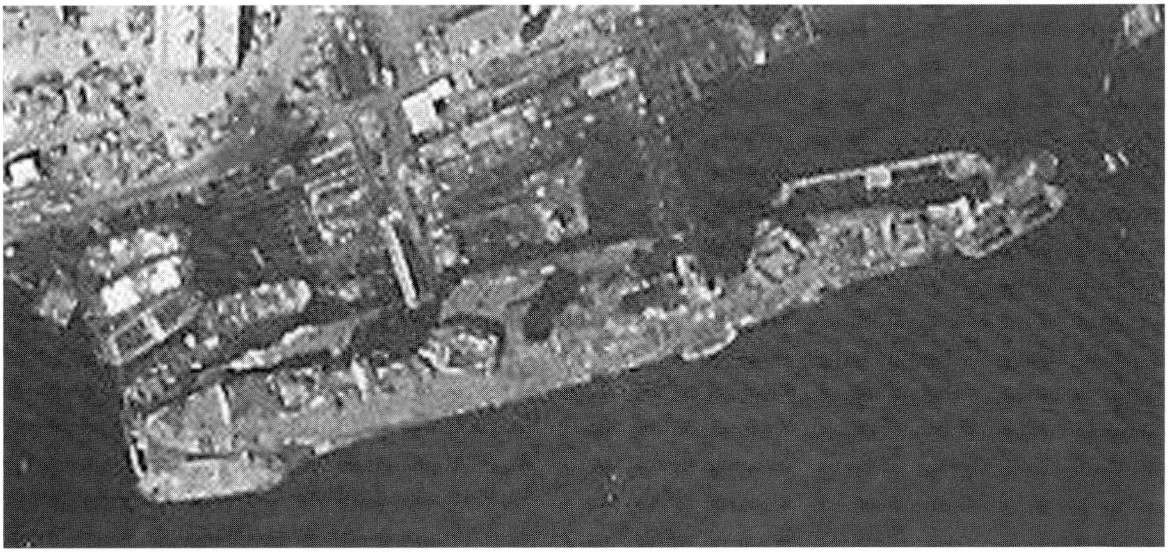

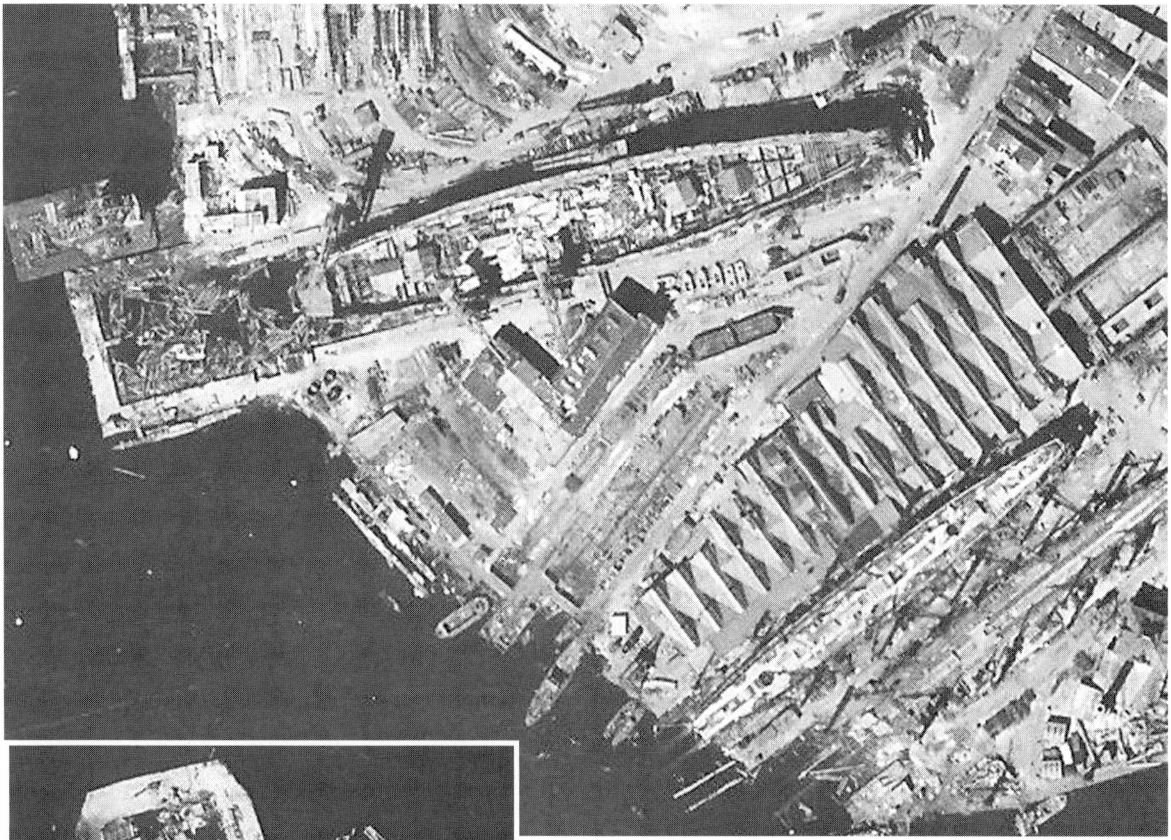

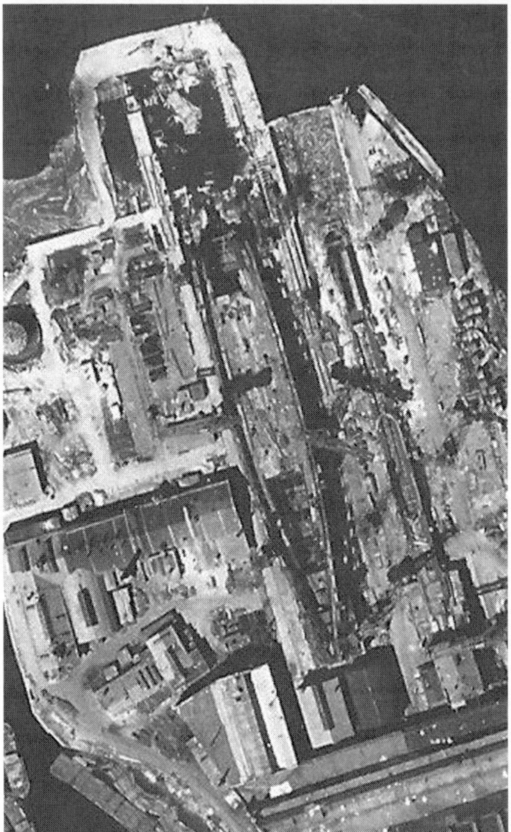

Above, the 884' long battleship, laid down in 1938. Conventional wisdom says she was to have 16" guns in three triple turrets—but it still looks to me that there are covers for four barbettes. I have seen no photos with turrets or guns installed.

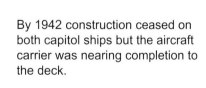

By 1942 construction ceased on both capitol ships but the aircraft carrier was nearing completion to the deck.

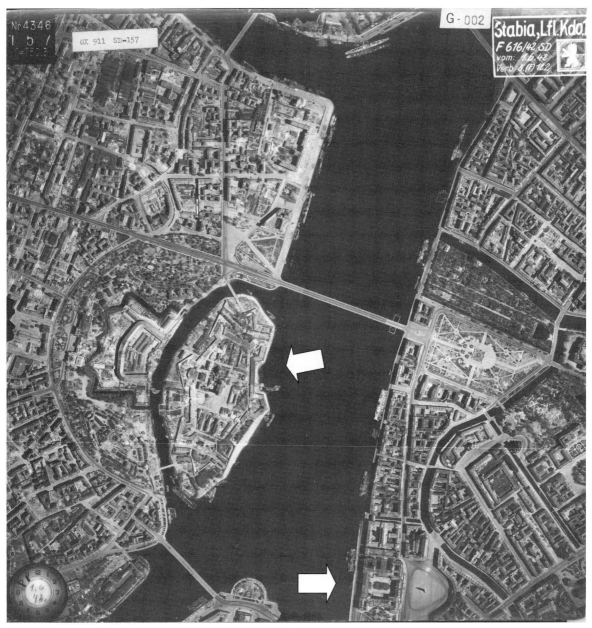

Still 1 June 1942, upstream from the last photos. Divide of the upper and lower Neva is at the top. This is the heart of Leningrad with Winter Palace at the right arrow and the Fortress of Peter and Paul at the left arrow.

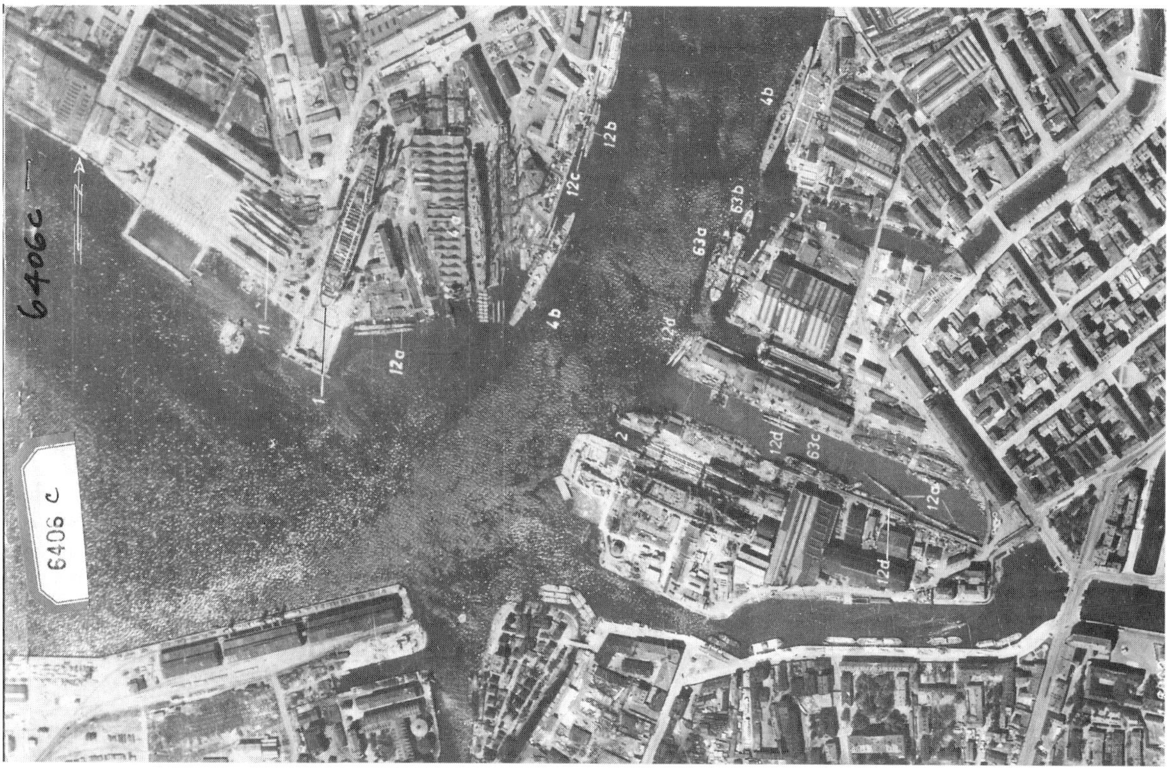
6406c
6406 c
1
2
4a
4b
11
12a
12b
12c
12d
63a
63b
63c

26 June 1941 (four days after the invasion began).
Baltic and Marti Shipyards with the vessels Germans watched most intently.
BB at annotation '1'
CV at annotation '2'
CA in building at annotation '4a'
CA afloat at annotations '4b'

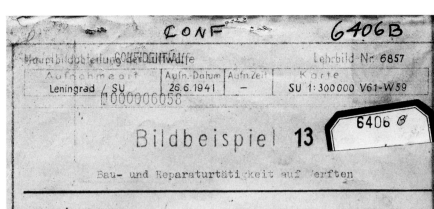

Hauptbildabteilung der Luftwaffe CONFIDENTIAL   Lehrbild Nr. 6857

Aufnahmeort	Aufn. Datum	Aufn.zeit	Karte
Leningrad / SU	26.6.1941	–	SU 1:300000 V61-W59

1000000058

Bildbeispiel 13   6406 B

Bau- und Reparaturtätigkeit auf Werften

Auswertung:

Auswertezahl   Gattung

1	=	1 Schlachtschiff, etwa 240 m lang, auf der Helling
2	=	1 Flugzeugträger, über 200 m lang, auf der Helling (Achterschiff noch nicht fertig)
4 a	=	1 Schwerer Kreuzer, ähnlich "Kirow"-Kl. ... lang
4 b	=	2 schwere Kreuzer der "Kirow"-Kl. in Ausrüstung
11	=	3 Zerstörer auf der Helling
12 a	=	4 U-Boote, 95 m lang
12 b	=	1 U-Boot, 80 m lang
12 c	=	1 U-Boot, 73 m lang
12 d	=	5 U-Boote, 60 m lang
63 a	=	1 ansch. Eisbrecher, 90 m lang
63 b	=	1 Fracht- und Fahrgastschiff (vermutlich Wohnschiff), etwa 8 000 BRT

Beurteilung:

Die Kenntnis von Gattung, Größe und Bauzustand der auf Werften liegenden Feindschiffe ermöglicht der eigenen Führung wertvolle Schlüsse. Luftbilder feindlicher Werften mit Neu- und Umbauten sind daher stets führungswichtige Unterlagen.

So konnte in diesem Luftbild zweier Bauwerften von Leningrad eins der auf den Helgen liegenden halbfertigen Großkriegsschiffe einwandfrei als Schlachtschiffneubau angesprochen werden (1), während es sich bei (2) wahrscheinlich um den Neubau eines Flugzeugträgers handelt.

In dem hier erkennbaren Bauzustand haben die Rümpfe von Flugzeugträger und Schlachtschiff zwar noch die ähnlichen Umrißformen, auch ihre Länge erschwert die gattungsmässige Unterscheidung. Dagegen sind die Wallgänge eines Flugzeugträgers schmaler gehalten als beim Schlachtschiff. Außerdem fehlen die beim Schlachtschiff erkennbaren runden Unterbauten für die schweren Geschütztürme. Beides trifft für das Schiff (2) zu, das somit als Flugzeugträger anzusprechen ist.

DTI 752.415

German PI Report for the preceding photograph.

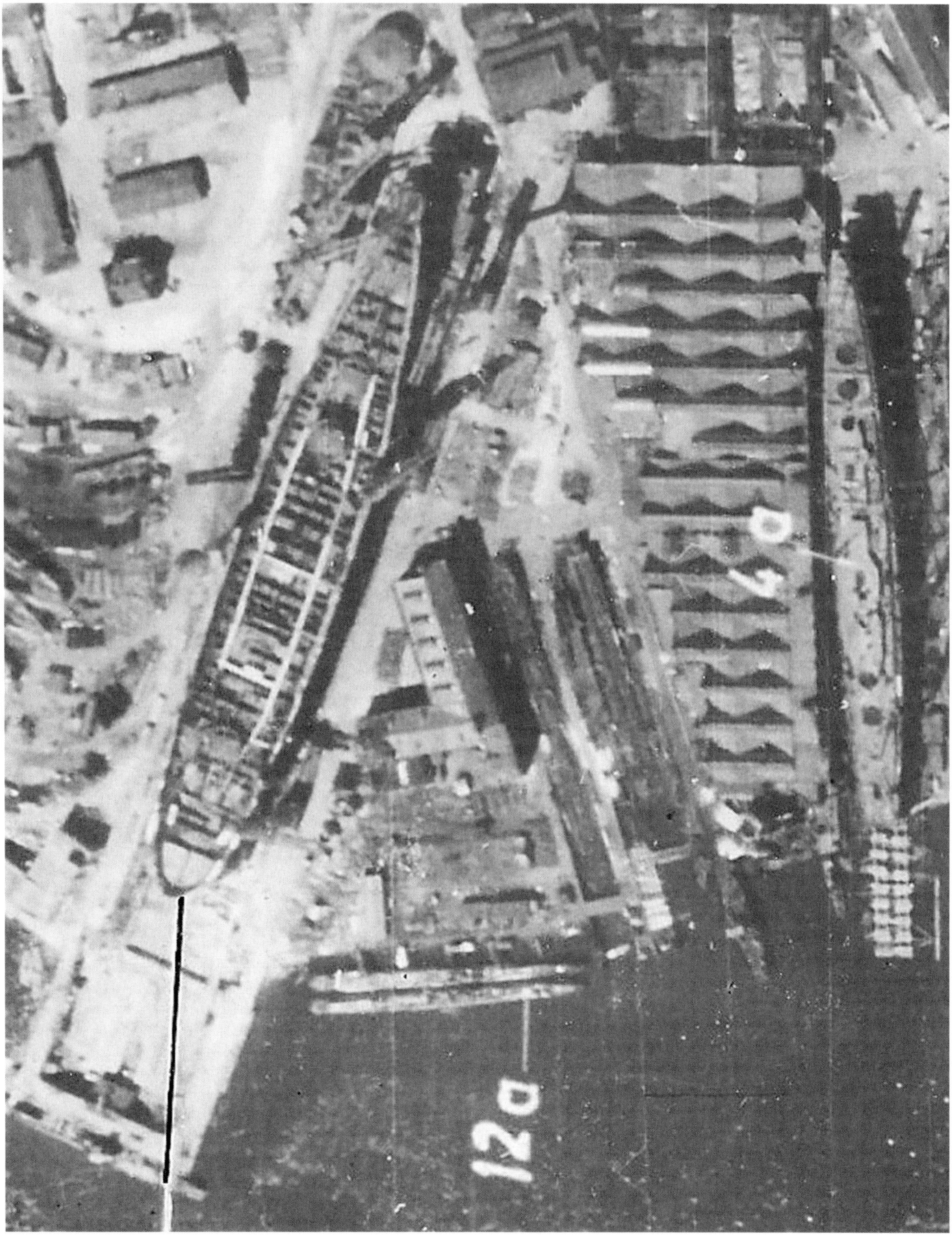

Enlargement of 26 June imagery. The stern turret cover is removed revealing no barbette at that location. So it WAS three turrets on the hull after all. Three barbettes are uncovered on the *Kirov* cruiser at right.

Soviet sappers planting mines
in front of an anti-tank barrier,
probably Leningrad, 1941.

The caption said this was Luftwaffe
bombing of a Soviet tank 'Lager'
(camp).

NO 36-1 #146

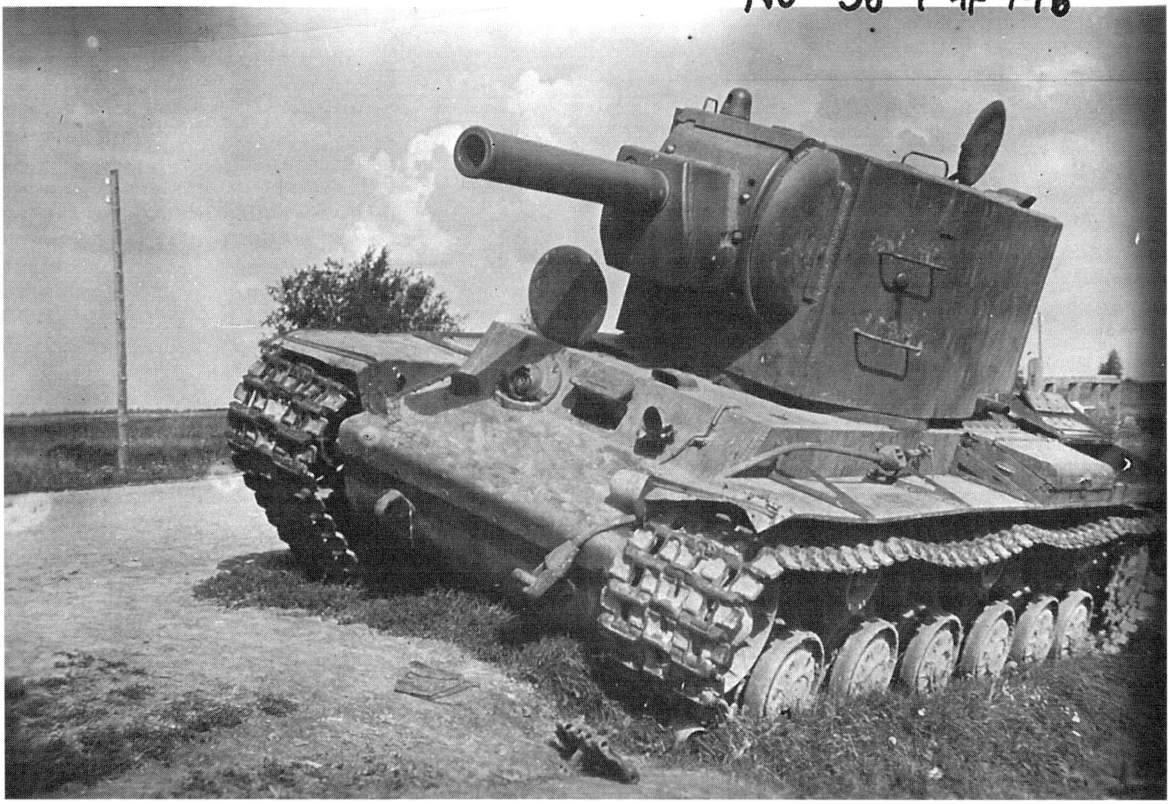

Abandoned Soviet KV-2, south of Leningrad.

Destruction in Leningrad suburbs, fall 1941.

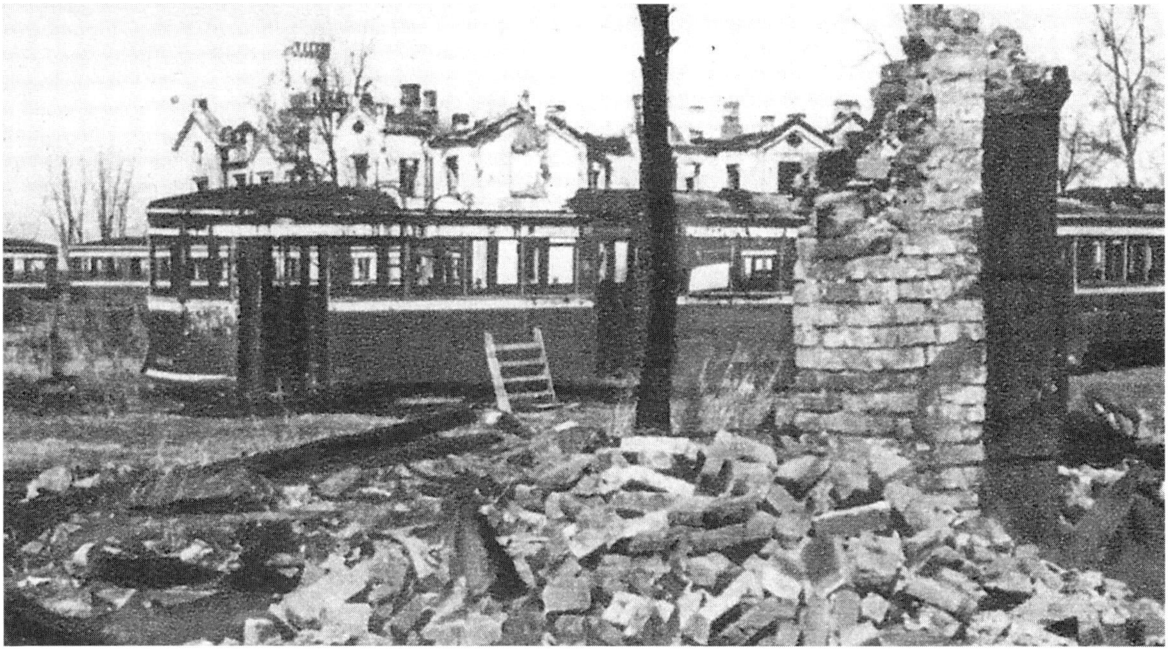

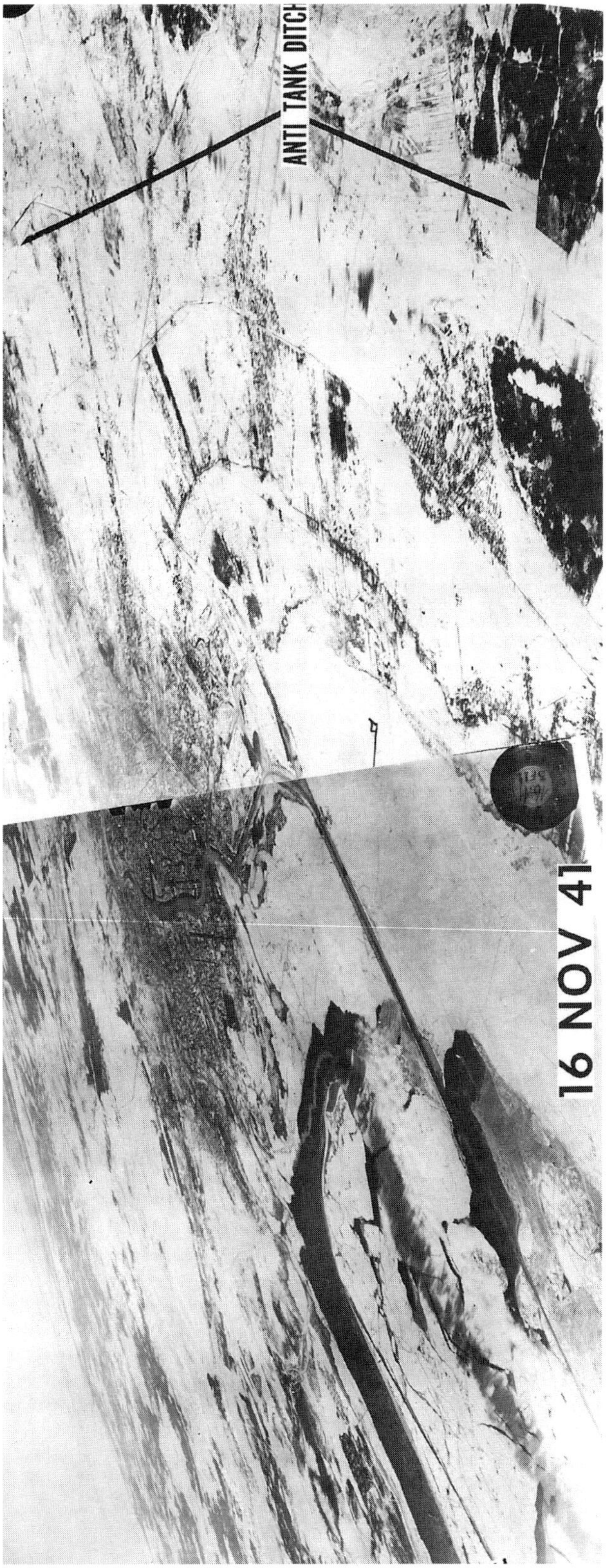
ANTI TANK DITCH
16 NOV 41

Enlargement of my wall display mosaic of Leningrad, looking northeast. Ice breakers have kept channels open to the Baltic.

Leningrad was besieged from 8 September 1941 to 27 January 1944 with only crossing Lake Ladoga remaining open.

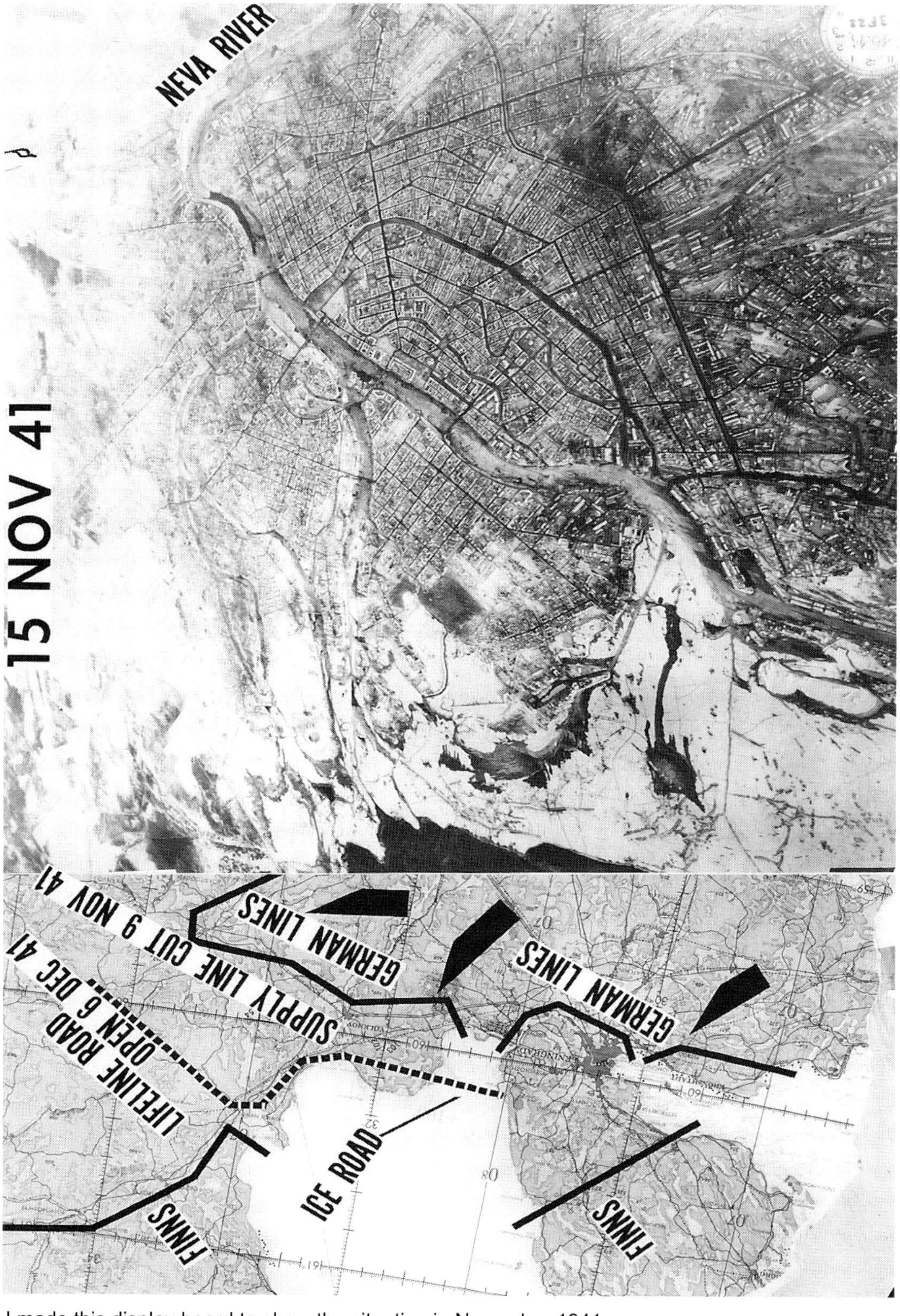
15 NOV 41
NEVA RIVER
GERMAN LINES
SUPPLY LINE CUT 9 NOV 41
GERMAN LINES
LIFELINE ROAD
OPEN 6 DEC 41
ICE ROAD
FINNS
FINNS

I made this display board to show the situation in November 1941.

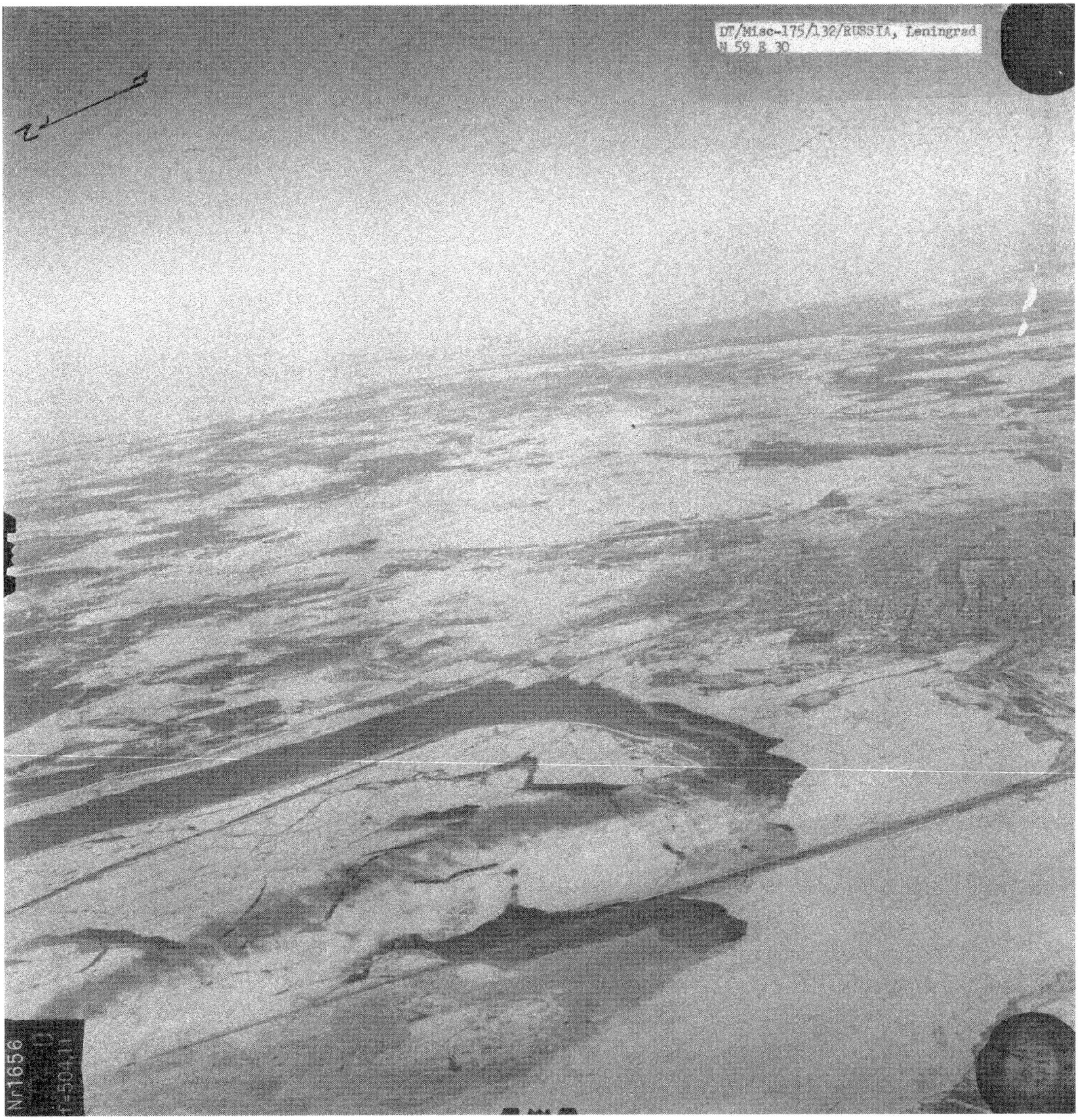
DT/Misc-175/132/RUSSIA, Leningrad
N 59 E 30
Nr1656

Besieged Leningrad (center right), looking northeast from just off shore, 16 November 1941. Ice breakers have kept a channel clear into the Baltic (crossing the foreground). Lake Ladoga is the dark shape in the distance (upper right). Long-time foes, the Finns, had already sealed off the Karelian Isthmus to the northwest. When German troops reached the south bank of Ladoga on 8 September, Leningrad was surrounded. When the lake froze, relief could reach the city by skirting German lines.

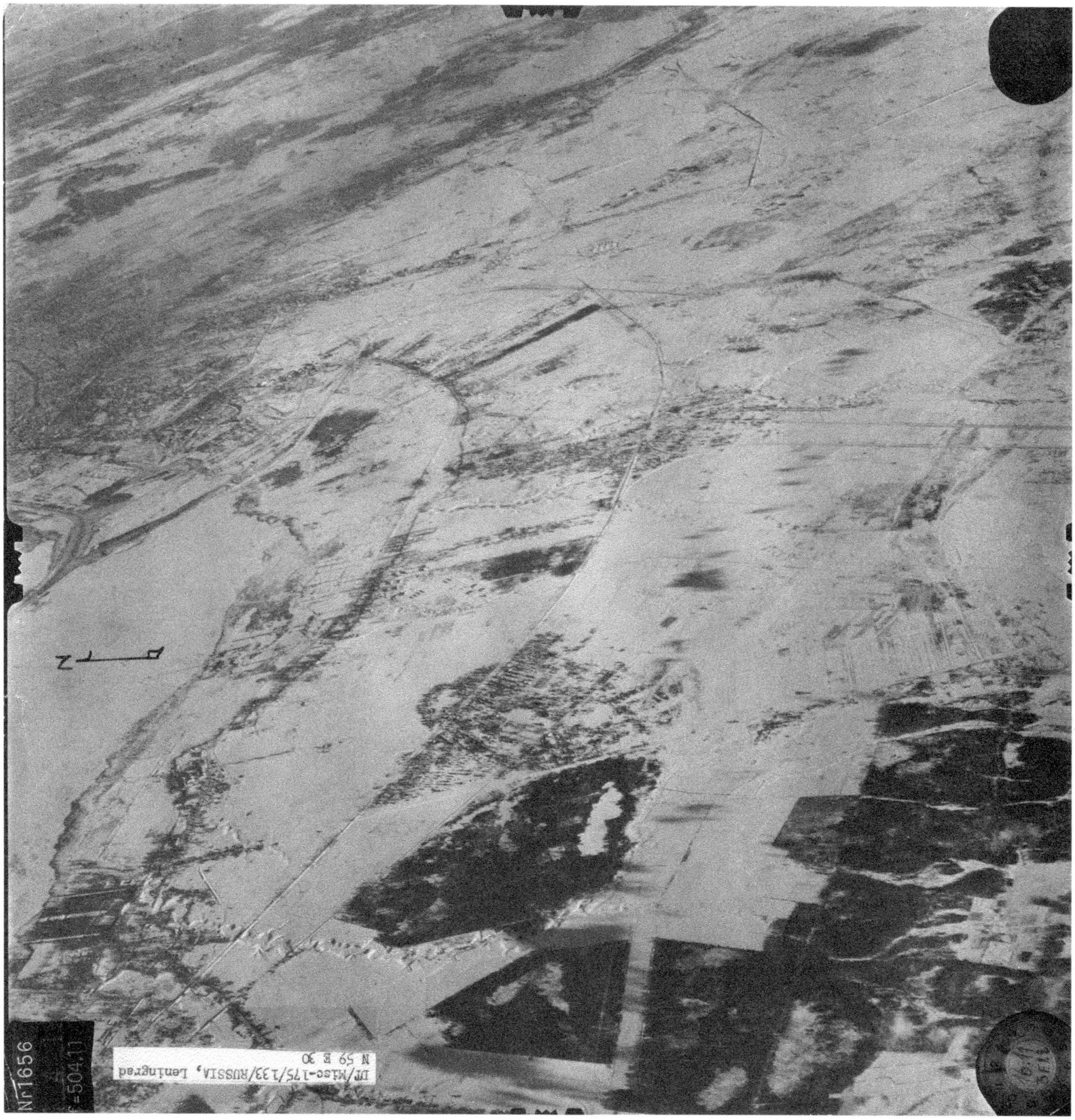
Nr1656
DT/Misc-175/133/RUSSIA, Leningrad
N 59 E 30

Another look from the same 16 November mission, still looking northeast but from about 15 miles south-southwest of Leningrad (upper left). German and Soviet troops are down there, but they don't have enough movement or activity (smoke, tracks, craters) for us to see them.

German target study of one of the airfields hurriedly scraped out to defend Leningrad. Kipuja was about 45 miles east of the city. The longest cleared area, 4300 feet, is plenty long enough for fighters and there may be five parked at the upper right end of the runway (can't be sure, they are just dark dots on this 26 June 1942 imagery reproduced on a printing press).

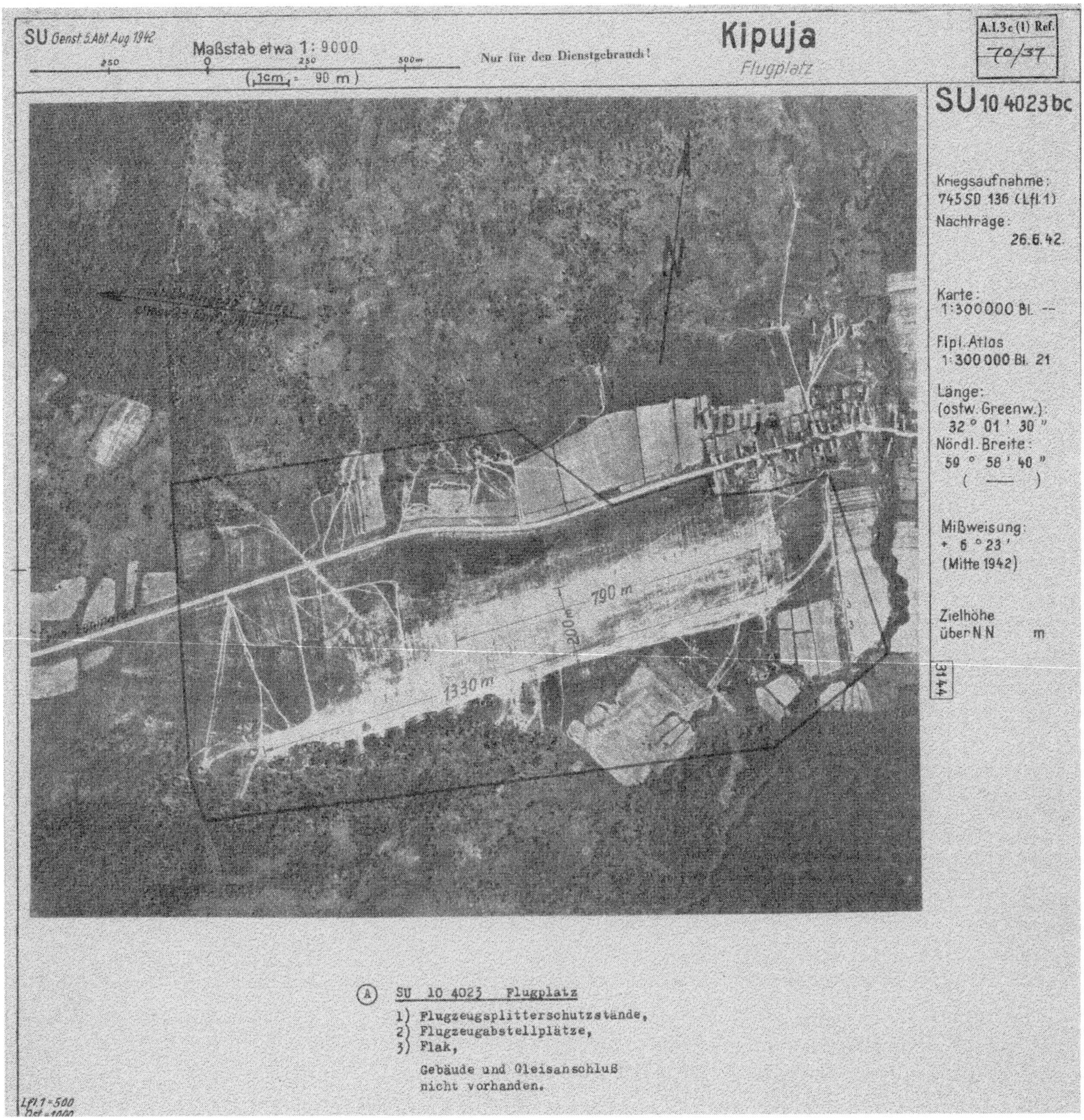

SU Genst 5.Abt Aug 1942
Maßstab etwa 1: 9000
250 0 250 500m
(1cm = 90 m)
Nur für den Dienstgebrauch!
Kipuja
Flugplatz
A.I.3c(I) Ref.
70/37
SU 10 4023 bc
Kriegsaufnahme:
745 SD 136 (Lfl.1)
Nachträge:
26.6.42
Karte:
1:300000 Bl. --
Flpl. Atlas
1:300 000 Bl. 21
Länge:
(ostw. Greenw.):
32° 01' 30"
Nördl. Breite:
59° 58' 40"
Mißweisung:
+ 6° 23'
(Mitte 1942)
Zielhöhe
über N N m
3144
N
Kipuja
790 m
200 m
1330 m
A SU 10 4023 Flugplatz
1) Flugzeugsplitterschutzstände,
2) Flugzeugabstellplätze,
3) Flak,
Gebäude und Gleisanschluß
nicht vorhanden.

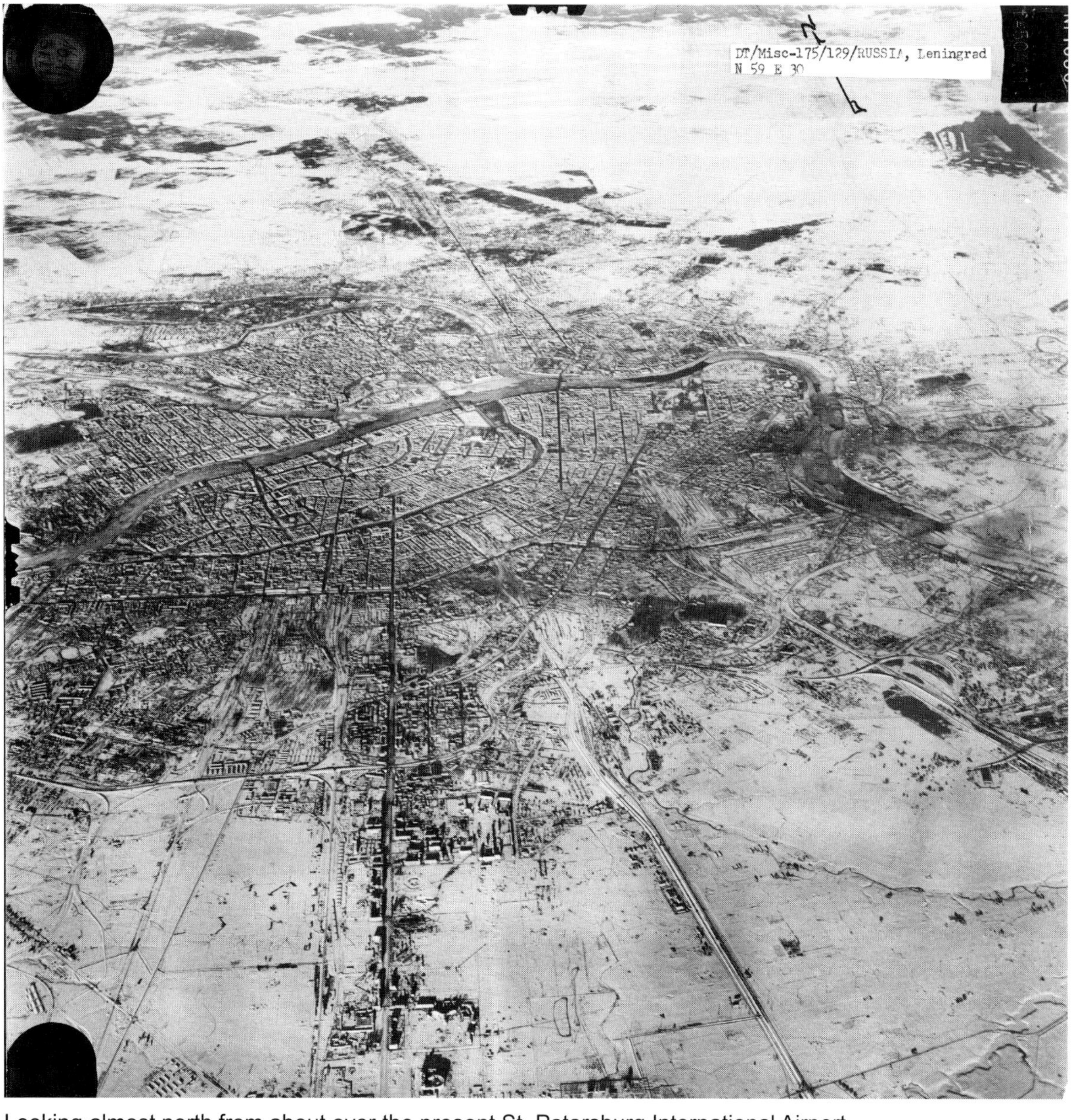
DT/Misc-175/129/RUSSIA, Leningrad
N 59 E 30

Looking almost north from about over the present St. Petersburg International Airport.

The siege began in September 1941. Soviet forces cut a corridor through to Leningrad on 18 January 1943 and the siege was lifted on 23 January 1944.

It cost the Germans over half a million casualties. The Soviets lost three and a half million plus six hundred thousand civilians to enemy action, starvation and cold.

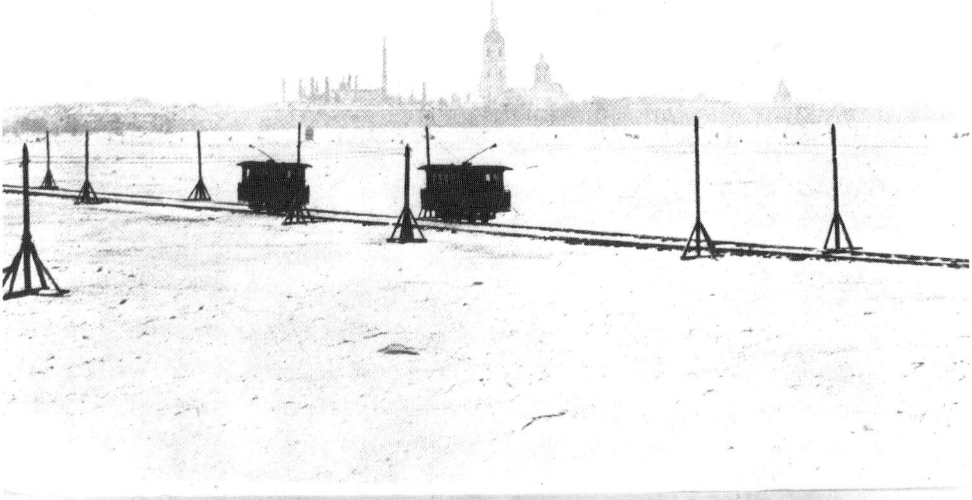

USSR. 59.55N - 30.15E. Leningrad.
Cat. 70. Streetcar tracks across the ice on the Neva river. In background, Peter-Paul fortress seen from the southwest. Source - Mil.Geo. Leningrad. GMDS H29/ID2.20, 1941, page 95.

Using the ice was nothing new to Leningrad. The besieged city established 'ice roads' over Lake Ladoga to get supplies.

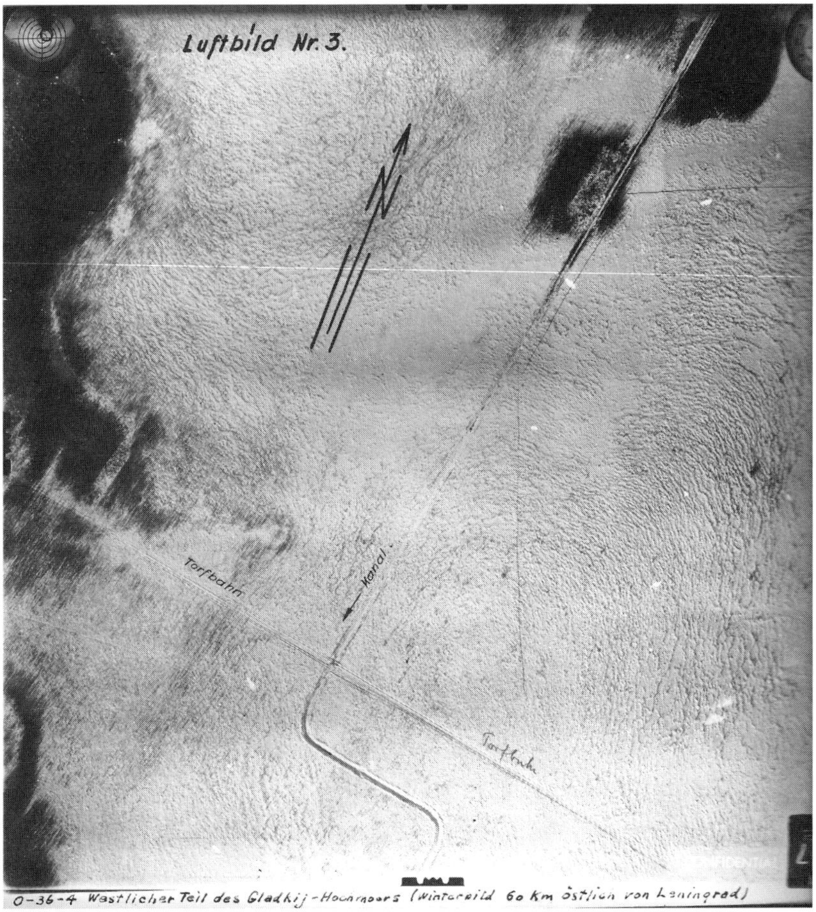
Luftbild Nr. 3.
Torfbahn
Kanal
0-36-4 Westlicher Teil des Gladkij-Hochmoors (Winterbild 60 km östlich von Leningrad)

An ice road near Leningrad. Luftwaffe bombing regularly disrupted the ice life-lines, killing thousands of people and sinking tons of supplies by breaking up the ice.

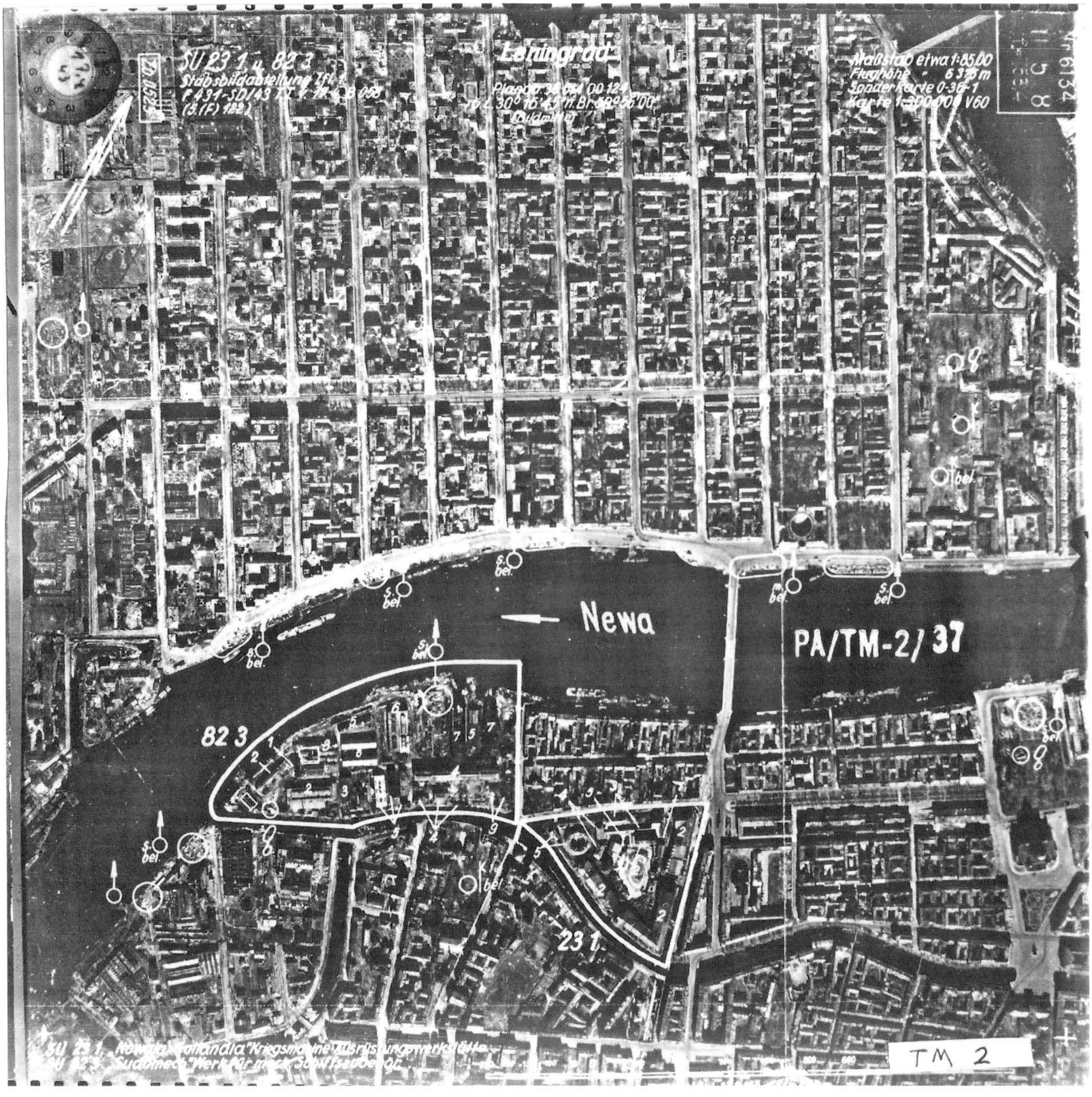
Leningrad
Newa
PA/TM-2/37
82 3
23 1
TM 2

Sudomech Shipbuilding Works, 17 April 1943. Annotated circles mark bomb hits. Big shipyards are just down the Neva (to the left).

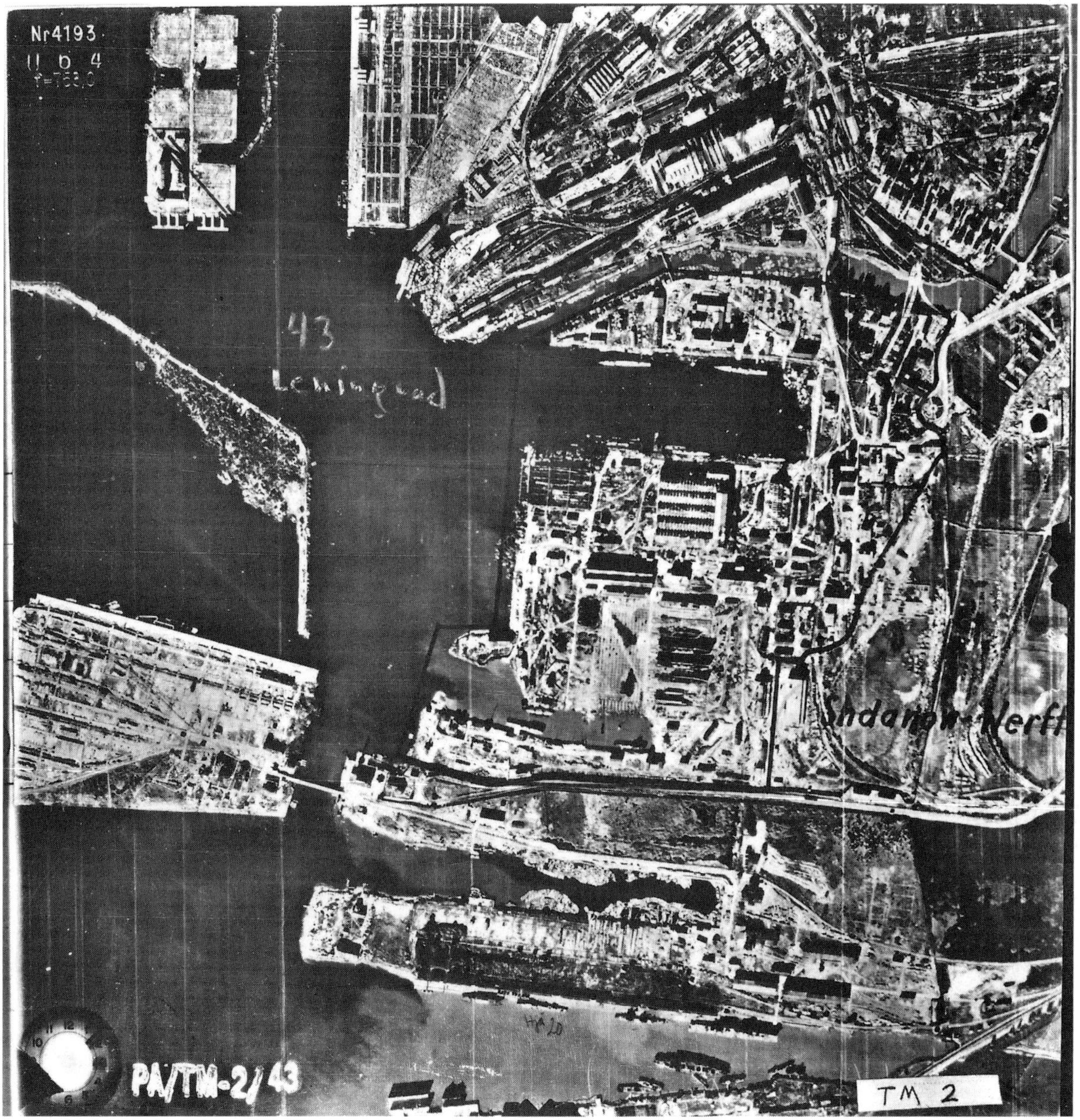
Nr4193
43
Leningrad
Shdanow-Werft
PA/TM-2/43
TM 2

Merchant ship basins one mile south of the Neva River mouth, 1943. This is another German Target Study also apparently used by American targeteers.

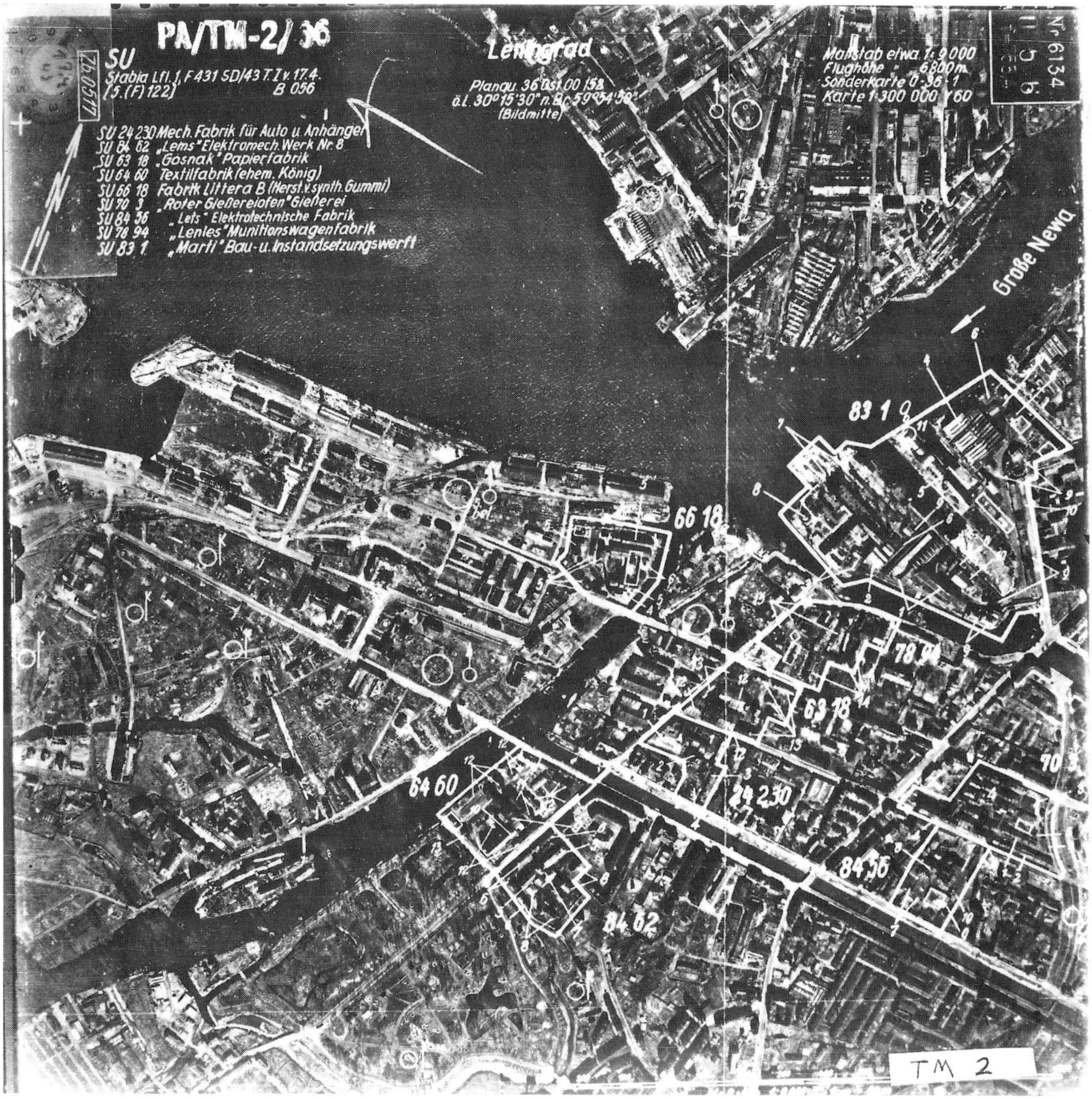
PA/TM-2/36
SU
Stabia Lfl. 1, F 431 SD/43 T. I v. 17.4.
[5.(F) 122]
B 056
SU 24 230 Mech. Fabrik für Auto u. Anhänger
SU 84 62 „Lems" Elektromech. Werk Nr. 8
SU 63 18 „Gosnak" Papierfabrik
SU 64 60 Textilfabrik (ehem. König)
SU 66 18 Fabrik Littera B (Herst. v. synth. Gummi)
SU 70 3 „Roter Gießereiofen" Gießerei
SU 84 56 „Lets" Elektrotechnische Fabrik
SU 78 94 „Lenles" Munitionswagenfabrik
SU 83 1 „Marti" Bau- u. Instandsetzungswerft
Planqu. 36 Ost 00 158
ö.L. 30°15'30" n.Br. 59°54'50"
(Bildmitte)
Nr 6134
Flughöhe " 6800 m
Sonderkarte 0-36-1
Karte 1:300 000 Y 60
Große Newa
83 1
66 18
78 94
63 18
64 60
24 230
84 56
84 62
70
TM 2

North is up and right. A more detailed target breakdown of the upper end of the Neva Riva ship canal (upper left) and mouth of the Neva, 17 April 1943. Location of the previous photo is down and left. Baltic and Marti Shipyards are at upper right.

Circles mark bomb or shell hits/craters.

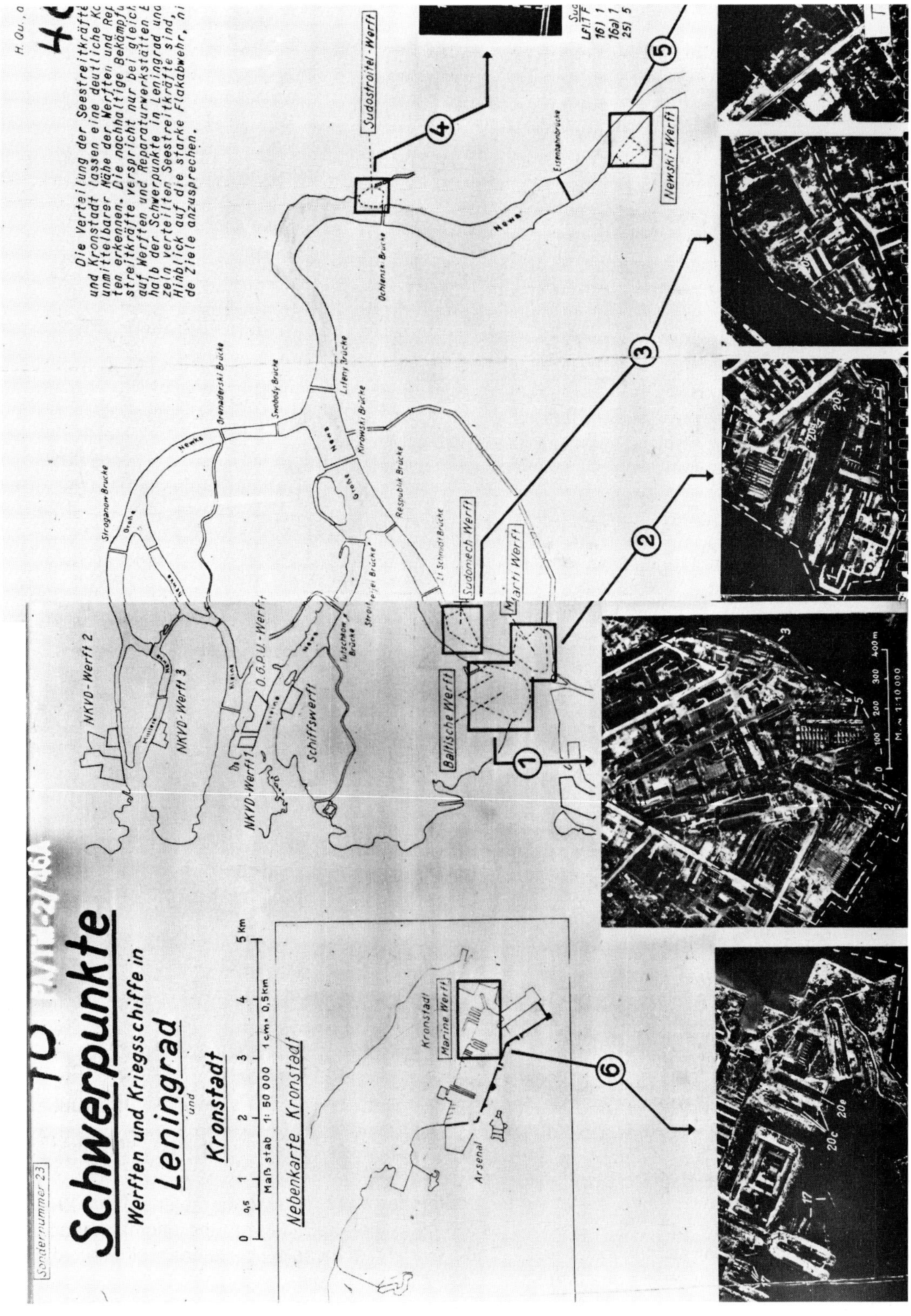
Sondernummer 23
Schwerpunkte
Werften und Kriegsschiffe in Leningrad und Kronstadt
Maßstab 1: 50 000 1cm = 0,5km
Nebenkarte Kronstadt
Kronstadt
Marine Werft
Arsenal
NKVD-Werft 2
NKVD-Werft 3
NKVD-Werft 1
O.G.P.U.-Werft
Schiffswerft
Baltische Werft
Sudomech Werft
Marti Werft
Sudostroitel-Werft
Newski-Werft
Newa
Stroganow Brücke
Grenaderski Brücke
Swobody Brücke
Liteny Brücke
Kirowski Brücke
Republik Brücke
Lt Schmidt Brücke
Ochtensk Brücke
Eisenbahnbrücke
Die Verteilung der Seestreitkräfte
und Kronstadt lassen eine deutliche Ko
unmittelbarer Nähe der Werften und Rep
ten erkennen. Die nachhaltige Bekämpfu
streitkräfte verspricht nur bei gleich
auf Werften und Reparaturwerkstätten b
halb der Schwerpunkte in Leningrad und
zeln verteilten Seestreitkräfte sind,
Hinblick auf die starke Flakabwehr, ni
de Ziele anzusprechen.
M. ~ 1:10 000

German PI Report showing all the shipbuilding and fitting out facilities in Leningrad.

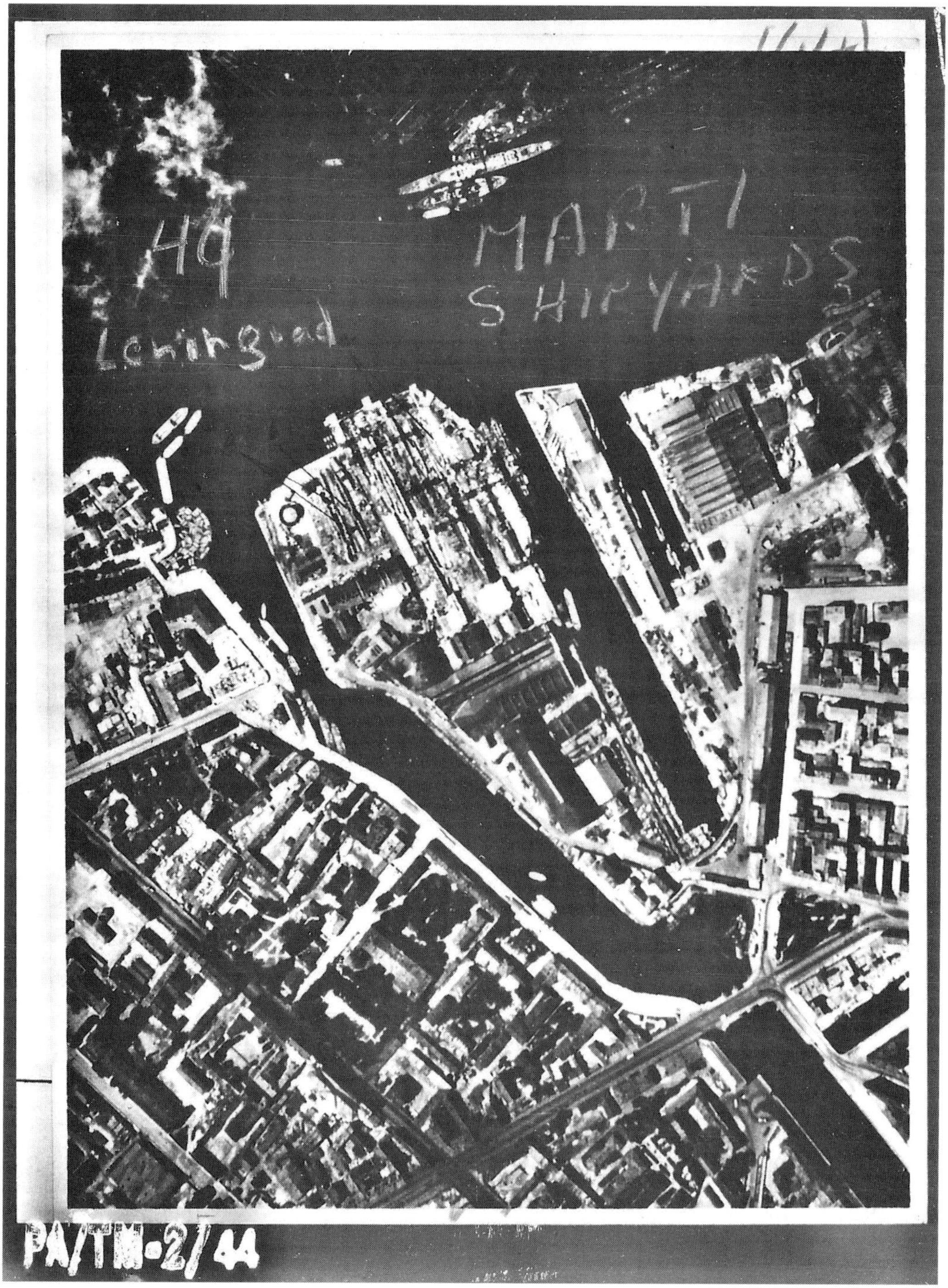
Hq
MARTI
SHIPYARDS
Leningrad
PA/TM-2/44

Original film date is unknown, but sometime after September 1943. This target material from 1944 suffers from a problem typical of much DT imagery—it is too many generations from the original negative. Each copying picks up more contrast and loses detail. The Neva end of these slipways has a different shape than seen earlier and the familiar shape of a large hull (Aircraft carrier) appears missing.

The grease pencil annotation was made by a US technician after the war.

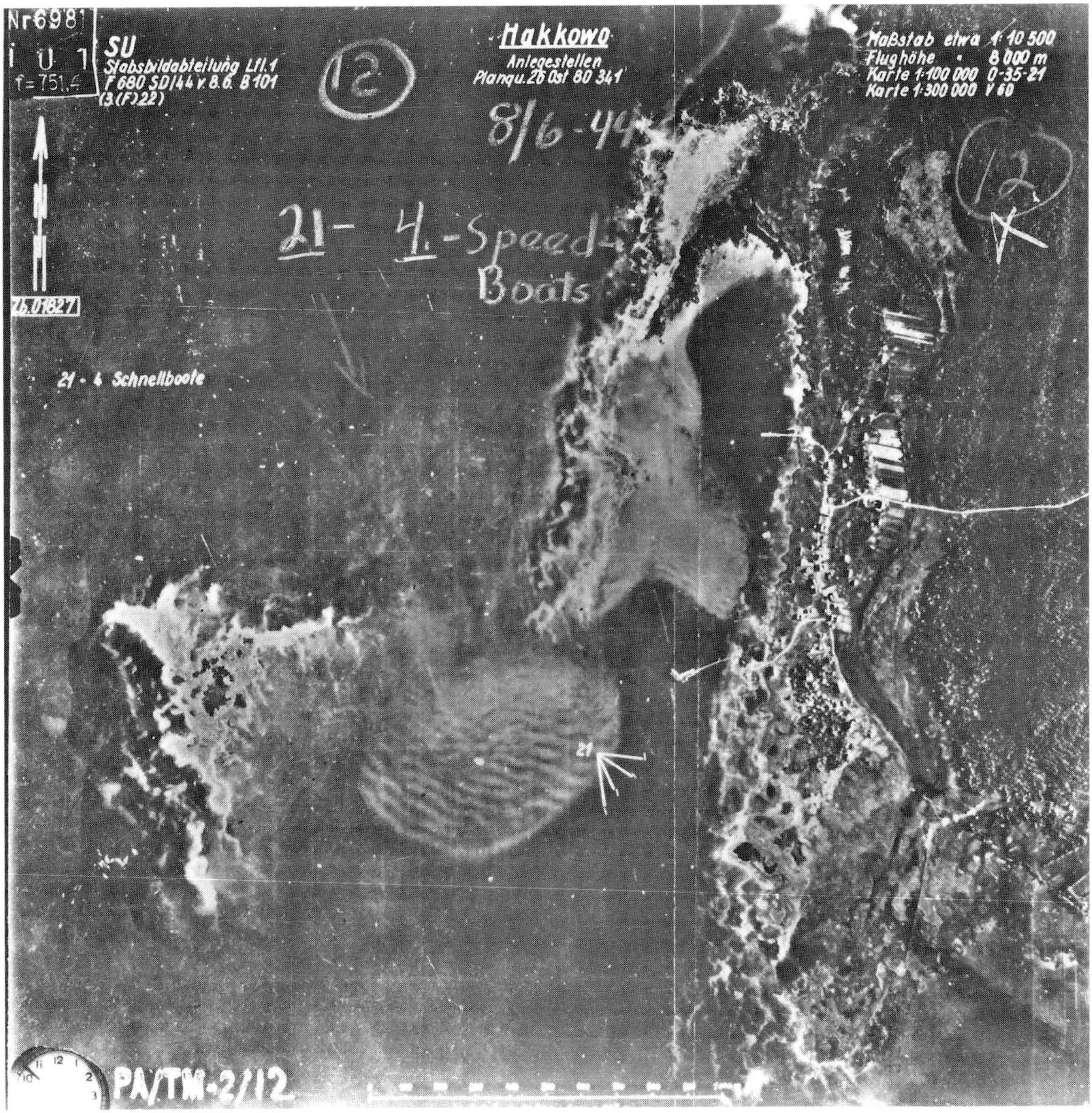
Nr 6981
SU
Stabsbildabteilung Lfl.1
F 680 SD/44 v. 8.6. B 101
(3.(F)22)
12
Hakkowo
Anlegestellen
Planqu. 26 Ost 80 341
8/6-44
Maßstab etwa 1:10 500
Flughöhe 8 000 m
Karte 1:100 000 0-35-21
Karte 1:300 000 V 60
12
21- 4.-Speed-
Boats
21 - 4 Schnellboote
21
PA/TM-2/12

A German target graphic with American post-war processing markings. I read the taking date as 8 June 1944. This is Gakkovo, 80 miles west of Leningrad. T-34s were at their gates but German PIs were still looking at minutia. In this case four Motor-Torpedo boats, enlarged at right.

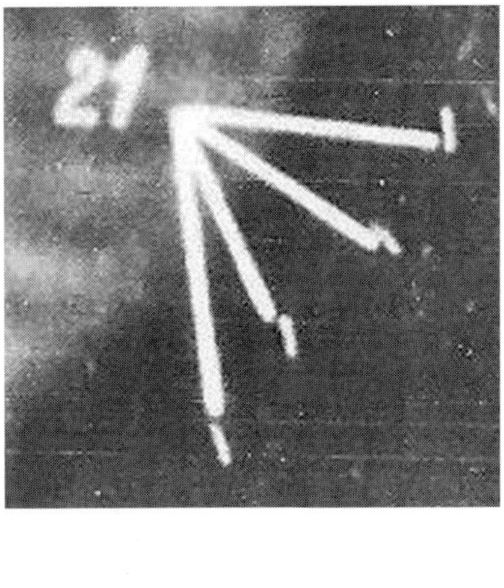
21

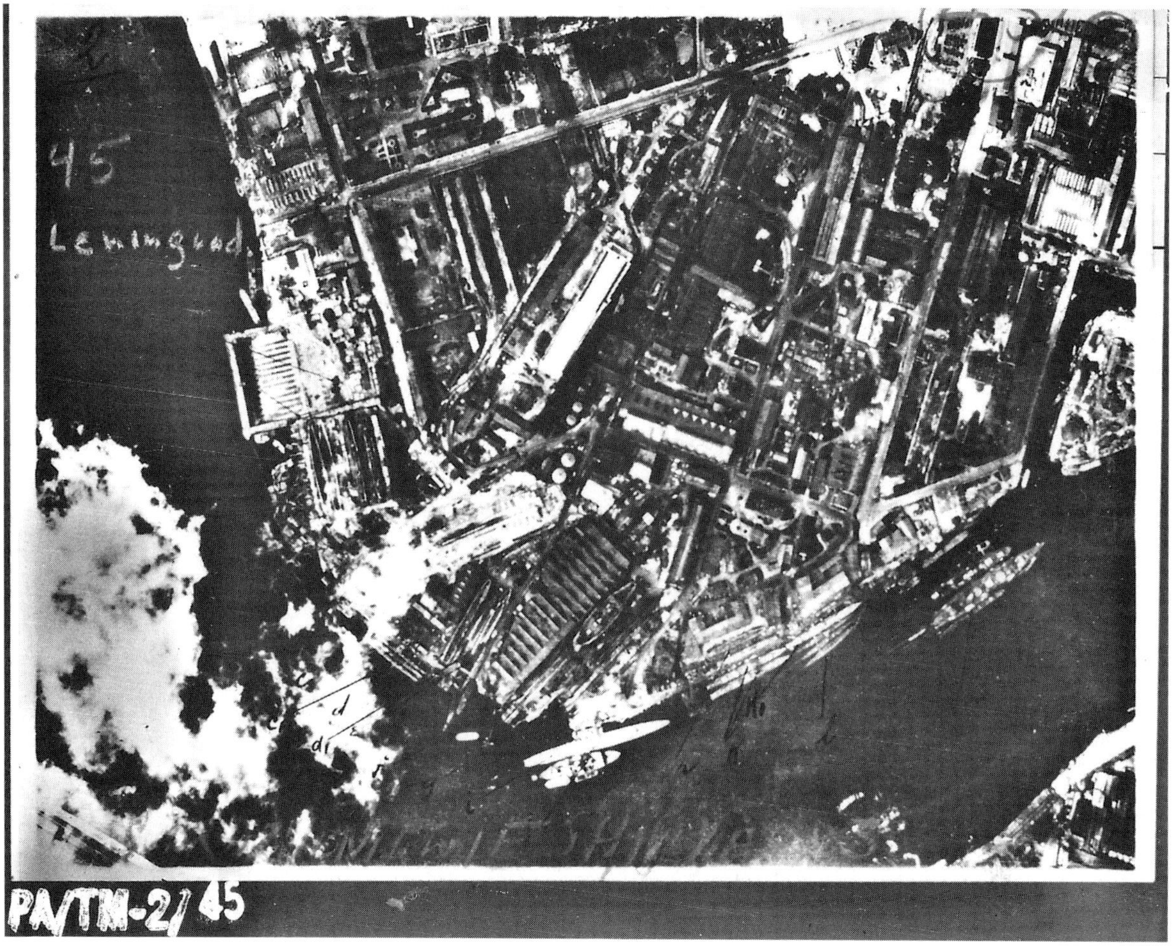
45
Leningrad.
PA/TM-2/45

Another example of too many generations of copying, this time compounded by cloud. With the FEBA some 200 miles to the west and moving west fast, it is hard to imagine what German Intelligence hoped to learn at Leningrad in 1945 (though the imagery may have been from many months earlier). At right, *October Revolution* is afloat in the river. An unfinished *Kirov* cruiser is in the same quayside location we've seen June 1941. The *Kirov* cruiser building on ways next to the battleship is gone, replaced by a hull half the length and three times the width, possibly an icebreaker. I can't see the battleship building ways well, but what I can see doesn't look right for the big hull. Some sources claim the hull was floated off to make room on the building way for other work. If it was moved, I don't have the right coverage to locate it.

MURMANSK

With Krieg's Marine so powerful in the Baltic, ice-free ports on Barents and White seas were crucial to survival of the USSR. Germany performed regular recce and stationed naval and air elements in northern Norway to interdict convoys heading for Russian ports.

Murmansk is a rail and road-served ice-free port located 25 miles south of the Barents Sea on the Tuloma River. It was founded in 1915.

A.I.3c (1) Ref.
Geheim!
S.U. 45 12c ZR.
Murmansk
Genst. 5. Abt. April 1941
1:300 000 Bl. 36
Kola-Bucht
1212
Basis Hk.
8393 Neue Werft im Bau
10108
Wasserturm
Siedlung
4512
Selený Hk.
Liegeplatz der Trawler
Abraham HK
MURMANSK
Stand der Uboote
Marine Pier
Schiffsrep.-Werkst.
8394
4951
Kl. Werft
Öltanks
83167
N
Maßstab 1:25000
S.U. 70108 Flughafen (See?)
" 1212 Kriegshafen
" 4512 Hafenanlagen
" 4951 Funkstelle
S.U. 8393 Schiffsbau-Werft Nr.2
" 8394 "Glawrybi"-Werft Nr.1
" 83167 Reparatur-Werft

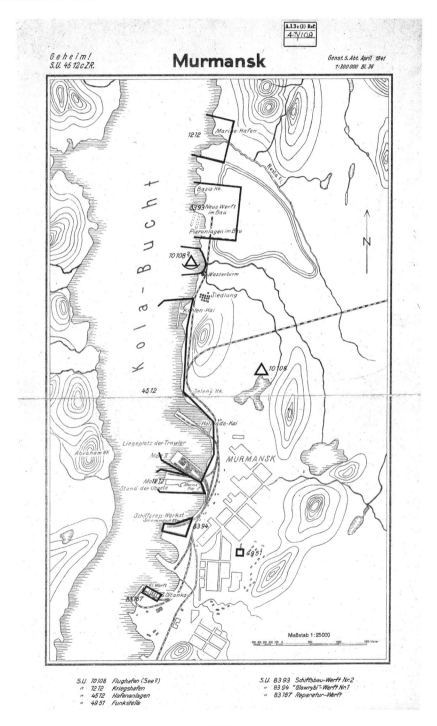

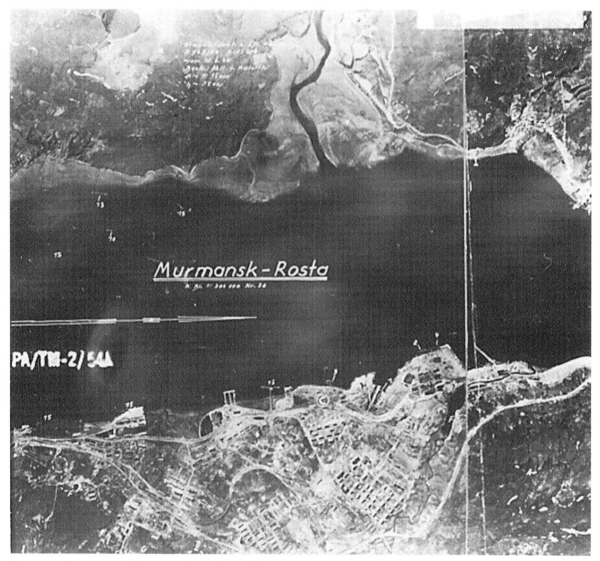

Murmansk - Rosta

PA/TW-2/54A

German photorecon of Murmansk continued throughout the war. This date is hard to read but I think it is 22 June 1943. Submarines were initially successfully interdicting Atlantic convoys to the Soviet Union. German surface ships and terrible weather were also hazards for merchant seamen rounding North Cape. Luftwaffe attempts to destroy Murmansk and ships anchored there were less successful.

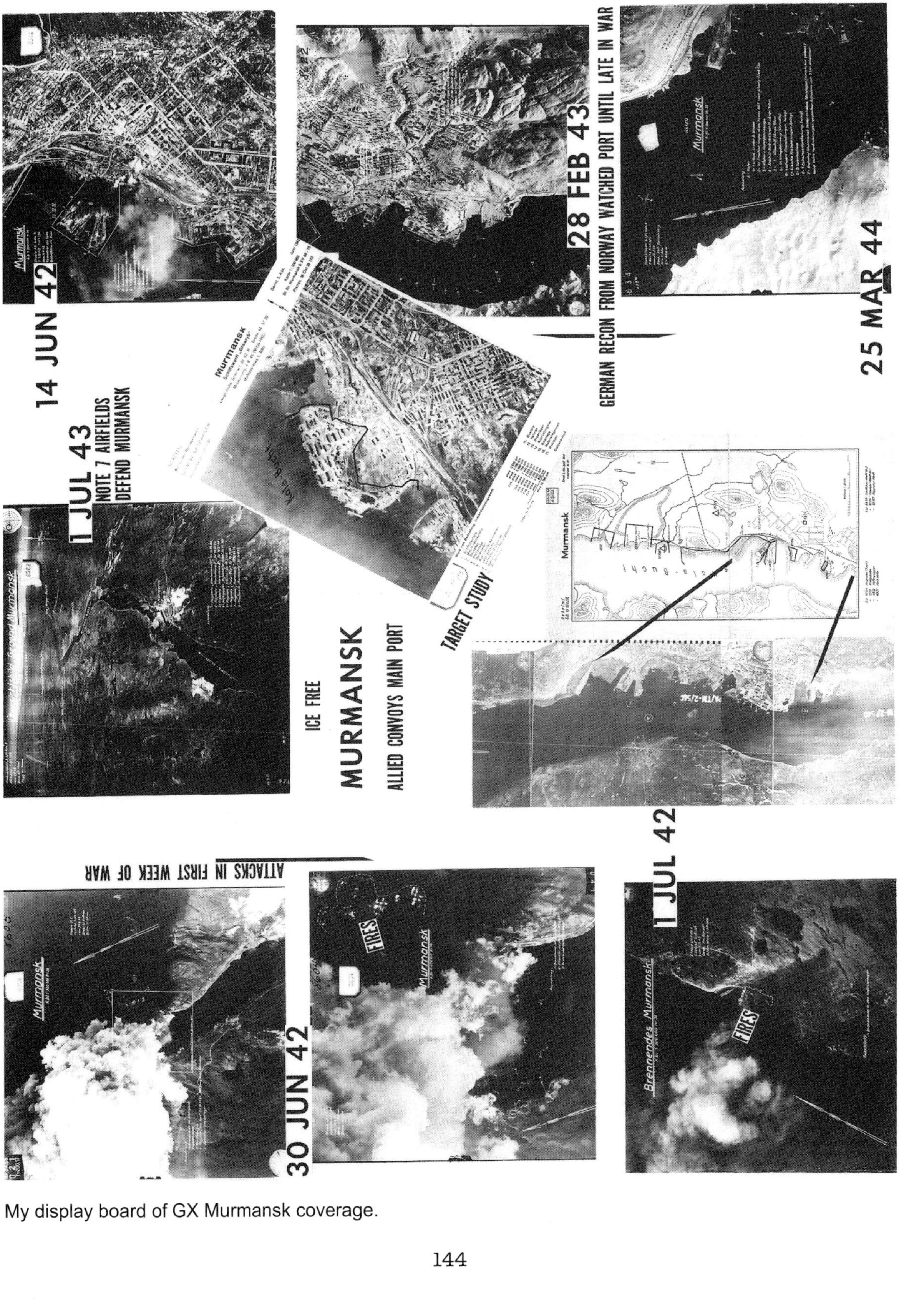
14 JUN 42
Murmansk
1 JUL 43
NOTE 7 AIRFIELDS
DEFEND MURMANSK
28 FEB 43
GERMAN RECON FROM NORWAY WATCHED PORT UNTIL LATE IN WAR
25 MAR 44
Murmansk
Kola-Bucht
TARGET STUDY
ICE FREE
MURMANSK
ALLIED CONVOYS MAIN PORT
1 JUL 42
ATTACKS IN FIRST WEEK OF WAR
30 JUN 42
Murmansk
FIRES
Murmansk
FIRES
Brennendes Murmansk

My display board of GX Murmansk coverage.

ARKHANGELSK

Four hundred miles southeast of Murmansk, on the White Sea, is the mostly ice-free port of Arkhangelsk. There has been a port on the Divna River mouth since before ninth-century Vikings used it as a route into central Russia.

This was a favorite termination for WW II Atlantic Convoys because it was farther from German bomber bases in Norway.

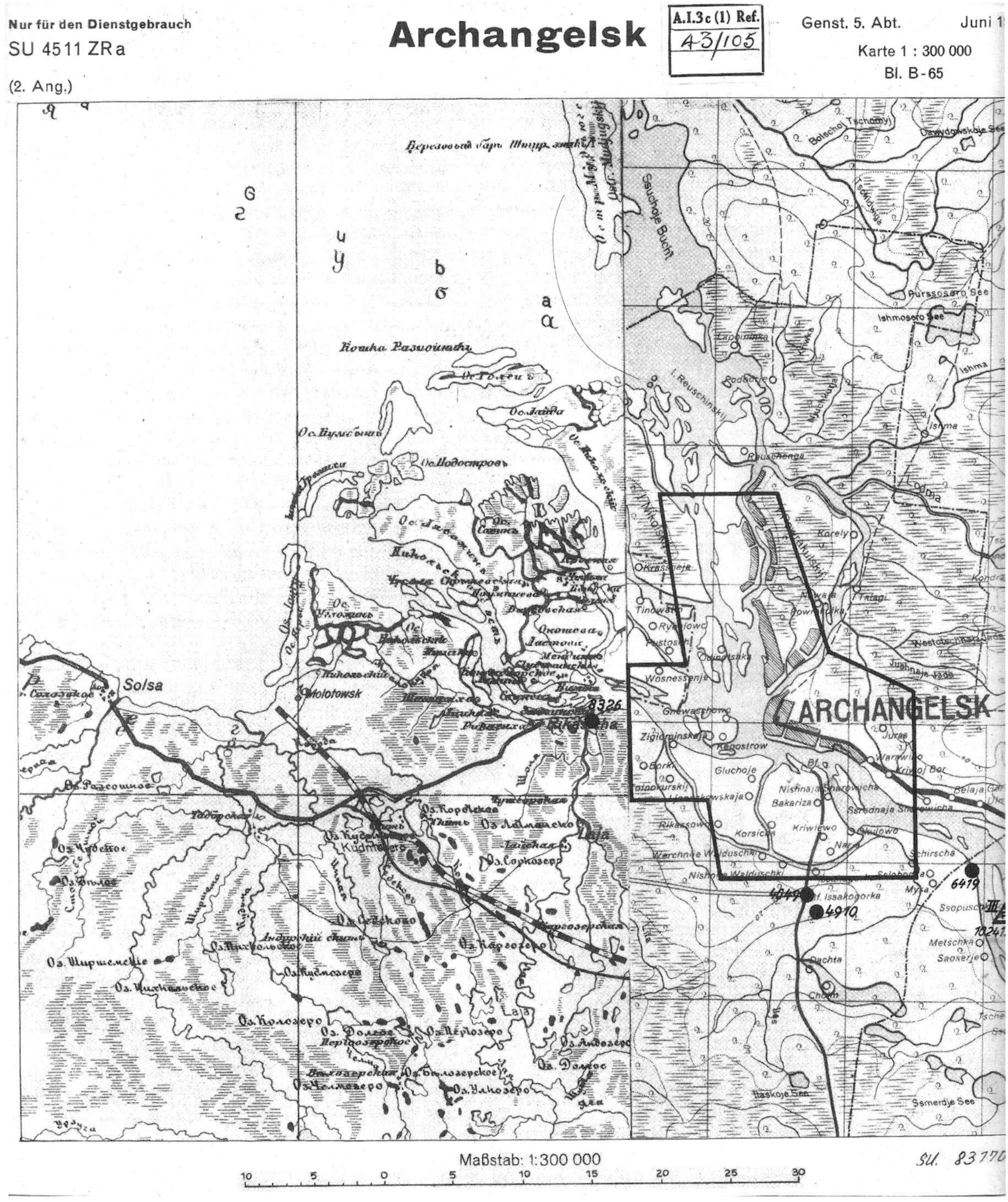

Nur für den Dienstgebrauch
SU 4511 ZRa
(2. Ang.)
Archangelsk
A.I.3c (1) Ref.
43/105
Genst. 5. Abt.
Karte 1 : 300 000
Bl. B-65
Ssuchoje Bucht
Pursso See
Ishmosero See
Ishma
Reuschenga
Korely
ARCHANGELSK
Solsa
Molotowsk
Kudmosero
Wosnessenje
Kegostrow
Gluchoje
Bakariza
Korsica
Kriwlewo
Nishni Wolduschki
Issakogorka
Ssopusch
Metschka
Saoserje
Dachta
Chorm
Smerdje See
Maßstab: 1:300 000
10 5 0 5 10 15 20 25 30
SU. 83770

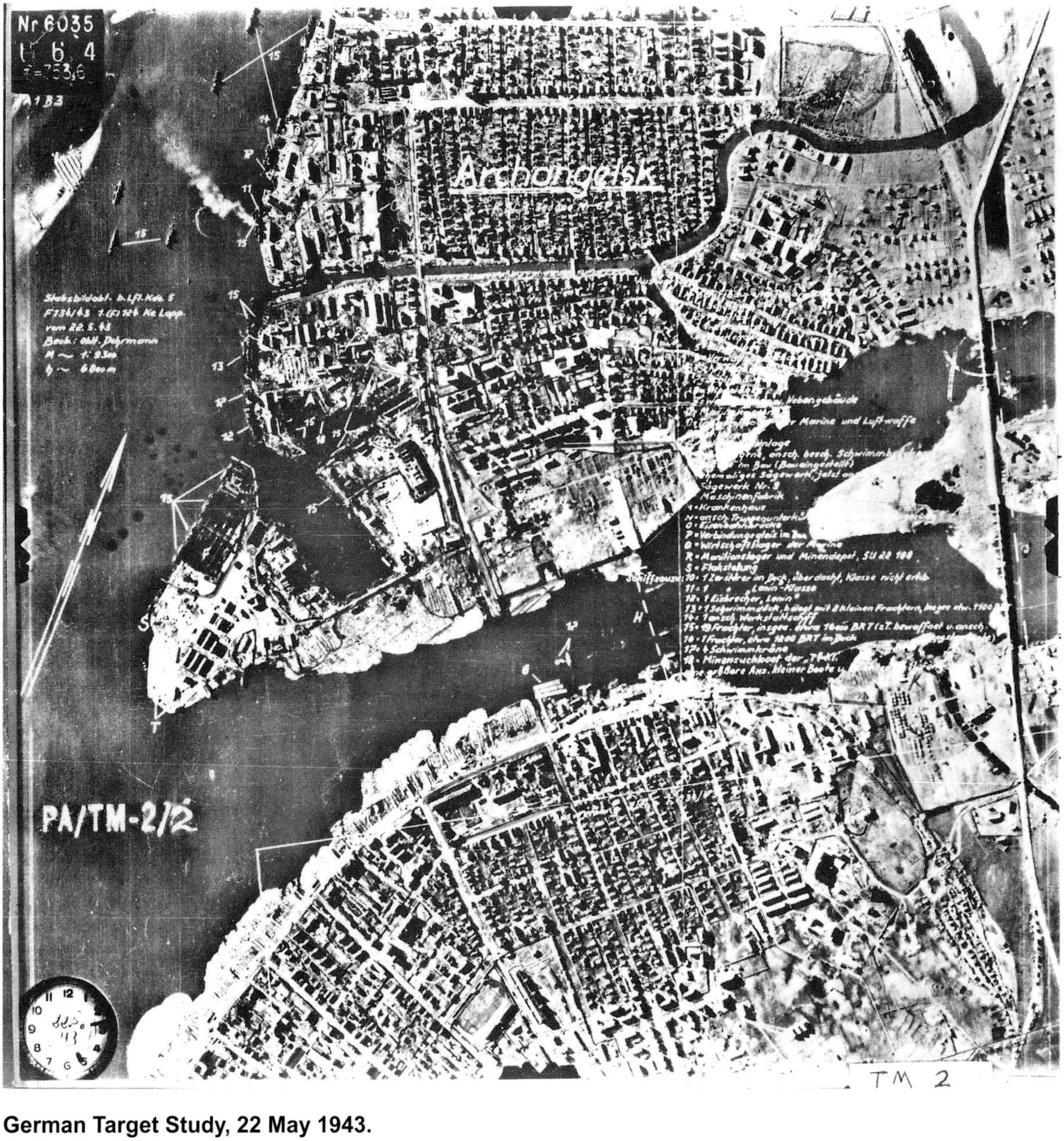
Nr 6035
Archangelsk
PA/TM-2/2
TM 2

German Target Study, 22 May 1943.
Forty convoys braved the gauntlet to reach Soviet Arctic ports. Over four million tons of supplies were delivered including 5,000 tanks and 7,000 aircraft. Ninety-eight cargo ships and eighteen warships were sunk during transit. Convoy PQ17, July 1942, lost twenty-four of thirty-six ships setting out from Iceland bound for Arkhangelsk.

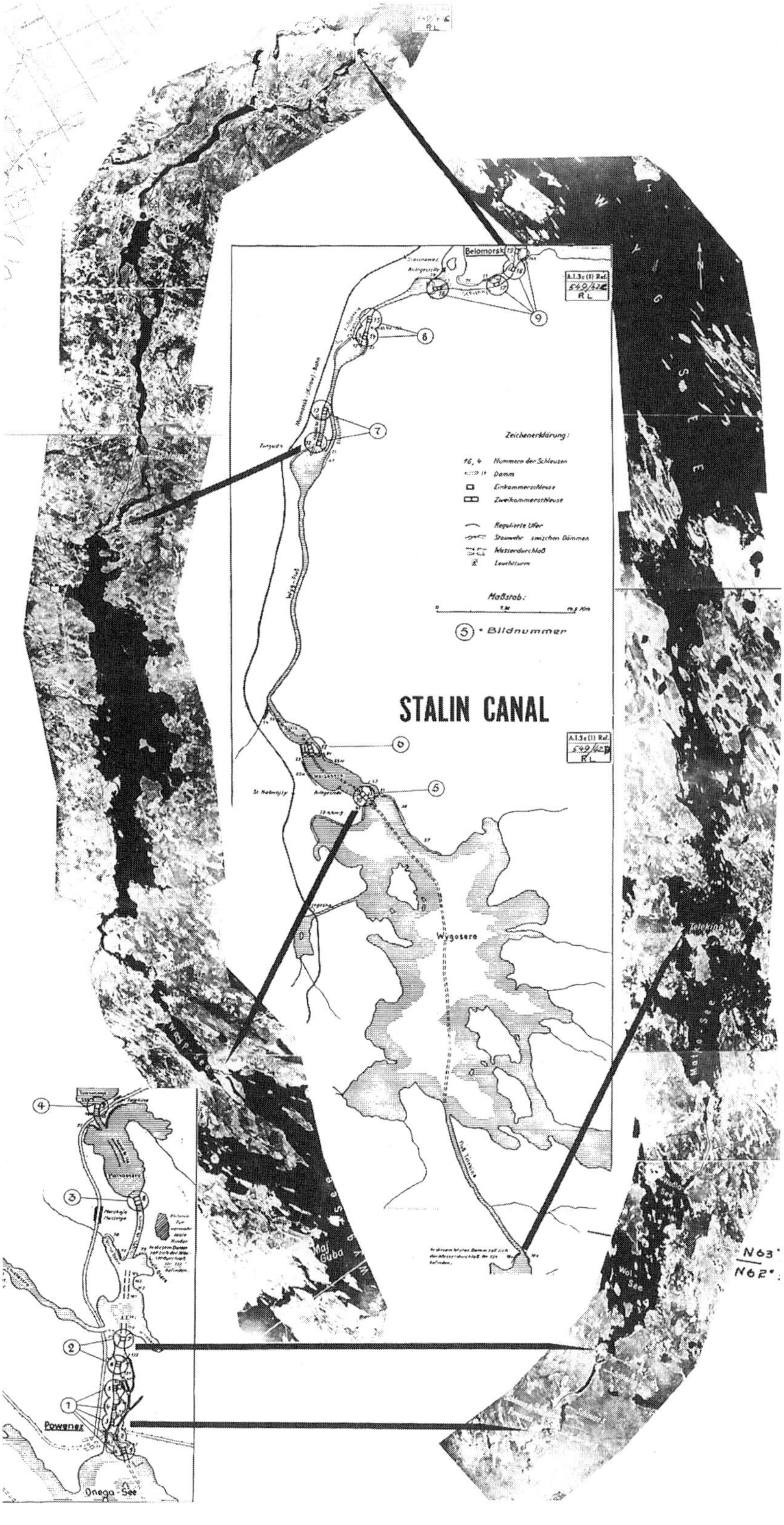
STALIN CANAL
Belomorsk
Zeichenerklärung:
Maßstab:
Bildnummer
Wygosero
Telekino
Powenez
Onega-See
N63°
N62°

STALIN CANAL
Another supply route south from Arctic ports was a canal completed in 1933 with 126,000 gulag (convict) laborers. It allowed goods to go from Ice-free Belomorsk, on the White Sea, to Powenez on Lake Onaga, then to the Svir River, on to Lake Ladoga, to the Neva River and thence to the Baltic.

Of course the Luftwaffe was interested in this supply line and photographed it often.

I put the imagery and associated map into one of my wall displays.

When I put this together I probably knew the material dates—but it was four decades ago and I didn't record it.

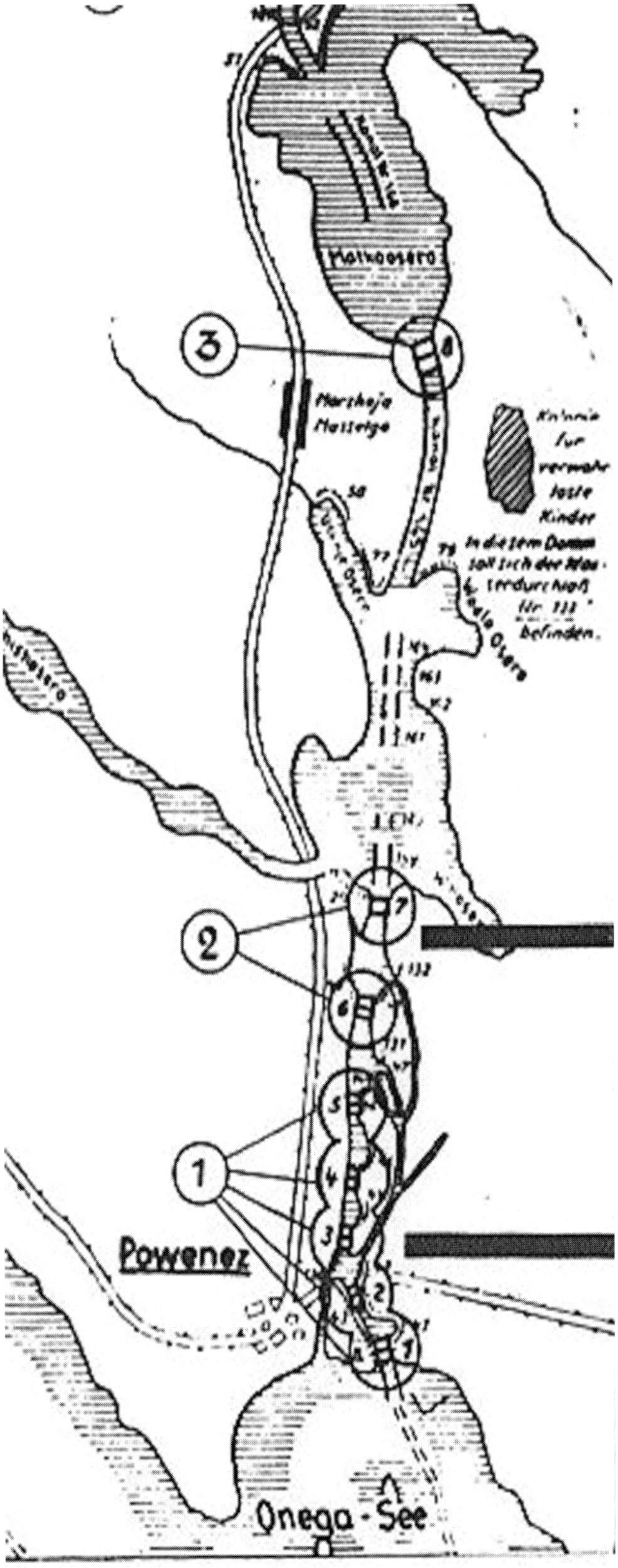
3
2
1
Powenez
Onega-See

The Stalin Canal concept made clever use of the many lakes and rivers available. One can only imagine the work with primarily hand labor. Seven locks stacked near Powenez (at left) was an obvious choke-point.

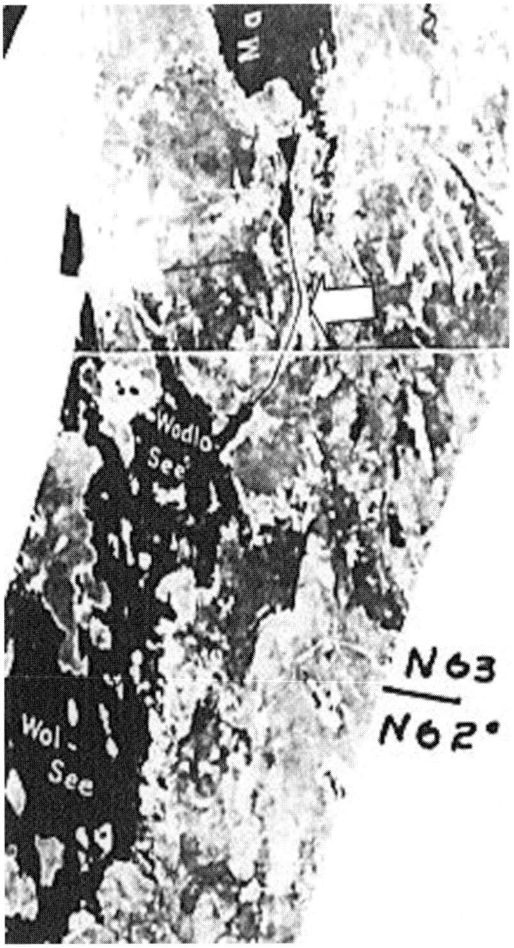
Wodlo-See
Wol-See
N63
N62°

Above, a two mile section of canal at larger scale (arrow). Unfortunately the canal was dug too shallow for large or heavy loads; however it was still valuable for critical supplies since it used many natural waterways, making it difficult for the Germans to interdict.

Chapter V

SCHWARZMEER

The Black Sea region was important to communications as German forces progressed east and south into the oil rich Caucuses. German ally Romania controlled the western Black Sea but Crimea, particularly Sevastopol, was the key to northern and eastern waters. Kerch was as critical to land advances past the Don as was Rostov. An open German flank to the south would have invited counterattack.

In addition, Soviet bombers from Crimea were attacking oil fields in Romania, threatening a resource Germany desperately needed.

To take the Caucuses one had to control Crimea and to control Crimea you had to take Odessa, the major port to its northwest.

German and Romanian forces attempted to do that beginning on 5 August 1941 with the Romania's 4th Army doing the heavy lifting. Attackers were stunned to be repelled and paused to reinforce. Attackers eventually outnumbered Soviet defenders by nearly 3 to 1.

Soviet warships provided on-shore fire support and prevented encirclement of Odessa. They also evacuated defenders to Crimea when it was obvious the city was lost.

The Soviets tried several attacks on German and Romanian flanks to pull forces from the city, including hastily mounting operations by parachutists that resulted in loss of most of the force and didn't stem enemy advances. All that did was extend the siege to 73 days.

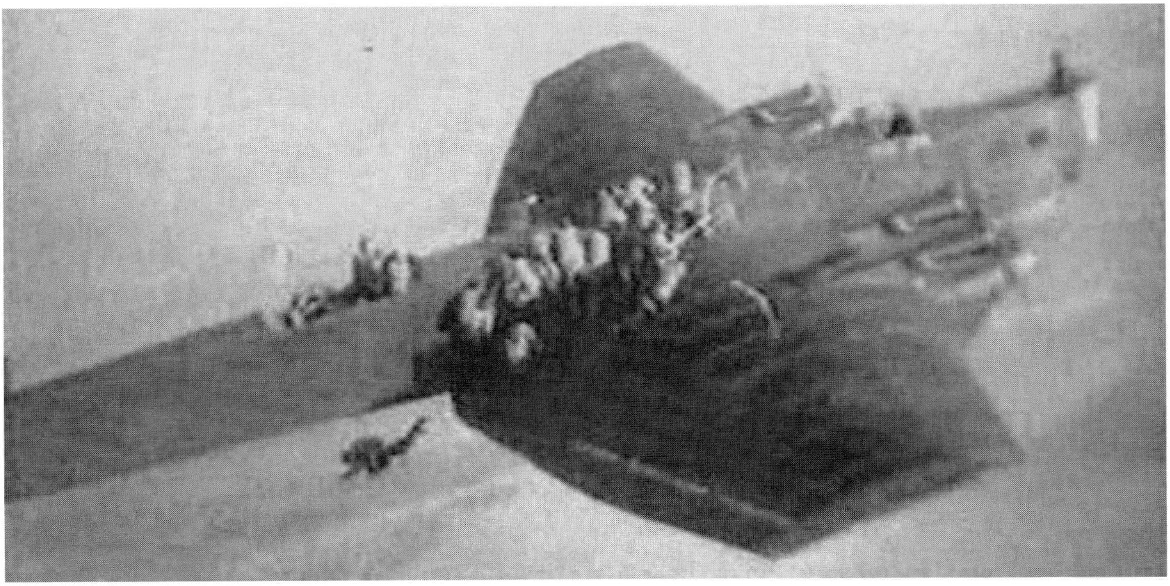

Soviet paratroops jumping from an obsolete Tupolev TB-3.

Four separate assaults gradually pushed defenders back into Odessa's suburbs. Lines finally broke on 16 October.

Attackers suffered 93K casualties taking Odessa, mostly Romanian and mostly wounded. Defenders lost roughly 50K men.

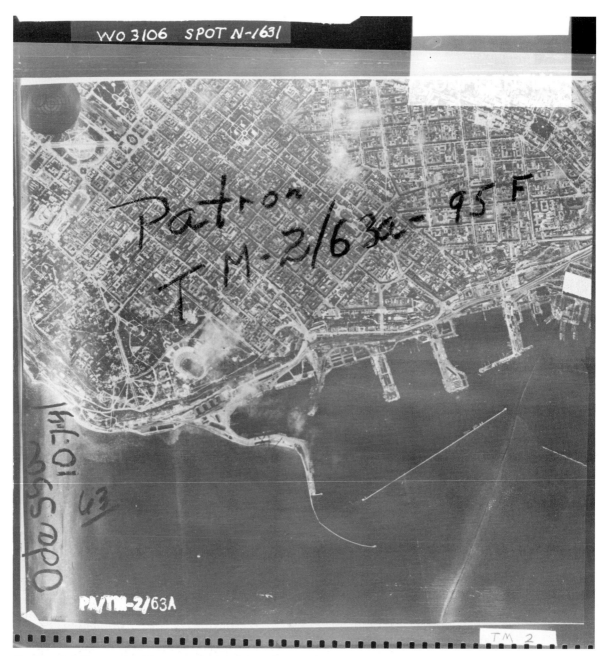

German Intelligence had been getting aerial coverage of Black Sea ports since early spring, but they began concentrated aerial photoreconnaissance of major ports and Crimea the day after Barbarossa began. By the time ground forces reached Odessa and Crimea, every fort, every installation, every strong point and battery had been mapped, analyzed and was known to Wehrmacht planners. Above, Odessa 10 July 1941, a month before ground forces arrived. There is little vehicular activity and the port has small vessels with only four freighters in the 350' range.

I've seen coverage in 1944 that shows little or no damage in the city beyond some along the water front. I conclude, unlike Stalingrad, most of the fighting was outside the city proper.

Marks on the photo above show it was used for target study by the Germans and by Allied Intelligence during the Cold War. Unfortunately it was copied several times, losing resolution with each generation.

Can't leave Odessa without a look at its most famous landmark.

The Boulevard steps were completed in 1840 and rise 88 feet from the waterfront to inland heights. Steps are 41 feet wide at the top and 71 feet at the bottom, giving the 200 stairs (now 192) an illusion of greater length than their 630 feet. The slope is designed so one doesn't see the landings from the bottom or the stairs themselves when viewed from the top.

The steps became the Potemkin Stairs officially in 1955 but were widely known as such after being featured in Sergei's 1925 silent movie *The Battleship Potemkin*, which tells the story of a 1905 naval mutiny that laid groundwork for the Russian Revolution.

Czarist soldiers marching steadily down those stairs using bayonets and rifle fire to disperse helpless civilians is an unforgettable scene.

Twenty-four year old Lyudmila Pavlichenko began her career as a sniper fighting in a target-rich environment around Odessa.[1] Her weapon of choice was a 7.62mm M1891/30 Mosin-Nagant bolt-action rifle. She went on to fight during the siege of Sevastopol where she was wounded by a mortar round in June 1943. Her record was 309 confirmed kills, including 36 German snipers. By the time she recovered from wounds, Lyudmila had such notoriety that she was never allowed in combat again. She was feted on Bond Tours in the US, Canada and Britain, staying in the White House overnight.

---

[1] The Soviets readily accepted women in direct combat rolls, using some 800,000 as snipers, tank crews, machine gunners, and aviators. Two female fighter pilots became aces at Stalingrad.

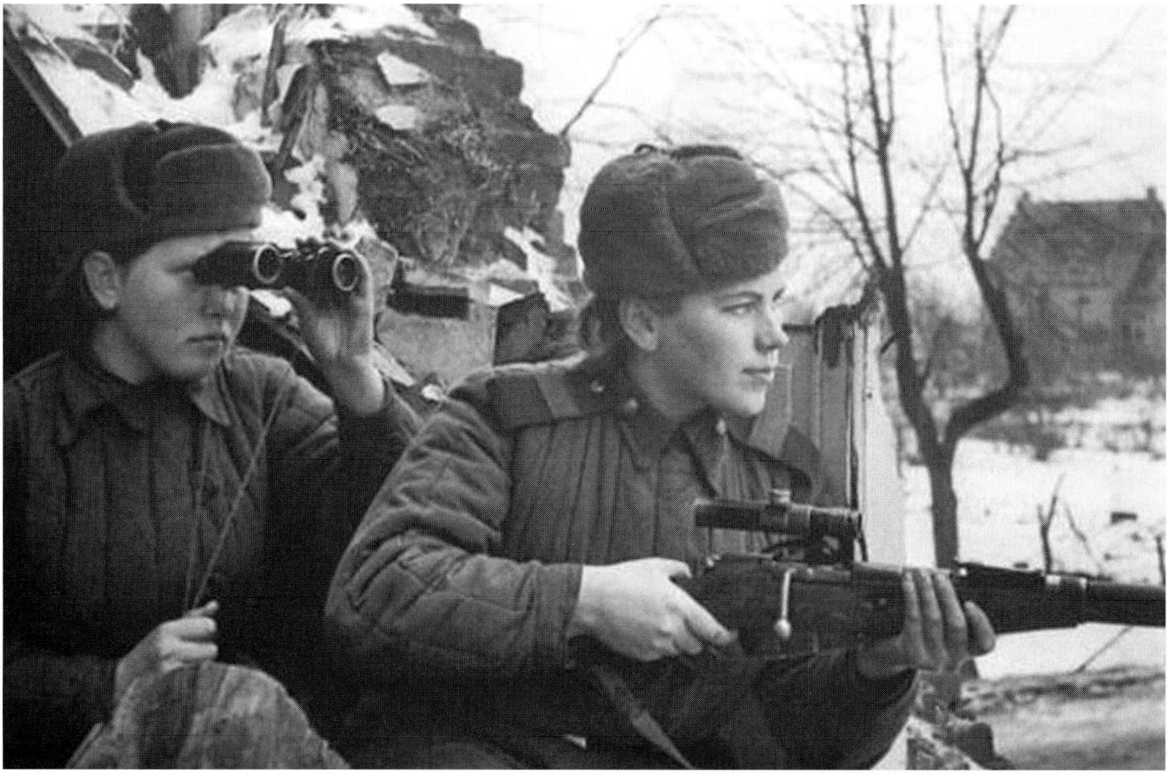

Sniper Pavlichenko and her spotter in an obvious PR photo.

Taking Odessa proved costly in lost manpower and time, but German and Romanian forces moved directly on to Crimea.

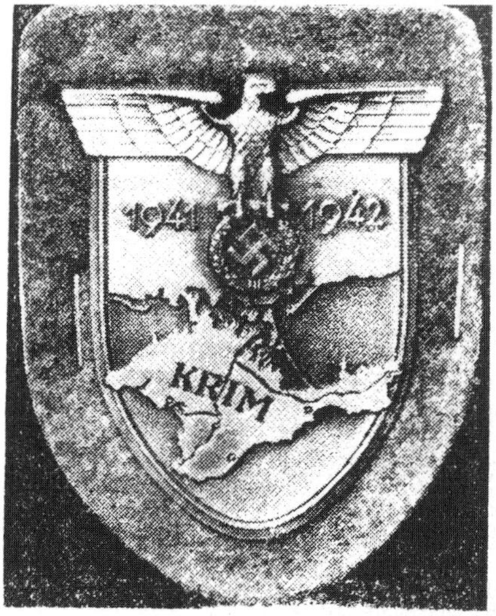

1941 1942
KRIM

Der Krim-Schild

Zur Erinnerung an die heldenhaften Kämpfe auf der Krim hat der Führer, wie berichtet, den Krim-Schild gestiftet, der zur Uniform am linken Oberarm getragen wird

007.345

Vormarsch im großen Donbogen

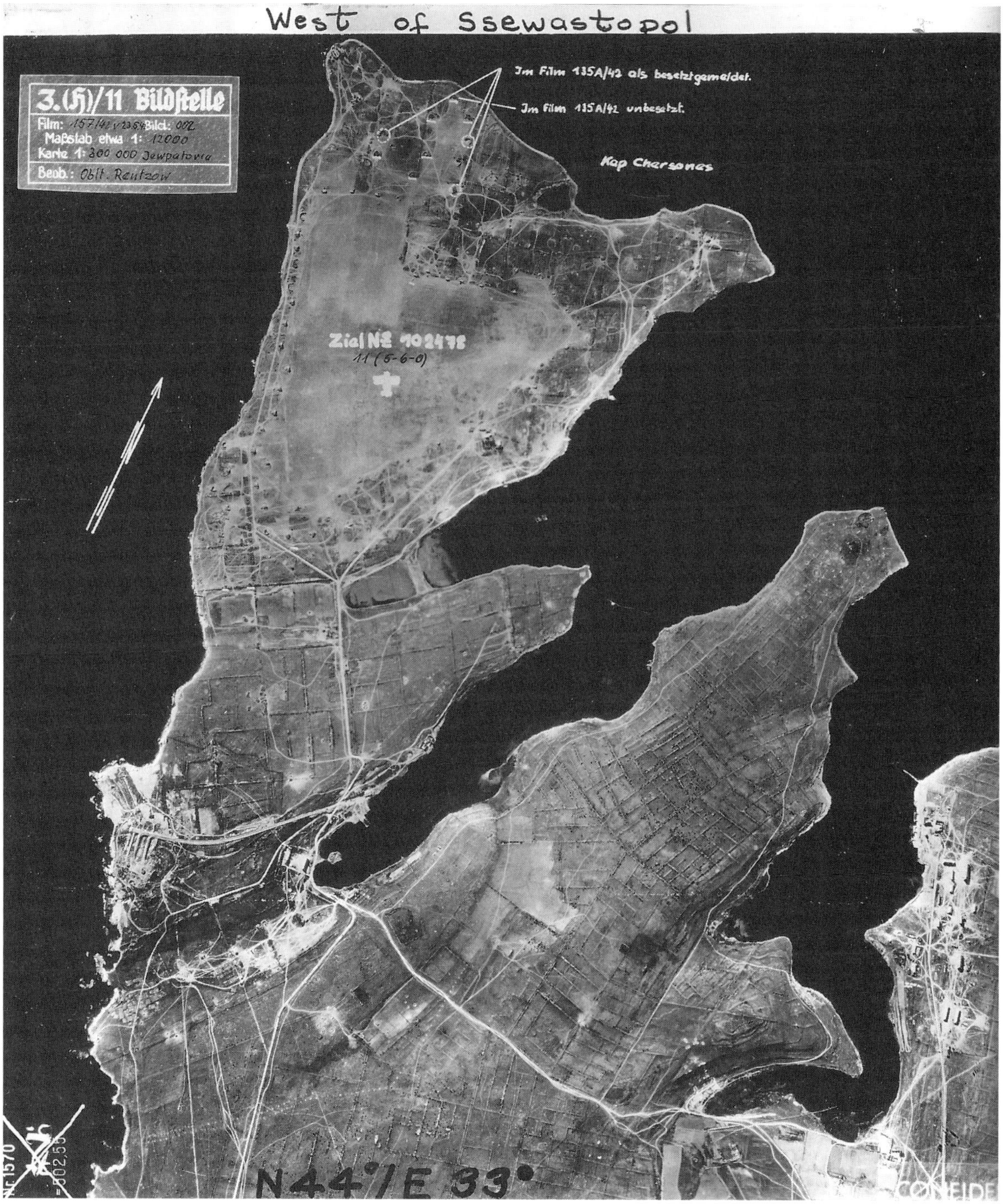
West of Ssewastopol
3.(H)/11 Bildstelle
Film: 157/42 v 23.6.42 Bild: 002
Maßstab etwa 1: 12000
Karte 1: 300 000 Jewpatoria
Beob.: Oblt. Reutzow
Im Film 135A/42 als besetztgemeldet.
Im Film 135A/42 unbesetzt.
Kap Chersones
N44°/E 33°

Aside from the port, another reason to take Crimea was to stop Soviet planes flying from bases like this one on Cape Charsones at Crimea's western tip. There are eighteen revetments and at least sixteen 1930s-style 'T-shaped' hangarettes, each designed to hold one light plane. This has the look of a civil aviation field. Imagery of 23 June 1942 has annotations for three 'reported unoccupied' and six 'unoccupied' (white line under revetment). I disagree. It looks to me like there are single-engine aircraft in three or four of those revetments.

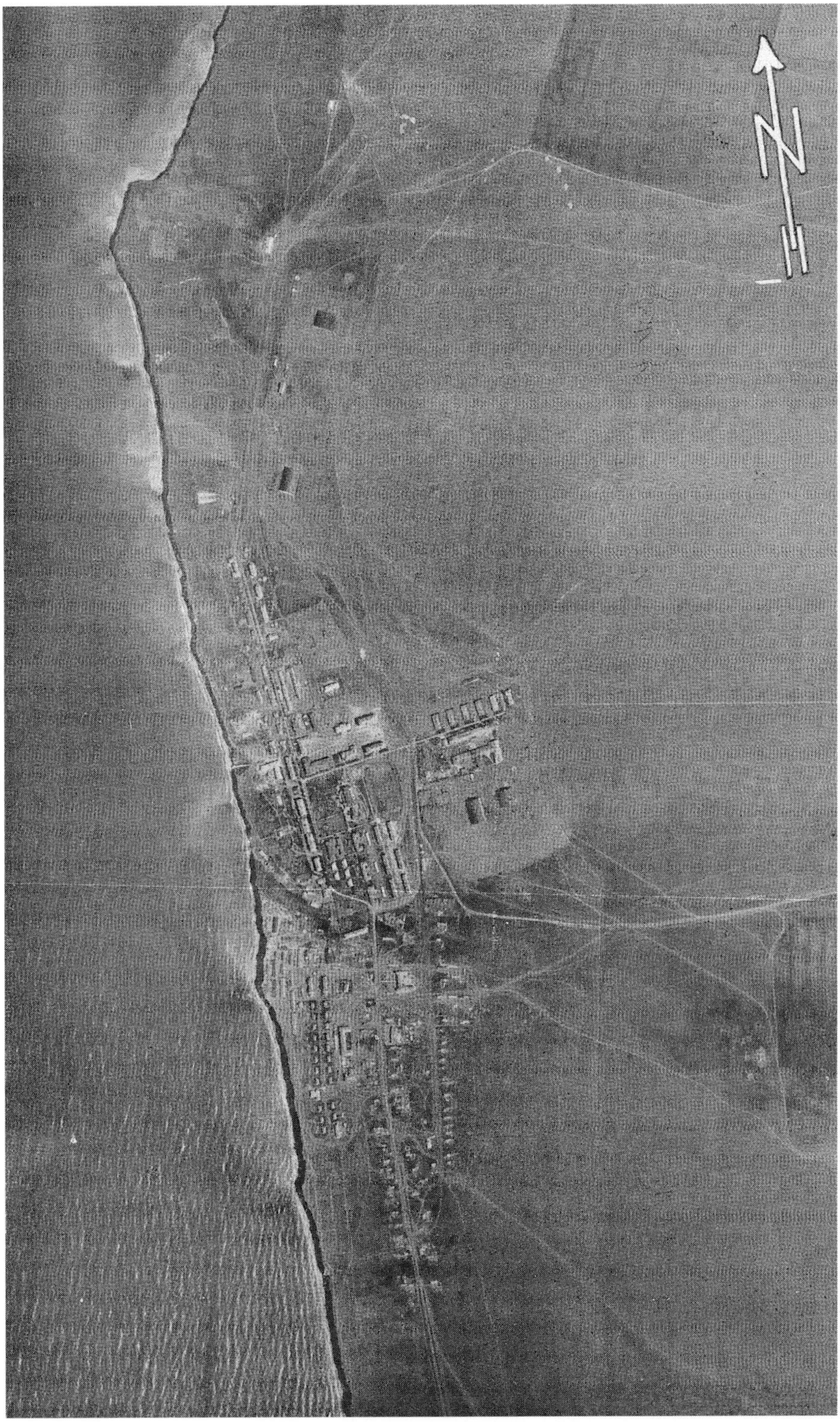
N

This airfield is 12 miles north of Severnaya Bay. It has only four obvious hangars but is laid out like a military base and has a grass landing ground large enough to take anything the Soviets could put in the air.

FOLLOWING BIG GUNS

The Black Sea's northern coast was the right flank of German land forces moving toward the Caucasus and oil. Aside from a few well-established fortifications at key locations, the major threat to German advances were Soviet land armies and guns of heavy ships of the Soviet Black Sea Fleet.

These ships were used to transport or evacuate troops and support isolated Soviet defense forces. Ranging from Odessa to the Caucasus, they could harass German troops with on-shore fire missions. There were no answering German warships so the Soviet Navy had relatively free rein, the only counter force being the Luftwaffe and/or occupation of their haven ports.

3. Schwarzmeer-Flotte
Schlachtschiffe
1) Sewastopol (ex Parischskaja Kommuna)
6 3
23000 t
18 Kn
27
184
Schwere Kreuzer
2) Molotow (wie Maksim Gorki)
6 6
8550 t
36 Kn
18
191
Erläuterung:
6 … 3 = 6 schwere, 3 mittlere Flak (leichte Flak nicht angegeben)
Weitere Angaben: 4. Anlagenheft zur LDv 91/3 und Weyers Taschenbuch der Kriegsflotten
3) Woroschilow (wie Kirow)
6 6
8550 t
36 Kn
191
18
Leichter Kreuzer
5) Krasny Krym
6
6600 t
29 Kn
16
4) Krasny Kawkas
8 6
8030 t
30 Kn
16
163

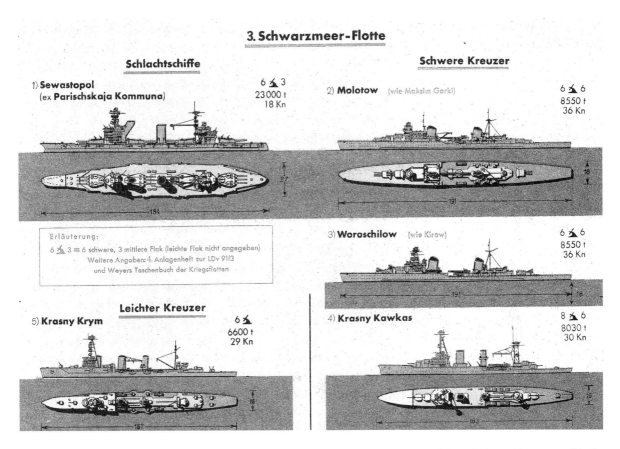

Of particular concern for advancing German forces were the twelve 12" guns of *Parizhskaya Kommuna* (Paris Commune), a 1911 battleship. In the 1930s she got modern 12", secondary and AAA gun upgrades, a catapult and aircraft. She also received a longer false bow to make her more seaworthy. She was then assigned to the Black Sea Fleet.

Other main naval threats were 1937 Nikolaev-built heavy cruisers *Molotov* and *Voroshilov*, each with nine 7.1" guns.

All of the big-gun ships were husbanded carefully by the Soviets to avoid loss. Most Black Sea Soviet naval actions involved destroyers, mine layers and motor torpedo boats, which the Soviet Navy had in superior numbers to Romanian and Italian vessels in the region.

Home port of the Soviet Black Sea Fleet was Sevastopol and German photorecon watched regularly. The imagery below was collected one day after Barbarossa began, three months before the German advance into Crimea. Considering the distance (at least +700 miles from the FEBA), this mission may have been flown from Romania (230 miles west).

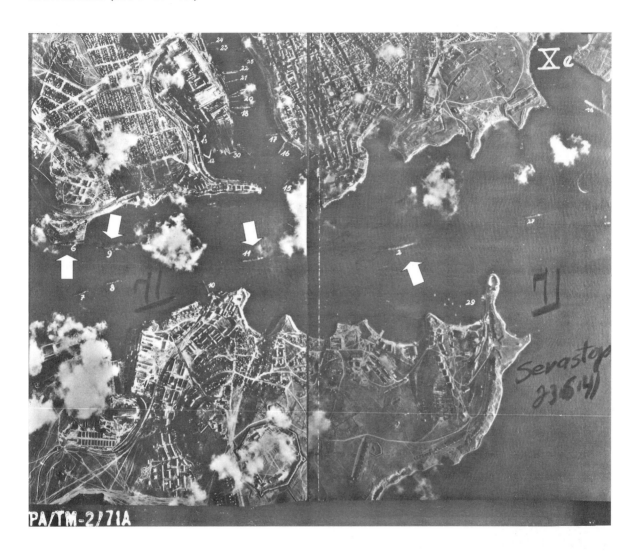

These two photos are a classic Detailed Report, forensically identifying even minor ships. There was probably a corresponding report dissecting functions on shore.

I've oriented the photo with north up (which the German PI didn't do). He did annotate ships in traditional PI fashion starting with the highest threat. Since there is no '1' showing, I infer that battleship *Parizhskaya Kommuna*, if present, is higher up Severnaya Bay (to the right) on frames of this imagery series I don't have.

Annotation 2 (left arrow) is probably one of the two modern heavy cruisers (*Molotov* or *Voroshilov*). Scale is too small, and she is underway, so I can't get a good length measurement. Note six float planes up and left from that first arrow. Next arrow (annotation 11) may be a Flotilla Leader (large destroyer). I believe annotation 9 is 1914 vintage heavy cruiser *Krasny Kavkaz* (Red Caucasus). Annotation 6 is probably one of the mid-30s heavy cruisers. Destroyers are at 7, 8 and 10.

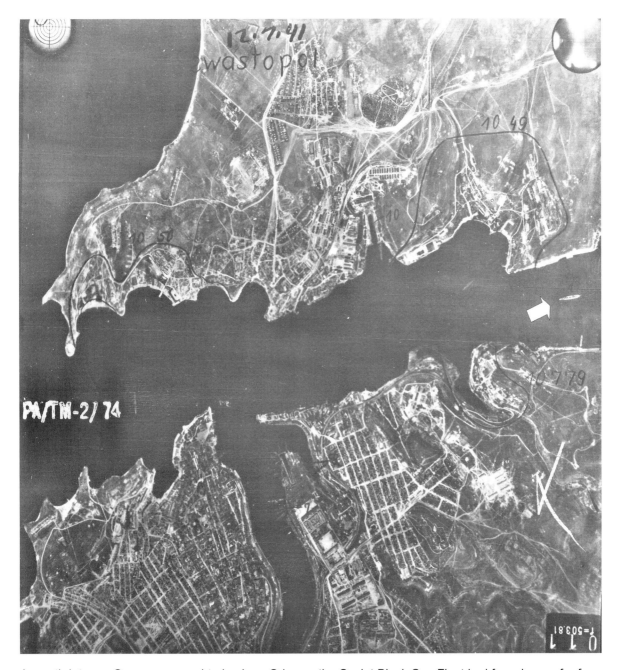

A month later as Germans moved to besiege Odessa, the Soviet Black Sea Fleet had few places of refuge and no way to be reinforced. To make matters worse, only Nikolaev and Sevastopol could perform heavy repairs such as changing gun barrels.

On 12 July 1941 Severnaya Bay was empty except for the battleship (arrow), though at least four large probable merchant ships are moored in bays to the south.

Some of the smaller warships may have been off assisting defense of Odessa.

The seaplanes were gone, never to return.

It doesn't look like Sevastopol had been bombed yet.

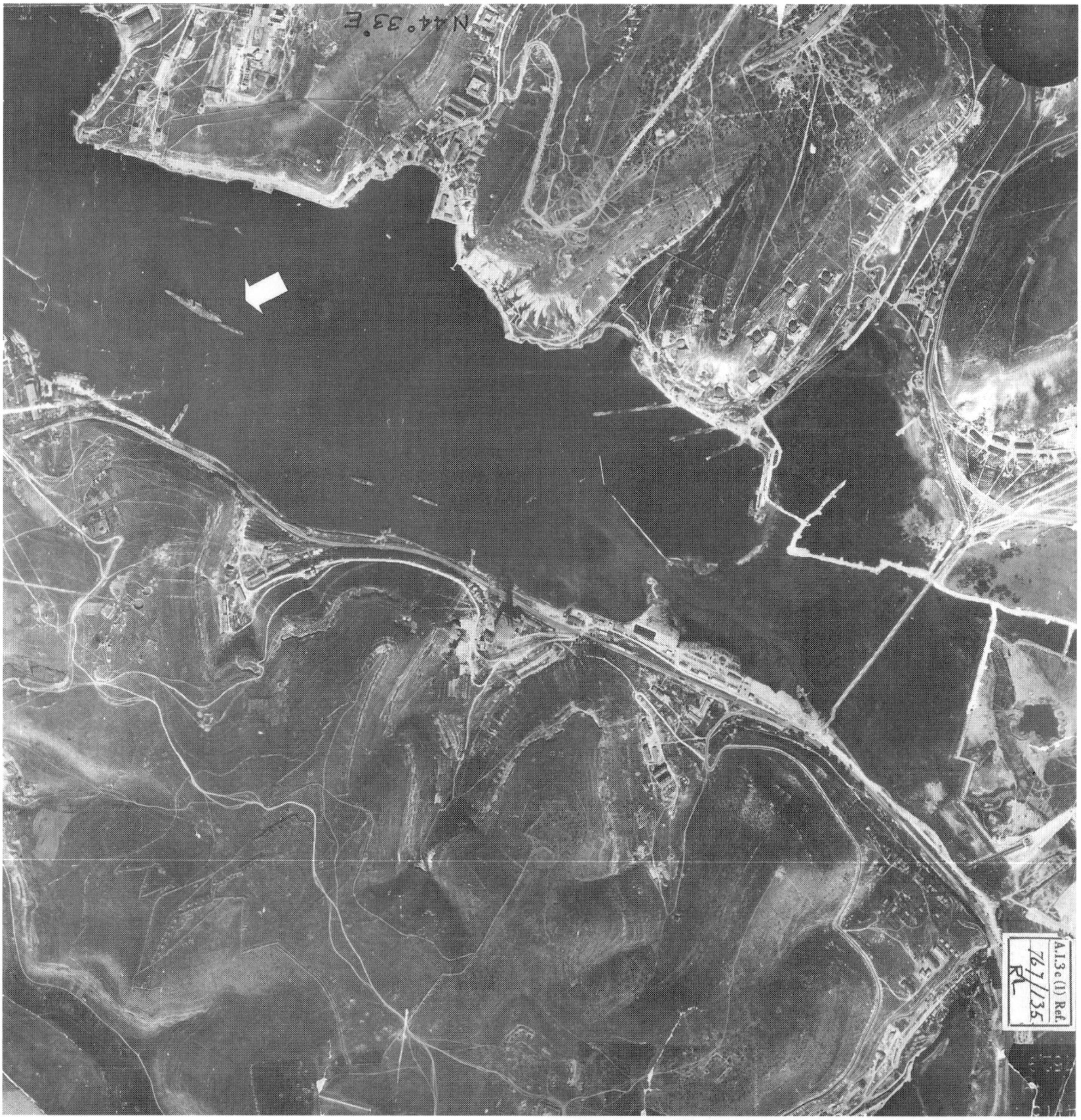
N44°33'E
A.13c (1) Ref.
767/135

Parizhskaya was in the upper bay again in September, anchored adjacent to a fuel depot (north bank) and with a small tanker probably transferring fuel.

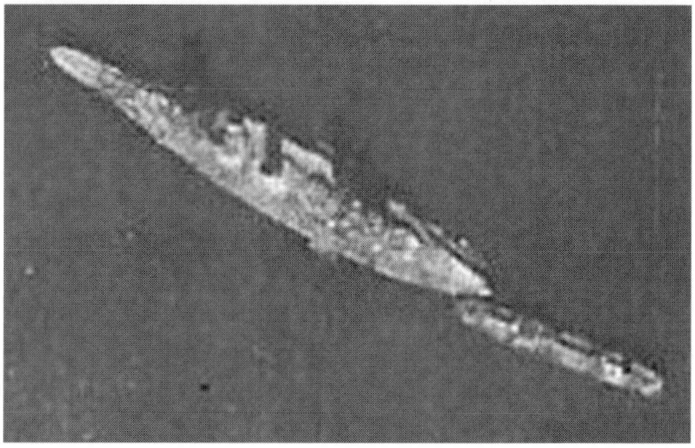

Here's what she looks like enlarged. Shadows show superstructure shapes.

A catapult and aircraft are reportedly on the third turret but I don't see them.

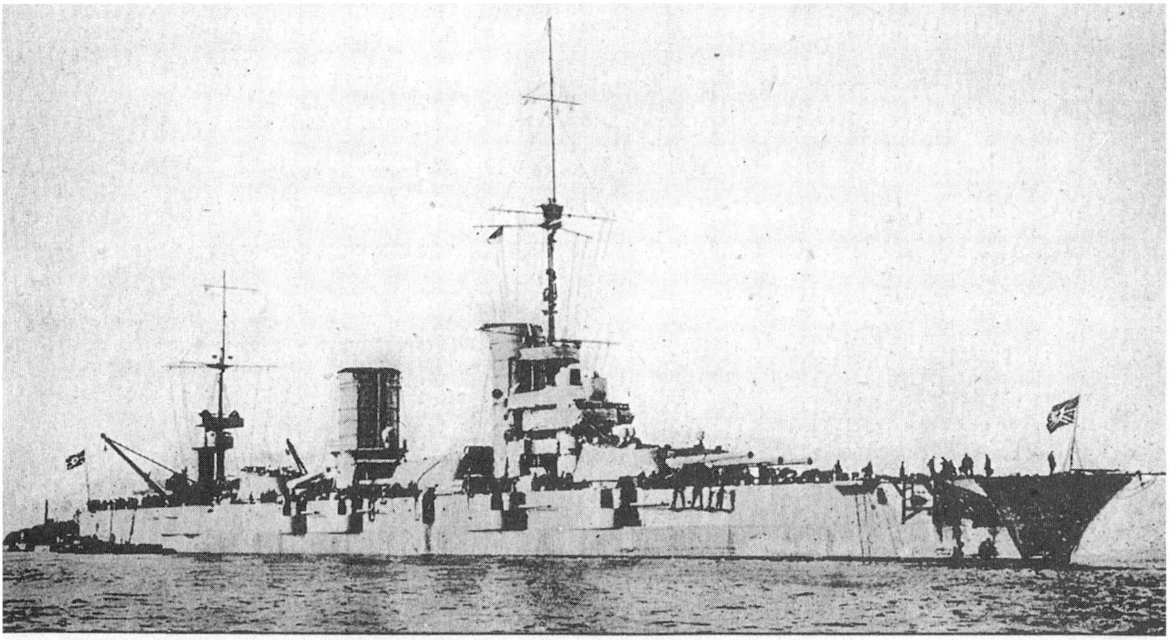

PARISKAYA KOMMUNA (Now has tripod foremast, aircraft and catapult). 1930 *Photo.*

Four turrets evenly spaced along a hull (center turrets have guns turned toward the after stack) were typical early *post-Dreadnought* Russian naval architecture. Definitely designed for broadsides, this ship was ideal for on-shore fire missions in 1941.

Below, also from a contemporary *Jane's all the World's Ships*. This drawing shows the ship before casemate guns were removed and tripod masts and longer false bow added.

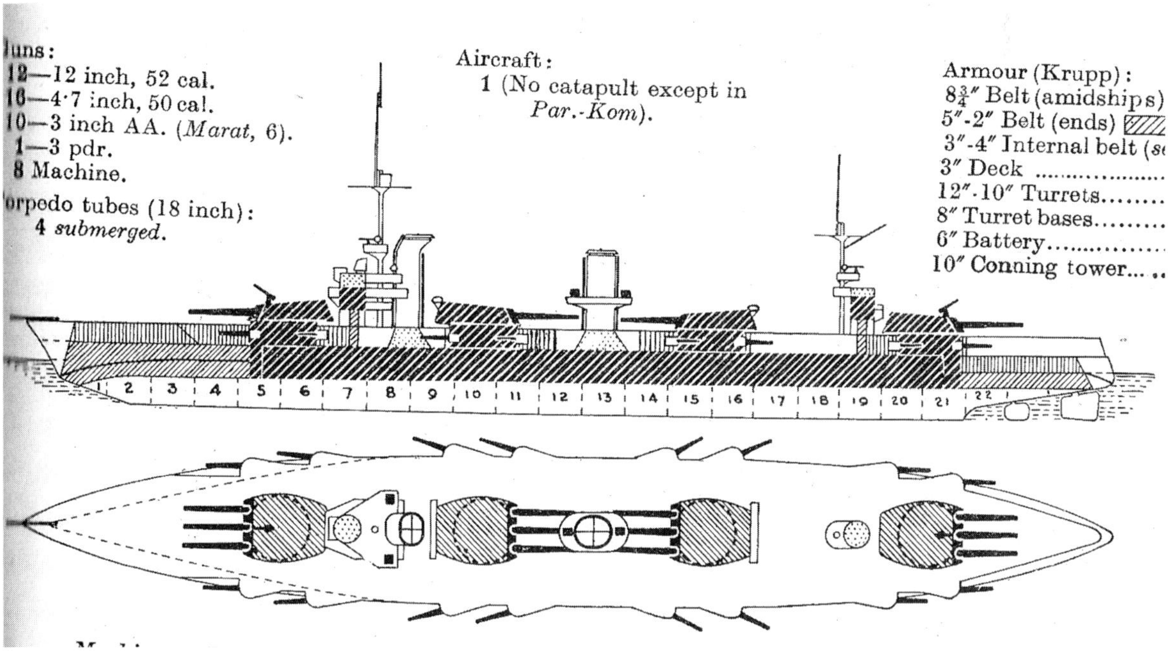

Guns:
12—12 inch, 52 cal.
16—4·7 inch, 50 cal.
10—3 inch AA. (*Marat*, 6).
1—3 pdr.
8 Machine.
Torpedo tubes (18 inch):
4 *submerged*.
Aircraft:
1 (No catapult except in *Par.-Kom*).
Armour (Krupp):
8¾" Belt (amidships)
5"-2" Belt (ends)
3"-4" Internal belt
3" Deck
12"-10" Turrets
8" Turret bases
6" Battery
10" Conning tower
1 2 3 4 5 6 7 8 9 10 11 12 13 14 15 16 17 18 19 20 21 22

SEWASTOPOL M:etwa 1:9800 SOWJETISCH Okt. 1941

A.I.3c (1) Ref. 7651

SCHLACHTSCHIFF (MARAL?) IM SCHUTZE VON NELZSPERREN

Lange 181 m. Breise 26.5 m. Stopellauf 29.6 m.

Bestückung 12 - 30.5 cm. in 4 Drillingstürme
16 - 12 "
2 - Flugzeuge NP64260

Tanker am Schlachtschiff

Wasserflugzeughalle mit Kasernenneubauten

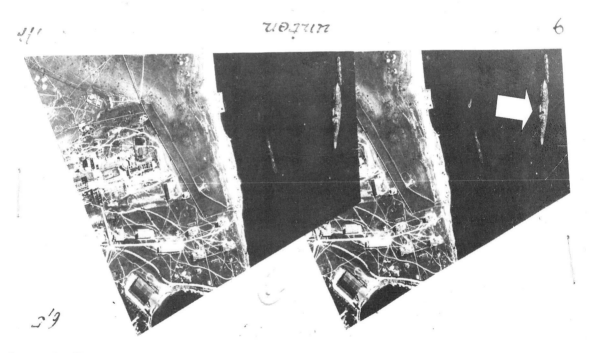

German Intelligence produced this stereo target study in October, using the same September imagery I used above. This graphic miss-identifies *Parizhskaya Commune* as *Maral*, a nonexistent ship (probably meant *Marat*, another *Gaugut-Class* battleship).[2] The PI correctly reports two main gun sizes and notes two aircraft (I still don't see them). I do see the two seaplanes (large and small) on land in front of a hangar at lower left. On this imagery North is left.

[2] Four *Gaugats* were built at Leningrad as Russia's first dreadnoughts, all launched in 1911. They were given appropriately Communist names in the early 1920s. Ironically, *Paris Commune* was originally named *Sevastopol*.

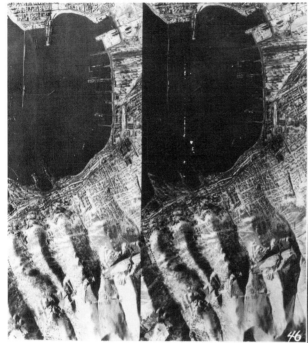

Fig. 1.

Novorossisk, Russia. Figures 1 and 2 of this Port show a comparison between small and large scale photography of the same area. In Fig. 1 only a few of the ships and port facilities are distinct enough for detailed interpretation while in Fig 2 individual ships and installations such as the Battleship, Tanker, Floating Dry Dock, Merchant Vessels, Small warships, etc. are easily distinguished.

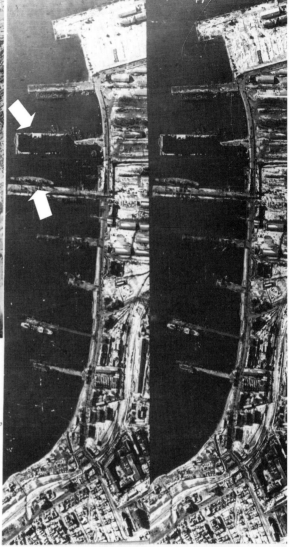

Fig. 2.

Another stereo study, this time Novorossiysk. US Intelligence used October 1941 GX imagery after the war to illustrate differences and advantages of large and small scale. My arrows show the floating drydock and battleship. North is to the right on this graphic.

With rapid German advances in Crimea, in October 1941 *Parizhskaya* was moved here to be out of Luftwaffe range. As German forces began their assault on Crimea and besieged Sevastopol, *Parizhskaya* returned to Severnaya Bay and executed fire missions on 28-29 November, shelling enemy troop concentrations up to 20 miles away. She didn't remain any place long enough to present an easy target for the Luftwaffe.

BUCHT VON SEWASTOPOL SOWJETISCH Herbst 1941

A.I.3c (1) Ref. 765/.

Wasserflughafen
Mun. Lager NP64264
Kasernen, Kriegsmarineschule
Tanklager
Industrie oder Kraftwerk
Schlachtschiff "Pasisehskaja Kommuna"

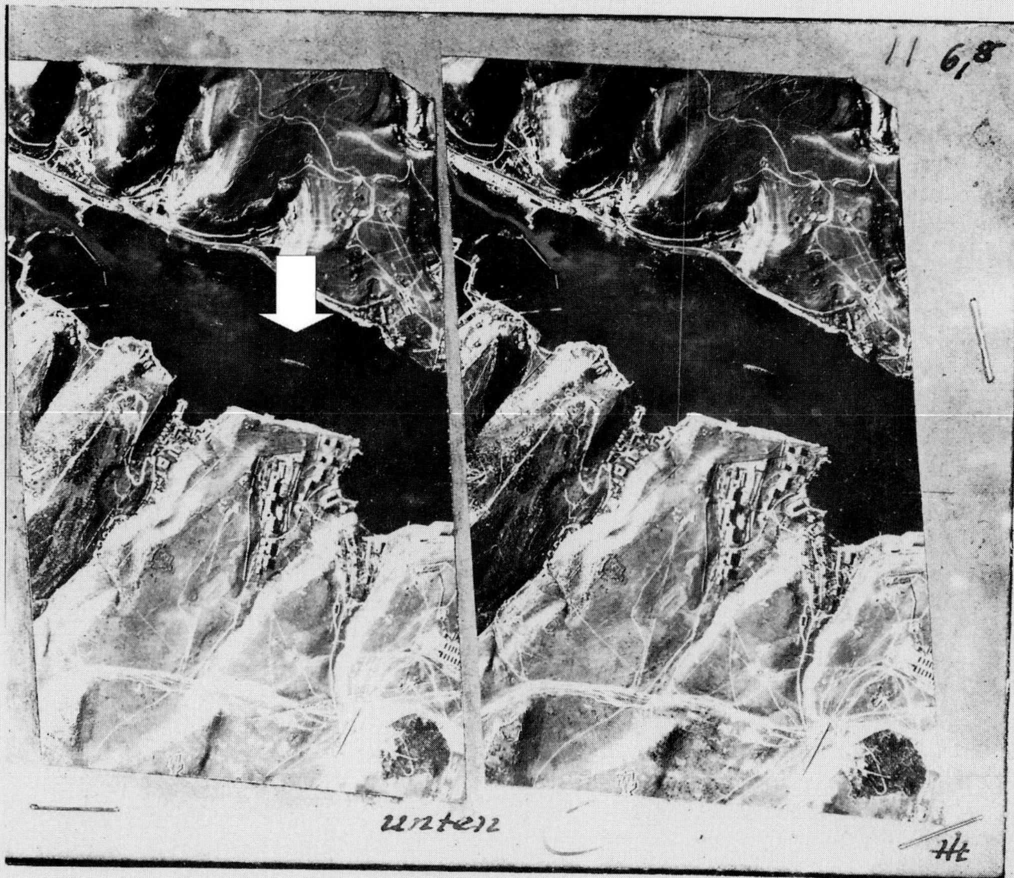
11 6,8
unten
Ht

SEVASTOPOL

This German stereo graphic has the battleship correctly identified and at her customary anchorage off the fuel depot in 'autumn' 1941. North is down.

Misnamed heavy cruiser *Krasny Kavkaz* was also in the bay on 12 November 1941. This stereogram shows her alongside a quay on the south side of Severnaya Bay.

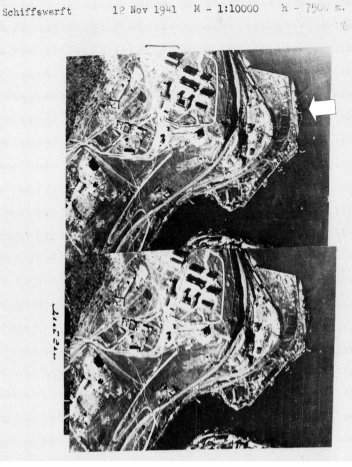

SEVASTOPOL — SCHWERER KREUZER "KRASNY KANUKAS"

8000 to Waflerverdrängg, 4/19 cm. Geschütze (Sowjetische)

Schiffswerft   12 Nov 1941   M — 1:10000   h — 7500 m.

A.I.3c (1) Ref.
765.

Enlarged at right, with four 7.1" main guns in four separate turrets *Kavkaz* is definitely the bottom end for a heavy cruiser (usually 8 to 12 8" guns). Seems like half the things in USSR were named Red something.

The battleship was back in the Bay for fire missions defending Sevastopol. On 29-31 December she left with heavy cruiser *Molotov*. Knowing she was a prize target for Stukas the battleship never remained in one place long but performed more on-shore fire from Severnaya Bay on 4-5 January. On 12 January, 26-28 February and 20-22 March the battleship supported Soviet landing attempts on Crimea's southeast coast. The battleship left for Poti to refit and to replace worn-out gun barrels. She didn't come out again.

Poti, Georgia, imagery of April 1942. Annotation 1 is battleship *Paris Commune*. A modern heavy cruiser is 2. Light cruisers are 3. Number 4 is likely a sub. Different classes of tanker are marked 5, 6 and 7. In an annotation mistake, number 5 is reused at upper right for a passenger liner. Annotation 8 is probably old heavy cruiser *Krasny Kavkaz*. Drydocks are marked 9.

For readers matching images with Google maps, this area (particularly the river) is significantly changed since 1942.

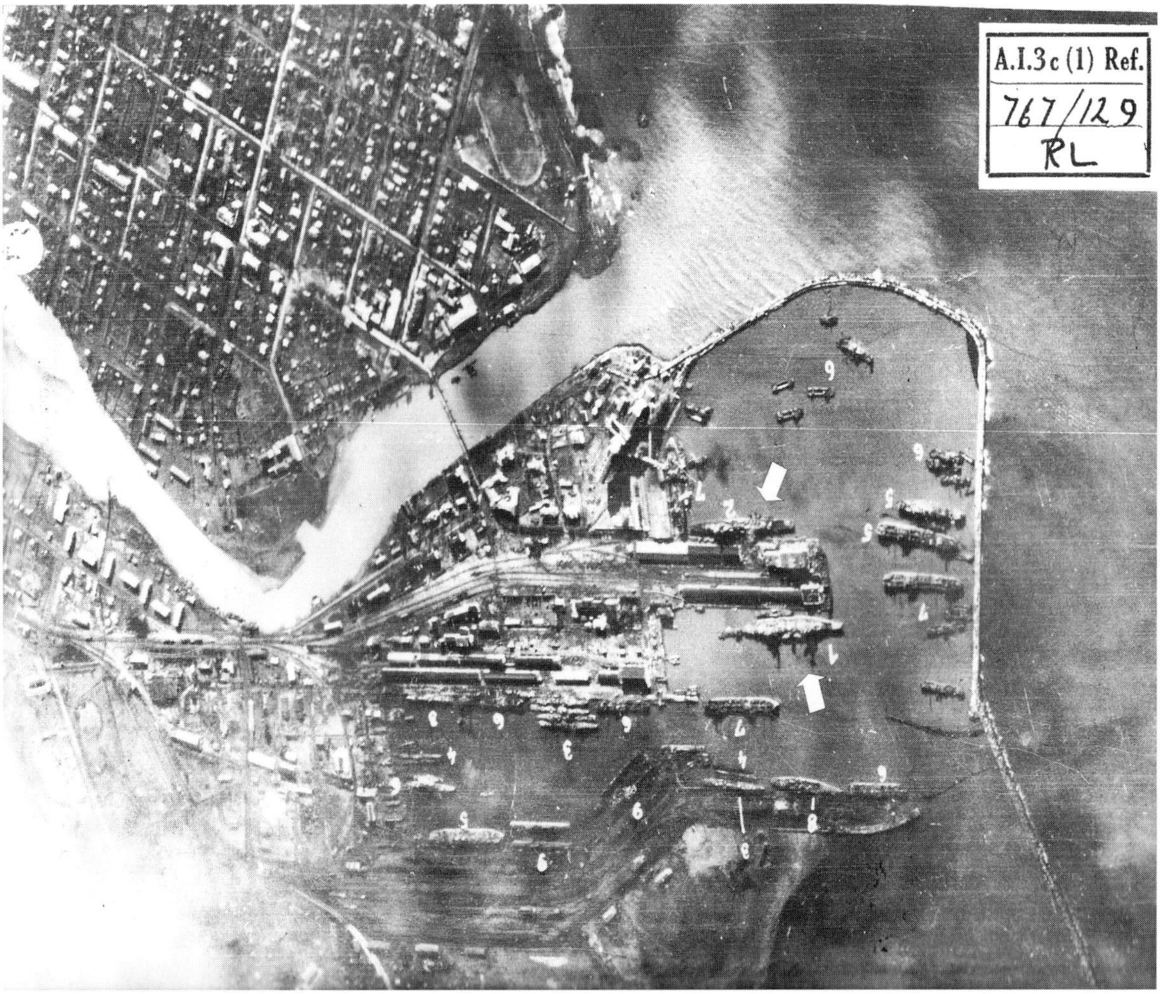
A.I.3c (1) Ref.
767/129
RL

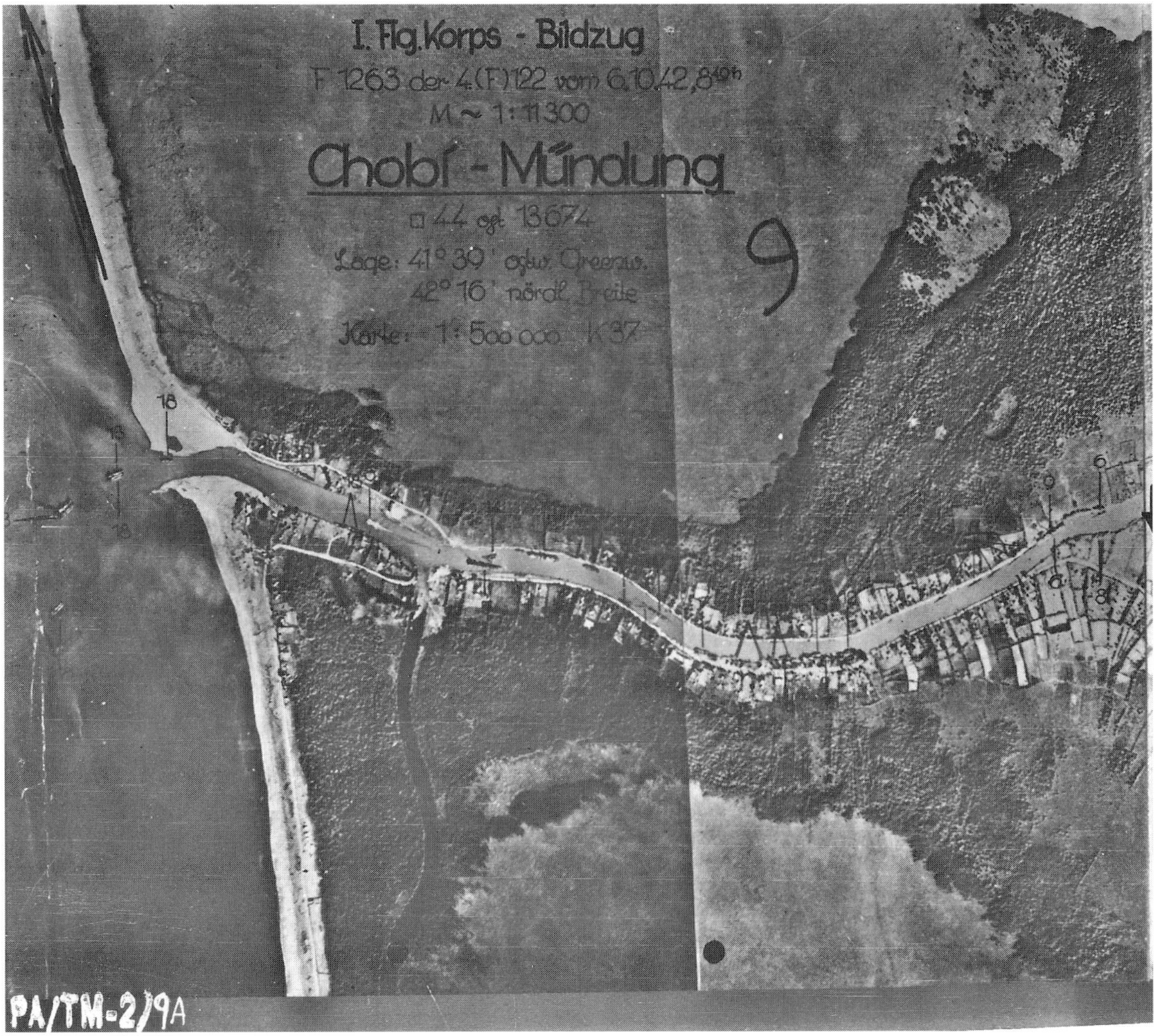
I. Flg.Korps - Bildzug
M ~ 1:11300
Chobi - Mündung
Lage: 41° 39' östl. Greenw.
42° 16' nördl. Breite
Karte: 1:500 000 K37
9
PA/TM-2/9A

On 6 October 1942, Luftwaffe aerial recon covered Chobi-Mundung, a small river port 6 miles north of Poti. I'm going to assume the larger port was also covered on this mission, but I haven't seen that imagery. This detailed study identifies and annotates small freighters, barges, tankers and oil barges. Oil was coming down practically every river in Georgia and the Germans could see it, they just couldn't reach it.

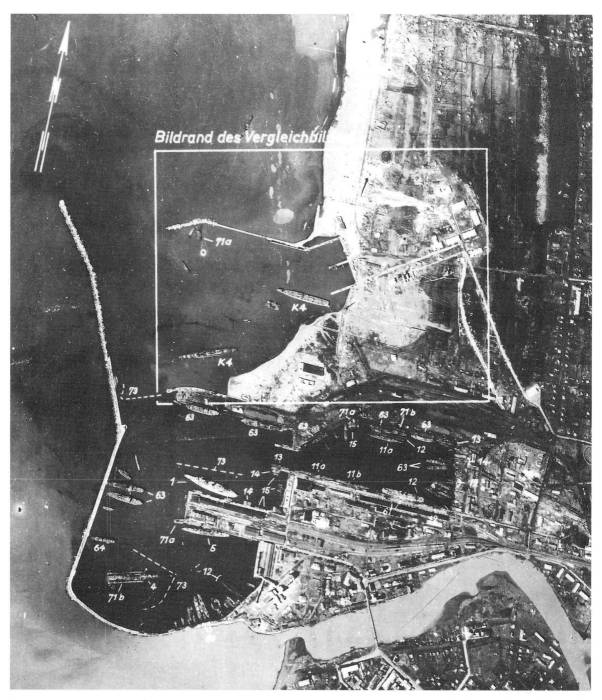

By 8 April 1943 Poti had become haven for most of the Soviet Black Sea Fleet. This PI apparently didn't look at the April 42 report because he annotated the battleship (1) incorrectly as *Petropavlovsk*. She's in the same location as always, just turned to face out.

Heavy cruiser *Kirov* is at (4); light cruiser *Krasny Krim* (5); two cruiser hulls (K4); three destroyers (11); seven U-boats (12); twenty-three M, R and S-boats (13-15); twelve freighters (63); a tanker (64); twenty coastal freighters (67); three floating cranes (71a); two floating drydocks (71b), and three torpedo nets (73).

AROUND THE BLACK SEA

The major Black Sea port and ship builder was Nikolaev (Nikolaeu to the Germans). That strange but successful location for building major ships, including warships, is 15 miles up the Inhul River from open water. The river winding on Nikolaev's north side is the Bug.

This GX imagery is marked as target material. This time a study of the city itself. Shipyards are along the Inhul River, just beyond the lower left corner of this frame.

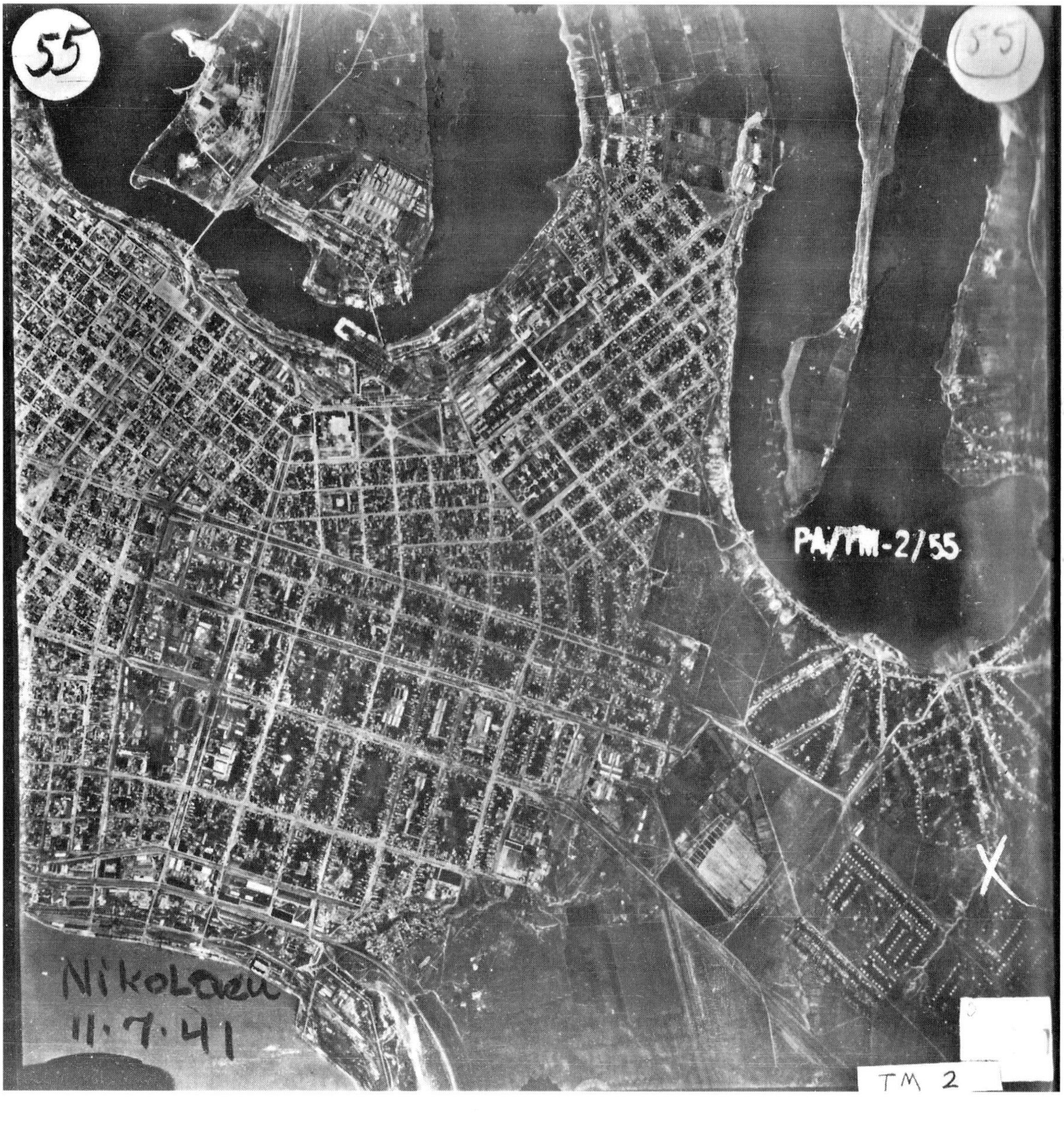
55
PA/TM-2/55
Nikolaeu
11.7.41
TM 2

USSR. 46.58N - 32.00E. Nikolayev.
Cat. 93. Black Sea Naval Base shipyards: Submarines on ways. Source:
C. I. A. Photograph No. 37320. 1941. CONFIDENTIAL.

2210.733. A. F.

Submarines under construction at Nikolaev destroyed by retreating Soviets to keep them from German hands.

HAV ... RINT?

AREA 13 - USSR - EUROPEAN RUSSIA - NIKOLAEV. App: 46° 57' N. -
32° 00' E. Southern Yard. Close-up view under battleship hull
on building way No. 0, showing buckled section of bottom plat-
ing where Russians had burned away keel-blocks prior to their
evacuation of Nikolaev in 1941. Print #55. Encl. (D).
ONI(H1) #459588.

This photo and its US explanation are from Office of Naval Intelligence (ONI) files. Date is unspecified but is probably shortly after the event. Its source may have been an American Naval Attaché traveling with German forces as a neutral observer before the US entered WW II against Germany on 11 December 1941.

A sister of the battleship building at Leningrad, if launched she would have been *Sovetskaya Ukraina* (*Soviet Ukraine*) and would have out-classed any other warship in the Black Sea.

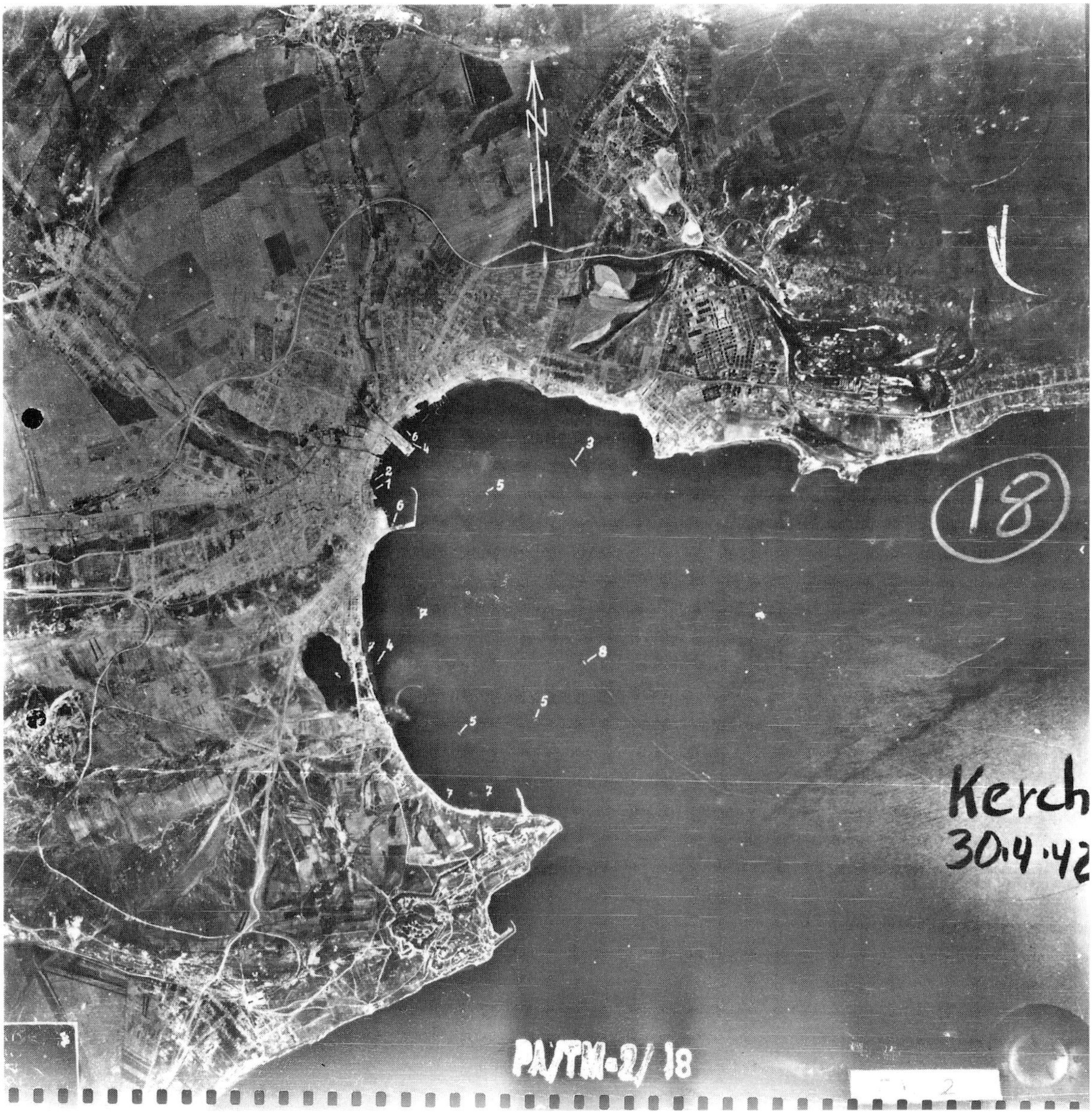
18
Kerch
30.4.42
PA/TM-2/ 18

Kerch (Kertsch to the Germans), on the eastern tip of Crimea, was another major Black Sea port and German objective because it controlled access to the Sea of Azov and headwaters of the Don. This high altitude German imagery of 30 April 1942 shows no major ships in Kerch Bay. White annotations are German and made on the negative. The black writing is probably American grease-pencil added after the war.

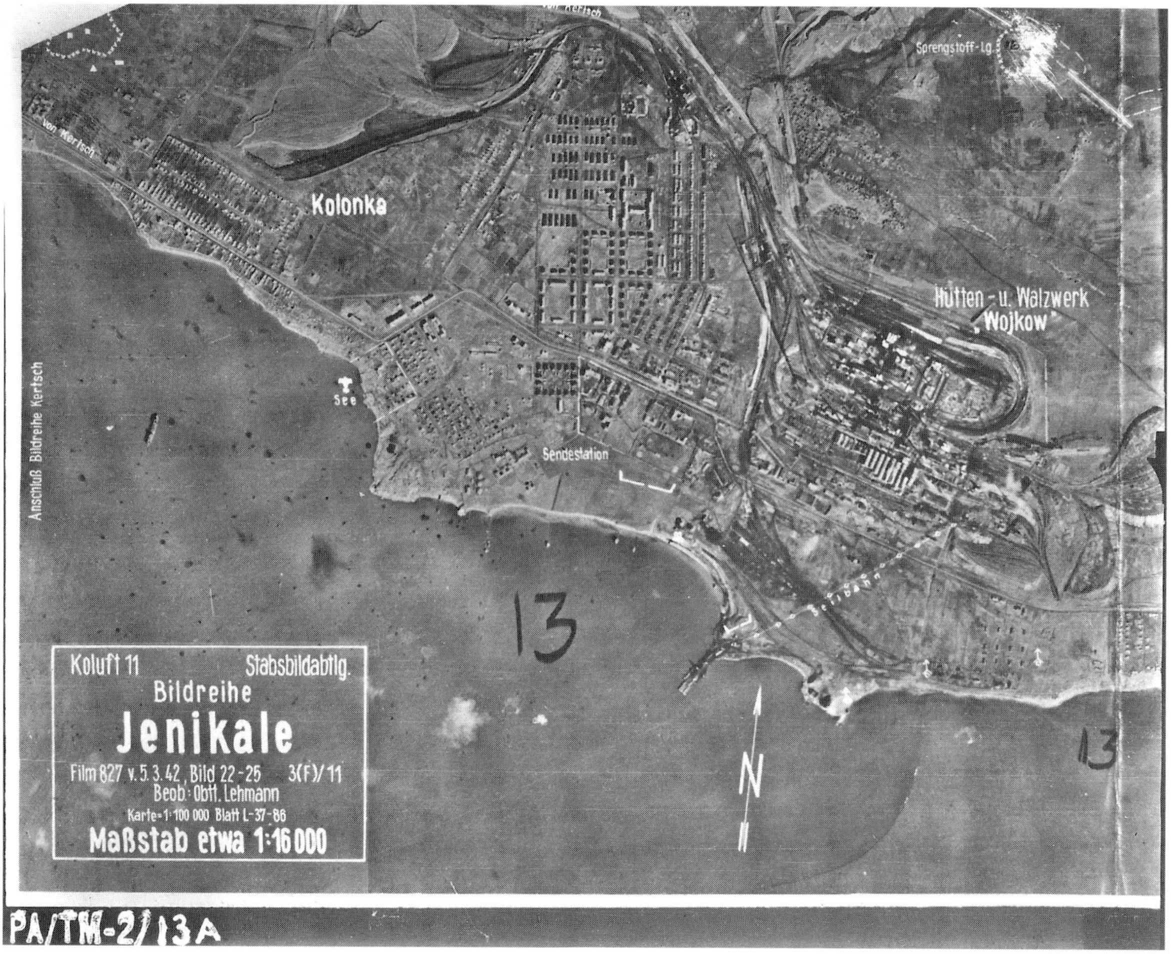
Sprengstoff-Lg.
von Kertsch
Kolonka
Hütten- u. Walzwerk
„Wojkow"
Anschluß Bildreihe Kertsch
See
Sendestation
13
Koluft 11 Stabsbildabtlg.
Bildreihe
Jenikale
Film 827 v. 5.3.42, Bild 22-25 3(F)/11
Beob: Oblt. Lehmann
Karte=1:100 000 Blatt L-37-86
Maßstab etwa 1:16000
N
13
PA/TM-2/13A

Kerch also had heavy industry. This German target study of a rolling mill east of the city uses imagery from 5 March 1942 (it is just up and left from the grease penciled '18' on the previous photo). A funicular railway runs from wharf to factory. There are no aircraft at the seaplane station (airplane symbol off shore). The annotation at upper right is labeled explosive storage and the left one seems to be a defended camp with what may be two regiments indicated inside and a battalion outside. There are two anti-aircraft gun positions noted near the coast at lower right.

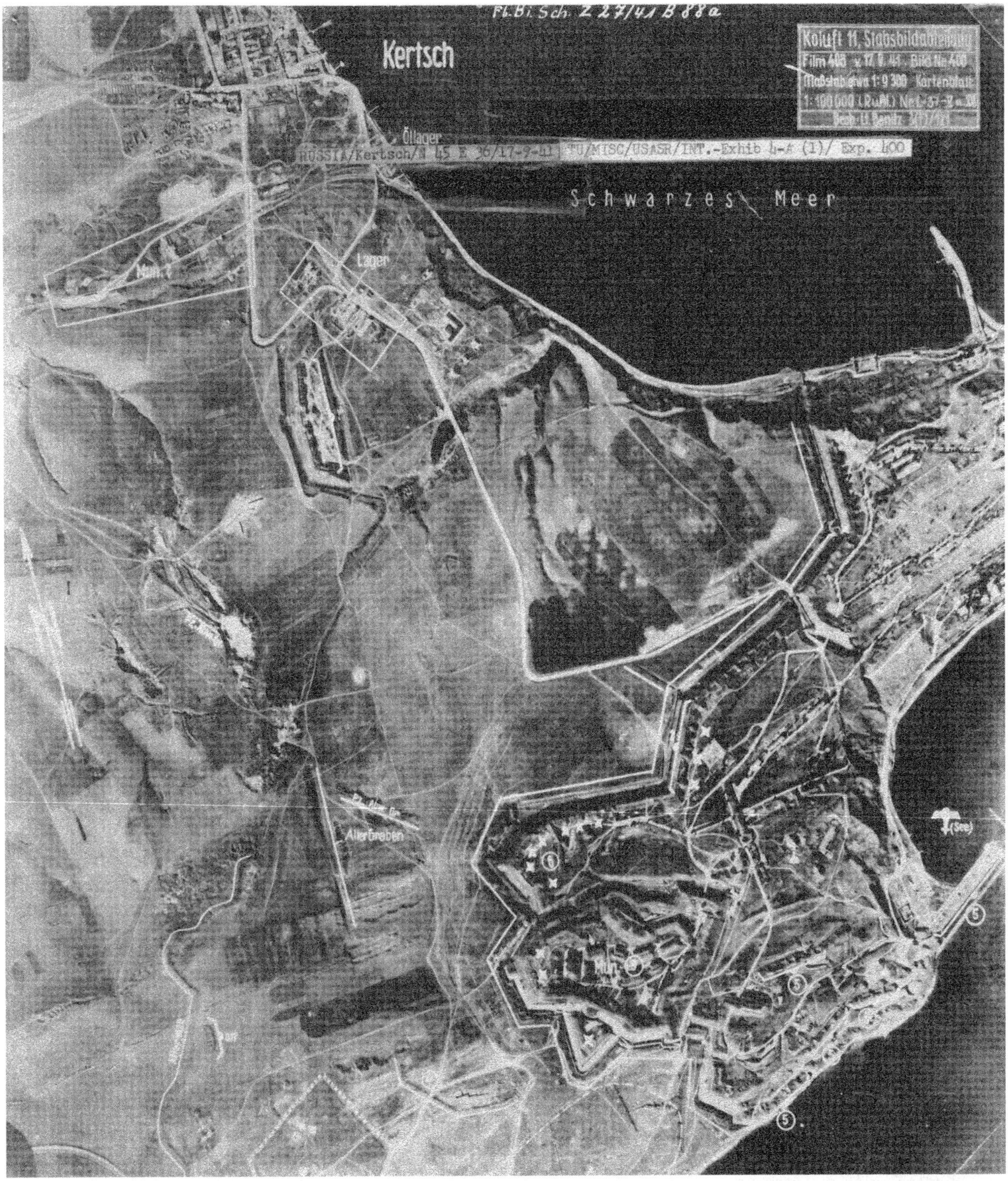
Kertsch
Schwarzes Meer
Lager
Öllager

A large-scale look at Kerch, 17 September 1941. German PIs outlined the anti-tank ditch and walls that were major defenses for seventeenth-century Fort Totlaben on White Cape at the easternmost end of Crimea.
A seaplane base is also noted at right, but I don't see any aircraft.

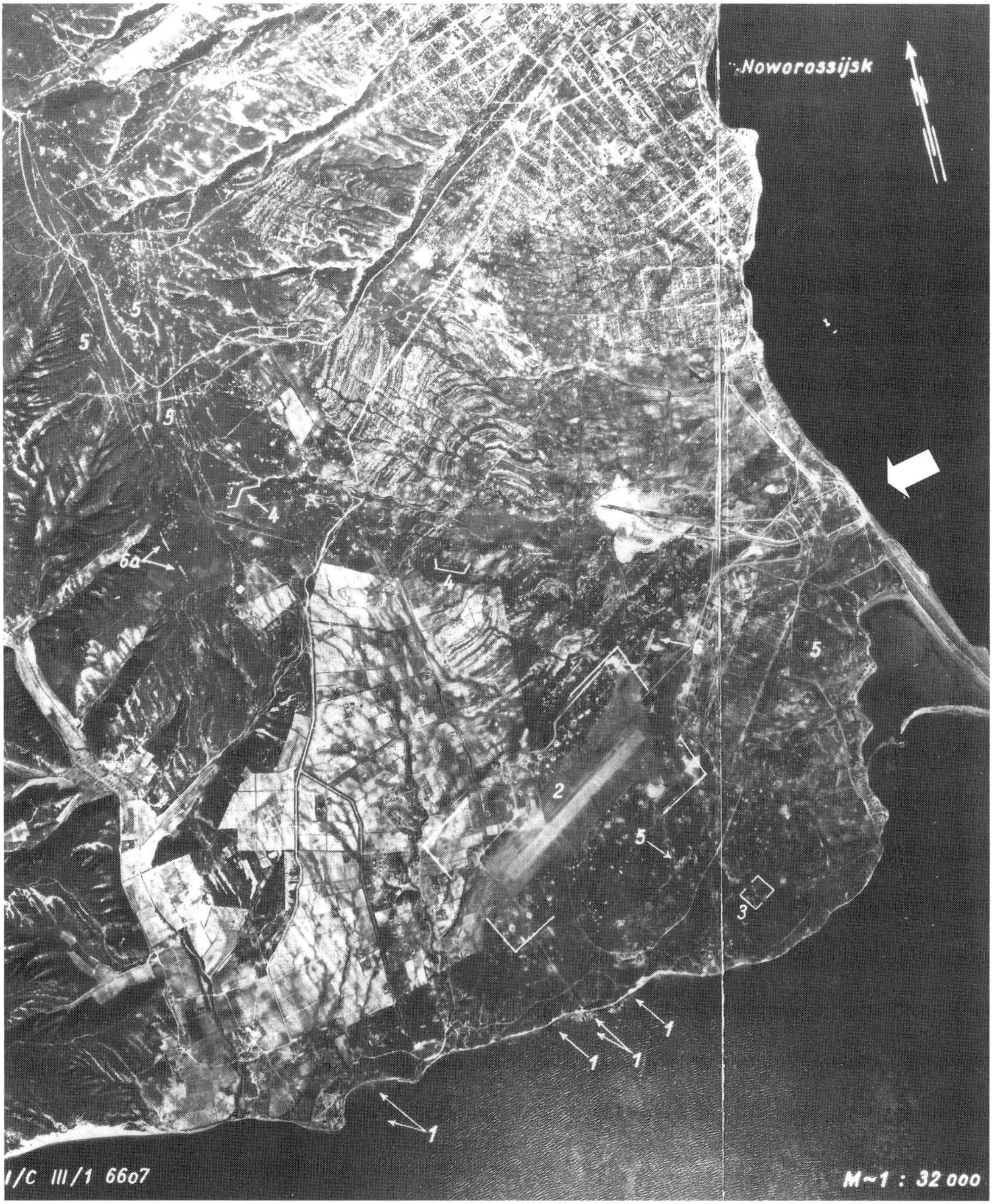
Noworossijsk
5
5
5
4
6a
4
5
2
5
3
1
1
1
1
/C III/1 66o7
M~1 : 32 000

Driving Germans back in the Caucasus, Soviet forces hoped to add pressure by outflanking Novorossiysk with amphibious landings. The night of 3 February 1943 a force too small for the job was put ashore at Cape Myskhako (annotations 1 in this report attachment), 3 miles south of the city. A decoy landing was put ashore the same night (my arrow).

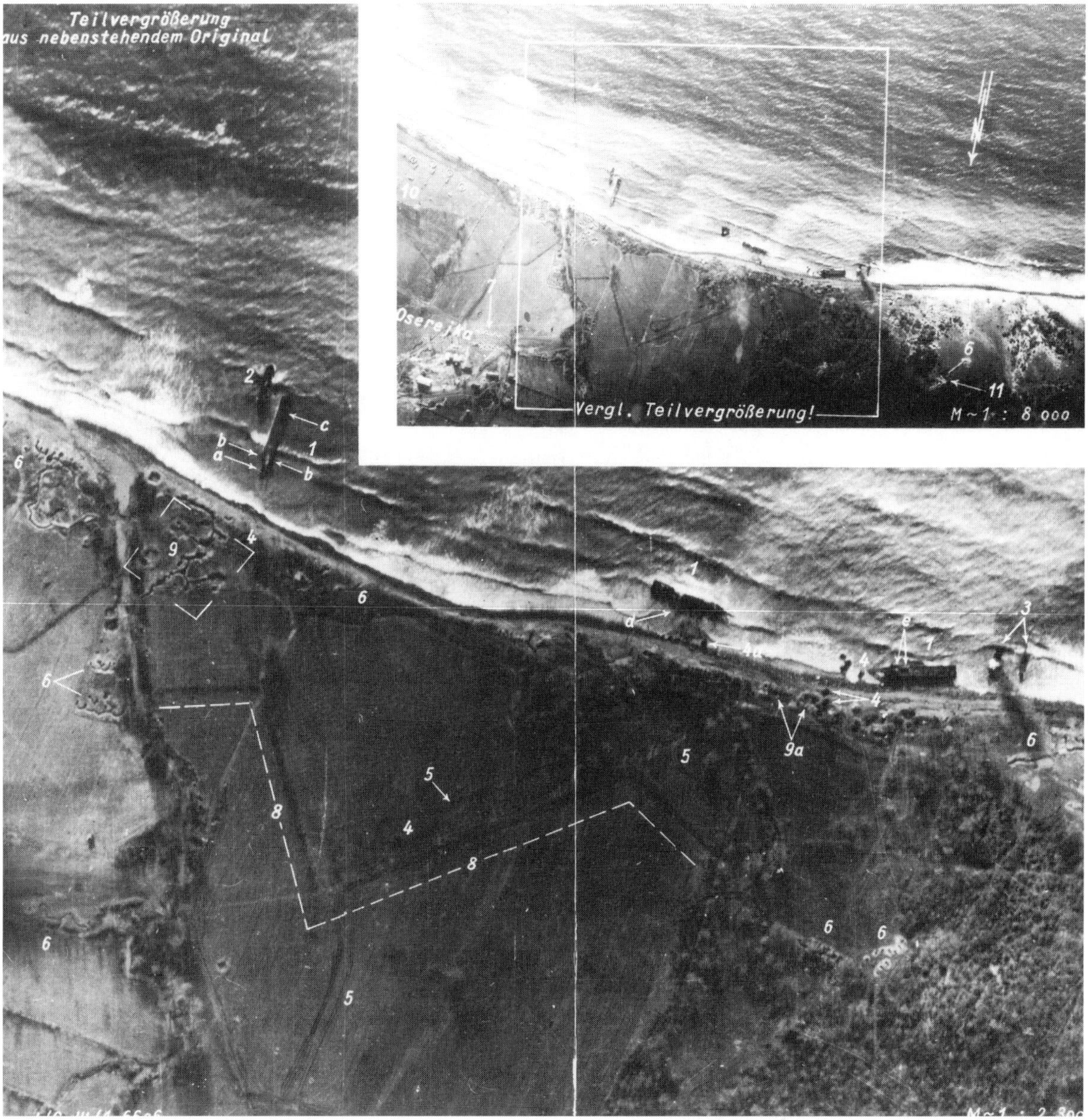
Teilvergrößerung
aus nebenstehendem Original
Oserejka
Vergl. Teilvergrößerung!
M ~ 1 : 8 000

Many sources say the Cape Myskhako landing was 5 February 1943, but a German report on the action, and this imagery were dated 4 Feb. Imagery flown the same day proves this part of the invasion was over quickly. North is down.

Boats (landing barges, tugs and support vessels) used are annotated 1, 2 and 3. Tanks are at 4. On the upper graphic the nearest town is marked 7. Annotation 5 is ground deemed good for tanks, i.e., where a landing might be expected. The good ground is blocked by 8, an anti-tank ditch. Infantry positions are at 6, 7 are barbed wire lines and artillery is at 9, 9a, 10 and 11.

Apparently anticipated, the landing was an ambush. When this landing failed, the Malaya Zemlya decoy landing closer to Novorossiysk (my arrow on the preceding photo) became the main landing. Eight hundred Soviet Naval Infantry held out there until the city was retaken by other Soviet forces on 6 February.

I can't explain why the previous broad area vertical imagery of 4 February shows evidence of one landing and not the other.

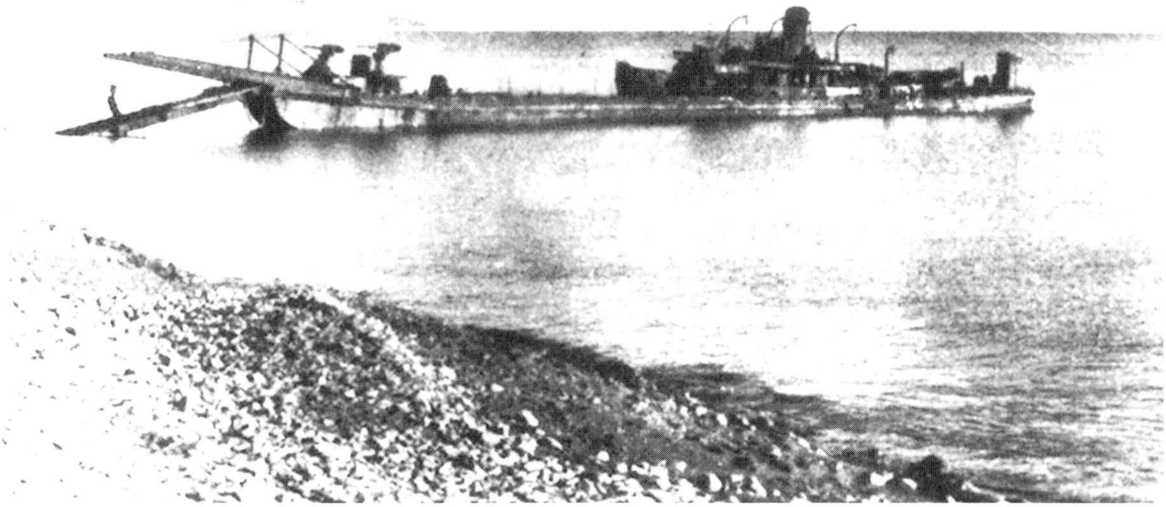

Landing barge and tug at Cape Myskhako.

Moving farther west, a barge with American-made M3 'Stuart' tanks onboard and one on shore. That's a German 5cm Pak 38 anti-tank gun in the foreground.

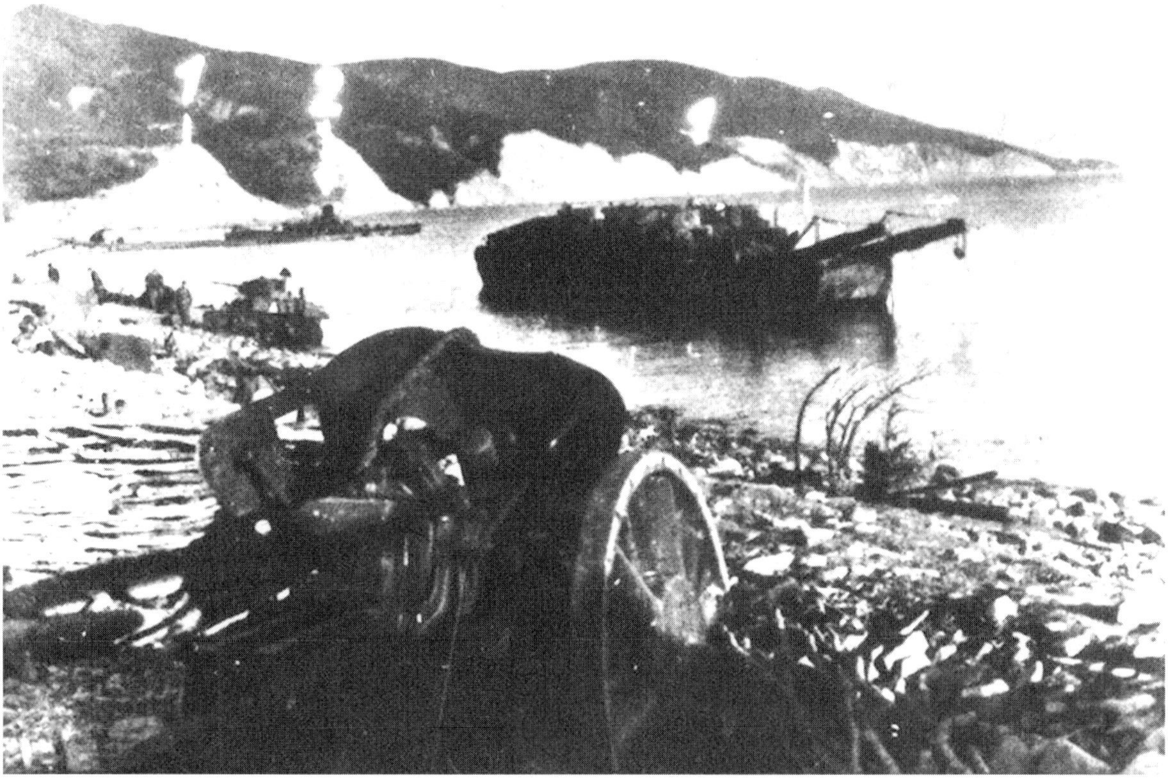

Soviet soldiers were trying to get a troop of M3 General Stuarts ashore to outflank Kerch.

Using the vertical imagery shown earlier, a German PI noted a total of thirteen tanks on the barge or in the water. Another five were annotated on shore in the vertical shot (annotation '4s').

It looks to me like seven or eight more clustered on shore just off the beach.

Combat damage isn't apparent. It looks like they were abandoned when it was obvious the Germans had been waiting for the landing.

SEVASTOPOL

The Black Sea prize for both sides was the port of Sevastopol. Severnaya Bay's large, sheltered anchorage and strategic location made this place valuable since the sixth-century. Greeks, Romans, Tatar Mongols and Tsarist Russians had all fought to take or defend it. The famous 1854 Charge of the Light Brigade was 2 miles south of Severnaya Bay. Sevastopol's position at the southwest tip of Crimea let naval vessels based there dominate the northern Black Sea and ports from Romania to Georgia.

German commanders had originally thought of Crimea as a mop-up campaign after the Don was crossed and Soviet Armies were in retreat east and into the Caucasus, but it didn't work out that way. When the August 1941 rush to take Odessa turned into a siege, Soviet ships evacuated 32,000 troops to reinforce Sevastopol, causing German planners to rethink. It was obviously dangerous to leave a large enemy force intact in Crimea behind German armies moving farther east.

We know German photo recce of Sevastopol began before the invasion and repeatedly covered the port. This is probably coverage of August 1941. The bay is empty and smoke defenses actually highlight major targets rather than protect them. Sevastopol city is mainly south of the bay.

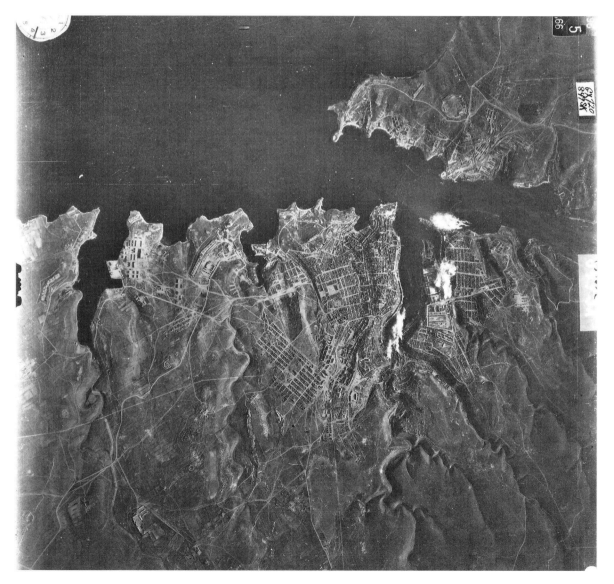

Smoke to hide targets or confuse attacking bombers was a typical tactic early in WW II. It was mostly futile.

Enlargement shows the northern smoke originated from small boats. This is the entrance to Pivdenna Bay, the Naval Base. The lower cloud is over two large drydocks and next to the Naval Arsenal.

Aerial reconnaissance was used to catalog and study every fortification around Sevastopol, and there were many, some dating back to the Crimean War (1854-55) and a few to the eighteenth-century.

SEWASTOPOL, FORTIK W. SOWJETISCH

Nov. 1941

A.I.3c (I) Ref.
765

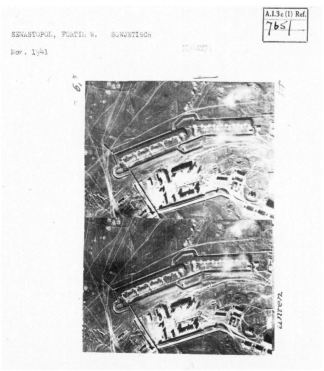

The fortification left is about l.5 miles west of Pivdenna Bay. It's designed to fire at ships approaching Severnaya Bay and the city from the west. On this November 1941 German stereo study, north is to the right.

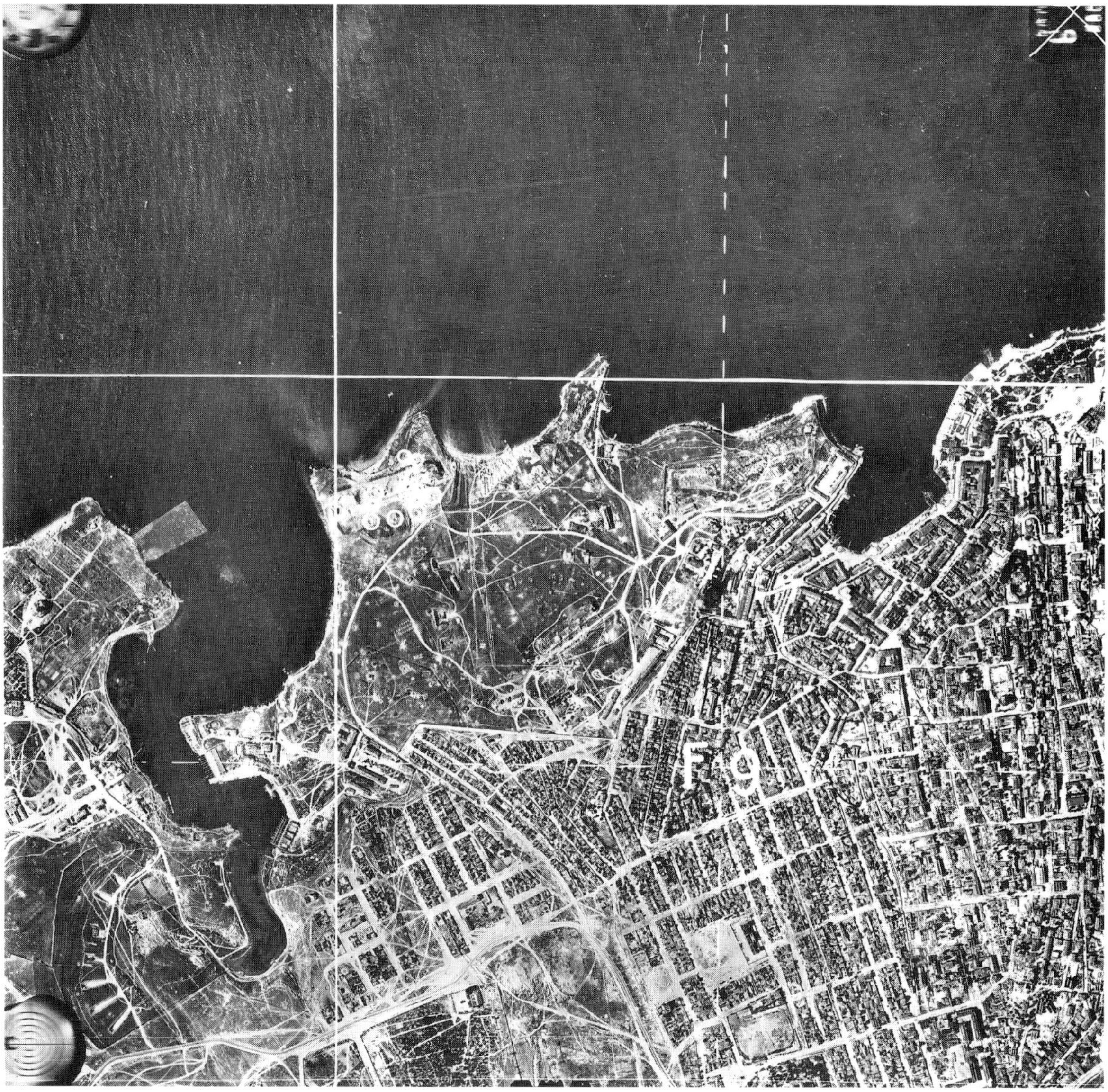
F 9

Sevastopol south side forts gridded off for bombing and reporting, showing bomb damage, November 1941.

There were several outer defense lines, mostly trenches. Actual forts with concrete and steel protecting modern artillery were in an arc about 5 miles inland, many of them on strategic heights occupied since the Crimean War.

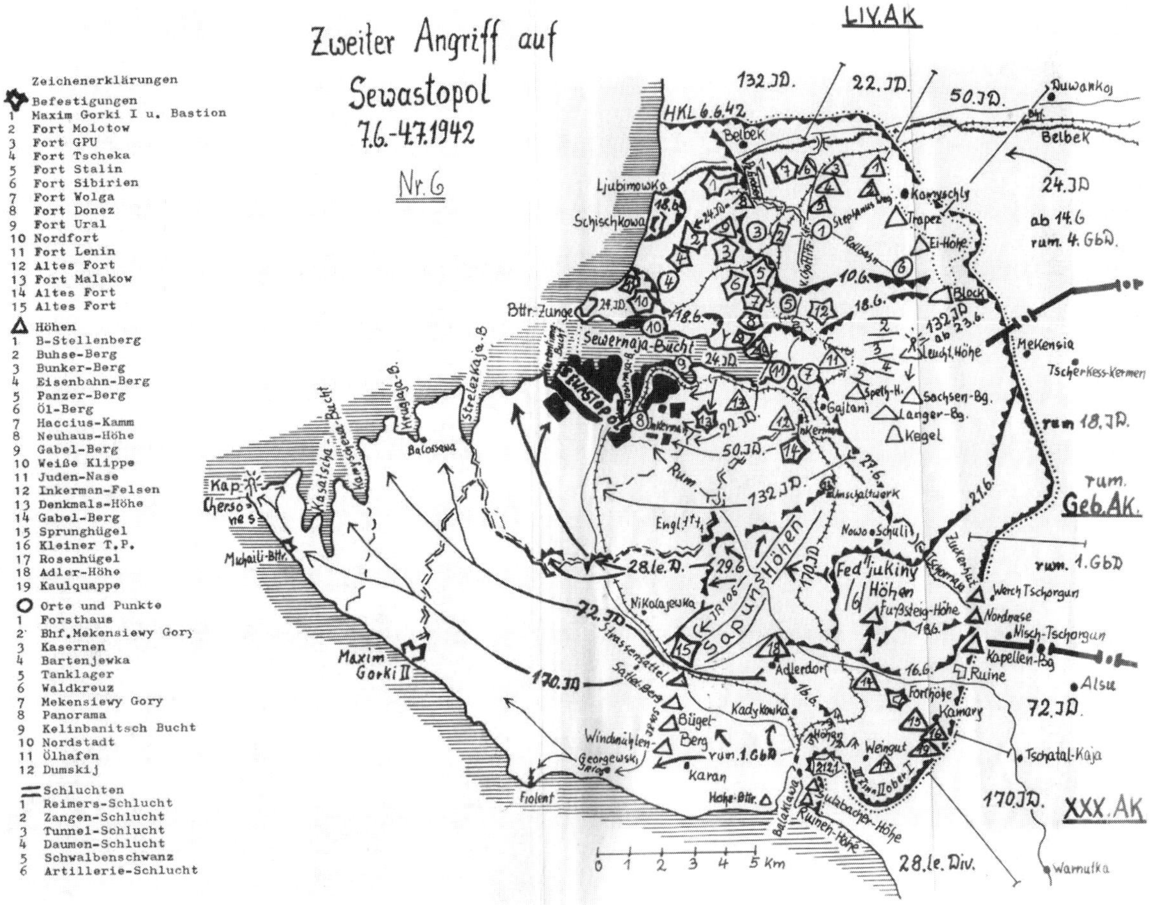
Zweiter Angriff auf
Sewastopol
7.6.-4.7.1942
Nr. 6
LIV.AK
Zeichenerklärungen
Befestigungen
1 Maxim Gorki I u. Bastion
2 Fort Molotow
3 Fort GPU
4 Fort Tscheka
5 Fort Stalin
6 Fort Sibirien
7 Fort Wolga
8 Fort Donez
9 Fort Ural
10 Nordfort
11 Fort Lenin
12 Altes Fort
13 Fort Malakow
14 Altes Fort
15 Altes Fort
Höhen
1 B-Stellenberg
2 Buhse-Berg
3 Bunker-Berg
4 Eisenbahn-Berg
5 Panzer-Berg
6 Öl-Berg
7 Haccius-Kamm
8 Neuhaus-Höhe
9 Gabel-Berg
10 Weiße Klippe
11 Juden-Nase
12 Inkerman-Felsen
13 Denkmals-Höhe
14 Gabel-Berg
15 Sprunghügel
16 Kleiner T.P.
17 Rosenhügel
18 Adler-Höhe
19 Kaulquappe
Orte und Punkte
1 Forsthaus
2 Bhf. Mekensiewy Gory
3 Kasernen
4 Bartenjewka
5 Tanklager
6 Waldkreuz
7 Mekensiewy Gory
8 Panorama
9 Kelinbanitsch Bucht
10 Nordstadt
11 Ölhafen
12 Dumskij
Schluchten
1 Reimers-Schlucht
2 Zangen-Schlucht
3 Tunnel-Schlucht
4 Daumen-Schlucht
5 Schwalbenschwanz
6 Artillerie-Schlucht
132.ID.
22.ID.
50.ID.
Duwankoj
HKL 6.6.42
Belbek
24.ID
ab 14.6 rum. 4. GbD.
Ljubimowka
Schischkowa
Kamyschly
Trapez
Ei-Höhe
Block
Bttr. Zunge
Sewernaja-Bucht
Mekensia
Tscherkess-Kermen
Sewastopol
Gajtani
Sachsen-Bg.
Langer-Bg.
Kegel
rum. 18.ID.
Balaklawa
50.ID.
132.ID.
rum. Geb.AK.
Kap Chersones
Michaili-Bttr.
Engl. Friedhof
Nowo Schuli
Fed'jukiny Höhen
Sapun Höhen
28.le.D.
170.ID
72.ID
Nikolajewka
Fußsteig-Höhe
Werch. Tschorgun
Nordnase
Nisch-Tschorgun
rum. 1.GbD
Maxim Gorki II
170.ID
Strassensattel
Sattel-Berg
Adlerdorf
Kapellen-Bg.
Ruine
Alsu
Forthöhe
Kamary
72.ID.
Kadykowka
Bügel-Berg
Windmühlen-Berg
Georgewski
Weingut
rum. 1.GbD
Karan
Tschatal-Kaja
Fiolent
Höhe-Bttr.
170.ID.
XXX.AK
Ruinen-Höhe
28.le.Div.
Warnutka
0 1 2 3 4 5 Km

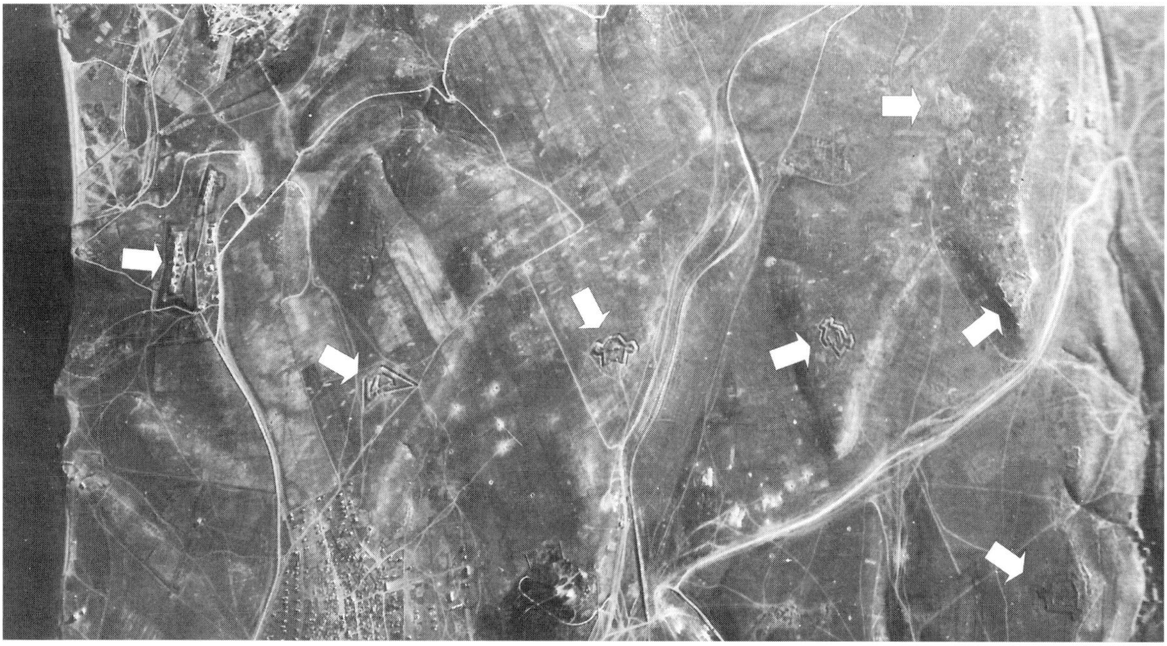

Going east from the coast are: Shishkov Fort, Ft. Molotov (disabled 6 June-taken 12 June), Ft. GPU, Ft. Sibirien and Ft. Stalin. Higher is an unnamed fort, lower is Ft. Volga (taken 17 June). Most are roughly a mile north of Severnaya Bay. Non-standardization of fort shape is because each took advantage of its unique hill or ridge and fields of fire.

Both of these photos are from 7 May 1942.

Enlargement of Ft. Stalin. A strategic location overlooking a main road (shadow gives an idea of the height and steepness). Originally made in 1855, the fort was upgraded and hardened in the 1930s. It had four 76mm AA guns that held German Infantry at bay for several days. Bombed by Stukas on 12 June, it fell on 13 June.

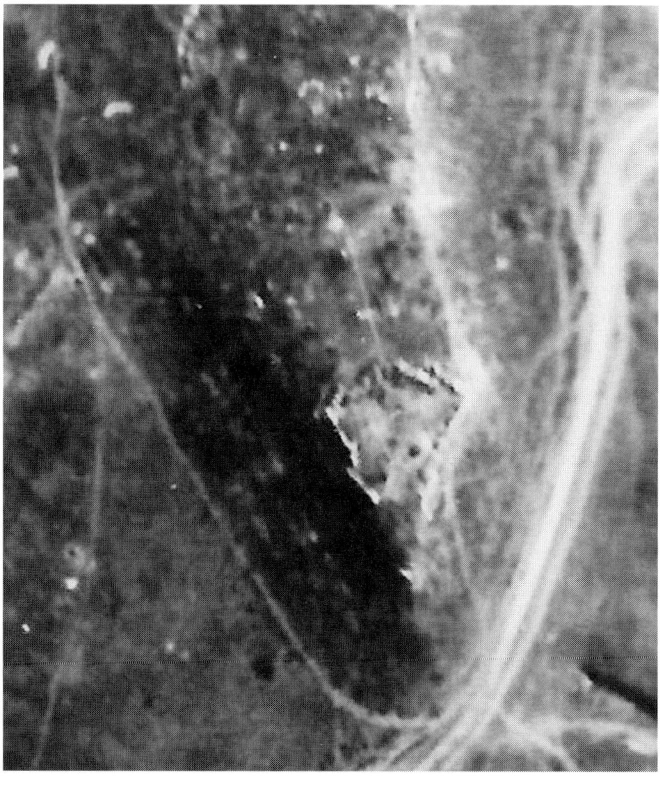

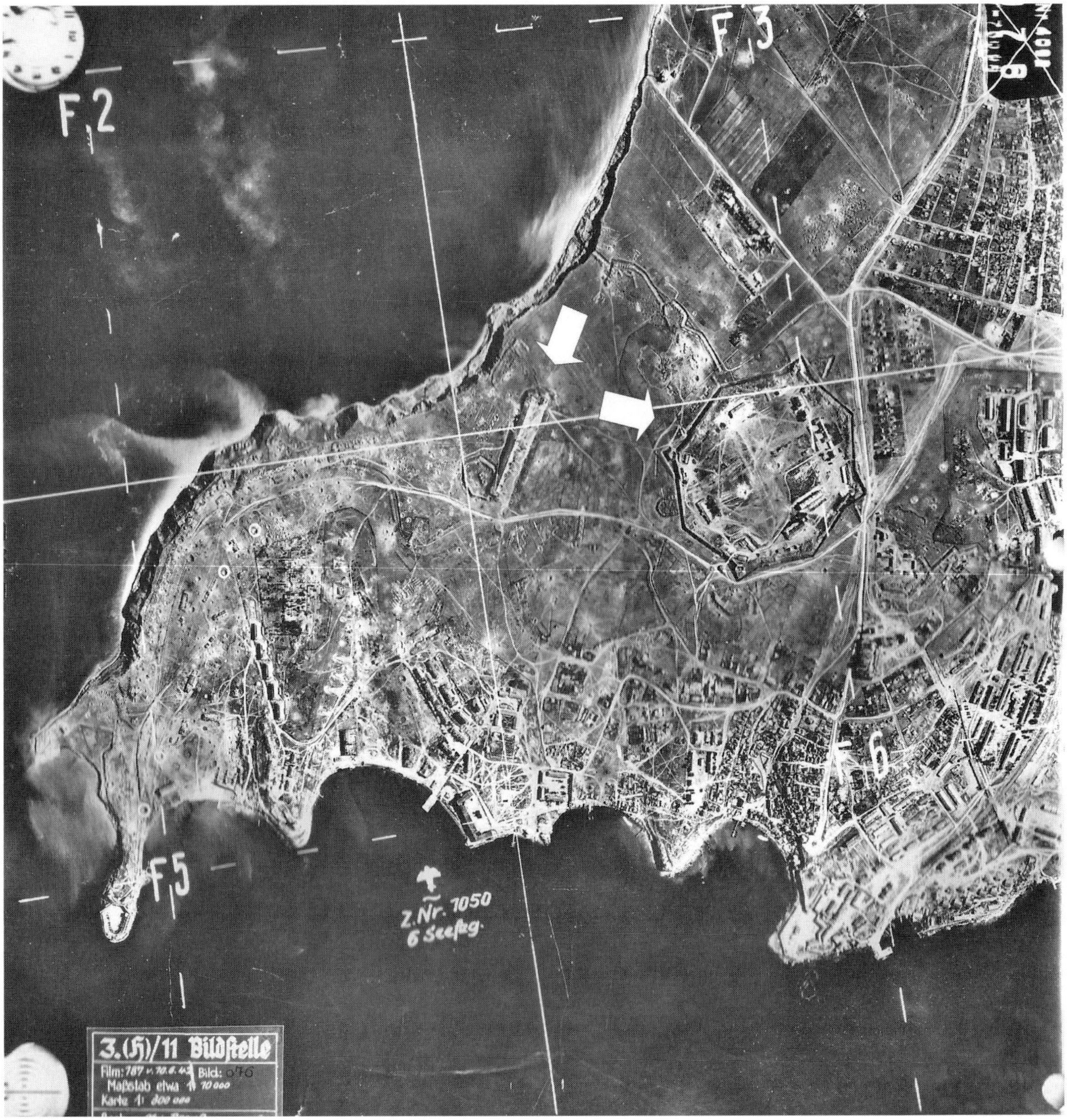
F 2
F 3
F 5
6
Z.Nr. 1050
3.(H)/11 Bildstelle

Left arrow is Ft. Lenin with four 76mm anti-aircraft guns, defended by a wide anti-tank ditch and machine-guns in thirty-two concrete bunkers plus seven armored cupolas, 10 June 1942. One of the last inner defenses, it fell to German Infantry on 21 June 1942.

Right arrow is the eighteenth-century North Fort, support base for Fort Lenin. It also had formidable bunkers and was defended by anti-aircraft, anti-tank and machine guns and successfully held off attackers for two days. It also fell on 21 June.

On this 10 June 1942 coverage there are bomb or shell craters all over the area. Some have been circled by a German photo interpreter to indicate new since the previous coverage.

At far left is a seventeenth-century fort extending into Severnaya Bay designed for muzzle-loading naval guns. Above it is what the German map (above) called Battery Zunge. Both defenses faced west. Zunge and the ancient fort south of it were repeatedly attacked by artillery and air.

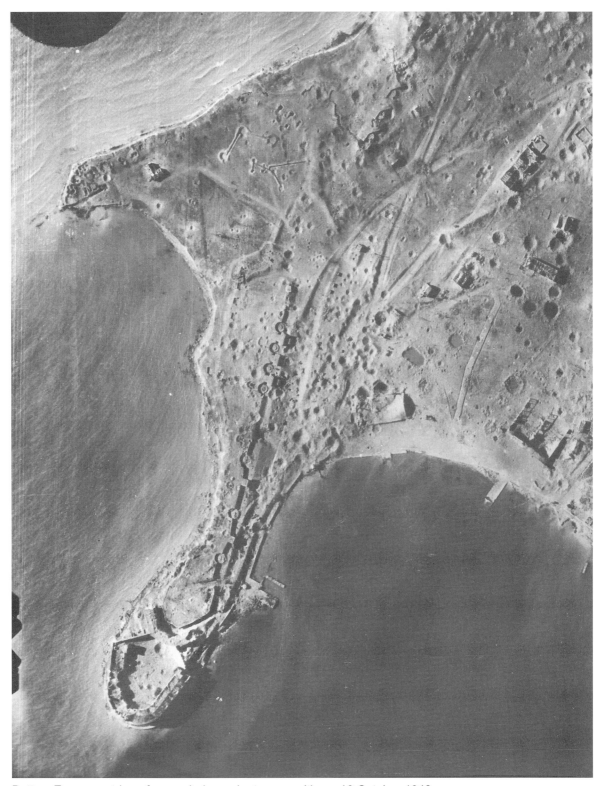

Battery Zunge, a string of seven independent gun positions, 16 October 1942.

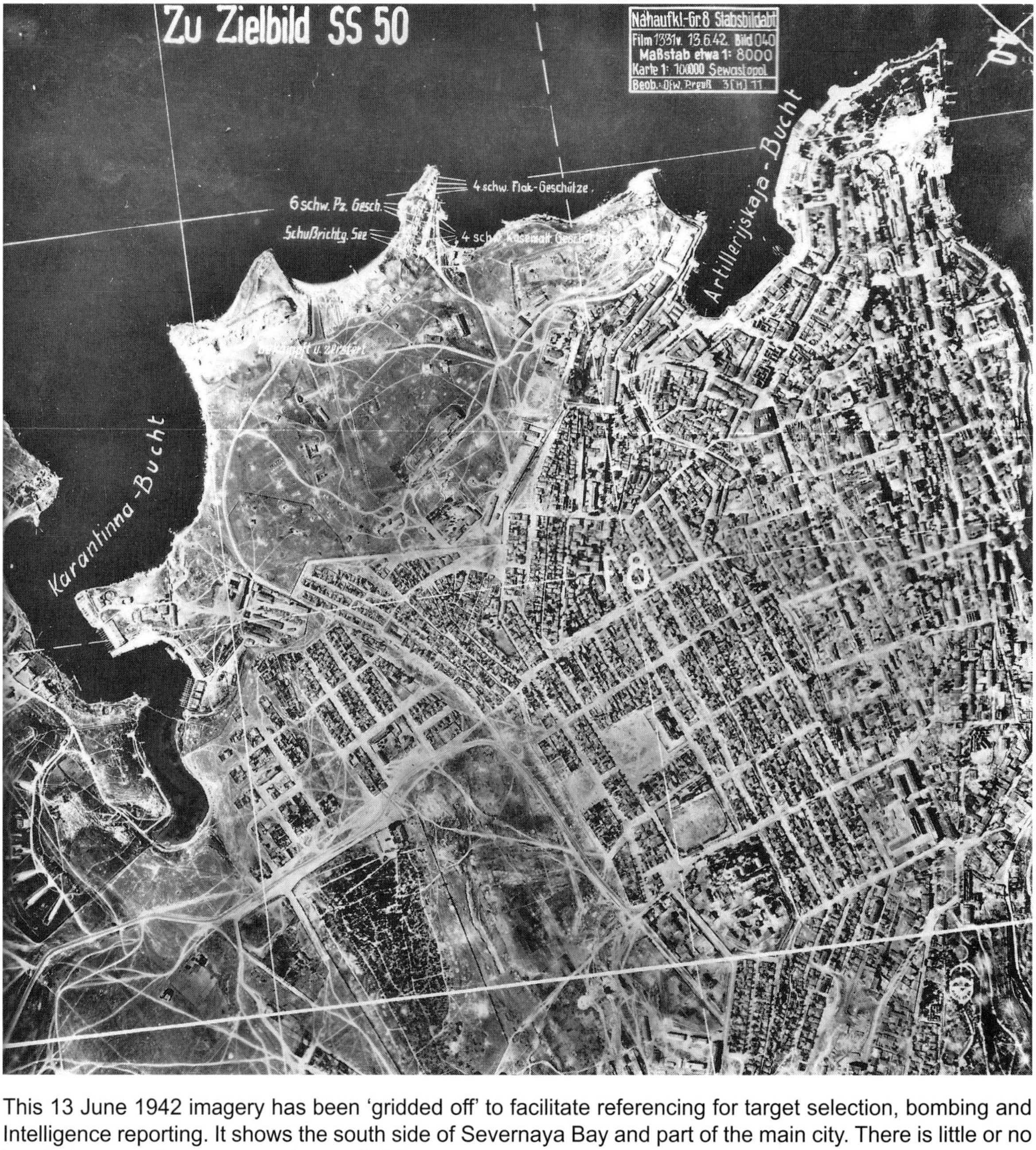
Zu Zielbild SS 50
Nahaufkl.-Gr.8 Stabsbildabt
Film 1331v. 13.6.42. Bild 040
Maßstab etwa 1: 8000
Karte 1: 10000 Sewastopol
Beob.: Ofw. Preuß 3(H) 11
4 schw. Flak-Geschütze.
6 schw. Pz. Gesch.
Schußrichtg. See
Artillerijskaja-Bucht
Karantinna-Bucht

This 13 June 1942 imagery has been 'gridded off' to facilitate referencing for target selection, bombing and Intelligence reporting. It shows the south side of Severnaya Bay and part of the main city. There is little or no bomb damage showing except around defenses.

4 schw. Flak-Geschütze
6 schw. Pz. Gesch.
Schußrichtg. See

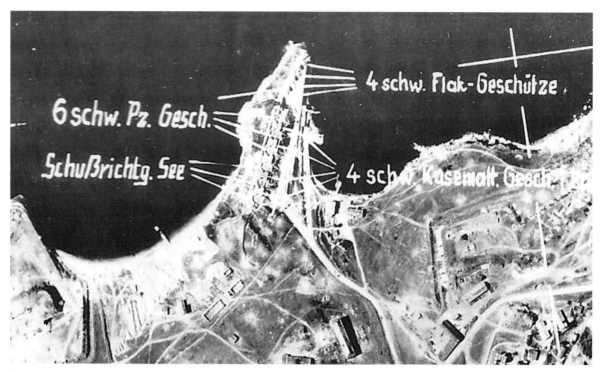

Enlargement of the previous image shows annotations for six heavy guns (probably at least 76mm) which could only fire west toward open water. Four heavy anti-aircraft guns were sited to defend the port and four heavy guns in casemates (probably anti-tank guns) were positioned to defend the installation from landward assault. A rangefinder installation supported the heavy coast artillery.

Annotations demonstrate the thoroughness and detail skills of German photo interpreters, and their primary interest in Soviet defenses.

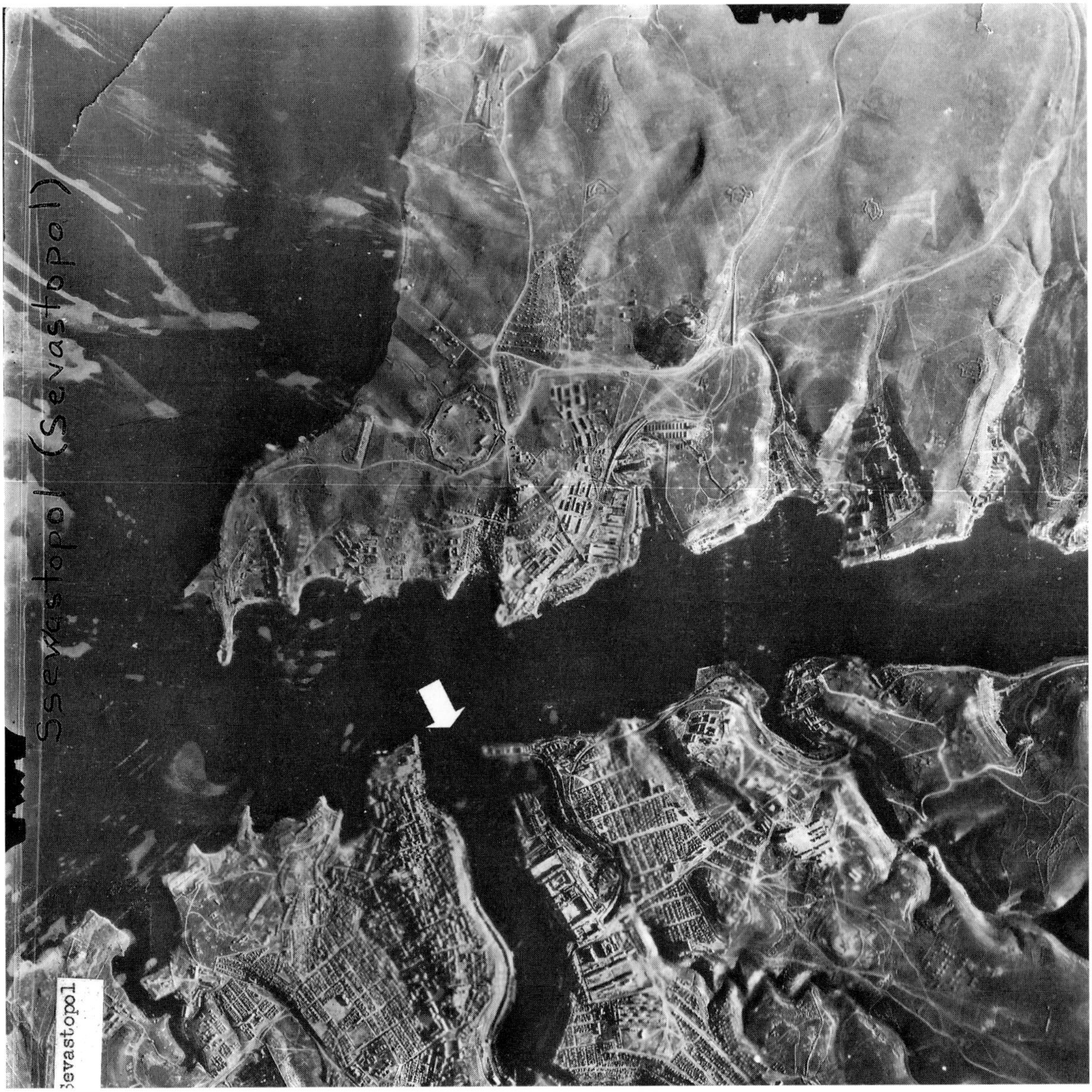
Ssevastopol (Sevastopol)
Sevastopol

Severnaya Bay runs east to west. My arrow indicates Pivdenna Bay, home of the Black Sea Fleet, naval yards and Arsenal.

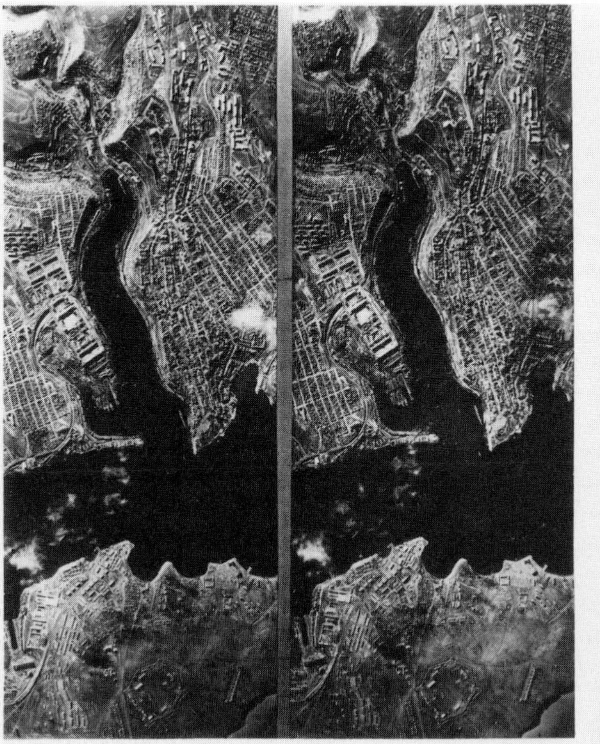

Fig 3

Sevastopol, Crimea. 1942.
Figures 3 and 4 further illustrate the comparison between small and large scale photography. In Fig 4 considerable damage, from air attack, is visible to various installations. The ships and submarines in the dry docks can be clearly seen on this large scale photography.

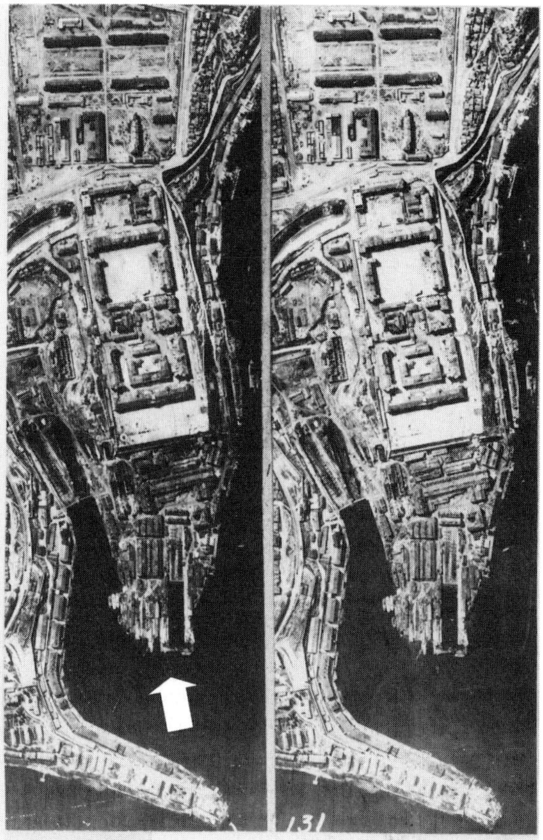
131

C.F.L. 754.17

Fig 4

CONFIDENTIAL

This post-war US stereogram (likely a teaching tool) uses GX imagery to illustrate advantages of large scale. The imagery is from at least 1943. North is down. It covers the head of Pivdenna Bay and Sevastopol's Naval Base. My arrow indicates the 'look angle' for the next photo. Up and left of my arrow are two large drydocks, both with their gates closed. The east dock looks like it has been pumped dry. Large buildings straight up from the arrow are Sevastopol's Naval Arsenal.

USSR. 44.35N - 33.34E. Sevastopol'.
Cat. 47. Battered shipyards on the Bukhta Severnaya and other industries
behind the shipyards. July 1942. Source: AMS Photograph No. 12244.

Taken just days after Sevastopol fell to German forces. The camera was apparently in a building on the peninsula just below my arrow on the previous image. I suspect this unattributed photo was part of a series acquired from a Romanian naval source (you'll see a couple more in this chapter).

We see an empty drydock and wrecked hull of a probable minesweeper and a destroyer on building ways.

This is an Italian CB-class mini-sub somewhere in Severnaya Bay (my guess, based upon the background, is looking north from near the mouth of Pivdenna Bay). Six mini-subs were sold to Romania in 1943 and operated in the Black Sea. The sub had a crew of four and we see three on the boat. Apparently the fourth crewman had a camera and in 1943 was taking typical tourist photos at Sevastopol.

There is no indication how US Intelligence got hold of those images, but I've used several.

German Bomber Attack on Sevastopol 1942
(Berliner Illustrieste Zeitung, Dec 31

Upper reaches of Pivdenna Bay, looking southeast. Bombing appears to be mostly in the town. Smoke over the Arsenal (on left) may be a passive defense.

The photo was in a Berlin newspaper. American Intelligence probably picked up this German 'open source' in a neutral country.

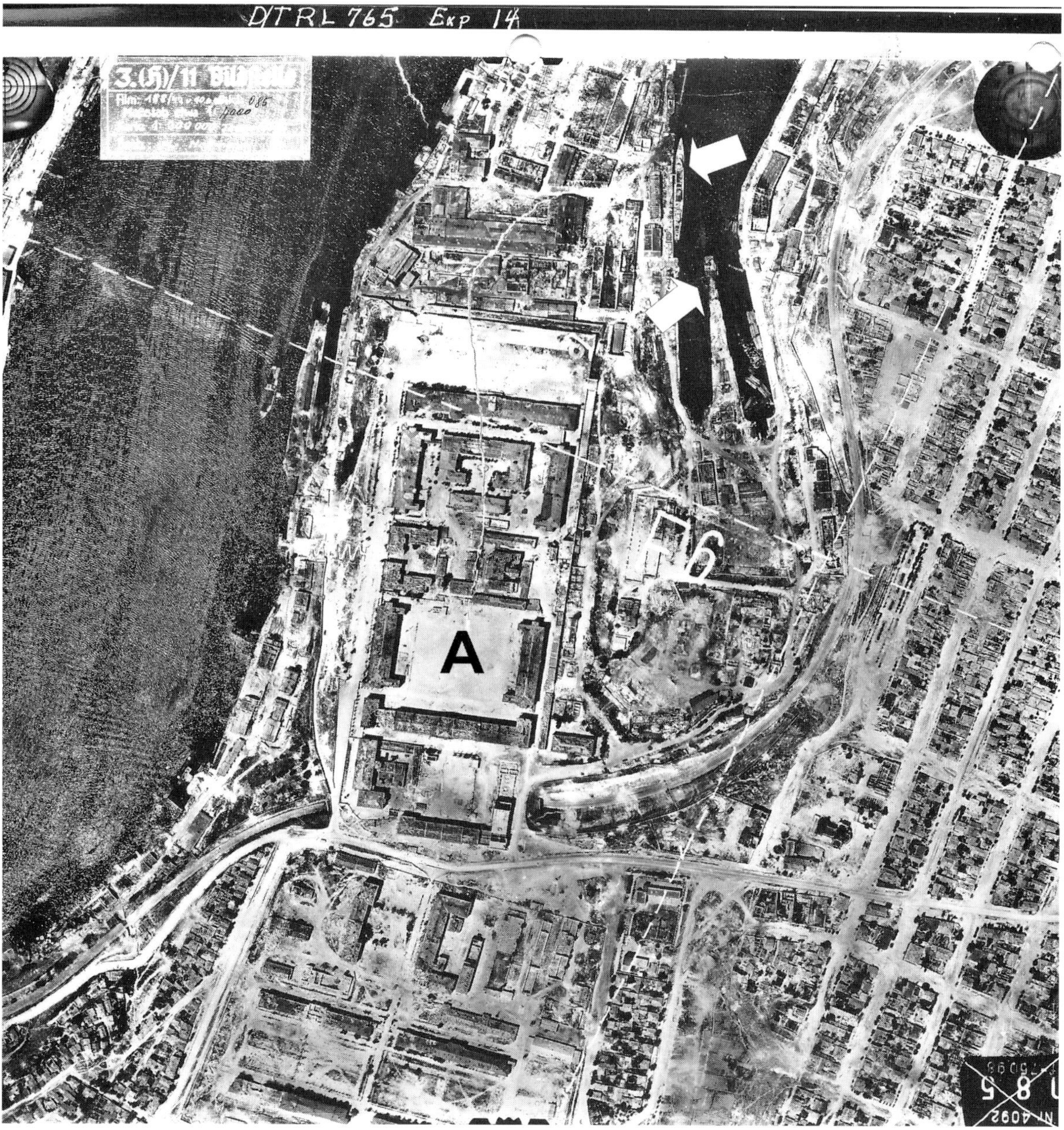
A

The same area in a vertical view, 10 May 1942. My upper arrow indicates a destroyer beside the quay apparently unfinished or damaged. Lower arrow is my best guess for the taking position and angle of the photograph two pages hence. Both west and east drydocks are open to the bay. I put a black 'A ' on the Naval Arsenal main parade ground. Burned buildings can be seen to the south (photo bottom) but few craters. Perhaps Luftwaffe attacks were with incendiaries?

Right, building damage north of the Arsenal.

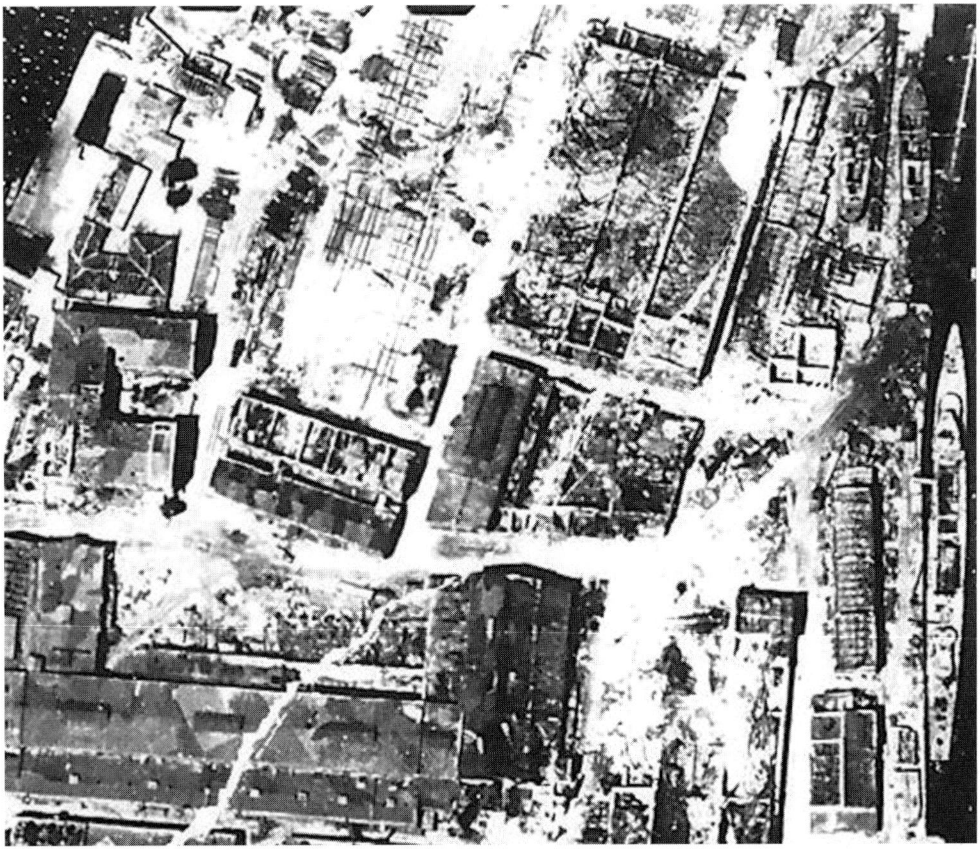

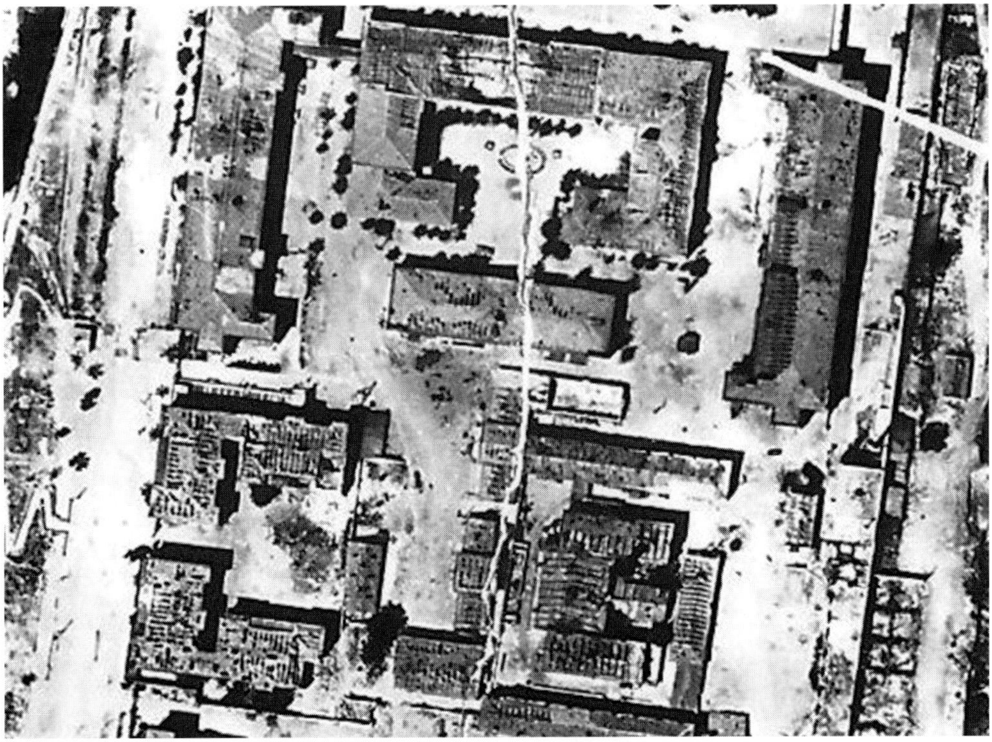

Left, a closer look at damage south of the Arsenal, 10 May 1942.

AREA 13 - USSR - EUROPEAN RUSSIA - SEBASTOPOL. App: 44° 37' N. - 33° 35' E
View taken from the naval dockyard near the "Arsenal", camera bearing 40°
showing western drydock and boats in eastern drydock. Print #21 taken
May 1943. Enc.(A). ONI(Y5) #467935.

Shot one year later from the location indicated on the 10 May 1942 vertical photo. I think this is another of my 'Romanian tourist' photos. It looks northeast across the upper end of west and east drydocks with more activity than in 1942. The west dock is empty but I think I'm seeing passenger ship deck ventilators behind that camouflage netting in the background. It appears a large vessel is in the east drydock, possibly a multi-deck passenger ship like *Abkhaziya*. Note treatment to hide the size and shape of the stack. Sorting out the ship outline is also confused by houses and other structures on high ground beyond the drydock.

To get into Crimea, German ground forces had to first get through the four-mile wide defended Isthmus of Perekop. For over twenty-five centuries that location had been fortified to keep people out of Crimea or to keep people living there from getting out.

The Wehrmacht broke through on 27 September and surged south into Crimea.

Below, a rare aerial photo of aircraft in action. Three Stukas bombing near Fort Perekop on the Tatar Ditch, 29 April 1941.

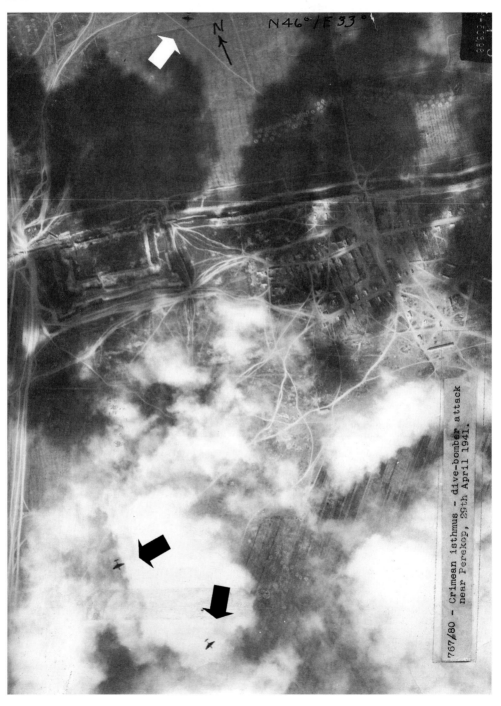

767480 - Crimean isthmus - dive-bomber attack near Perekop, 29th April 1941.

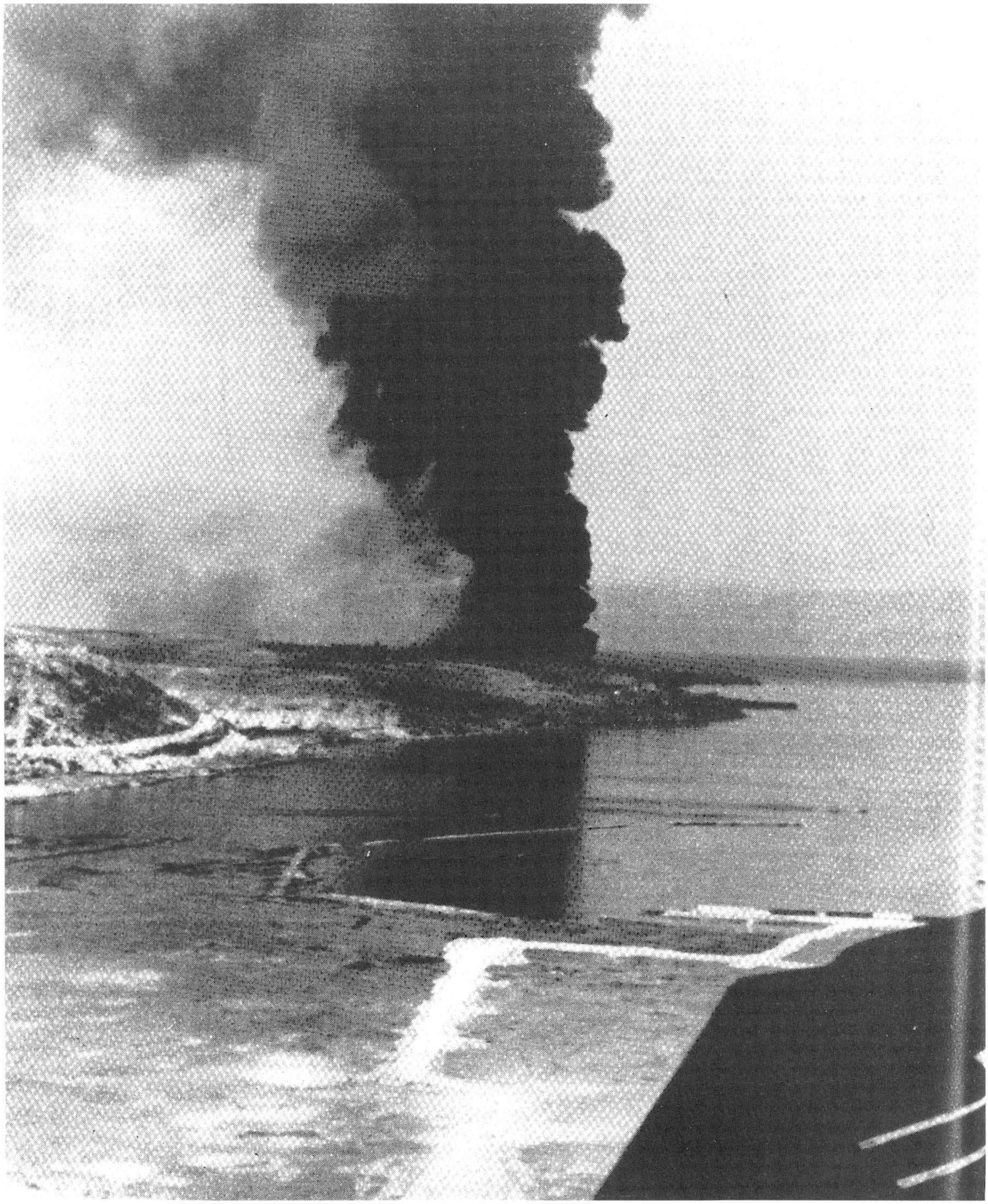

A German plane over Inkerman at the upper end of Severnaya Bay looking west. Smoke is coming from something close to the Naval Base, probably May 1942.

With Kerch diversionary landings suppressed in May, German air and land effort focused on Sevastopol — but the defense lines wouldn't break.

Severnaya Bay in the foreground and what look to be defensive smoke (not fires from bombing) over the Naval Base. Half-tone printing says this photo is from a German 'open source'. It was titled Sevastopol 1943. That doesn't make sense since Sevastopol fell to German land forces in July 1942. Perhaps it's the acquisition date thing again, but it's a good shot so I'm using it.

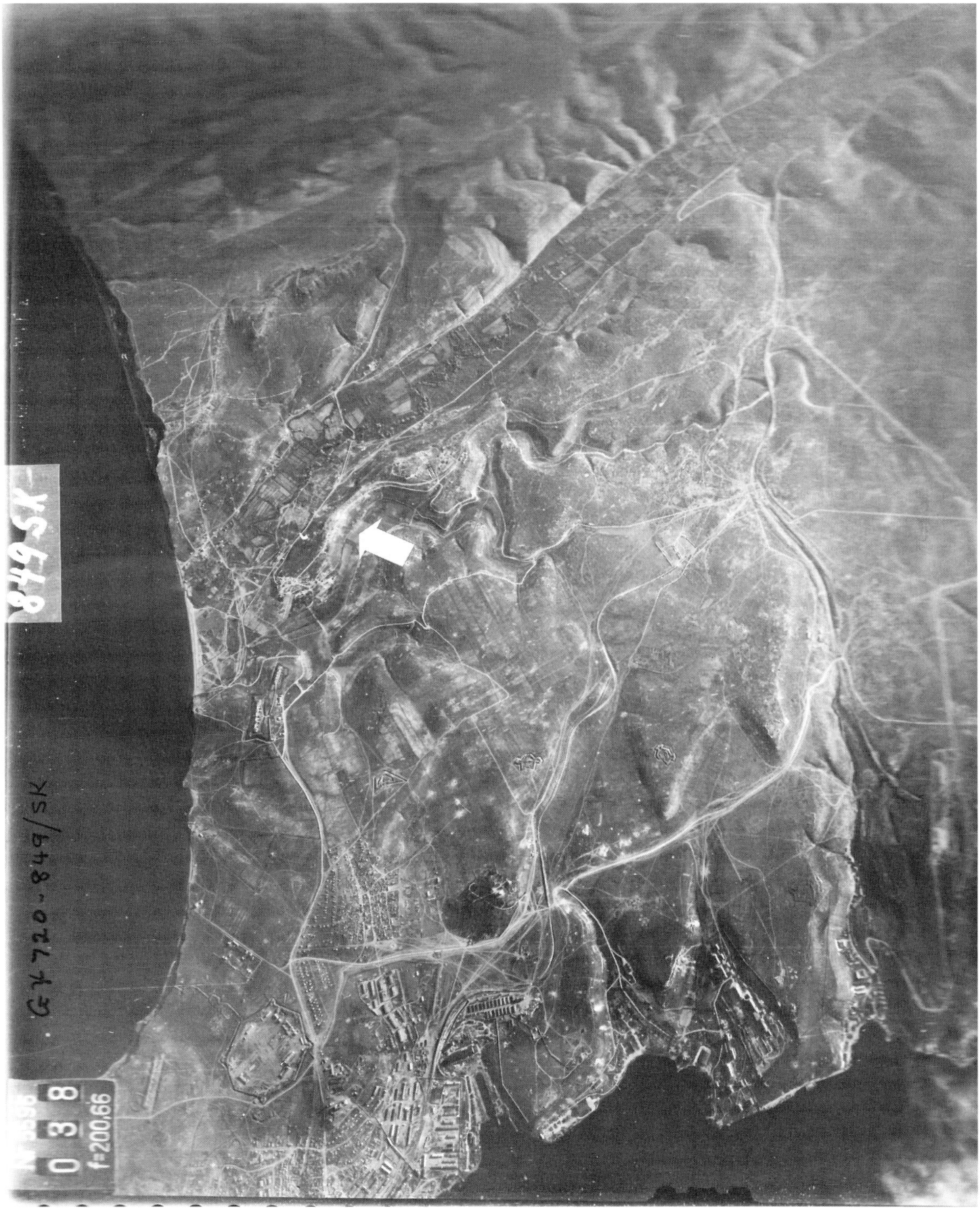
849SK
038
f=200,66

Struggling south in Crimea against determined resistance, everything except Sevastopol was in German hands by 16 November.

A major obstacle to breaking Sevastopol's inner defense line was fire from Battery 30 (aka Maxim Gorky) with four 30.5cm (12") guns in two battleship-style turrets.

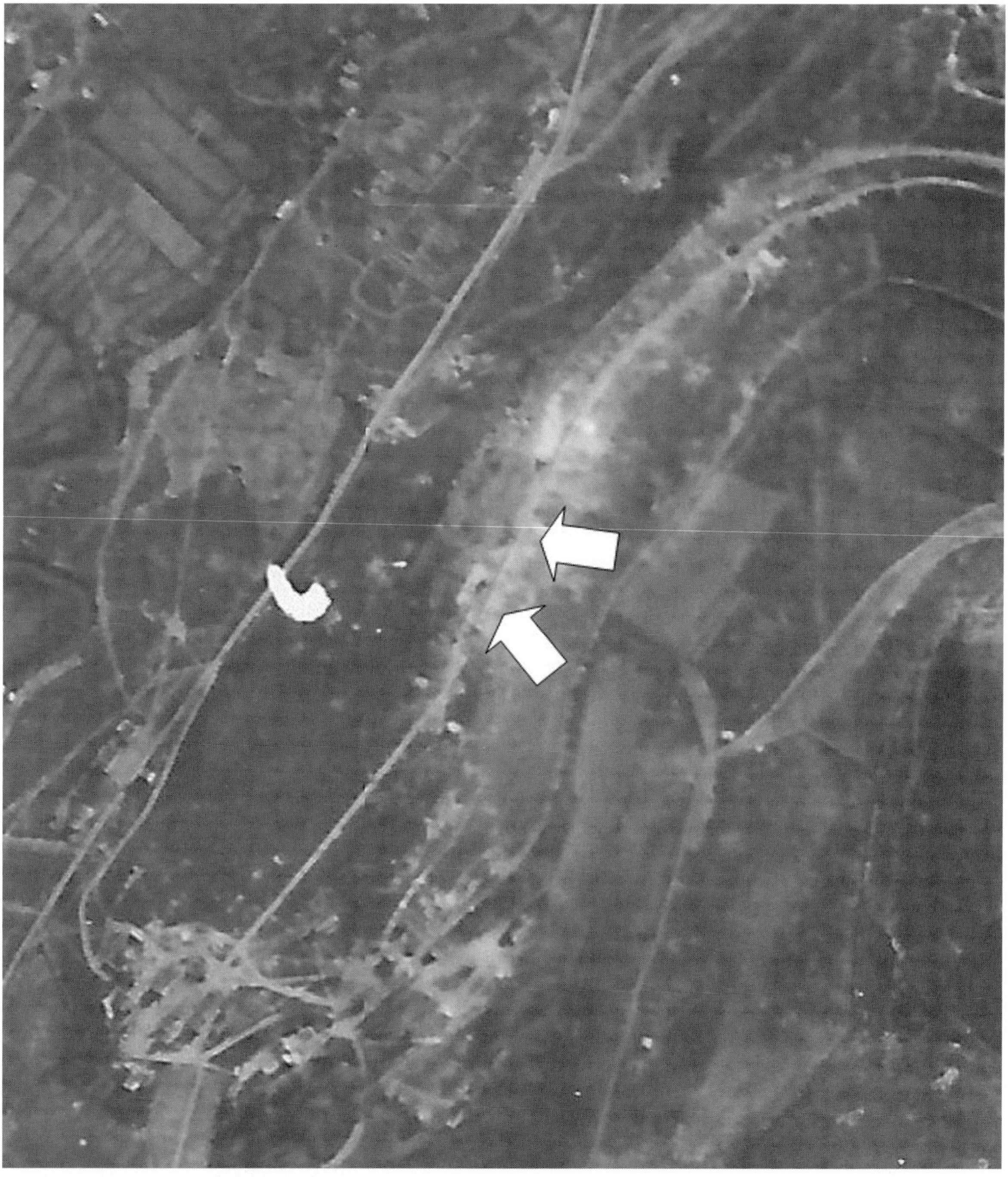

Enlargement of the previous image. The camouflaged twin turrets are darker shapes just left of the road. Located on a ridgetop, they were equally effective firing to sea or inland, which is how they helped stall several German advances on the city. Battery 30 was a thorn in German sides and a big factor in stringing out Sevastopol's siege to 250 days.

Several Soviet amphibious landings near Kerch that had to be snuffed out also side-tracked German the main effort temporarily.

That white 'C' shape behind Battery 30 isn't mine. I don't know if it means anything.

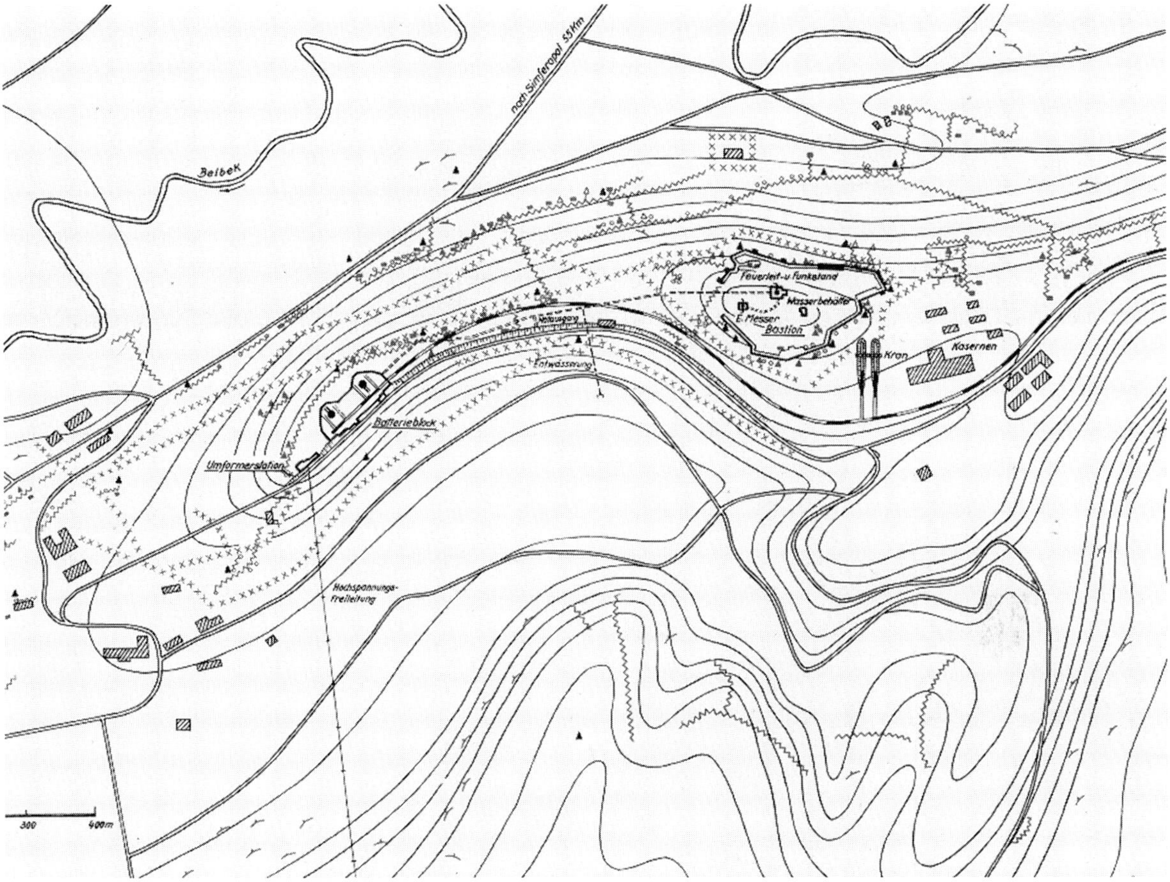
Belbek
nach Simferopol 55Km
Feuerleit-u Funkstand
Wasserbehälter
E. Messer
Bastion
Kran
Kasernen
Batterieblock
Umformerstation
Entwässerung
Hochspannungs-
Freileitung
300
400m

For comparison with the imagery, a German map of Battery 30 (left center). Contour lines show how the steep ridge gave 'Maxim Gorki' a wonderful field of fire and natural defense.

One of the twin turrets firing. The first fire mission was on 1 November and these guns helped stall the first German offensive on Sevastopol. Anything within 26 miles could be a target.

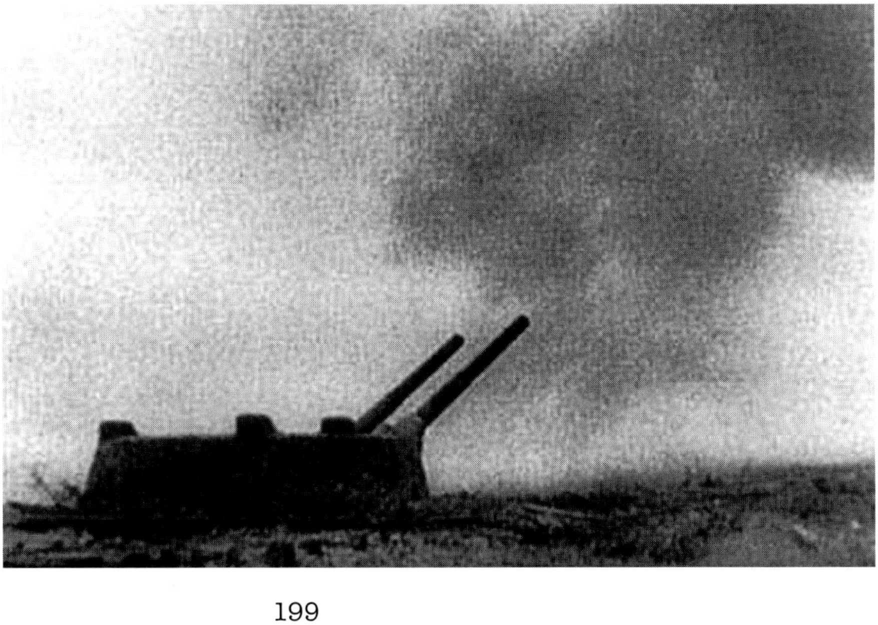

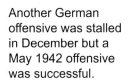

Another German offensive was stalled in December but a May 1942 offensive was successful.

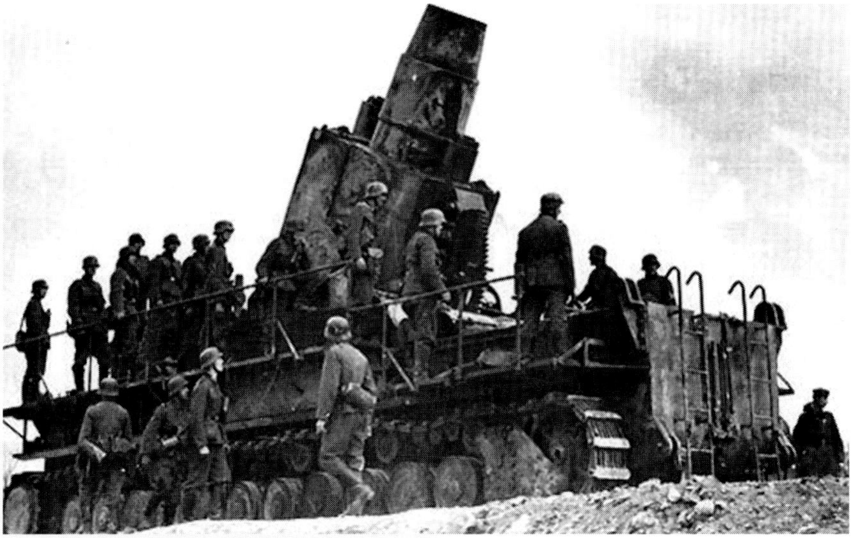

Battery 30 was attacked by two 60cm 'Thor' self-propelled mortars, one of which scored hits with its 2.7 ton shells on 6 and 7 June 1942. Range was inside 6 miles so accuracy was good.

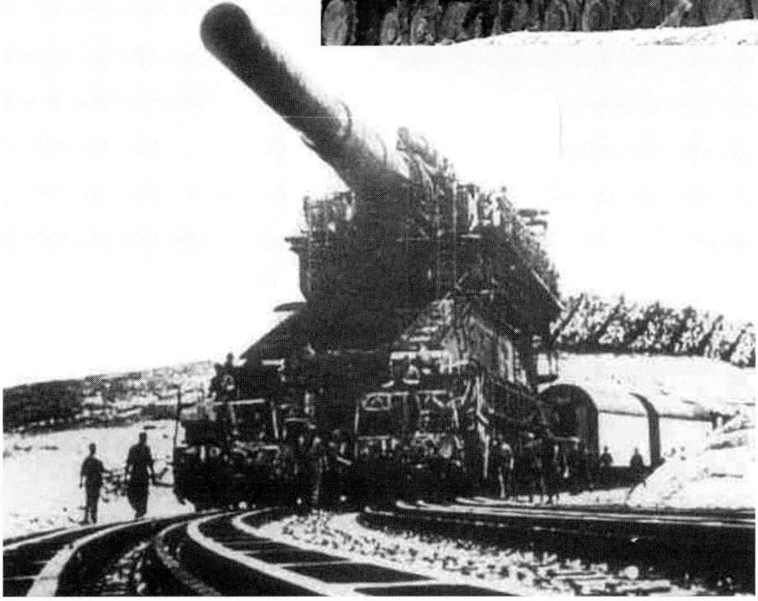

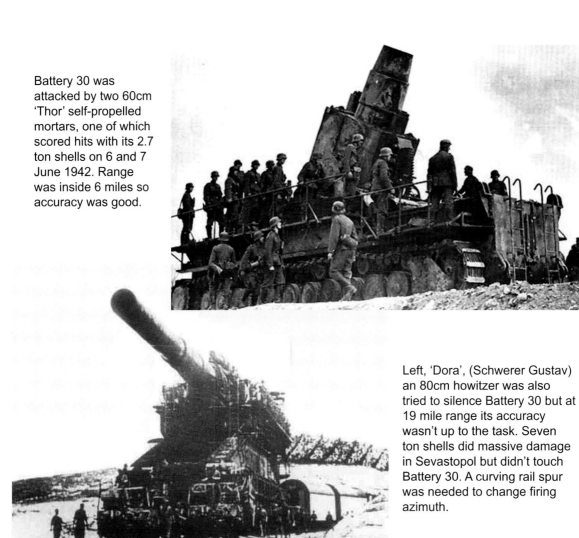

Left, 'Dora', (Schwerer Gustav) an 80cm howitzer was also tried to silence Battery 30 but at 19 mile range its accuracy wasn't up to the task. Seven ton shells did massive damage in Sevastopol but didn't touch Battery 30. A curving rail spur was needed to change firing azimuth.

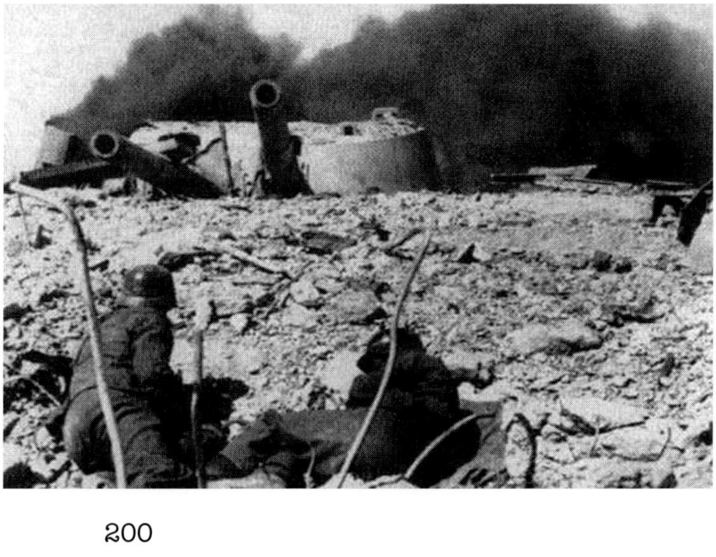

German infantry took the Battery on 21 June. With Battery 30 gone, Sevastopol's inner defenses were quickly breached and defense of the city began to collapse.

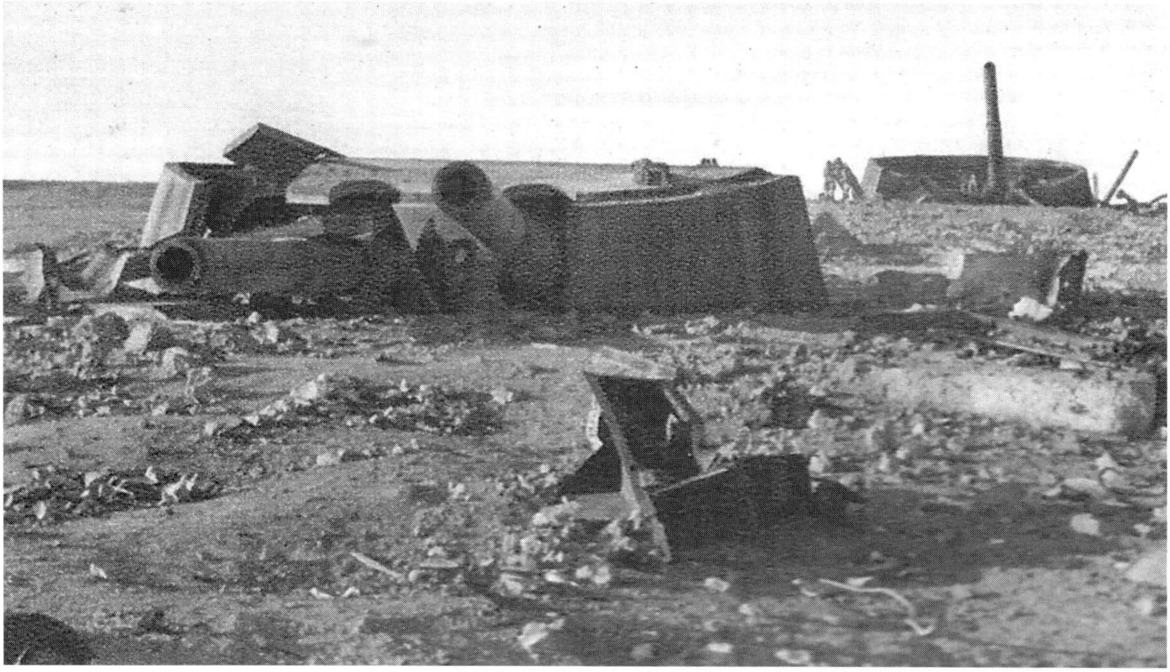

Buckled 406mm armor plate and split barrels show both turrets out of action in June 1942, but fire from Thor and Dora only put one gun in one turret out of action (left in near turret). The big damage was done by Soviet demolition as gun crews withdrew from the position on 21 June.

There's my Romanian navy tourist again. It's a good look at that armor plate.

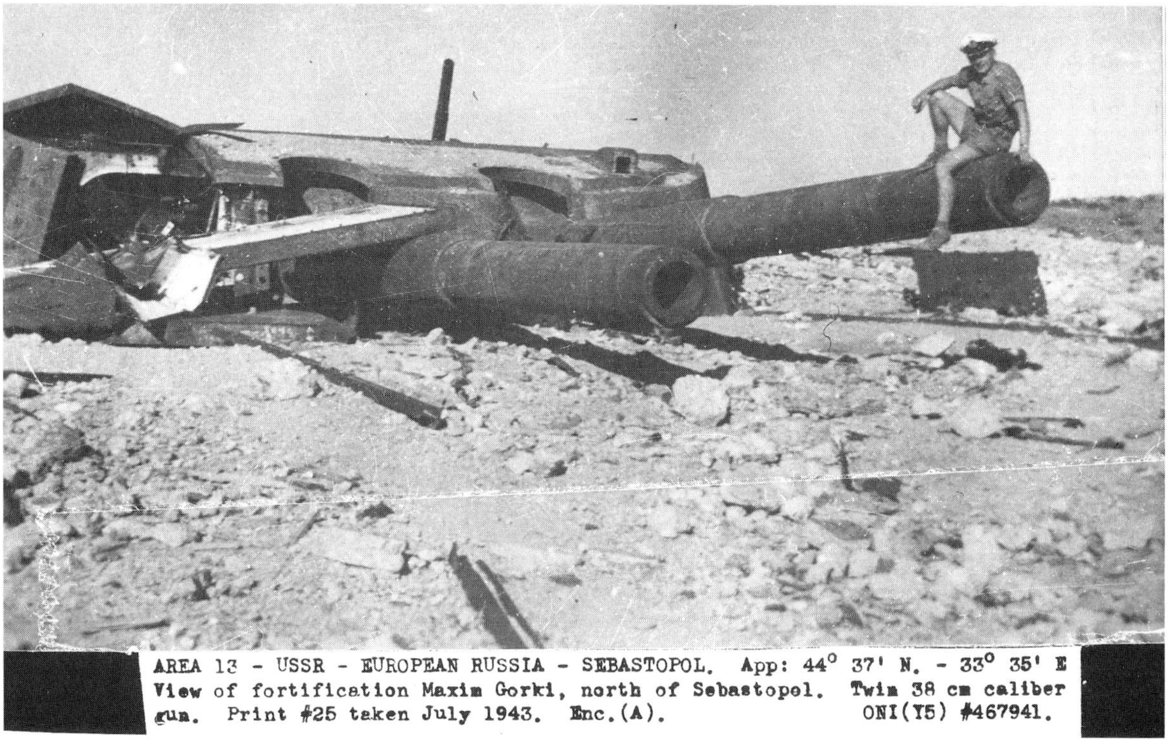

AREA 13 - USSR - EUROPEAN RUSSIA - SEBASTOPOL. App: 44° 37' N. - 33° 35' E
View of fortification Maxim Gorki, north of Sebastopol. Twin 38 cm caliber gun. Print #25 taken July 1943. Enc.(A). ONI(Y5) #467941.

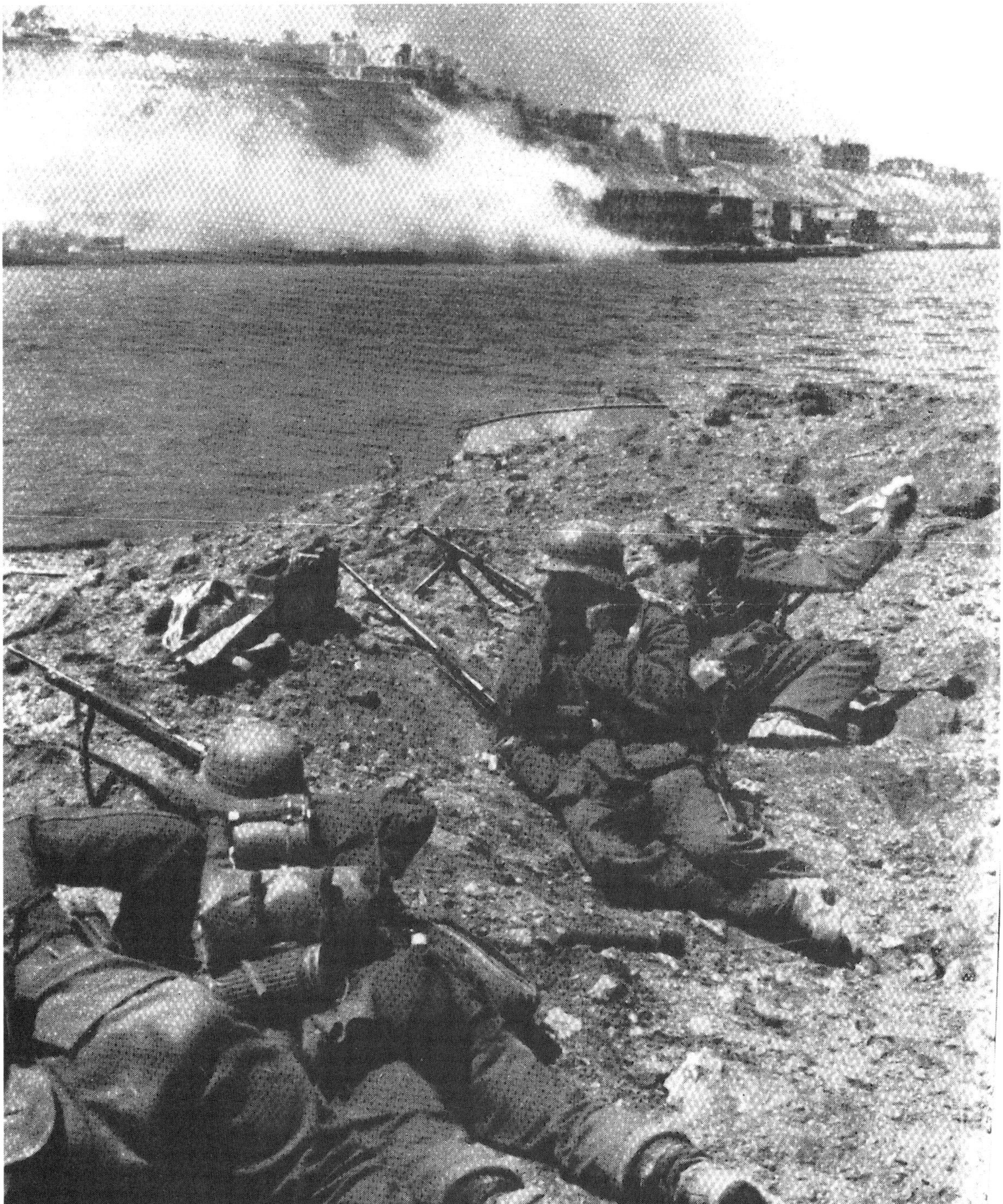

The caption on this photo said 'Sevastopol from across the bay, 1943'. Those troops are on the west side of Pivdenna Bay looking at the Naval Arsenal. I don't know how to put this in context. The city surrendered on 4 July 1942 and those aren't summer uniforms. Perhaps the 1943 date was when US Intel acquired the image and it actually dates from fall of 1941?

It could also be from the Soviet retaking of Sevastopol in 1944.

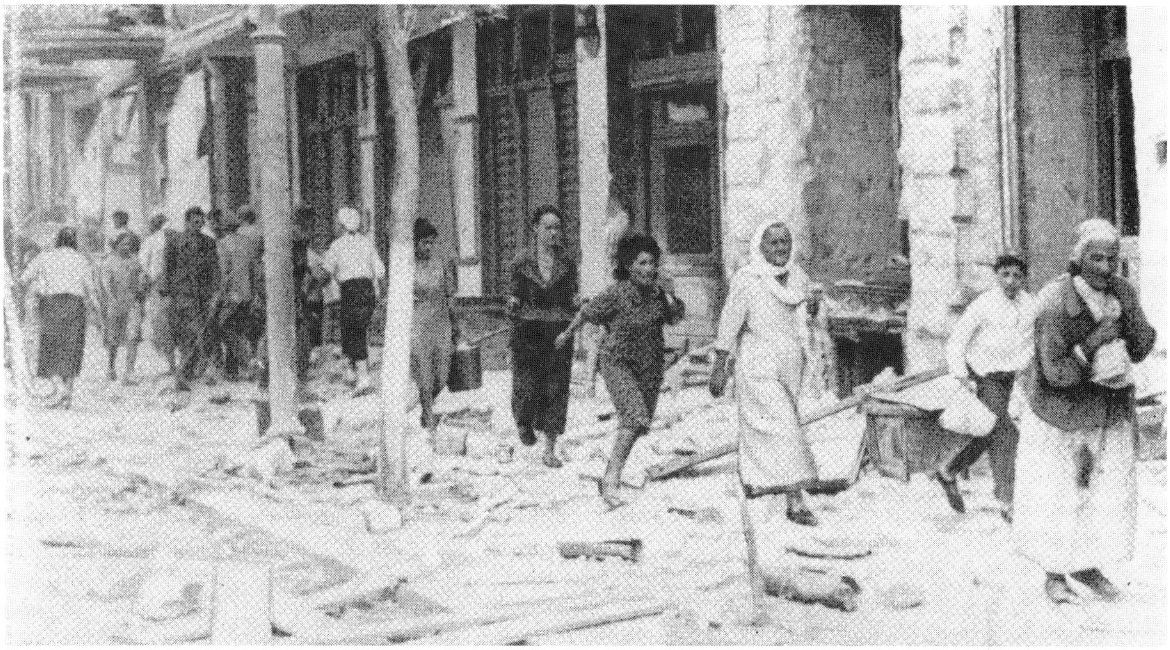

Photo taken by a German soldier or combat photographer in June 1942. The caption said 'Sevastopol people out of shelters'.

Below, obviously an official German photo, we probably acquired it from a magazine in a neutral country. The caption read, 'Sevastopol conquerors', 1943'.

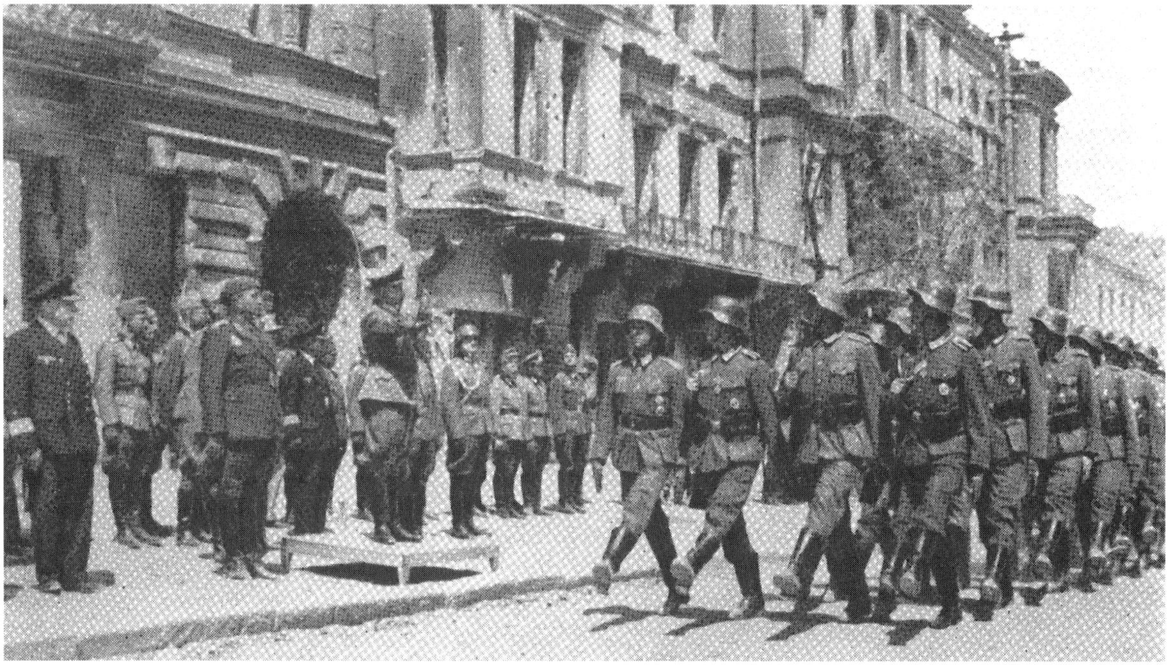

Sevastopol cost Romania and Germany over 71,000 casualties and led to weakness in armies going to Stalingrad and the Caucasus. Note the Romanian officer to the right of the German reviewer.

Soviets lost 156,000 men defending Sevastopol.

They took it back in May 1944.

Chapter VI

1942

Progress in 1941 was astounding, with the front pushed east 1200 miles in five months. Soviet defenders were knocked off balance by well planned, well executed initiatives that never gave them time or opportunity to regain solid footing. Cold and snow slowed German progress during the winter of 1941-42, and most changes in the FEBA were straightening lines. In spring came mud, giving Soviet forces more time to regain their feet and organize defenses. During winter months Soviet massed artillery fire became legendary.

German Infantry suiting-up for winter combat.

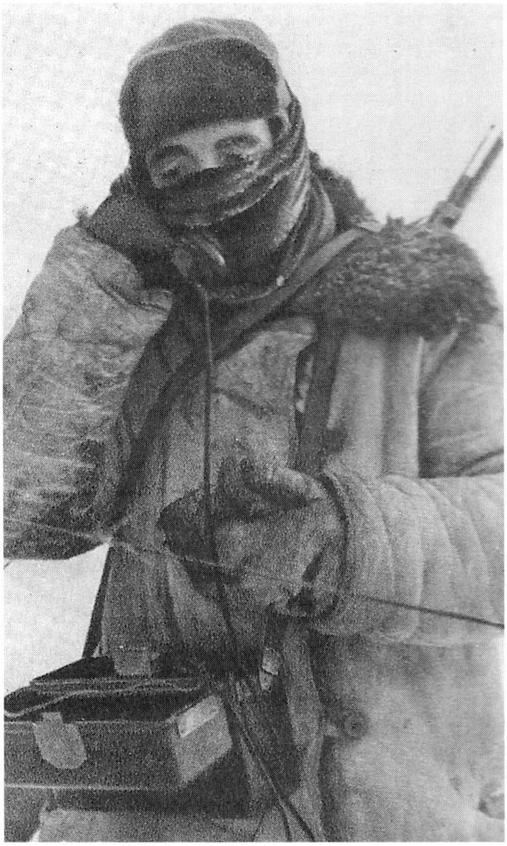

The Wehrmacht wasn't really prepared for a Soviet winter—individual soldiers certainly weren't.

Left, a German soldier with a field telephone. Nothing and nobody really works well at 40 degrees below zero. Combat didn't cease that winter but it certainly slowed. In spring the FEBA was still aligned generally north-south between 100 and 200 miles short of the Don.

The caption 'Forward Observation Post' is in Russian but the binocular periscope looks German to me. A photographer shooting from in front of their supposedly camouflaged position suggests a publicity photo.

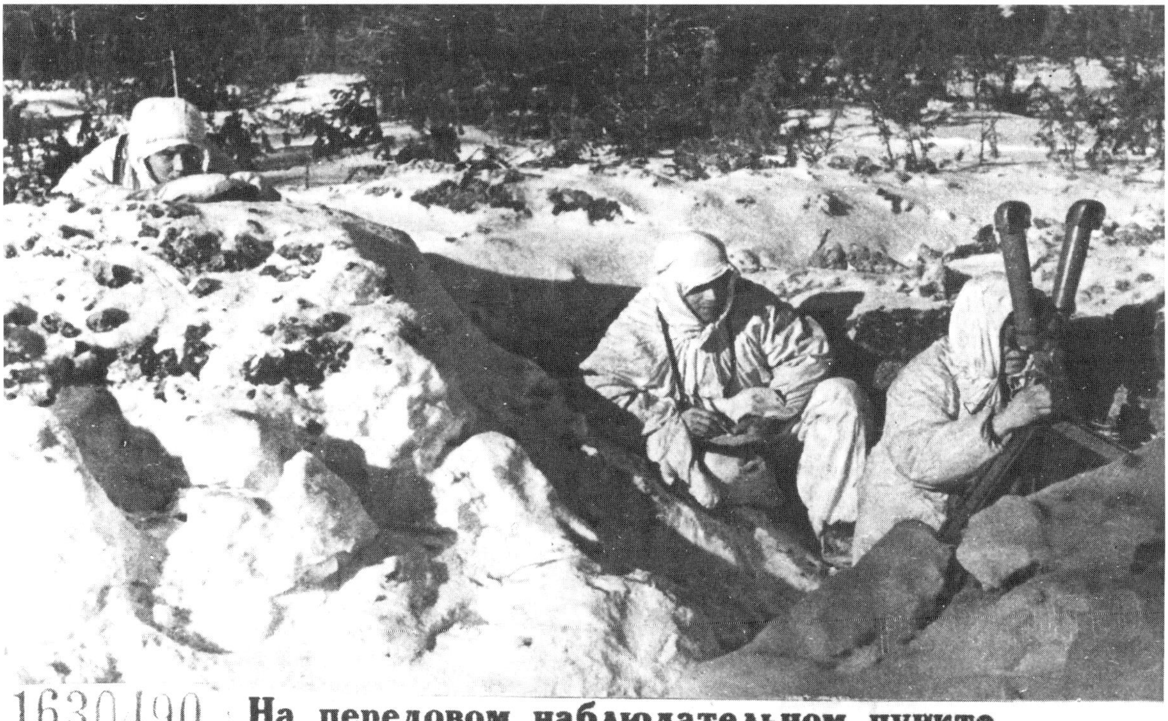

1630490 **На передовом наблюдательном пункте**

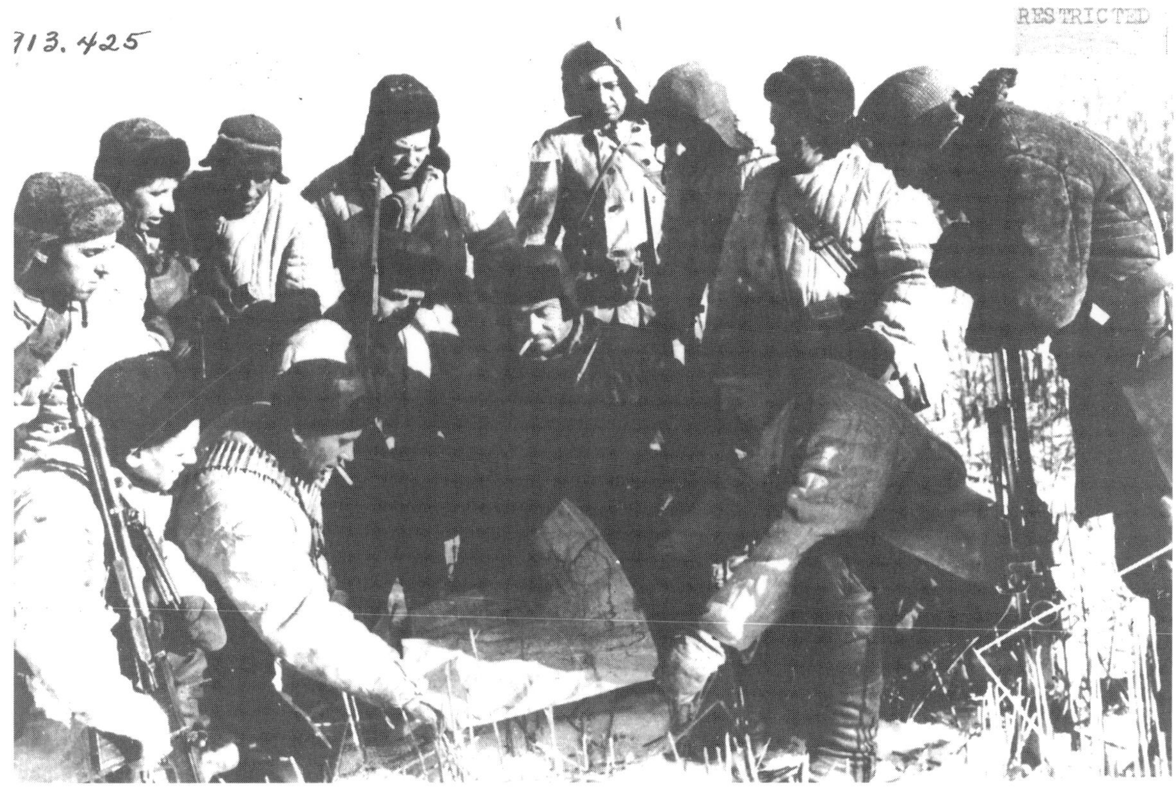
713.425
RESTRICTED

No question about these guys being Soviets. Variations in uniform and weapons cause me to suspect these are partisans, not regular Infantry.

Soviet T-60 scout tanks in a publicity shot (all waving to the camera). T-60s weighed 6.3 tons and carried a 20mm main gun in a turret left of center. They were on a par with German PzKfw IIs but no match for PzKfw IIIs or IVs.

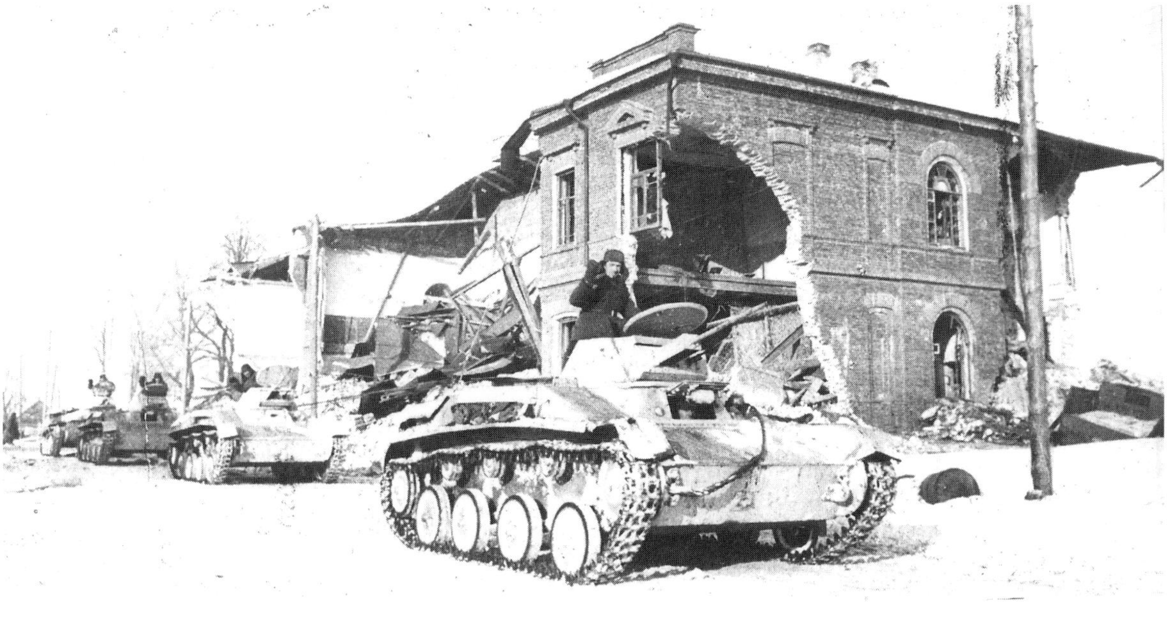

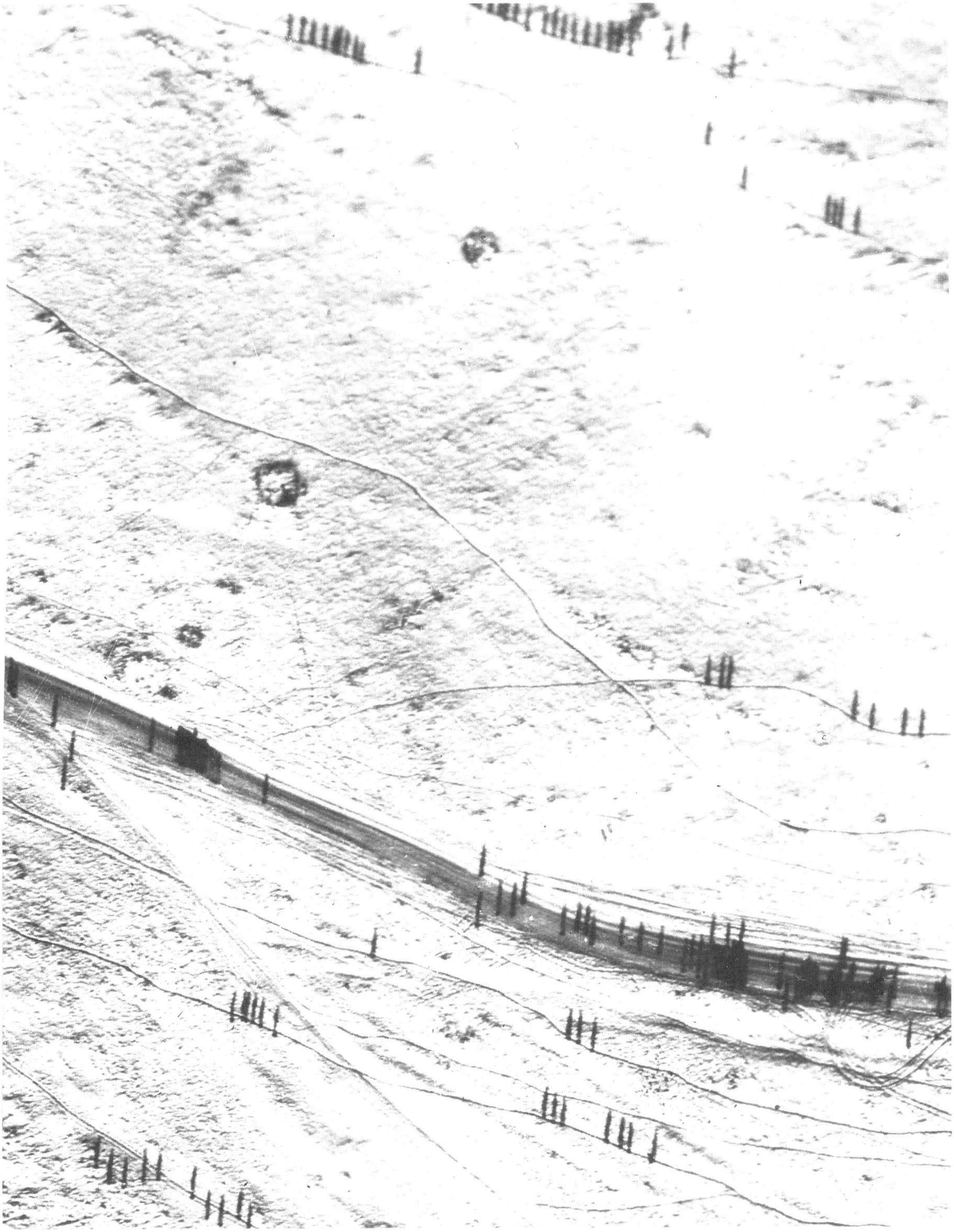

Photo interpreters rarely see people on the ground but shadows permitted a good count on this Soviet troop movement.

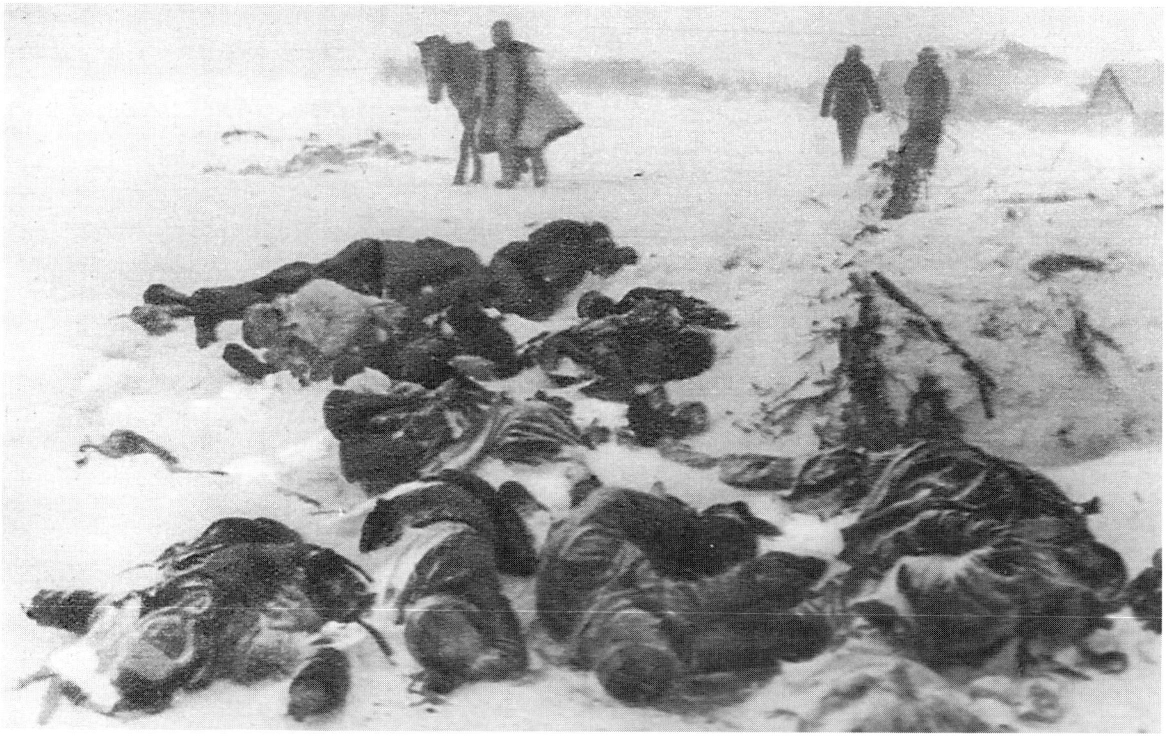

Men on both sides died of wounds or cold each night and were simply taken out of their tents or huts and left for attention later. The ground was too hard for burial.

So much for the myth of German mechanized warfare. Soldier's hands steadying their prone comrade suggest the troop is wounded. I doubt this squad started out that morning with the horse and cart.

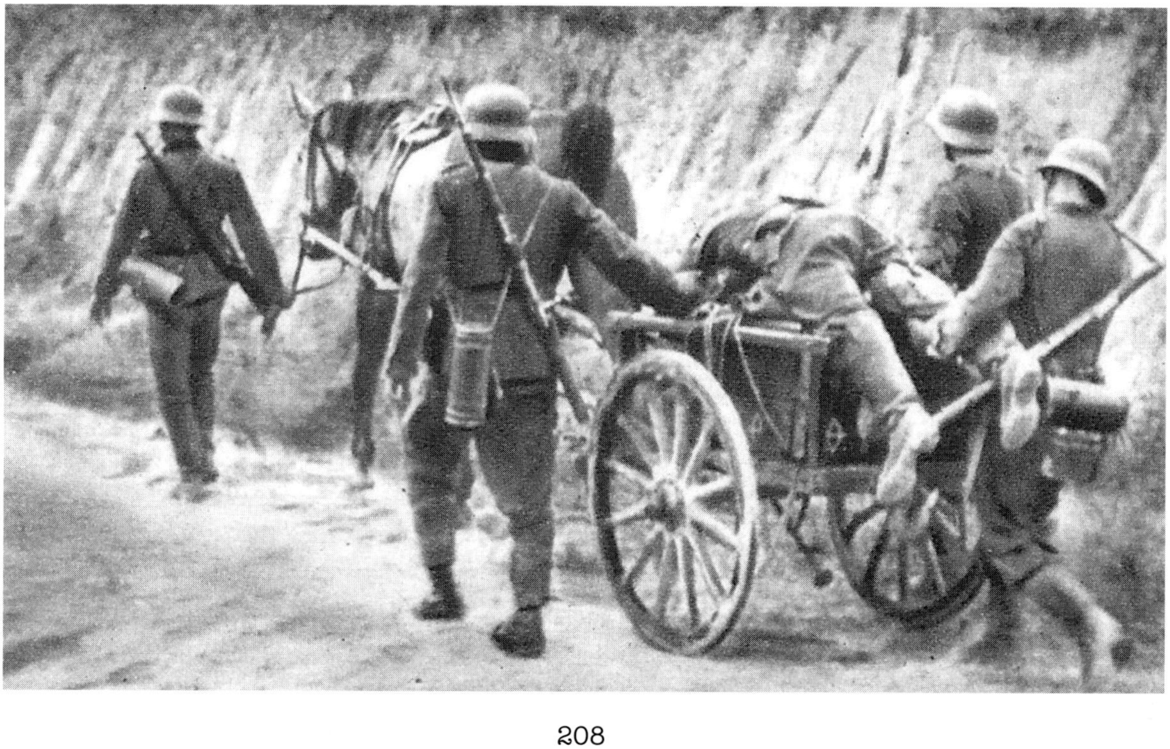

More horses probably commandeered to move supplies in the snow. I think these are Germans but they are using traditional Russian sleighs, yokes and harness.

This photo and post-war explanation deal with a unique 'Pange' breed of horse found in Russia.

Xb6/b6

Sychevka

Troika, a sleigh, drawn by 3 horses of the "Panje" type, which adapt themselves well in that part of the country. They are very sturdy and ꭓꭓꭓꭓꭓꭓꭓꭓꭓꭓꭓ undemanding animals, and can withstand the cold over 30 centigrade in the open, when protected from wind. Load capacity of a "Panje" sleigh with 2 horses is: circa 3-500 kilograms ꭓꭓꭓꭓ 2-4 "Panje" sleighs can be substituted for a German military field carriage. For this reason the "Panje" sleighs were more maneuverable than a German field carriage on impassable roads. The "Panje" horses also served well as pack animals.

Ssytschewka

gespannt mit 3 Panjepferden, den dem Lande angep

den.leichter Schlag, aber ungemein genügsam u.

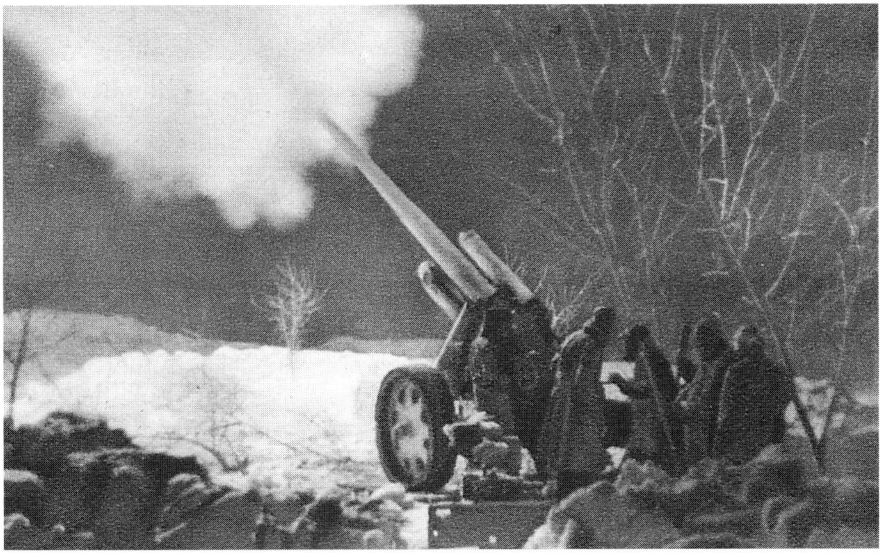

Left, German 15cm Kanone 18 firing at long range, winter 1941-42.

Right, Steppes in winter. SdKfz 142 Sturmgeschutz III (75mm self-propelled artillery) on the Donez Front., 1942.

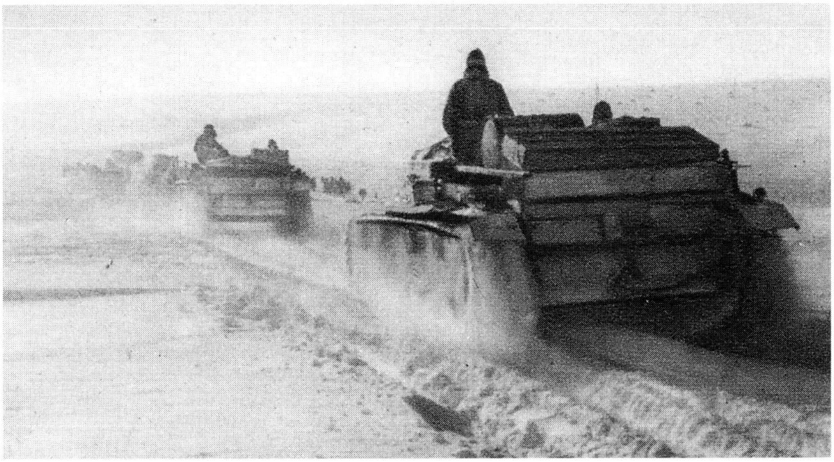

Below, Soviet spotter and sniper with a PTRD-41 anti-tank rifle. The 14.5mm round could penetrate side armor on PzKfw IVs and older AFVs. A shell exploding in the background means this photo may be from real combat.

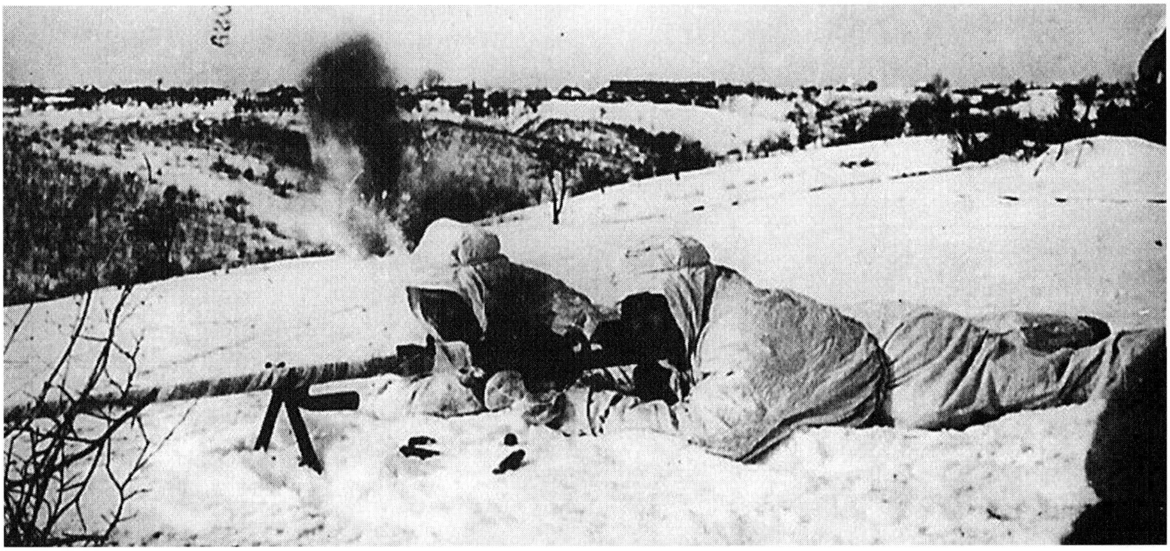

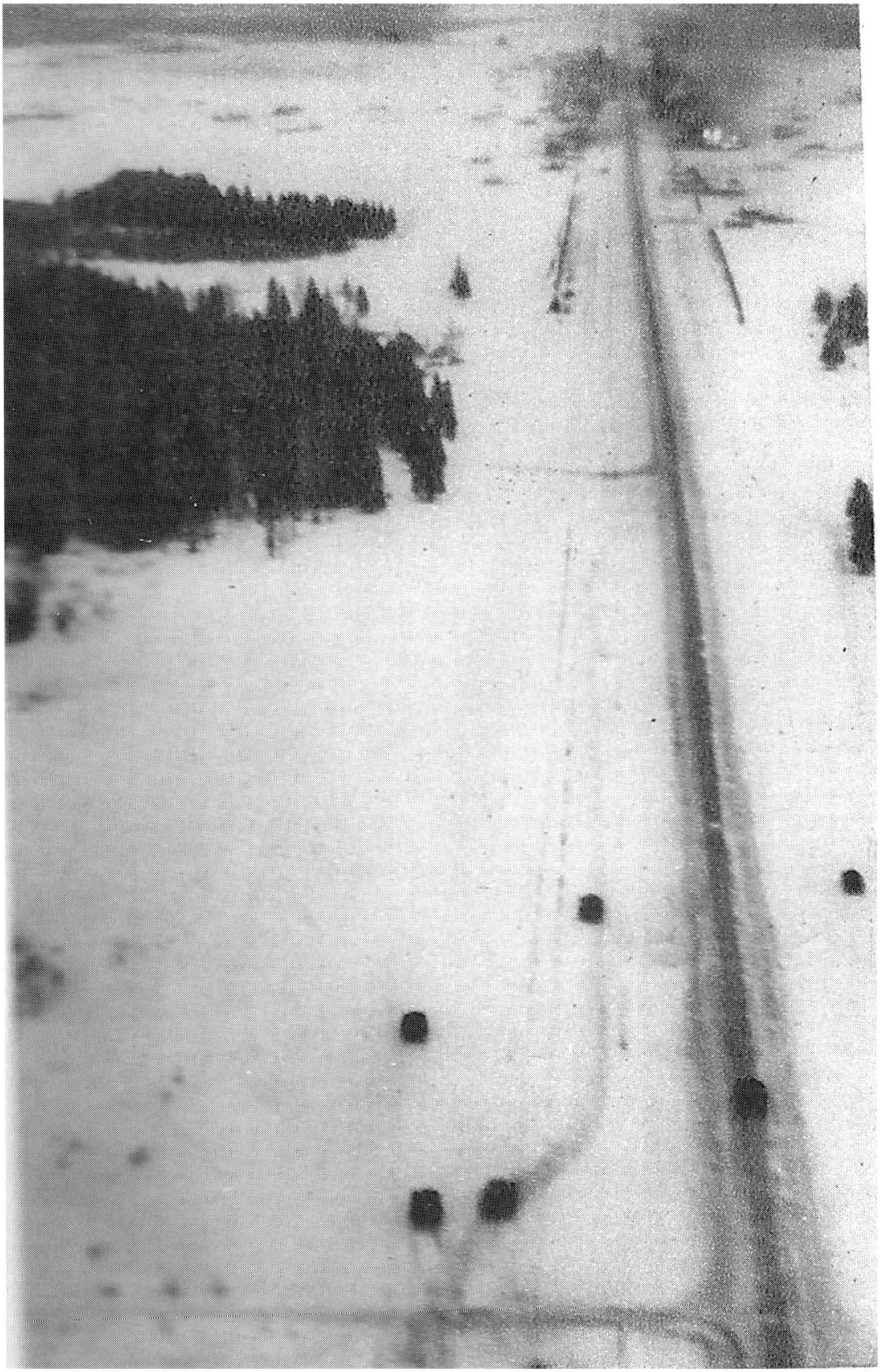

A burning village and Panzers on the road to Moscow, 1942.

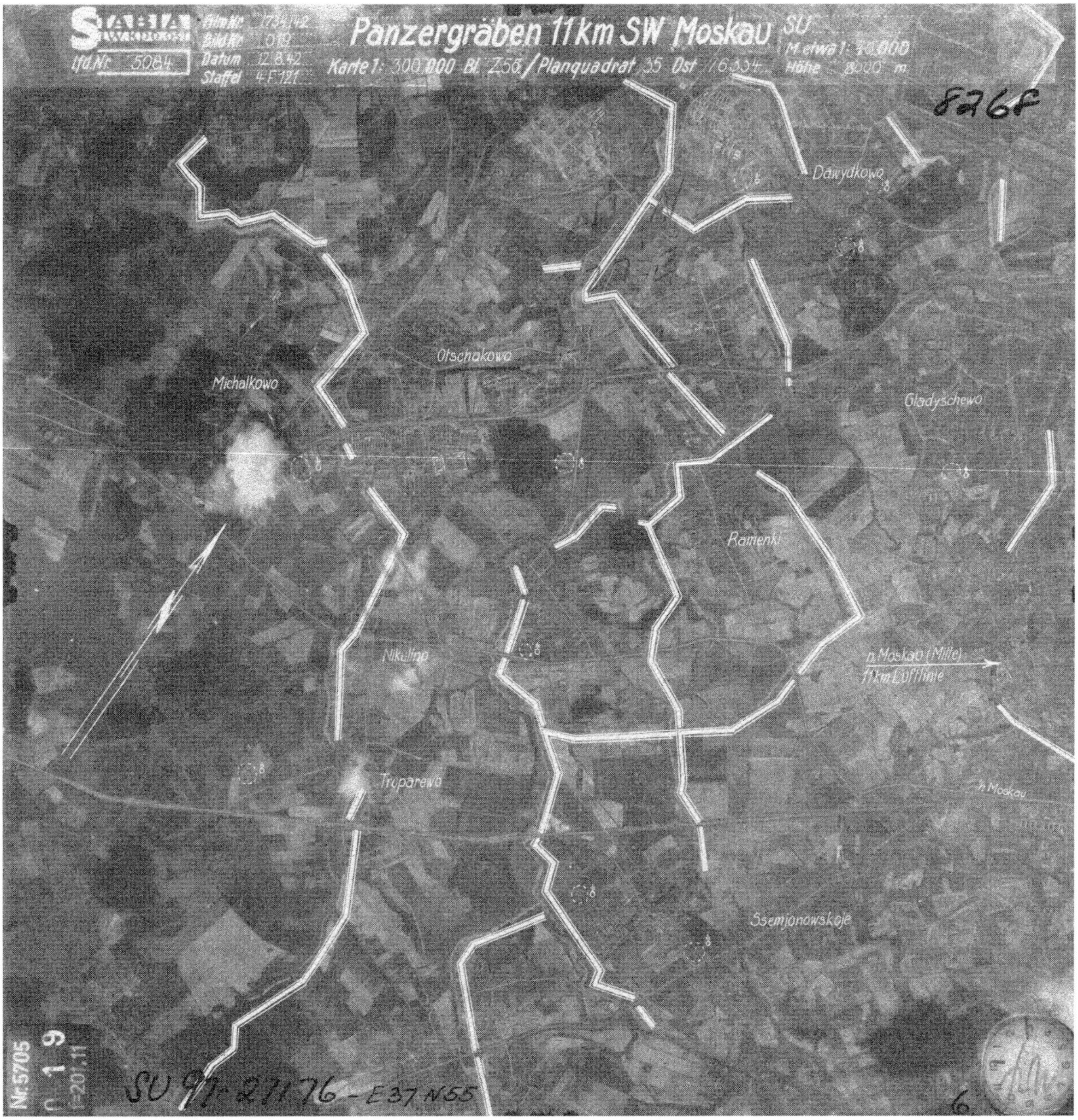
Panzergräben 11km SW Moskau
Otschakowo
Michalkowo
Dawydkowo
Gladyschewo
Ramenki
Nikulino
Troparewo
Ssemjonowskoje
n. Moskau (Mitte)
11km Luftlinie
n. Moskau

German photo interpreters marked these Soviet anti-tank ditches 6.8 miles southwest of Moscow, 12 August 1942.

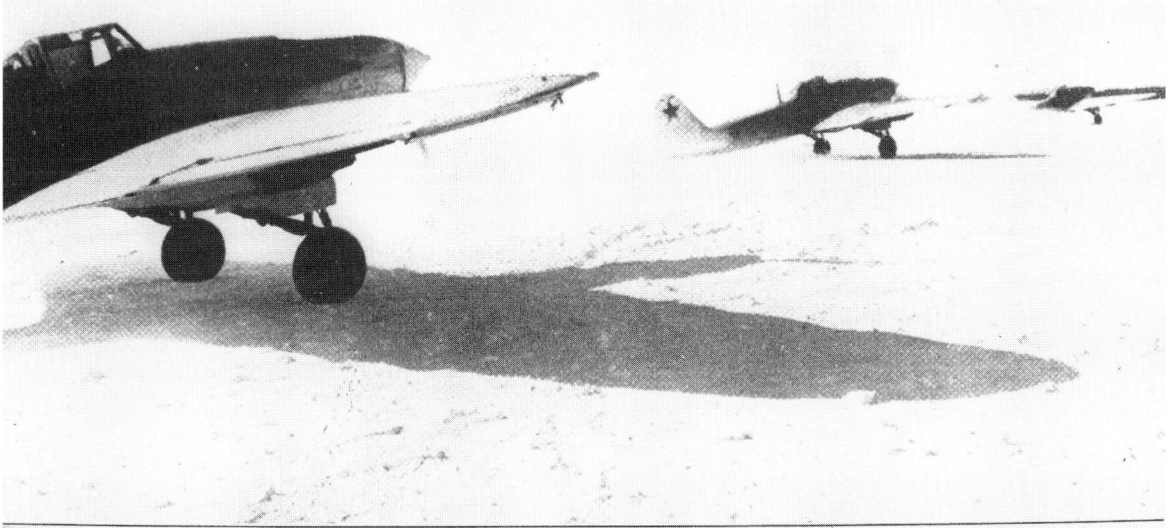

923.966 FRONTISPIECE 2. IL-2 Ground-Attack Aircraft fitted with Rocket Bombs leaving a Russian Airfield.

Rugged, reliable IL-2 Sturmoviks (the name means ground attack aircraft) had two or three cannon and two machine guns. Armor protecting motor and crew made the plane particularly effective in low altitude (150-200') wave attacks that happened so fast defenders seldom saw them coming and had few ways to stop them.

A 250kg bomb loading on a Tupolev SB-2. Introduced in 1935, the plane was a star in Spain but obsolete by 1942. Note absence of a wheel on the strut at right—this plane is on skis.

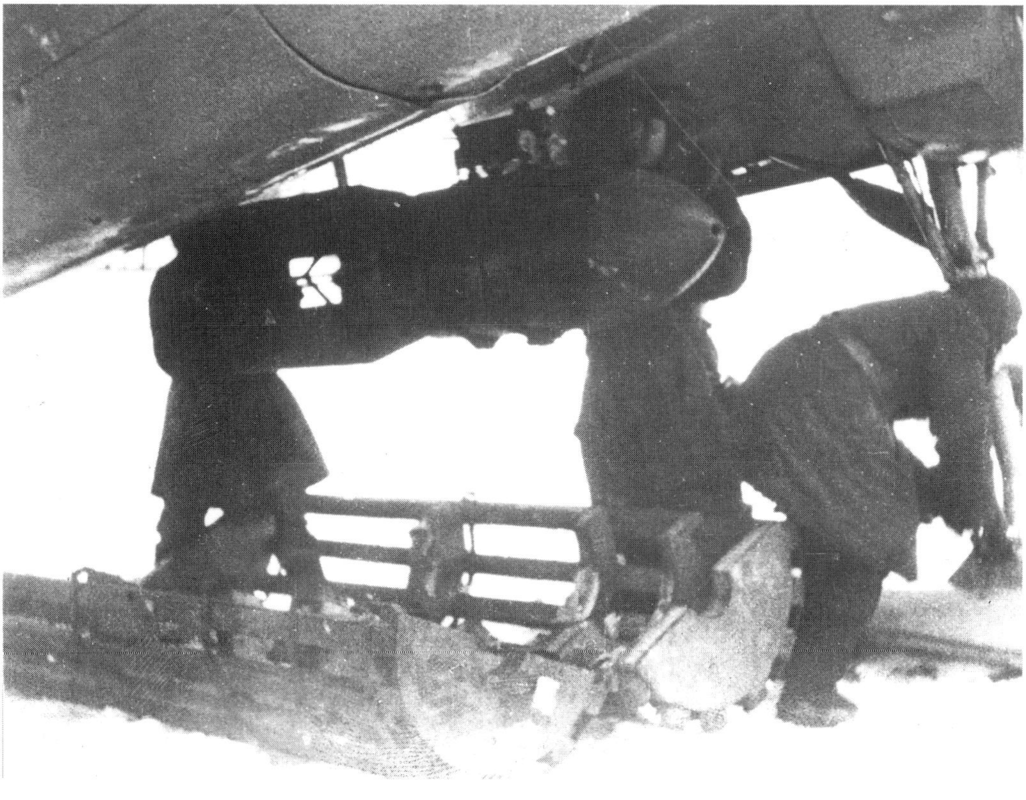

A Soviet crew recovering usable parts from a crashed Tupolev SB-2. Date and location unknown.

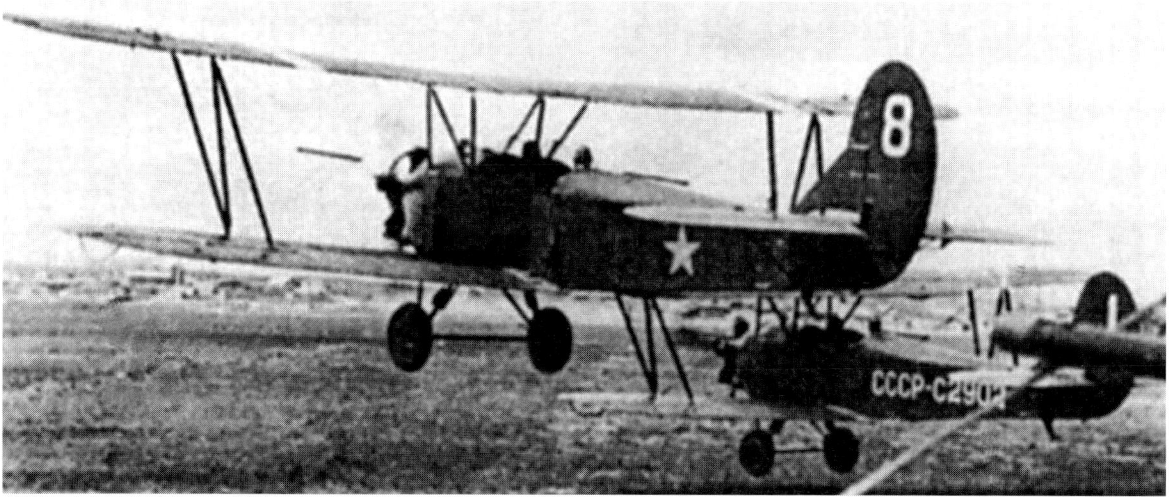
8

Necessity forced the Soviets to use anything possible to push back against German advances. An imaginative initiative was creation of three squadrons of females. The 588th was a Night Bomber unit with all female pilots, navigators and mechanics flying 1928 vintage Polikarpov Po-2 bi-planes. The plane was originally intended for pilot training and crop-dusting, so there were a lot of them available in the Soviet Union.

Carrying six 50kg bombs, they would throttle back and silently glide over German lines, attacking to harass and deny sleep. All that was heard from the ground was wind whistling in their guy-wires and struts, earning them the name 'Nachthexen' (Night Witches). Night bombing with small bombs did little real damage but could kill a few troops, destroy a few vehicles or stocks of stores each night.

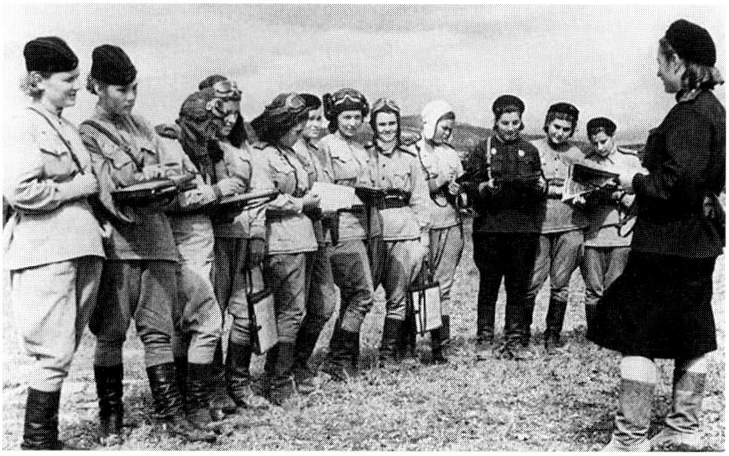

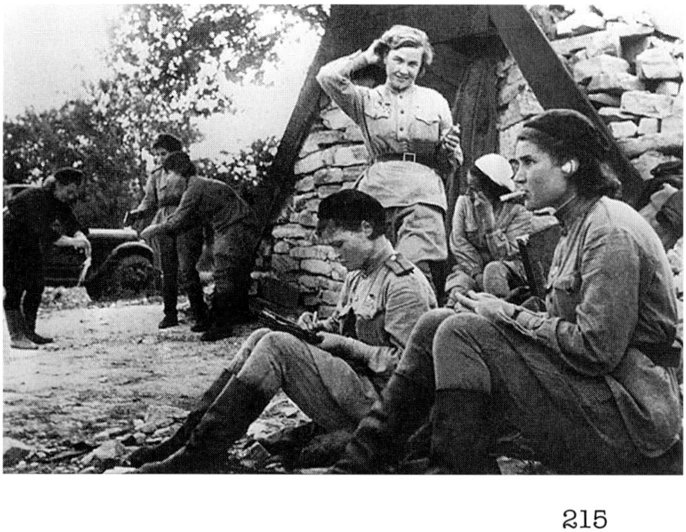

Their most important result was keeping ground troops on edge. German soldiers hated the witches. You never knew when and where they would be in the dark overhead, and you couldn't stop them.

With cruise speed slower than German fighter stall speed, they were almost impossible to bring down from the air. It was an automatic Iron Cross for a Luftwaffe pilot who could down a Night Witch. Hedge-hopping and exceptional maneuverability also made them fleeting targets for ground fire.

Among other fronts, the Hexen flew at Stalingrad, in the Crimea, Taman Peninsula and Caucasus. Operating from small, unimproved fields near the front, flights were short and multiple sorties each night were the rule. 588th Regiment ended the war with every pilot logging over 800 combat misions.

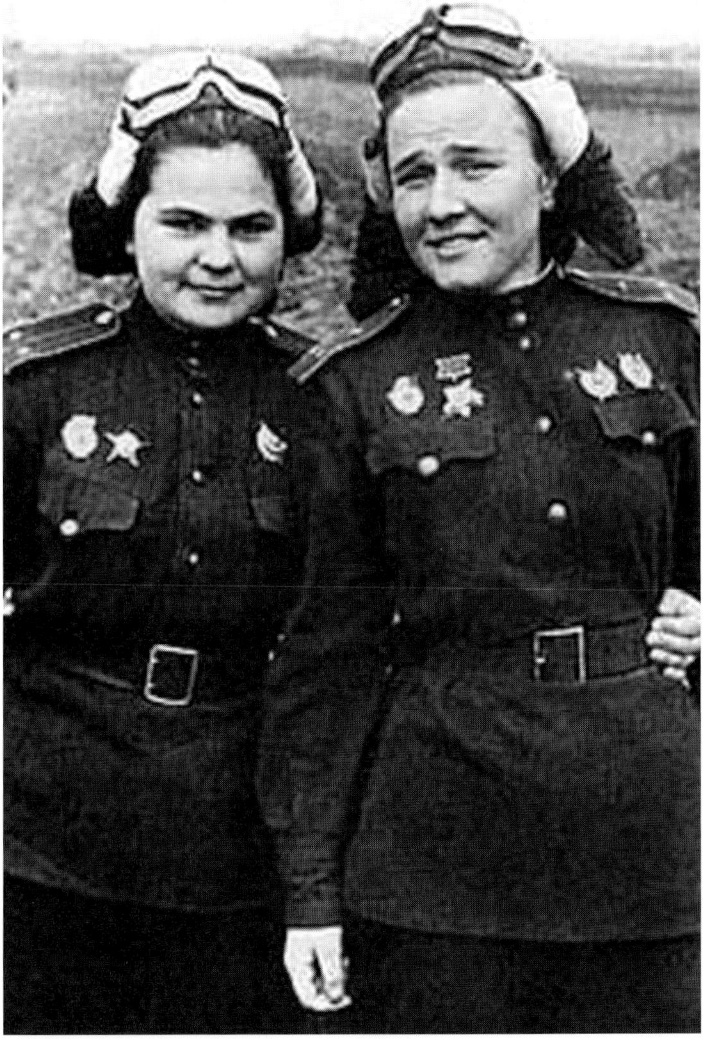

Katya Ryabova and Nadya Popova flew eighteen bombing sorties in a single night.

Below, a captured Po-2 examined by German soldiers, Ukraine, 1941.

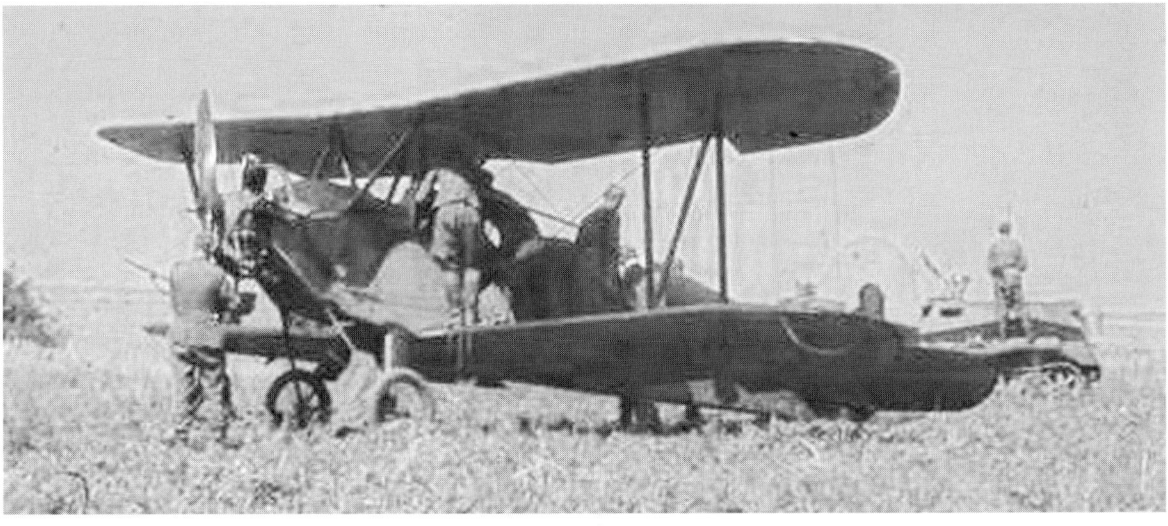

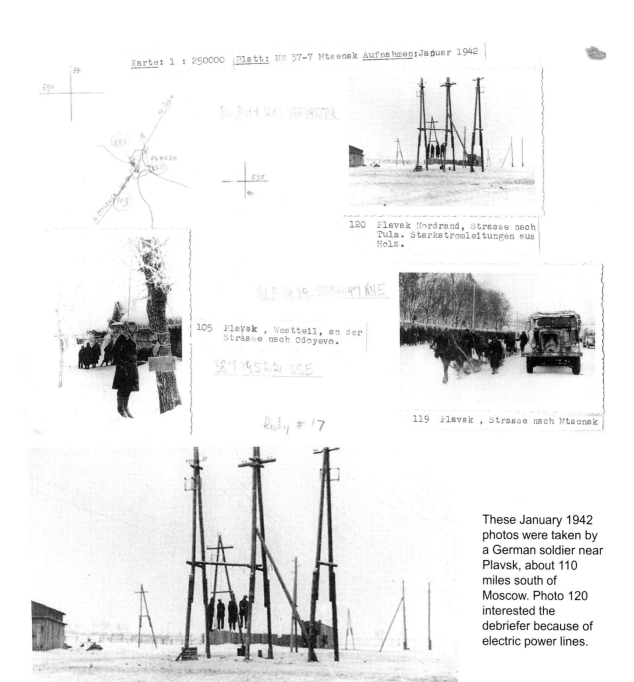

Karte: 1 : 250000 Platt: NN 37-7 Mtsensk Aufnahmen: Januar 1942

N. TULA
PLAVSK
N. MTSENSK
105
120
119
596
595

120 Plavsk Nordrand, Strasse nach Tula. Starkstromleitungen aus Holz.

105 Plavsk , Westteil, an der Strasse nach Odoyevo.

119 Plavsk , Strasse nach Mtsensk

Ruby #17

120 Plavsk Nordrand, Strasse nach Tula. Starkstromleitungen aus Holz.

These January 1942 photos were taken by a German soldier near Plavsk, about 110 miles south of Moscow. Photo 120 interested the debriefer because of electric power lines.

No comment was made on photo 105. The sign on the tree says 'Partisan' in Russian.

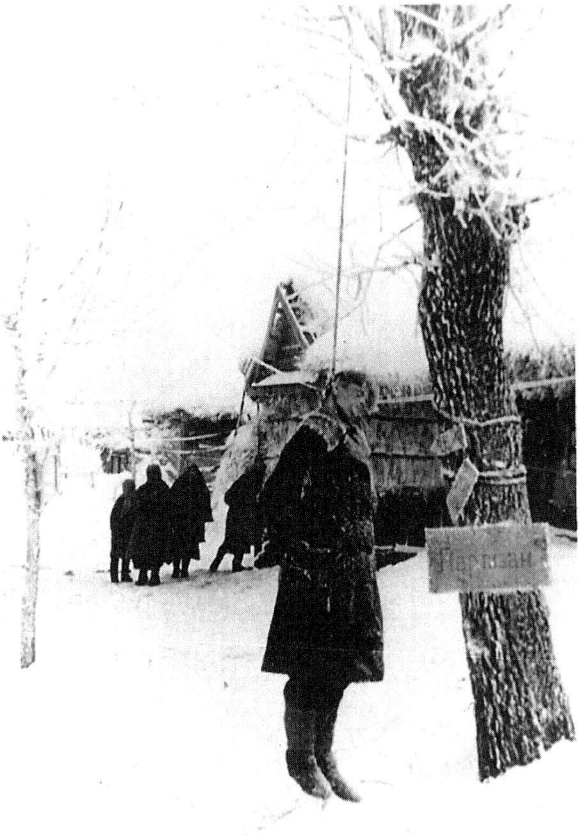
Партизан

Photo 119 is enlarged below. Three horses with traditional sled, halter and harness caught my eye. I presume those are German soldiers with the horses. Solid lines of people along the road all heading in the same direction suggest PoWs.

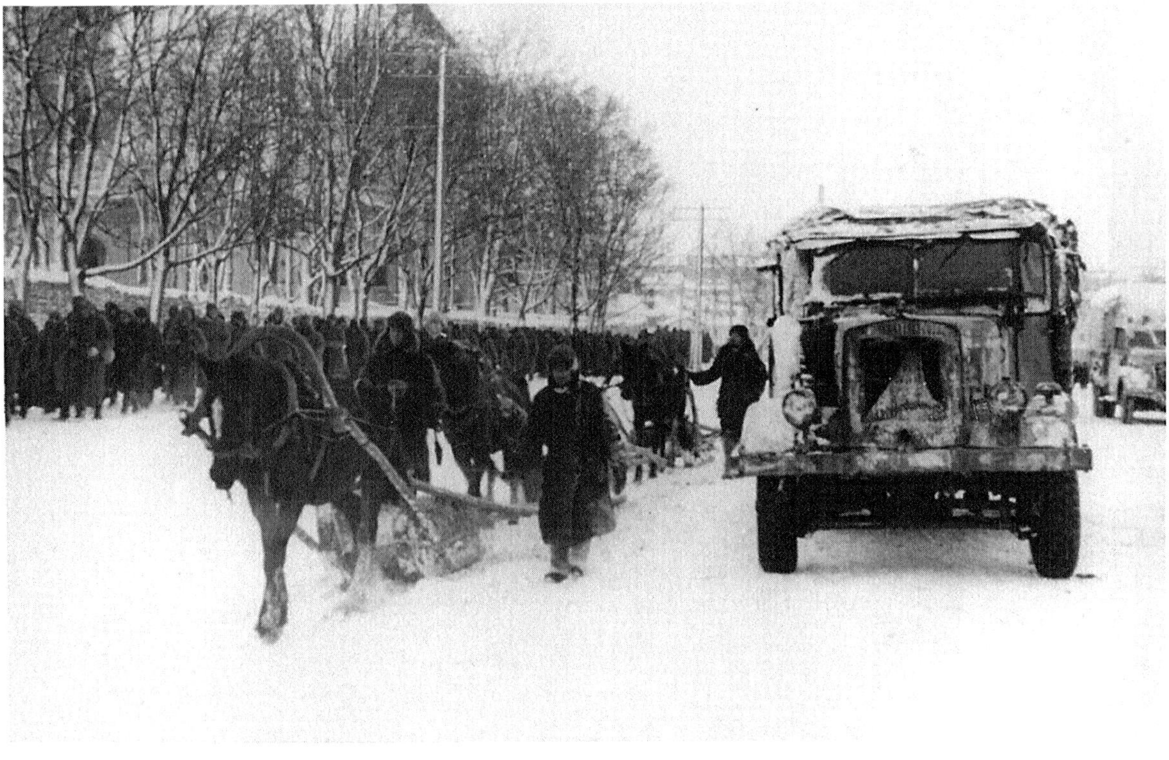

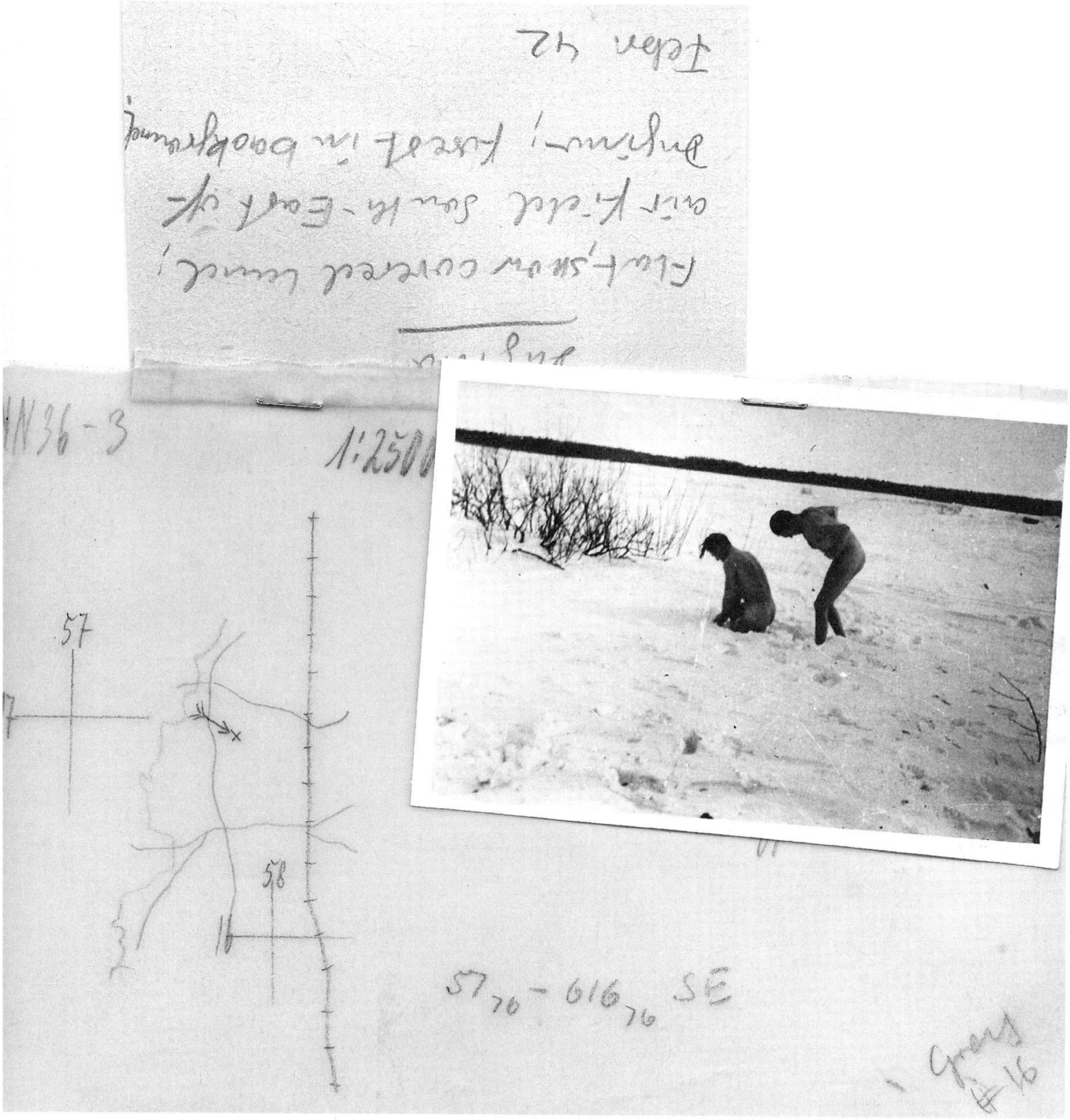
57
58

Soldiers do what they have to do. Trying to keep clean, about 40 miles north of Vyazma, February, 1942. A US Intel analyst wrote, ‘Flat, snow covered land; airfield south east of Dnjinv (hard to read, now probably Voronoye); forest in background.’

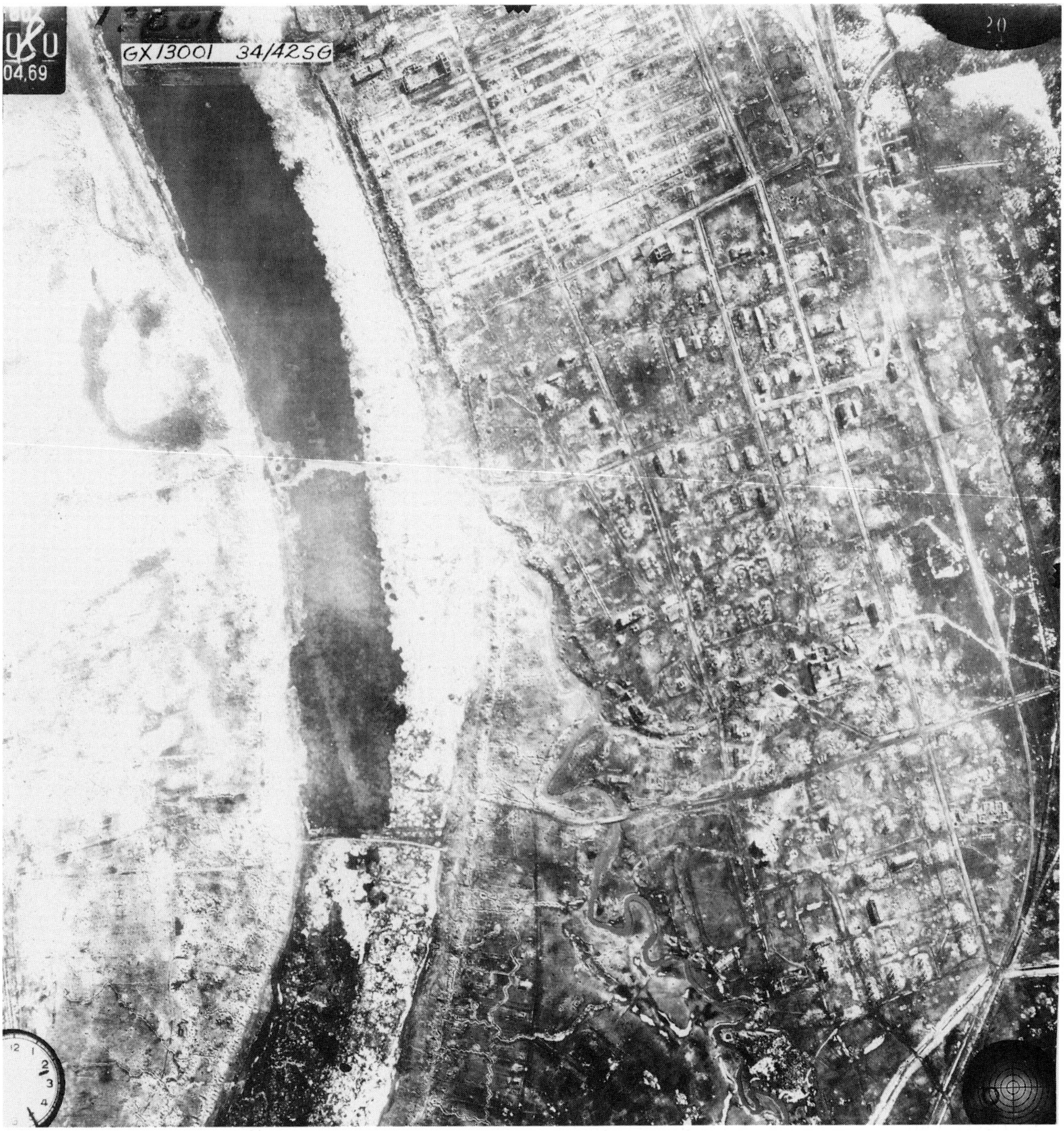
GX13001 34/42SG
04,69

Ice in the river and snow blanketing the town, winter 1941. I believe this is north of Novgorod. There is a lot of trenching along the bank (at photo bottom).

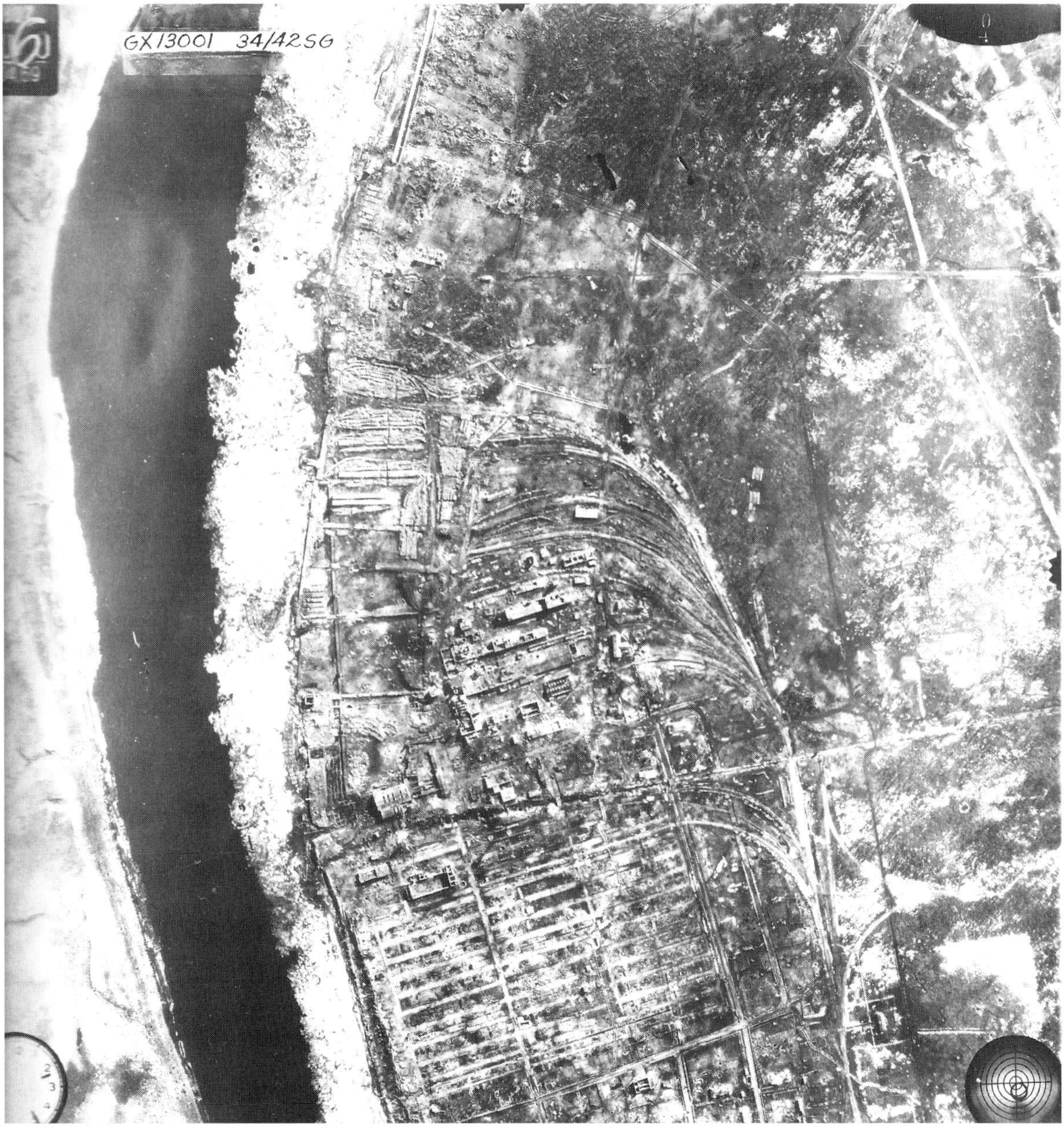
GX13001 34/42SG

The next photo north shows destroyed buildings in what was once a large factory complex. There are perhaps 200 rail cars on the numerous rail spurs curving toward the river and large piles of what is probably raw material between tracks and the river, but I can't tell what was made here. If I had to guess I'd say something to do with food processing. At upper right we see a bit of a classic Soviet fighter base design—single runway with a taxiway swinging wide to connect the ends (see a complete one in Chapter VII). I don't see any activity on the airfield or in the town.

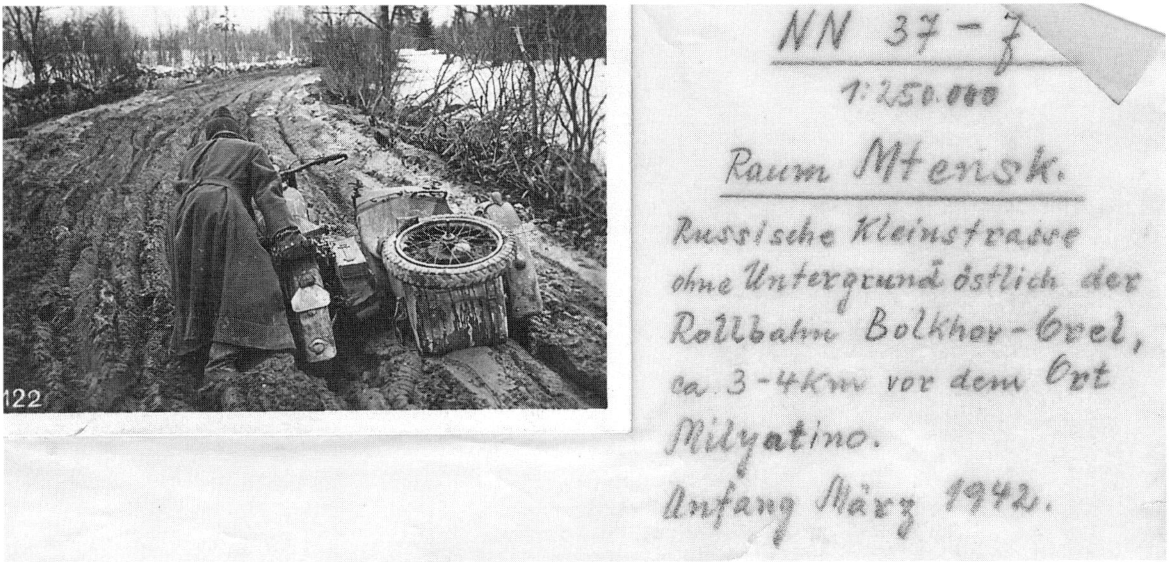
122
NN 37-7
1:250.000
Raum Mtensk.
Russische Kleinstrasse
ohne Untergrund östlich der
Rollbahn Bolkhov-Orel,
ca. 3-4Km vor dem Ort
Milyatino.
Anfang März 1942.

When snow and frozen ground changed to spring, General Mud ruled battle. This is a secondary road near Mtensk, 20 miles NNE of Oryol, March 1942.

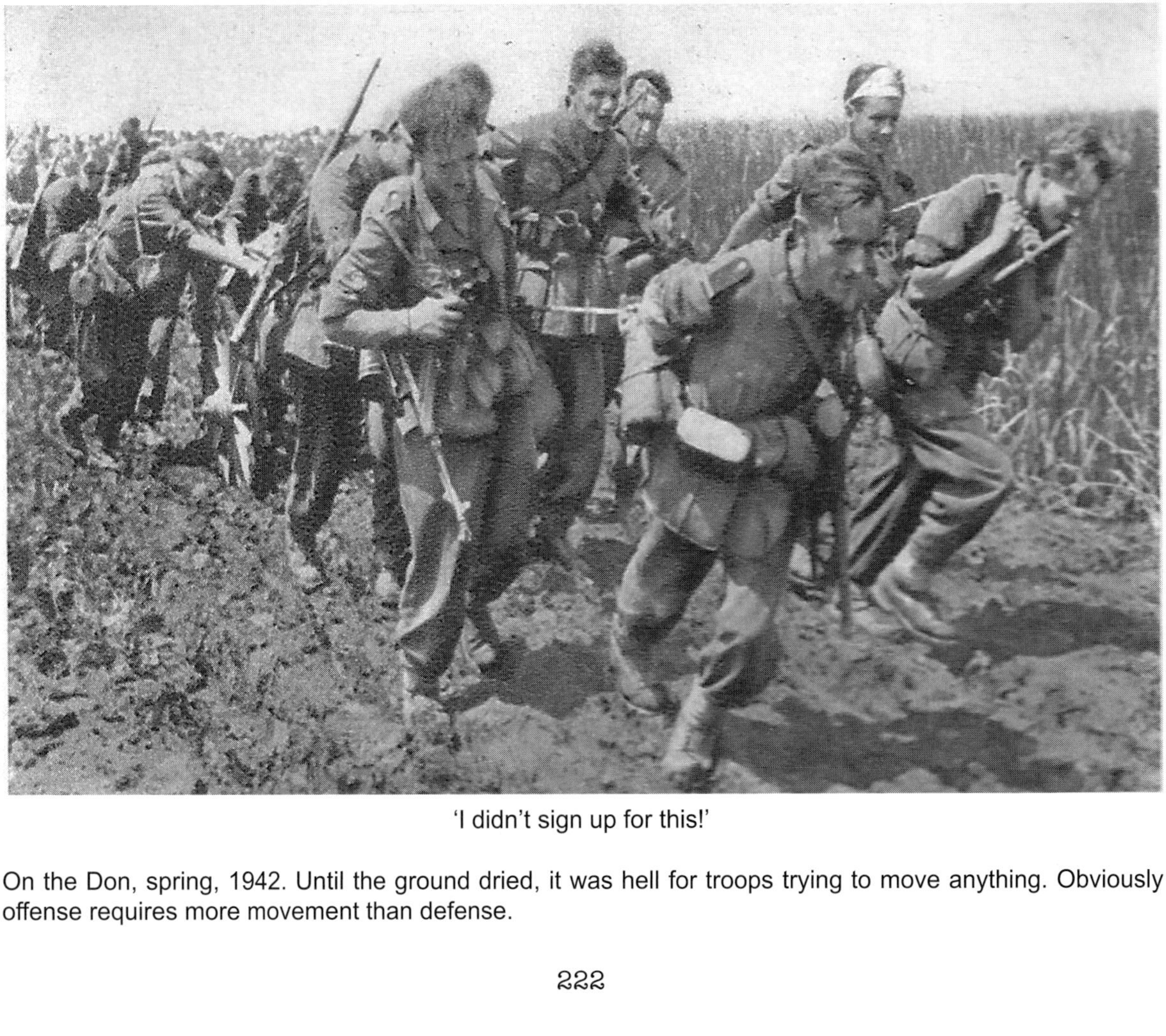

'I didn't sign up for this!'

On the Don, spring, 1942. Until the ground dried, it was hell for troops trying to move anything. Obviously offense requires more movement than defense.

Juli 1942

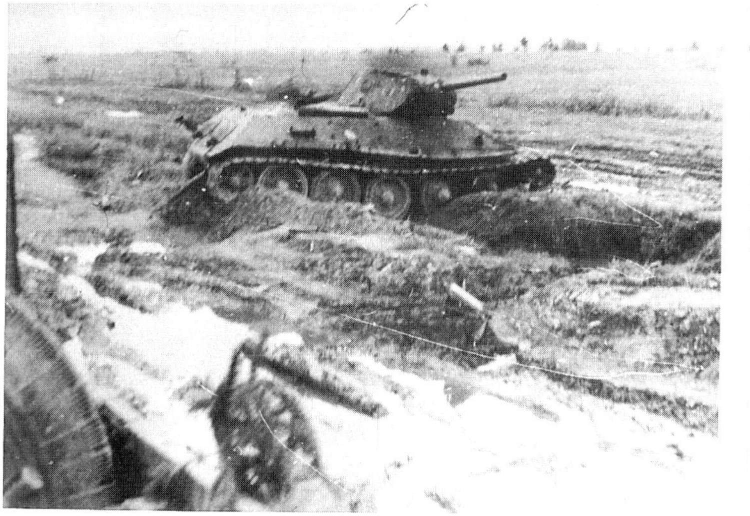

Gelände westl. von Ort Yasil'yershchina

NO 36-7

Even wide tracks of the much vaunted Soviet T-34 medium tank could succumb to 'The General'. A German soldier in a passing truck photographed this bogged tank east of Oryel (Orel), July 1942.

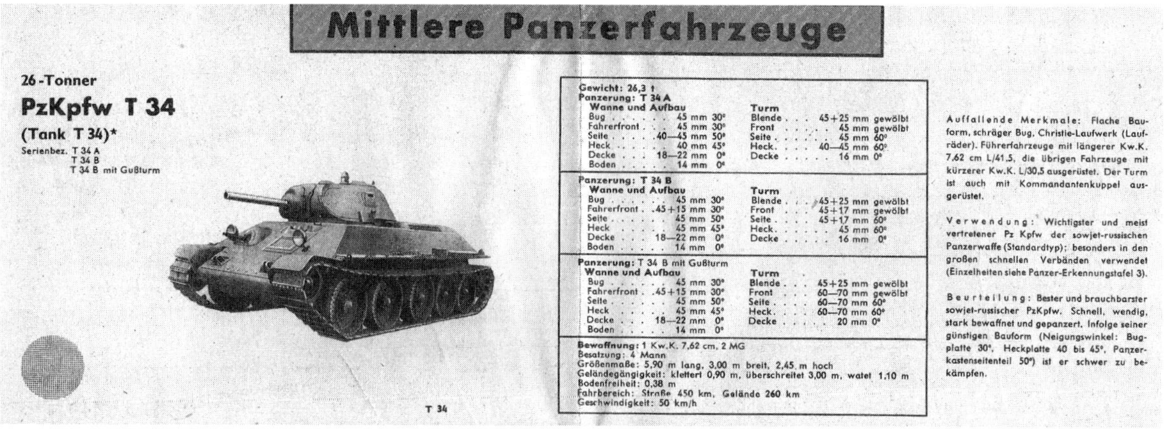

Mittlere Panzerfahrzeuge

26-Tonner

PzKpfw T 34

(Tank T 34)*

Serienbez. T 34 A
T 34 B
T 34 B mit Gußturm

T 34

Gewicht: 26,3 t

Panzerung: T 34 A

Wanne und Aufbau		Turm	
Bug	45 mm 30°	Blende	45+25 mm gewölbt
Fahrerfront	45 mm 30°	Front	45 mm gewölbt
Seite	40—45 mm 50°	Seite	45 mm 60°
Heck	40 mm 45°	Heck	40—45 mm 60°
Decke	18—22 mm 0°	Decke	16 mm 0°
Boden	14 mm 0°		

Panzerung: T 34 B

Wanne und Aufbau		Turm	
Bug	45 mm 30°	Blende	45+25 mm gewölbt
Fahrerfront	45+15 mm 30°	Front	45+17 mm gewölbt
Seite	45 mm 50°	Seite	45+17 mm 60°
Heck	45 mm 45°	Heck	45 mm 60°
Decke	18—22 mm 0°	Decke	16 mm 0°
Boden	14 mm 0°		

Panzerung: T 34 B mit Gußturm

Wanne und Aufbau		Turm	
Bug	45 mm 30°	Blende	45+25 mm gewölbt
Fahrerfront	45+15 mm 30°	Front	60—70 mm gewölbt
Seite	45 mm 50°	Seite	60—70 mm 60°
Heck	45 mm 45°	Heck	60—70 mm 60°
Decke	18—22 mm 0°	Decke	20 mm 0°
Boden	14 mm 0°		

Bewaffnung: 1 Kw.K. 7,62 cm, 2 MG
Besatzung: 4 Mann
Größenmaße: 5,90 m lang, 3,00 m breit, 2,45 m hoch
Geländegängigkeit: klettert 0,90 m, überschreitet 3,00 m, watet 1,10 m
Bodenfreiheit: 0,38 m
Fahrbereich: Straße 450 km, Gelände 260 km
Geschwindigkeit: 50 km/h

Auffallende Merkmale: Flache Bauform, schräger Bug, Christie-Laufwerk (Laufräder). Führerfahrzeuge mit längerer Kw.K. 7,62 cm L/41,5, die übrigen Fahrzeuge mit kürzerer Kw.K. L/30,5 ausgerüstet. Der Turm ist auch mit Kommandantenkuppel ausgerüstet.

Verwendung: Wichtigster und meist vertretener Pz Kpfw der sowjet-russischen Panzerwaffe (Standardtyp); besonders in den großen schnellen Verbänden verwendet (Einzelheiten siehe Panzer-Erkennungstafel 3).

Beurteilung: Bester und brauchbarster sowjet-russischer PzKpfw. Schnell, wendig, stark bewaffnet und gepanzert. Infolge seiner günstigen Bauform (Neigungswinkel: Bugplatte 30°, Heckplatte 40 bis 45°, Panzerkastenseitenteil 50°) ist er schwer zu bekämpfen.

By late 1942 German Intelligence knew a great deal about the T-34, maybe more than they wanted to know. Many German generals considered it the best tank of the war.

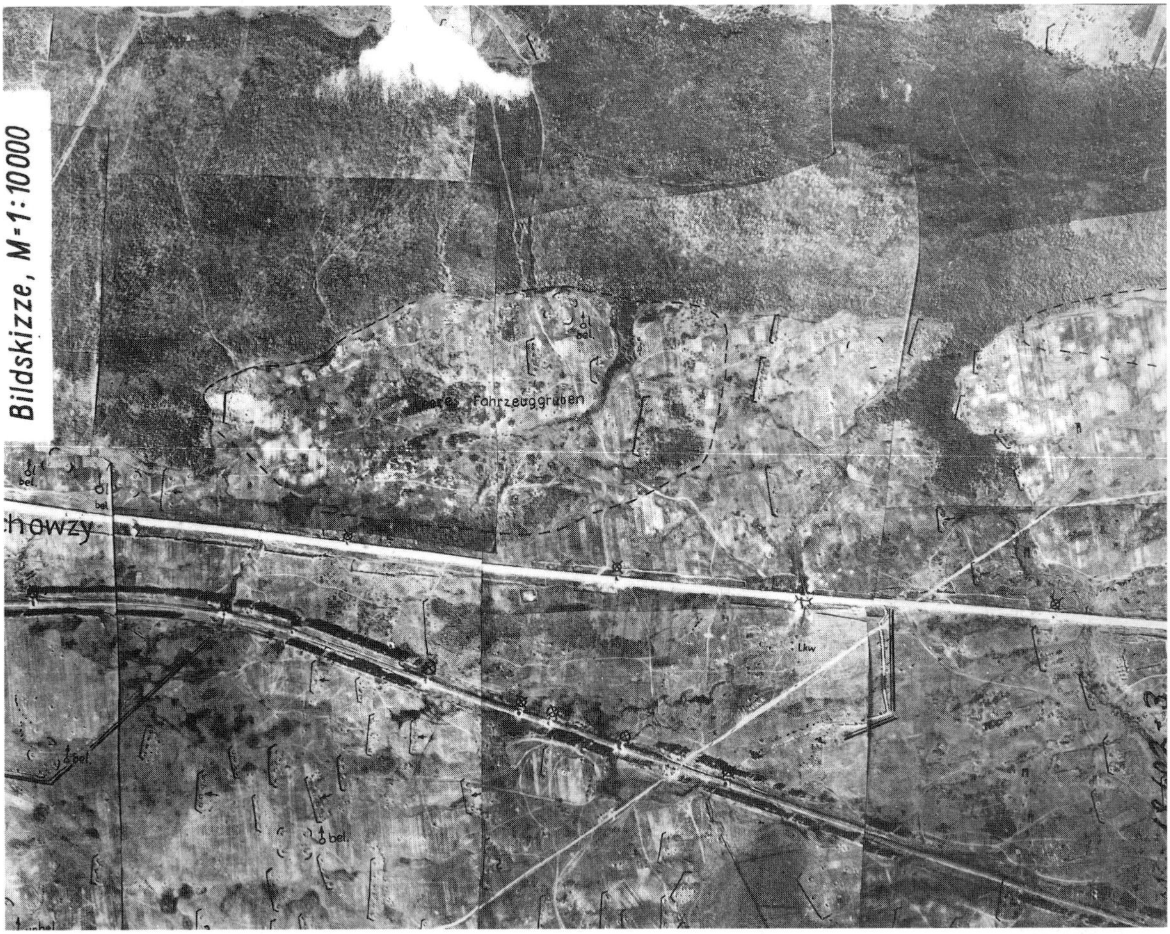
Bildskizze, M=1:10000
Fahrzeuggruben
Lkw

The Luftwaffe was so confident of air superiority it was flying mapping coverage—back and forth in a regular pattern to cover an area completely with stereo imagery. German Intelligence made this uncontrolled mosaic from a dozen different exposures to show Soviet defenses ahead of German troops.

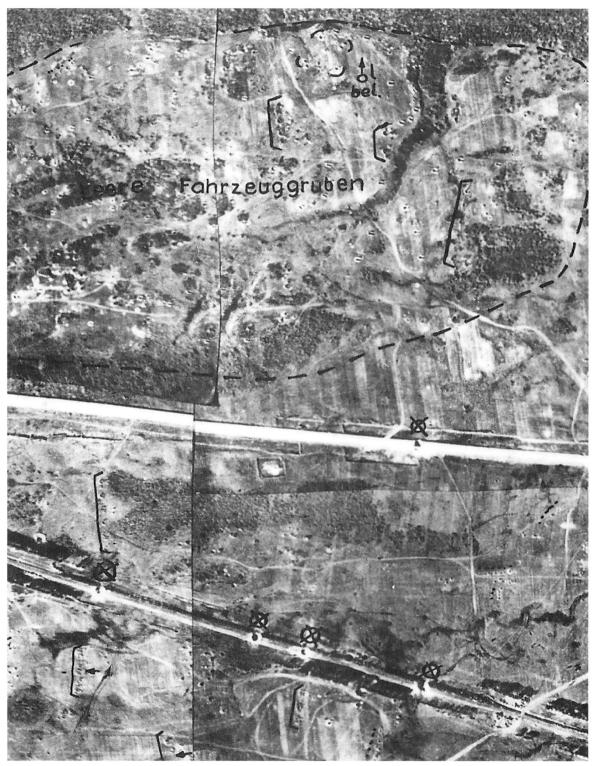

Enlargement of the previous photo shows retreating Soviet demolition on the rail line ('Xs' at bottom), unoccupied vehicle and gun positions including a four-gun light AAA position at top center.

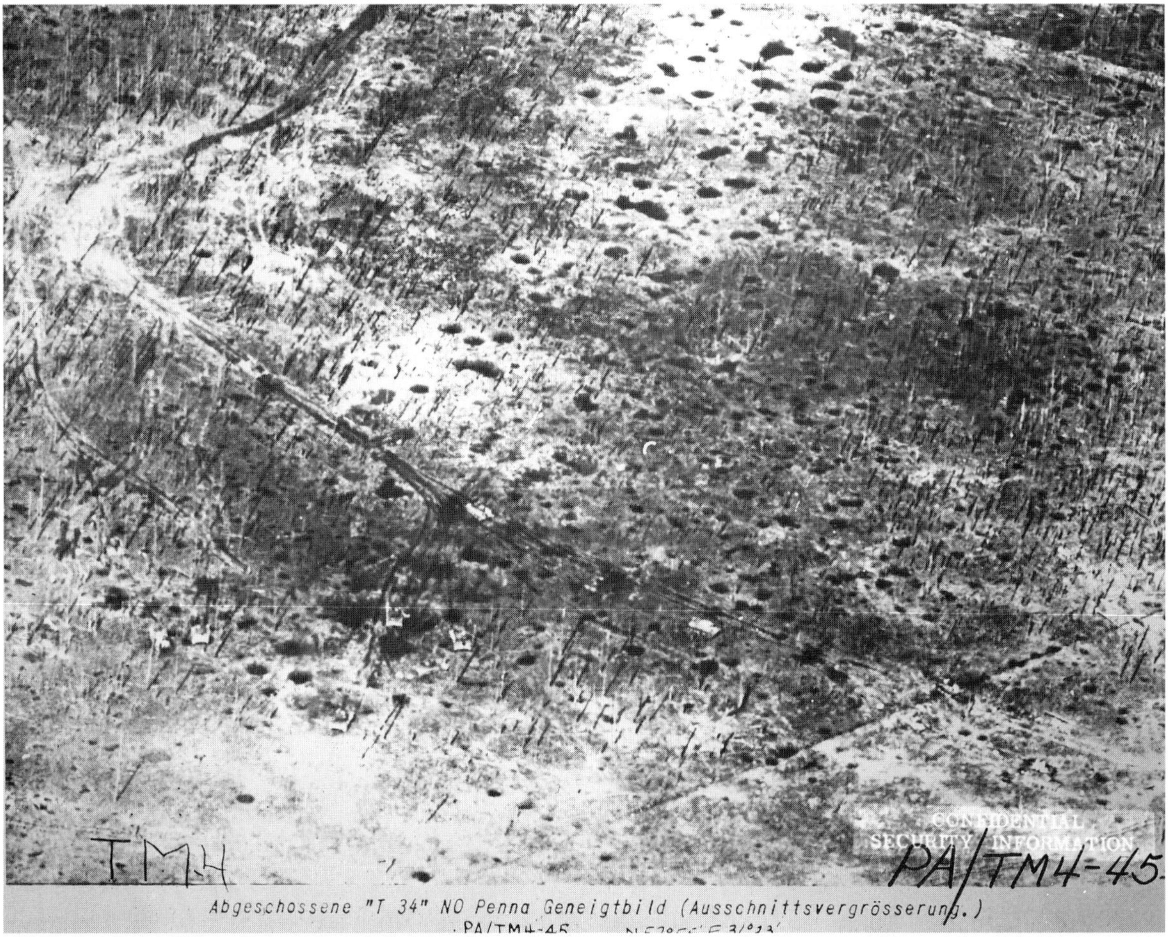
T-M-4
CONFIDENTIAL
SECURITY INFORMATION
PA/TM4-45
Abgeschossene "T 34" NO Penna Geneigtbild (Ausschnittsvergrösserung.)

Eleven T-34s maneuvering in swampy woods southeast of Staraja Russa.

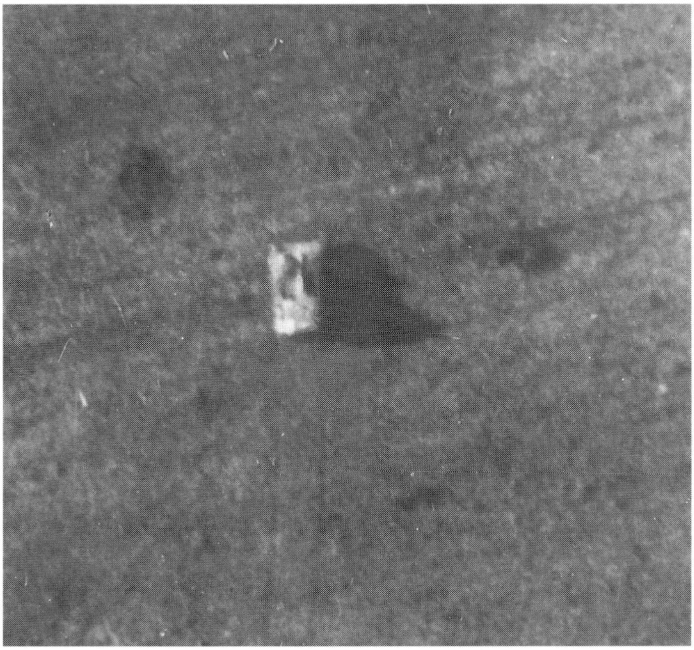

The shadow showing a high structure at the rear says this isn't a tank. It is probably a Soviet BA-20 armored car. We don't often get this good a look at that kind of equipment in the field.

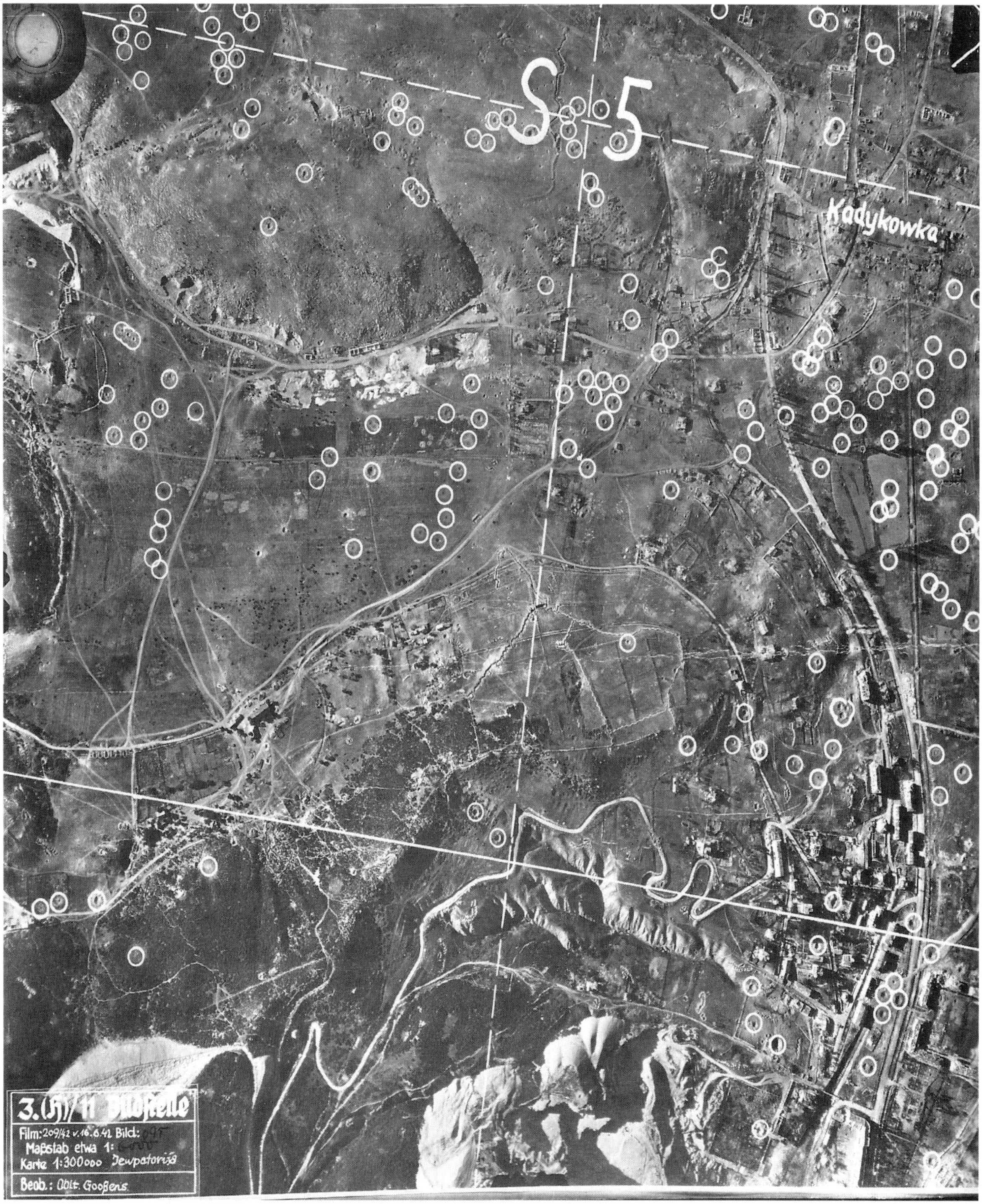
S 5
Kadykowka
3.(H)/11 Bildstelle
Film: 209/42 v.16.6.42 Bild:
Maßstab etwa 1:
Karte 1:300000 Jewpatorija
Beob.: Oblt. Goossens

Marking bomb and artillery fire craters, Kladokova, 45 miles southeast of Moscow, 16 June 1942. Gridding-off the area makes counting and referencing easier for a PI or bomber.

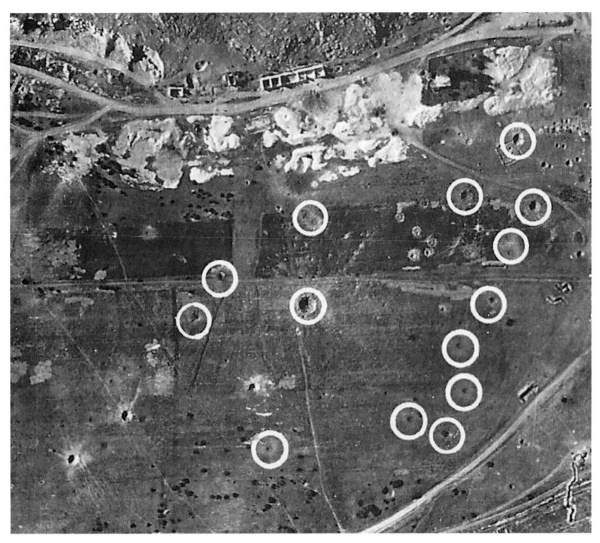

Enlargement of the 16 June 1942 imagery above. A ragged string of craters the same size (at right) probably says He 111 bombing. A lone large one (center) might be a 500kg bomb from a Ju 87. Not noting three obvious craters at lower left suggests the circles indicate damage since some previous date.

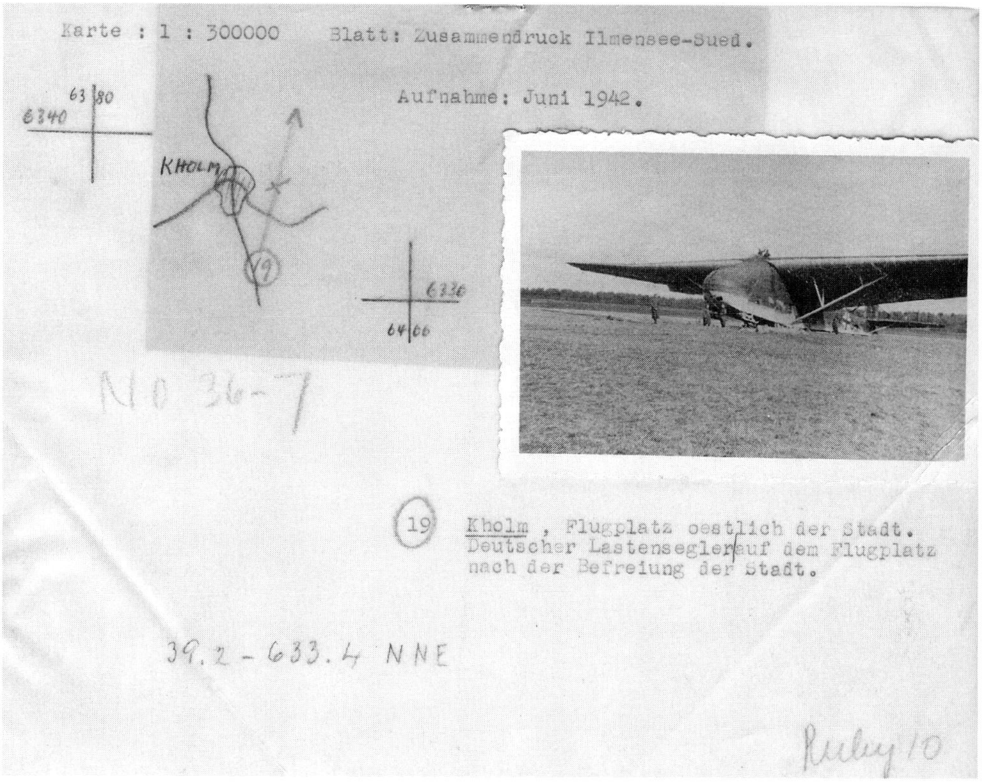
Karte : 1 : 300000 Blatt: Zusammendruck Ilmensee-Sued.

Aufnahme: Juni 1942.

63|80
6340
KHOLM
19
6330
64|06

NO 36-7

(19) Kholm , Flugplatz oestlich der Stadt. Deutscher Lastensegler auf dem Flugplatz nach der Befreiung der Stadt.

39.2 - 633.4 NNE

A huge Messerschmitt Me 321 glider used to supply German troops at Kholm, 50 miles SSW of Staraja Russa. Troops standing around suggests this landing wasn't a regular happening.

Searching for Soviet landmines, never a popular assignment.

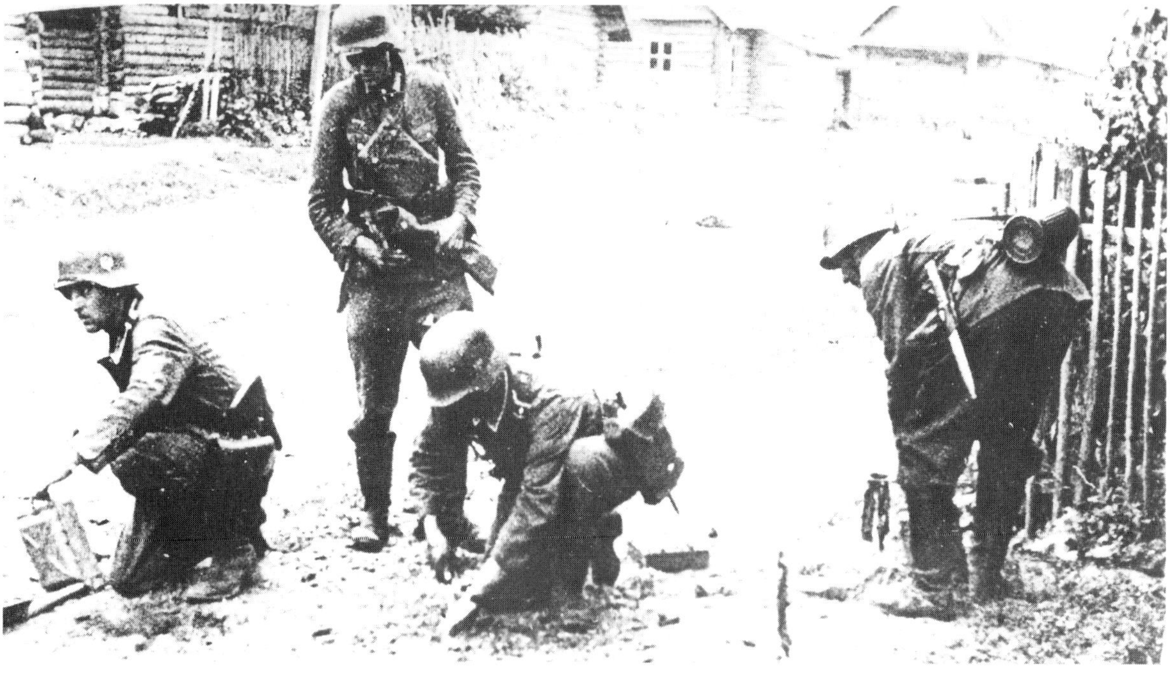

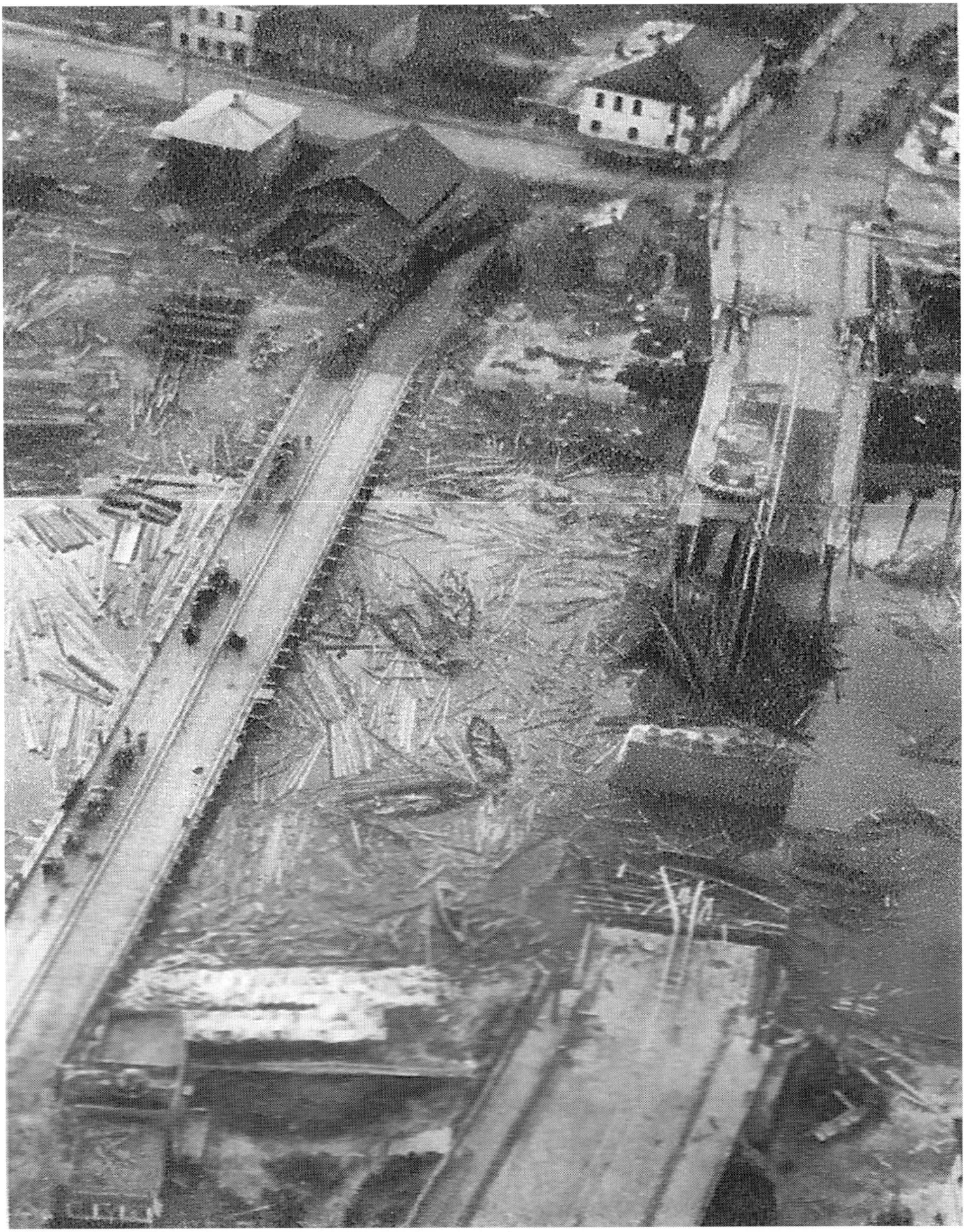

Staraja Russa, just south of Lake Ilman, the destroyed bridge was replaced by a field bridge. No vehicles are in sight but several hand and horse-drawn carts are on the bridge. Three groups of people are at the far approach and two more in town appear headed for the bridge.

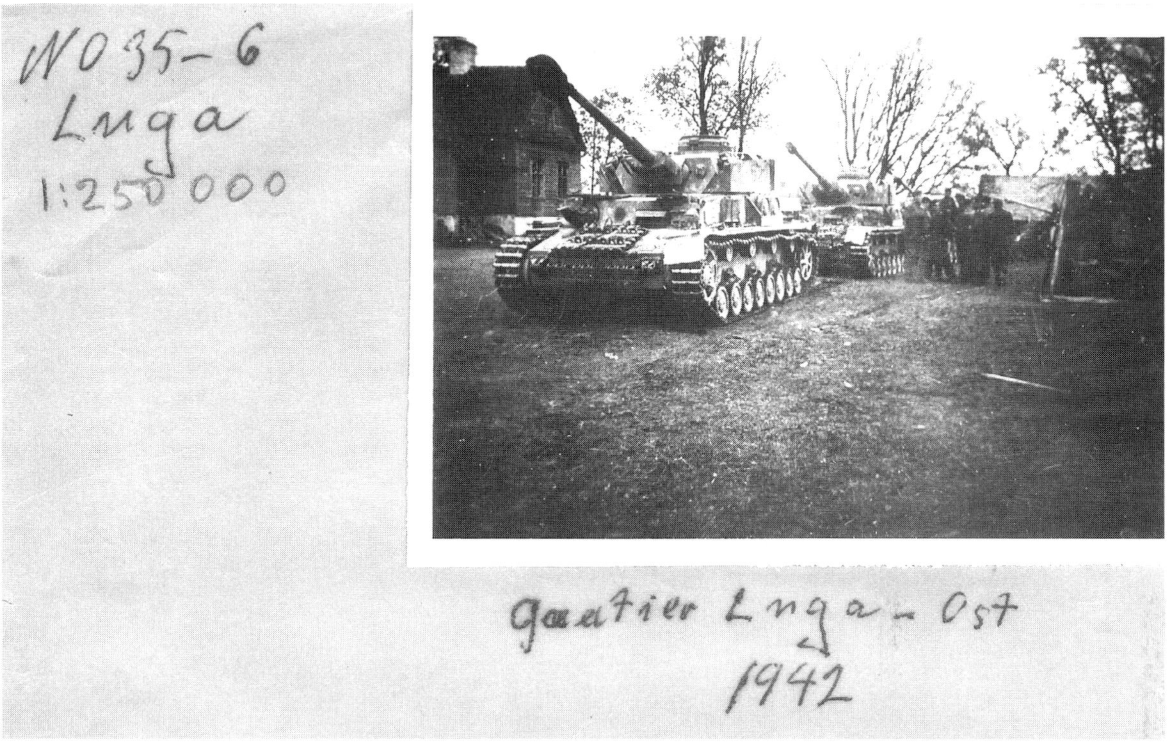
WO35-6
Luga
1:250 000
Luga - Ost
1942

Above, PzKfw IVs with new 75mm guns resting at Luga, 65 miles south of Leningrad, 1942.

Below, PzKfw IIIs at Vayzma, 130 miles WSW of Moscow, September 1942.

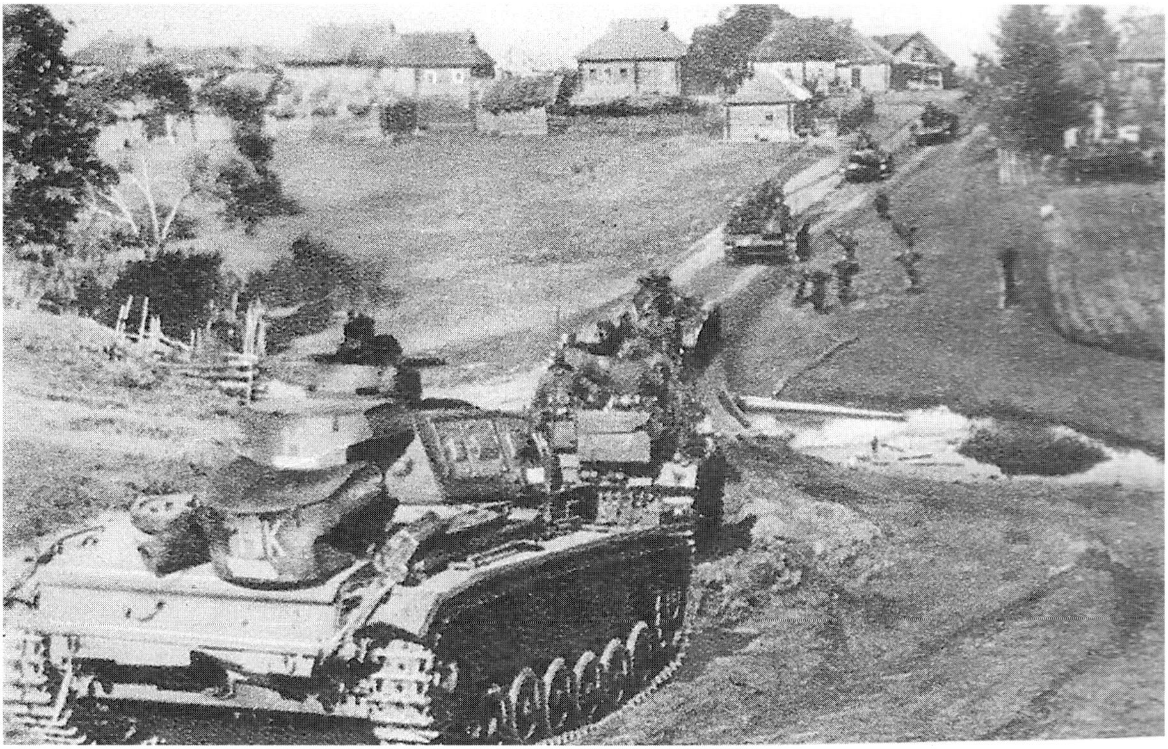

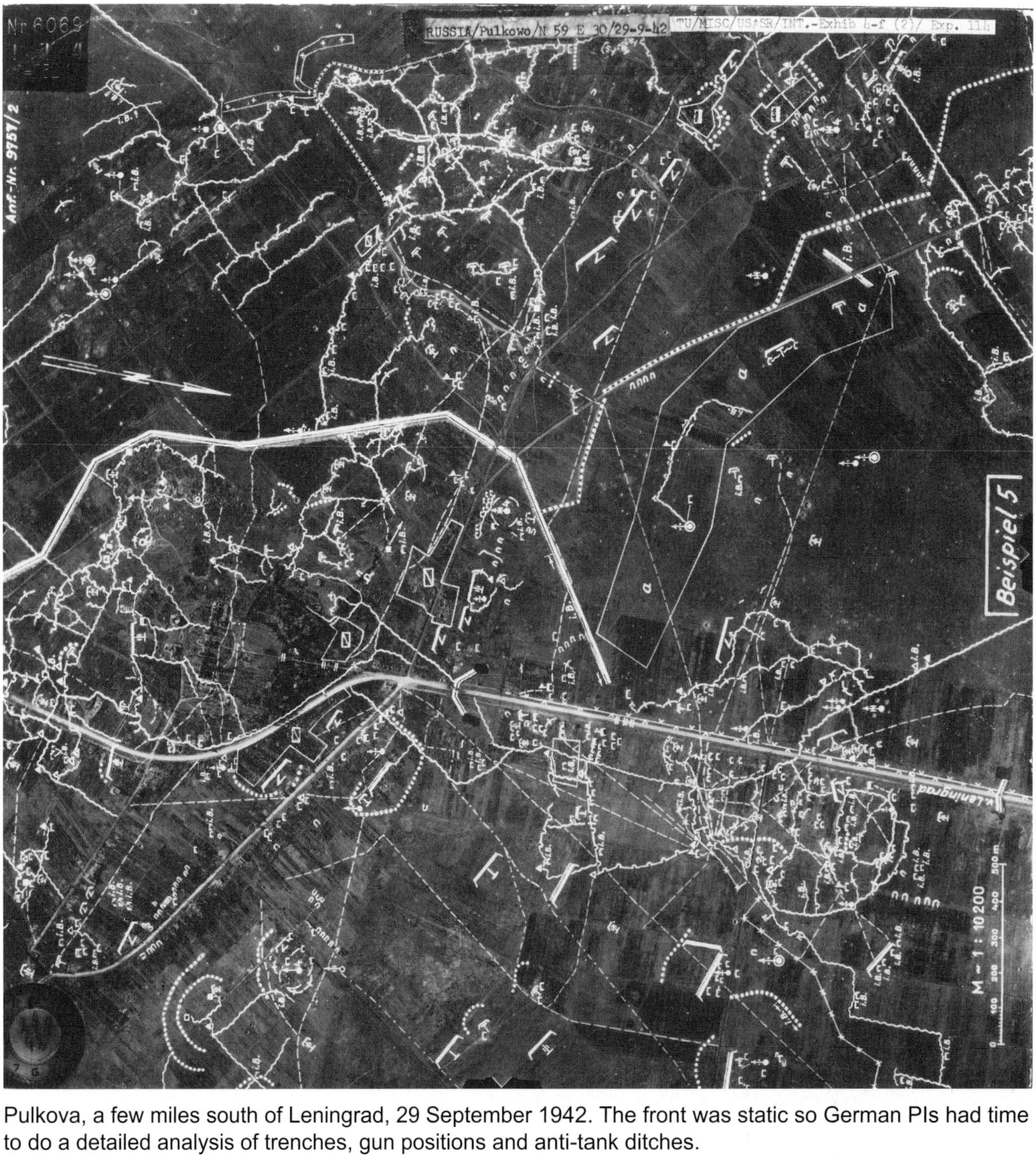
RUSSIA/Pulkowo/N 59 E 30/29-9-42
TU/MISC/US/SR/INT.-Exhib 4-f (2)/ Exp. 114
Beispiel 5
M - 1 : 10200

Pulkova, a few miles south of Leningrad, 29 September 1942. The front was static so German PIs had time to do a detailed analysis of trenches, gun positions and anti-tank ditches.

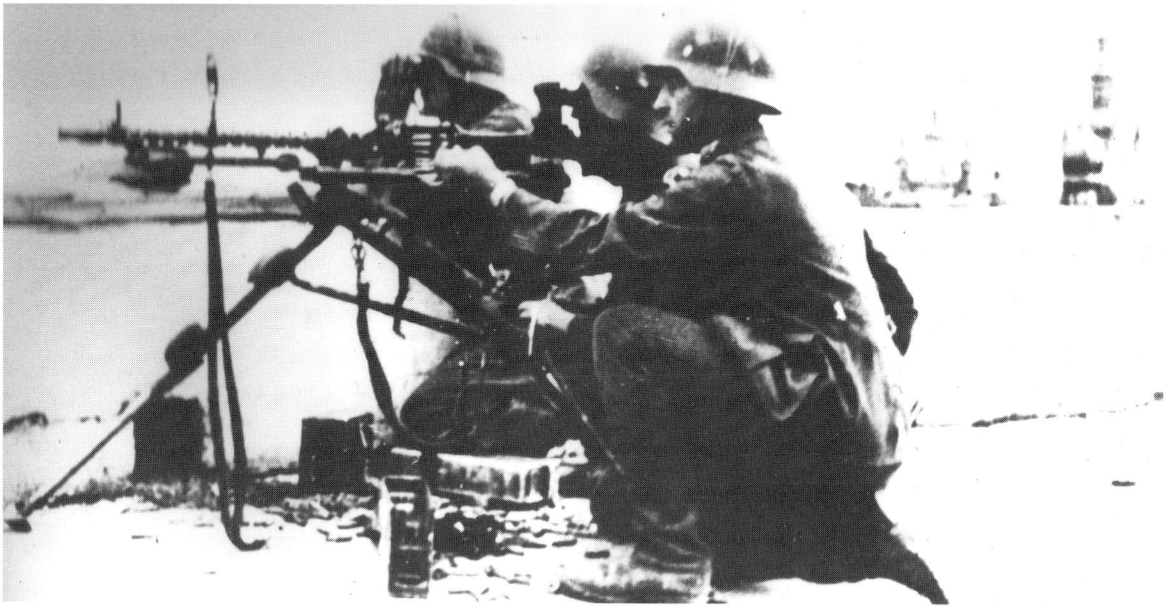

I like this photo of an Mg 34 team with a Russian Orthodox Church in the background, but come on, no one in his right mind engages an enemy that exposed. If they aren't posing for a photo or simply zeroing –in their weapon, they're crazy.

Below, more likely the real thing. A 152mm Soviet M1935 Br-2 gun loading. The small crane lifts a 107 lb. projectile on its cart to the breach then folds back along the trail after the round is rammed home (in progress). Another shell cart and projectile are on the ground at left. Next a powder charge will be loaded—it looks like the soldier at photo center is holding it in his hands. The gun will then be elevated and fired to a range of up to 15 miles. Note tracks instead of wheels on the gun.

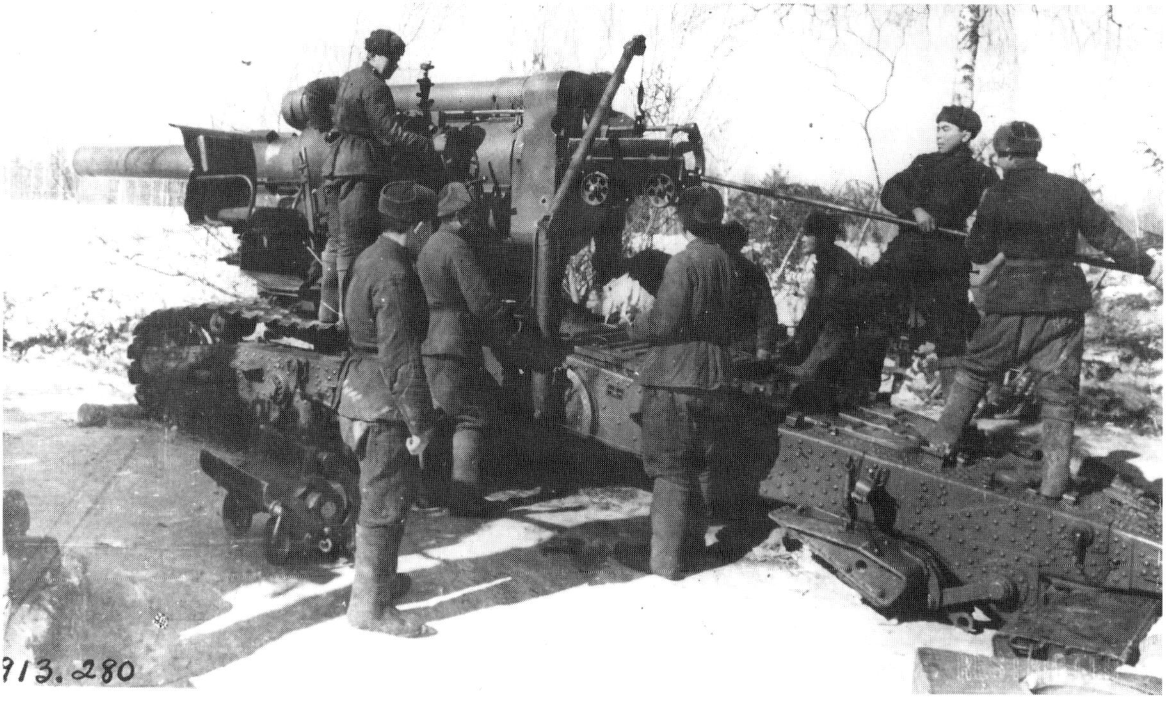
913.280

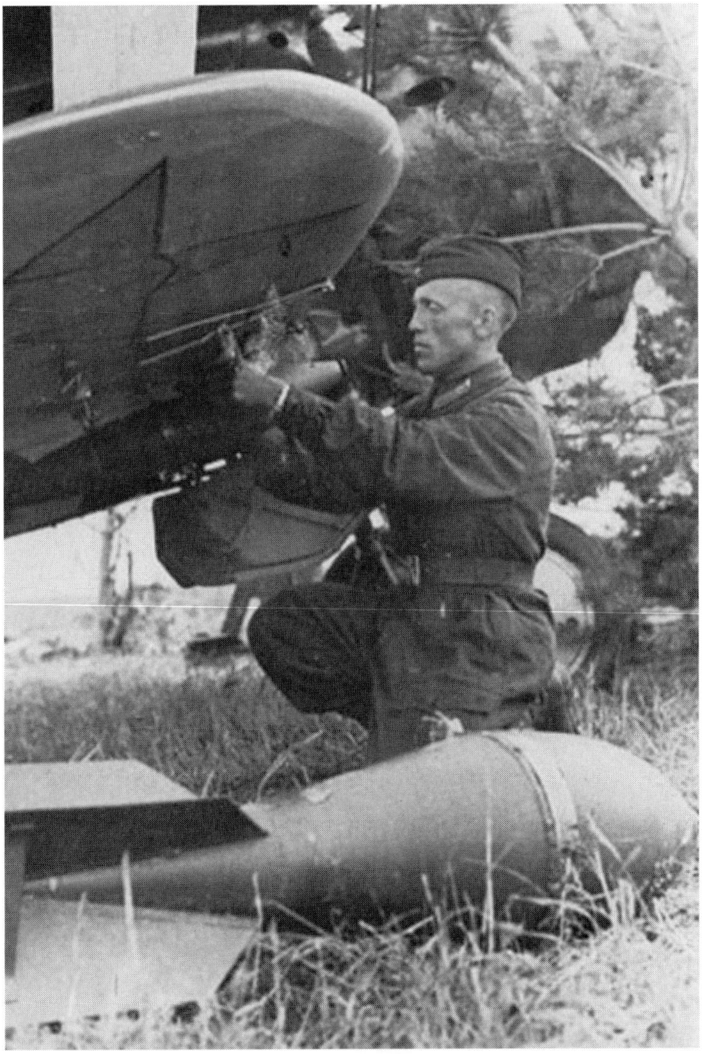

With good weather in early 1942, fighting time began again and the Red Air Force was struggled back. No longer competitive as a fighter plane, this I-15 is being loaded with 50kg bombs (foreground).

Obsolescent I-16s still flew against faster (but less maneuverable) Bf 109s and FW 190s, playing for time as new Soviet fighters were hurriedly developed and rushed into production.

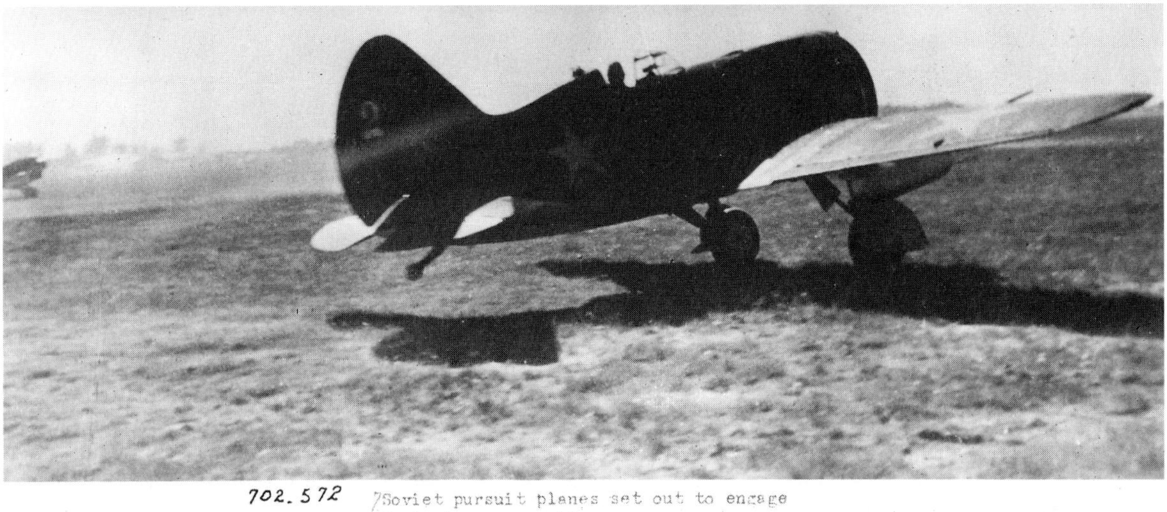

702.572 7Soviet pursuit planes set out to engage against enemy machines.

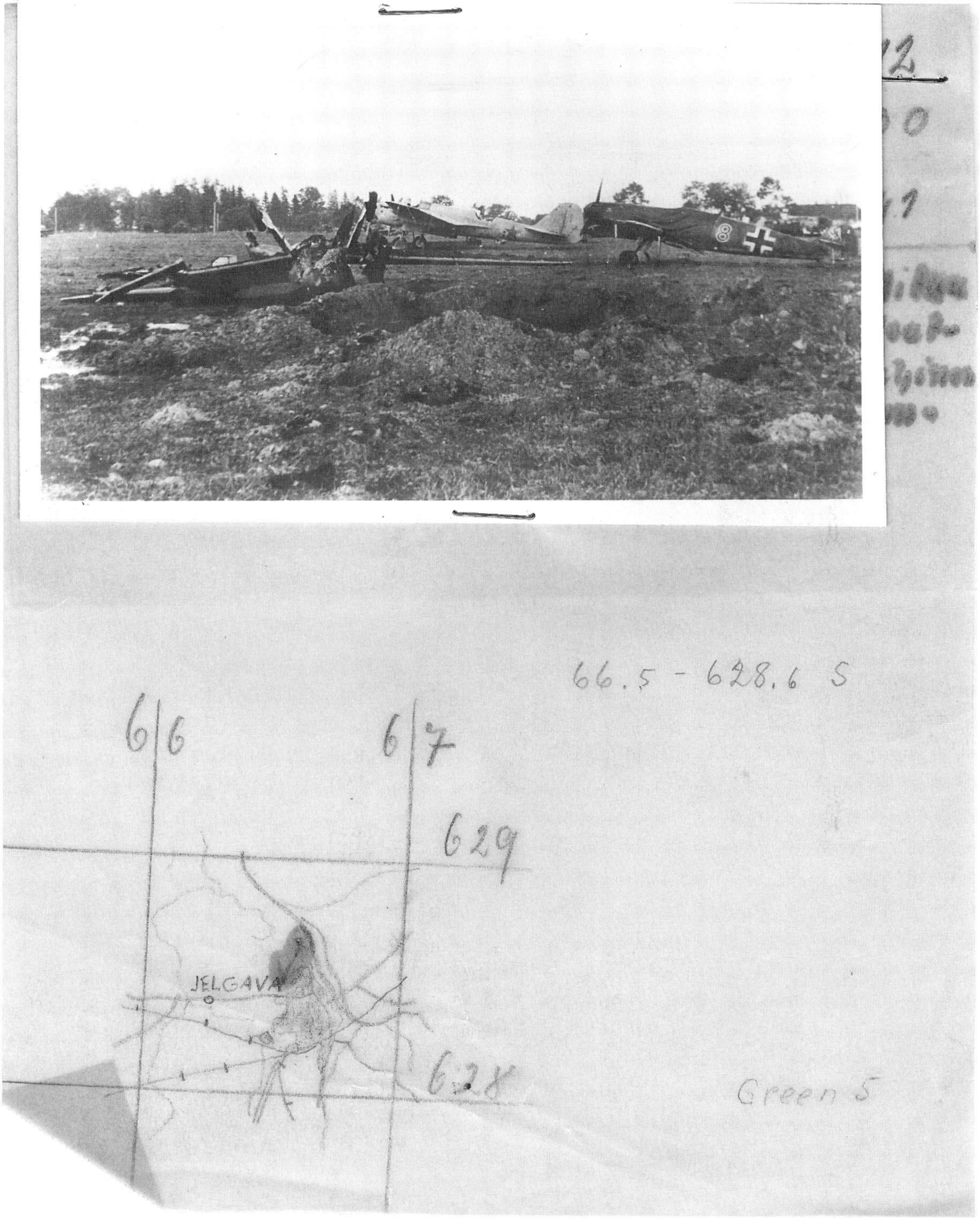
66.5 - 628.6 S
66
67
629
JELGAVA
628
Green 5

Jelgava is 20 miles southwest of Riga, Latvia. A Bf 109G is flipped on its back beside where it was parked, which is now a crater. I doubt that resulted from enemy action. More likely a mishap loading a bomb. Another 109G is in the background. Further back is a Soviet SB-2M with its dorsal turret removed. Nine out of ten Soviet bombers were SBs when Barbarossa began.

Another rare look at a pre-war or early war Il-2 single seater. Because of combat losses to German fighters, in 1942 the antenna was relocated and cockpit extended to add a rear gunner.

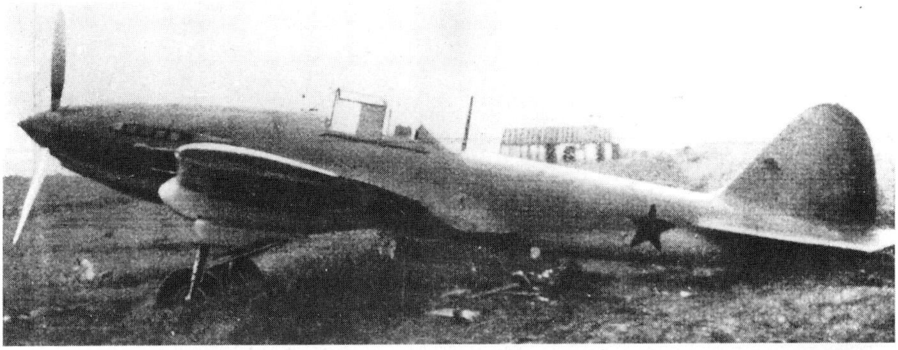

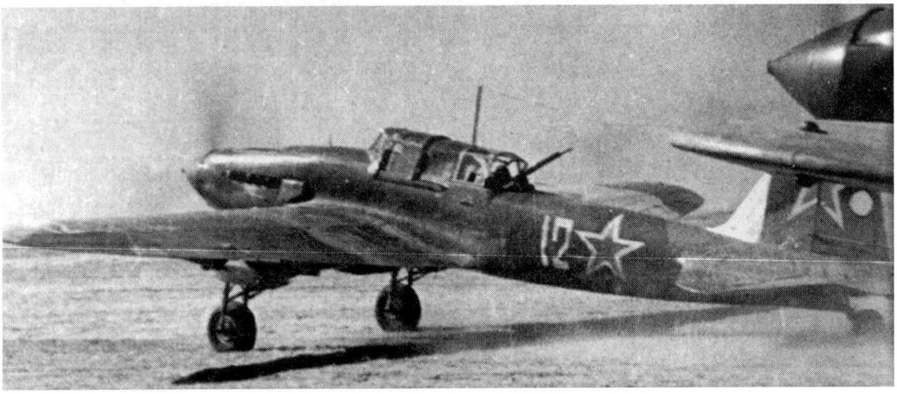
12

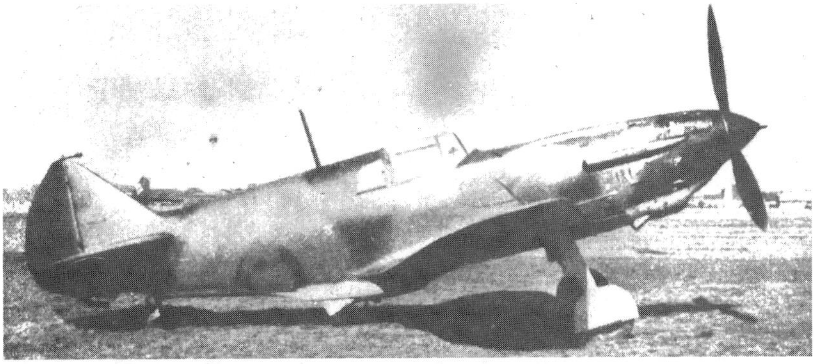

Left, wood-frame Lavochkin-Gorbunev-Gudkov LaGG-3. A good looking ship but underpowered. Slow and with a poor rate of climb, at the time it had one of the best bursts of fire with a 20mm canon firing through the propeller hub and two 12.7mm machine guns. Introduced in 1941, it was considered obsolete a year later.

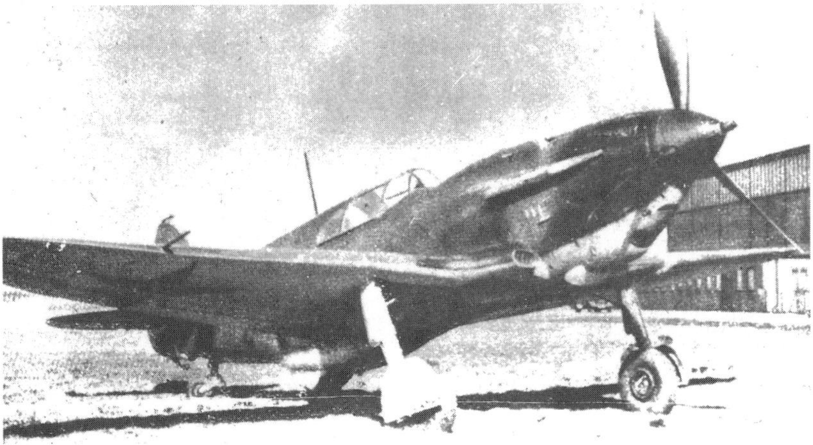

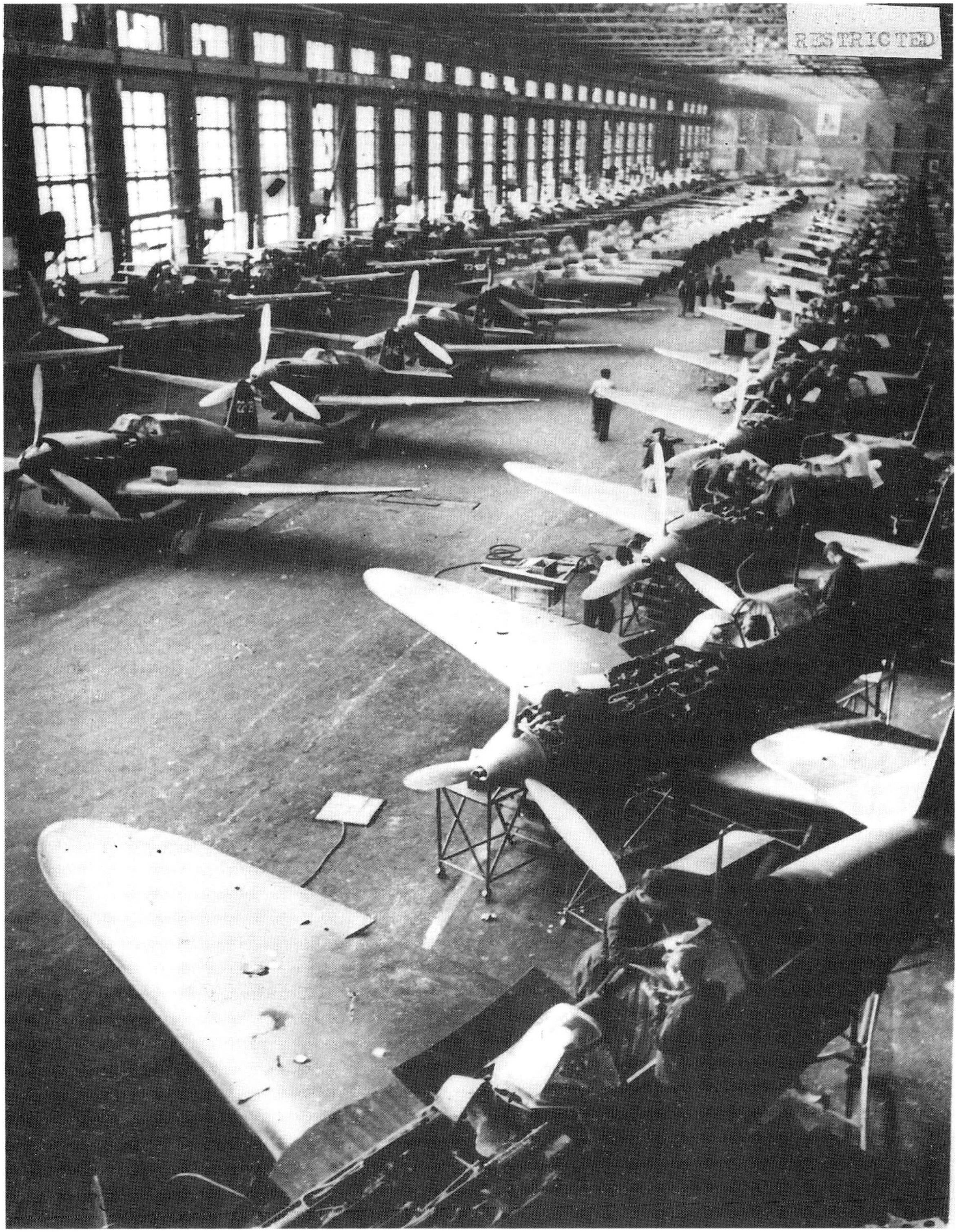
RESTRICTED

Despite flaws, in 1942 LaGG-3s were cranked out in large numbers, hoping that quantity would become quality.

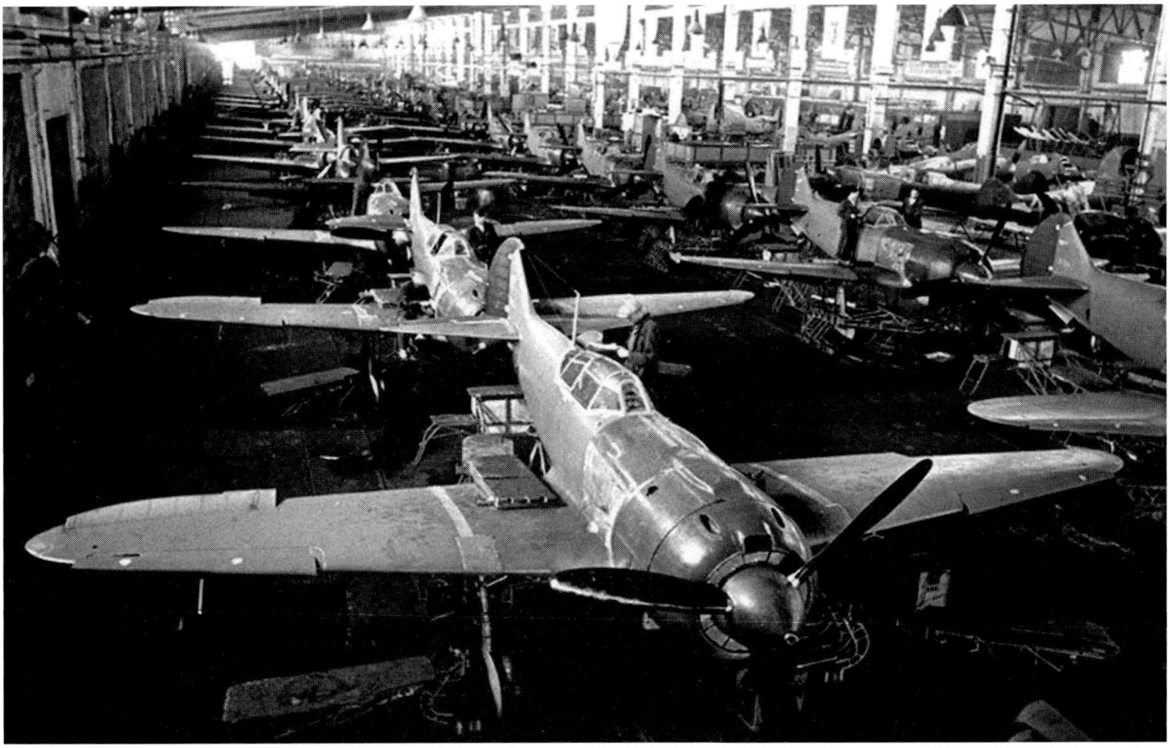

Faults of the LaGG-3 were corrected to produce the Lavochkin La-5F in 1942. This turned out to be one of the best Soviet fighter planes. The factory is at Gorki.

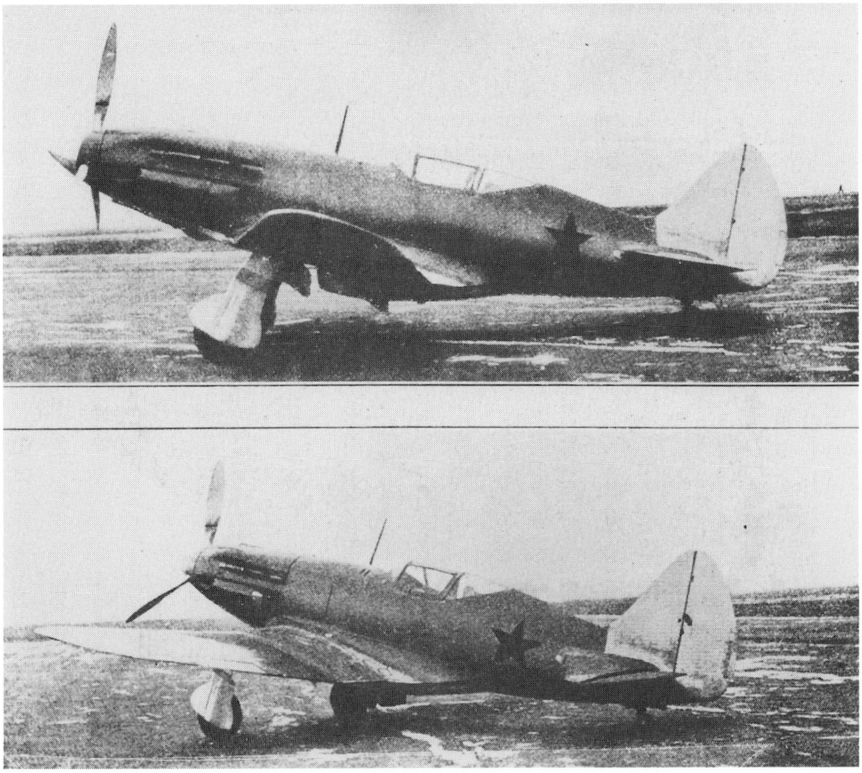

Left, Mikoyan-Gurevich MiG-3. Fast at altitude, it was inferior nearer the ground where the war was being fought and its single 12.7mm and twin 7.62 machine guns were light armament compared to enemy fighters.

PE-2 (PE-3)

24

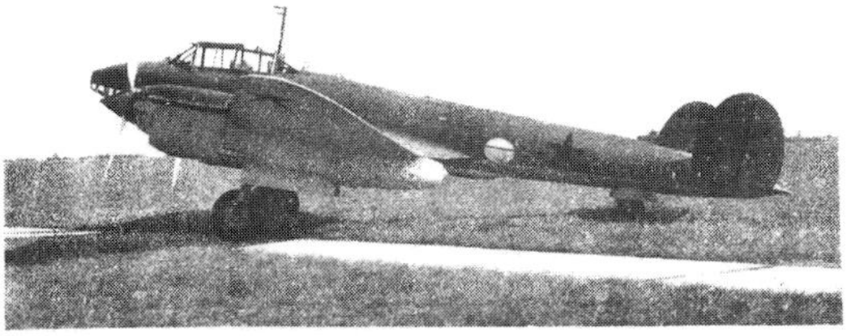

Left, Luftwaffe Intelligence followed Soviet bomber developments. The fast, rugged Petlyakov PE-2 ground attack bomber was considered one of the best of its type in the war.

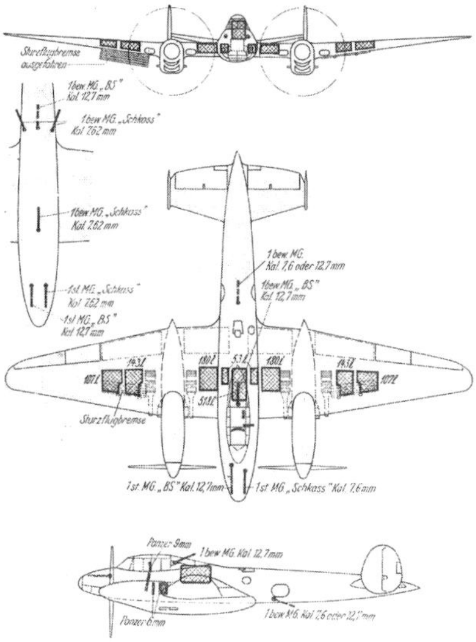

Verwendung: Kampf-u. Fernaufklärungsflzg.
Besatzung: 3 (PE-3 = 2 Mann)
Motor: M-105R
Höchstgeschwindigkeit: 480 km/h in 6000 m
Gipfelhöhe: 9000 m
Reichweite: 1200 km (PE-3 2000 km)
Bombenlast: 600 kg
Bewaffnung u. Panzerung: siehe Skizze
Bemerkungen: Sturzflugtauglich, PE-3 Fernaufklärer mit größerer Betriebsstoffmenge und geänderter Bewaffnung.

Right, an SB-2 crew briefing—pilot, navigator and gunner, 1942. 'Kick the tires and we'll go that way.' Obviously a publicity shot, but the crew and plane are probably the real deal.

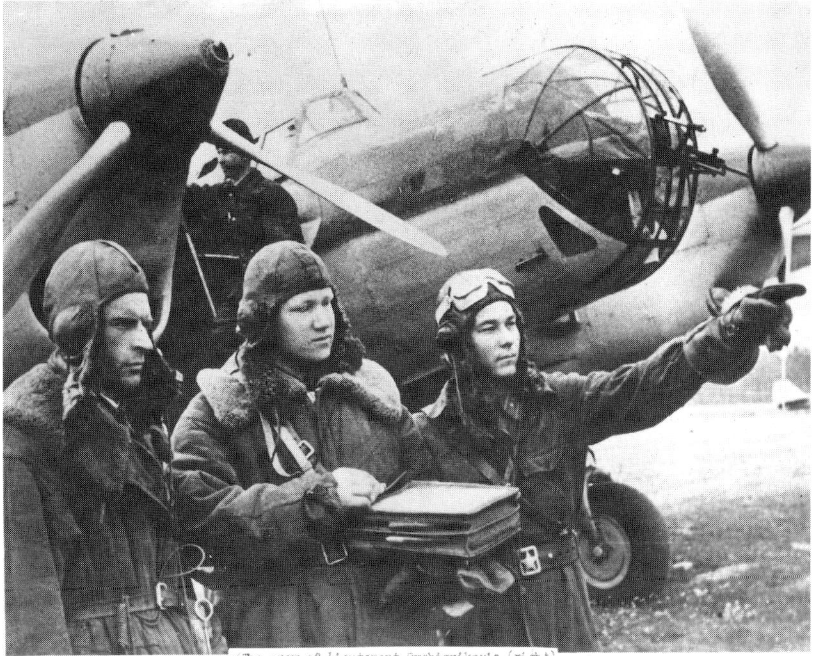

702.571 The crew of Lieutenant Ovchinnikov's (right) plane set down route of the flight it is about to make.

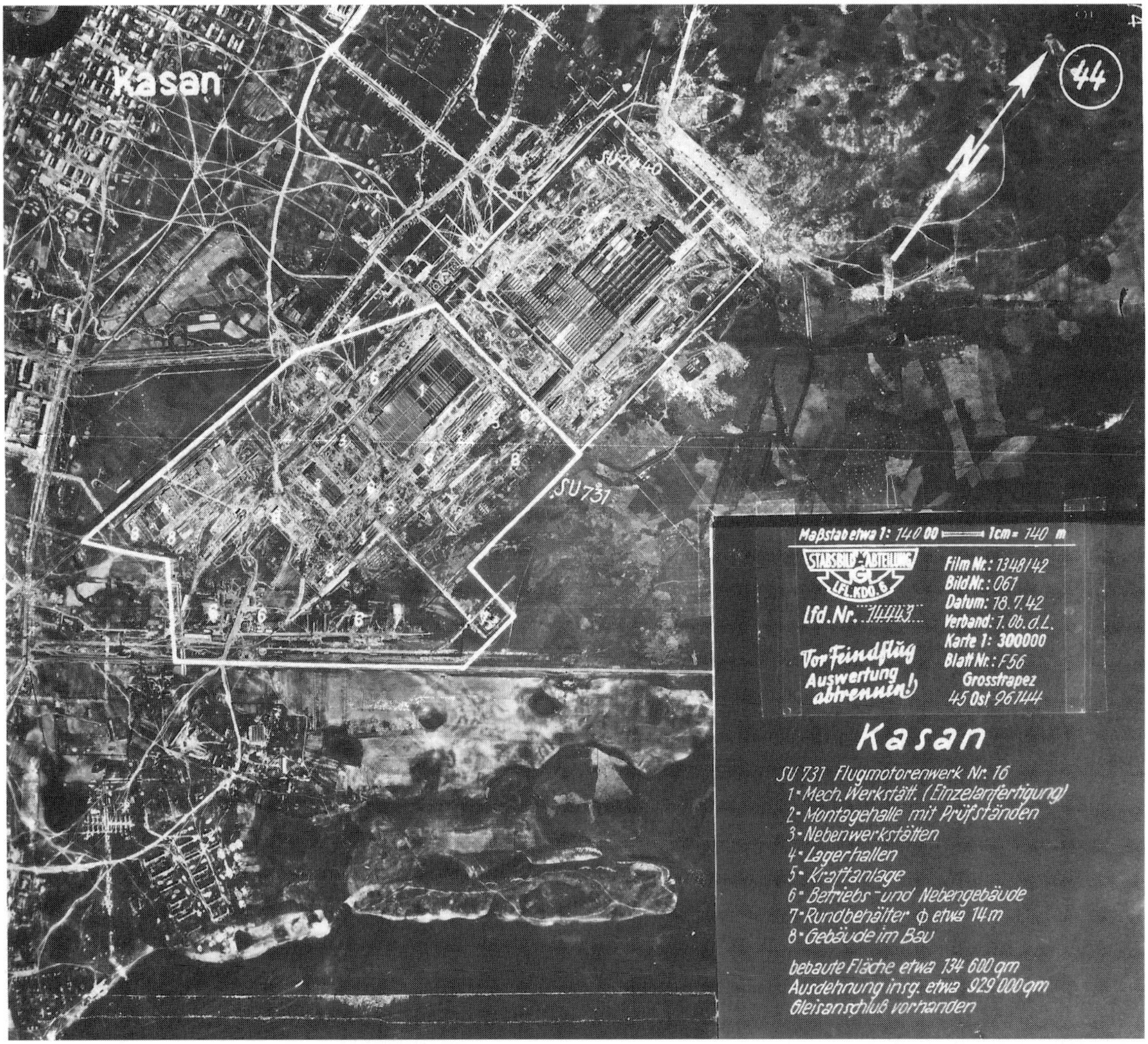
Kasan
SU 731
44
N
Maßstab etwa 1: 140 00 1cm = 140 m
STABSBILD-ABTEILUNG G LFL. KDO. 6
Lfd. Nr. 14443
Vor Feindflug Auswertung abtrennen!
Film Nr.: 1348/42
Bild Nr.: 061
Datum: 18.7.42
Verband: 7. Ob. d. L.
Karte 1: 300000
Blatt Nr.: F56
Grosstrapez
45 Ost 96144
Kasan
SU 731 Flugmotorenwerk Nr. 16
1 - Mech. Werkstätt. (Einzelanfertigung)
2 - Montagehalle mit Prüfständen
3 - Nebenwerkstätten
4 - Lagerhallen
5 - Kraftanlage
6 - Betriebs- und Nebengebäude
7 - Rundbehälter ϕ etwa 14m
8 - Gebäude im Bau
bebaute Fläche etwa 134 600 qm
Ausdehnung insg. etwa 929 000 qm
Gleisanschluß vorhanden

German target study of an aircraft motor plant, Kasan, 18 July 1942. I'd bet the US Strategic Air Command also used this one in the late 1940s and early 1950s.

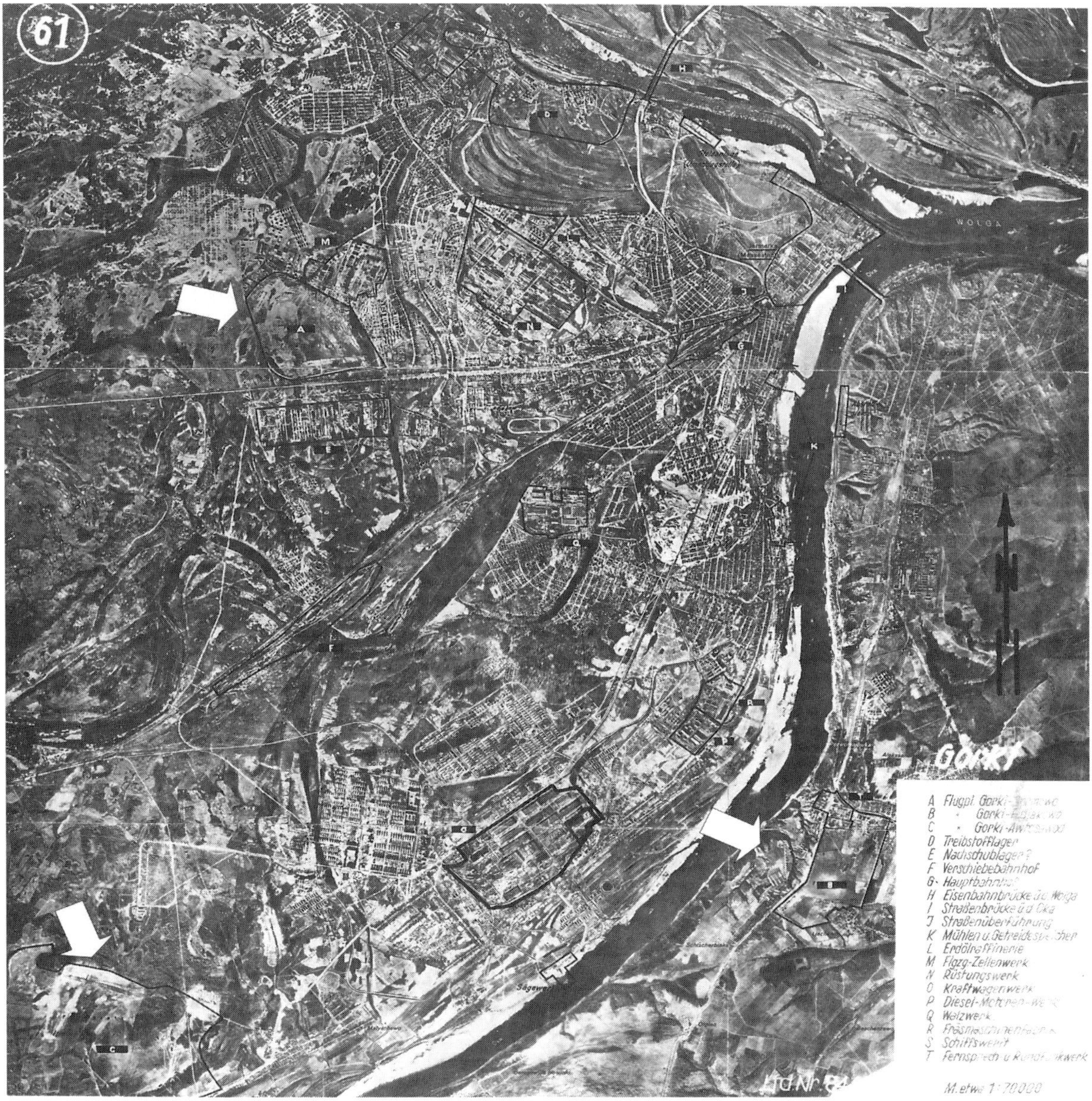
61
WOLGA
GORKY
A Flugpl. Gorki-
B Gorki-
C Gorki-
D Treibstofflager
E Nachschublager?
F Verschiebebahnhof
G Hauptbahnhof
H Eisenbahnbrücke
I Straßenbrücke
J Straßenüberführung
K Mühlen u. Getreide
L Erdölraffinerie
M Flgzg-Zellenwerk
N Rüstungswerk
O Kraftwagenwerk
P Diesel-
Q Walzwerk
R
S Schiffswerft
T Fernsprech
M. etwa 1:70000

Gorki and some of its factories. There were three airfields noted, all with natural landing surfaces (arrows). German annotation M is an aircraft parts works.

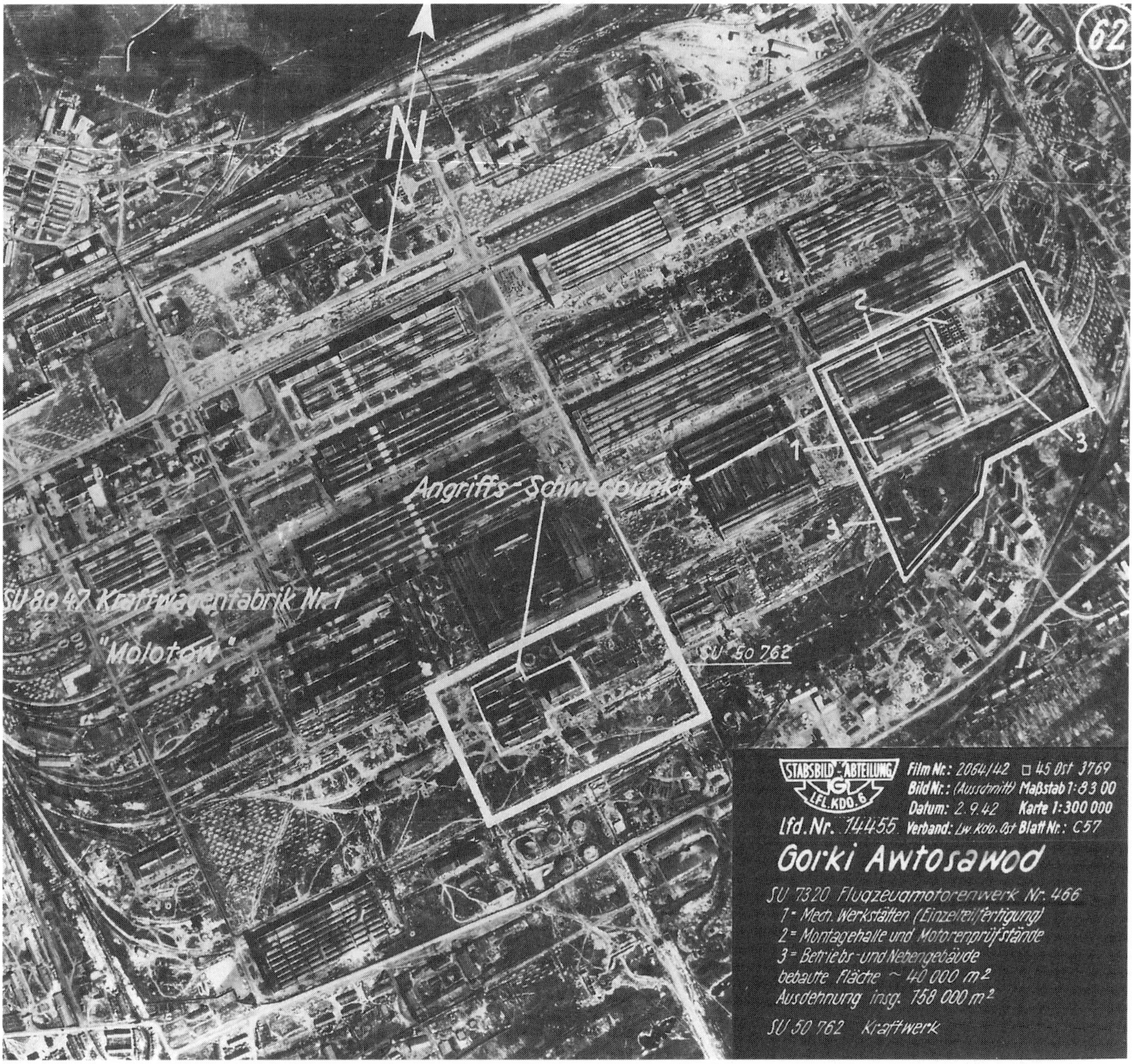
62
N
Angriffs-Schwerpunkt
SU 80 47 Kraftwagenfabrik Nr. 1
"Molotow"
SU 50 762
1
2
3
STABSBILD-ABTEILUNG
G
LFL. KDO. 6
Film Nr.: 2064/42 □ 45 Ost 3769
Bild Nr.: (Ausschnitt) Maßstab 1:8300
Datum: 2.9.42 Karte 1:300 000
Lfd. Nr. 14455 Verband: Lw. Kdo. Ost Blatt Nr.: C57
Gorki Awtosawod
SU 7320 Flugzeugmotorenwerk Nr. 466
1 = Mech. Werkstätten (Einzelteilfertigung)
2 = Montagehalle und Motorenprüfstände
3 = Betriebs- und Nebengebäude
bebaute Fläche ~ 40 000 m²
Ausdehnung insg. 158 000 m²
SU 50 762 Kraftwerk

German target study of an airplane motor factory, Gorki. Imagery is from 2 September 1942.

Note the PI annotated the 'Angriffs Schwerpunkt' showing the key points to attack. Target SU (for Soviet Union) 50 762 is a power plant. SU 7320 is an aircraft motor factory with '1' being individual parts fabrication; '2' motor assembly and testing; and 3 is offices and out-buildings.

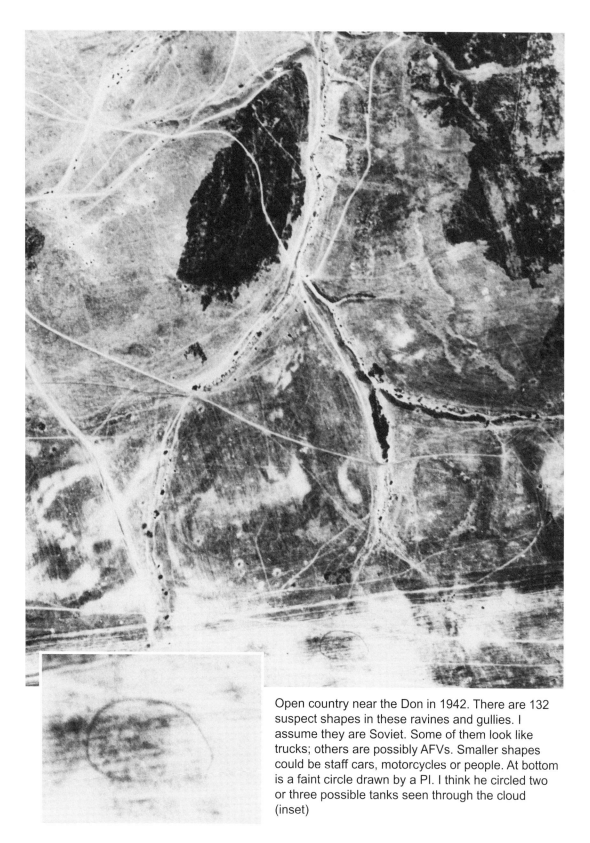

Open country near the Don in 1942. There are 132 suspect shapes in these ravines and gullies. I assume they are Soviet. Some of them look like trucks; others are possibly AFVs. Smaller shapes could be staff cars, motorcycles or people. At bottom is a faint circle drawn by a PI. I think he circled two or three possible tanks seen through the cloud (inset)

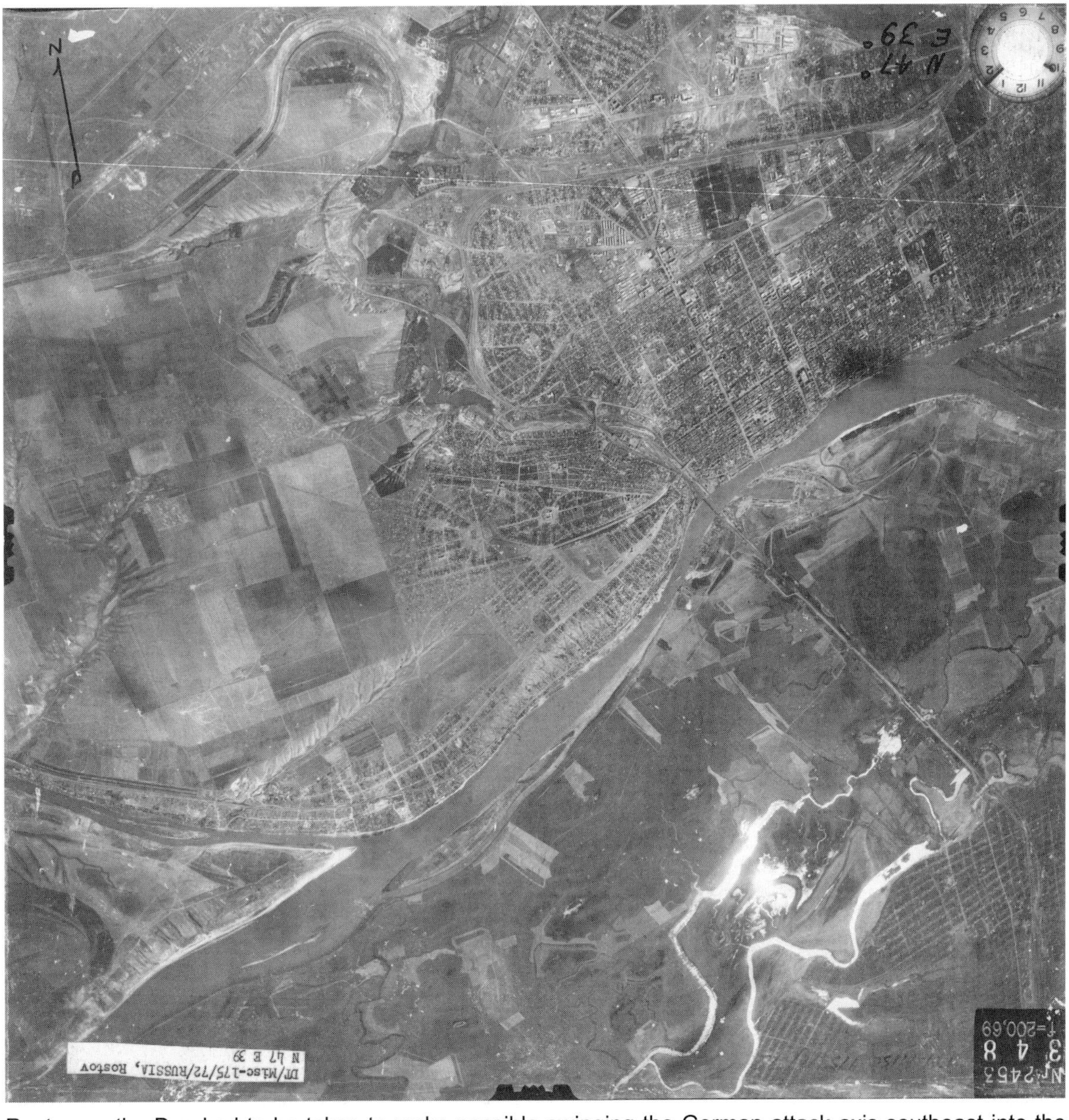
DT/Misc-175/72/RUSSIA, Rostov
N 47 E 39

Rostov on the Don had to be taken to make possible swinging the German attack axis southeast into the Caucasus to capture those oil fields, 14 April 1942. There is no sign of damage in or around the city at this date. Note the way the rail line loops heading west (photo top). Those loops show what had to be done to conquer the steep gradient directly west of Rostov.

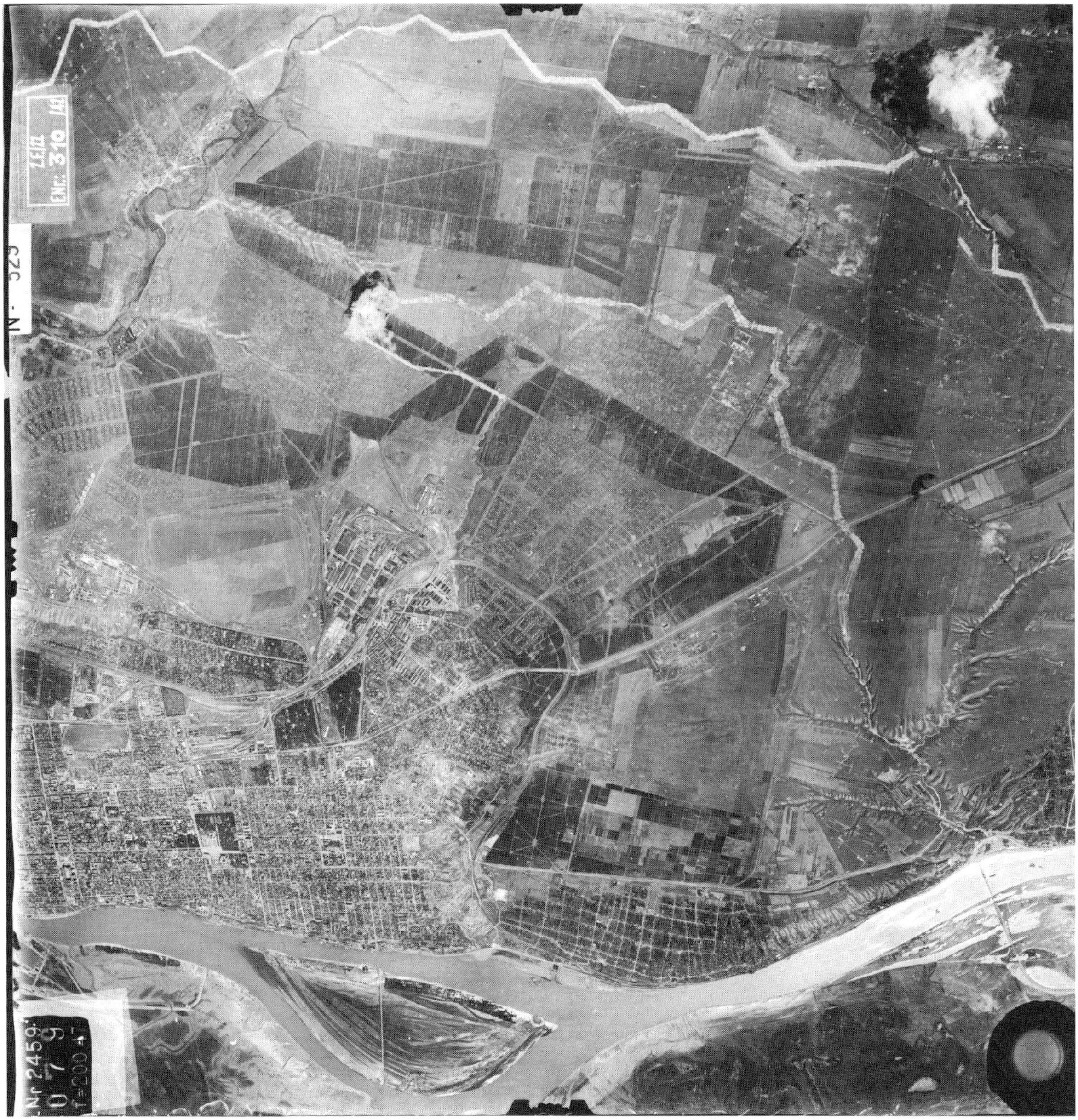

East of the preceding photo, Rostov on 7 May 1942. Still no sign of bombing, even on the sod airfield just north of town, but we see an outer line of anti-tank ditching apparently completed and an inner line under construction.

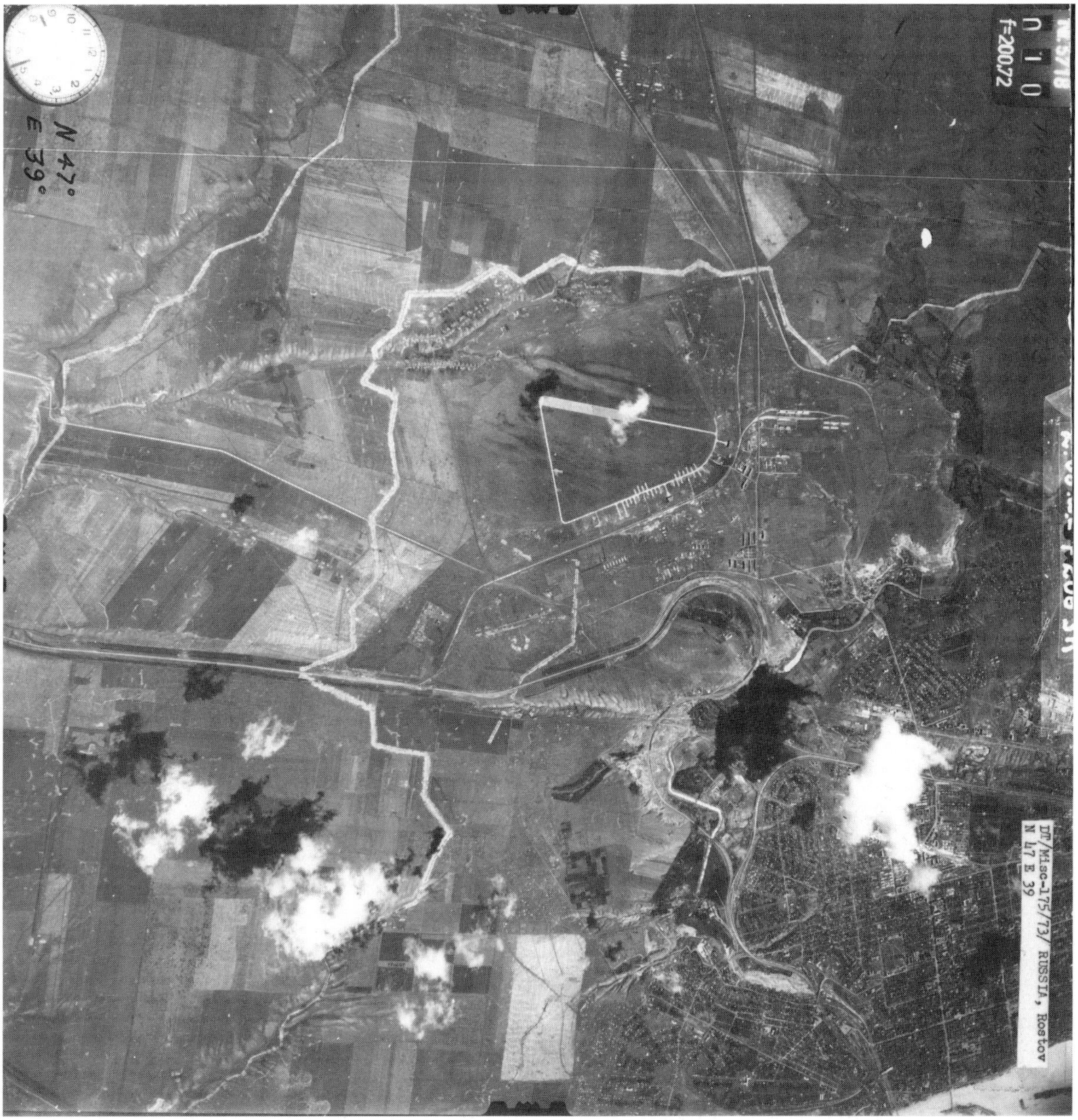
N 47°
E 39°
f=200.72
DT/Misc-175/73/ RUSSIA, Rostov
N 47 E 39

West of the preceding imagery, Rostov on 2 June 1942. Still no sign of enemy action nor is there any activity on the airfield. The outer anti-tank defense line appears near completion and there is another line of ditching even farther north. The inner defense line hasn't yet reached this far west. German ground forces were over a month away and steadily advancing.

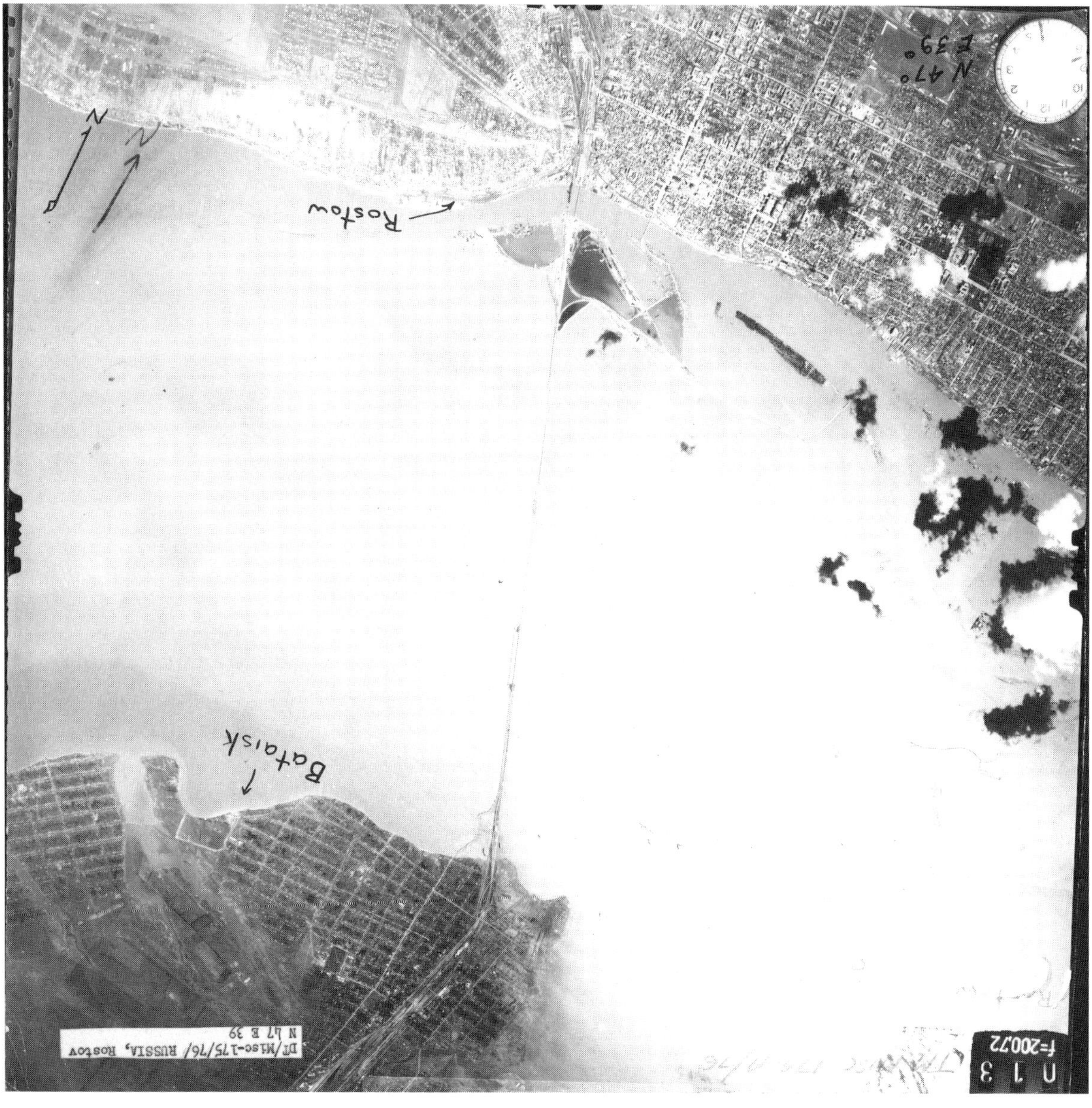
N 47°
E 39°
Rostow
Bataisk
DT/Misc-175/76/ RUSSIA, Rostov
N 47 E 39
f=200,72

What a difference a week makes. Rostov, 9 June 1942. Now we see why that rail bridge from Bataisk to Rostov was so long. There was little hope of major German forces (armor and heavy artillery) getting to the south/east bank until the Don subsided.

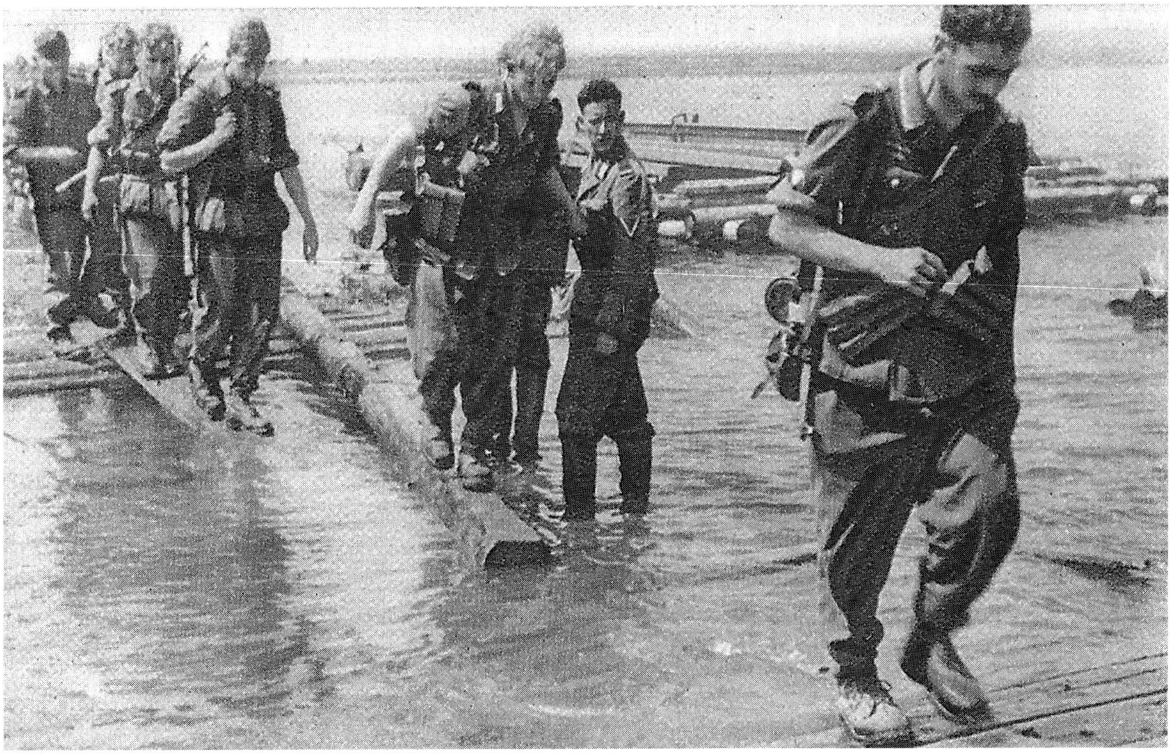

German soldiers crossing the Don at Rostov using makeshift rafts, July 1942. The river behind them is still in flood and this is obviously not an assault crossing. Apparently an Infantry bridgehead had already been established.

July 1942, German soldiers crossing a rail line on the upper Don near Voronezh. That looks like a burned out boxcar (goods wagon) in the background.

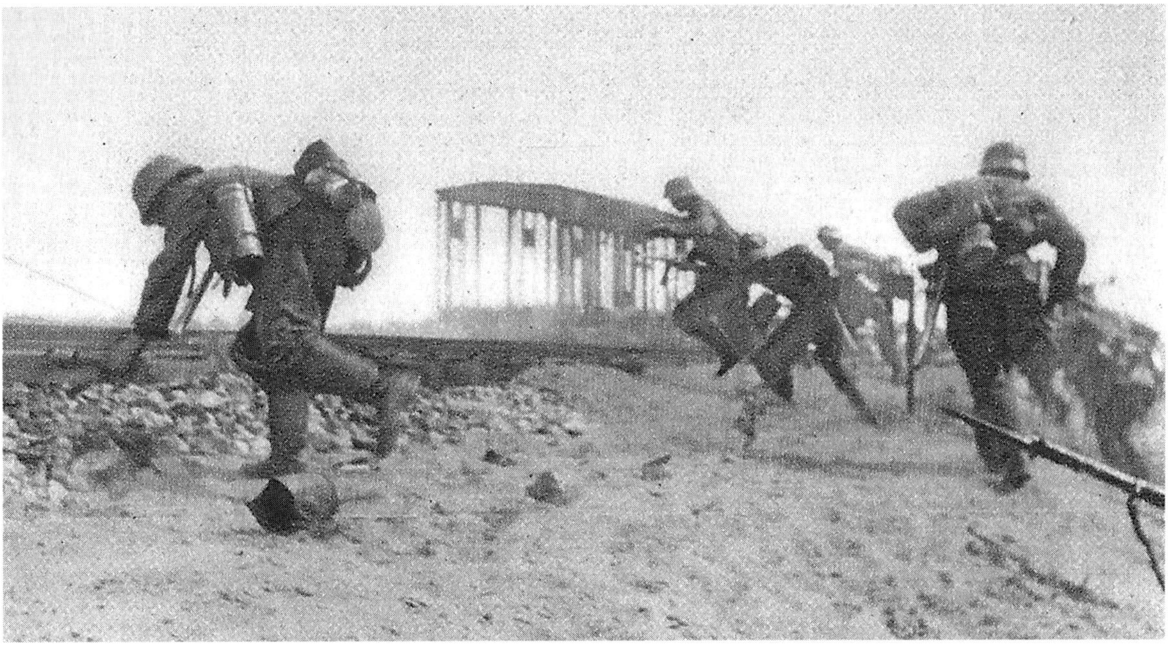

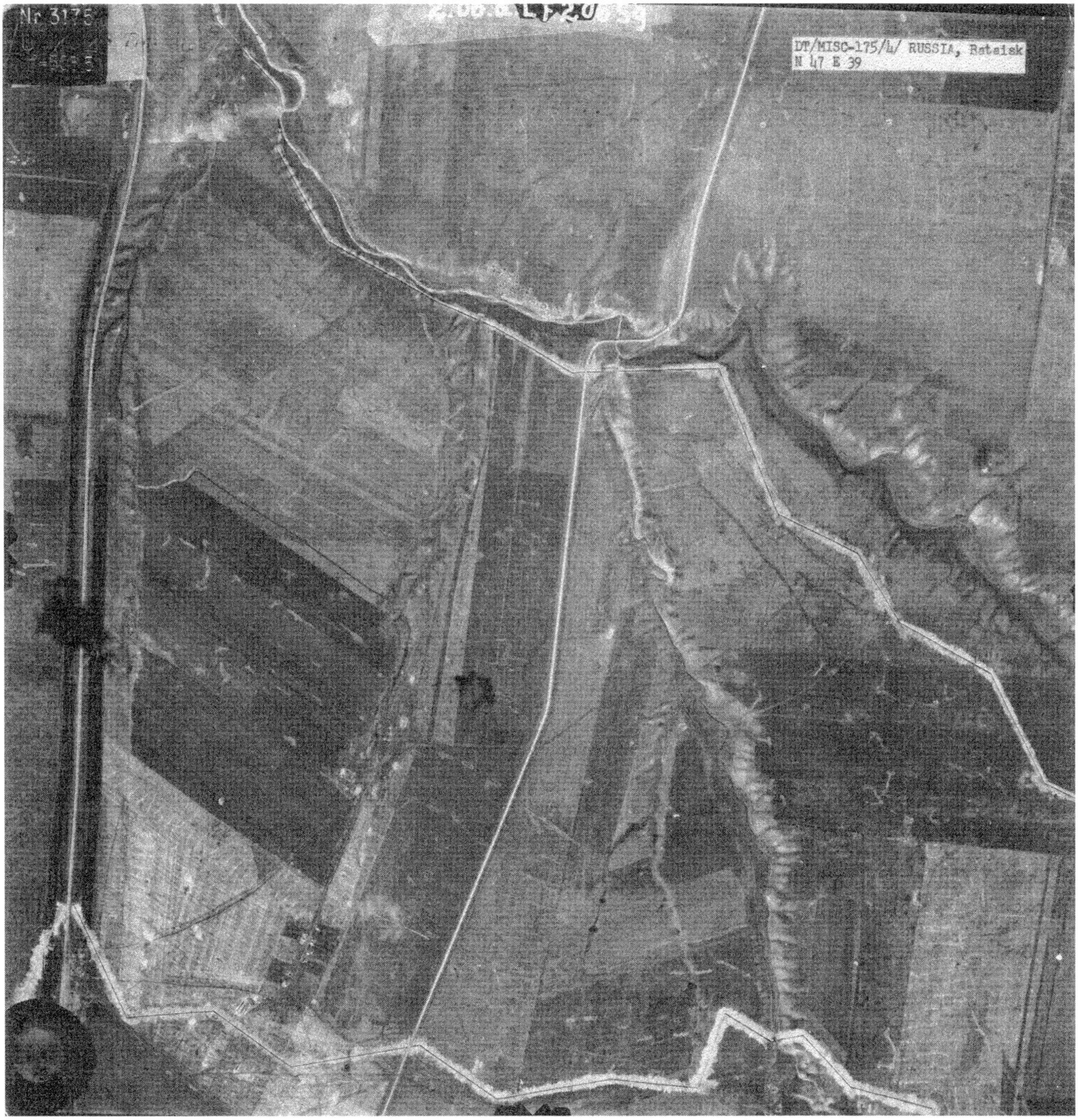
DT/MISC-175/4/ RUSSIA, Bataisk
N 47 E 39

Defenses at Bataisk, on the Don's south bank opposite Rostov, 2 June 1942. German forces reached the Don on 26 July and were on the south bank in August—1,500 miles from the start line in Poland. Soviet resistance was stiff, but the Red Army was cleared from the west/north bank by 10 August. Continuing last-ditch defensive struggles east of the Don slowed and eroded German strength. Germany Army Group A turned south into the Caucasus, leaving von Paulus' Sixth Army weakened and alone just when it was starting its push toward the Volga and Stalingrad.

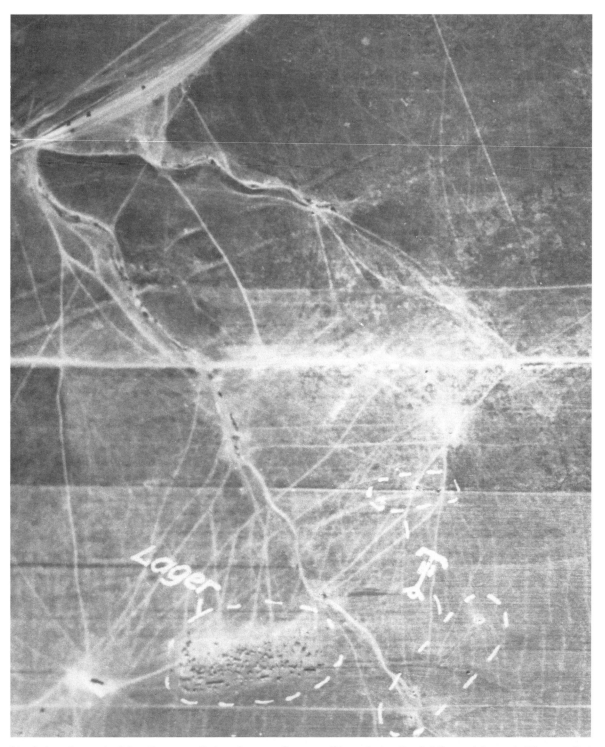

Much terrain east of the Don was flat and open. German PIs noted a Soviet 'Lager' (camp). The symbol indicates a light anti-aircraft artillery position (37mm). Not noted were vehicles on the road at upper left, apparently heading for the camp.

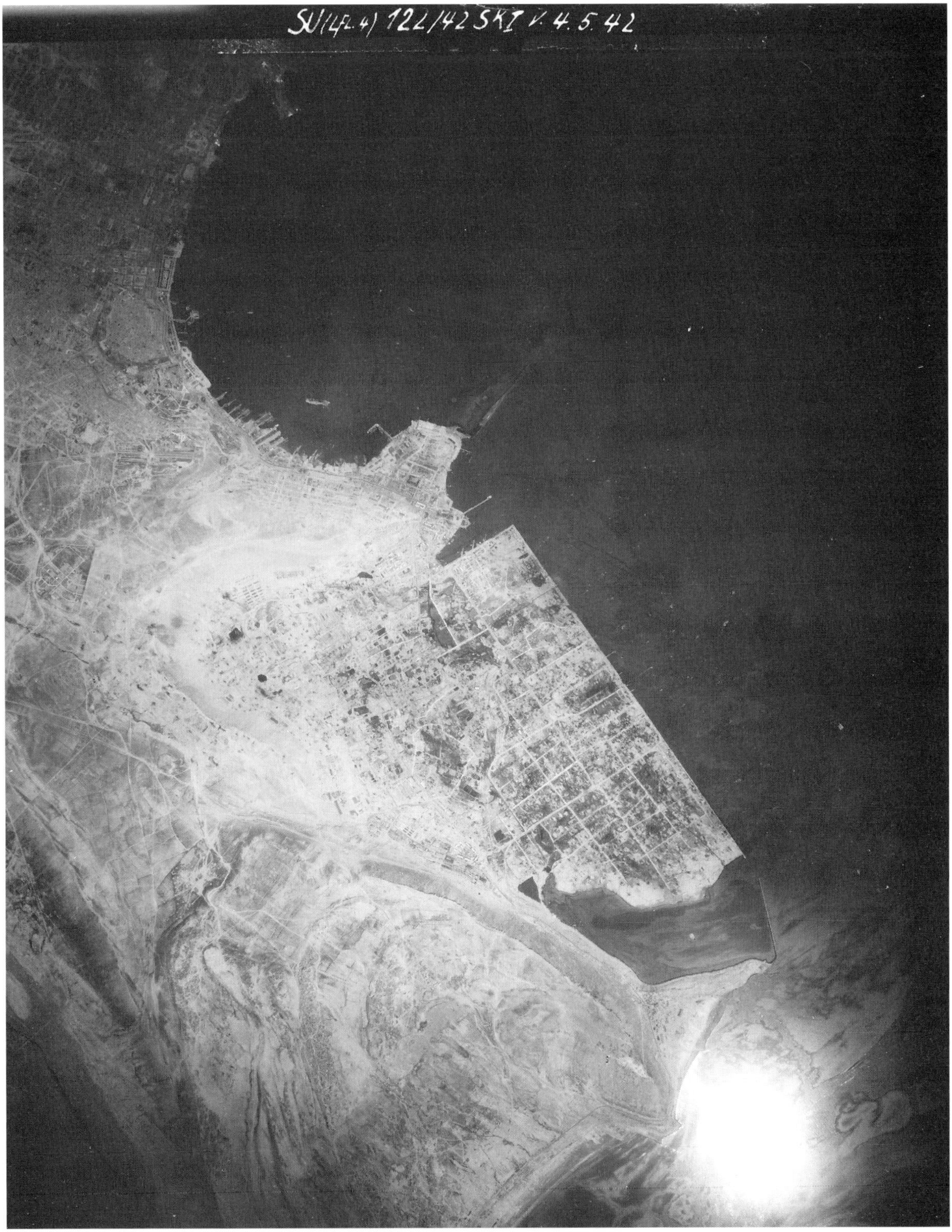
SU(LFL.4) 122/142 SKI V. 4.5.42

German aerial reconnaissance continued to watch oil sources. Baku, 4 May 1942. German troops made it to the mountains of Georgia but not into Azerbaijan—and Baku was almost 200 miles farther.

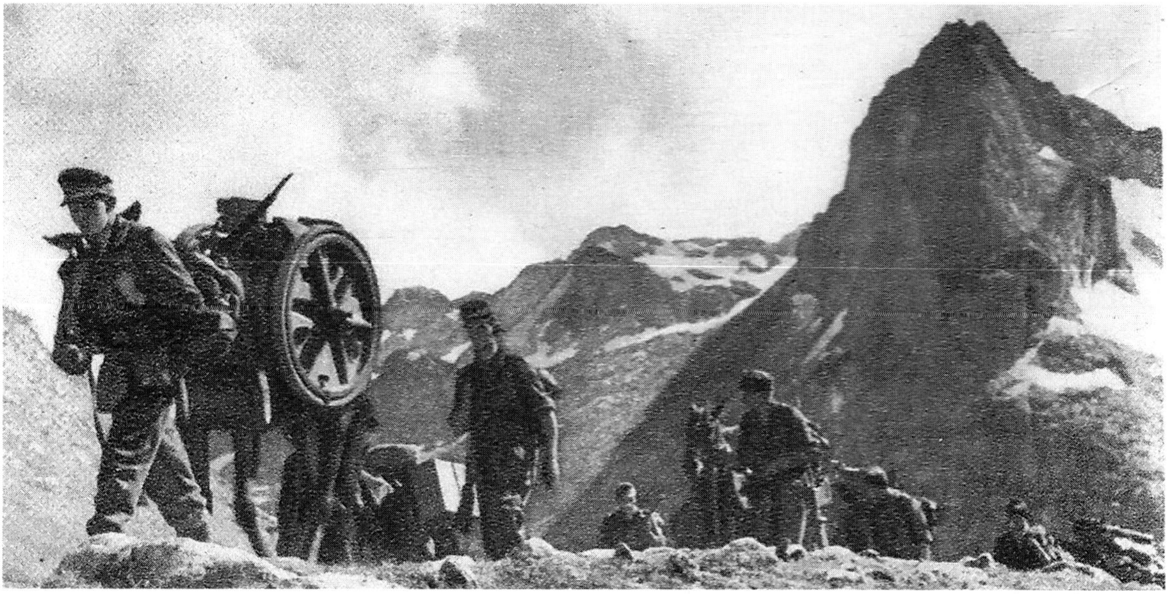

August 1942, German mountain troops in the Caucuses. That wheel identifies this as crew for a 7.5cm Gebirgsgeschütz 36 (mountain howitzer). The 1,650 lb. gun was broken down into mule-capable loads. It could fire a 12.7 lb. round to 10K yards.

In mid-August a German pilot photographed Mt. Elbrus, highest point in the Caucuses.

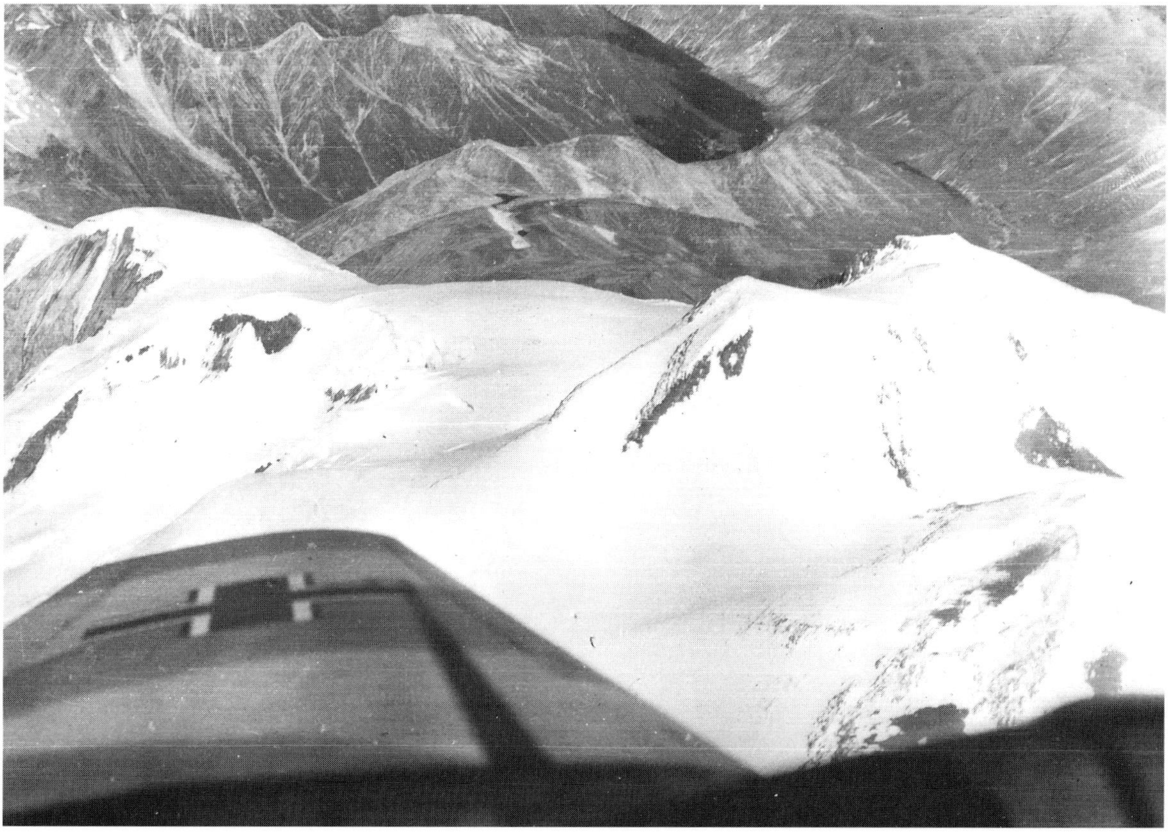

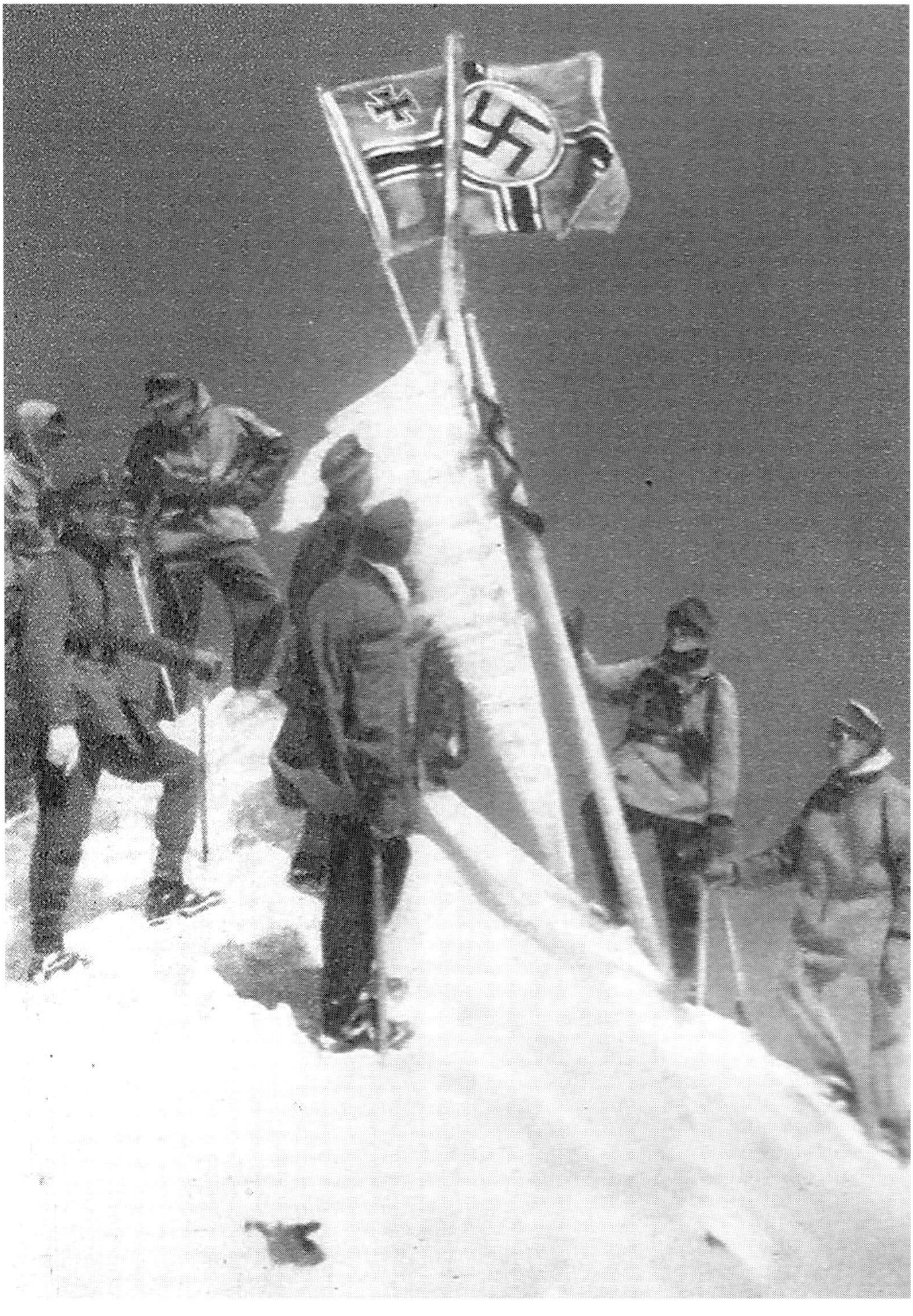

Troops of 1st Mountain Division planted their flag on Mt. Elbrus on 21 August 1942. This was intended to symbolize their imminent attainment of Barbarossa's objective—control of oil-rich lands farther south.

It was not to be. The Wehrmacht thrust out of Poland fourteen months earlier had driven Red Armies steadily east, but was nearing the end of its reach.

Chapter VII

STALINGRAD

Most photos in this book were found during random inspections of dormant Intelligence files or sorting through unlabeled boxes to see what was in them. Stalingrad was different. That battle didn't end war in the east… but it decided it. I made an effort to find photos of Stalingrad, focusing on the city. One hundred thirty six GX missions had imagery somewhere in Degree Square 48N44E. I found so many aerial and ground photos of the city and environs that I couldn't include them all. Some aerial overage (even late in the siege) was taken in long strings and some had repeated overlapping passes (mapping coverage). Obviously, Luftwaffe fighters were keeping the skies clear and the ease of German aerial reconnaissance collection around Stalingrad indicates a complete lack of, or disdain for, enemy air defenses.

I've selected images that help tell the story and show Stalingrad at various times through the German siege and Soviet counter siege. I've looked at a LOT of WW II imagery while writing eight books featuring aerial recce but these photos are curious in several respects. A PI doesn't expect to see people, scale and resolution are usually inadequate. But we do expect to see activity; tracks, vehicles, equipment and gun positions. I was used to European coverage where there is usually plenty of activity to occupy a PI's interest.

Much German coverage of Stalingrad has both the scale and quality to show activity, but seeing equipment at Stalingrad is rare. In fact, the streets are eerily clean and bare. There are rail cars in yards and factories but no crowds of people in markets, no buses, no cars, no trucks delivering goods. That would be expected during bombing and shelling in September but it is also true in April when German forces had yet to cross the Don. It gradually dawned on me that life on the Volga was akin to Europe in mid-1800s. Many industries were built here but workers lived in small dwellings or giant government provided apartment blocks. And apparently everyone walked to work.

Based upon what I'd read I expected to see Panzers destroyed during attacks near the Tractor Factory or attacking Pavlov's House. Tank battles were going on but where were they? Where were the damaged/destroyed Panzer hulls? I saw them in Normandy, why not here? Perhaps battle here was more intensely an Infantry war than I'd thought.

Of course aerial reconnaissance wants to look at what will be, not what was. It doesn't usually look at one's own forces or close combat. Recce is normally laid-on to see ground ahead of a force, to map/assess enemy defenses and capabilities. It is also used to identify critical enemy logistic and support locations, sometimes far behind the FEBA, so key things can be bombed. Once Sixth Army was surrounded, Stalingrad presented German Commanders a very different situation. Radio reports from inside the Kessel (cauldron), people coming out by air and aerial recce were the only sources of information on events inside the pocket. That recon led to images included here. I was awed to hold photos held, interpreted and marked by fellow PIs 73 years earlier during an event that significant.

Why was this city so important?

Stalingrad was key to the lower Volga River and northeast anchor of the critical drive into oil-rich Caucasus. Sixth Army was the German left flank. It was also the high-point of an amazing campaign that had advanced deep into the Soviet Union in a year. After failure at Stalingrad, German advances in the east were over.

Stalingrad's 190 day siege (actually Soviets besieged then Germans besieged) is one of the longest in modern history and certainly one of the bloodiest. During the battle both Hitler and Stalin demonstrated their ruthless attitude toward their people. Hitler ordered his troops to stand fast and not try to break-out even after when fighting on was hopeless. Stalin gave the same order and also commanded that civilians not evacuate the city while they still might have.

The massive German offensive toward Stalingrad began on 28 June 1942 but for nearly a year German Intelligence had been hard at work reaching out over the line of advance to cover the city.

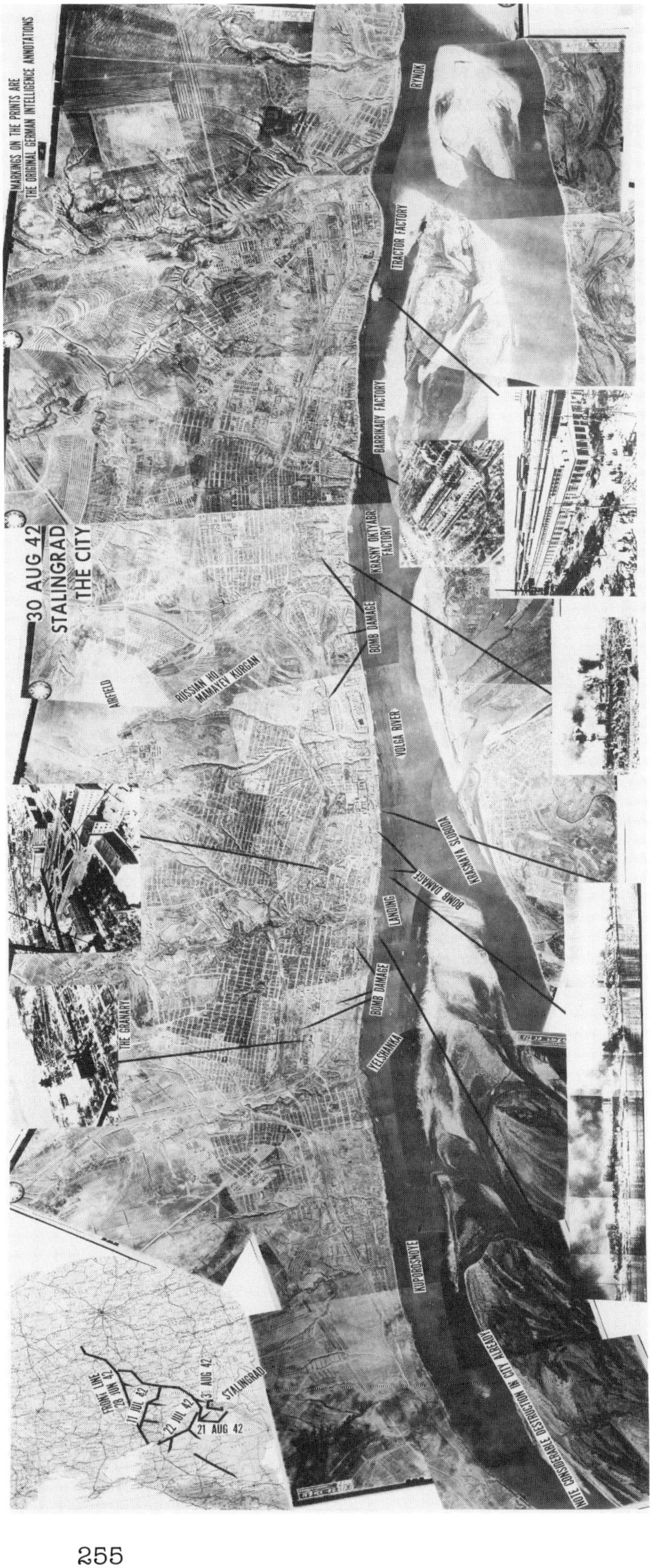
MARKINGS ON THE PRINTS ARE THE ORIGINAL GERMAN INTELLIGENCE ANNOTATIONS
30 AUG 42
STALINGRAD
THE CITY
RYNOK
TRACTOR FACTORY
BARRIKADY FACTORY
KRASNY OKTYABR FACTORY
BOMB DAMAGE
RUSSIAN HQ MAMAYEV KURGAN
AIRFIELD
VOLGA RIVER
KRASNAYA SLOBODA
BOMB DAMAGE
LANDING
BOMB DAMAGE
THE GRANARY
YELSHANKA
KUPOROSNOYE
QUITE CONSIDERABLE DESTRUCTION IN CITY ALREADY
FRONT LINE 28 JUN 42
11 JUL 42
22 JUL 42
31 AUG 42
21 AUG 42
STALINGRAD

My Stalingrad Mosaic made for a NARA Modern Military History Symposium used 30 August 1942 imagery.

Below is a German Target Chart for 'Red Barricade' Ordnance and Munitions Works.

Photo Interpreters have expertly dissected the installation so planners could decide where, and with what, to bomb. Analysis was based upon imagery of 1 November 41 (National Archives holdings start in January 1942). A post-war 'DT/RL' tag indicates this was from the Dick Tracy collection and probably used by USAF Intelligence targeteers during the Cold War. Annotated numbers are in black and hard to see.

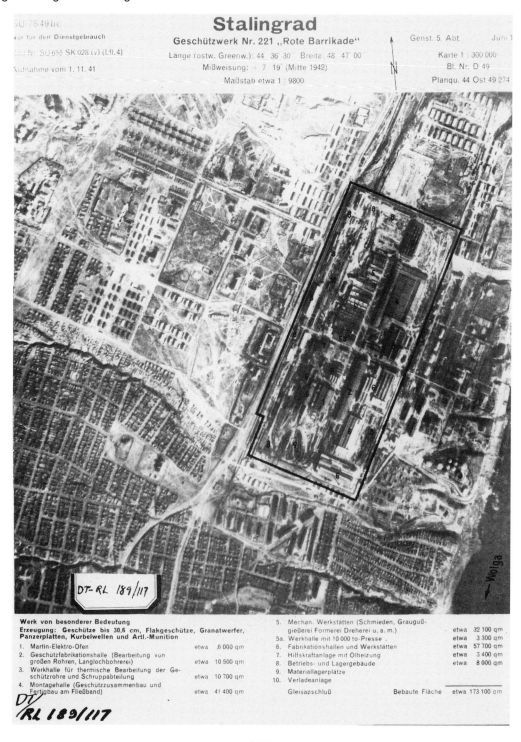

Stalingrad
Geschützwerk Nr. 221 „Rote Barrikade"

Länge (ostw. Greenw.): 44° 36′ 30″ Breite: 48° 47′ 00″
Mißweisung: ÷ 7° 19′ (Mitte 1942)
Maßstab etwa 1 : 9800

Genst. 5. Abt.   Juni 1
Karte 1 : 300 000
Bl. Nr. D 49
Planqu. 44 Ost 49 274

DT-RL 189/117

DT/RL 189/117

Werk von besonderer Bedeutung
Erzeugung: Geschütze bis 30,6 cm, Flakgeschütze, Granatwerfer,
Panzerplatten, Kurbelwellen und Artl.-Munition

1. Martin-Elektro-Ofen	etwa	6 000 qm
2. Geschützfabrikationshalle (Bearbeitung von großen Rohren, Langlochbohrerei)	etwa	10 500 qm
3. Werkhalle für thermische Bearbeitung der Geschützrohre und Schruppabteilung	etwa	10 700 qm
4. Montagehalle (Geschützzusammenbau und Fertigbau am Fließband)	etwa	41 400 qm

5. Mechan. Werkstätten (Schmieden, Grauguß-gießerei Formerei Dreherei u. a. m.)	etwa	32 100 qm
5a. Werkhalle mit 10 000 to-Presse	etwa	3 300 qm
6. Fabrikationshallen und Werkstätten	etwa	57 700 qm
7. Hilfskraftanlage mit Ölheizung	etwa	3 400 qm
8. Betriebs- und Lagergebäude	etwa	8 000 qm
9. Materiallagerplätze		
10. Verladeanlage		
Gleisanschluß	Bebaute Fläche etwa	173 100 qm

A German light plane flying low near Gorodishche looking at fires in the city to the southeast, probably in late August 1942. This shows ground poor for Panzers and ideal for defense northwest of Stalingrad.

Once the city was reduced to rubble, it too was good defensive ground and used as such by each side as German momentum shifted from offense to defense later in the year.

SU 70 154 (76 133) bc
ur für den Dienstgebrauch
ild Nr. SU 655 SK 028 (v) (Lfl. 4)
ufnahme vom 1. 11. 41

Stalingrad

Metallurgisches Werk „Krasny Oktjabr"

Länge (ostw. Greenw.): 44° 34' 30'' Breite: 48° 46' 00''
Mißweisung: + 7° 19' (Mitte 1942)
Maßstab etwa 1 : 9500

Genst. 5. Abt. Juni 1
Karte 1 : 300 000
Bl. Nr. D 49
Planqu. 44 Cst 49 273

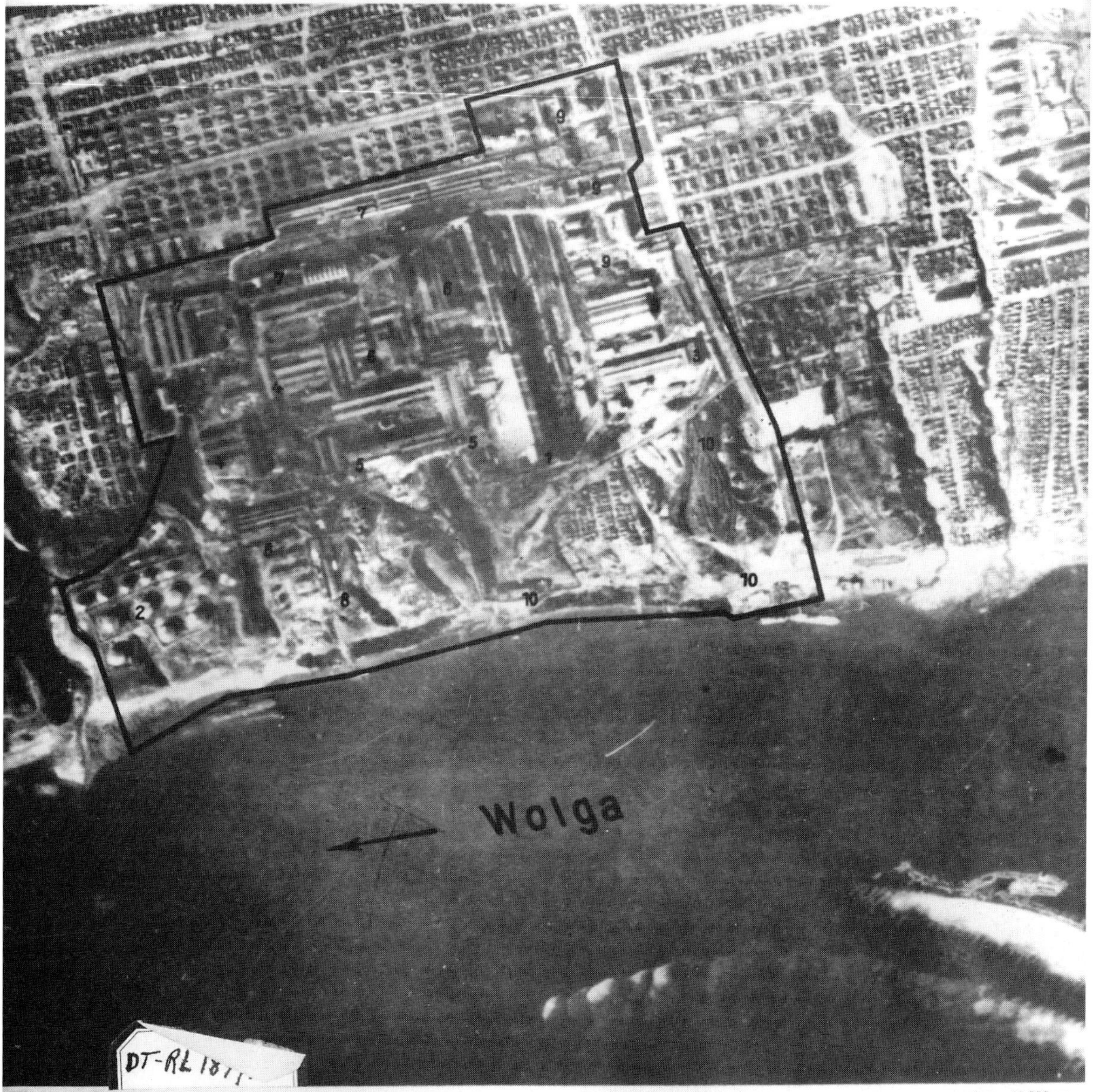
Wolga
DT-RL 1811

Werk von Bedeutung
Erzeugung: Rohstahl, Walzware, Ferrolegierungen, Federstahl, Konstruktionsstahl, Einzelteile für Kraftwagen, Traktoren- und Flugzeugbau, Panzerplatten, Kriegsgerät

1.	Siemens-Martinöfen	etwa	21 900 qm
2.	Betriebsstoffbehälter ⌀ etwa 33 m und 26,50 m		
3.	Fabrikationsabteilung für Panzerzüge	etwa	16 300 qm
4.	Walzwerke	etwa	24 700 qm
5.	Drahtfabrikationshallen	etwa	42 000 qm
6.	Fabrikations- und Werkhallen	etwa	47 700 qm
7.	Geschoßfabrik	etwa	56 000 qm
8.	Eisengießerei	etwa	11 900 qm
9.	Verwaltungsgebäude	etwa	17 600 qm
10.	Werkstätten und Nebengebäude	etwa	5 200 qm
	Bebaute Fläche	etwa	243 300 qm

Gleisanschluß

DT/

'Red October' Steel Plant, 1 November 1941 imagery. German ground forces were 300 miles west and coming on fast when this Target Study was made.

Pre-war photo titled 'An unidentified Public Utility'.
I think this is the SW corner of Dzerzhinsky Traktor Factory.

65 64 bc
für den Dienstgebrauch
Nr SU 655 SK 025 (v) (Lfl. 4)
Aahme vom 1. 11. 41

Stalingrad

Erdölraffinerie mit Krackanlage?
und Treibstofflager
Länge (ostw. Greenw.): 44 33' 15"   Breite: 48 44' 00"
Mißweisung: + 7 21' (Mitte 1942)
Maßstab etwa 1 : 10 300

Genst. 5. Abt.   Juni 1?
Karte 1 : 300 000
Bl. Nr. D - 49
Planqu. 44 Ost 49 411

Refinery and oil storage depot just north of town center. Volga barge traffic was still active, 1 November 1941.

Stalingrad hat besondere Bedeutung für den Erdölumschlag vom
Wolgatanker zum Kesselwagen

1.	Destillationsanlage	etwa 4 100 qm
2.	Umschlaghalle	etwa 2 400 qm
3.	Ansch. Pumpenhäuser	etwa 1 200 qm
4.	105 Treibstoffbehälter ≈ etwa 10—20 m	
5.	Rohölbecken	
	Gleisanschluß	Bebaute Fläche etwa 7 700 qm

UT-RL 189/116

189/116

259

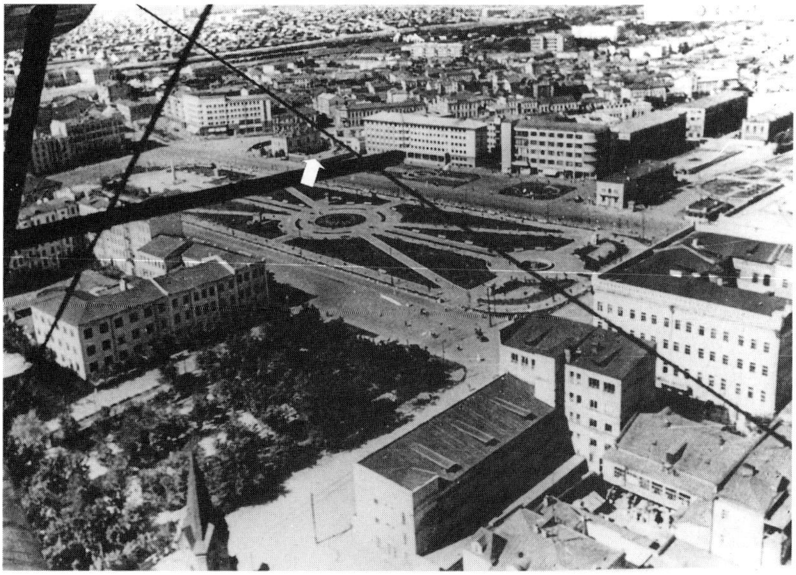

Red Plaza, Stalingrad's central square, looking north.

Photo from 1930s. It looks like the Univermag Department store is under construction at upper left of the Plaza (arrow).

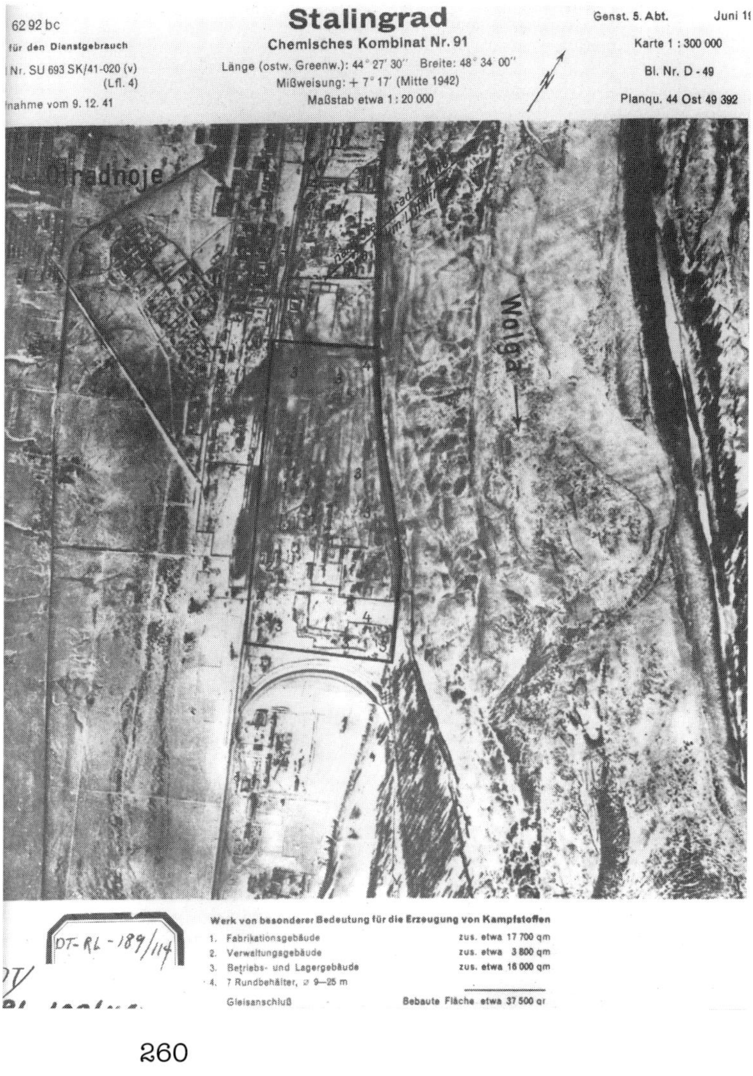

62 92 bc
für den Dienstgebrauch
Nr. SU 693 SK/41-020 (v)
(Lfl. 4)
nahme vom 9. 12. 41
Stalingrad
Chemisches Kombinat Nr. 91
Länge (ostw. Greenw.): 44° 27' 30" Breite: 48° 34' 00"
Mißweisung: + 7° 17' (Mitte 1942)
Maßstab etwa 1 : 20 000
Genst. 5. Abt.
Juni 1
Karte 1 : 300 000
Bl. Nr. D - 49
Planqu. 44 Ost 49 392
Otradnoje
Wolga
DT-RL-189/114
Werk von besonderer Bedeutung für die Erzeugung von Kampfstoffen
1. Fabrikationsgebäude zus. etwa 17 700 qm
2. Verwaltungsgebäude zus. etwa 3 800 qm
3. Betriebs- und Lagergebäude zus. etwa 16 000 qm
4. 7 Rundbehälter, ⌀ 9—25 m
Gleisanschluß
Bebaute Fläche etwa 37 500 q

This Target Graphic is of a large chemical plant on the south side of the city.

On 9 December 1941 the Volga was starting to ice.

SU 80 95 b c

Nur für den Dienstgebrauch

Bild Nr. SU 659 SG 028 (v)
(Lfl. 4)

Aufnahme vom 5. 11. 41

Stalingrad

Traktorenwerk „Dsershinski"

Länge (ostw. Greenw.): 44° 37' 00'' Breite: 48° 47' 30''
Mißweisung: + 7° 19' (Mitte 1942)
Maßstab etwa 1 : 7800

N

Genst. 5. Abt.
Karte 1 : 300 000
Bl. Nr. D 49
Planqu. 44 Ost 49

Wolga
DT-RL-189/118

Werk von besonderer Bedeutung. Erzeugung: Schwere Panzerkampfwagen, Raupenschlepper, Geschutztraktoren

1.	Montagehallen	zus. etwa	47 800 qm	11.	Lagergebäude
2.	Fabrikationsgebäude für Pz.-Motore	etwa	21 800 qm	12.	Unterkunftsgebäude
3.	Montagehallen (Pz.-Fertigbau am Fließband)	etwa	36 000 qm	13.	Schalt- und Transformatorenanlage
4.	Eisen- und Stahlgießerei	etwa	30 000 qm	14.	Verwaltungs- [illegible] Gebäude
5.	Modellbauhalle für Eisengießerei	etwa	11 000 qm	15.	Betriebs- [illegible]
6.	Graugußgießerei	etwa	4 500 qm	16.	2 Rundbe[illegible] etwa 50 m
7.	Modellbauhalle für Graugußgießerei	etwa	1 800 qm	17.	Materiallager
8.	Schmieden, Preß- und Stanzwerke	etwa	23 900 qm	18.	Kohlenlager
9.	Reparaturwerk	etwa	17 500 qm		Bebaute Fläche etwa [illegible]
10.	Werkstätten	etwa	4 450 qm		Gleisanschluß

German Target Graphic of the Tractor Factory. This imagery was flown 5 November 1941, probably a 1000 mile mission at that time.

This complex at the north end of the Factory Area had retooled to make T-34 tanks.

Some of the hardest fighting occurred here early on and it was the last German strong point when Soviet forces retook Stalingrad.

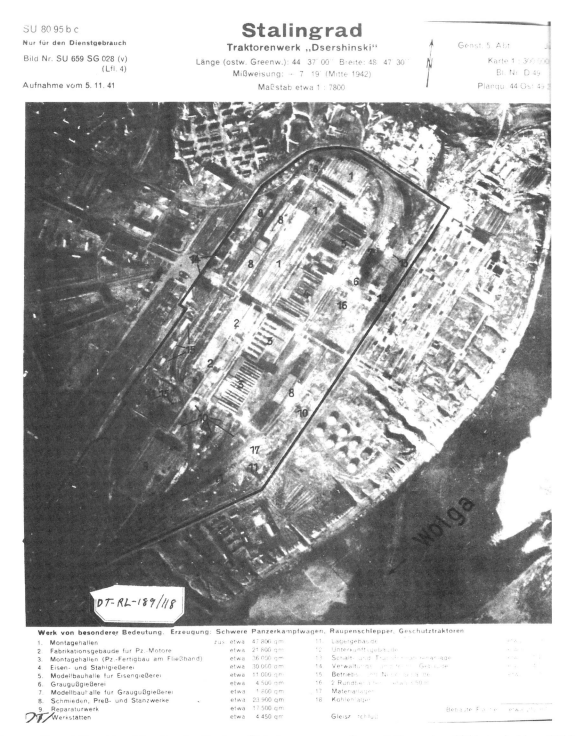

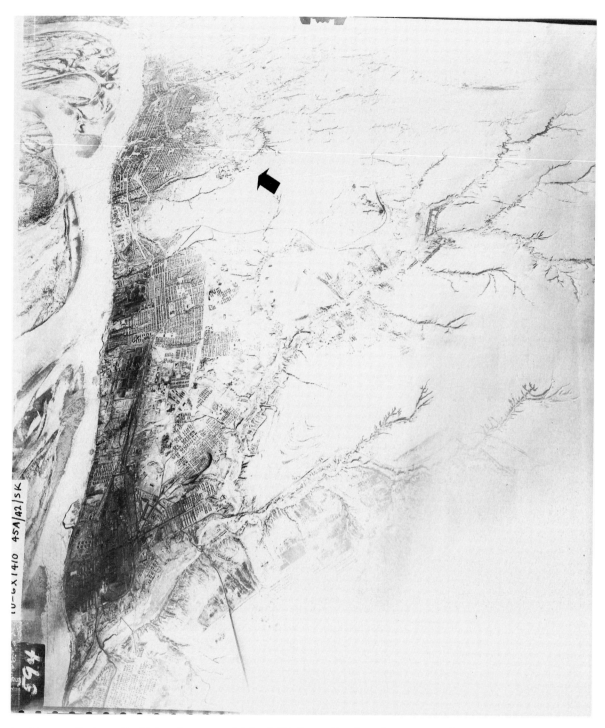

Looking south down the Volga. Imagery of 4 April 42 shows the river frozen over. Oncoming German ground forces were still west of the Don. The arrow indicates Stalingradski Flying School's landing ground, pointing at its three hangars.

Stalingrad city is between the airfield and river. The Factory District is along the river between the city and lower left. It is 25 miles from South Stalingrad to the Dzerzhinsky Factory.

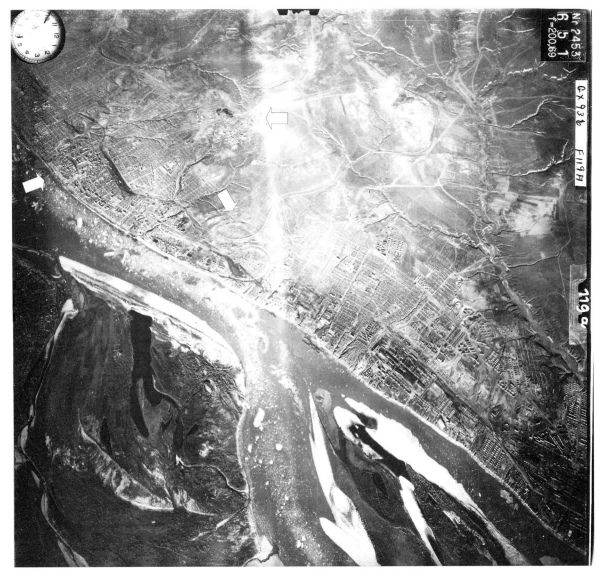

Looking at Stalingrad from above the east bank of the Volga on 20 April 1942. Leftmost arrow points toward Red Plaza, city center. Beyond it is Railway Station #1 and the main rail yard. The Factory District runs north along the river to Dzerzhinsky Traktor Factory on the far right.

The next arrow up indicates Mamayev Kurgan. Hill 102 was some of the most hotly contested ground in the city. It has been said that ground is saturated with more blood, bone and metal than any other spot on earth.

Stalingradski Airfield is indicated by the upper arrow.

Still no signs of ground defenses being created to the west.

From what I saw in film plots, Luftwaffe high-altitude photoreconnaissance missions were over Stalingrad regularly in the spring of 1942.

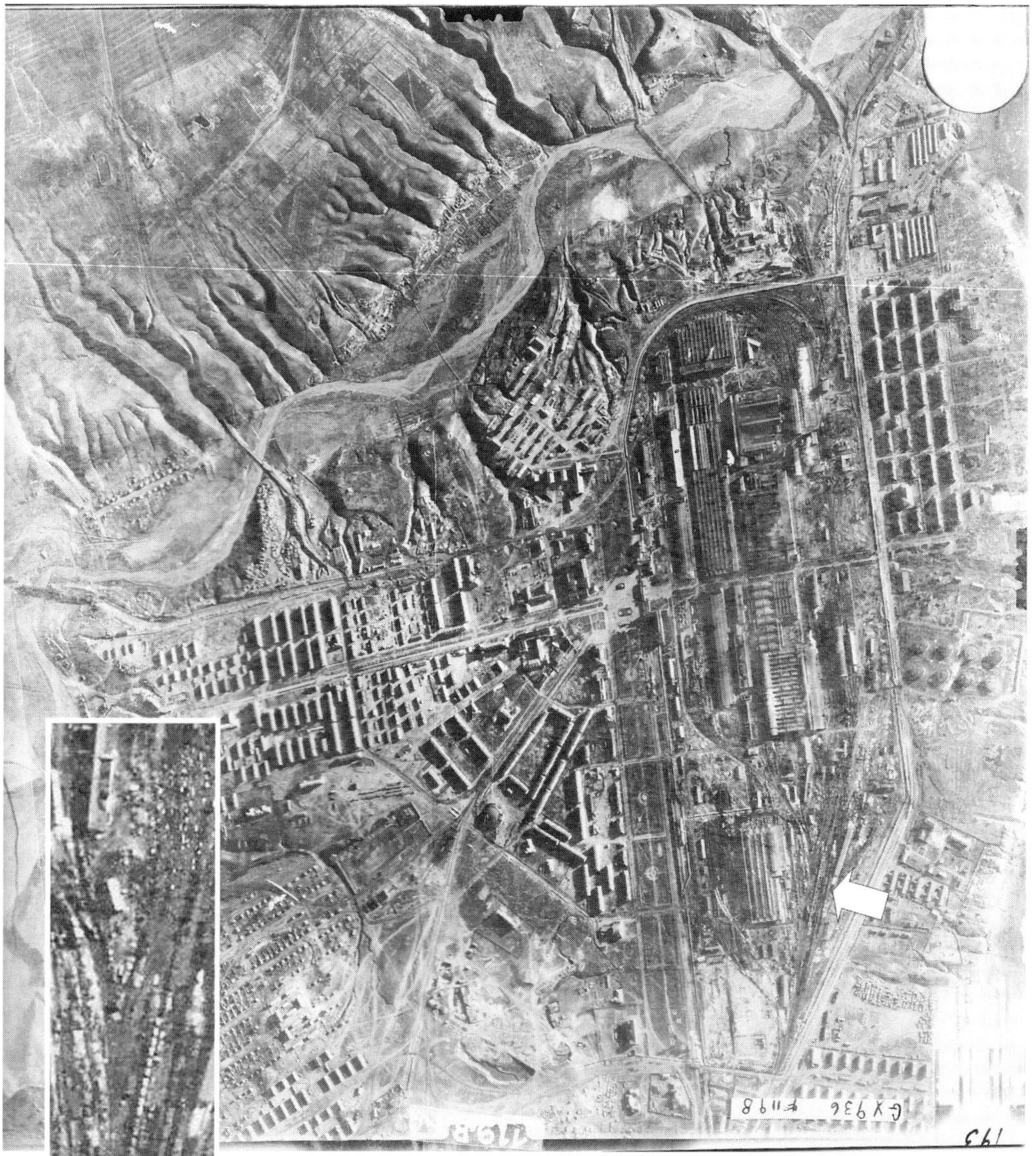

Above, the Tractor Factory, 20 April 42. Steep gullies and broken ground to the north show why Soviet planners didn't think German Panzers would attack from that direction.

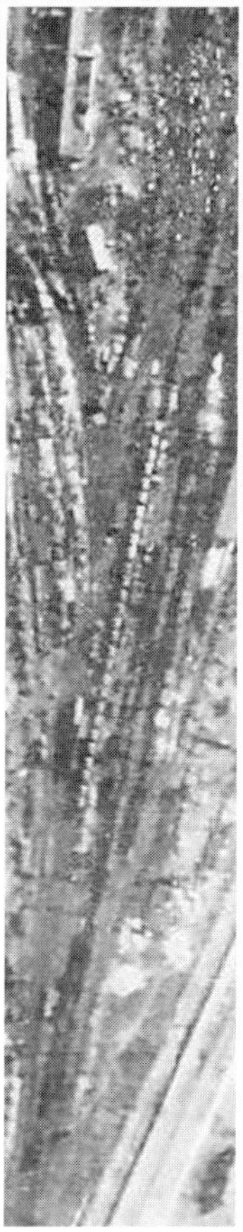

Location of the enlargement at left is indicated by my arrow above. Can't say for certain but those twenty-eight light-colored rectangular objects on rail cars are the right length/width ratio for tanks or tractors under tarps (two to a car).

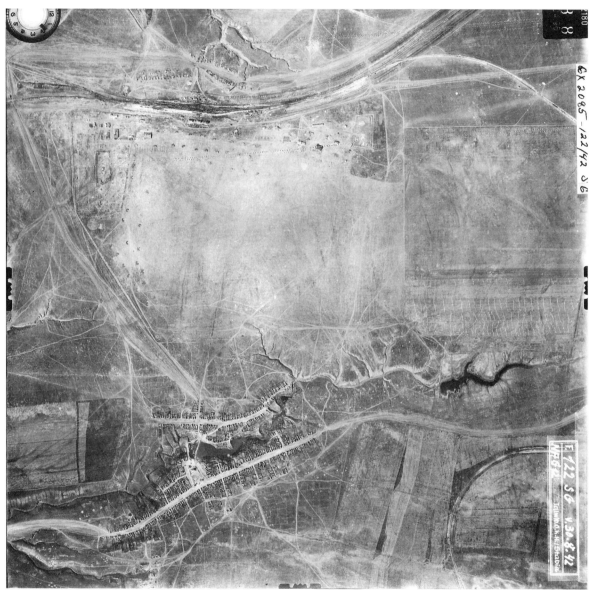

Airfield 10 miles south-southeast of Stalingrad, 30 August 1942. Forty earthen revetments and no aircraft. Matching with maps I believe this is Peschanka Airfield. It was probably in German hands at this time.

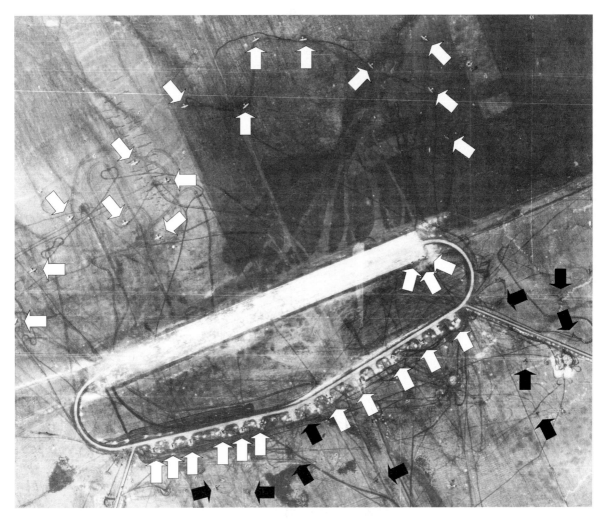

Another Soviet airfield near Stalingrad, 20 April 1942. When I got this enlargement in 1977 I didn't dream I'd write a book, so I didn't pay attention to the actual location. All I have is 'north of Stalingrad' written on the back. The airfield design is typical for the Red Air Force. We saw a corner of one near Novgorod in Chapter VI and you'll see one being built at Gumrak later in this Chapter.

This airfield is loaded. I'm comfortable calling the six upper right arrows probable Tupolev DB-2s, even the camouflaged aircraft. The other nine above the landing strip may be the same, but the horizontal stabilizer shape bothers me.

Three single-engine, single-seat fighters are on strip alert at the right end of the runway. They look like narrow wings and inline engines, so they are definitely not Polikarpovs.

Six airplanes on hardstands may be Petlyakov Pe-2 light bombers.

Ten black arrows show aircraft scattered out of convenient use on unpaved surfaces. Some of those are probably utility aircraft. Others are likely under repair or being cannibalized for parts.

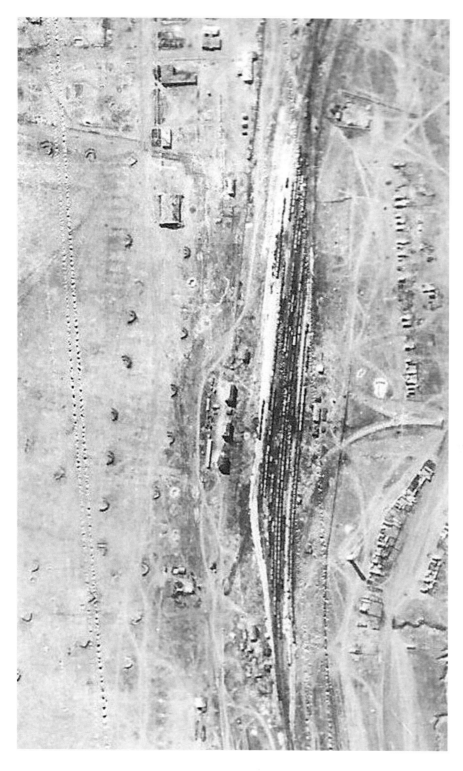

Peschanka enlarged shows no damage to the airfield or facilities. Nor do the small towns to north and south show signs of fighting or vehicle tracks. The rail yard may have been strafed, but we see no cars off the rails or strewn about as with a bombing run.

Those lines of black dots crossing the lower part of this image are emulsion scratches on the original negative caused by poor film processing equipment.

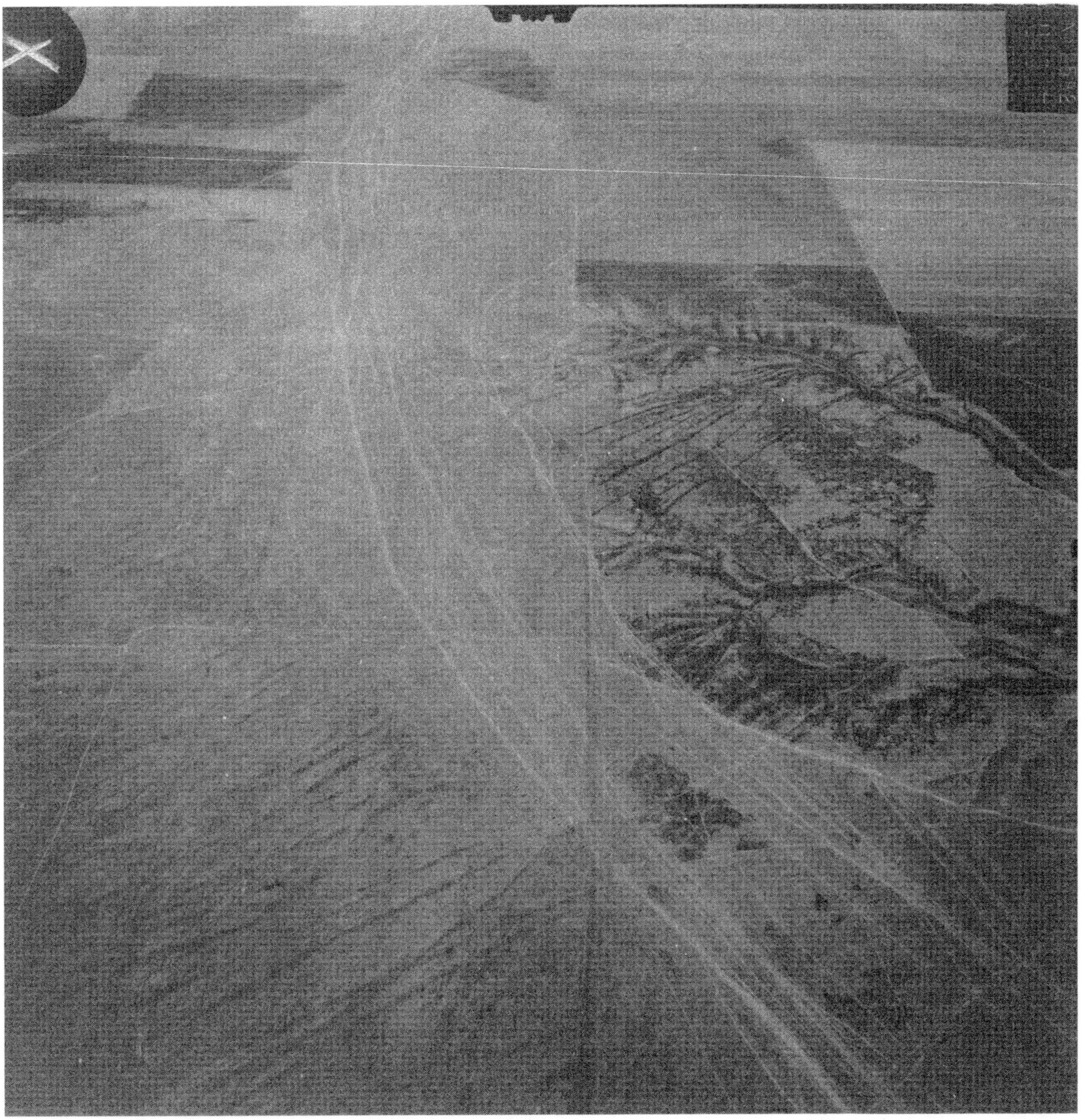

The northwestern approach to Stalingrad, 28 August 1942. Perfect tank country; flat, open and few places to mount a defense. Many parallel tracks show this is firm ground with good load-bearing capacity. No sign of German or Soviet activity.

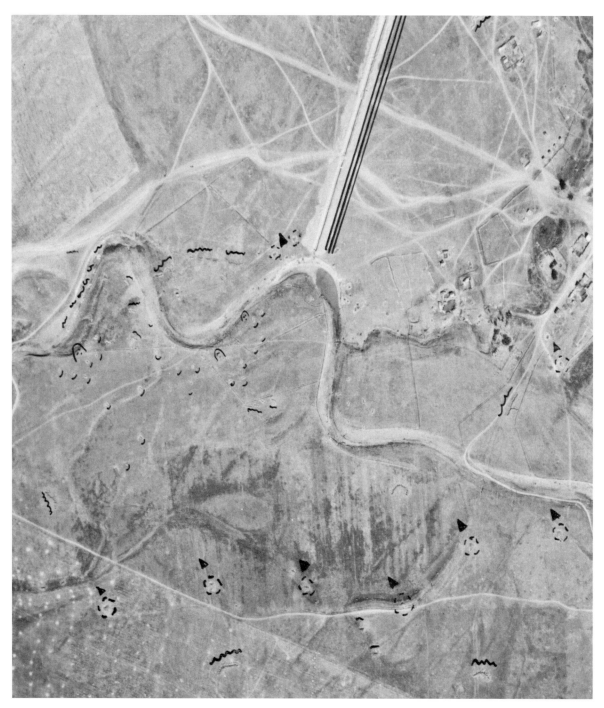

The actual assault on Stalingrad is accepted as beginning on 22 August. What was German aerial recon looking at? This is about 25 miles NNW of the city. A thin Soviet defense line was established mostly just south of a small river, flanked by an anti-tank ditch to the north. German PIs marked dashed circles on the print to show 'lagers' (camps). Solid triangles mean battalion-sized (they may be small barracks). There are 18 of them. Other annotations show trenches and revetments for artillery. There is no visible activity, though about half of the gun positions appear occupied.

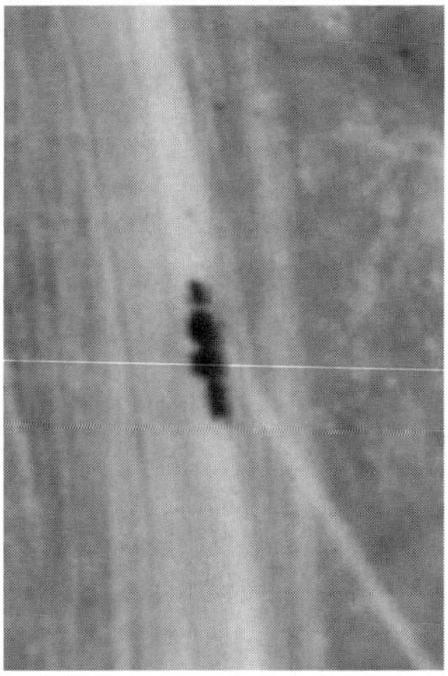

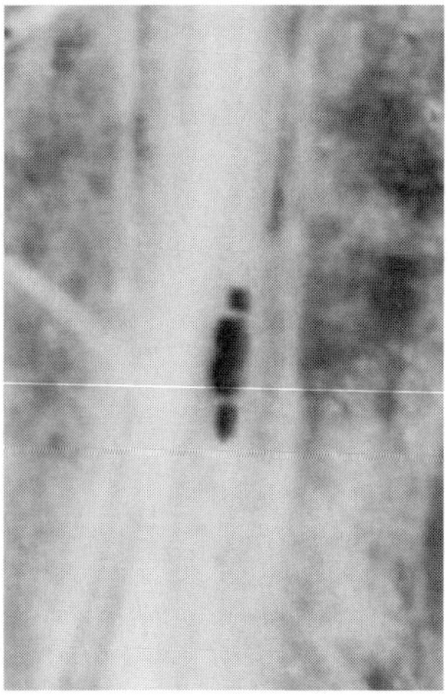

A road in the same area as above on the same day is a puzzle. Seeing vehicular traffic in aerial imagery of USSR was unusual and here was a surfeit on a short section of road. If this was Soviet commerce they were almost in the arms of oncoming Barbarossa forces. If it's a German convoy it's farther east than generally expected—and badly spread out. Origins and destinations are obscure because vehicles were on both arms of road splits at top and bottom of the photo.

The left enlargement shows one of vehicles is clearly much larger than ordinary 20 foot-long 4 x 2 fixed-frame trucks. It appears to be towing. The only vehicles I know of that size in Russia at the time would be German tank transporters (the Soviets had none). Enlargement at right (from other imagery) shows three distinct sections.

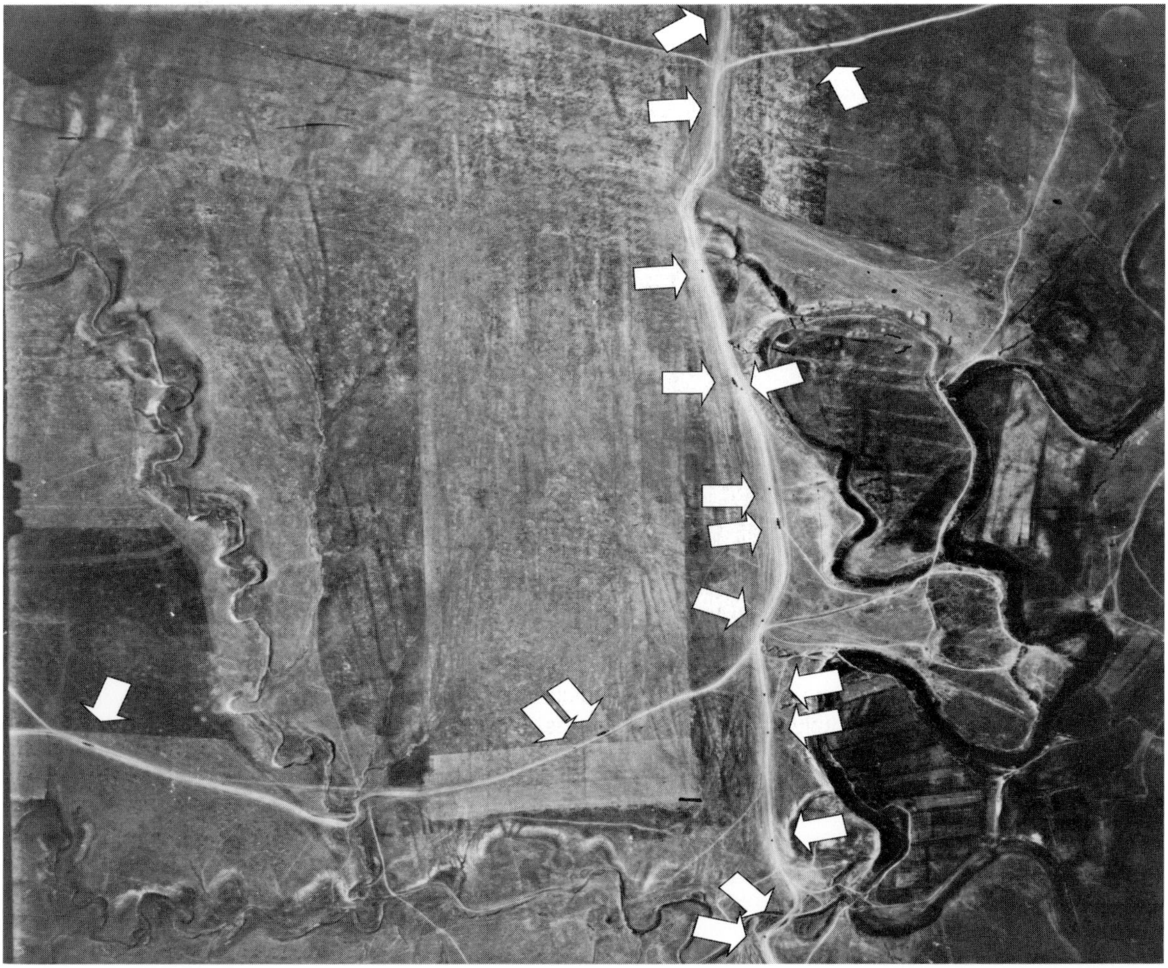

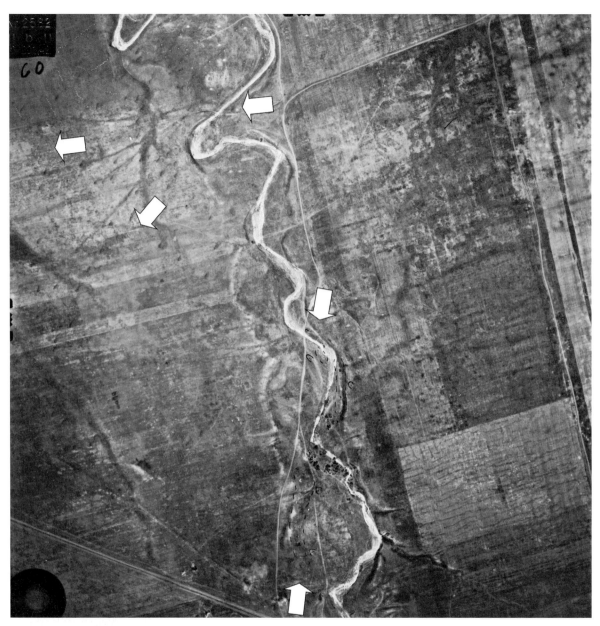

Another location NNW of Stalingrad on 22 August 1942. The two bottom arrows show a static defense line along a small river. A photo top is something more difficult to interpret. Tracks on the ground look to me like things I've seen in Normandy, Italy and Belgium. I suggest this MAY show AFV (Armored Fighting Vehicles), probably armored cars, crossing the river (upper arrow) and fanning out in the fields (far left arrows showing axis of deployment. If I'm right, the origin east of the river and direction of movement suggests Soviet equipment.

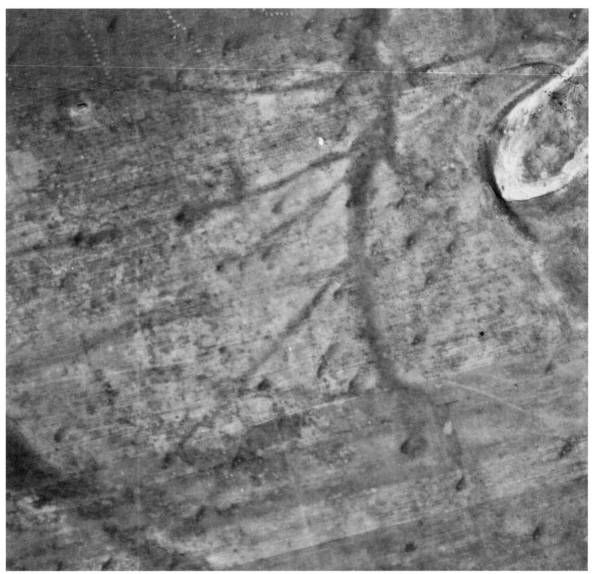

If I'm correct with the ID, this enlargement from upper left of the previous photo shows some 30+ vehicles all heading down and left. Note shapes at end of tracks and some shapes following in the same tracks. Tracks don't show the 'kink' characteristic of skid turns by a fully tracked vehicle. Some shapes leave no tracks, leading me to guess they are light, probably armored cars like BA-10s.

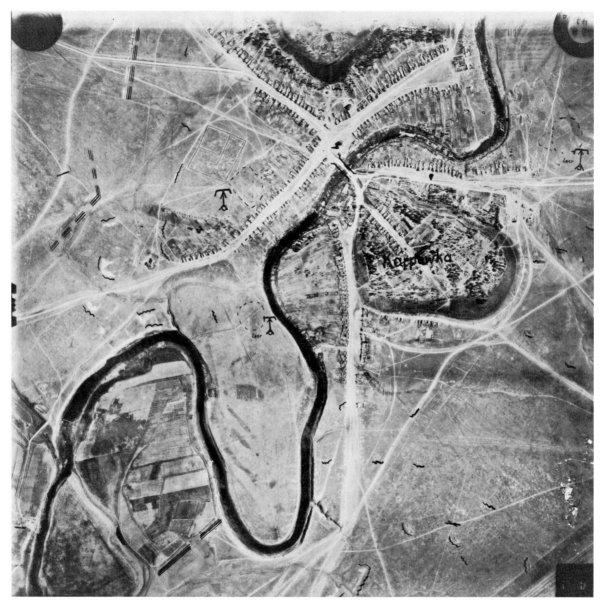

Karpovka, 30 miles west of Stalingrad, 22 August 1942. This would become the site of a Stalingrad support airfield (which was overrun by Soviet infantry on 13 January 1943). German annotations show the area is defended by three five-gun anti-aircraft batteries (probably 37mm guns).

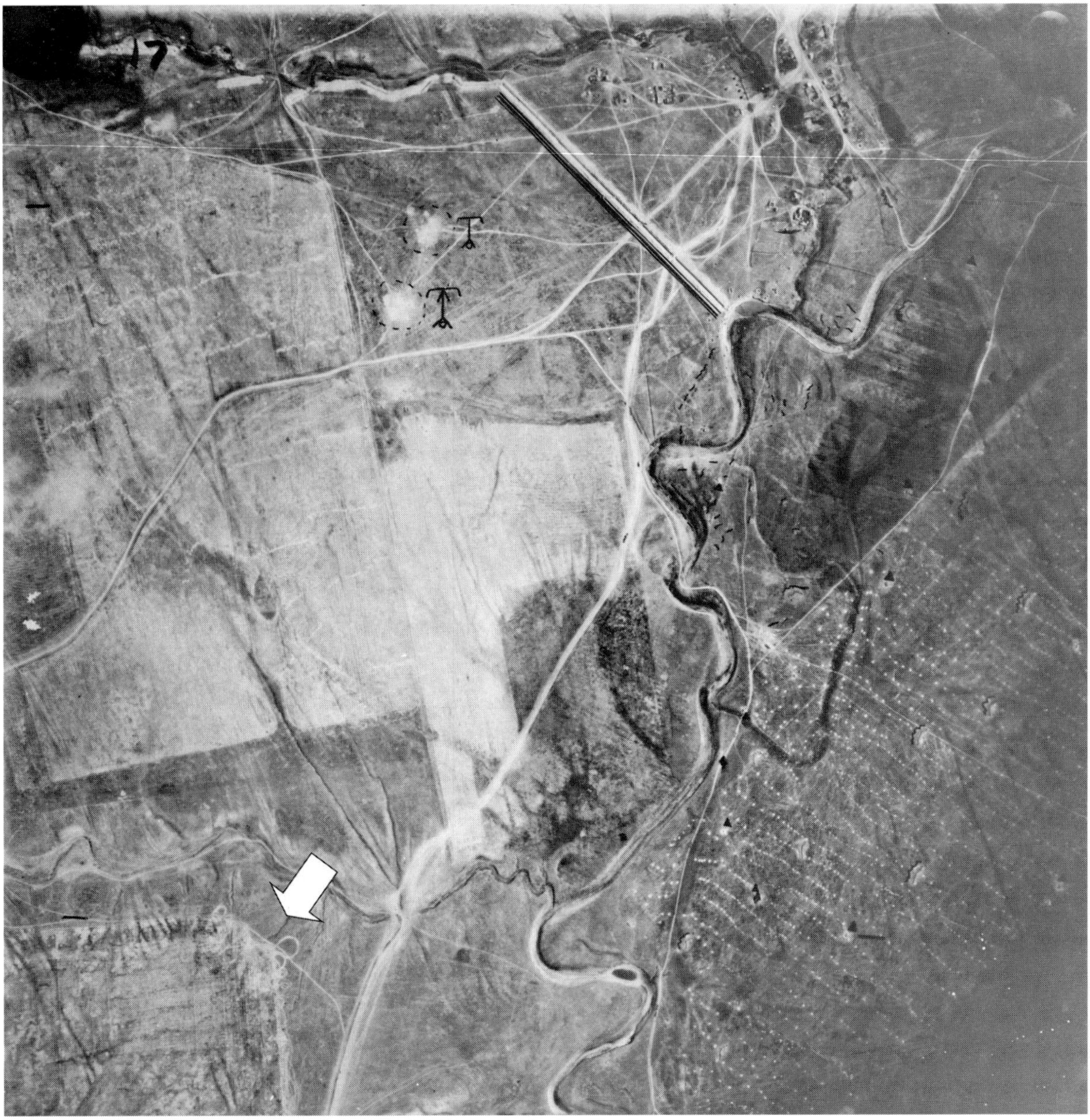

Near Karpovka, 22 August 1942. This area is defended by an anti-tank ditch and two anti-aircraft positions. The upper light guns are probably machine guns and the lower is probably a five-gun 37mm battery. My arrow at lower left shows track activity I would look at long and hard as a PI. Large diameter circles indicate rigid frame vehicles or long loads.

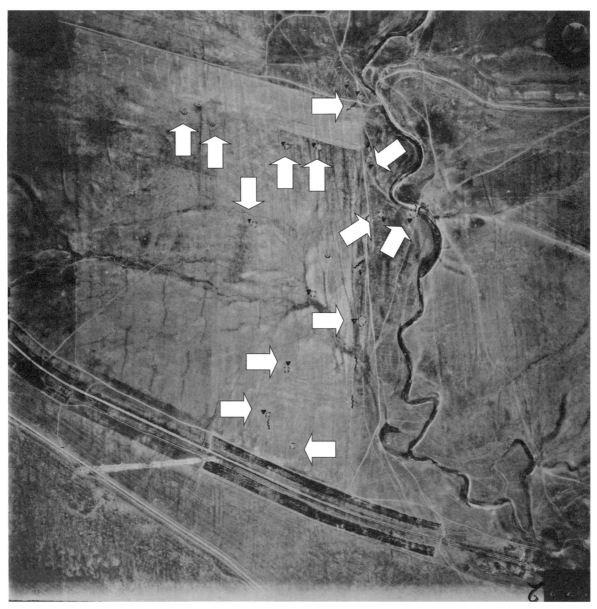

Arrows show German PI annotation for 'lagers' (camps). The symbols indicate battalion size, but they seem a little small for that. This is near Kotluban, 25 miles northwest of Stalingrad, 22 August 1942.

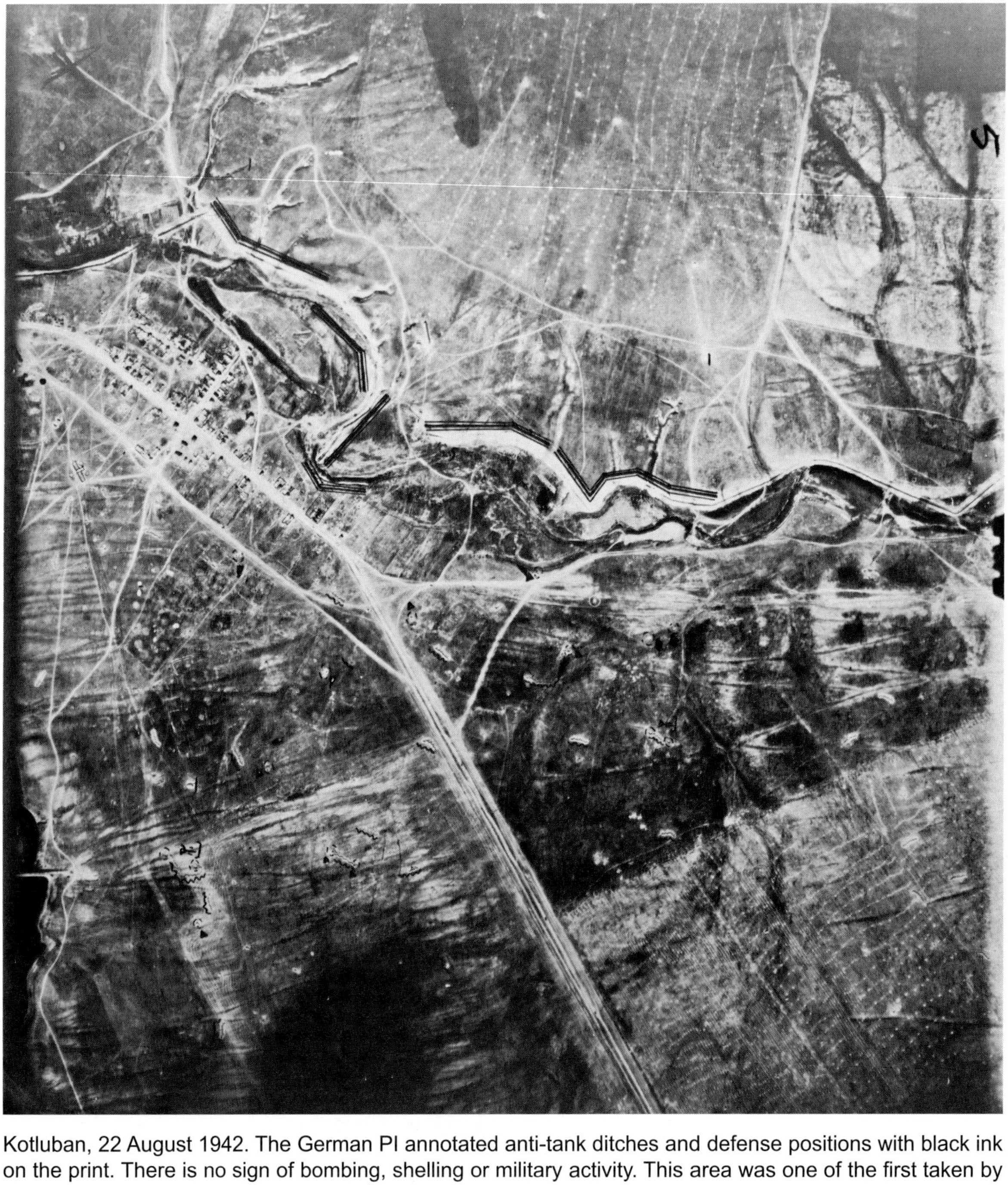

Kotluban, 22 August 1942. The German PI annotated anti-tank ditches and defense positions with black ink on the print. There is no sign of bombing, shelling or military activity. This area was one of the first taken by German forces on the way east to Stalingrad and one of the key areas lost on the retreat back west.

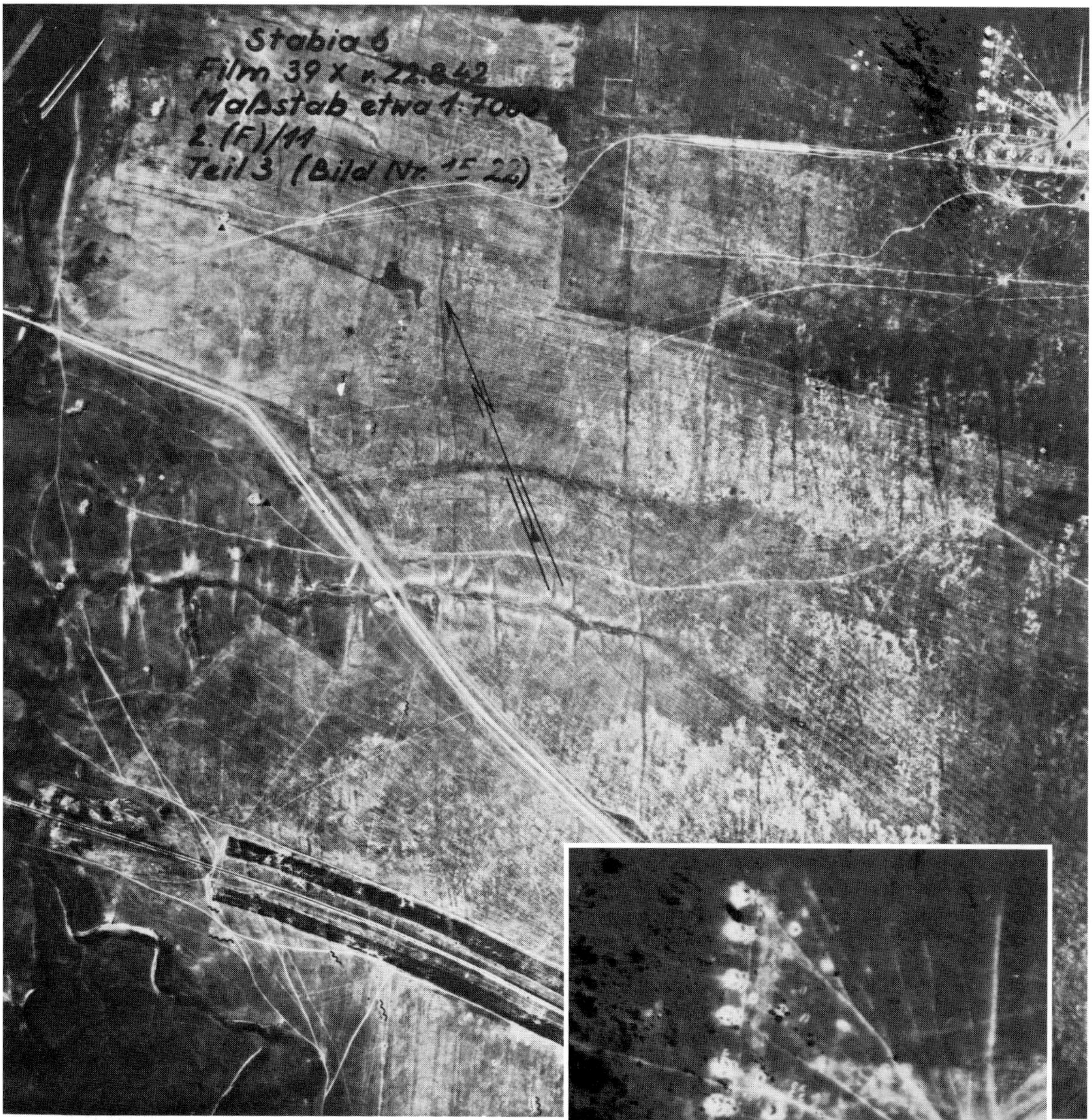
Stabia 6
Film 39 X v. 22.8.42
Maßstab etwa 1:7000
2.(F)/11
Teil 3 (Bild Nr. 15 22)

Near Kotluban, 22 August.
German PIs didn't annotate the activity at upper right.

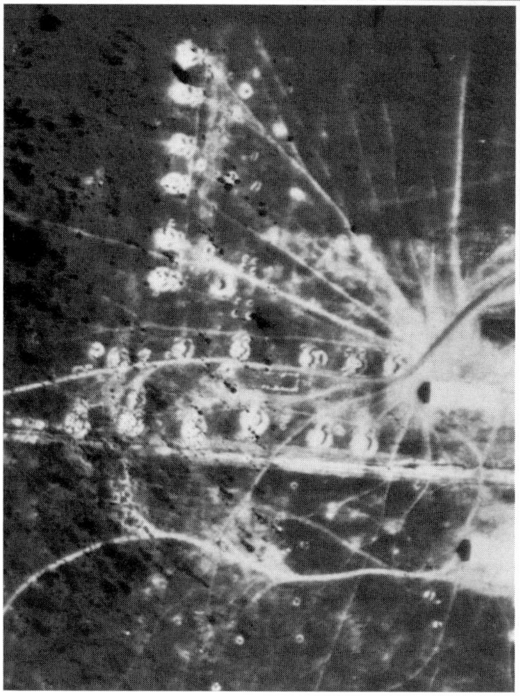

Enlarged (at right) that looks like a six-gun heavy artillery battery position. Revetments along the road would be for prime movers to tow the guns.

I can't tell if the position is occupied.

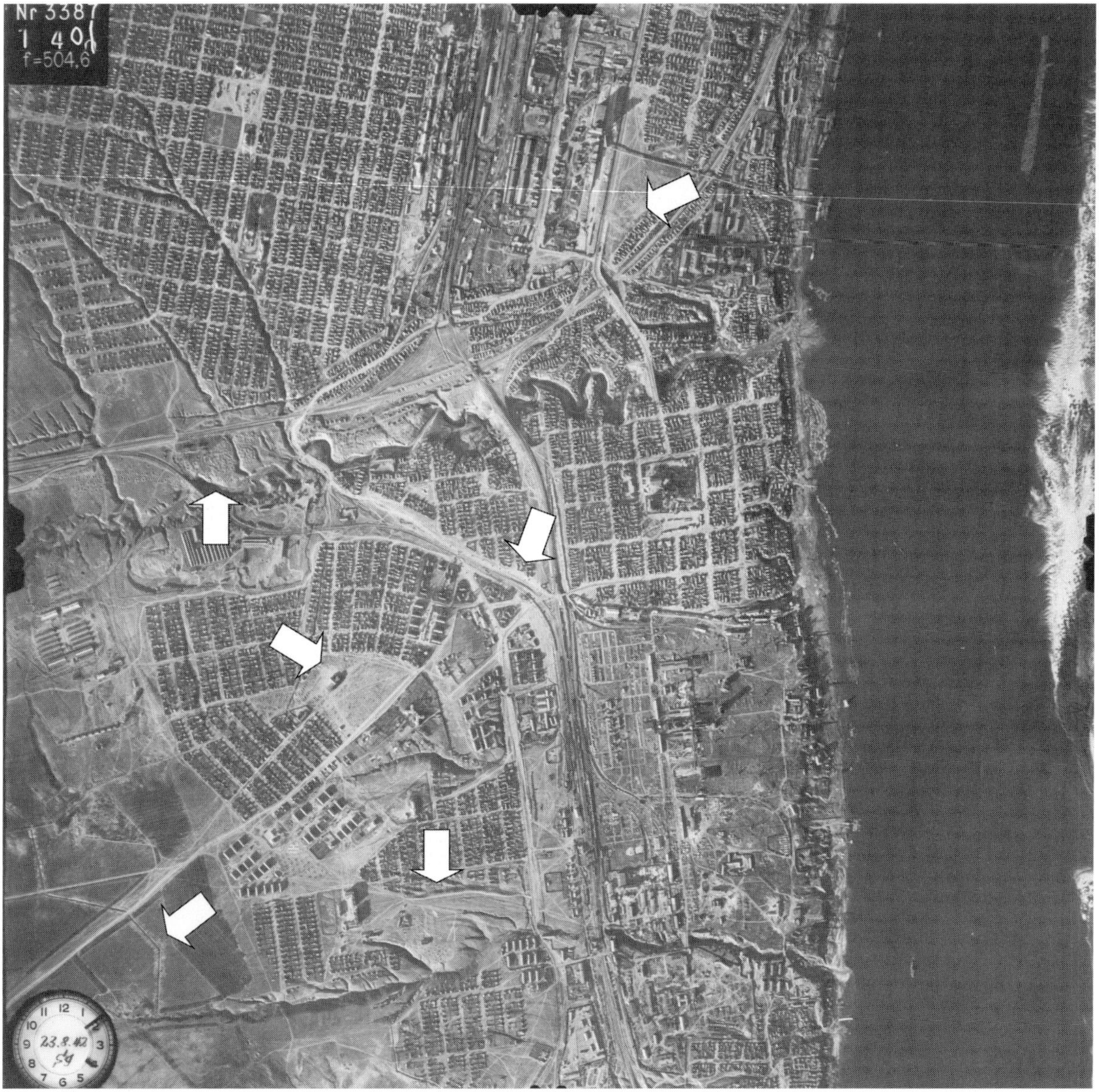
Nr 3387
1 40
f=504.6
23.8.42

South Stalingrad, 23 August 1942, the only active defense showing on this frame is a light anti-aircraft gun position in a cleared area just east of the well-known Grain Elevator (upper arrow). The towering building's shadow shows just up and left from my arrow and a line from there to the shore was a pipe to transfer grain to Volga River barges.

A small anti-tank ditch is at the lower left arrow.

Other arrows show clusters of pits and dug-outs to shelter personnel.

There are no apparent provisions for ground warfare.

There is no sign of bomb or fire damage. This was the day traditionally used as the start of the Siege of Stalingrad.

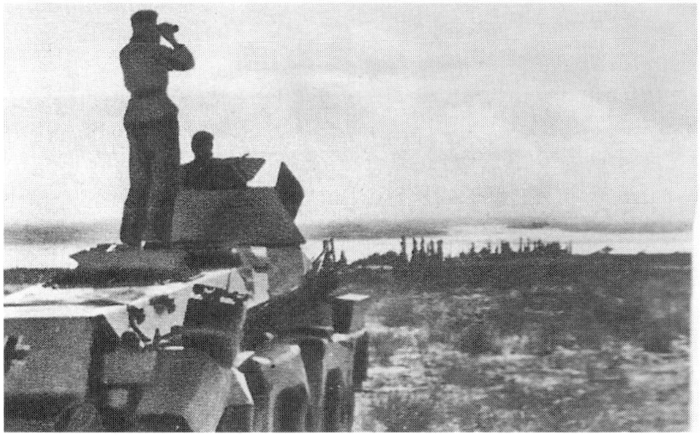

North of Stalingrad, German soldiers overlooking the Volga from a Panzer Division's SdKfz. 232 (8-rad) Armored Reconnaissance vehicle, late August 1942. Once the river was reached encirclement of Stalingrad began, and Soviet 62nd and 64th armies were steadily pushed east against the river inside the city.

Southwest fringe of Stalingrad, 30 August 1942, a week after the German attack began. That anti-tank ditch under construction (between arrows) hasn't progressed much. There are shell/bomb craters south of the ditch and numerous fox-holes amid buildings north of the ditch.

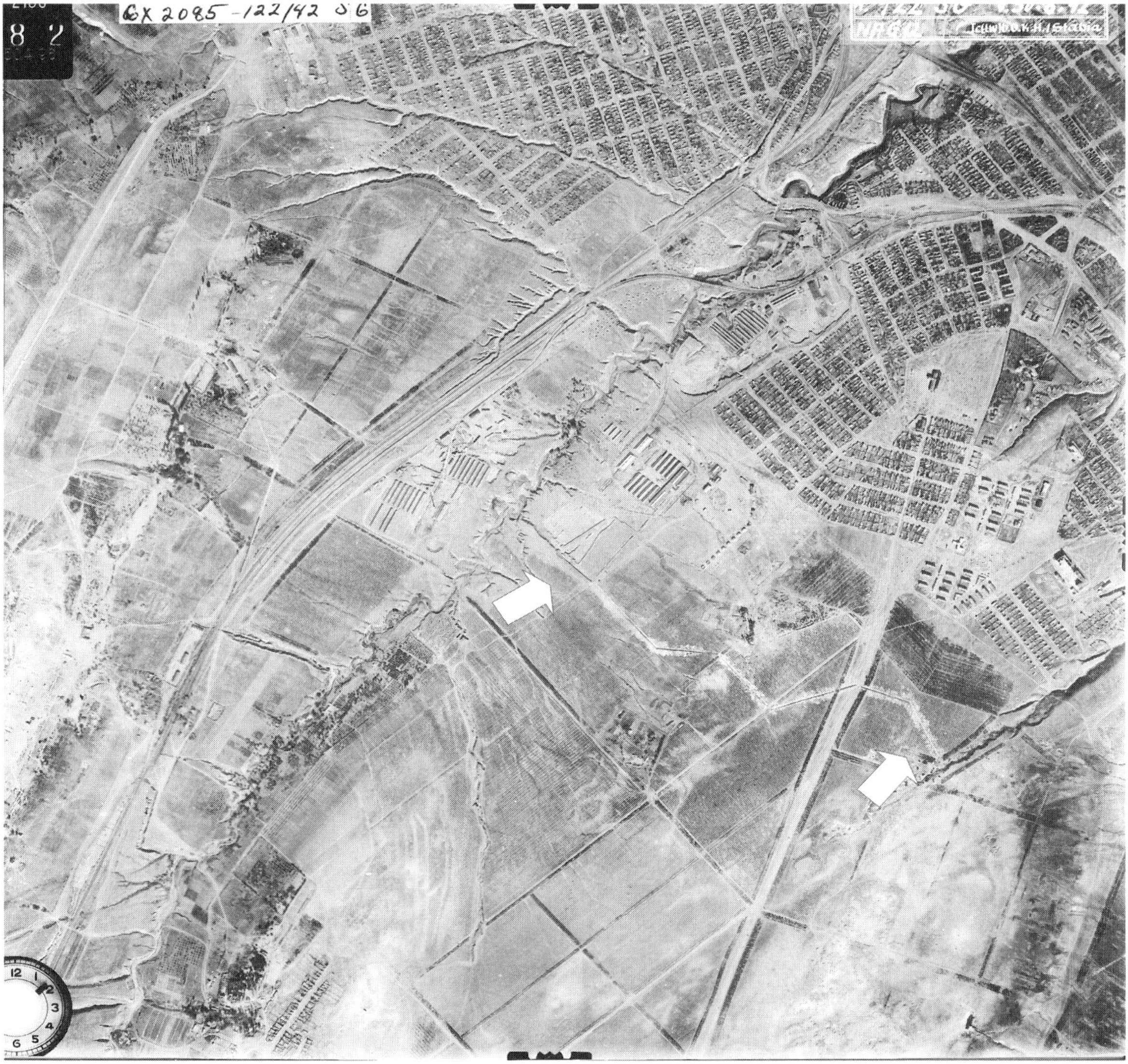

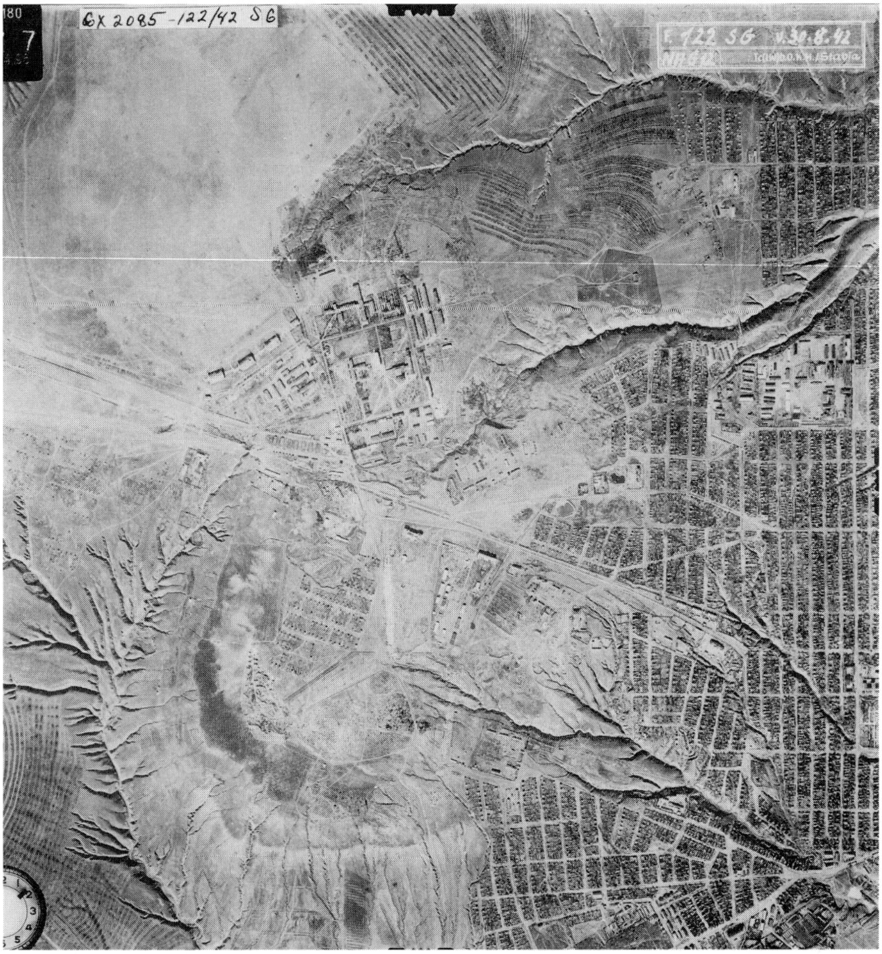
GX 2085 -122/42 SG

Stalingradski Airfield & Flying School (upper left), 3 miles west of the river, 30 August 1942.

Enlargement shows thirty-nine revetments, three possible single-engine aircraft. There are bomb hits on all three hangars.

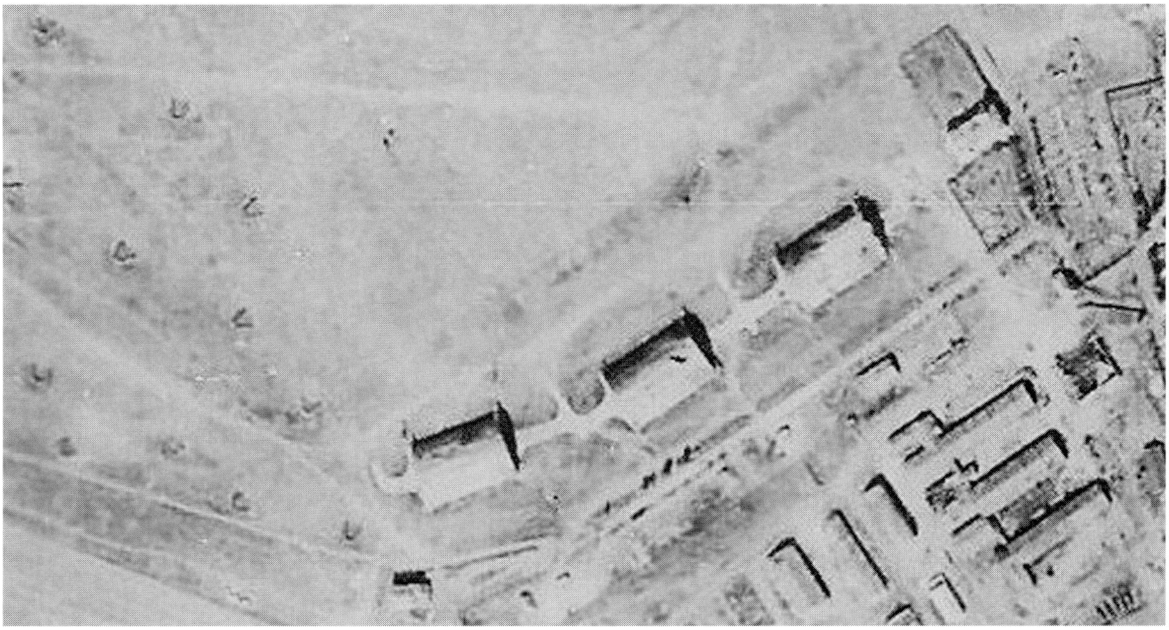

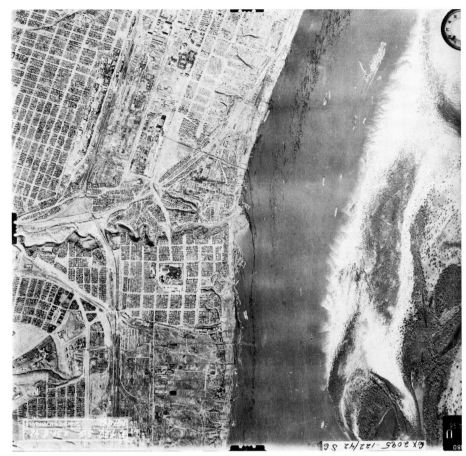

South side of the city, 30 August 1942 (one week after the photo three pages earlier).

Top left center is the iconic Grain Elevator, enlarged at right. The AAA position to its right is occupied. Compared with surrounding buildings, long shadows show the height of this structure.

Buildings on all sides have been destroyed by fire, artillery and bombing but there is no evidence of ground warfare as yet.

From 17 to 21 September this area saw some of the bitterest back-and-forth fighting early in the siege of Stalingrad. The Grain Elevator so epitomized battle in Stalingrad that General von Paulus intended to use it on a victory patch he wanted created.

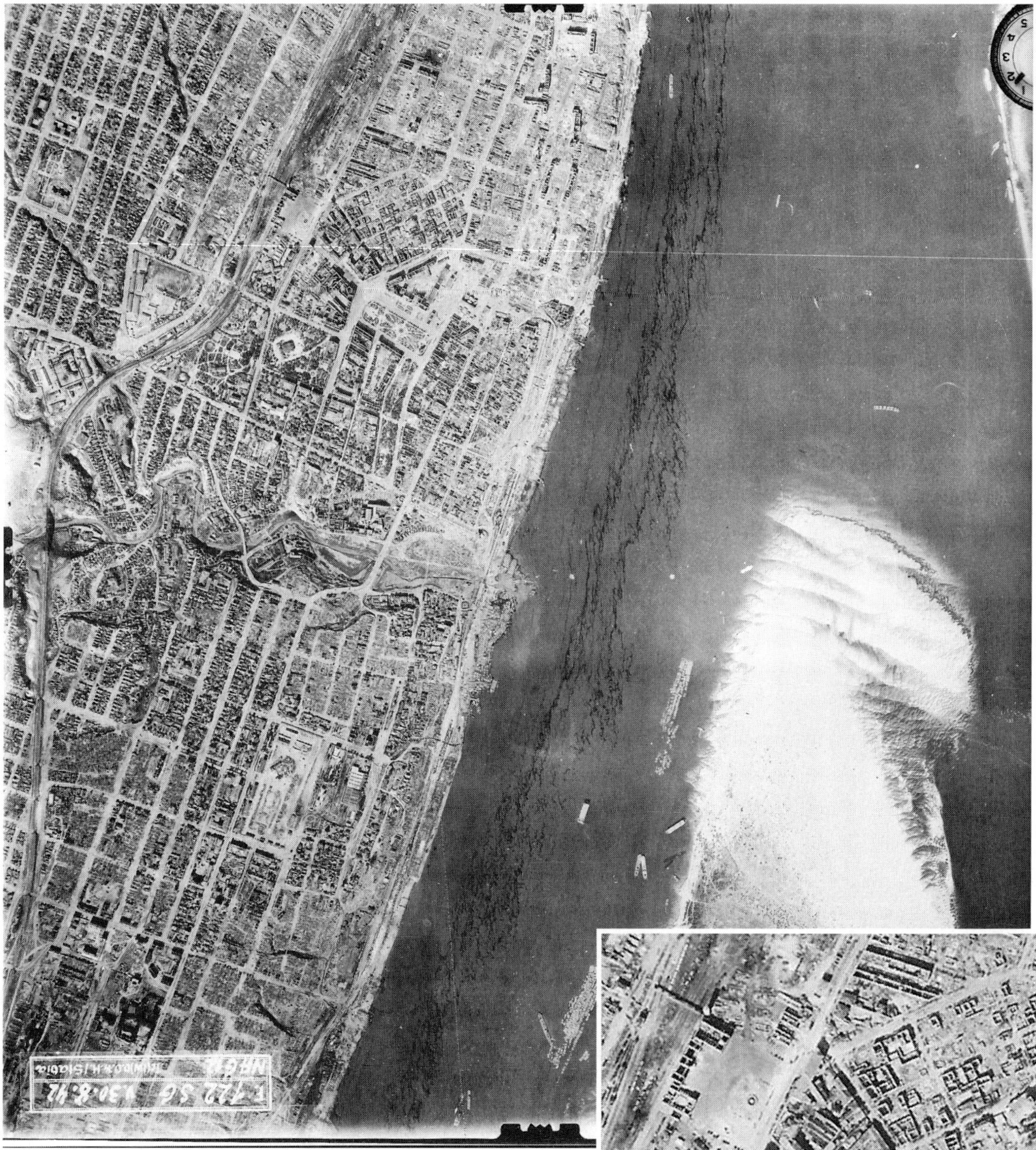

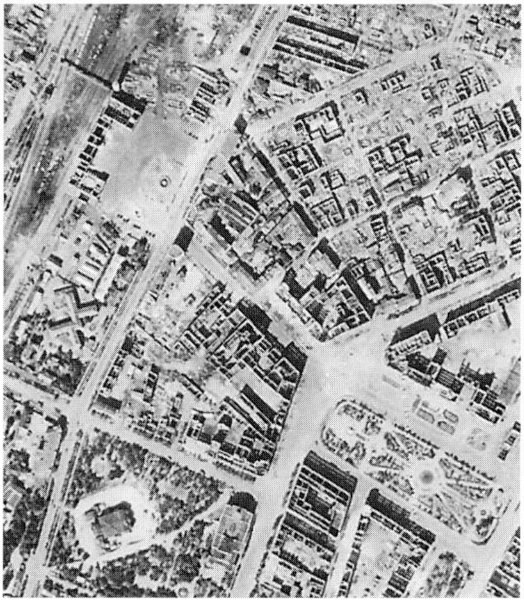

City center, 31 August 1942. Compare with the pre-war photo (earlier in chapter). Enlargement at right shows Red Plaza and road angling to RR Station #1. German troops weren't here yet, but at the height of battle that railroad station changed hands fourteen times in six hours.

Bombing began on 23 August and burned out many buildings (we are looking inside walls missing roofs). Absence of craters or rubble indicates fire destroyed this area. The rail yard has also been bombed.

North of Red Plaza. Enlargement of 31 August 1942 coverage. Station # 1 is lower left. Rail service in and out of Stalingrad is clearly over for the duration. Dwellings just south of here still have roofs and appear untouched. Buildings east and west of the rail yard are either burned-out or blasted into rubble.

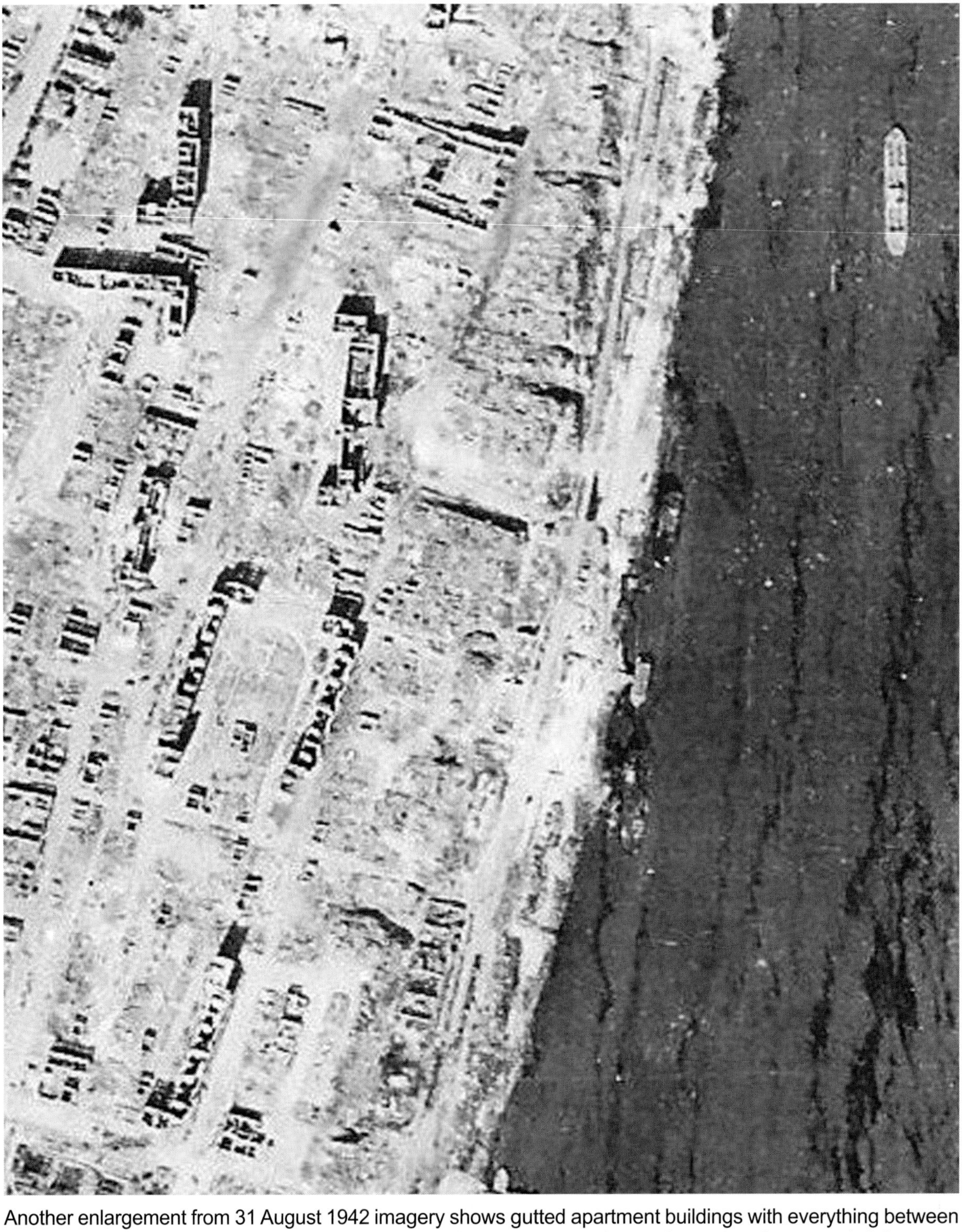

Another enlargement from 31 August 1942 imagery shows gutted apartment buildings with everything between the dour but sturdy concrete multi-storied communal structures bombed or burned to the ground. A firestorm resulting from bombing on 23 August did much of that damage.

German troops were fighting in the outskirts of Stalingrad by this time.

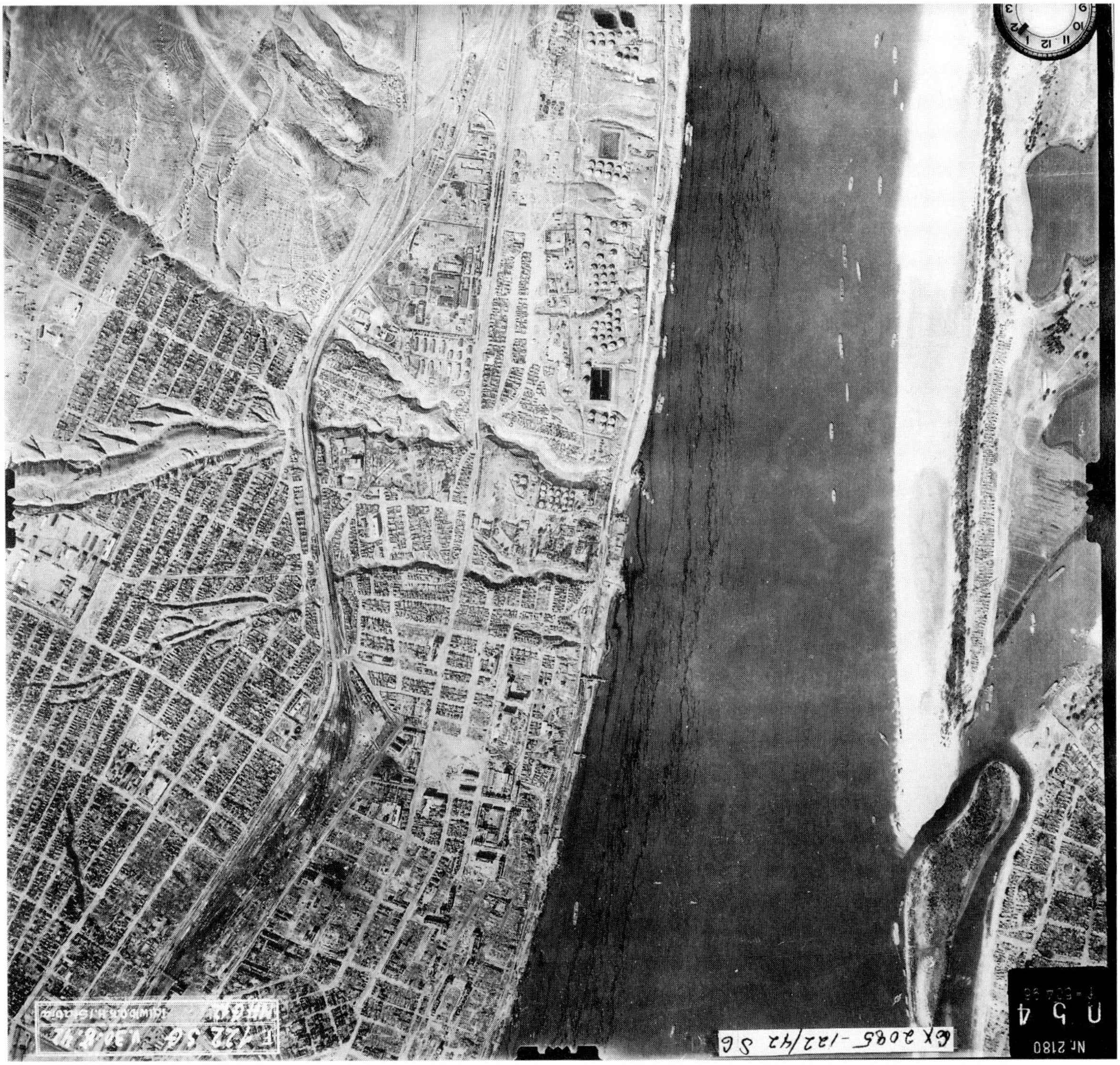

North side of the city, 30 August 1942. The attack had begun but Soviets still held Stalingrad at this time and Volga River barge traffic was still active. The rail yard at lower left has been bombed and there is destruction in residential areas to the east and west of the yard. However, I count eighty-one untouched fuel storage tanks near the river from photo center to top.

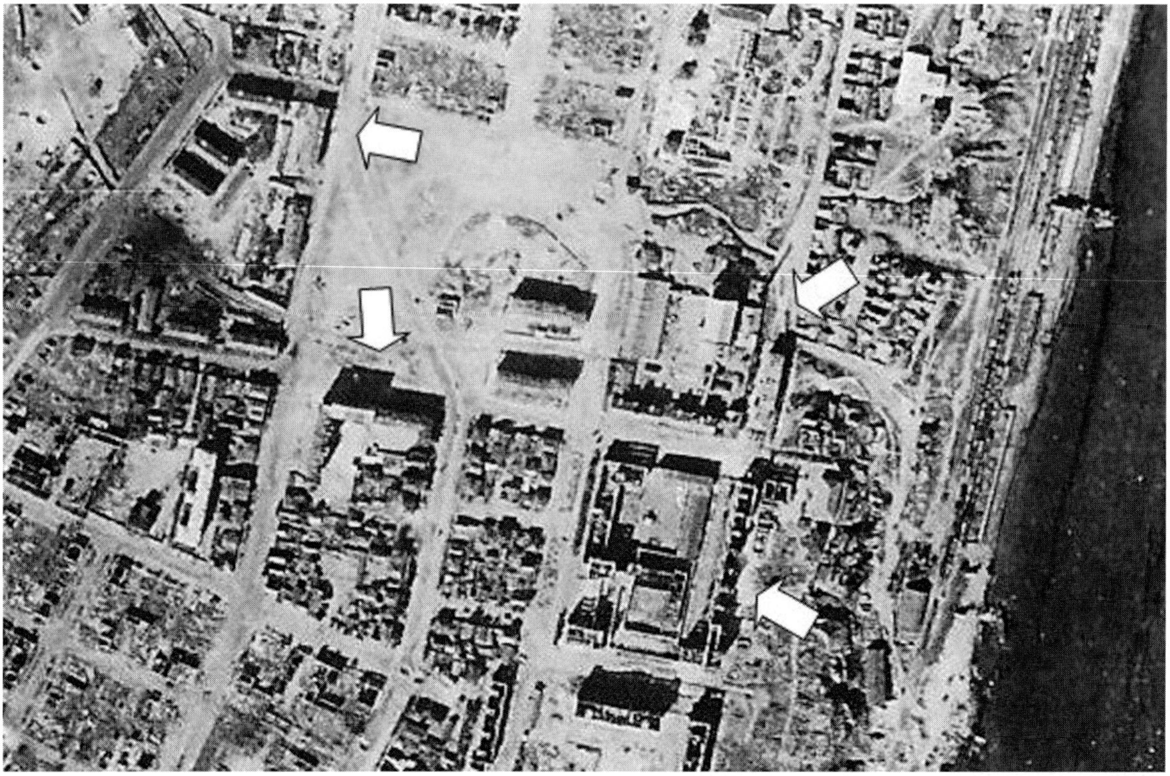

9th January Square, 30 August 1942
According to a German map, clockwise from upper left arrow: a General Store, Electric Sub-Station, Water Works, and Post Office.

The upper long building nearest square center is Pavlov's House where two dozen Soviet soldiers under Junior Sergeant Yakov Pavlov held out from 27 September to 25 November, keeping open a vital supply route to the Volga's east bank.

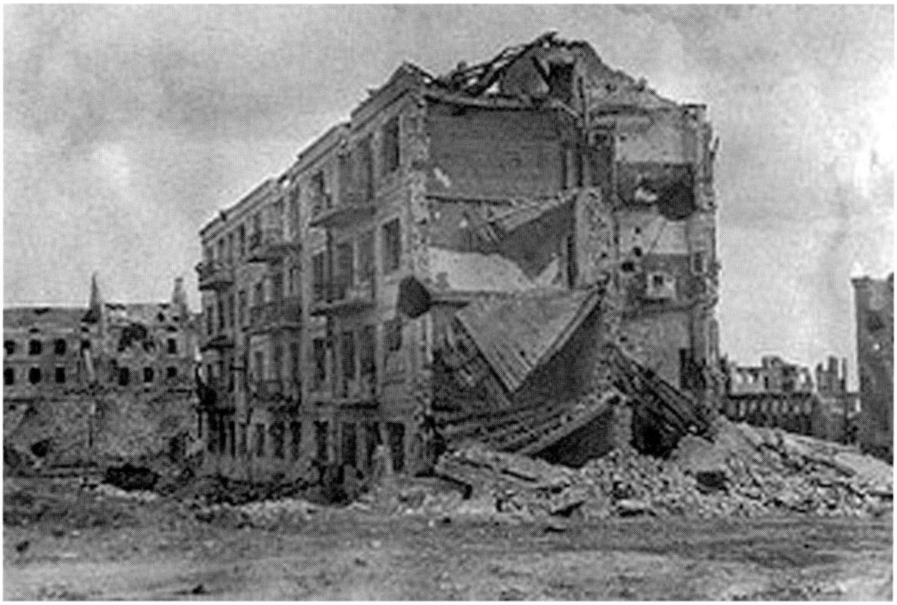

Left, Pavlov's House after the battle.

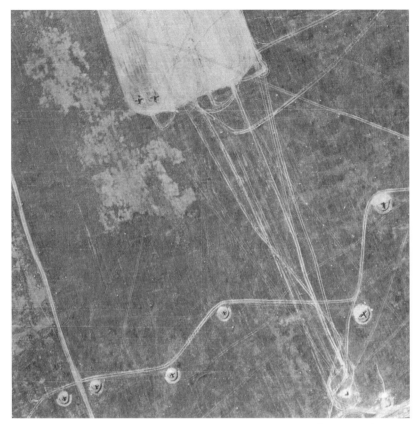

Newly bulldozed runway of a Soviet tactical airfield near Stalingrad, 30 August 1942. Left four revetments hold probable I-16s. Based upon cockpit position, the right two may be Yak-1Bs. Aircraft on strip alert are the right size for Il-2s. In another two weeks this was probably being used by Luftwaffe units.

Below, five probable Il-16 fighters on a decidedly ad hoc field near Stalingrad.

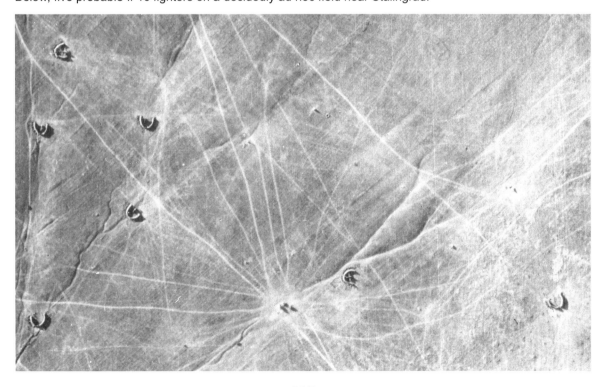

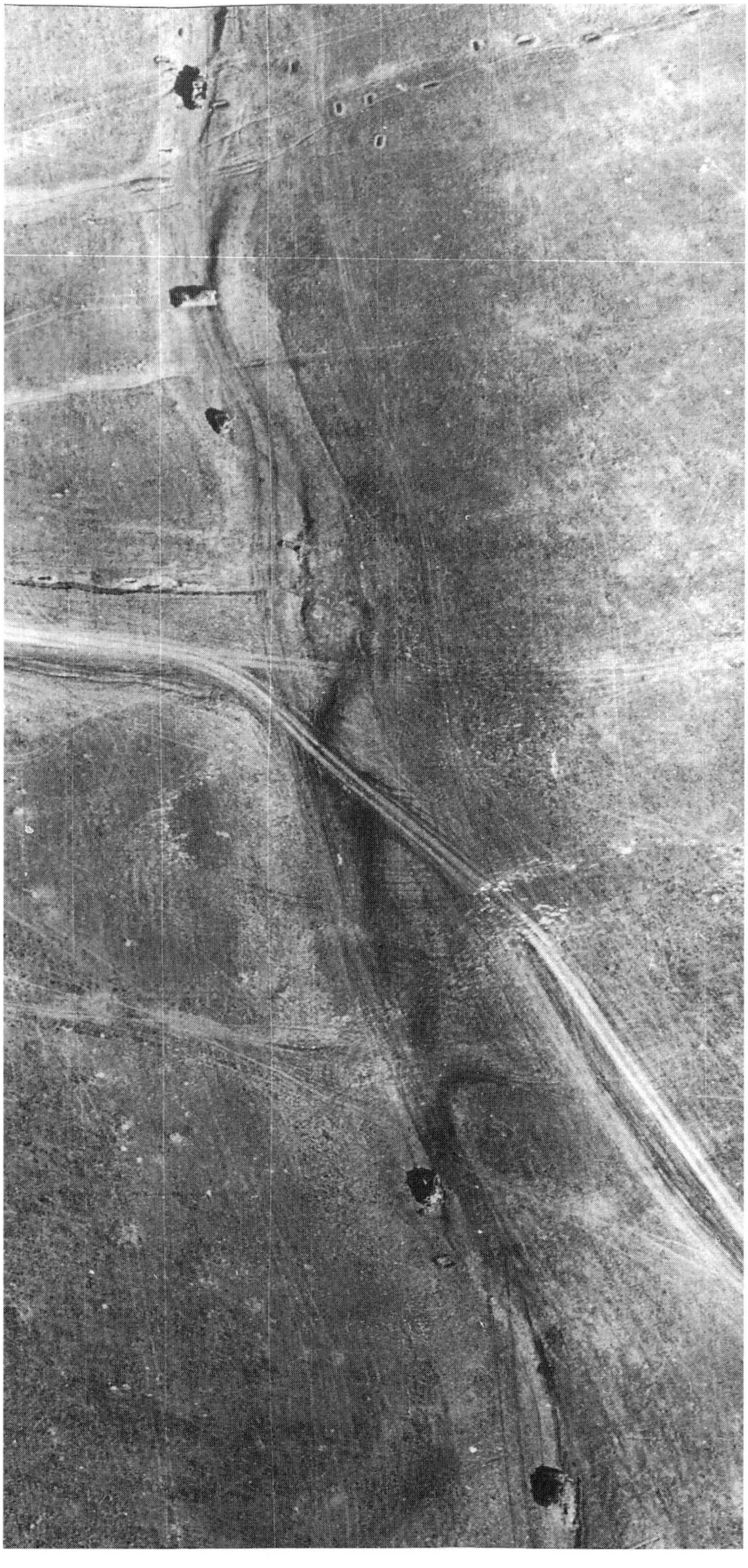

Probable German vehicles in a ravine west of the city, 30 August 1942 (awaiting the attack to begin).

From top; a half-track, tank, reconnaissance car, another half-track and a possible self-propelled assault gun.

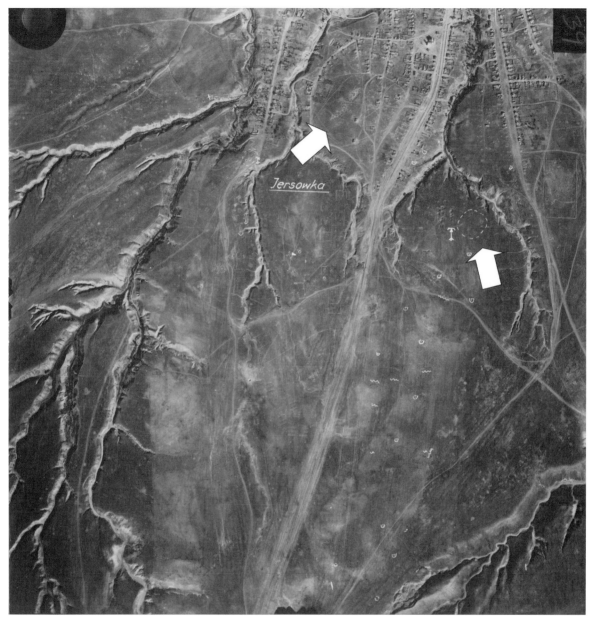

Jersovka, on the Volga 10 miles north of Stalingrad, 25 September 1942. The upper arrow points to clusters of personnel shelters (fox holes) between the settlements. Just left of the arrow is an annotation for a searchlight. The right arrow is a five gun light anti-aircraft battery. Small defense positions and slit trenches are annotated in white.

There is a single bomb crater at center left.

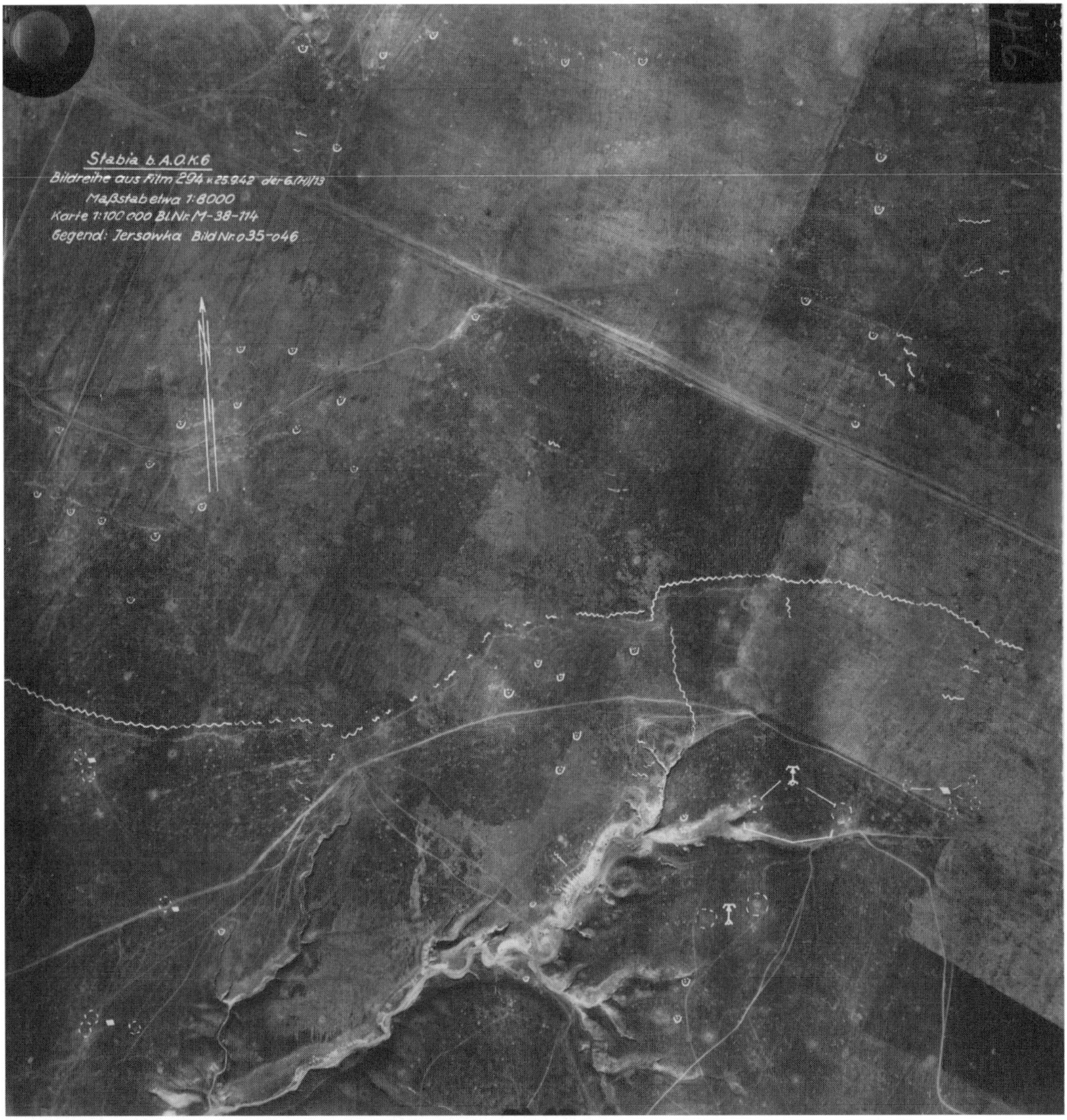
Stabia b. A.O.K.6
Bildreihe aus Film 294 v. 25.9.42 der 6.(H)/13
Maßstab etwa 1:8000
Karte 1:100 000 Bl.Nr. M-38-114
Gegend: Jersowka Bild Nr. 035-046

Near Jersovka, 25 September 1942. A number of slit trenches coalesce to form a defense line. Numerous fighting pits are scattered in open ground to the west. The line is supported by four medium anti-aircraft guns (76mm) in individual revetments.

East of the anti-aircraft guns a German PI annotated four armored vehicles (enlarged on the next page.)

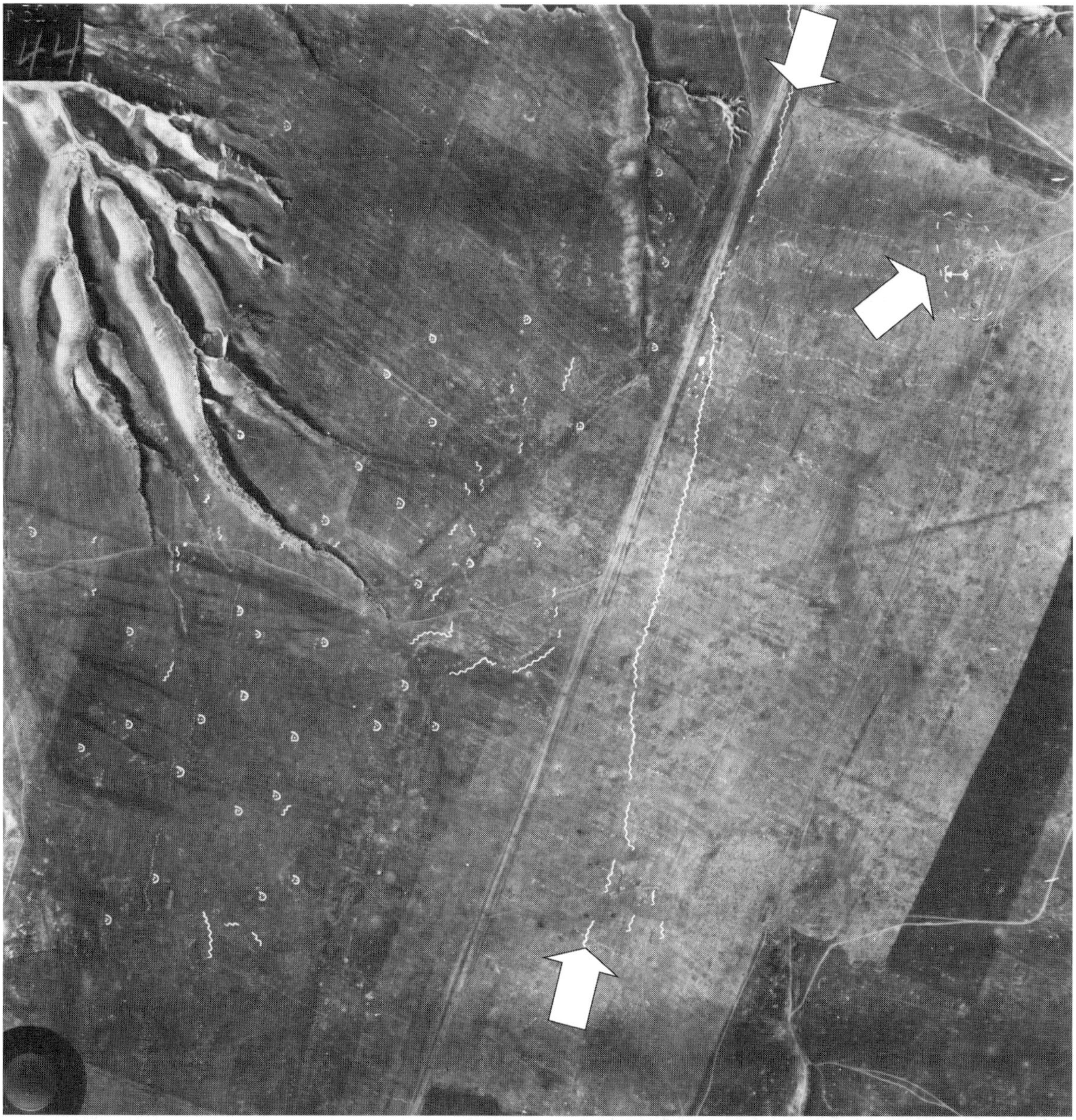

A long trench runs between the upper and lower arrows. Numerous fighting pits are in open fields to the west. The right arrow is an annotation for anti-aircraft guns but the revetments are positioned more typically for field artillery. They are occupied.

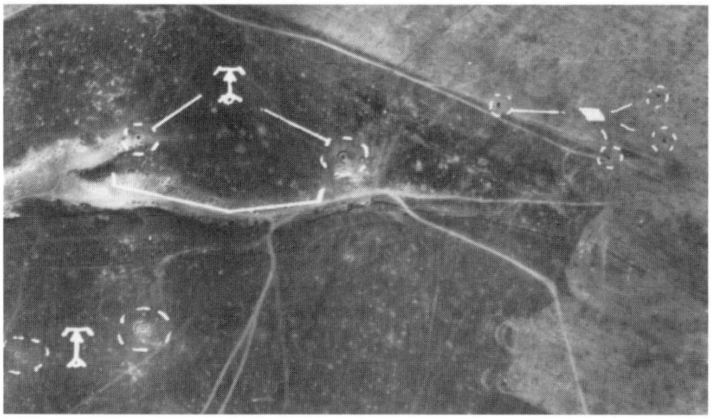

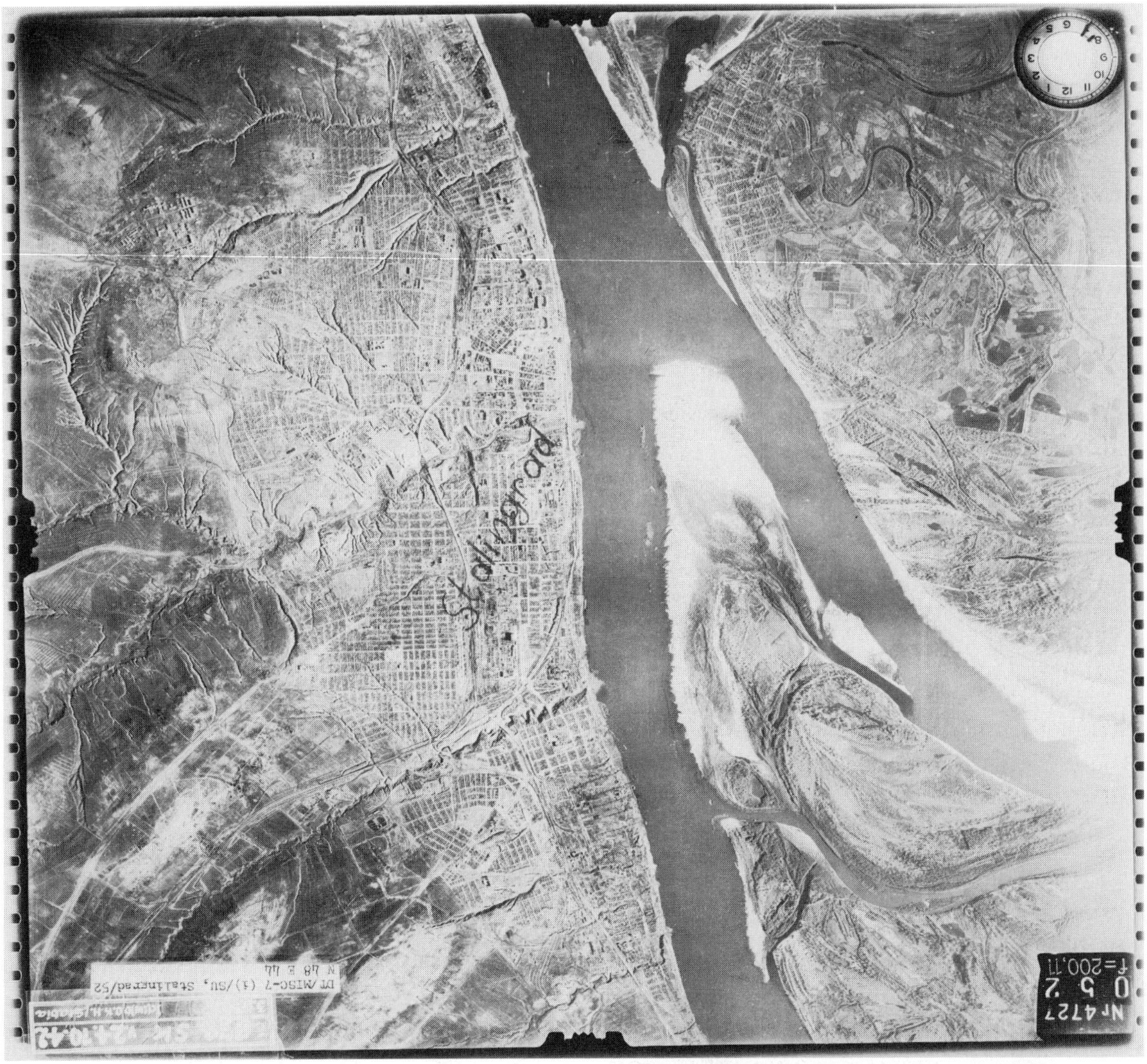
Stalingrad

Stalingrad on 24 October 1942. A German PI inked 'Stalingrad' in red on the original print. Soviet 62nd Army still held a narrow strip along the shore from the annotation to photo top.

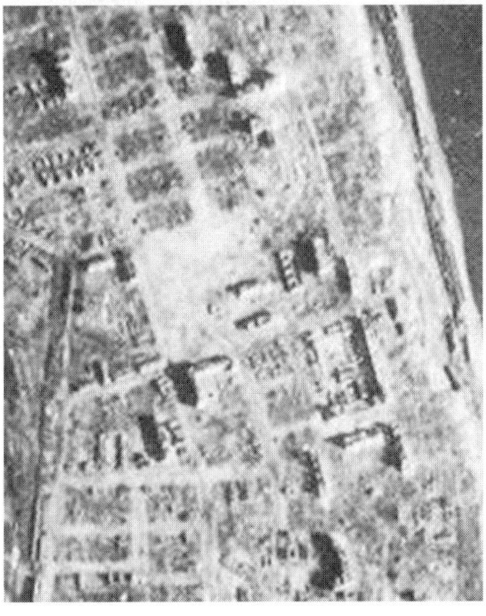

By 25 April everything around 9th January Square was destroyed but Sergeant Yakov Pavlov's team was only half-way through their heroic defense of what was left of a make-shift fortress in a four-story building.

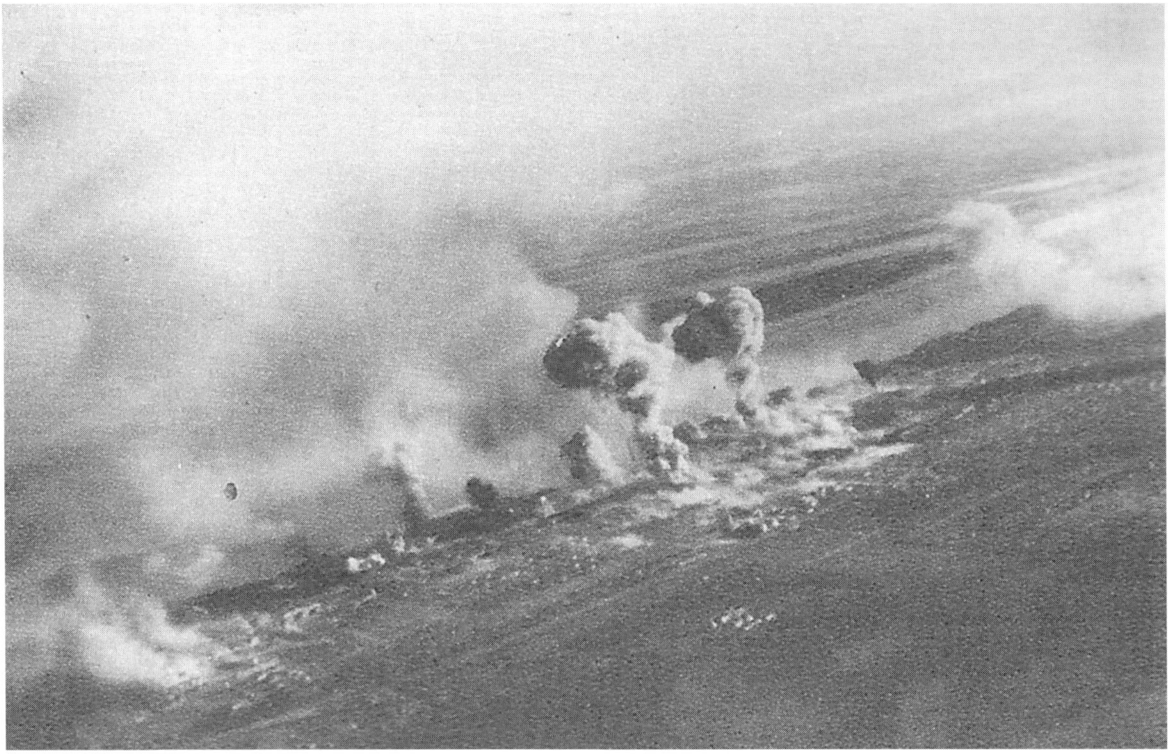

Before the siege was over, Stalingrad suffered more bombs than London during the Blitz. Photo probably September 1942.

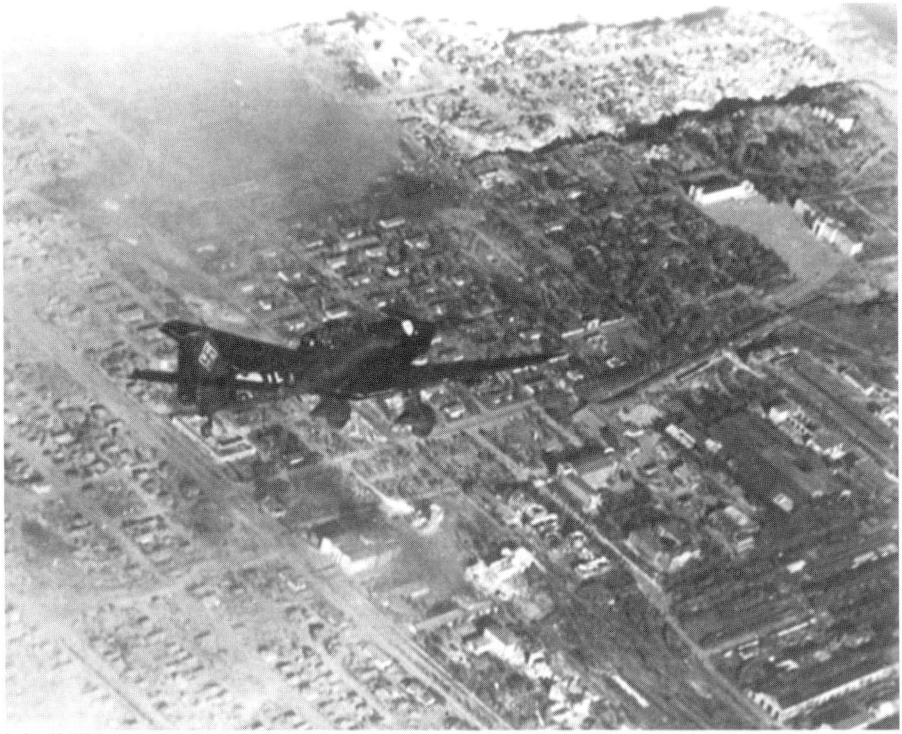

iv, Bild 183-J20510
1 Oktober 1942

Left, Krasny October Steel Plant is down and right. This Ju 87 apparently has its sights on Red Barricade Ordnance Plant at top, 1 October 1942. Stukas were particularly effective in silencing Soviet artillery firing from east of the Volga.

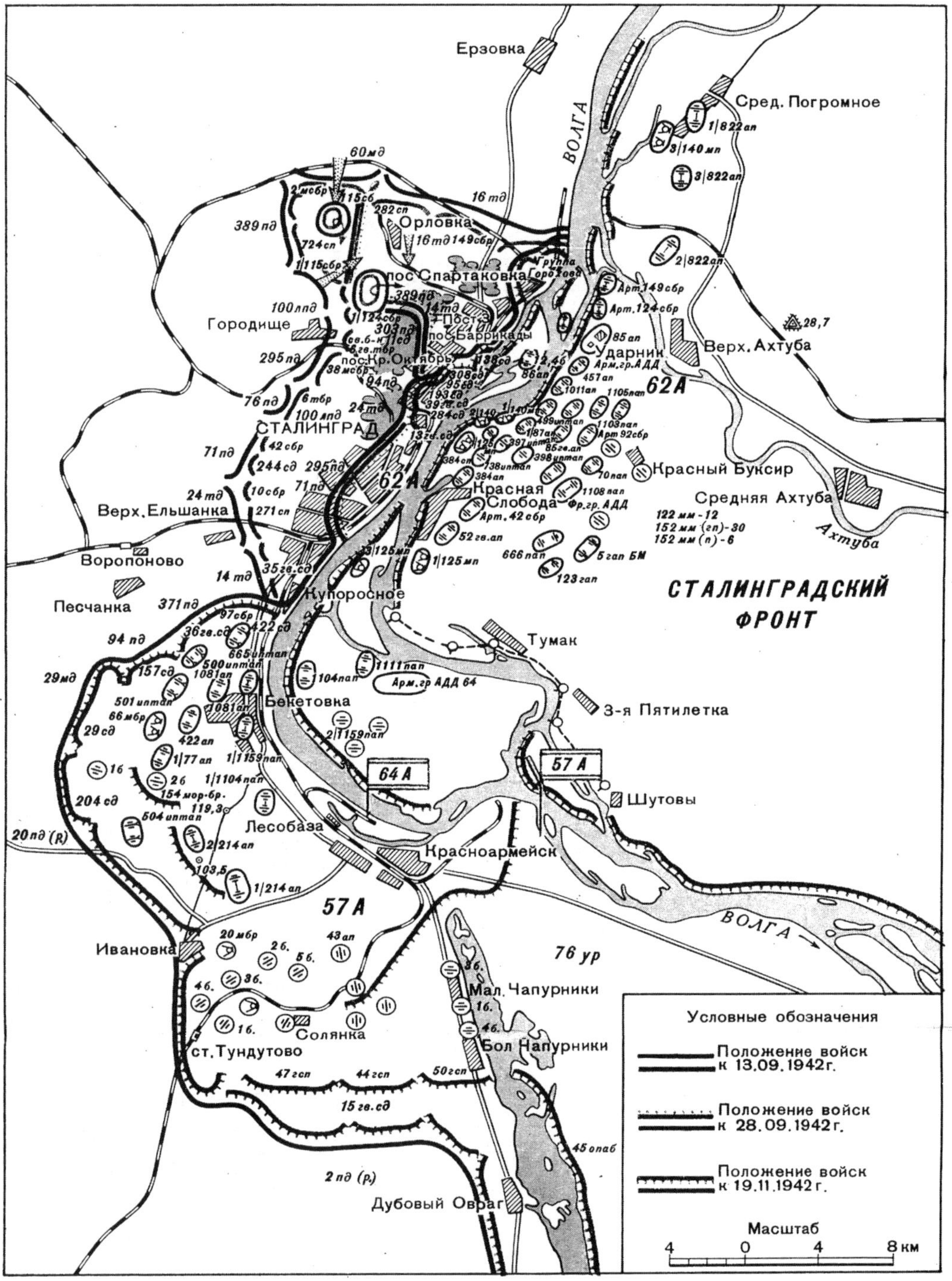
Ерзовка
Сред. Погромное
ВОЛГА
60мд
16тд
389пд
Орловка
пос.Спартаковка
Городище
100лпд
295пд
пос.Баррикады
пос.Кр.Октябрь
76пд
СТАЛИНГРАД
Верх. Ахтуба
Ударник
62А
71пд
24тд
Верх.Ельшанка
Красный Буксир
Средняя Ахтуба
Красная Слобода
122 мм - 12
152 мм (гп) - 30
152 мм (п) - 6
Ахтуба
Воропоново
14тд
Песчанка
371пд
Купоросное
СТАЛИНГРАДСКИЙ ФРОНТ
Тумак
94пд
29мд
Бекетовка
Арм.гр АДД 64
3-я Пятилетка
29сд
64А
57А
Шутовы
204сд
20пд (R)
Лесобаза
Красноармейск
57А
ВОЛГА
Ивановка
76ур
Мал. Чапурники
Солянка
ст.Тундутово
Бол Чапурники
15гв.сд
2пд (р.)
Дубовый Овраг
Условные обозначения
Положение войск к 13.09.1942г.
Положение войск к 28.09.1942г.
Положение войск к 19.11.1942г.
Масштаб
4 0 4 8км

Схема 12. Группировка артиллерии при обороне Сталинграда в сентябре — ноябре 1942 г.

A Soviet graphic covering 13 September to 19 November shows the 62nd Army almost pinched out and 64th Army encircled south of the city. The Red Army had amassed hundreds of heavy guns on the east bank to support fighting in Stalingrad.

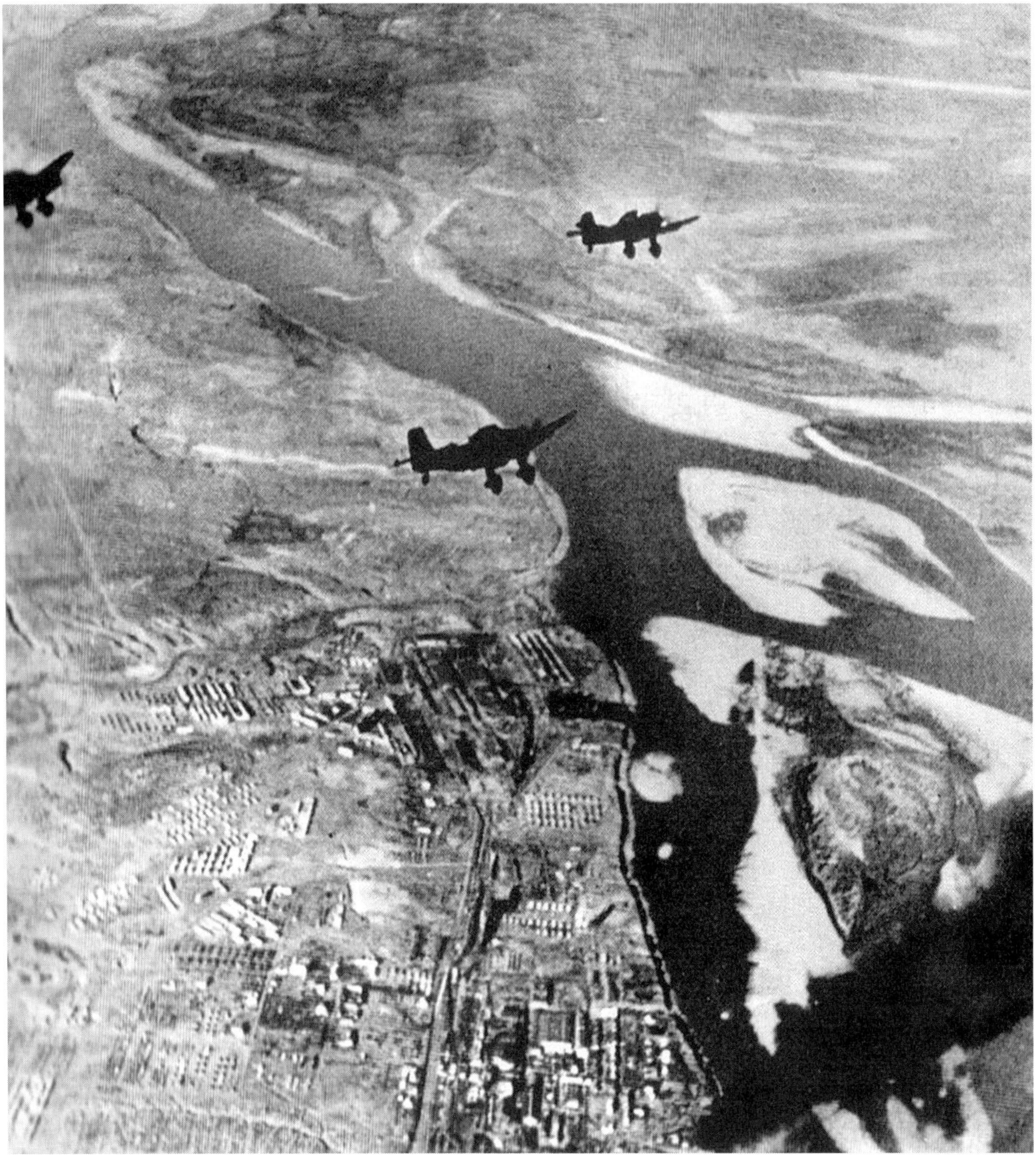

Stukas over Red Barricade Munitions Works, 1 October 42. Great photo, but the planes have apparently already dropped their bombs.

Four days later 900 Ju 87 and He 111 sorties all but leveled the Tractor Factory. Ten days after that over two thousand more sorties rained bombs into the Factory Area. Because they couldn't carry the loads of Lancasters and B-17s, Luftwaffe planes had to fly many back-to-back missions, straining equipment and aircrew, putting them in AAA range more frequently. More important, they couldn't effectively carpet bomb a large target with Ju 87s dropping bombs one at-a-time or He 111's spilling them out with little accuracy.

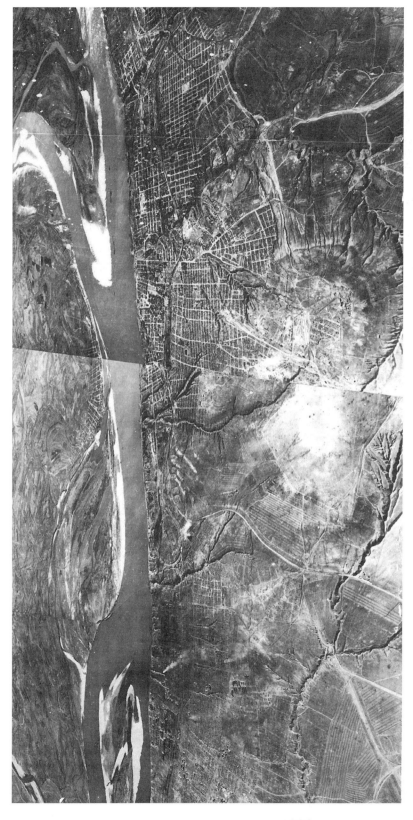

Looking southeast, my oblique Stalingrad mosaic uses 28 October 1942 imagery.

Turning the imagery so the Volga's east bank is at the top, Stalingradski airfield is the light area at lower center. Mamayev Kugan is just above it, closer to the Volga. The city is to the right. The Factory District is to the left.

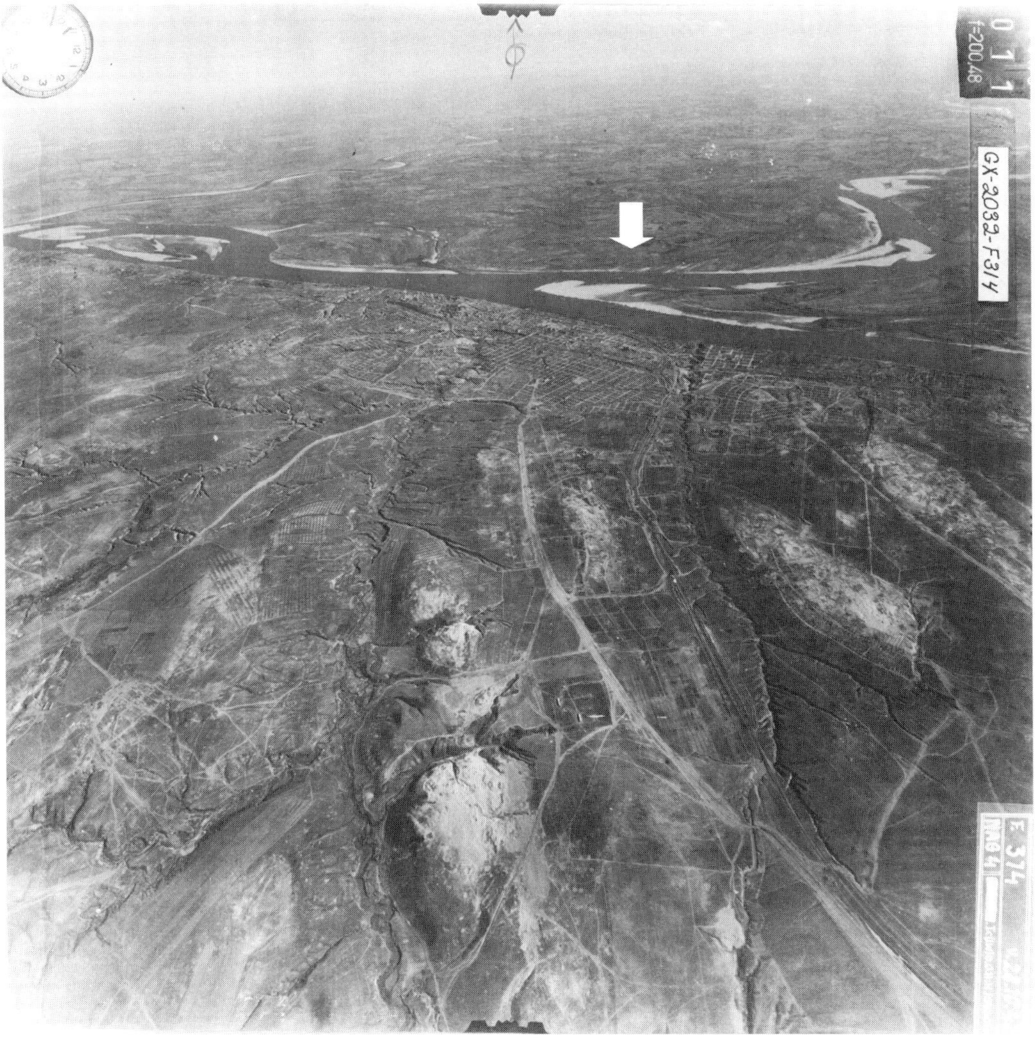
GX-2032-F314
f-200.48

Stalingrad, 28 October 42, looking northeast. The Tractor Factory is upper left. Sharp eyes will pick out the Grain Elevator near the river at right center (under arrow). The German army made no attempt to cross the Volga, and the east bank harbored Soviet reinforcements, supplies and heavy artillery that kept the 62nd Army alive in Stalingrad.

Below, photos from the east bank show devastation in the city's center.

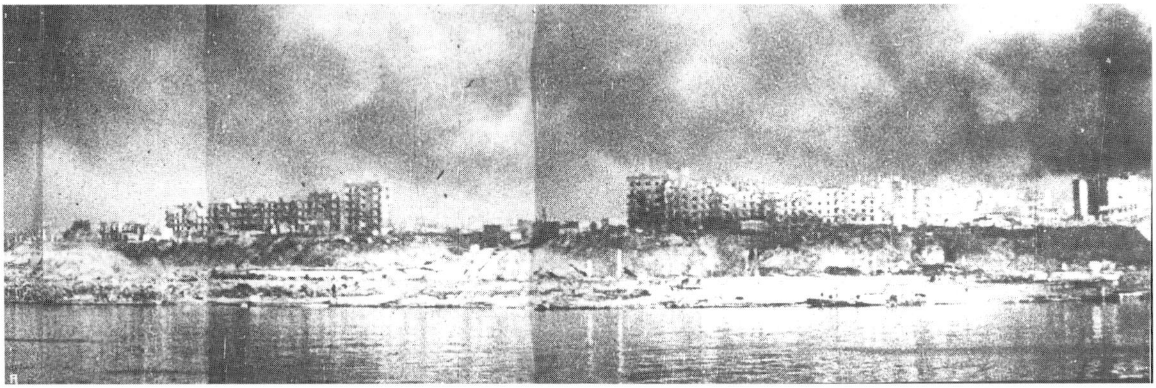

Red October Steel Plant under what is probably defensive smoke, 28 October 42. The other two longer plumes of gray smoke are fires.

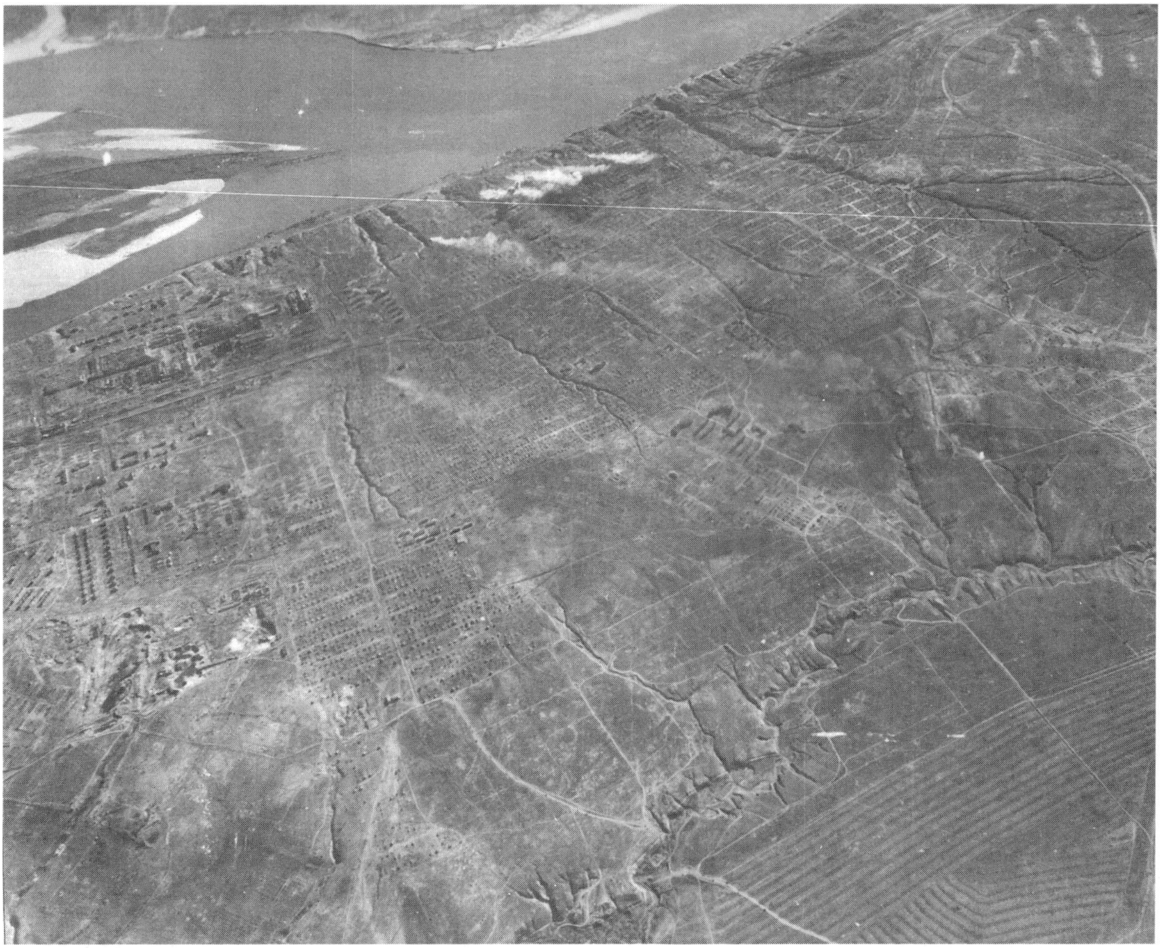

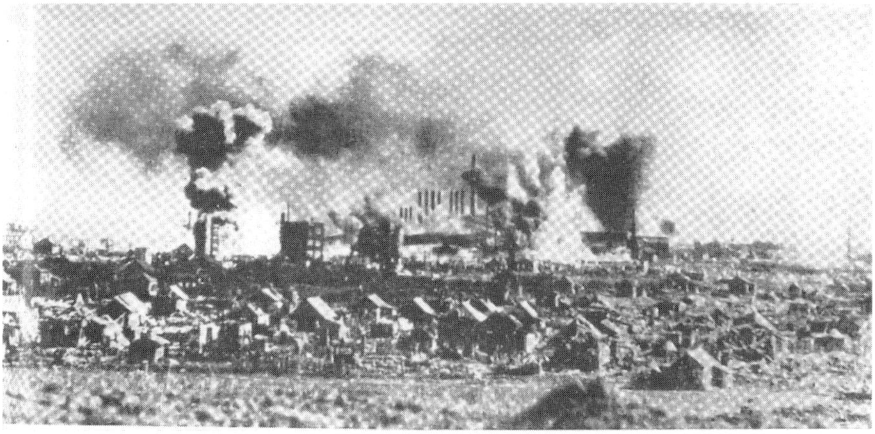

Left, the Steel Works being bombed viewed from the west. Workers housing in the foreground looks untouched.

USSR. 48.45N - 44.25E. Stalingrad.
Cat. 70. Panorama of city under bombardment. Source:
Communist party of Great Britain. The siege of Stalingrad,

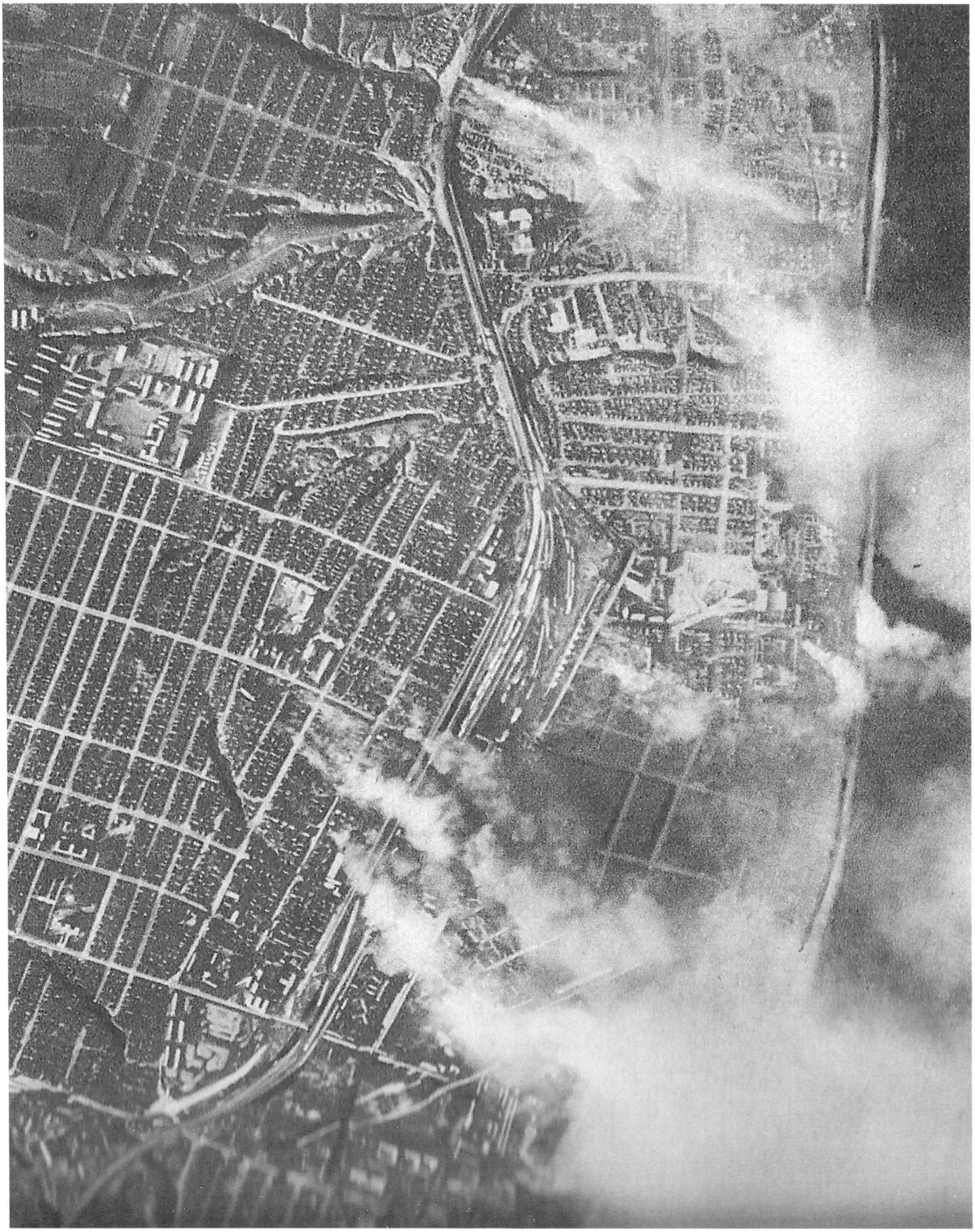

Bombing around Railroad Station # 1. The upper rail yard and buildings to the west look untouched, dating the photo close to initial bombing on 23 August. German heavy artillery was able to reach parts of the city by this time.

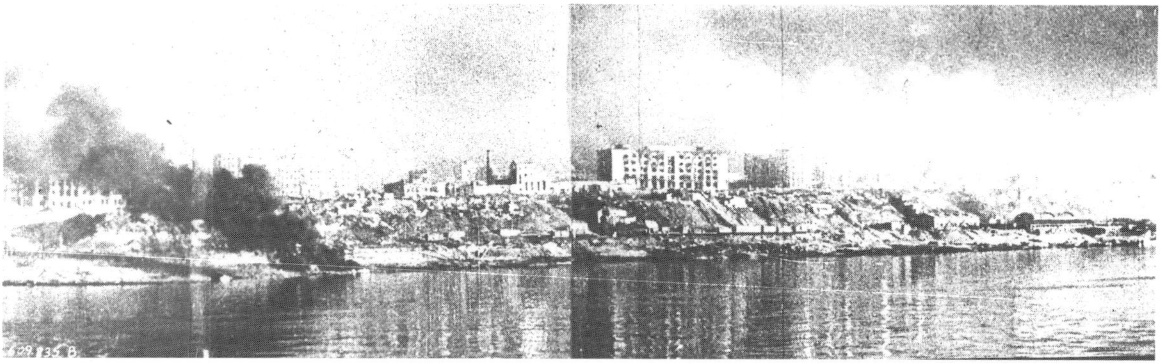

Another look at central Stalingrad's devastation from the east bank of the Volga.

City center, 4 November 1942.

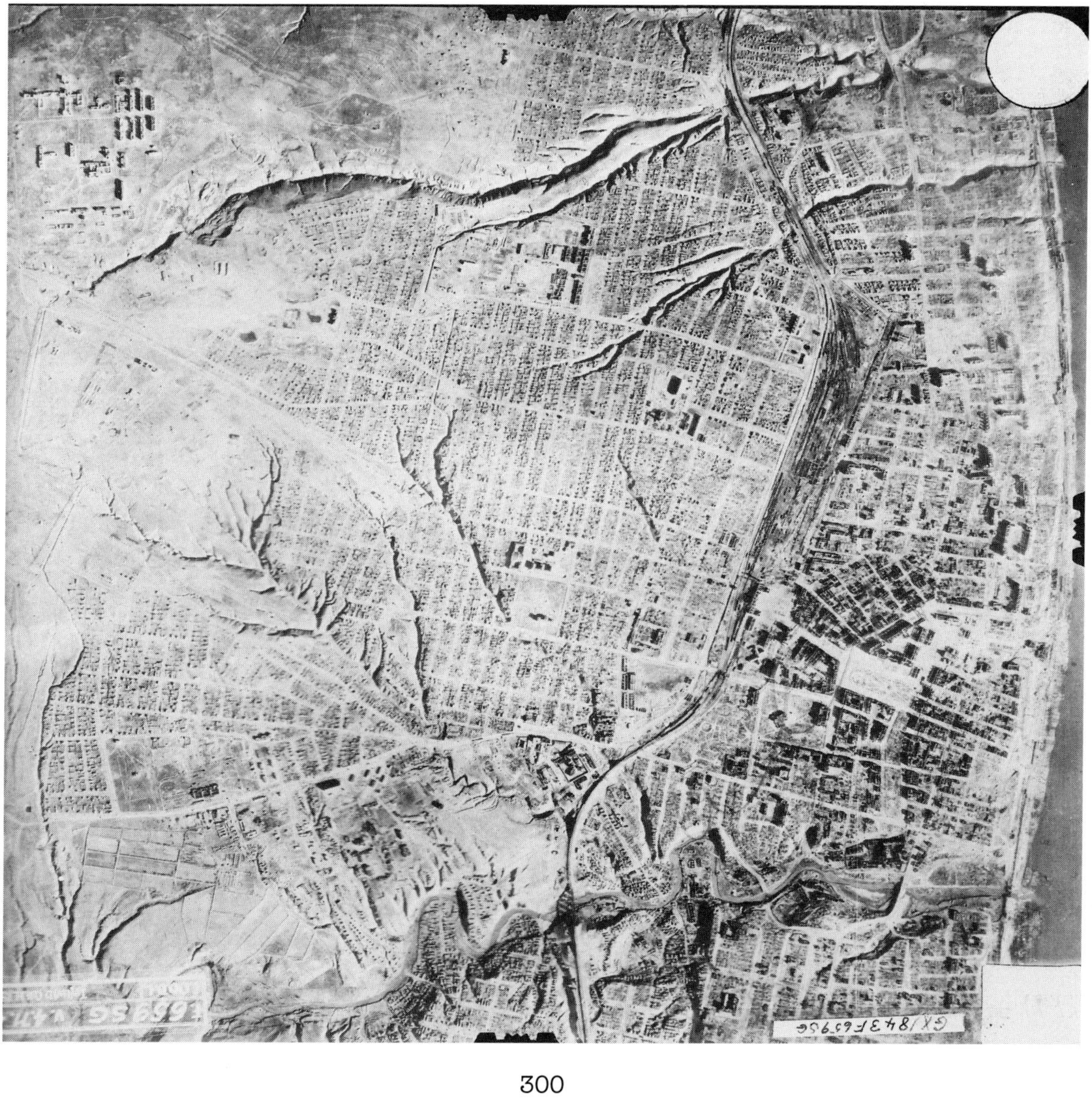

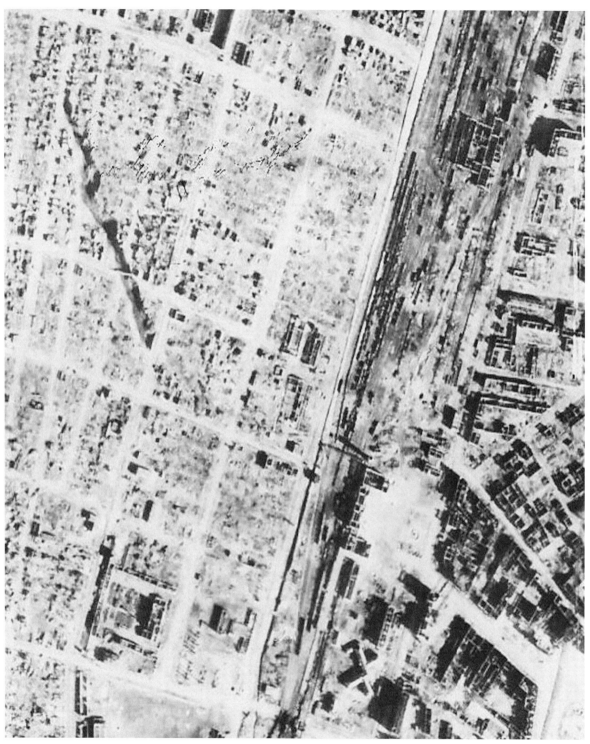

Enlargement of 4 November imagery shows buildings west of the rail yard completely destroyed and those east of the tracks gutted. Much fought-over Railway Station # 1 is the large 'U-shaped' structure at lower center. The station was in German hands at this time.

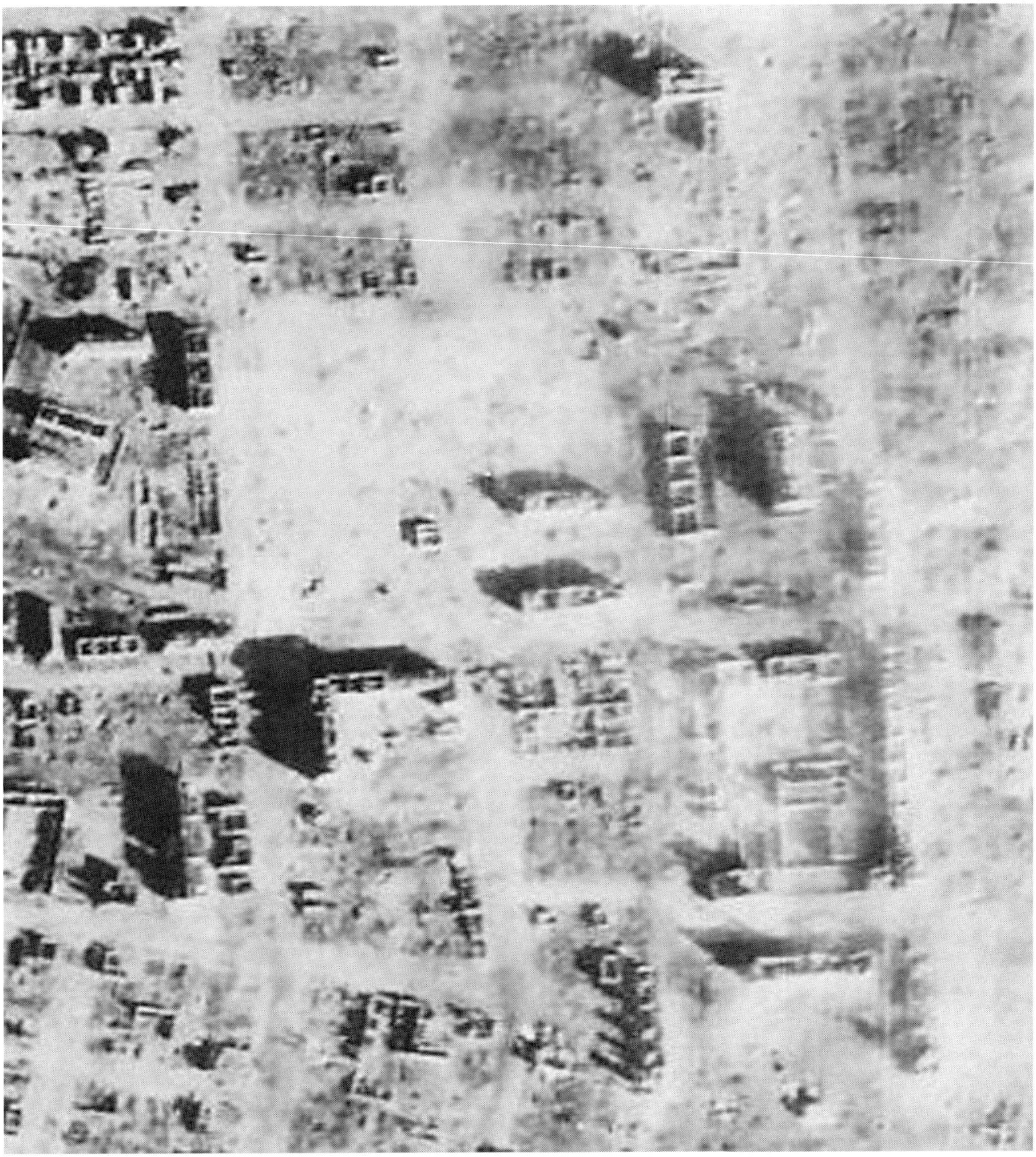

Enlargement of 9th January Square on 4 November 1942. Buildings to the west survived as shells only because of sturdy concrete construction. Pavlov's House still dominated the square. He had been reinforced with heavy machine-guns, light mortars and 14.5mm Anti-Tank Rifles that proved particularly effective shooting down from the building roof at less-protected upper decks of armored vehicles.

I expected to see barricades in cross-streets, damaged/destroyed vehicles and evidence of the intense combat after repeated German attempts to take Pavlov's House and punch through to the river.

This ad hoc fortress helped keep the narrow, dwindling Soviet pocket inside Stalingrad (between here and the Steel Plant) alive. Nineteen days after this photo was taken. the German Sixth Army was surrounded and being compressed east against the Volga.

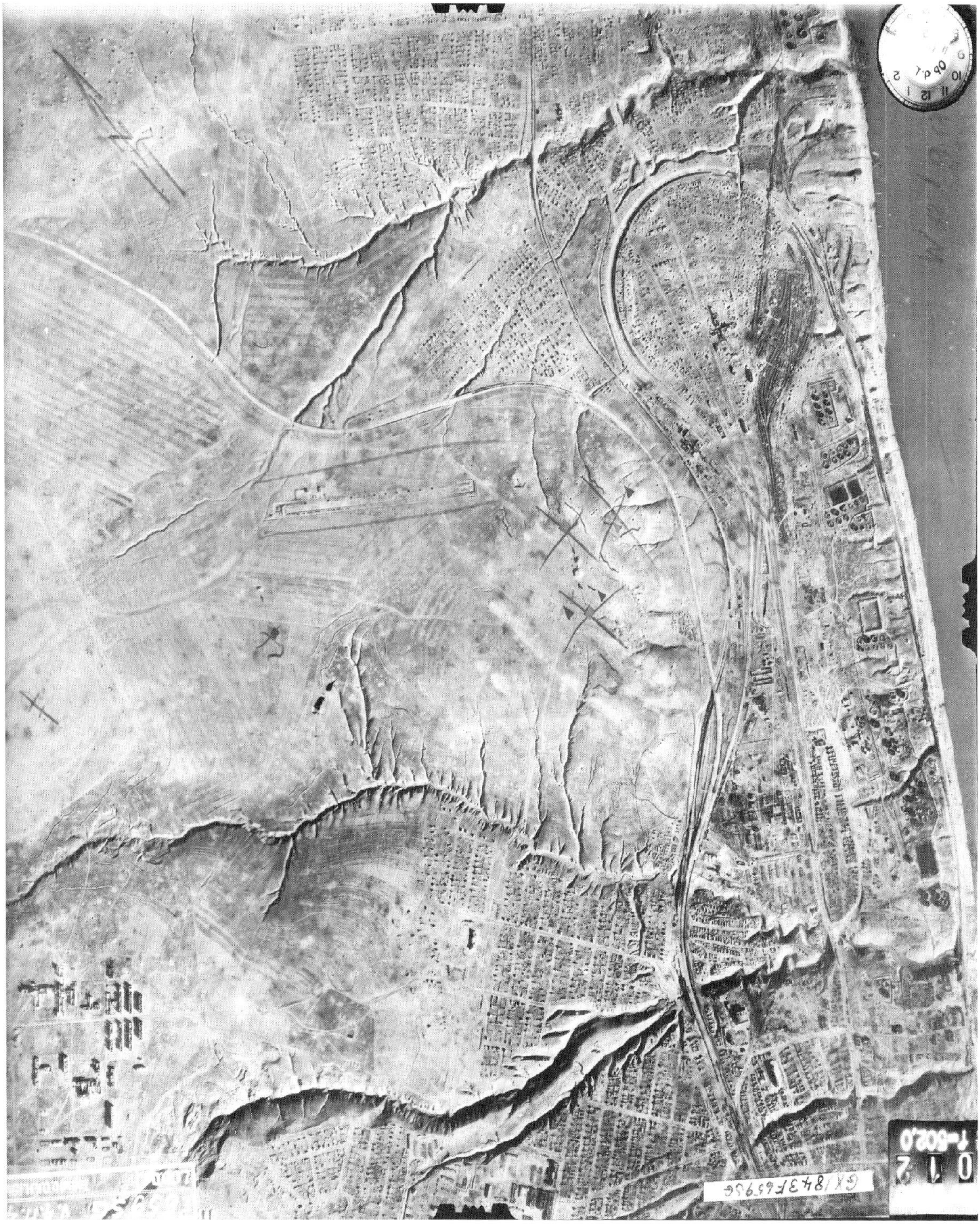

The bottom of the Factory District, 4 November 1942. Petroleum storage along the river was critical to Soviet survival (as long as barge traffic from the east bank was possible.)

'X' annotations made by a German PI show Order of Battle changes on Mamayev Kurgan.

I have no idea what that very long narrow building is for (outlined to the west).

Enlargement of the previous photo shows German PI markings for several defense line/positions. The PI also put 'Xs' on unit symbols indicating destruction of two Regiments (squares) and one Battalion (triangle) – presumably Soviet.

This is Hill 102 (Mamayev Kurgan), the much disputed highest ground near Stalingrad. Annotations indicate three Infantry Battalions still on the hill.

Soviet 13th Guards Rifle Division fought here (and at RR Station #1) on14-16 September. The Division lost 30% of its men on the first day. Only 320 of the original 10K strength survived retaking the hill.

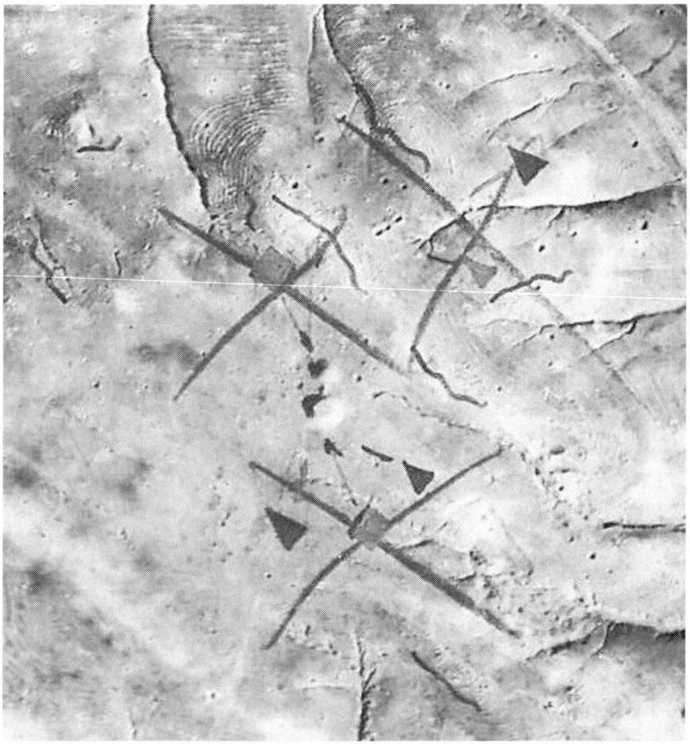

The undated photo below is identified as Stalingrad. It may be carnage at Mamayev Kurgan. Men standing in the upper right corner look German.

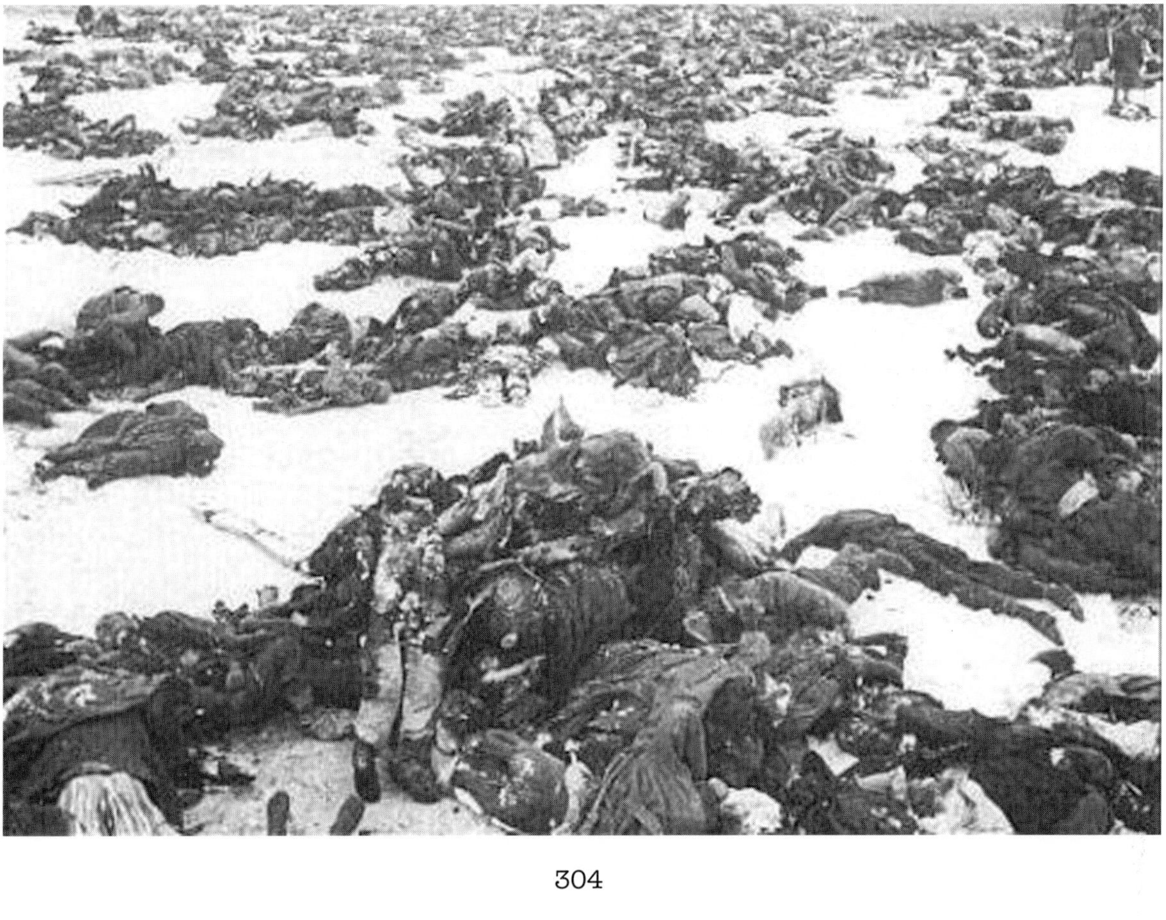

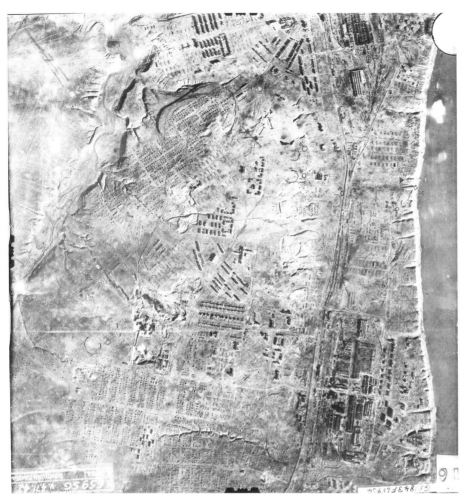

Soviet positions between Dzerzhinsky Traktor Factory and Red Barricade Ordnance Works, 4 November 1942. German forces squeezed remaining Soviet troops into two pockets and were systematically snuffing out resistance. Heavy Luftwaffe bombing made supply/reinforcement from east of the Volga increasingly tenuous. Sixth Army was itself in a pocket 19 days later and being backed against the river. Army HQ moved east from Golubinsky to Gumrak Airfield on 22 November 1942 and then into Univermag Department Store on Red Plaza in January.

Right. German defense position with an MG 34 machine gun. The caption read 'Picture came to US from London, November 26'.

Above, just south of the Tractor Factory. This was one of the last areas in the city still held by Soviet troops. Enlarged German annotations from the previous photo indicate two Regiments destroyed and a Battalion remaining. Near the shore are annotations for an Infantry Battalion and Platoon. Below them is a Searchlight unit. Closer to the tracks are three four-gun anti-aircraft batteries (probably 37mm).

A story I've heard for years goes; not expecting a ground attack from the north, defense of the important Tractor Factory was assigned to 1077th Anti-Aircraft Regiment. But 16th Panzer did attack from the north.

On 23-25 August, unsupported by Infantry and without armor-piercing ammunition, the thirty-seven 37mm AAA guns of 1077th Rgt (personnel strength probably about 300), destroyed 83 German tanks, 14 aircraft, and three battalions of infantry. Soviet gun crews held off advancing Germans until all guns and gunners were out of action and overrun. Only then did German soldiers discover the gun-crews were all female, many in their teens.

I dearly love the 1077th Regiment story. Standing fast in the face of certain death when retreat was possible, like 300 Spartans at Thermopylae or Texicans at the Alamo, touches something deep inside anyone who has worn a uniform. The courageous force being young women and girls makes the response more visceral. Unfortunately I am unable to photo-confirm the events as portrayed. Guns above aren't positioned to do the job.

Air defense of a factory making the vital T-34 tanks was to be expected. I've looked at a lot of Soviet 37mm guns from the air (in three wars) and I know where they'd have to be to defend the factory. The regiment would be five to seven batteries, each comprised of four or five guns in a circle in cleared areas with good fields of fire upward. They'd have to be within a half-mile of the factory to take advantage of their four-mile range. We have enough imagery to verify the order-of-battle at Dzerzhinsky and I don't see that many guns. Further, good air defense positions wouldn't work to oppose ground targets. True, the guns were mobile and could be readily relocated (even by hand for a short distance). They would have to be in lines with fields of fire to the front for ground defense. In that case they'd be on bluffs overlooking the valley north of Dzerzhinsky. I don't see any guns there.

In many photos earlier in this book you have seen typical positioning of anti-aircraft batteries. You've also seen that three batteries are the most we've noted in one place.

The aircraft and infantry kills claimed are believable but 83 tanks is a stretch. Trucks, half-tracks and armored cars destroyed are more likely. Tanks involved could have been Pz IIs and IIIs so a lucky HE hit on the side might do the job. Pz IVs heavier armor would be immune to 37mm HE fire.

Ironically, both sides in the famous combat used 37mm guns with the same range and reports suggest both had the wrong ammunition. The anti-aircraft guns had few/no armor piercing rounds and Pz IIIs 37mm guns, designed to kill tanks, were firing armor piercing rounds. Had the AA guns been firing AP, their higher muzzle velocity would have given them the advantage.

I'm not saying the 1077th 'last stand' didn't happen, but I seriously doubt it was in the city limits of Stalingrad defending Dzerzhinsky Traktor. More likely it was at Gumrak Airfield, 7 miles west-northwest of Red Plaza and 11 miles southwest of the Factory District.

Let's take a look at Gumrak.

There are no aircraft on the field. A typical Soviet fighter base 4000 foot hard surface runway was under construction. Facilities (A) were insignificant yet on 13 July 1942 the field was defended by a five-gun AAA battery to the north, a three-gun battery to the west and a possible three-gun position to the south. A total of 11 guns.

Maßstab etwa 1: 41 000
(1cm = 410 m)
14603
Stalingrad-Tumrak
SU 10 3312 bc
2. Ang.
Kriegsaufnahme:
389 044 (LN.4)
Nachträge:
13.7.42.
Karte:
Flpl. Atlas
1:300 000
Länge:
(ostw. Greenw.):
44° 22' 00"
48° 47' 00"
Mißweisung:
7° 19'
(Mitte 1942)
Zielhöhe
über N N m
nach Kalschalinskaja
flak
Tumrak
von Stalingrad
A
109
SU 10 3312 Flugplatz.
1) 1 Flugzeughalle etwa 1 300 qm
2) Unterkunfts-und Wirtschaftsgebäude etwa 3 200 qm
3) Baracken und Lagergebäude etwa 1 200 qm

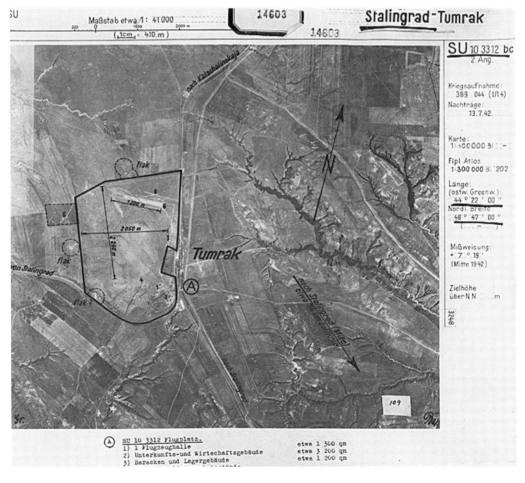

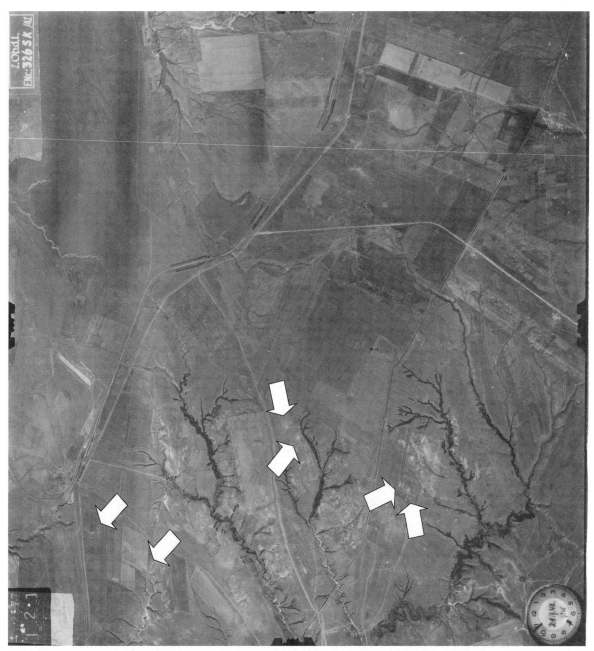

This photo is east of the Stalingrad-Don road/rail line on 24 July 1942. Stalingrad is 8 miles south. Gumrak airfield is at center left. Two arrows at lower left show the start and end of an incomplete anti-tank ditch. Other arrows show four anti-aircraft batteries moved in since the last German cover.

From right to left—five guns in a circle and three four-gun batteries. Revetment arrangement gives no doubt those are AAA not Field Artillery. They have good fields-of-fire to the north but none of those guns are well positioned to defend the airfield from air attack. The nearest are 3 miles from the runway (out at the effective range of their guns) and the farthest right arrows are a mile beyond being able to cover the airfield. All four batteries are on ridge tops and have good fields of fire north.

In the upper right corner, a German PI grease-pencil circled an area that appears to be a Soviet Infantry Company bivouacked in open fields.

308

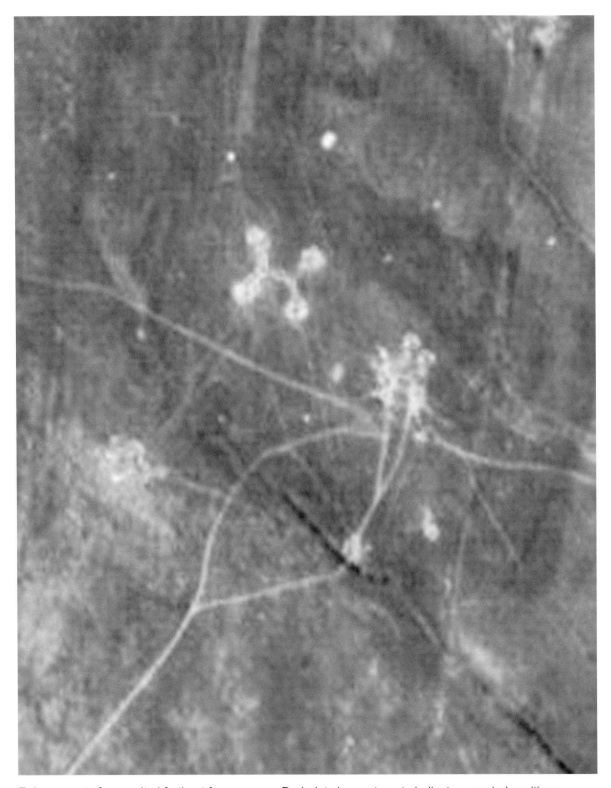

Enlargement of guns sited farthest from runway. Dark dots in revetments indicate occupied positions.

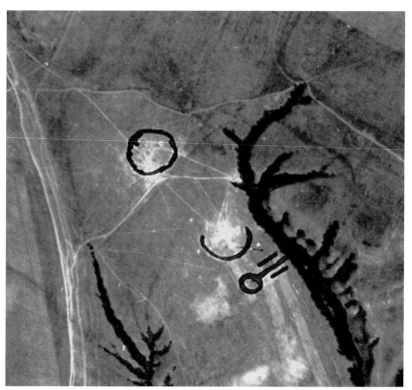

Annotations prove German Intel knew about those guns a month before the assault on Gumrak.

The four-gun batteries enlarged at left are nearest the runway but barely in range for coverage. So, what was their mission? The German PI annotated them as Light AAA. I agree. Revetment and circle size point to 37mm guns.

Note none of these gun positions show fox holes for crew protection or trenches for infantry that would make these strong points. They are clearly not set up as ground defense positions. They appear designed to be a trip wire—a typical Soviet trading of lives for time.

At right. Five-gun battery north of the runway. The annotations were made in red ink by a German PI in July 1942. This is a classic AAA configuration.

I submit we have found the 1077th Rgt. Positioned on open ridgetops a month in advance of German arrival, it must have dawned on even inexperienced gunners that they hadn't been sent here to defend Gumrak. If so, it was unforgiveable for their superiors not to supply them with armor piercing rounds. It also makes the gunners' courage more impressive.[1]

I realize this imagery doesn't prove the 1077th Rgt. event happened or happened here, but I've never seen anything that better matches the oft told scenario—and I've looked at thousands of frames of GX around Stalingrad.

1 Special thanks to NARA researcher Susan Strange for finding these annotated German prints.

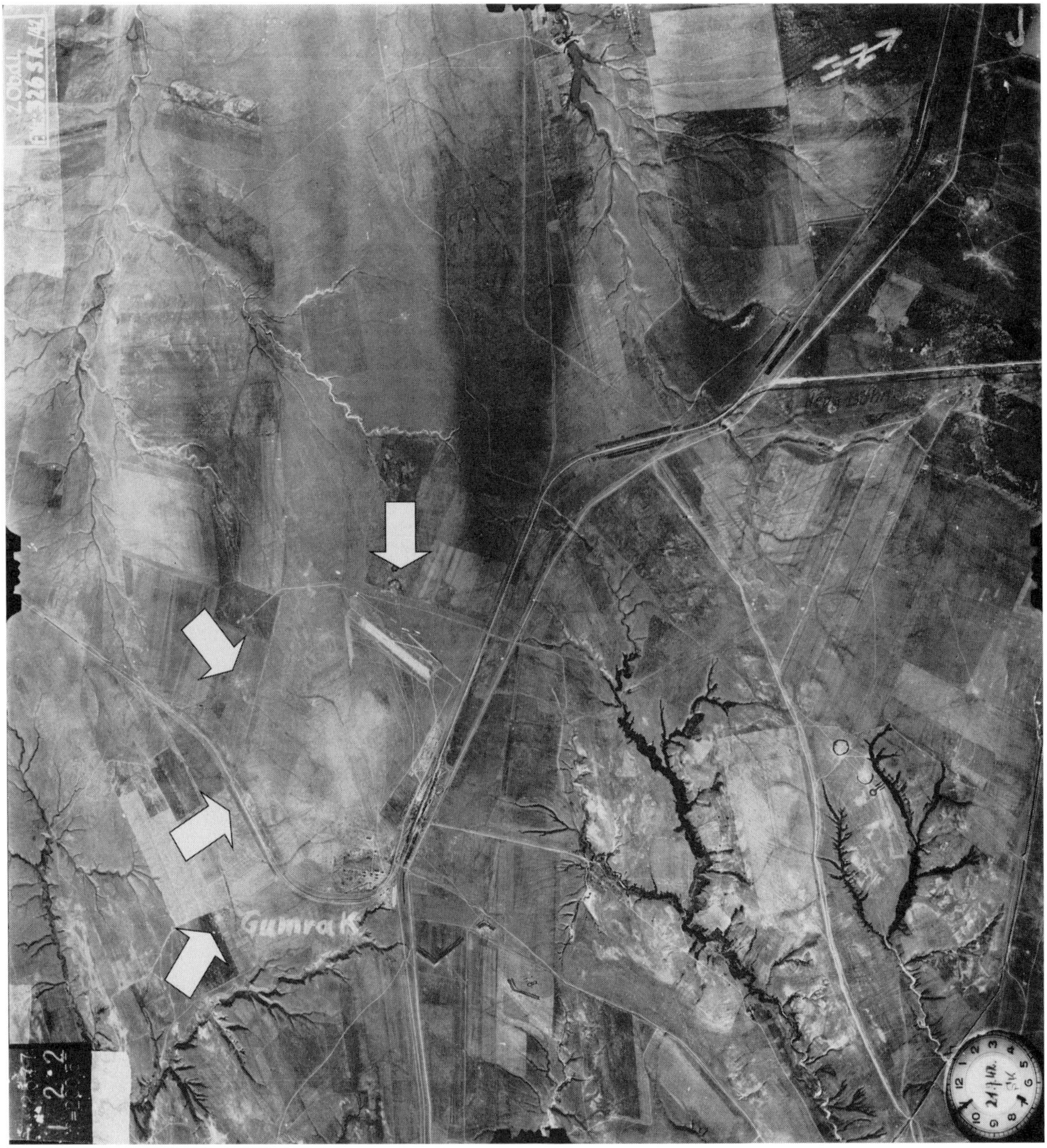
Gumrak

Four anti-aircraft batteries are west of the northeast road and rail lines on Gumrak, 24 July 1942. Is this the rest of 1077th Rgt? Sharp eyes will spot actual German PI annotations at original scale. These Light AAA guns are typically positioned for airfield defense. On the north is the five-gun circle enlarged on the previous page. Next down is a probable three-gun triangle, followed by another probable three-gun battery. Counting guns east of the road/rail line, a newly added four-gun battery (just left of the Gumrak annotation), made a total of 32 guns at Gumrak—a pretty close match to the 1077th story. I'd put money on this being the site of those heroic three days when female gunners stood their ground.

Unfortunately there are no aerial photos closer to, during or immediately after the German assault. Fernaufklärung photorecon units just didn't do that sort of coverage.

Gumrak guns were undoubtedly Soviet M1939 37mm[2].

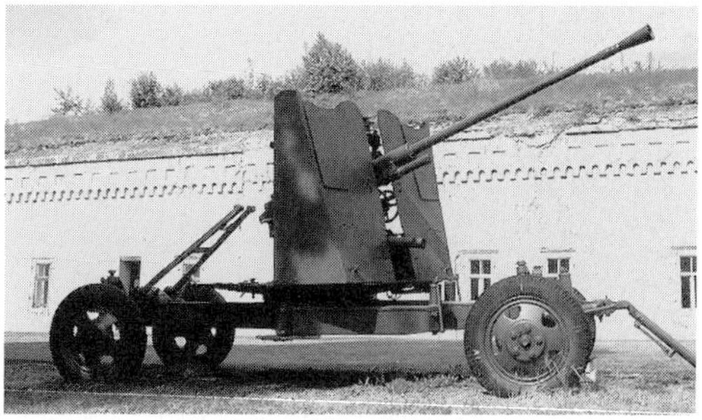

A crew of eight was kept busy loading five-round clips to keep up an 80 to 100 rounds per minute rate. Normal rounds had explosive charges. Traverse was excellent but slew-rate wasn't good against fast, low-flying aircraft like strafing Bf 109s. Slow flying, diving Stukas or horizontal bombing He 111s were easier targets. Effective altitude for the gun was 10,000 feet. Effective horizontal range was just over 2 miles. At 2.3 tons it was highly mobile.

Below, Gumrak field is at right. I see no air or ground defenses of any kind west of the airfield. Despite German forces just days away a train is at the center arrow, heading southwest to Gorkovskiy, 4 miles southwest of Stalingrad.

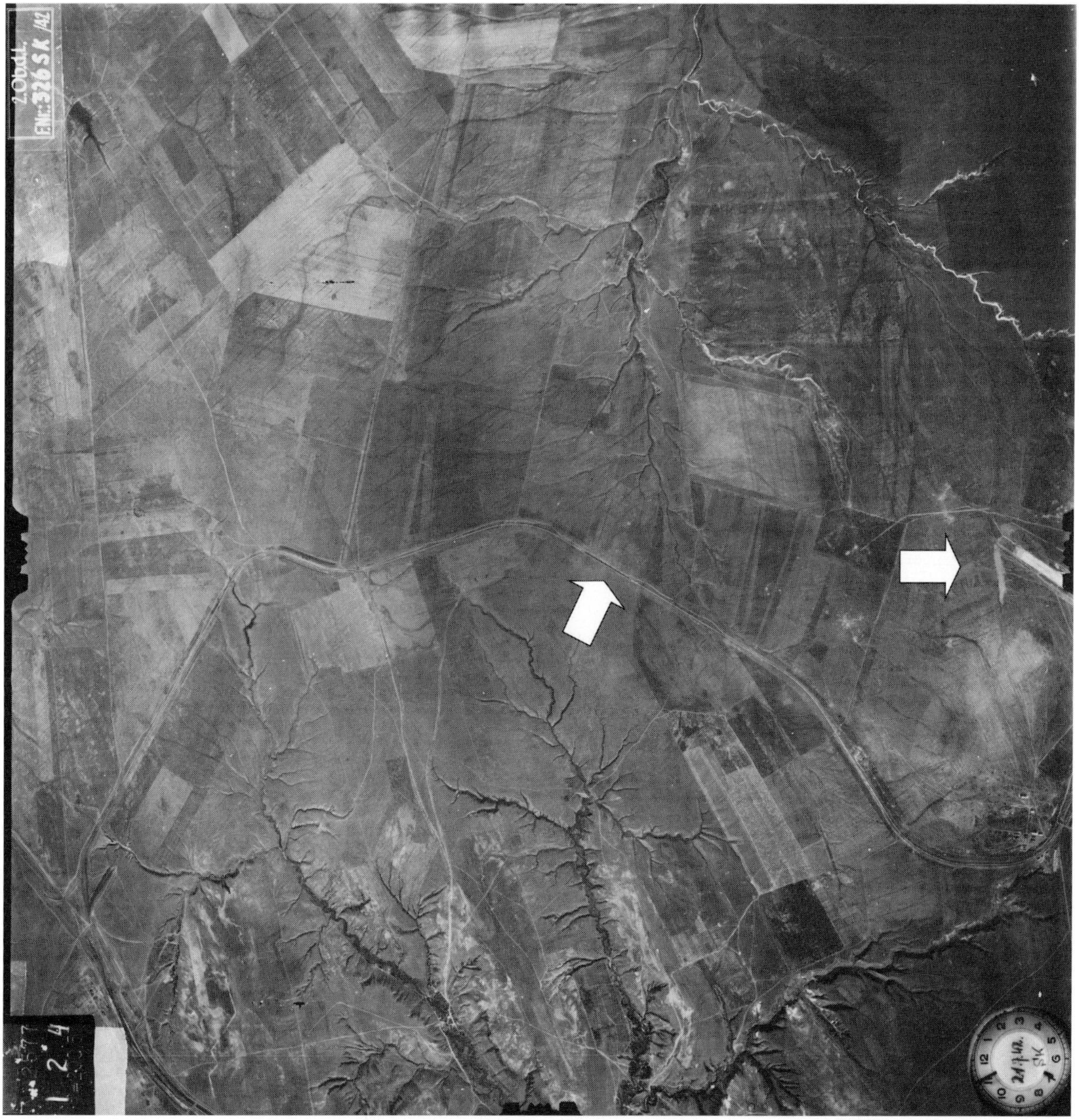
2.Obd.L.
FNr.: 326 SK /42

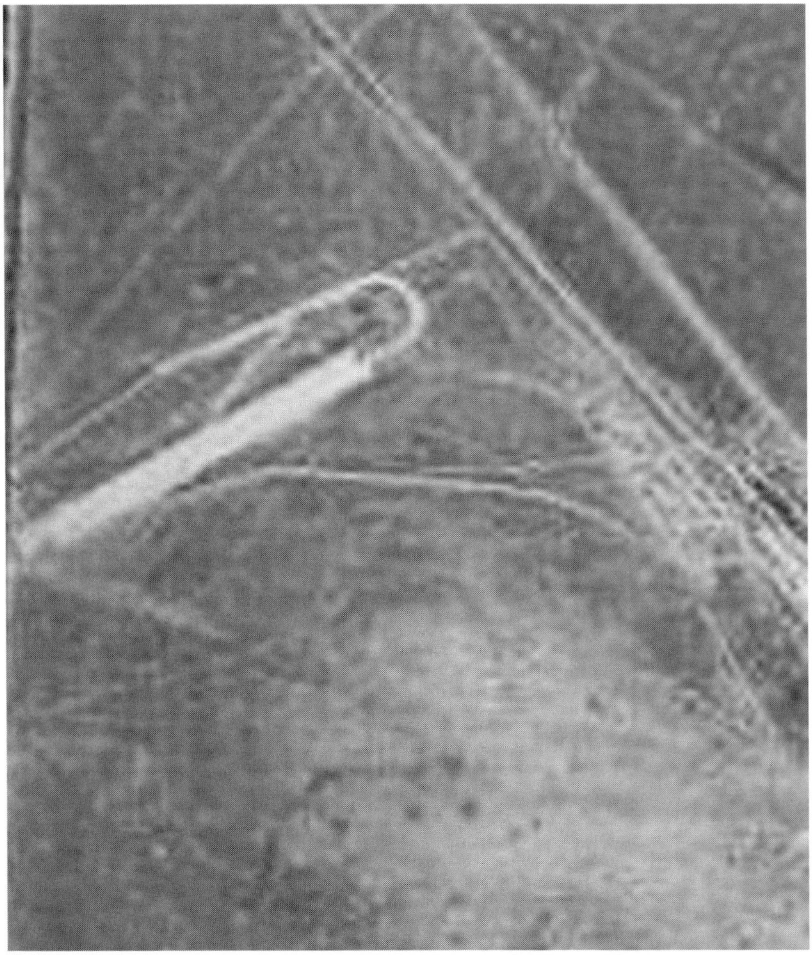

Gumrak in German hands on 17 September 1943, a Soviet-begun turn-around taxi-way is being finished. There is a new track north of the runway, but I expected to see tank tracks crossing the sod landing area. A half-dozen pock-marks on the field are the only signs of battle here.

Below, Soviet troops attacking in Stalingrad. Amid rubble, both sides were sucked into the 'Rat War' being waged building-to-building, room-to-room, even in the sewers. Even punishing cold didn't stop the fighting.

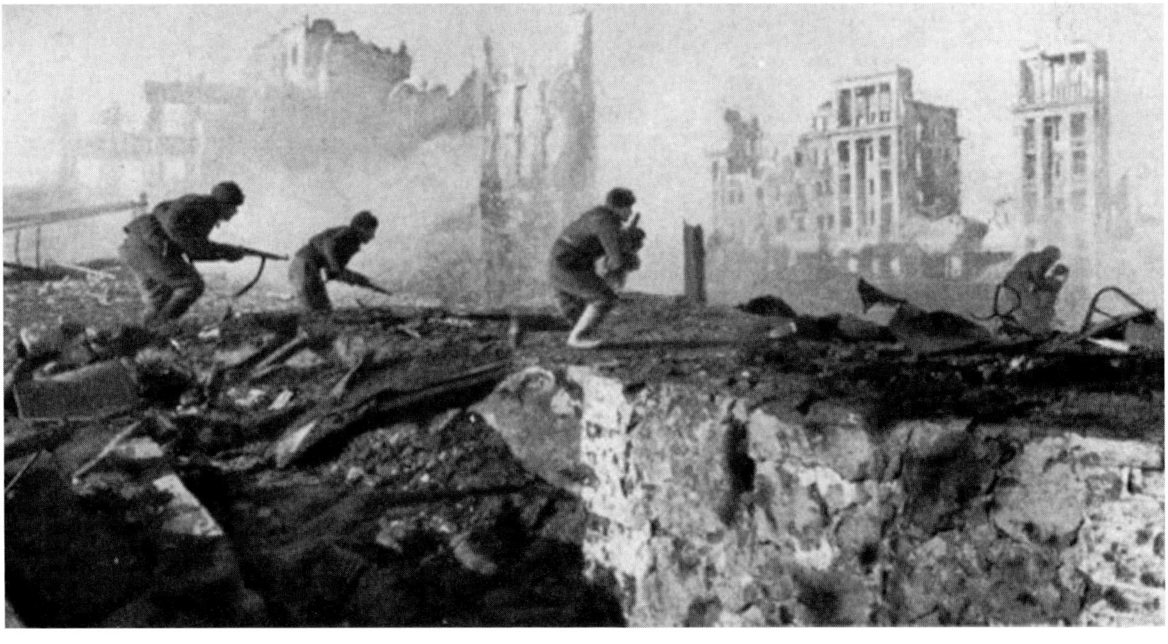

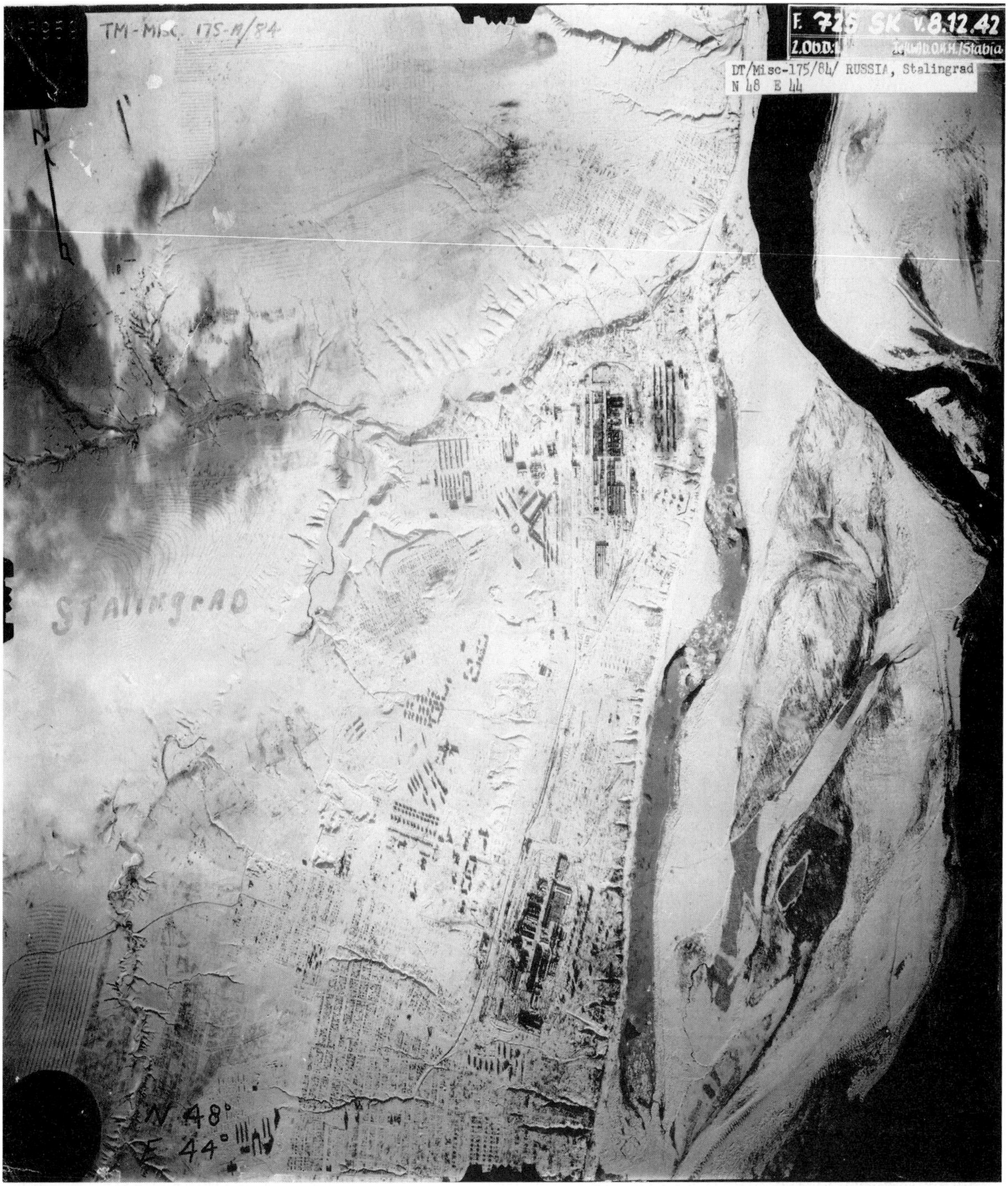
v.8.12.42
DT/Misc-175/84/ RUSSIA, Stalingrad
N 48 E 44
STALINGRAD
N 48°
E 44°

Back to where we were before the Gumrak sidetrack—the Traktor Factory and south to Red October gun factory, imaged on 8 December 1942. German troops were being steadily pushed into a pocket north and against the river. Snow covers all, and ice was forming in the river.

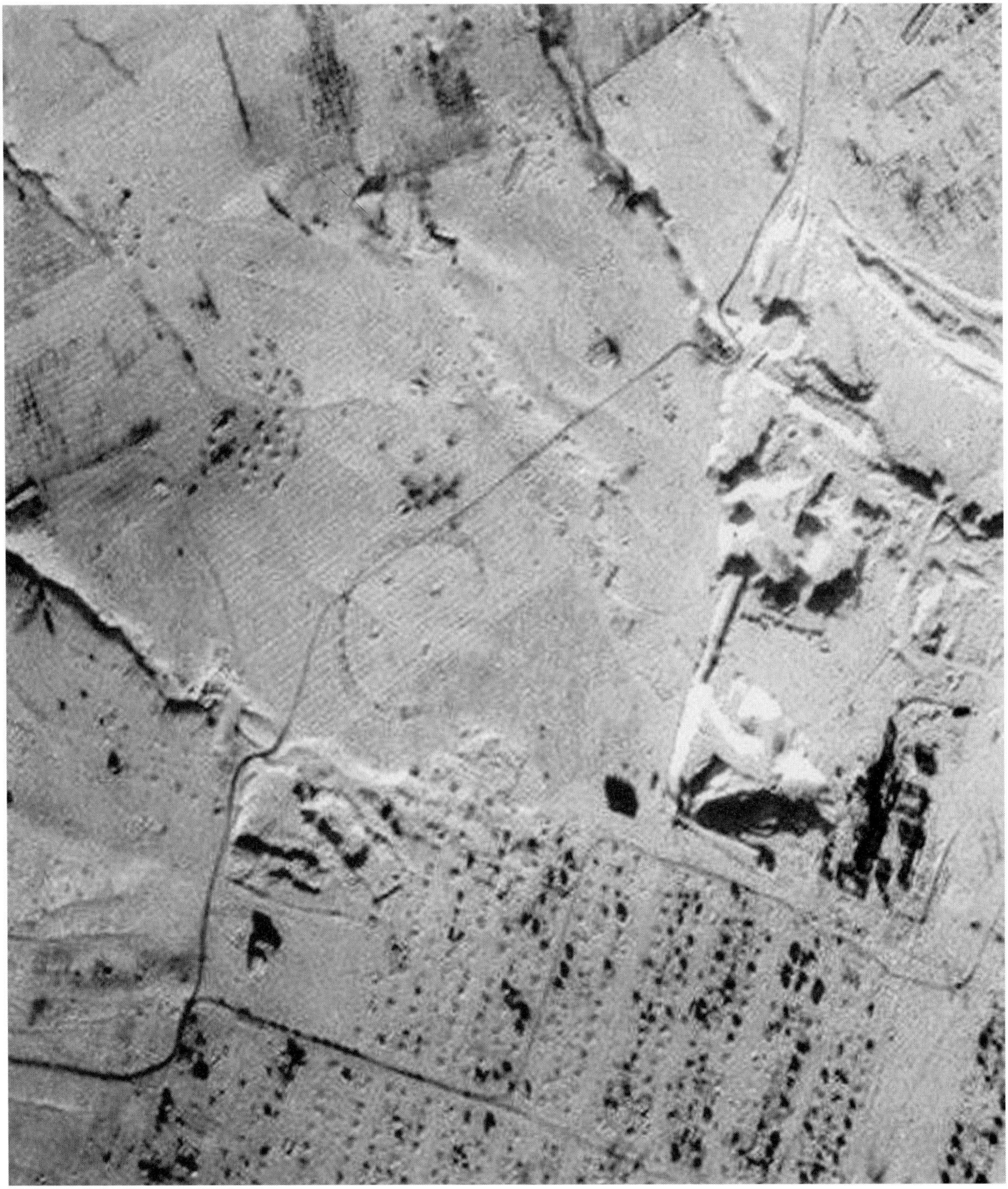

Enlargement of above. West of the Steel Plant a German PI circled a four-gun unoccupied AAA position (diameter of the circle suggests guns of at least 57mm?). Intense combat is going on down there but we don't see it. No tracks, no vehicles, no spots blackened by fire or explosions, no changes. Aerial photorecon doesn't do well with that sort of battle.

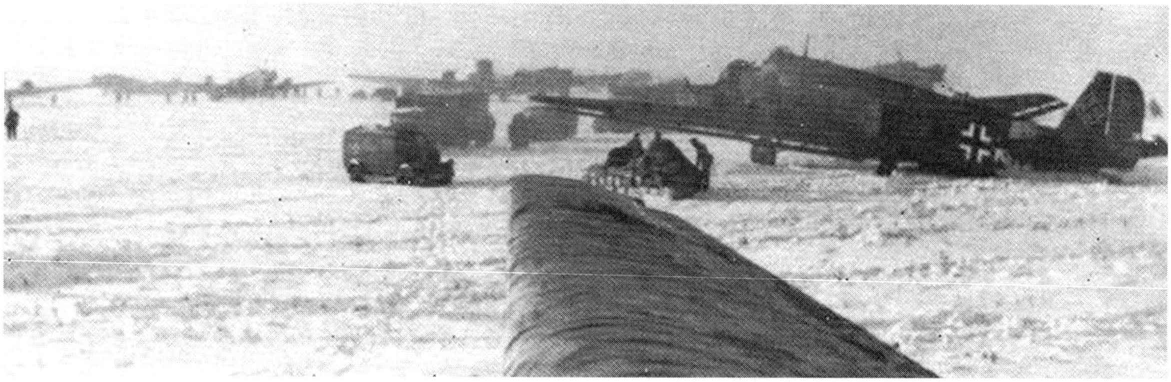

By 23 November, Soviet offensives had Sixth Army cut off. The only way in and out of the shrinking 'Kessel' was by air. The Ju 52 fleet wasn't large enough or fast enough and couldn't haul the needed tonnage to sustain Sixth Army. Desperate for food, 10,000 horses were slaughtered but that was just a Band-Aid on a gushing aorta. A third of Luftwaffe transports (800 aircraft) were lost to AAA fire and a resurgent Russian fighter force with better equipment.

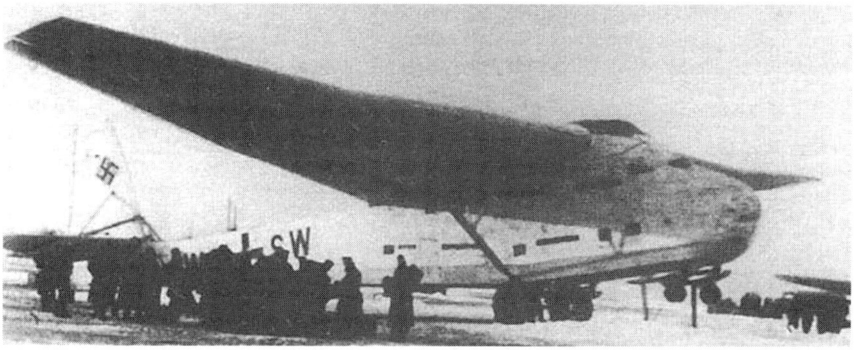

Huge Me 321 'Gigant' gliders carried a bigger load but required a large tow-plane. Their losses were also high.

Below, Me 323, six-engine version of the cavernous Messerschmitt glider, was more effective until Soviet artillery ranged on the available airfields Pitomnik was lost on 16 January, Gumrak on the 22nd. The last flight out of Stalingradski was a day later. With all seven fields overrun Sixth Army rapidly ran out of food, fuel and ammunition.

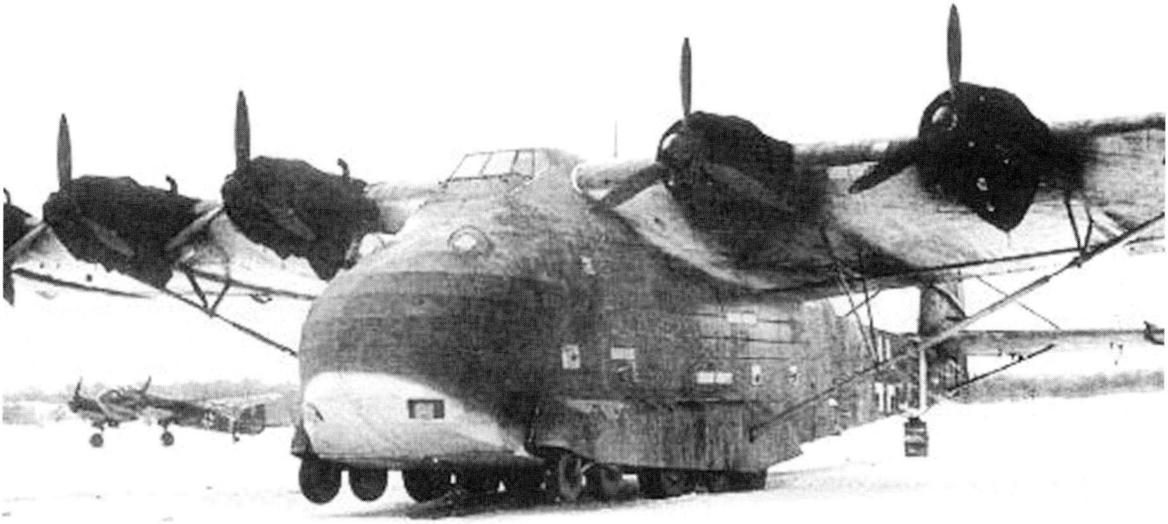

Luftwaffe losses were 488 planes (roughly seven a day) delivering 8350 tons of fuel, ammo, food and evacuating wounded from 24 November to 31 January. As airfields fell to Soviet advances it was finally recognized that Sixth Army couldn't be supported by air.

Nor were German ground forces outside the 'Kessel' strong enough to break the Soviet encirclement.

On 26 January Sixth Army was split in two pockets pressed against the Volga. The southern pocket surrendered on 31 January, the northern on 2 February 1943.

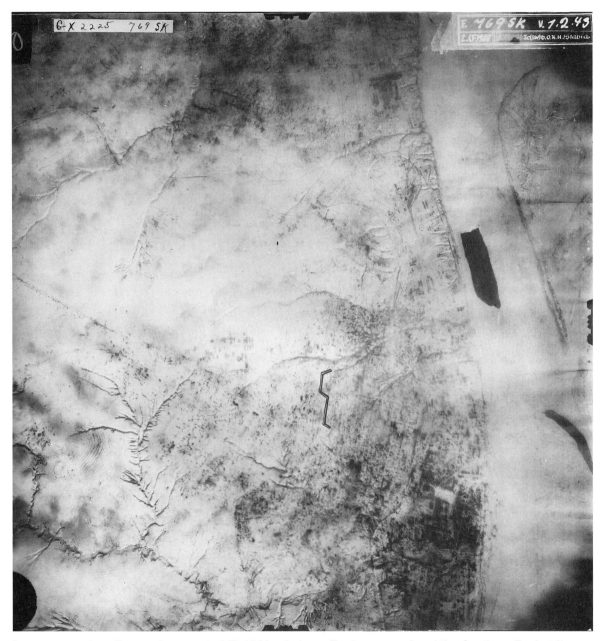

Imagery one day after newly promoted Field Marshal von Paulus surrendered the Southern Pocket (troops clustered around Red Plaza). A German PI drew in a defense line usually meaning an anti-tank ditch about half way between Stalingradski Airfield and Red Plaza (white rectangle near the river at lower right).

Irregular black shapes on the snow are craters from artillery rounds.

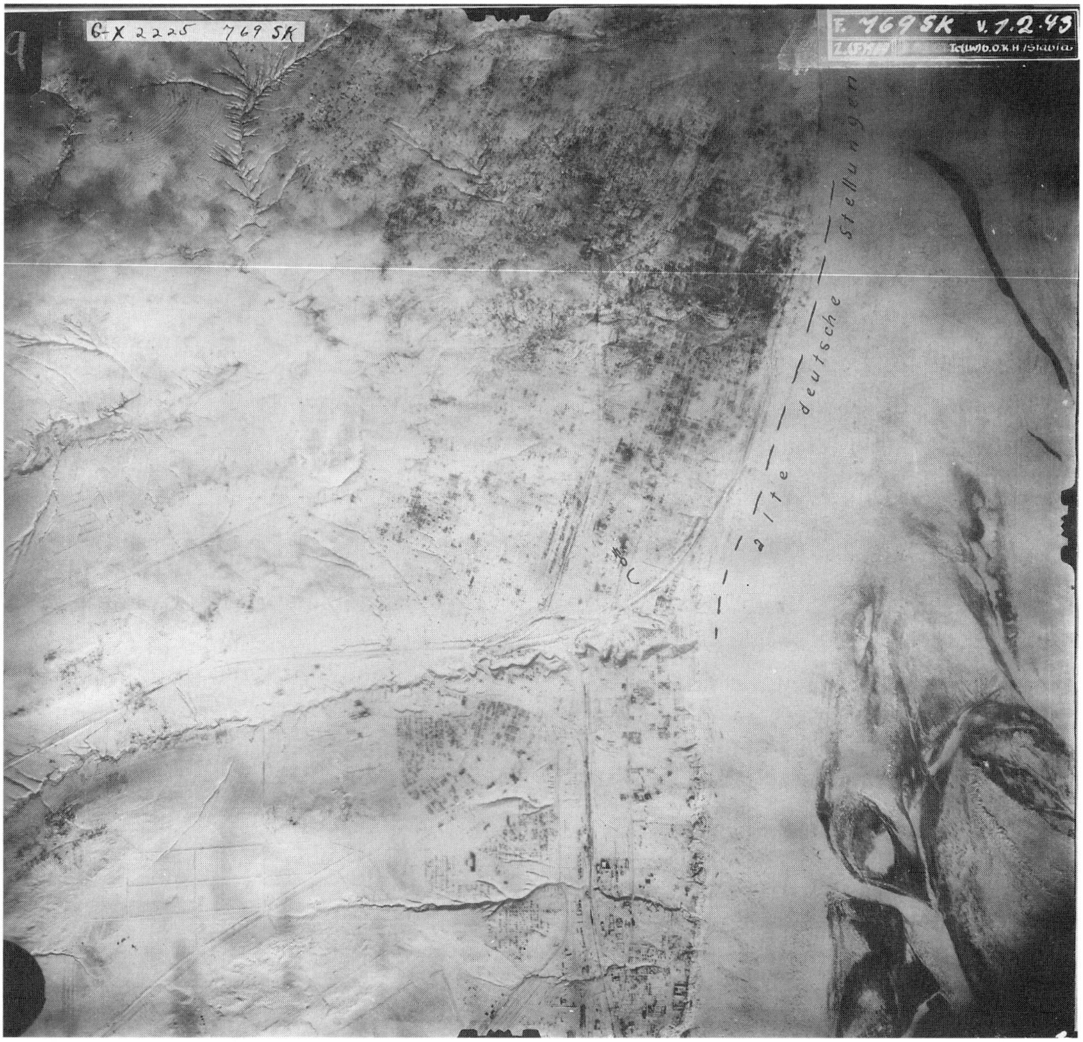
G-X 2225 769 SK
F. 769 SK v. 7.2.43
alte deutsche Stellungen

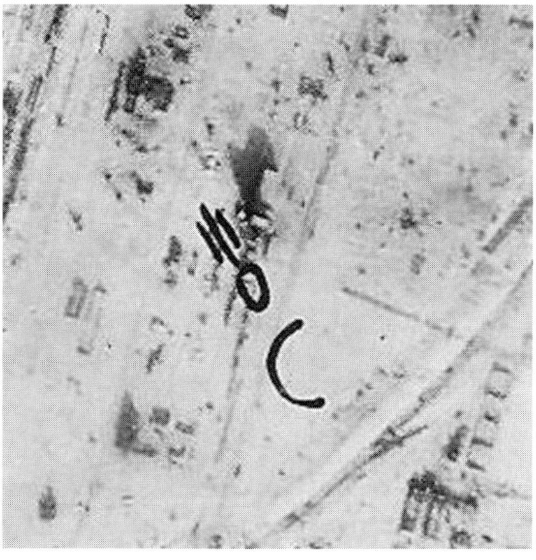

The next exposure heading south.
A German PI annotated ‘Old German Line’ on this imagery a day after Southern Pocket surrender. The only other annotation was near the unmistakable Grain Elevator shadow. A (presumably Soviet) three-gun light AAA battery inside the curve of the semi-circle.

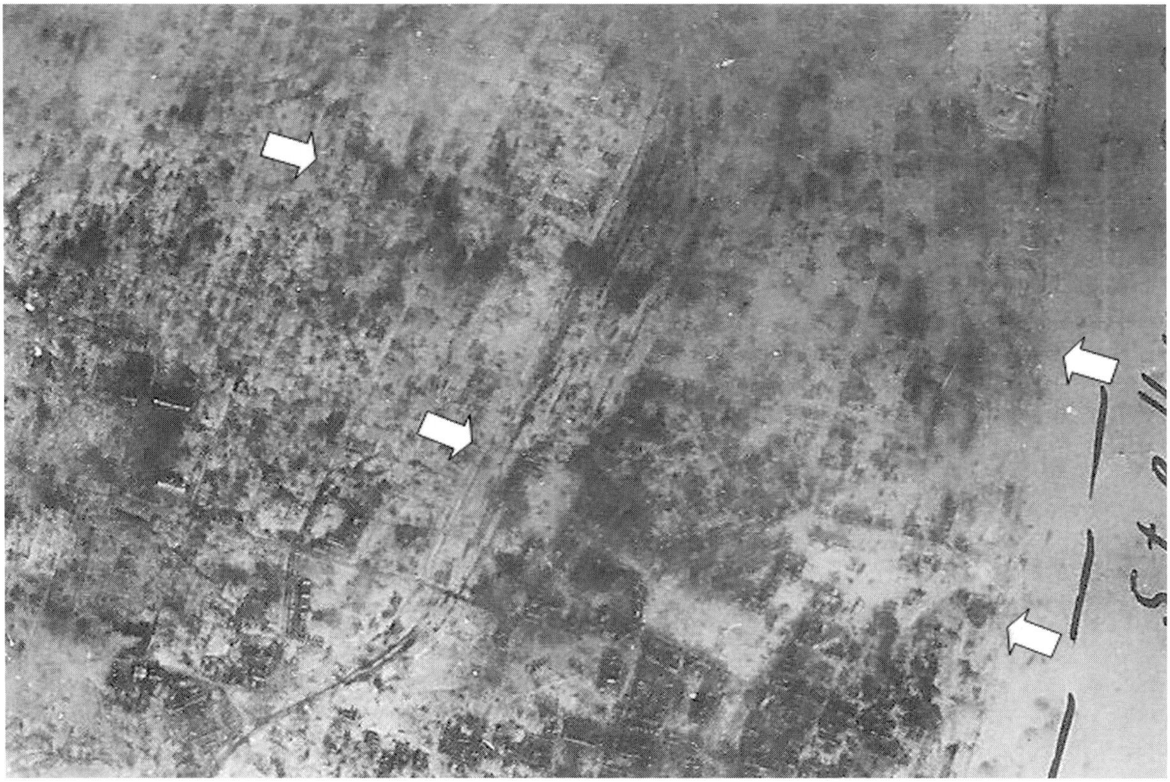

Maximum enlargement of previous 1 February 1943 imagery covering Stalingrad's center.

Comparing the two 1 February 1943 photos, it looks to me like two strings of bombs are going off (between arrows) crossing buildings near the river, Red Plaza, the rail yard and buildings to the west (bombers appear to be going east to west).

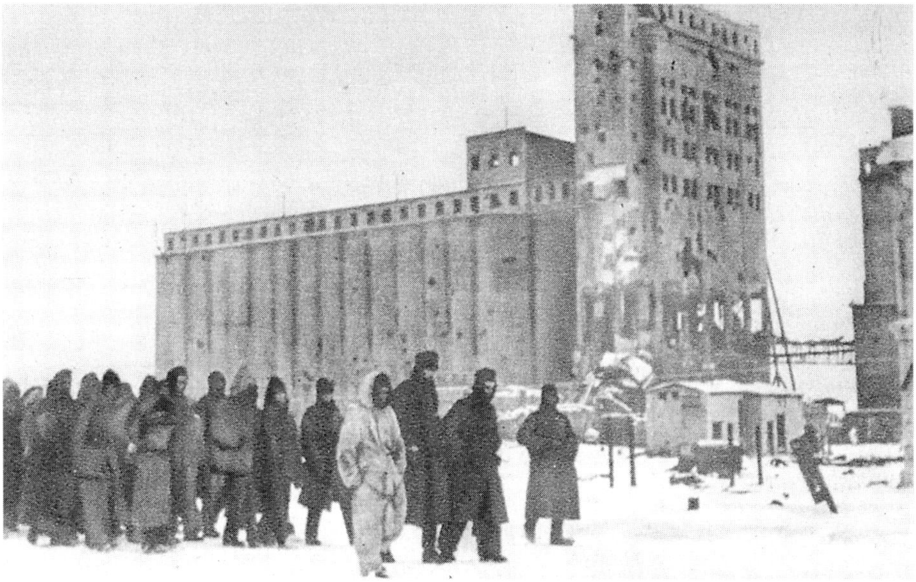

German PoWs being marched past the west side of the iconic much damaged massive Grain Elevator. Early February 1943.

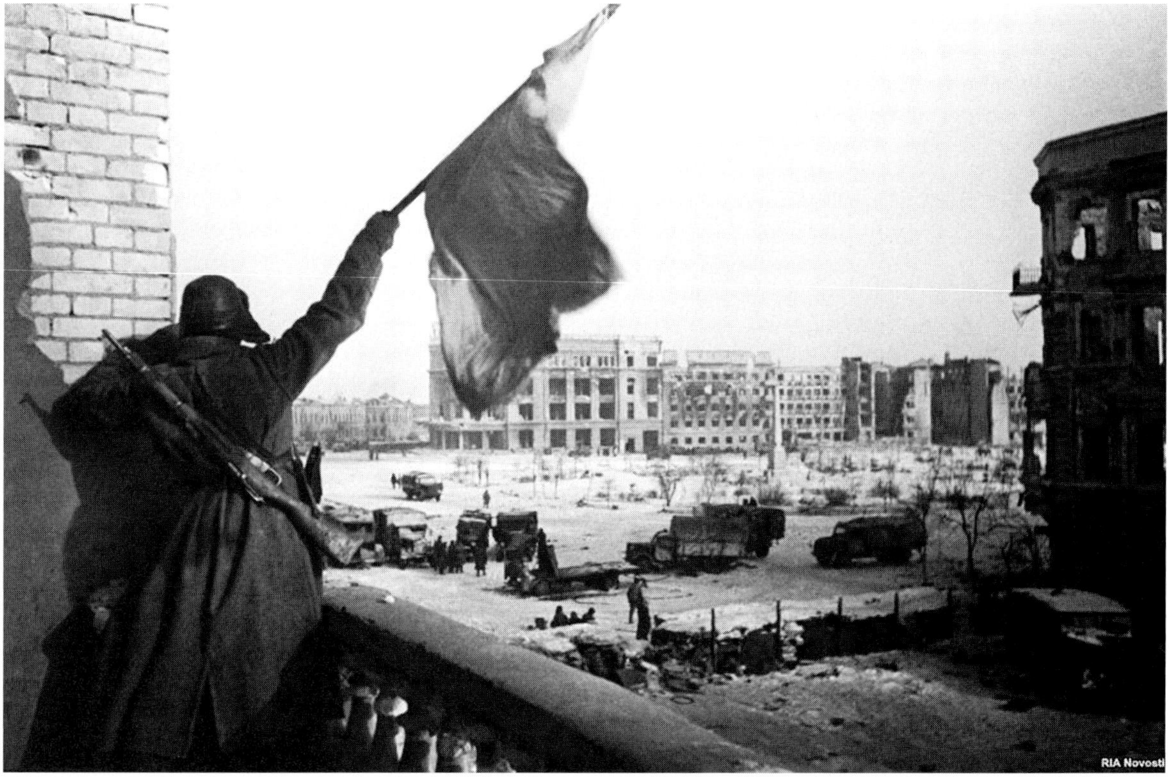
RIA Novosti

This photo of a Soviet soldier proudly waving the flag of victory over Red Plaza has been published many times but not explained. Directly under the flag is the entrance to Univermag Department Store. Sixth Army HQ was in that basement at the time of surrender.

Red Plaza from a light plane. Lack of rubble in the streets is further evidence of fire, not explosives, as the major cause of damage. Univermag Department Store is the acutely angled building at bottom center.

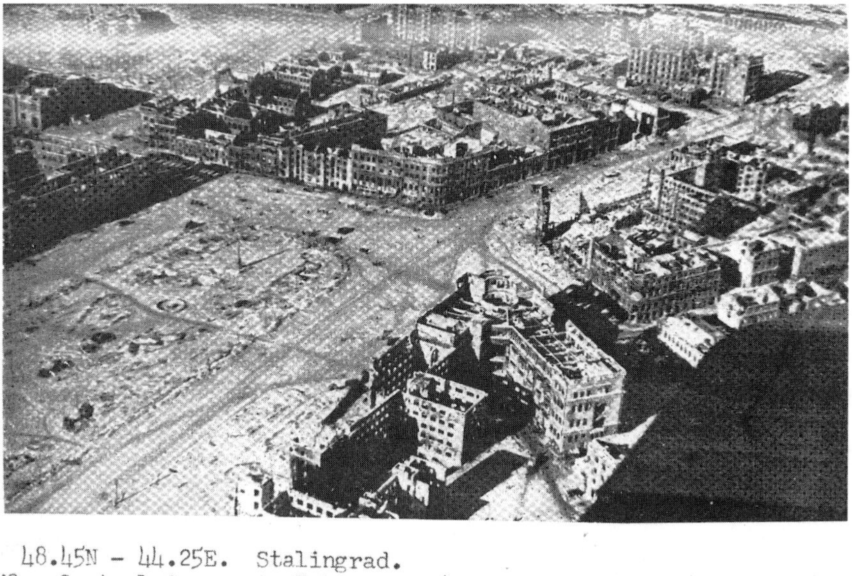

48.45N - 44.25E. Stalingrad.
'O. Central Square in February 1943. Source: Stalingrad.

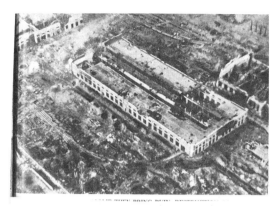

USSR. 48.45N - 44.25E. Stalingrad.
Cat. 00. Aerial view of unidentified factory. Source:
Communist party of Great Britain. The siege of Stalingrad,

Since small pockets of Soviet troops remained active along the Volga shore, I deem Stalingrad was never really taken by the Germans.

Every building in the city was destroyed but so was the German Sixth Army along with Hitler's hope of Caucasus oil and defeat of the Soviet Union.

USSR. 48.45N - 44.25E. Stalingrad.
Cat. 73. German PoWs marching out of the destroyed "Red October" steel plant. Date - 1949. Source: CIA 25099. CONFIDENTIAL.

2205.453. A. F.

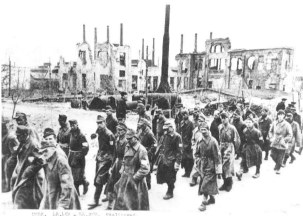

German PoWs exiting the ruins of Red October Steel Works.

USSR. 48.45N - 44.25E. Stalingrad.
Cat. 70. Central region of the city after its destruction

Burned and bombed-out hulks of workers housing.

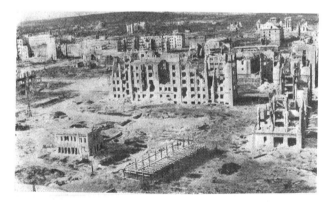

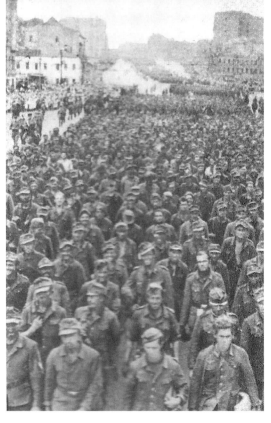

Field Marshal von Paulus surrendered between 110K and 91K men (depending upon your source). Only 5K made it back home (in 1950-1956).

As many as 10,000 German soldiers continued armed resistance near Stalingrad into March 1943.

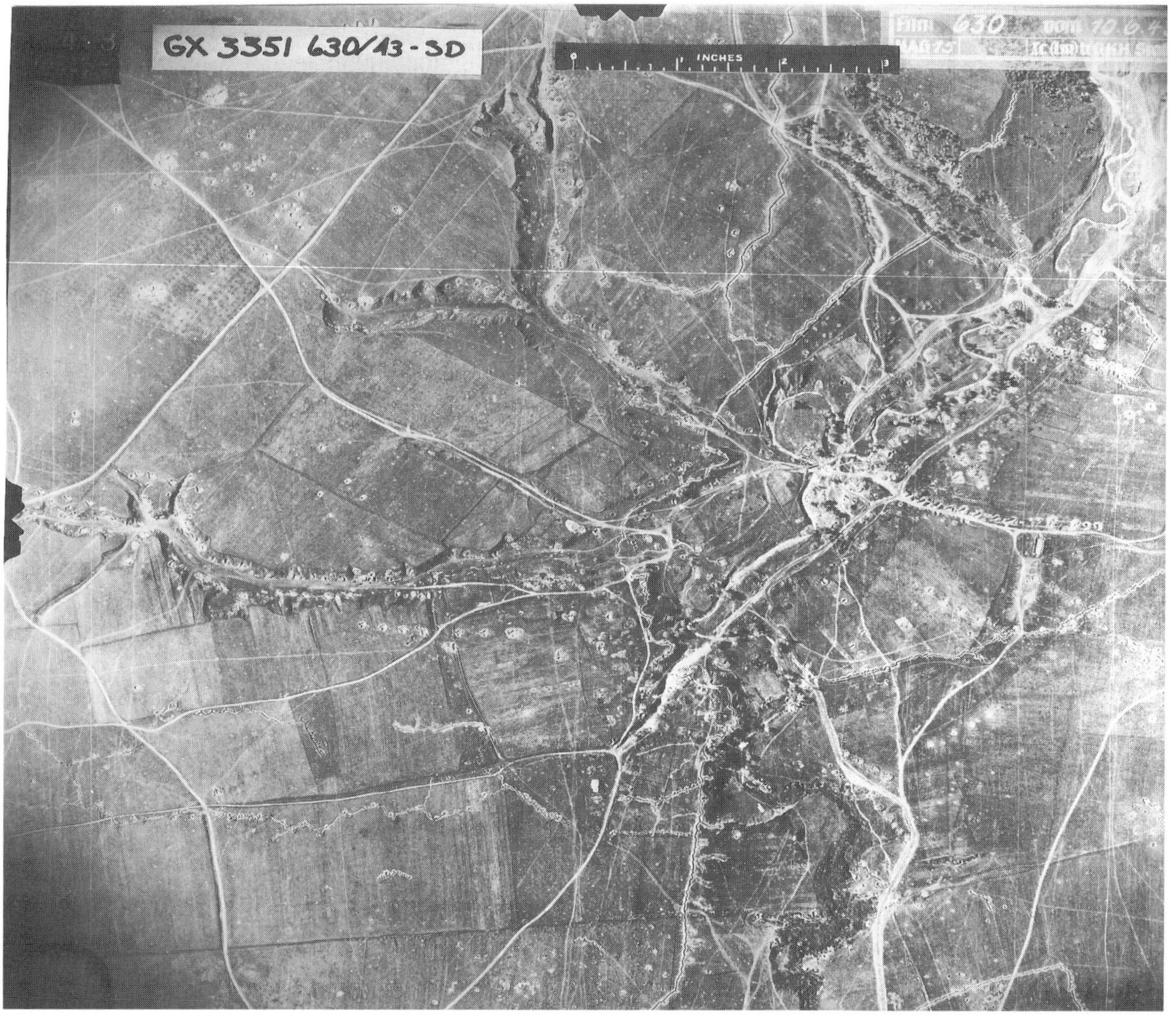
GX 3351 630/13 - SD
INCHES

Well into 1943 Luftwaffe aerial recon was covering areas around Stalingrad. These are abandoned Infantry and heavy artillery positions southwest of the city, 10 June 1943.

Below, enlargement.

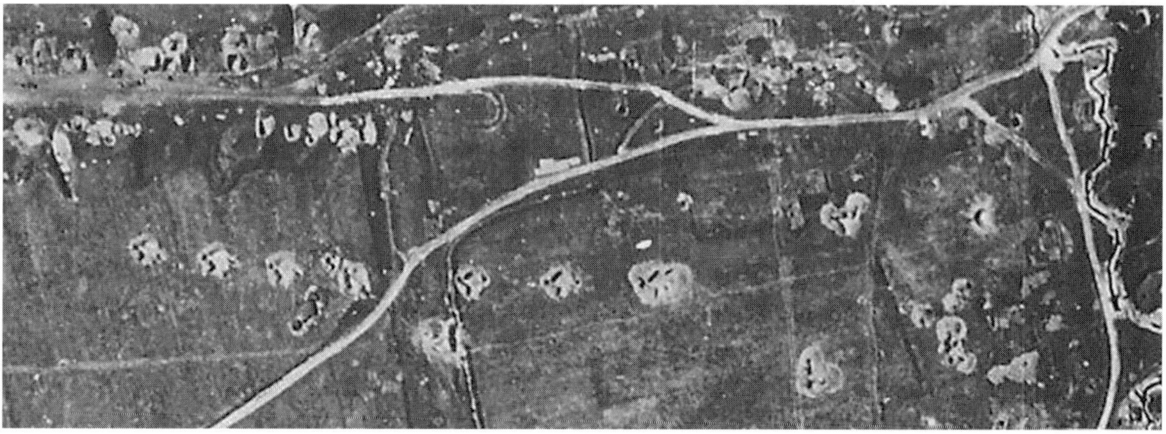

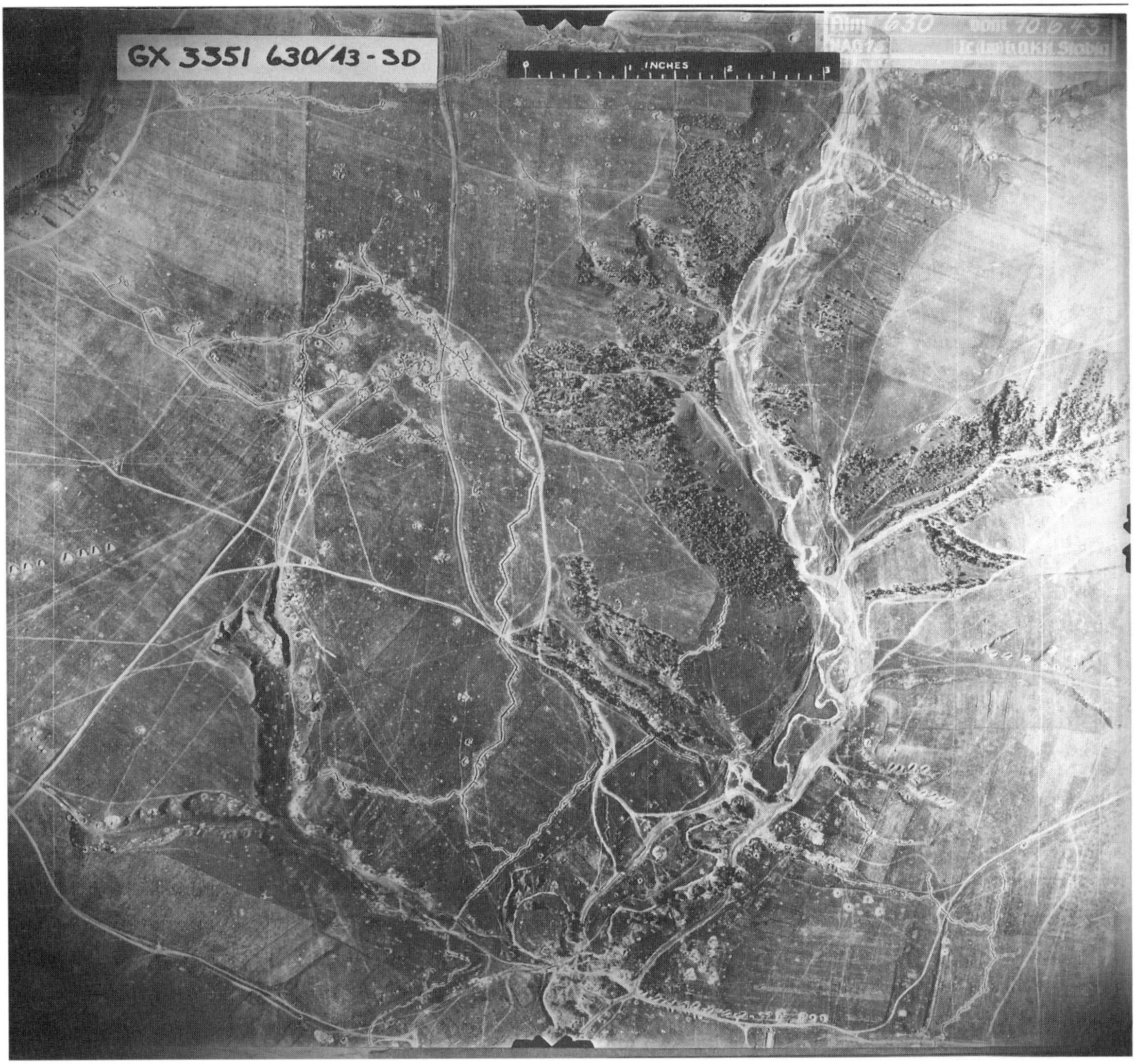
GX 3351 630/43-SD
0 1 INCHES 2 3

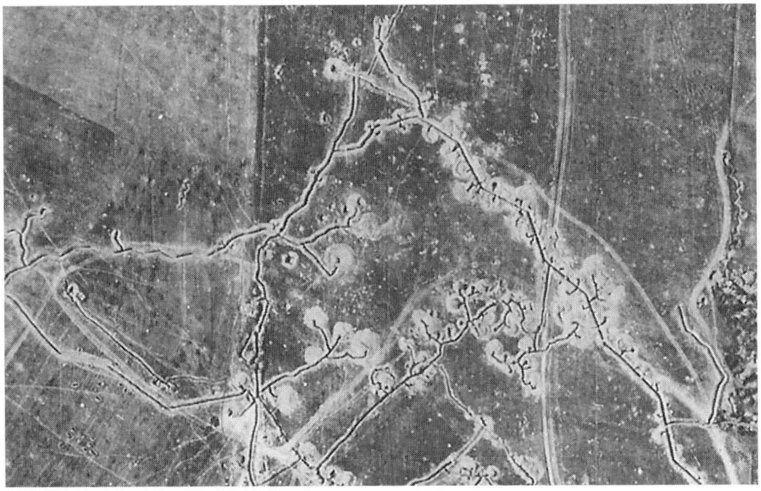

Same mission. Enlargement of a really elaborate Infantry strongpoint.

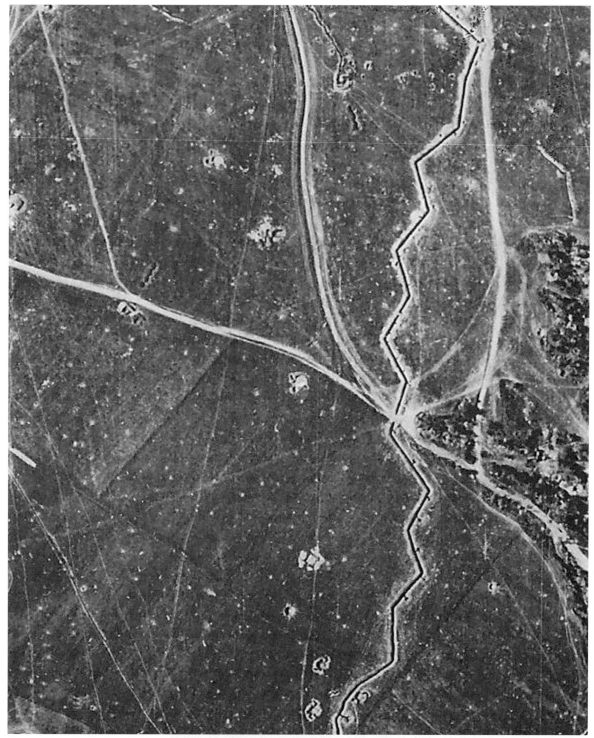

Anti-tank ditch and unoccupied artillery revetments, probably remnants of the two encirclement campaigns.
German, Romanian, and Italian casualties numbered 850,000.
Soviet losses at Stalingrad have been cited as 1,129,619 personnel.
We will probably never know the number of civilians who died.

Chapter VIII

1943 AND ON

Not everyone could see or admit after February1943 that Barbarossa was over. The twenty month, 1200 mile victorious Wehrmacht Vormarsch had failed, and there would be very little Vormarsching from then on. A magnificent army, and probably two generations of young men, had been squandered. Now they were being slowly destroyed by an enemy that was growing stronger while the Wehrmacht was weakening.

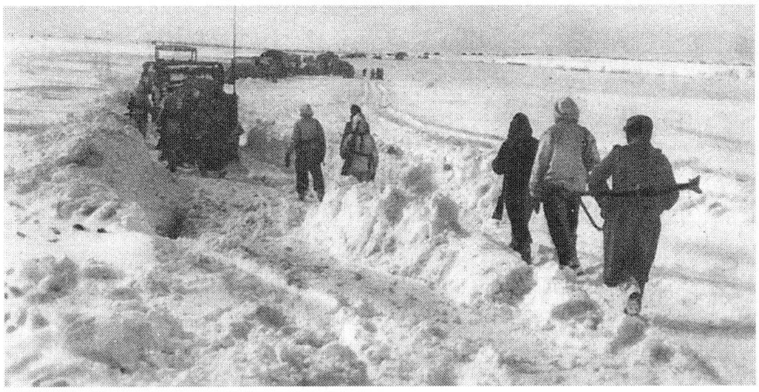

Retreat from Stalingrad was as painful as the winter had been for Sixth Army—endless, pointless, no hope of success.

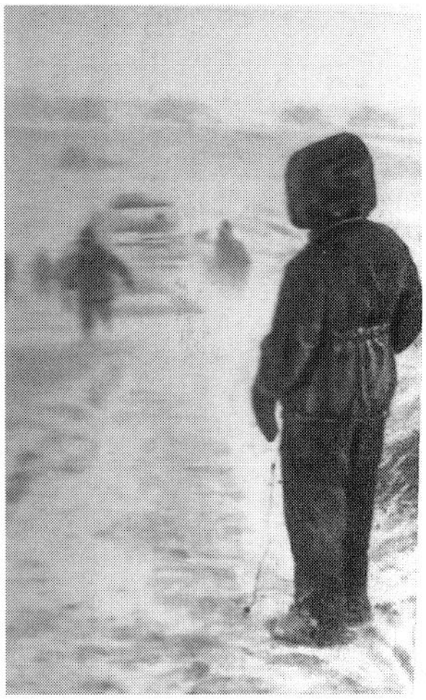

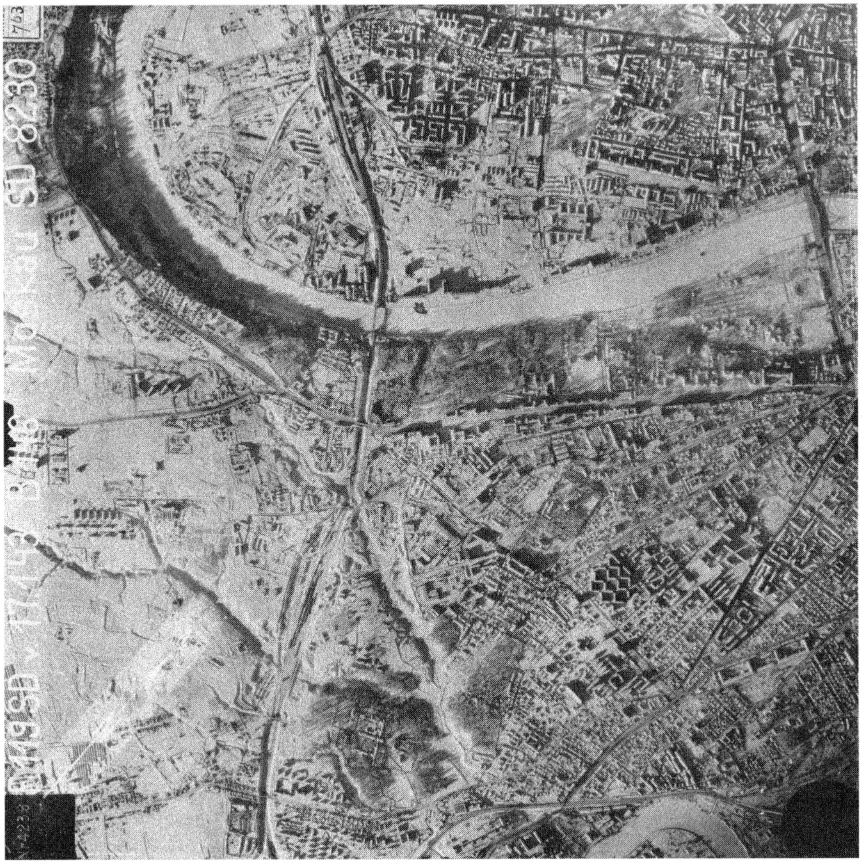

Meanwhile, the Luftwaffe photographed Moscow again on 17 July 1943—a city they couldn't take on the way east and wouldn't touch on the way west.

Peasants greet Soviet cavalry near Rostov, March 1943.

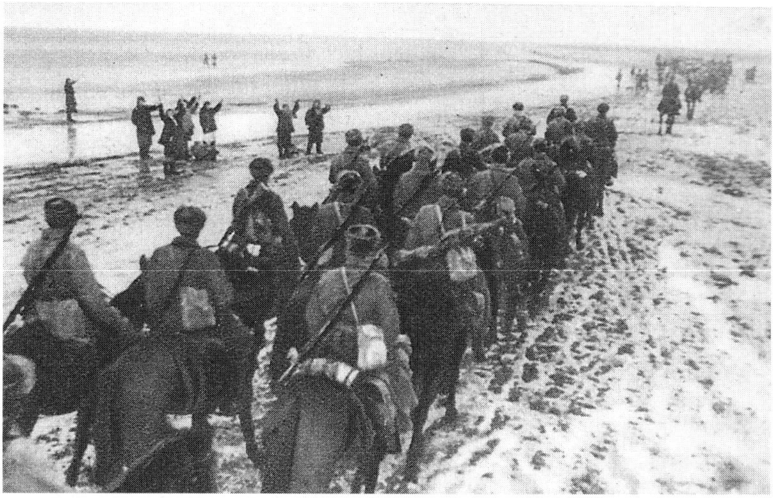

Below, 26 June 1943, south of Kursk, near Ssmirnoff. This is from a target study and meticulously annotates defense positions (trenches, machine-gun pits, and AAA guns). A perfect four-gun is in an open field at lower right.

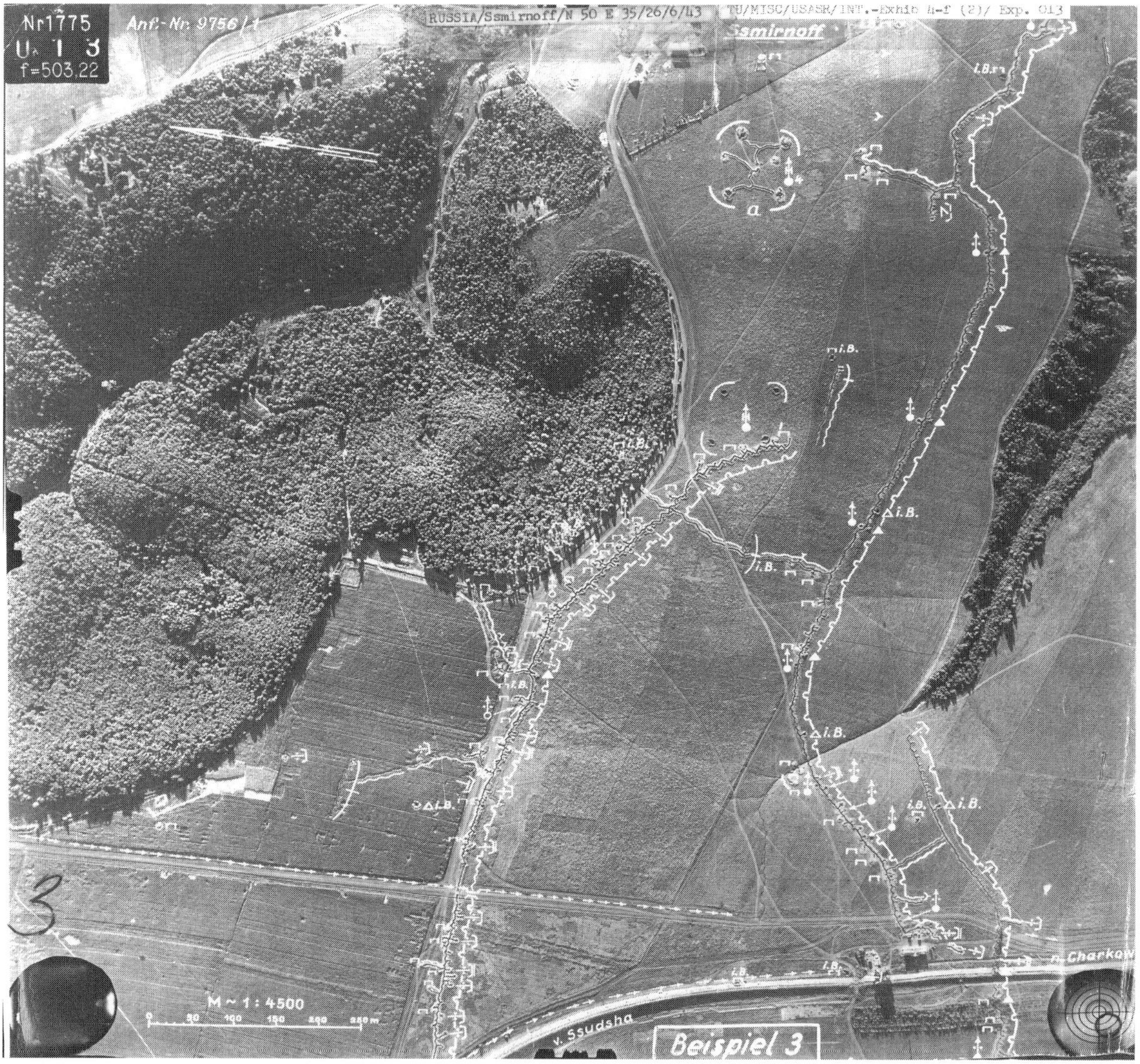
Nr1775
f=503.22
Anf.-Nr. 9756/1
RUSSIA/Ssmirnoff/N 50 E 35/26/6/43
Ssmirnoff
M ~ 1:4500
v. Ssudsha
n. Charkow
Beispiel 3

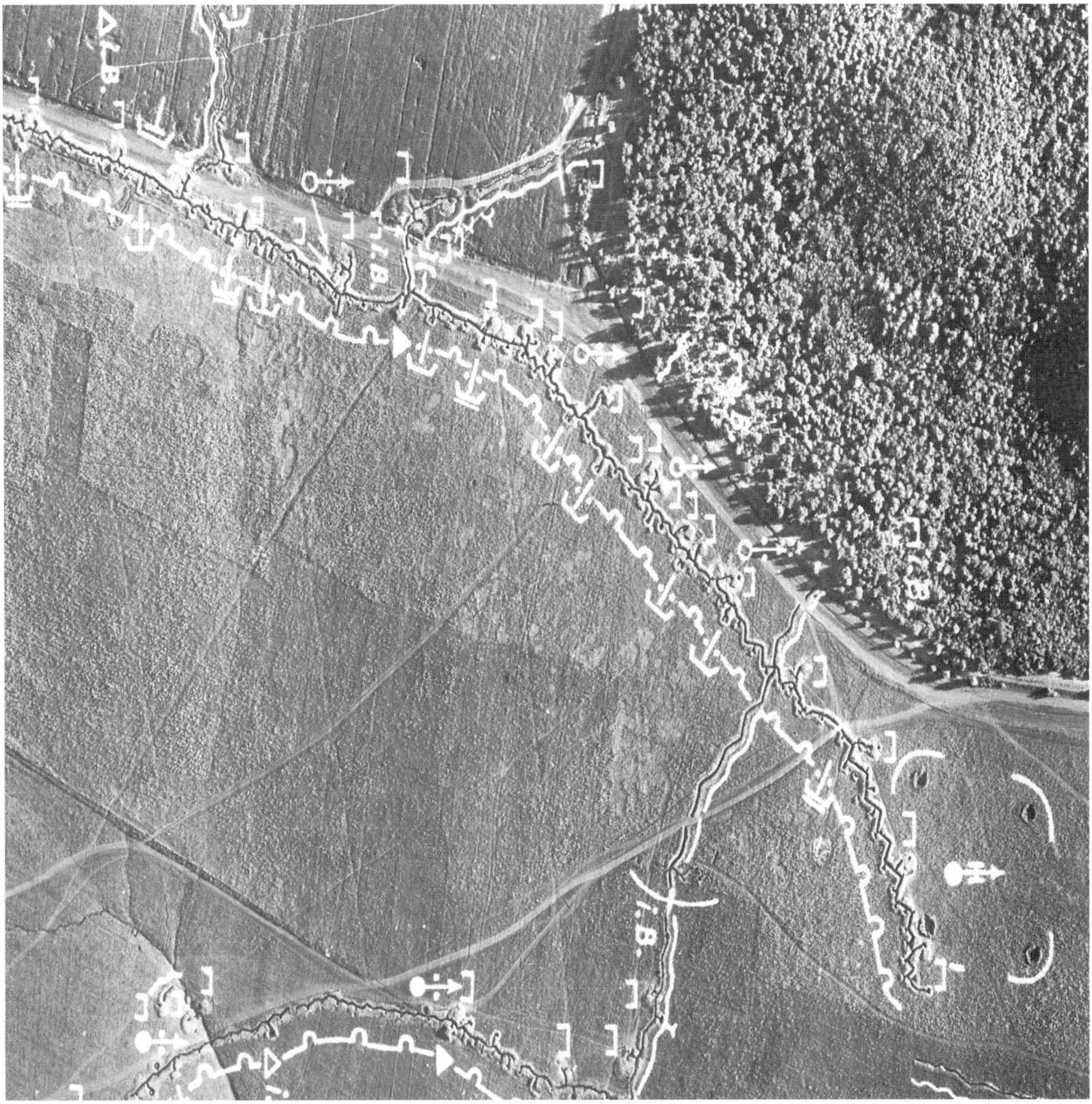

Arrows ending in circles are anti-aircraft guns. Bars along the arrow shaft indicate heavy guns (88mm), dots beside the shaft are for lighter guns down to 20mm. All those gun symbols along the trench line indicate heavy machine-guns. Ones with a thick or double line for a base (they look like a boat with a line of water) are anti-tank weapons.

Another symbol says this was Battalion strength, but I don't think anyone is down there.

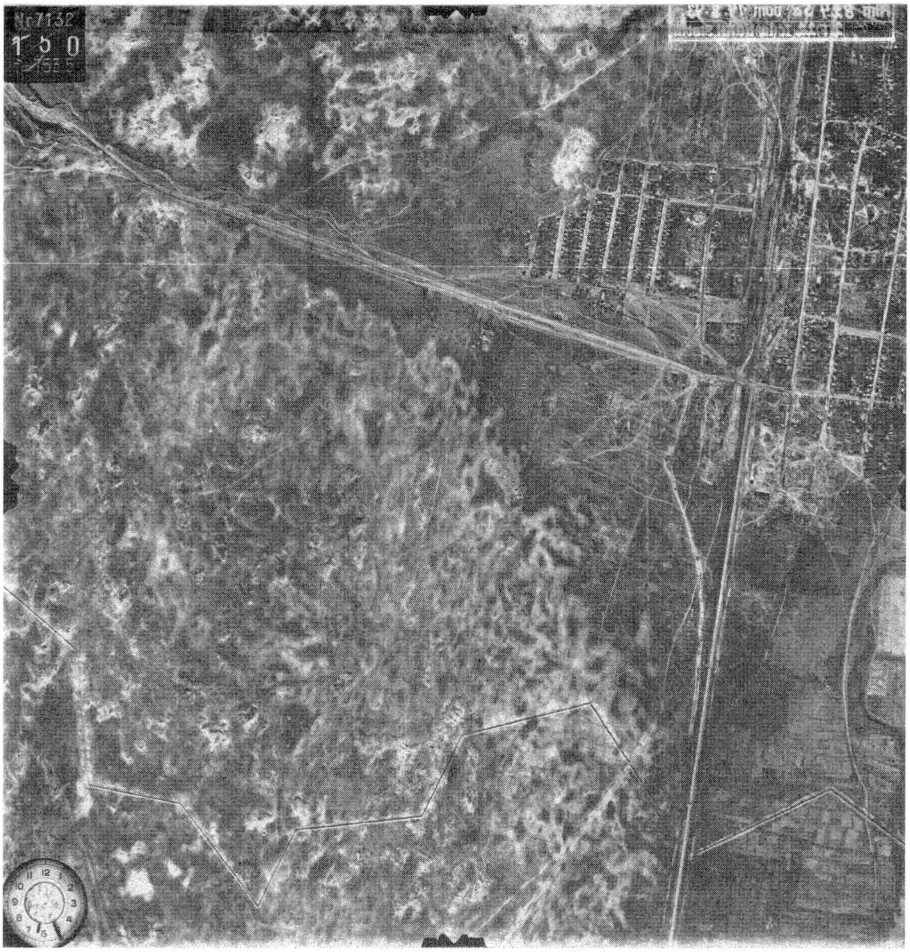
Nr7132

German ground forces were well west of Stalingrad and heading in the other direction on 14 August 1943, but this recon mission photographed anti-tank ditches southwest of the city. Why?

Enlarged below.

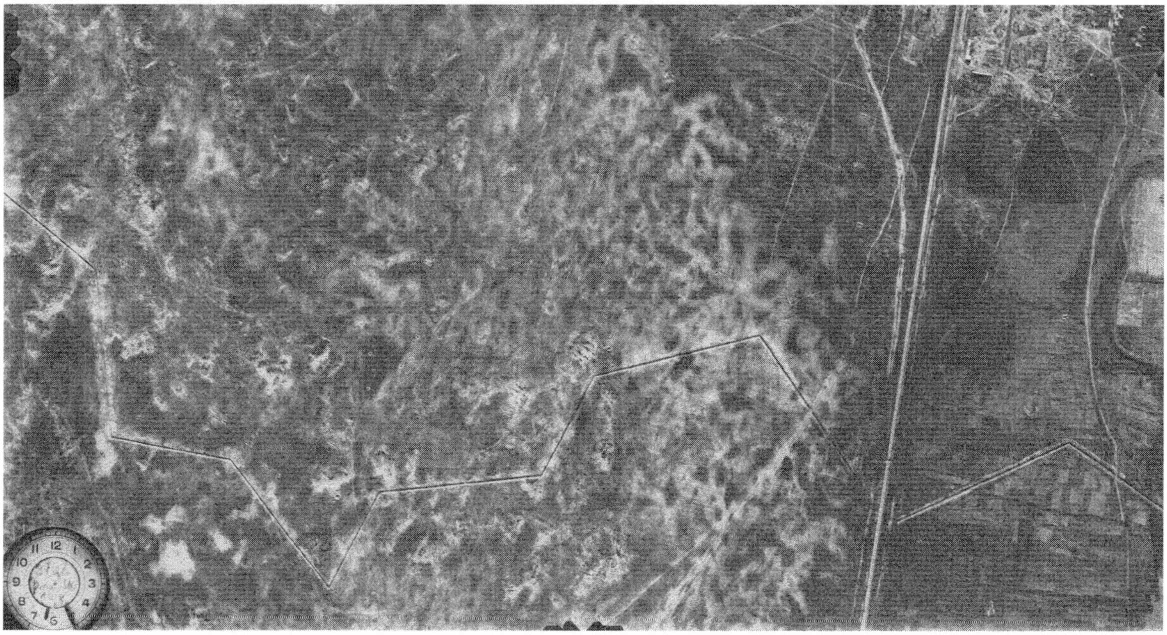

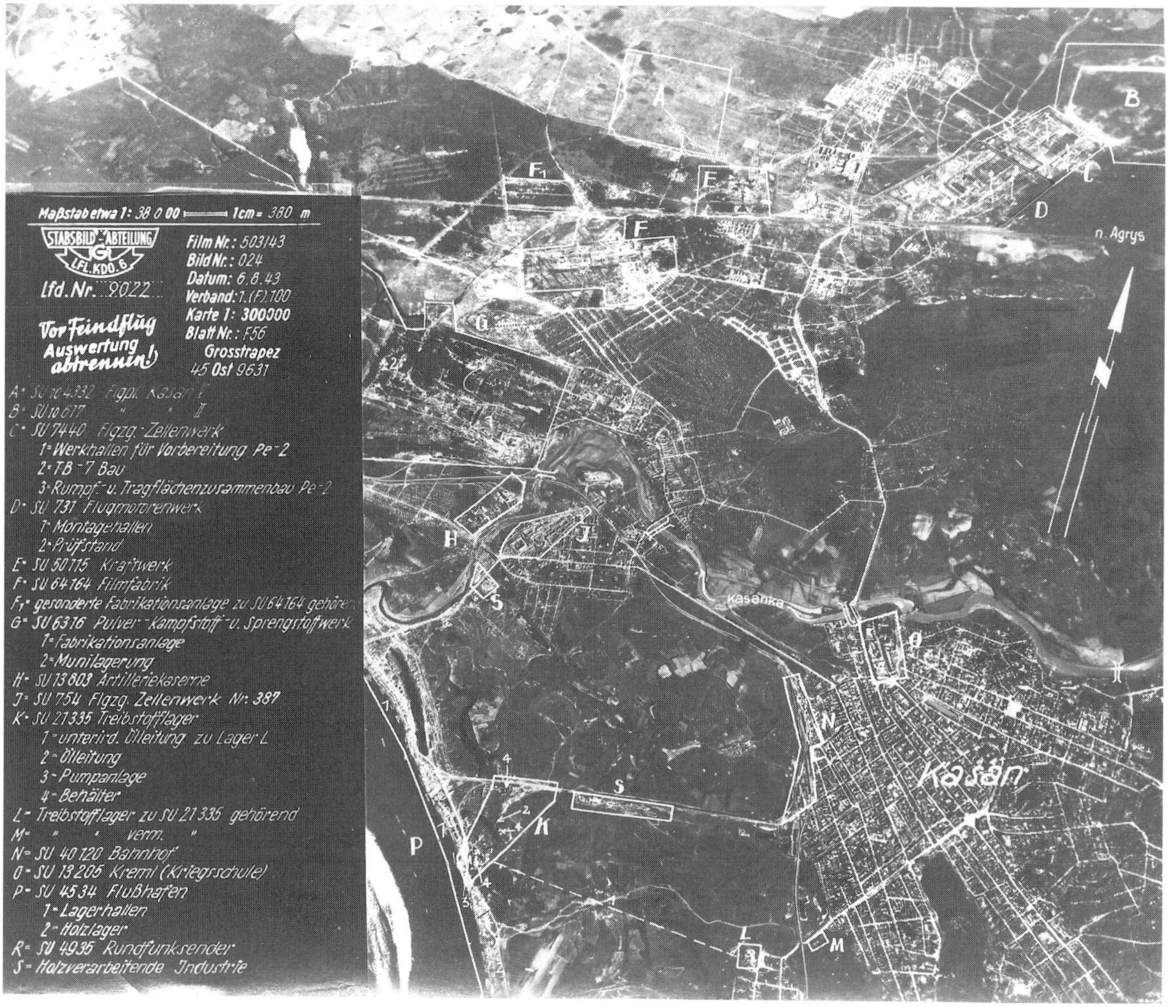
Maßstab etwa 1: 38 0 00 1cm = 380 m
STABSBILD-ABTEILUNG G LFL.KDO.6
Lfd. Nr. 9022
Vor Feindflug Auswertung abtrennen!
Film Nr.: 503143
Bild Nr.: 024
Datum: 6.8.43
Verband: 1.(F).100
Karte 1: 300000
Blatt Nr.: F56
Grosstrapez
45 Ost 9631
B= SU 10 617 " " II
C= SU 7440 Flgzg.-Zellenwerk
1= Werkhallen für Vorbereitung Pe-2
2= TB-7 Bau
3= Rumpf- u. Tragflächenzusammenbau Pe-2
D= SU 731 Flugmotorenwerk
1= Montagehallen
2= Prüfstand
E= SU 50 715 Kraftwerk
F= SU 64 164 Filmfabrik
F1= gesonderte Fabrikationsanlage zu SU 64 164 gehörend
G= SU 6316 Pulver- Kampfstoff- u. Sprengstoffwerk
1= Fabrikationsanlage
2= Munilagerung
H= SU 13 803 Artilleriekaserne
J= SU 754 Flgzg. Zellenwerk Nr: 387
K= SU 21 335 Treibstofflager
1= unterird. Ölleitung zu Lager L
2= Ölleitung
3= Pumpanlage
4= Behälter
L= Treibstofflager zu SU 21 335 gehörend
M= " " verm. "
N= SU 40 120 Bahnhof
O= SU 13 205 Kreml (Kriegsschule)
P= SU 4534 Flußhafen
1= Lagerhallen
2= Holzlager
R= SU 4935 Rundfunksender
S= Holzverarbeitende Industrie
Kasanka
Kasan
n. Agrys

Kasan, 6 August 1943. You have to admire this one. It is detailed PI work at its best—everything a targeteer could ask for. It is so detailed I suspect pre-war ground information must have been involved.

Right, enlargement of aircraft factory “C”.
1 = Pe-2 parts hall
2 = TB-7 hall
3 = assembly hall.

Aircraft motor works “D”.
1 = assembly hall
2 = test cells.

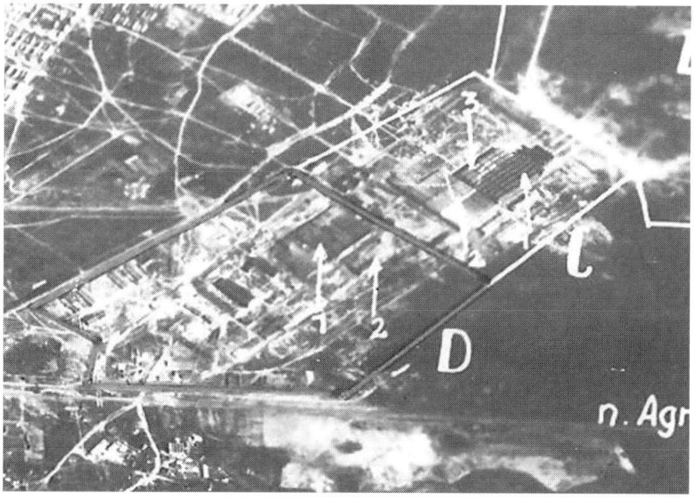
C
D

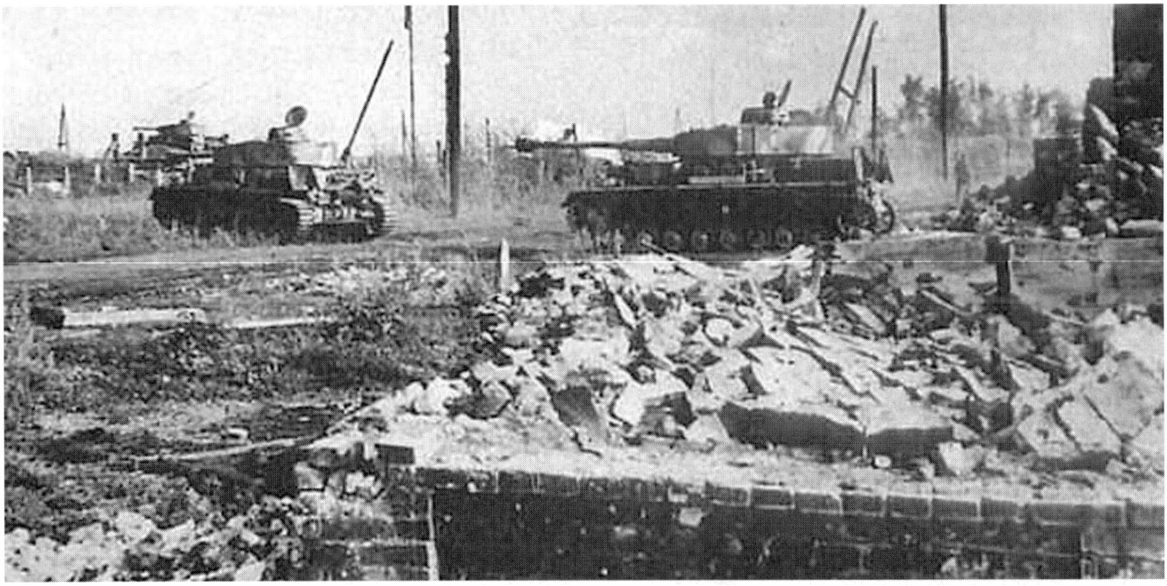

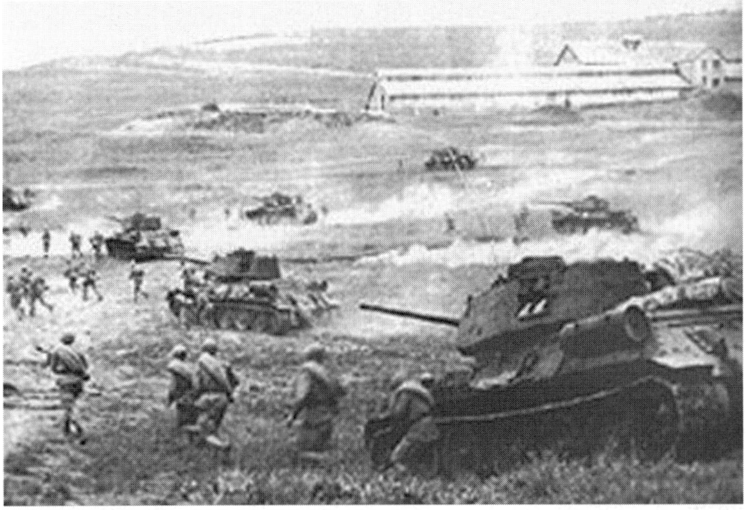

Meanwhile, at Kursk (280 miles southeast of Moscow) the last German offensive on the eastern front was underway. From 5 July to 23 August 1943 780K Germans with 780 tanks and 10K guns tried to encircle 1.9 million Soviets with 5K tanks and 25K guns.

Above, Pz IVs with high velocity 75mm guns move into battle.

Left, Soviet T-34s with high velocity 76.2 mm guns go into action with supporting infantry.

Below, the Soviets threw everything they had into the battle, including some obsolescent, under gunned US M3s.

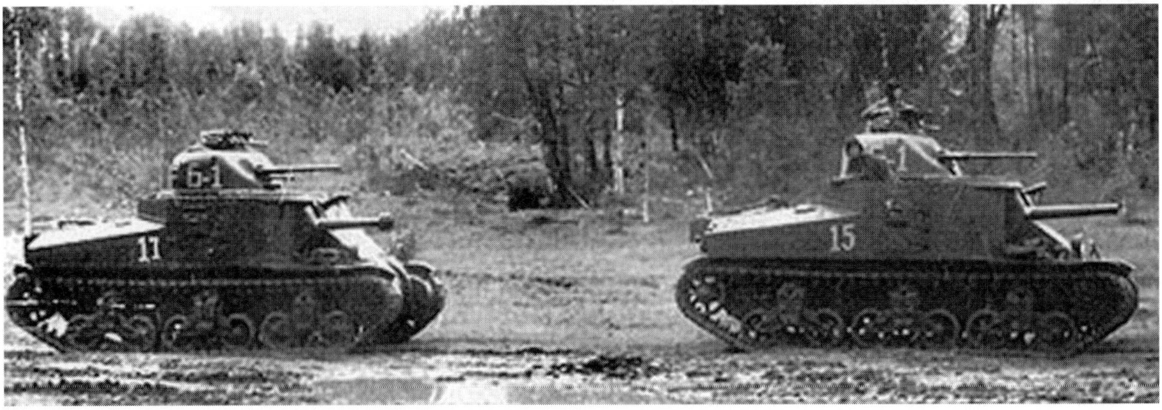
11
15

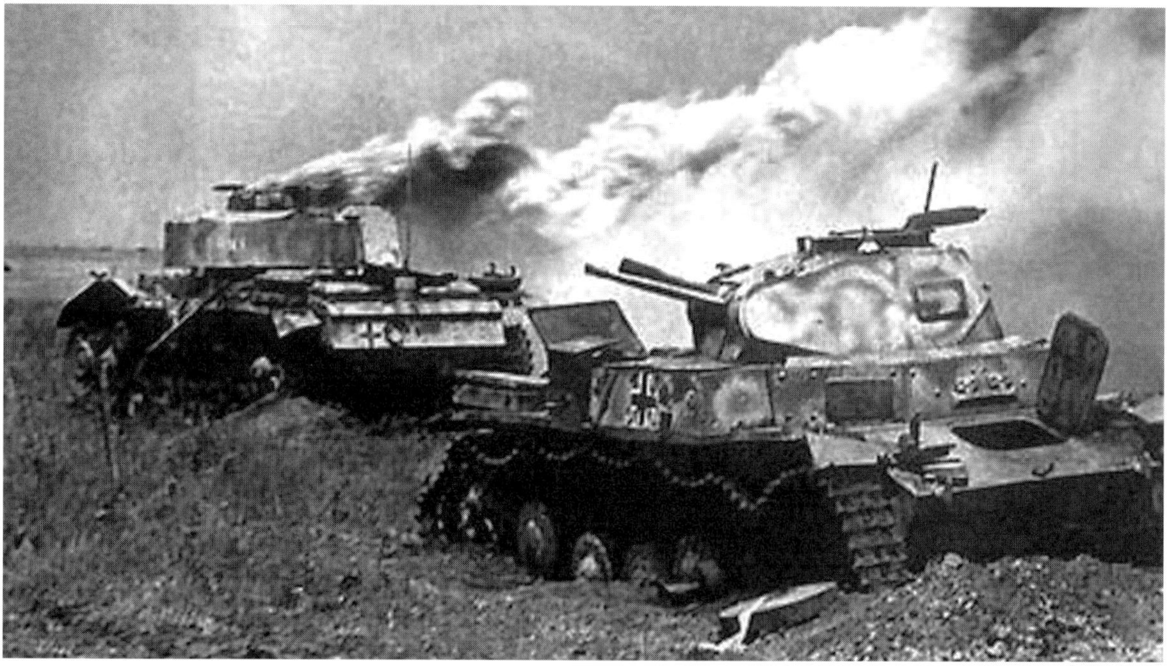

A burning Pz IV in front of an out of action Pz II, Olkhovatka, near Voronezh.

Kursk became several distinct battles and both sides were hurt badly. Soviet manpower losses were roughly four times German, and nearly all their tanks were lost. Soviet air losses were double Luftwaffe losses.

Casualties and loss of equipment in 49 days of combat around Kursk were crippling, but the Soviets could replace theirs.

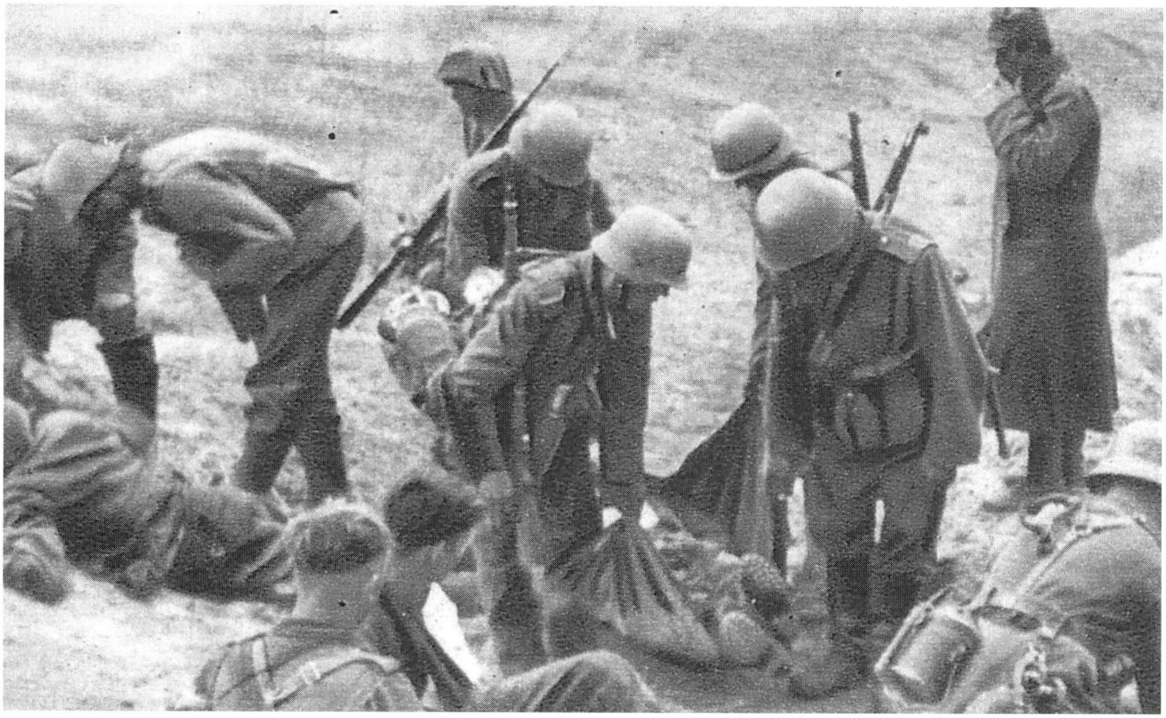

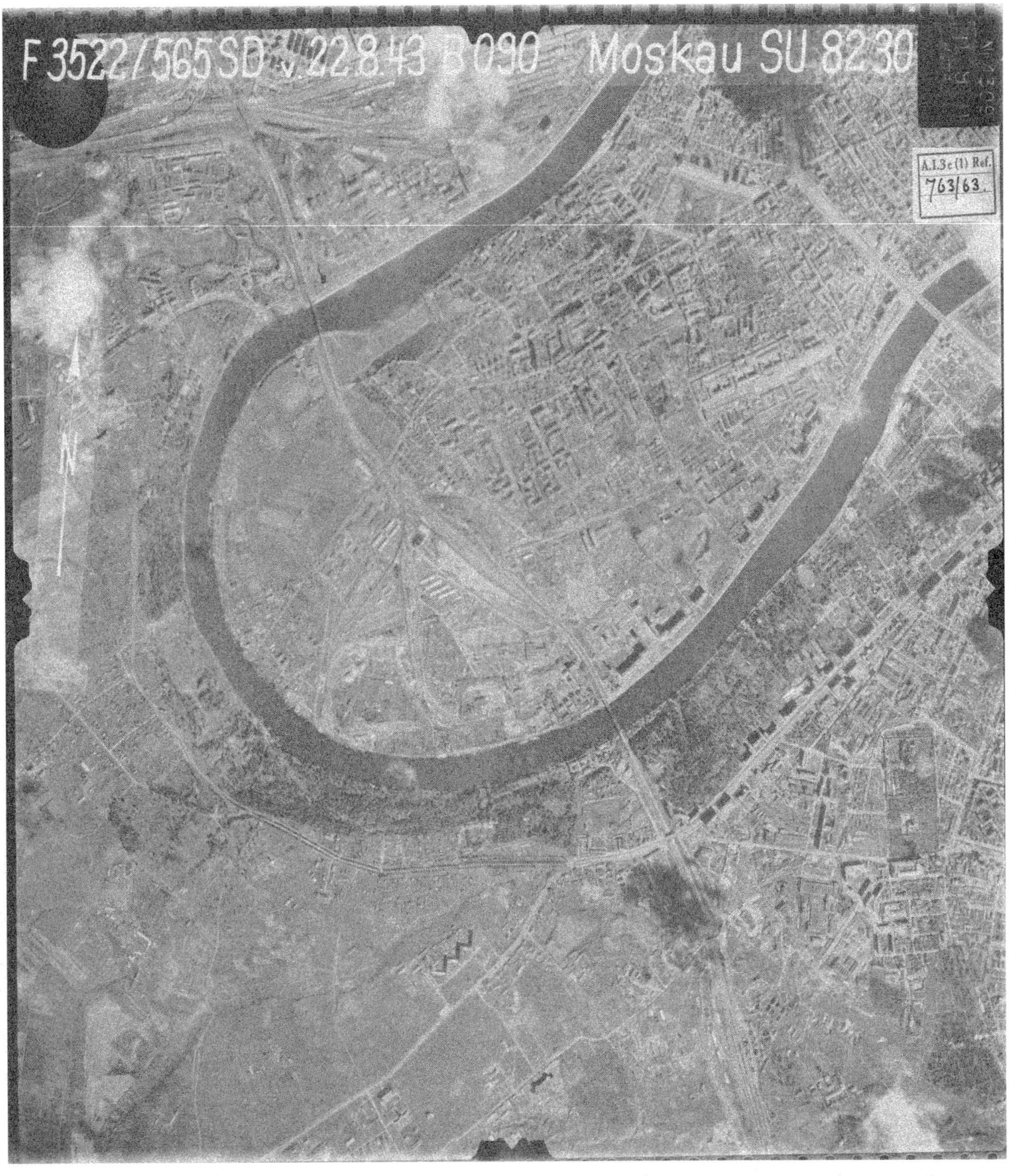
F 3522/565 SD v. 22.8.43 B 090 Moskau SU 82 30
A.I.3c (1) Ref.
763/63.
N

And, on 22 August, while one of the largest armored clashes of the war was wrapping up, German long range photoreconnaissance was back looking at the Moscow railroad yards. I wish they'd have flown a couple of sorties over the battle area around Kursk.

This photo shows something else. There is no bomb damage in this industrial part of the enemy capitol. Luftwaffe assets were stretched thin and losses over Kursk were hard to replace. Here is where the Luftwaffe's biggest mistake was obvious. In 1938-39 they should have developed a fleet of long-range heavy-load bombers like the Lancaster or B-24.

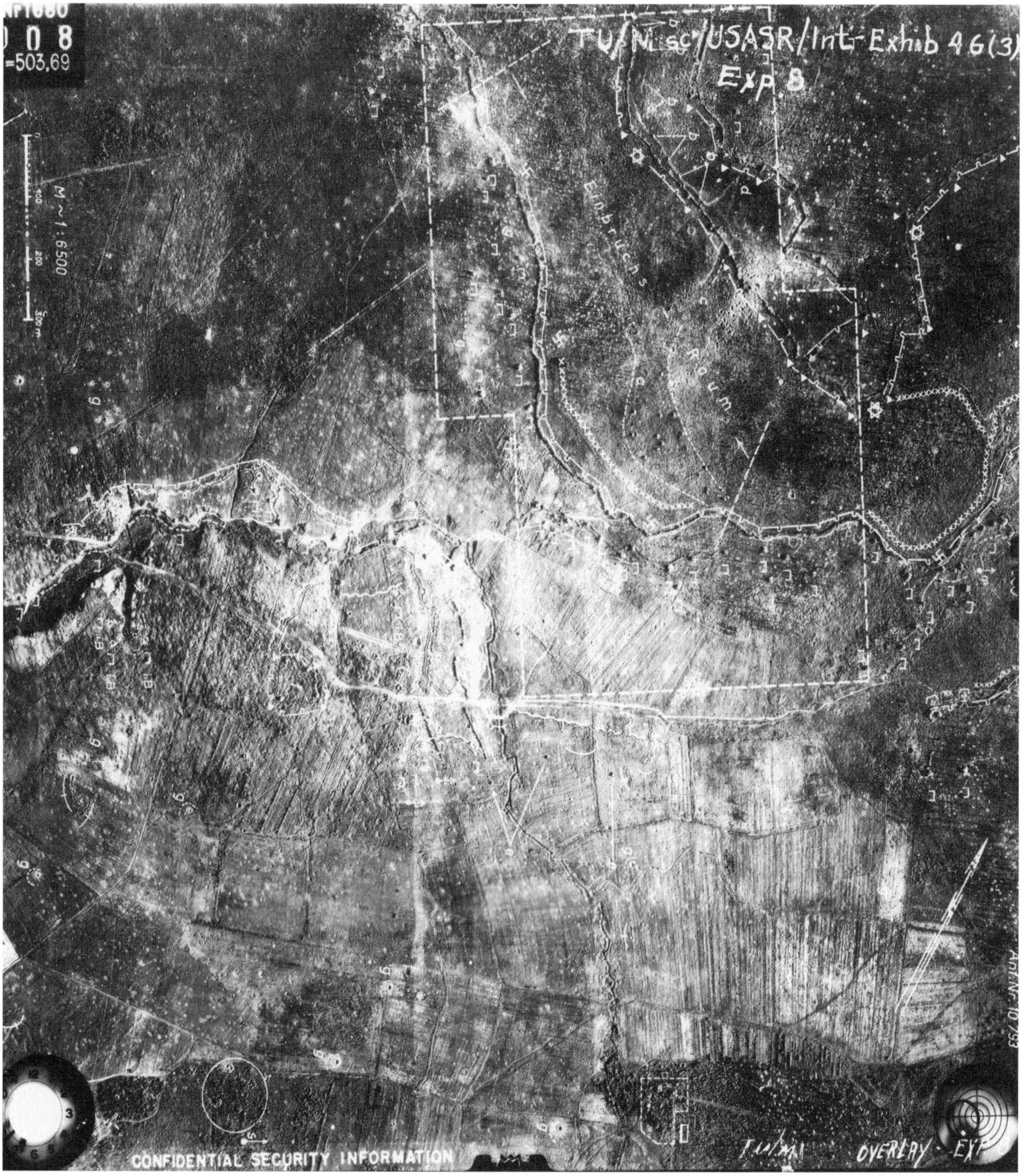
Einbruchs
Raum
M~1:6500
CONFIDENTIAL SECURITY INFORMATION
OVERLAY

Titled ‘Positions S. of Ilmensees’ the 22 August 1943 photo is actually near Staraja Russa just south of Lake Ilman. It must have been an attachment to a German After Action Report. Both Soviet and German lines are shown and the space between them annotated ‘Einbruchs Raum’; which I translate as Incursion Zone. Twenty Soviet tanks and armored cars are seen advancing.

As rare and interesting as combat is on reconnaissance imagery, American markings on the film tell me this small-scale print was important to US Intelligence, probably for its cartographic value.

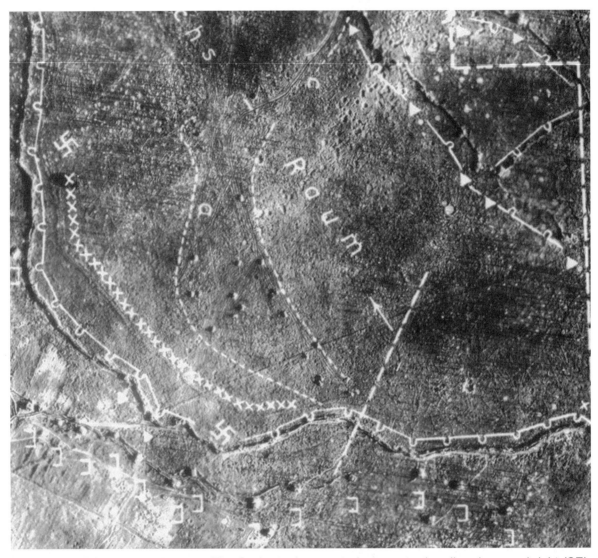

Enlargement of 22 August imagery. The Soviet tanks are at photo center heading down and right (SE), curiously presenting their sides to the German line.

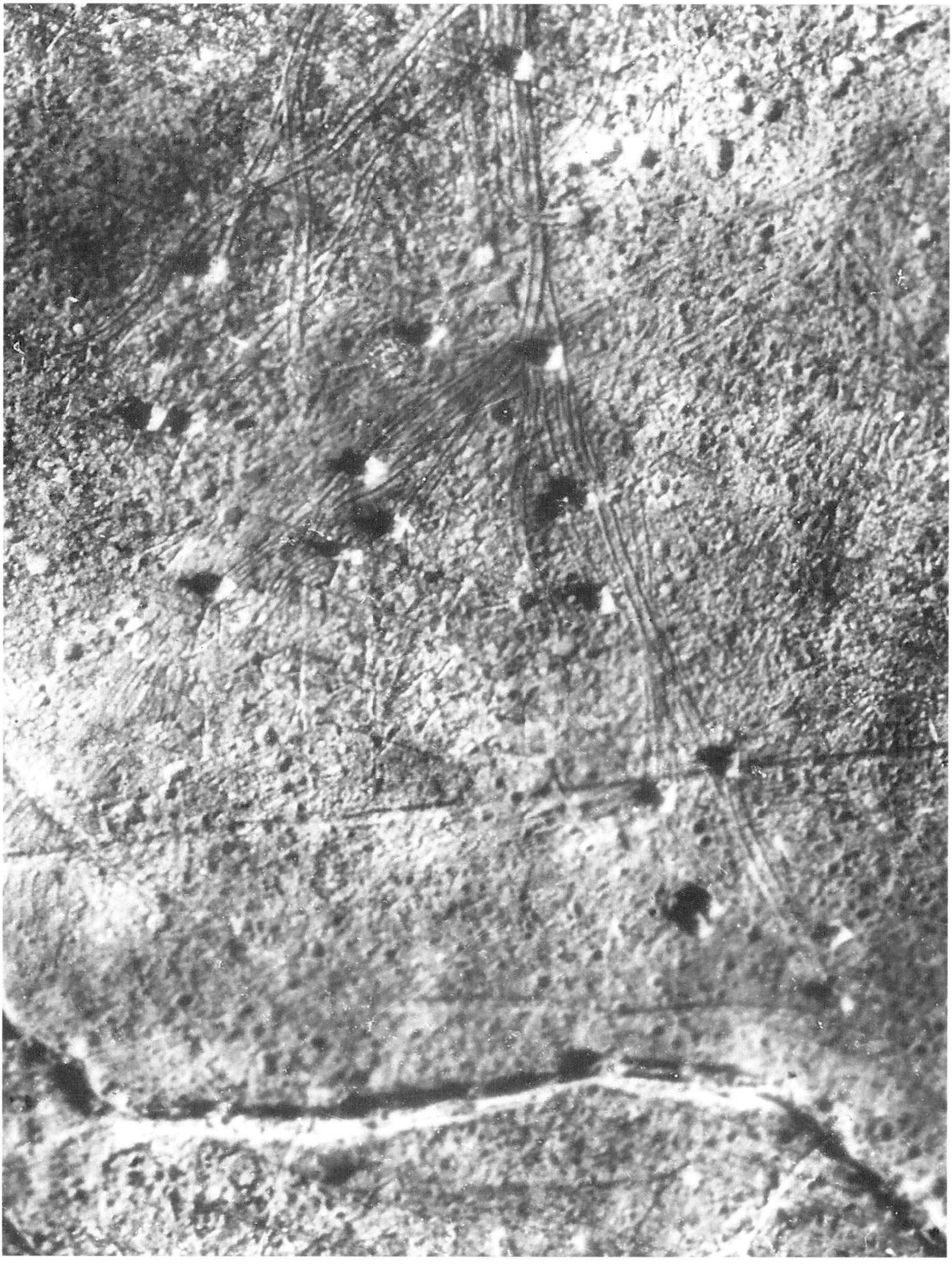

This is as good as I can get the AFVs. Shadows high in back are probably BA-10s.

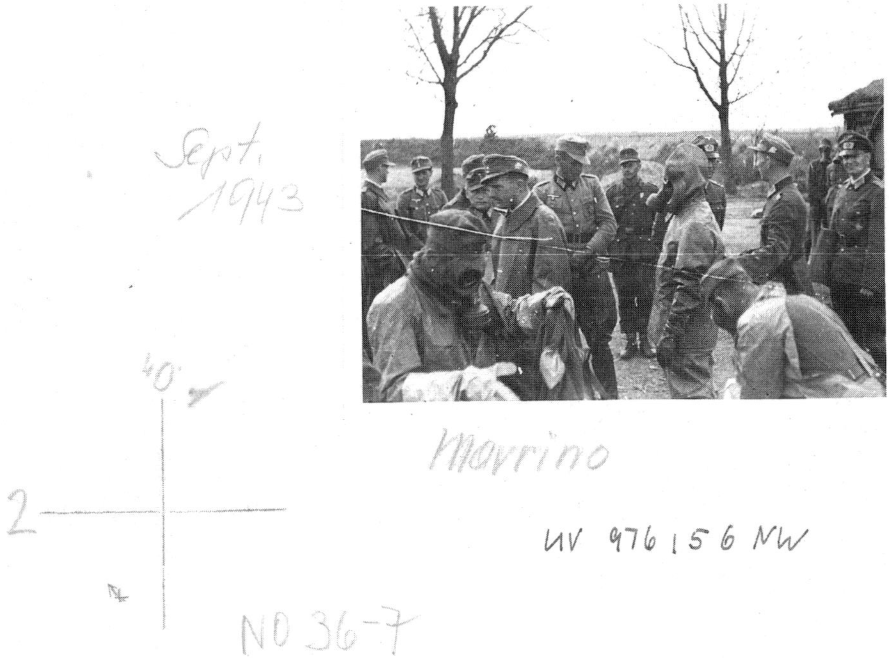
Sept. 1943
Morvino
UV 976 156 NW
NO 36-7

This is September 1943 at Morvino, south of Staraja Russa. Rubber chem suits either means chemical weapons disposal or recovery of long-buried bodies. The nearest man holds a garment that seems almost new. Faces don't show revulsion or anger, in fact some are smiling?

Below. Trust the troops to find an easier way to do something. First choice is be in the truck (you could sleep) second is commandeer a bicycle and let the truck pull you—beats walking. Heading northwest 8 miles out of Nevel (Newel to Germans), September 1943.

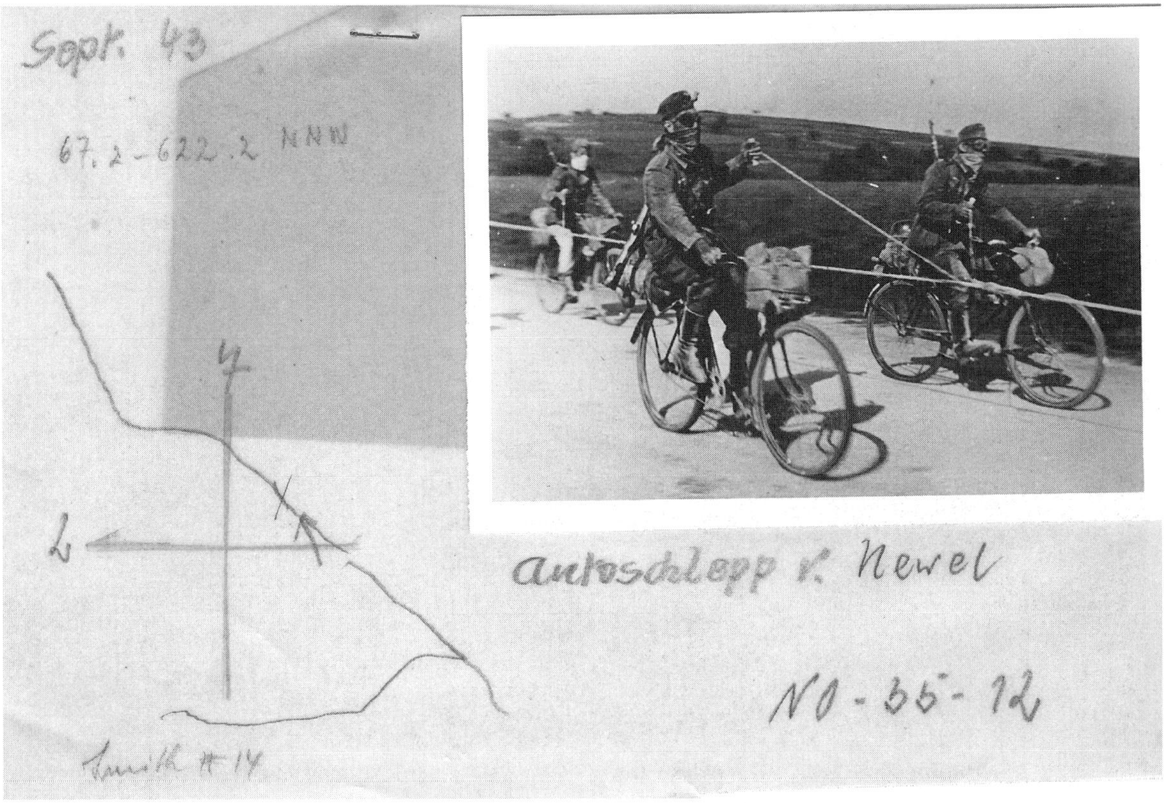
Sept. 43
67.2-622.2 NNW
Autoschlepp v. Newel
NO-35-12

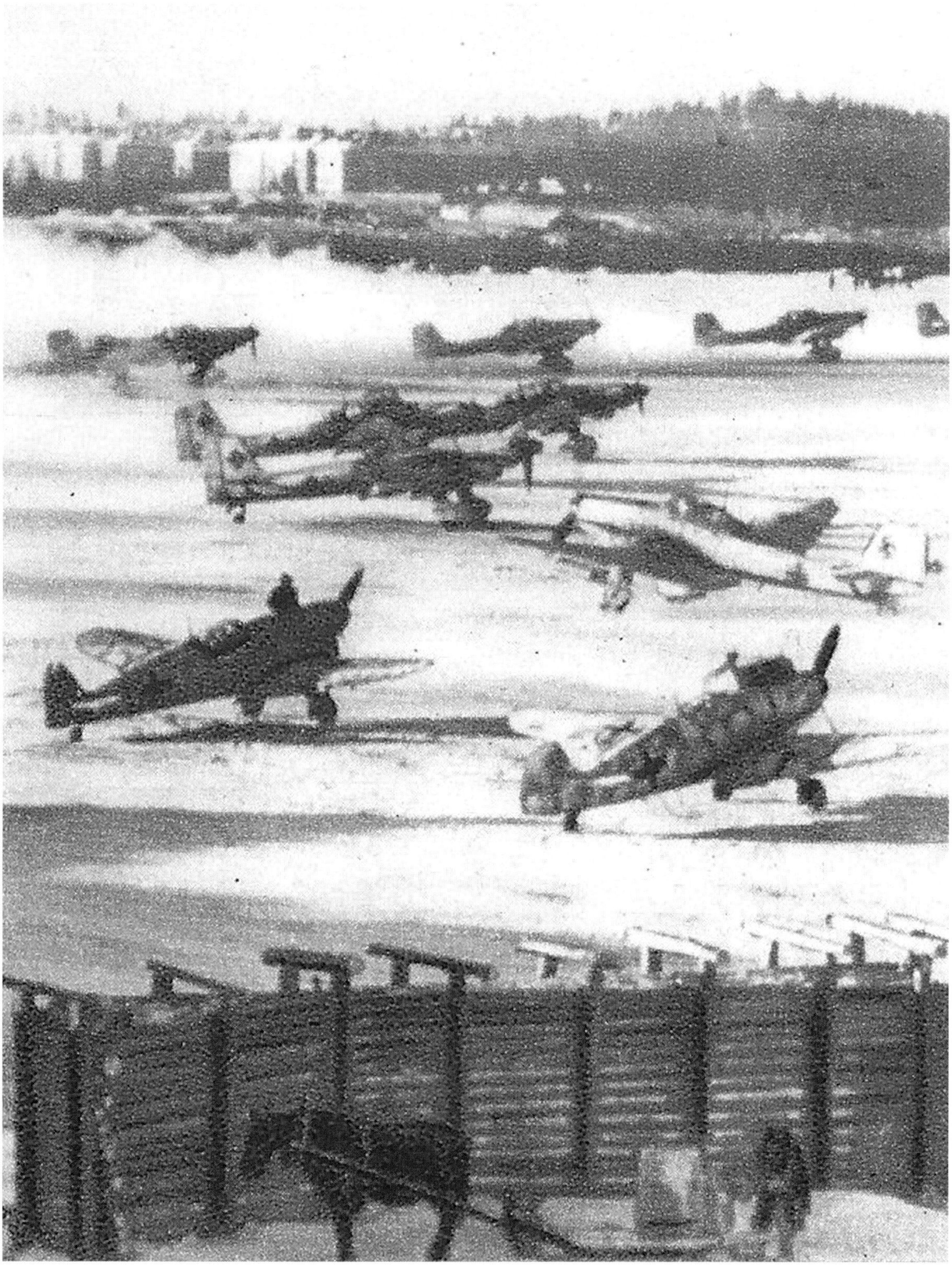
Eight Ju-87s and three Bf-109Gs, near Nevel, fall of 1943. This is almost back where Barbarossa began.

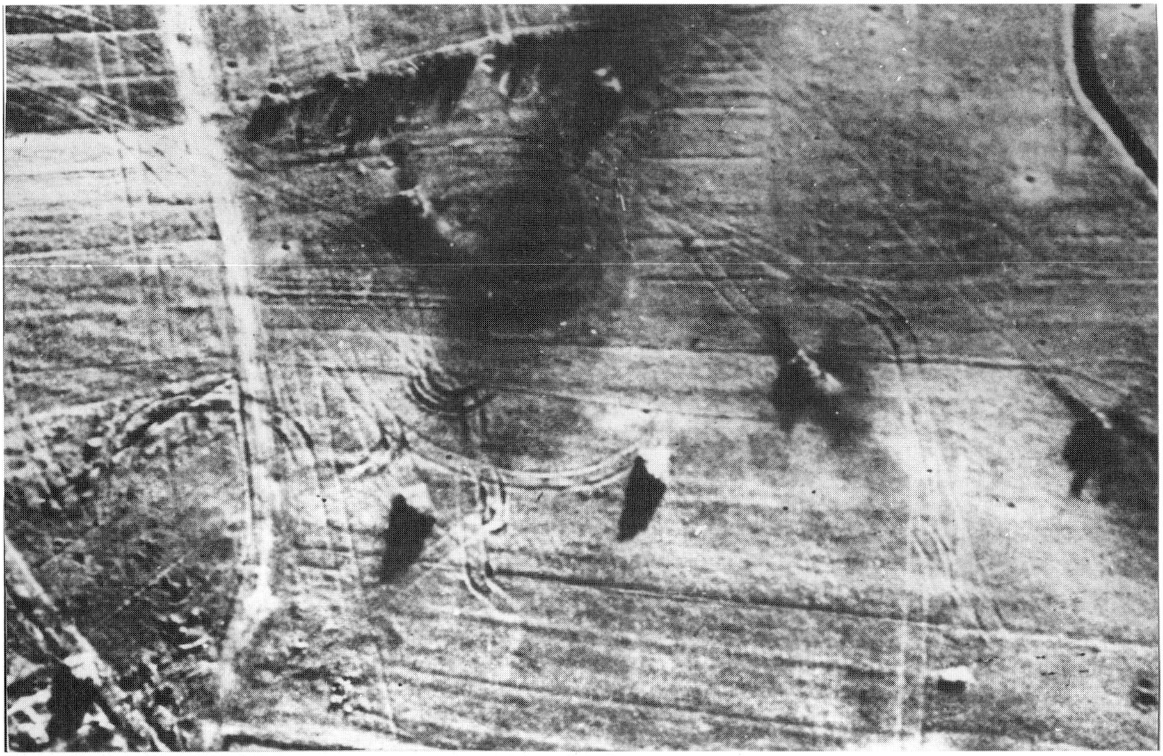

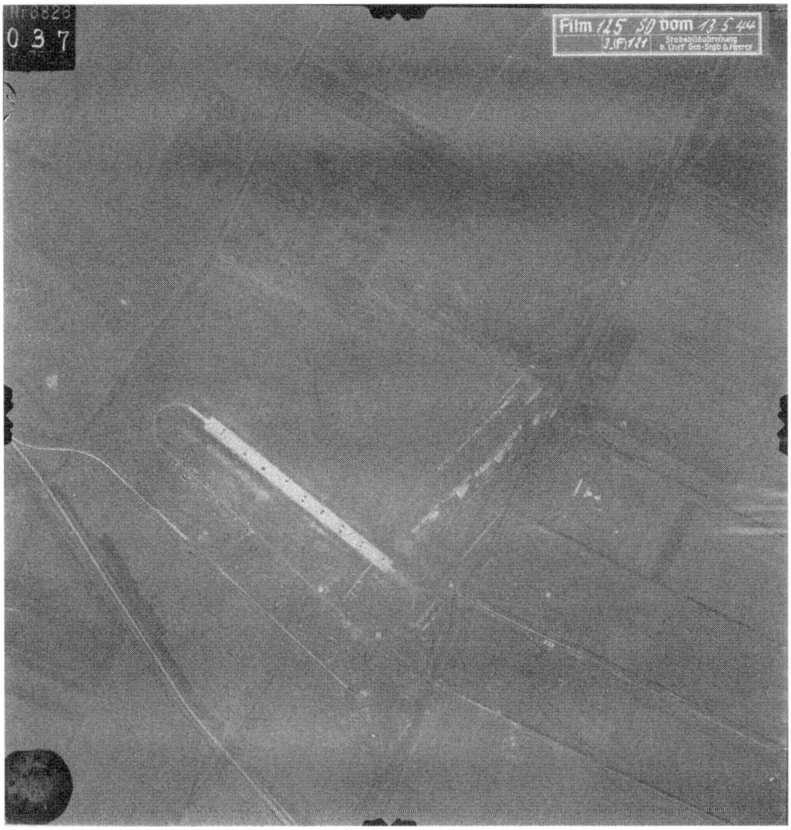
037
Film 125 50 vom 13.5.44
3.(F)121

Three Soviet light tanks (left) and three probable BA armored cars maneuvering near Nevel.

Left, sure sign of an army in retrograde—a sabotaged runway. Those dark spots are demolitions to make landing impossible, 13 May 1944.

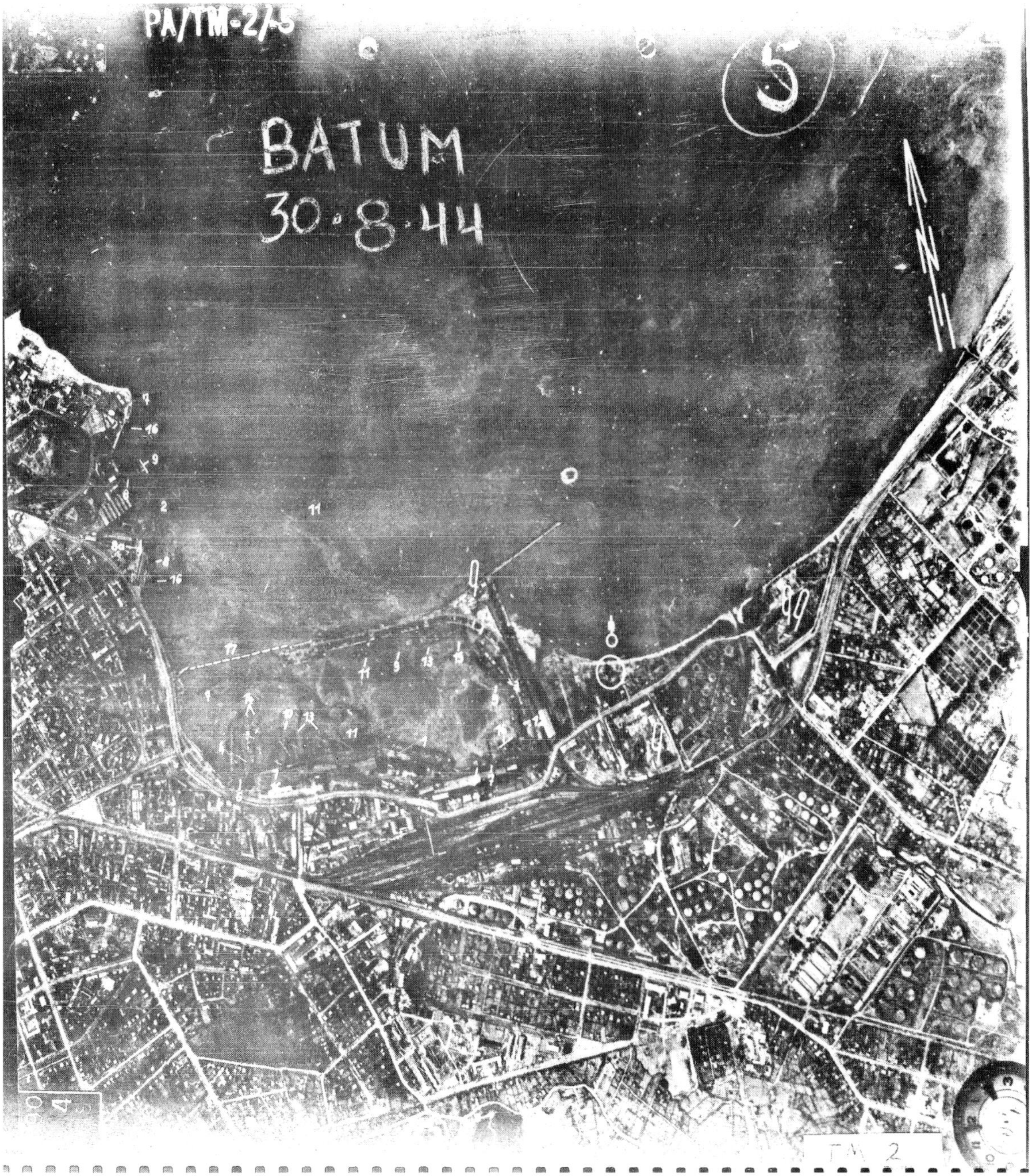
PA/TM-2/-5
BATUM
30.8.44
5
TM 2

This photo is almost humorous. On 30 August 1944 Batum was so far out of reach I doubt the Luftwaffe could even bomb it. What was to be learned by this reconnaissance? But anti-aircraft defenses and ships in port were all carefully noted.

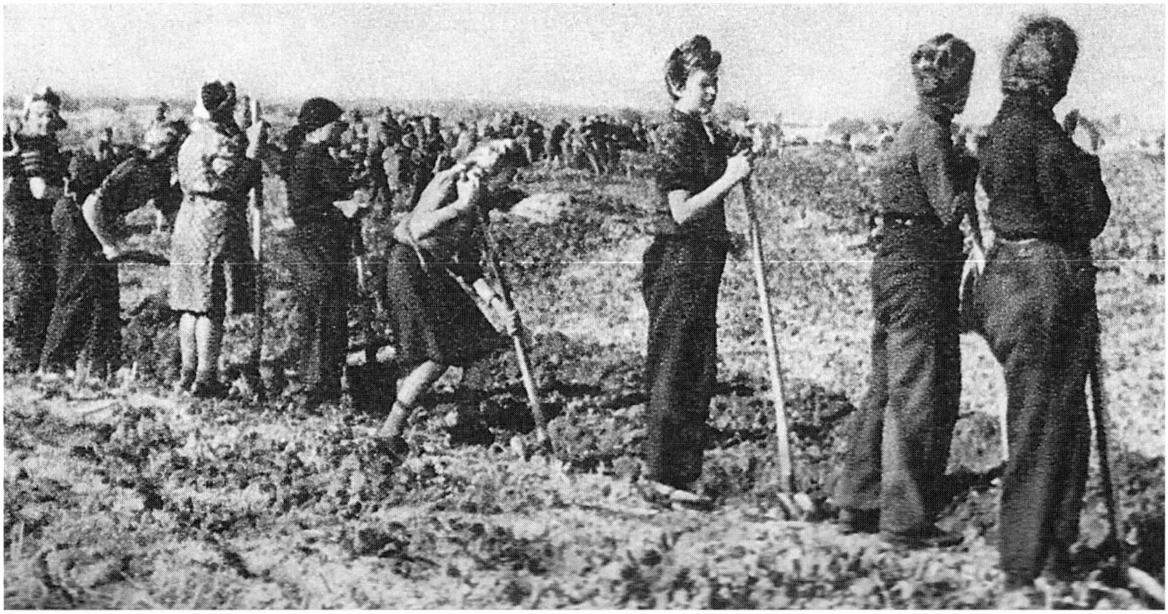

In 1944 it was German women who were digging anti-tank ditches.

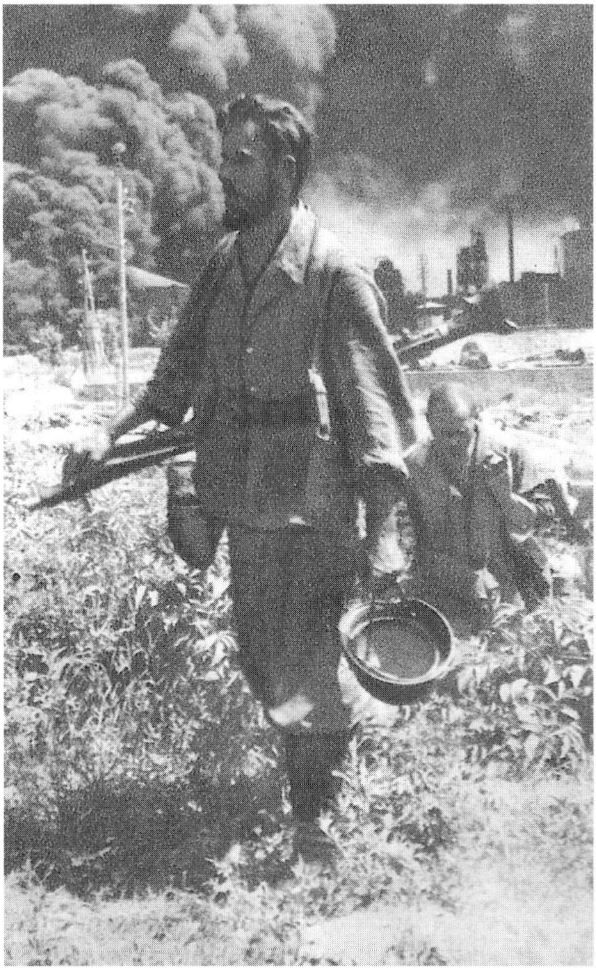

Left, fall of 1944. Novorossijsk is burning behind a MG34 gunner. The man kneeling behind him may be using a field radio-telephone.

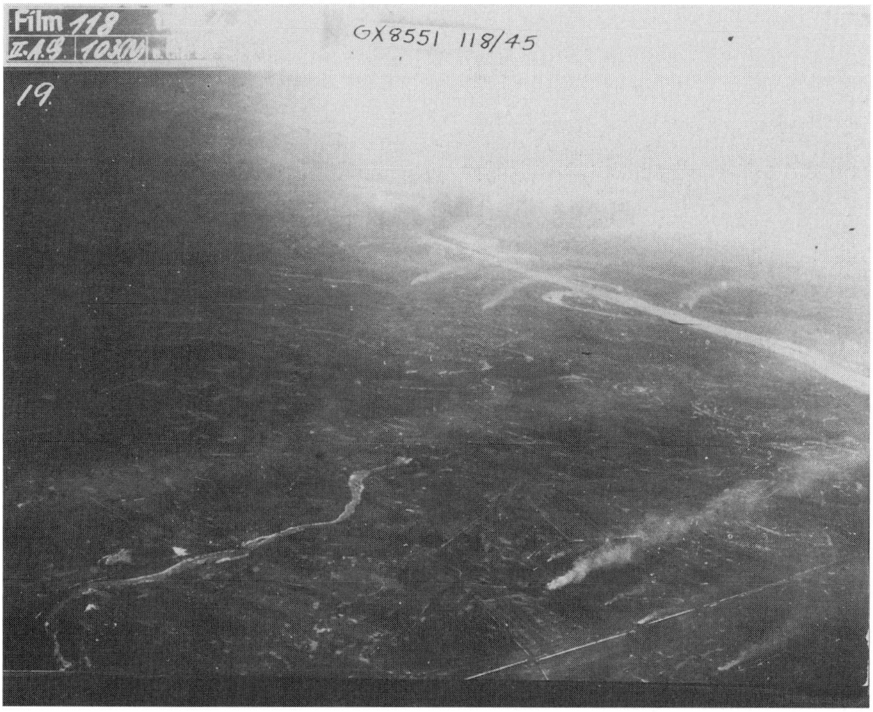
Film 118
GX8551 118/45
19.

South of Stettin, looking east over the Oder, 4 February 1945.

Below, same tactical recon sortie. Soviet tanks maneuvering. Halation off wet ground makes it impossible to count AFVs but there are at least 14 distinct tracks.

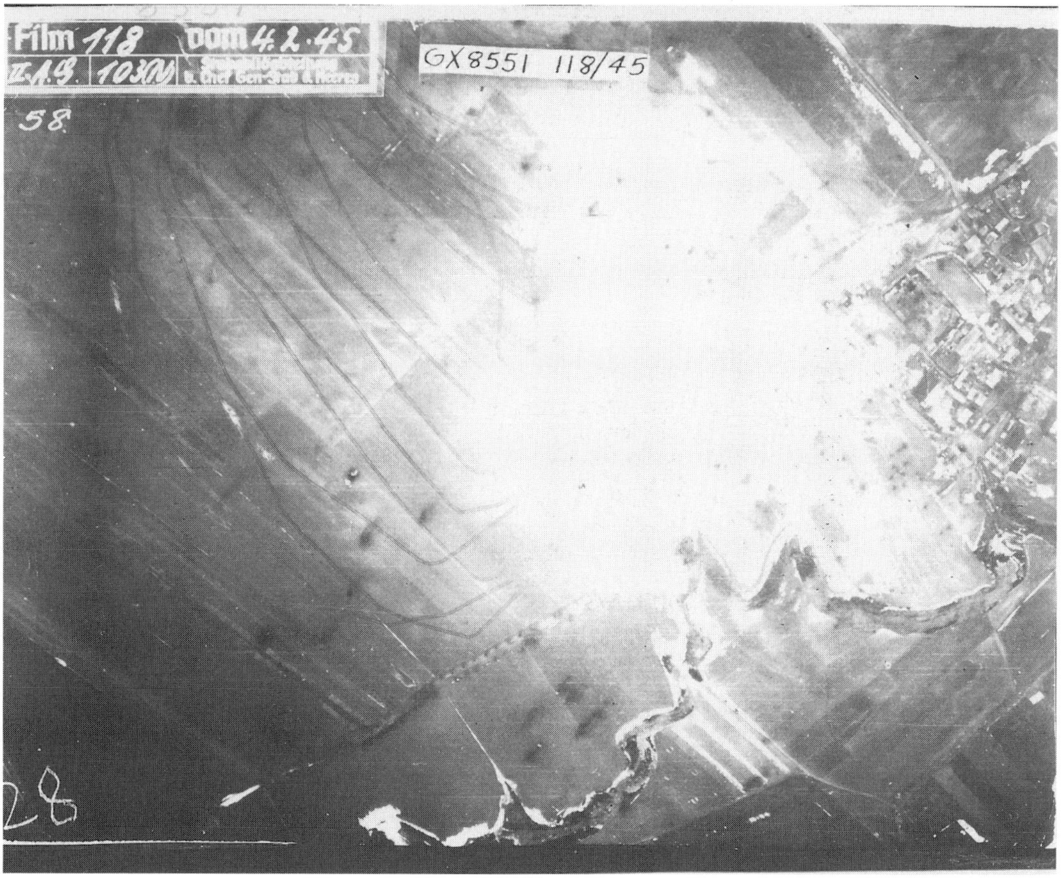
Film 118
vom 4.2.45
GX8551 118/45
58

Soviet troops with
German PoWs,
probably Germany in
1945.

German prisoners
walk past civilians,
probably in Poland.

USSR/RUSSIAN SFSR/MOSCOW- 5545N 3737E- AERIAL VIEW OF KREMLIN 1945
1820.264-AF   CONFIDENTIAL

Left, an Allied airplane got
permission to overfly
Moscow in May 1945.
Probably a transport
bringing in dignitaries.

MAY 1945

Hitler was gone.
Barbarossa was gone.
Red Square was decked out for celebration.

And all that wonderful German imagery was being scooped up by Allied Intelligence for the Cold War.

OBSERVATIONS

I feel confident saying that over the past 45 years I've probably looked at as much WW II German aerial imagery as anyone else, and I know I've just scratched the surface of the collection. My searches have been subject/location oriented, not systematic. What I've learned about that imagery is not scientific, just observations and impressions. I could easily be wrong on some of these assumptions.

First, it appears German PIs mainly worked from roll original negatives. That meant rapid first phase results but surrendered the advantage of stereo. Apparently prints were considered archival (where we have always considered the original neg the primary record). We know prints were used for mapping and Detailed Reports. There is plenty of evidence that prints were used for detailed studies where stereo was necessary. Dick Tracy is full of their annotated prints.

Second, the Dick Tracy collection I've seen is almost entirely copies of prints from original negs but most of them have been copied, sometimes through many generations. GX first generation prints are hardly ever annotated;[1] when they are it is usually a crude PI note—a place name, a circle or 'X' in pencil actually ON the print. DT images are frequently annotated, as you would expect from target materials, and the annotations are actually IN the neg images which generated the prints we have. That means prints were marked and subsequently copied. Annotations that show up in white were made on a neg (probably a dupe neg) in black ink and show white when the neg is printed. Annotations in black came from marks on prints two generations earlier.

Third, the base GX collection is first generation positive prints which seldom have annotations. What we do see as annotations are actually written ON the prints. They are often ad hoc notes made by photo interpreters as part of their exploitation. Many pencil and grease pencil annotations we see today on GX and DT were probably made by American PIs after the war as they plotted and indexed the prints or used them in Cold War work.

German aerial imagery collection sources were:

1. Fernaufklärung (long range reconnaissance), what we would call strategic reconnaissance. Those Gruppen (numbered 120 to 124) flew long range aircraft, usually at high altitude. Photo runs tended to be long and continuous. I have seen frame numbers in the 700s. Some missions made multiple passes over an area. This sort of imagery has a low 'WOW-factor'. It is business-like, comprehensive area coverage. Sometimes rows of plots lay together side-by-side in what is called 'mapping coverage'. Other times the collection track seems to wander, almost aimlessly, but a look at the map often proves they were following a river or road. In each case, the track was designed to let planners see specific ground the army would soon reach or to determine the status of enemy defenses/activity.

2. Nahaufklärung (near reconnaissance) units, flew shorter-range, light aircraft on lower altitude mission profiles, collecting both photo and visual reconnaissance at the tactical level. Their flights were always near the FEBA. That is usually the source of dramatic, action-type imagery that people like to see and even an amateur can understand.

3. Strike aircraft sometimes mounted aerial cameras but most of that sort of imagery came from aircrew using personal cameras. Images from bombing sorties are few, and fewer still in any sort of series, but they often got one or two photos showing a lot of action.

---

[1] I'm sure no annotations were ever allowed on the original negatives. It just isn't done.

What we know as GX imagery was from the first source and we are fortunate that so many entire/complete missions have survived as positive prints. Photos with taking-unit identifiers such as 1(F) 122 show their heritage. We see images that froze time somewhere over the surface of the earth seven decades ago. This is raw intelligence. No judgements or comments are made. Nothing is taken away or added. It is what it is. Many of those images are the base for DT materials, but the DT images are almost always processed intelligence (not necessarily finished intelligence).

Based upon what I've seen, unfortunately we have little or none of the short range imagery collection beyond shots extracted for briefing purposes—we used to call them 'happy snaps'. I have seen some of that, but most were single frames found in Intel Files (occasionally the foot square negatives). As far as I know, no complete tactical (Nahaufklärung) missions have survived, even as prints.

My guess is the reason for GX survival is that it was flown by units reporting to a central organization with a headquarters (Staaken Airfield at Berlin). Squadrons and Groups in the field must have processed and used the imagery in the field, then forwarded original negs to Staaken where they were printed again for subsequent distribution and use.[2] As the end of the war neared, the Wehrmacht master print file was stashed away in a barn, to be found by Allied troops. I didn't know until recently that prints found in 1945 were the German army copies. That brings up something everyone who has worked in Aerial Recon knows—it is tough to serve many masters with finite resources. The Luftwaffe wanted information on enemy Air Order of Battle, AA location and location of bombing targets. The German army wanted maps, identification of ground defenses and any indication of force build-up. The German navy wanted status of ports and location of ships.

The Luftwaffe had fine pilots, aircraft and cameras, but aircrews go where they are told and collect the imagery directed. I've never seen any of their Ops orders or planning documents, so I can only guess their overall recon intentions based upon what I see in plots and on my own experience.

Much as we might wish it, I don't think there are any surviving complete Luftwaffe aerial photo missions with profiles similar to RAF and USAAF low altitude sweeps over Normandy in June 1944 or Market Garden locations in September. What we see in those foot-square gray boxes suggests the long-range photo recon units stayed pretty much above 30K altitude and Germans didn't use aerial recce to document events in the field. Of course it may also mean those negs were not collected in 1945, their repositories not discovered, or destroyed in battle.

Future historians, are fortunate there are so many 'Barbarossa survivors'. I hope they make more use of them in understanding WW II in the East.

---

[2] This was not unlike the RAF centralized system at Medmenham or the USAAF handling of roll negs that eventually got film to DIA and my organization.

ADDENDUM

My 1977 Barbarossa mosaic.
This used a cache of ground photos found in US Army Intel cut-neg files, most of which are also used elsewhere in this book.

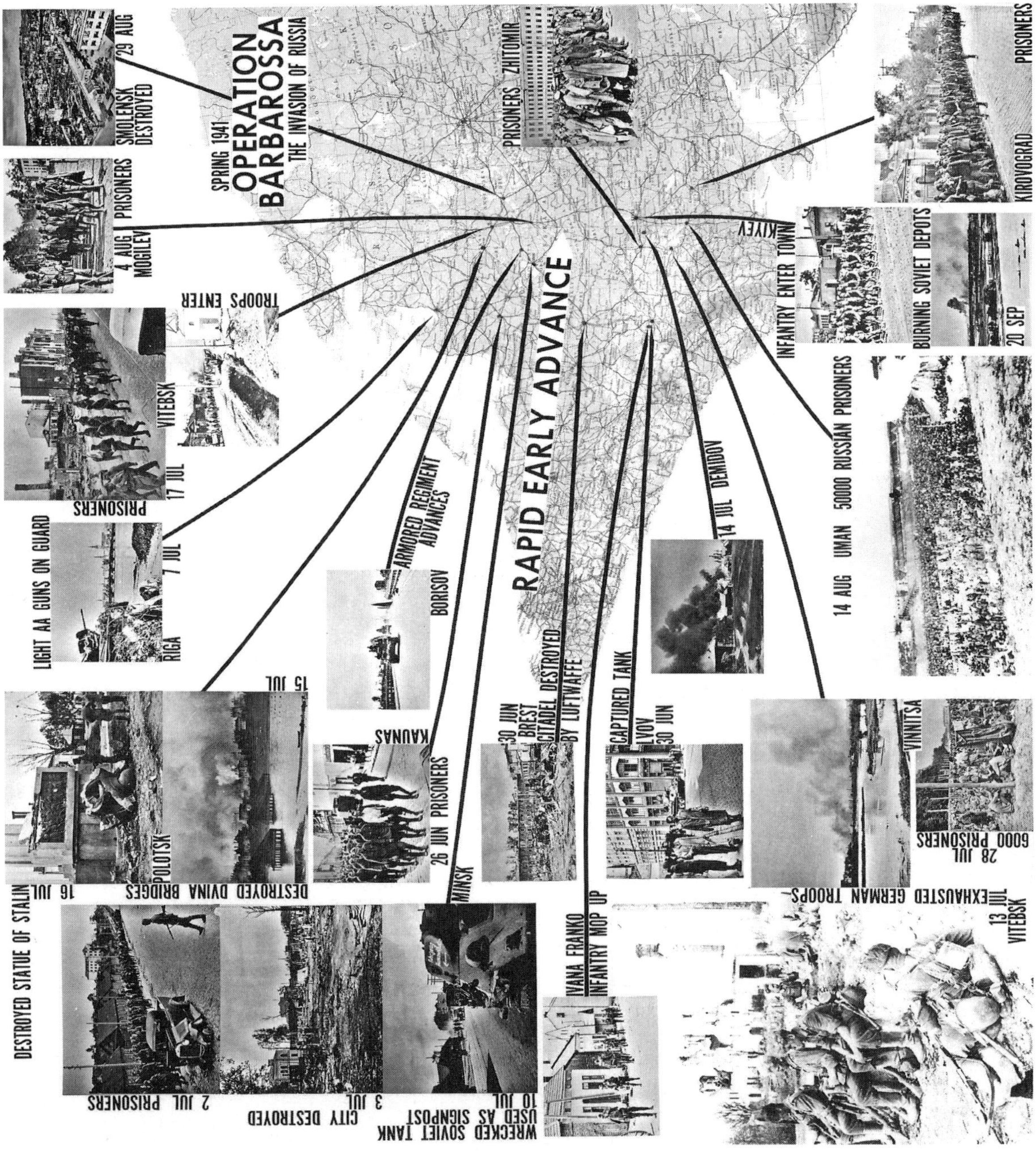
SPRING 1941
OPERATION BARBAROSSA
THE INVASION OF RUSSIA
SMOLENSK DESTROYED 29 AUG
4 AUG MOGILEV PRISONERS
TROOPS ENTER
VITEBSK 17 JUL PRISONERS
LIGHT AA GUNS ON GUARD
RIGA 7 JUL
PRISONERS ZHITOMIR
KIROVOGRAD PRISONERS
KIYEV
INFANTRY ENTER TOWN
BURNING SOVIET DEPOTS 20 SEP
14 AUG UMAN 50000 RUSSIAN PRISONERS
14 JUL DEMIDOV
RAPID EARLY ADVANCE
ARMORED REGIMENT ADVANCES
BORISOV
15 JUL
KAUNAS
26 JUN PRISONERS
30 JUN BREST CITADEL DESTROYED BY LUFTWAFFE
CAPTURED TANK LVOV 30 JUN
VINNITSA
28 JUL 6000 PRISONERS
13 JUL VITEBSK
EXHAUSTED GERMAN TROOPS
POLOTSK
DESTROYED DVINA BRIDGES
16 JUL
DESTROYED STATUE OF STALIN
MINSK
2 JUL PRISONERS
3 JUL CITY DESTROYED
10 JUL USED AS SIGNPOST
WRECKED SOVIET TANK
IVANA FRANKO
INFANTRY MOP UP

INDEX

UR=Soviet, GR=German, RO=Romanian, UK=British, US=American